The
Developing Child

Teacher Wraparound Edition

Ninth Edition

Holly E. Brisbane

Glencoe

New York, New York   Columbus, Ohio   Chicago, Illinois   Peoria, Illinois   Woodland Hills, California

Photo Credits

Tim Fuller, Morgan Cain & Associates, TM-21
Stock Market
    Jose L. Pelaez, TM-20

Internet Disclaimer

The following Internet listings are a source for extended information related to our text. We have made every effort to recommend sites that are informative and accurate. However, these sites are not under the control of Glencoe/McGraw-Hill, and therefore Glencoe/McGraw-Hill makes no representation concerning the contents of these sites. We strongly encourage teachers to preview Internet sites before students use them. Many sites contain links to other sites, and following such links may eventually lead to exposure to inappropriate material. Internet sites are sometimes "under construction" and may not always be available. Sites may also move or have been discontinued completely by the time you or your students attempt to access them.

The McGraw-Hill Companies

Send all inquiries to:
Glencoe/McGraw-Hill
3008 West Willow Knolls Drive
Peoria, Illinois 61614-1083

ISBN 0-07-846257-6 (Teacher Wraparound Edition)
ISBN 0-07-846256-6 (Student Edition)
Printed in the United States of America
2 3 4 5 6 7 8 9 071 07 06 05 04 03

TEACHER'S MANUAL CONTENTS

The Developing Child program includes all you need to enhance students' knowledge of child development, parenting, and child care skills. Program components include:

- **Student Edition.** The student text provides a broad, substantive introduction to child study. Choose from hundreds of review and application exercises designed to allow students to demonstrate their mastery of the material.

- **Teacher Wraparound Edition.** This daily resource tool includes complete lesson plans, teaching suggestions, and supplementary information that are "wrapped around" the pages of the student edition for easy, point-of-use reference.

- **Student Workbook.** Chapter study guides help guide students' reading and provide a valuable resource for review. Reinforcement activities for each of the text's 52 Sections help students apply their learning. A coordinated *Teacher Annotated Edition* of the *Student Workbook* has answers printed in color right on the student pages.

- **NEW** **Student Motivation Kit.** This collection of reproducible resources contains six individual booklets on special topics: *Nurturing Brain Development, Observations & Case Studies, Reteaching Activities, Enrichment Activities, Teen Parenting Skills,* and *Creative Activities for Children.* By using this resource, you can easily reinforce and expand text information and personalize the program to meet your individual course needs.

- **NEW** **Teacher Resource Guide.** The reproducible pages of this 320-page book include a correlation to the National FCS standards for Human Development and for Parenting, lesson plan organizers, Section quizzes, Chapter tests, authentic assessment options, and 8 sample color transparencies with teaching suggestions.

- **NEW** **Effective Instruction CD-ROM.** The CD-ROM contains three components to speed preparation and enhance learning. The lesson plans organizers, provided in Word for Windows® format, can easily be updated to match your teaching plans. With the **Exam***View*® *Test Generator*, you can create or modify Section quizzes and Chapter and Unit tests. PowerPoint® slides of all the color transparencies give you the flexibility of an electronic presentation format.

- **Transparency Package.** These 56 ready-to-use color transparencies focus on key chapter concepts. Coordinated teaching ideas are also included.

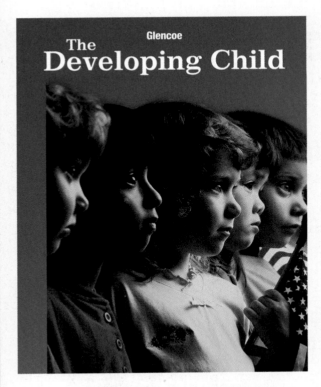

The Developing Child has a long tradition as the most current, comprehensive, and motivating textbook program for studying children and parenting. This Ninth Edition combines the best of the old with new research and topics.

- **Brain development research.** Research continues to unlock the mysteries of early brain development. These crucial findings and their application to parenting and child care are integrated throughout. A special brain logo in the text margin highlights related information.

- **Career options and employment skills.** Chapter career features help students realize the breadth of careers related to child development and care. Career planning is highlighted in Chapter 1. A new *Career Success Handbook* teaches the skills needed to find and succeed on a job and progress in a career.

- **Ages and stages.** The core of the text focuses on growth and development from conception to age twelve. Students learn about the physical, emotional, social, and intellectual development of infants, toddlers, preschoolers, and school-age children.

- **Real-life connections.** Throughout the text, students see how theory applies to everyday life. Links are made to parenting, family, community, and workplace, with opportunities for relevant skill development.

- **The family's role.** A child develops within a family setting. *The Developing Child* explains the influences of society, culture, parents, and other family members.

The Developing Child **is designed to maximize students' interest and learning about child development, parenting, and child care. It is also adaptable to your own course and the needs of your students.**

Flexible Organization

The Developing Child follows a logical structure, yet is easy to adapt to your specific course. The 20 Chapters are divided among 5 Units, with each Chapter subdivided into Sections. The Section arrangement simplifies sequencing of content. Cross-references help you make certain students have essential background information, regardless of the order of presentation you choose.

Engaging Presentation

The many photos of children and the striking visuals draw students into the book. Then the warm, interesting tone of the content keeps them reading. Thought-provoking questions and activities involve them in the learning process.

Vital Content

Understanding child development is essential for parenting and working with young children. To build this knowledge, *The Developing Child* opens with the importance of studying children, the role of families, and the responsibilities of parenthood. The core of the book outlines the development of children at different ages and stages, while maintaining emphasis on the whole child. The final unit addresses special concerns, such as children with disabilities, child abuse, health and safety, and working in an early childhood setting. A new *Career Success Handbook* focuses on entering and succeeding in the working world.

Special Features

Throughout the book, special features highlight and extend important topics. These features attract students' attention while also teaching essential skills.

The two-page "Parenting with Care" features highlight topics in greater depth. Follow-up activities help students apply the information and practice process skills.

Five experts address questions about issues that concern many parents and caregivers. The experts' range of experiences gives students a variety of perspectives.

Students learn about twenty careers related to children. Features include an interview with a person in that field plus basic information about required education and the outlook for the career area. Questions reinforce school-to-career competencies.

Brain development information is woven in three ways. Section 8-2 "The Developing Brain" describes brain development in infancy and how caregivers can enhance it. "The Developing Brain" features provide additional information culled from recent research. The brain logo appears throughout the book when brain development issues are discussed.

"Practicing Parenting" features provide guidance on special parenting issues, such as parent-child bonding and handling temper tantrums.

"Health Tips" and "Safety Tips" present health- and safety-related issues, ranging from hearing problems to toy safety.

"Infolink" references tell where in the text additional information can be found on a topic. This can be especially important when the Chapters are taught out of sequence.

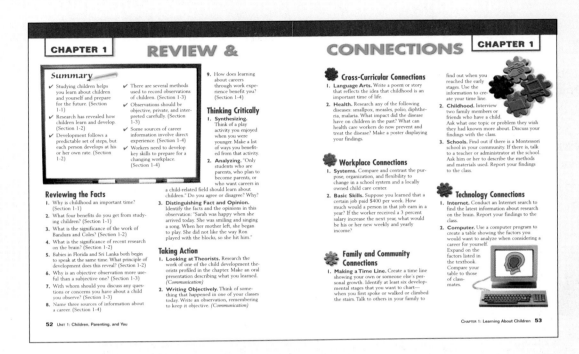

Chapter Review and Connections

Each Chapter concludes with a two-page "Review and Connections" section. These pages provide a wide variety of review and activity options for you to choose from:

- The **Summary** recaps important Chapter concepts. Each is identified with the Section in which it was presented.

- **Reviewing the Facts** includes recall and higher-level thinking questions on core Chapter concepts.

- **Thinking Critically** questions give students practice in analyzing, synthesizing, and evaluating Chapter content.

- **Taking Action** provides hands-on activities keyed to process skills—thinking, communication, management, and leadership.

- **Cross-Curricular Connections** activities show how the study of children is linked to other disciplines.

- **Workplace Connections** are activities that help your students apply Chapter content to work-based situations.

- **Family and Community Connections** are activities that extend beyond the classroom to the home or the community at large.

- In **Technology Connections,** students use technology to explore Chapter topics.

Answers to the "Chapter Review & Connections" material plus all caption questions can be found in the *Teacher Wraparound Edition.*

Section Elements

Each Section of the text serves as a self-contained lesson to maximize student learning. All Sections follow a similar structure.

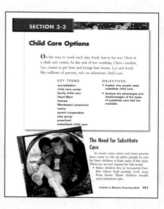

Section Opening Page

The Section begins with three elements that introduce students to the Section content:

- The **Introduction** summarizes the importance of the issue or developmental stage addressed in the Section.

- **Key Terms** highlights the chapter vocabulary terms. Vocabulary development is reinforced in the body of the text. When a "Key Term" is first used in the Section, it appears in **boldface type.**

- **Objectives** informs students what content and skills they are expected to learn from the Section.

Section Organization

Sections are clearly organized with headings that structure the material into major topics and subtopics. The text is interesting and readable, with specific examples used to clarify information.

Section Review

A two-part "Section Review" reinforces students' learning:

- **Check Your Understanding** questions are a set of review and application questions focused on key concepts in the Section.

- In **Putting Knowledge Into Practice,** students answer critical thinking questions and complete an activity that requires them to observe behavior and apply their findings.

The Career Success Handbook, Appendix, and Glossary

Several key elements at the end of the text expand the book's content and usefulness.

 ## Career Success Handbook

This new teaching aid gives specific information on beginning a career by finding a job, being a successful employee, and moving on to new challenges. These skills are applicable to teens' first jobs, as well as throughout their working life.

The "Finding a Job" section begins with locating job openings, continues through the application and resume process, and gives detailed information on interviewing successfully.

"Building Career Skills" explains the importance of communication, human relations, leadership, and teamwork skills. Managing multiple roles, handling performance reviews, and lifelong learning are also included.

"Leaving a Job" focuses on the legal and ethical aspects of changing jobs.

Appendix

The Appendix contains basic information on the male and female reproductive systems and a chart with information on various methods of family planning. Abstinence is emphasized as the only certain way of preventing pregnancy.

Glossary

All of the "Key Terms" are included and defined in the Glossary. After the definition, the Section in which the term appears is noted in parentheses.

The *Teacher Wraparound Edition* (TWE) is a highly comprehensive and usable teaching tool. Its "wraparound" presentation allows you to follow the Student Edition page by page, while keeping teaching notes at your fingertips. The reduced-size student pages are surrounded by lesson plans filled with teaching activities and information. In the Teacher's Manual that you are now reading, you will find charts and other resources useful in course and lesson planning, assessing student learning, and finding additional reference materials.

Unit Opening Pages

Every unit of the TWE begins with the following items:

- **Unit Objectives** are stated in behavioral terms.

- **Unit Overview** offers a précis on the content of each Chapter in the Unit.

- **Using the Poem** suggests ways to utilize the poem found on the Unit opening page as a catalyst for class discussion.

- **Introducing the Unit** identifies activities that can be used to launch the Unit.

- **Completing the Unit** includes extension, evaluation, and FCCLA activities.

- **Community as Classroom** provides suggestions for guest speakers and field trips.

Teaching the Chapter

The TWE material for each Chapter follows a similar structure. Introductory material appears on the Chapter opening pages. The "Chapter Review & Connections" pages have the "Assess" and "Close" portions of the Chapter-related lesson plan.

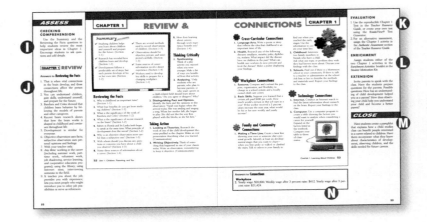

A Identifies the Chapter Sections

B Lists Chapter supplementary materials

C Summarizes the content of each Section

D Identifies Chapter objectives

E Suggests introductory activities

F Provides an activity using the scenario

G Explains the level codes for activities

H Identifies a resource relevant to the Chapter

I Suggests use of the summary and review questions

J Provides answers to "Reviewing the Facts"

K Identifies the Chapter test and authentic assessment options

L Provides enrichment and extension suggestions

M Gives a summary activity to close the chapter

N Provides any answers to activities on this page

Teaching the Section

The *Teacher Wraparound Edition's* core lesson plan for each Chapter is contained in the side columns of the Sections. This lesson plan follows a **Focus, Teach, Assess, Close** sequence, with specific activities appearing in each part.

The lesson plan applies to the main body of Section content. In addition, special text features such as "Practicing Parenting" have corresponding teaching suggestions in the TWE.

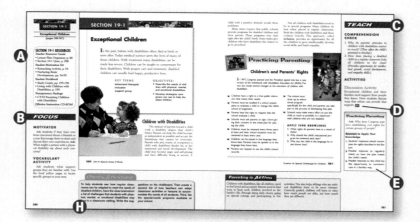

Ⓐ Identifies where all Section-related resources in the program can be found.

Ⓑ **Focus** section includes a motivator and a vocabulary activity.

Ⓒ **Teach** section provides comprehension questions and activities related to the page content.

Ⓓ Activities are labeled L1, L2, or L3 to indicate difficulty.

Ⓔ Special feature box expands use of the text feature.

Concluding the Section

Like the final two pages of each Chapter, the "Section Review" contains the **Assess** and **Close** portions of the Section lesson plan.

Ⓐ **Assess** gives options for reviewing content, evaluating students' knowledge, and reteaching, enriching, or extending Section content.

Ⓑ **Close** suggests a Section closure activity.

Ⓒ Answers to the Section Review appear at the bottom of the page.

Teaching the Student Edition Special Features

The special text features set off with design elements in the Student Edition have matching boxes with teaching suggestions in the *Teacher Wraparound Edition*.

Parenting With Care

- The two-page "Parenting with Care" features follow a lesson-plan structure:
- The "Focus" Section begins with a Motivator.
- The "Teach" Section includes "Comprehension Check" and "Activities."
- The "Close" Section contains a wrap-up activity that gives closure to study of the feature.
- On the bottom of the left page, a "Resources on…" box that refers to additional resources related to the feature topic.
- On the bottom of the right, "Answers to Following Up" gives answers to the questions at the end of the feature.

Ask the Experts

- Each of these features begins with a brief introductory activity that draws on students' own experience or prior knowledge about the topic addressed in the feature.
- Answers to the questions posed in the feature are given.

- "Applying What You've Learned" suggests an activity for reinforcement and application.

CAREER OPPORTUNITIES

- For "Career Opportunities" features, a bottom-of-the-page box gives an activity to provide practice in school-to-career skills.

Practicing Parenting

- *Teacher Wraparound Edition* material is similar for these four features. Each includes an introductory activity plus answers to the feature questions.

Highlighting Key Topics

In addition to the lesson plans, some of the special topical boxes in the *Teacher Wraparound Edition* highlight and expand on key topics in child development and parenting. Others suggest activities or teaching strategies.

The Developing Brain

 With this supplemental information on the brain, you can enhance students' understanding of the importance of brain development in childhood.

DID You Know?

This symbol indicates additional information or fascinating sidelights on issues related to the text discussion. Use these as part of your teaching or as a springboard for further discussion.

ISSUES IN TEEN PARENTING

You will likely deal with teen parenting as a topic for discussion, but you may also have teen parents in class. The material presented is designed to discourage additional teen pregnancies and to help parenting teens develop good parenting skills. Recurring themes include maturity and responsible decision making. Choose those topics that are appropriate for your class and community.

ISSUES IN CHILDREN'S HEALTH

"Children's Health" boxes provide supplementary information on special health issues such as children and organized sports and how children display anger.

LEARNING STYLES

Individual students learn best in different ways. Some may be primarily verbal learners, while others are visual learners or kinesthetic learners. These boxes suggest ways to accommodate students' different learning styles.

Management/Leadership Skills

These boxes reinforce the text information with activities that promote good management practices and family, school, and community leadership skills.

MULTIPLE INTELLIGENCES

Use this information to teach how young children with different intelligences may respond to the same stimulus. Some show how an idea might be presented to children of different intelligences. The information relates to children of the age under study.

Observing & Participating

This symbol indicates a suggested activity related to observing or working with children—skills directly related to the study of children.

Parenting in Action

Look to these boxes for information and activities related to typical situations that parents must respond to.

Student Workbook

The Student Workbook for *The Developing Child* reinforces understanding and application of text content. The Workbook includes the following:

- **Study Guides.** Every text chapter has a coordinated study guide that can be used to guide students' reading and later help them review important chapter concept. The study guide for each chapter is divided into sections that correspond to those in the text.

- **Activities.** A one- or two-page activity is provided for each text Section. These worksheets engage students in a variety of activities from completing time lines to interpreting observations.

Pages in the Student Workbook are perforated for easy removal. Please note that *The Developing Child* Student Workbook is a consumable product to be used by only one student. Reproducing pages for multiple use is a violation of copyright law.

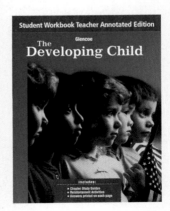

Student Workbook Teacher Annotated Edition

Answers to all worksheets can be found in the *Student Workbook Teacher Annotated Edition*. They are printed in color on each Workbook page.

NEW The *Student Motivation Kit* contains six separate booklets, each focusing on a specific topic. A transportable file holds all six, providing convenient storage and mobility. All materials may be reproduced for classroom use with *The Developing Child* text.

Nurturing Brain Development

This newly revised 86-page booklet provides reproducible supplementary information and activities that can expand students' knowledge of early brain development. It can be used to add depth to text information.

Observations & Case Studies

This booklet begins by introducing students to various types of observations, followed by an observation activity worksheet for each chapter. The "Learning Through Participation" section provides information and useful forms for experiences working with children in an early childhood setting. The "Case Studies" activities provide real-life simulations for students to deal with. An answer key is included.

Creative Activities

This excellent resource provides more than 70 activity ideas for students working with children ages two to six in a child care or early childhood class setting. Activities are organized into four categories: Art; Games, Thinking, and Sensory Activities; Science and Nature Activities; and Drama and Music. Each activity is keyed by age level and skills learned, plus a materials list. 128 pages.

Reteaching Activities

The Reteaching booklet presents key material in a new way for students who have not fully grasped content. One activity is provided for each text Section. A full answer key shows answers to activities in place on reduced-size student pages.

Teen Parenting Skills

This booklet contains effective teacher and student materials that offer teens support and help them develop effective parenting skills. The importance of finishing high school and becoming a self-sufficient adult are stressed.

Enrichment Activities

Activities suitable for higher-level students or more in-depth learning are included in this booklet. There are two activities for each text Chapter. Topics range from the practical—how to prepare a resume—to the theoretical—ideas about intellectual and moral development.

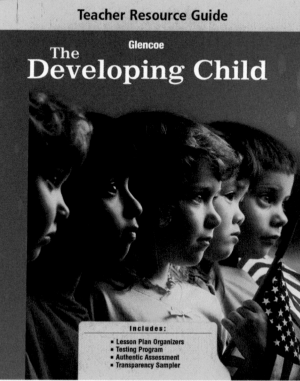

Teacher Resource Guide

Glencoe

The Developing Child

Includes:
- Lesson Plan Organizers
- Testing Program
- Authentic Assessment
- Transparency Sampler

Teaching with *The Developing Child*

The introductory section of the *Teacher Resource Guide* includes planning guides and a wealth of materials and suggestions to help you use *The Developing Child* program effectively and successfully.

Lesson Plan Organizers

A convenient one-page lesson plan is provided for each Section of *The Developing Child Student Edition*. The lesson plan uses a convenient checklist format. You can easily note the materials in the *Teacher Wraparound Edition, Student Motivation Kit, Student Workbook, Teacher Resource Guide,* and *Transparency Package* that you will use in teaching each Section to your students. Section objectives are included and lesson plans follow the **Focus, Teach, Assess,** and **Close** format.

Testing Program

The Testing Program section provides two types of ready-to-reproduce testing instruments—a one-page quiz for each text Section and an expanded, comprehensive test for each Chapter. Each quiz includes objective questions that assess students' mastery of terminology, concepts, and principles. The Chapter tests include a variety of objective question formats and essay questions that give students an opportunity to synthesize and apply their learning. An Answer Key provides answers for all quizzes and tests.

Authentic Assessment

The authentic assessments give an alternative way to evaluate students' learning. One alternative assessment is provided for every text Chapter. This section begins with background on the philosophy behind authentic assessment, the mechanisms for assigning and evaluating such assessments, and the use of portfolios. After the assessments for each Chapter, student assessment lists and rubrics are provided for various types of authentic assessment products, such as newspaper articles, public service announcements, and videos.

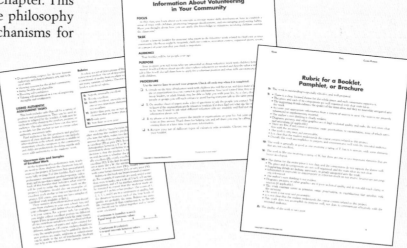

NEW Effective Instruction CD-ROM

The CD-ROM contains three components in an electronic format to simplify planning and teaching tasks. The lesson plan organizers are provided in a Word for Windows® format so they can easily be updated and printed. With the **Exam**View® *Test Generator*, you can create or modify Section quizzes and Chapter tests. The test generator also contains Unit tests and additional questions for each text Chapter. PowerPoint® versions of all 56 color transparencies simplify electronic presentations.

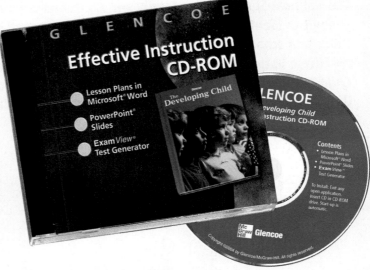

Transparency Package

The *Transparency Package* includes 56 ready-to-use full-color transparencies. The photos, drawings, and charts on these transparencies are effective tools for focusing students' attention, increasing comprehension, and extending learning. They can be used to introduce topics, reinforce concepts, stimulate discussion, and sharpen critical thinking skills. An accompanying booklet provides, for each transparency, a list of objectives, a warm-up activity, discussion questions, and related activities to help make the transparencies true teaching tools.

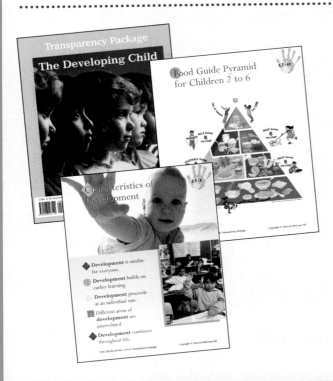

The National Standards for Family and Consumer Sciences Education respresents the first attempt to identify core standards common to areas of study nationwide. While individual states and school districts have their own courses and course curricula, most do incorporate these basic standards. The following charts show how and where *The Developing Child* student text matches these standards. The text is correlated to both the Human Development standards and the Parenting standards. Numbers shown in the chart are Section designations in the textbook.

Human Development Standards

	Chapter 1	Chapter 2	Chapter 3	Chapter 4	Chapter 5	Chapter 6	Chapter 7	Chapter 8	Chapter 9	Chapter 10
12.1: Analyze principles of human growth and development across the life span.	1-1 1-2	2-1 2-2	3-1	4-1	5-1	6-1	7-1 7-2 7-3	8-1 8-2	9-1 9-2	10-1 10-2
12.2: Analyze conditions that influence human growth and development.	1-2	2-1 2-2	3-1	4-2	5-1 5-2 5-3	6-1 6-3	7-2 7-3	8-1 8-2 8-3 8-4	9-1 9-2	10-1 10-2
12.3: Analyze strategies that promote growth and development across the life span.	1-1 1-2	2-2	3-2	4-2	5-1 5-3	6-1 6-2 6-3	7-2 7-3	8-1 8-2 8-3 8-4	9-1 9-2	10-1 10-2

Incorporating Process Skills

The process skills of **Thinking, Leadership, Communication,** and **Management** are integrated throughout the content and activities of *The Developing Child* program. These skills are highlighted for easy identification. Every Chapter offers dozens of opportunities for skills development and practice.

Child development and parenting knowledge is useful only if it can be applied to diverse situations. That is why you will find **Problem Solving** skills also incorporated and developed in *The Developing Child.*

▶ Human Development Standards (continued)

	Chapter 11	Chapter 12	Chapter 13	Chapter 14	Chapter 15	Chapter 16	Chapter 17	Chapter 18	Chapter 19	Chapter 20
12.1: Analyze principles of human growth and development across the life span.	11-1 11-2	12-1 12-2	13-1 13-2	14-1 14-2	15-1 15-2	16-1 16-2	17-1 17-2 17-3 17-4	18-2	19-1 19-2	
12.2: Analyze conditions that influence human growth and development.	11-1 11-2	12-1 12-2	13-1 13-2	14-1 14-2	15-1 15-2	16-1 16-2	17-1 17-2 17-3 17-4	18-1 18-2	19-1 19-2 19-3	20-1 20-2
12.3: Analyze strategies that promote growth and development across the life span.	11-1 11-2	12-1 12-2	13-1 13-2	14-1 14-2	15-1 15-2	16-1 16-2	17-1 17-2 17-3 17-4	18-2	19-1 19-3	20-1 20-2

▶ **Parenting Standards**

	Chapter 1	Chapter 2	Chapter 3	Chapter 4	Chapter 5	Chapter 6	Chapter 7	Chapter 8	Chapter 9	Chapter 10
15.1: Analyze roles and responsibilities of parenting.	1-1 1-2	2-2	3-1 3-2	4-2	5-1 5-3	6-1 6-2 6-3	7-2 7-3	8-1 8-2 8-3 8-4	9-1 9-2	10-1 10-2
15.2: Evaluate parenting practices that maximize human growth and potential.	1-1 1-2	2-2	3-2	4-2	5-1 5-4	6-1 6-2 6-3	7-2 7-3	8-1 8-2 8-3 8-4	9-1 9-2	10-1 10-2
15.3: Evaluate external support systems that provide services for parents.	1-2 1-4	2-1 2-2	3-1 3-2 3-3	4-1 4-2	5-2 5-3	6-1 6-2 6-3	7-1 7-2	8-1 8-3	9-2	10-2
15.4: Analyze physical and emotional factors related to beginning the parenting process.	1-1 1-2	2-1 2-2	3-1 3-2 3-3	4-1 4-2	5-1 5-2 5-3 5-4	6-1 6-2 6-3	7-1 7-2 7-3	8-3	9-1 9-2	10-1 10-2

Parenting Standards (continued)

	Chapter 11	Chapter 12	Chapter 13	Chapter 14	Chapter 15	Chapter 16	Chapter 17	Chapter 18	Chapter 19	Chapter 20
15.1: Analyze roles and responsibilities of parenting.	11-1 11-2	12-1 12-2	13-1 13-2	14-1 14-2	15-1 15-2	16-1 16-2	17-1 17-2 17-3 17-4	18-1 18-2	19-1 19-2 19-3	20-1
15.2: Evaluate parenting practices that maximize human growth and potential.	11-1 11-2	12-1 12-2	13-1 13-2	14-1 14-2	15-1 15-2	16-1 16-2	17-1 17-2 17-3 17-4		19-1 19-2 19-3	
15.3: Evaluate external support systems that provide services for parents.	11-2		13-2	14-1 14-2	15-1	16-1 16-2	17-1 17-4	18-1 18-2	19-1 19-2 19-3	
15.4: Analyze physical and emotional factors related to beginning the parenting process.	11-1 11-2	12-1		14-1	15-1	16-2	17-2	18-1 18-2	19-1 19-2 19-3	

SCOPE AND SEQUENCE

This chart shows how major themes are woven throughout *The Developing Child*. You will find it useful for planning your course and for correlating *The Developing Child* to your curriculum. Numbers shown in the chart are text Section numbers.

	Ch 1	Ch 2	Ch 3	Ch 4	Ch 5	Ch 6	Ch 7	Ch 8	Ch 9	Ch 10
Brain development	1-2		3-1 3-2		5-1 5-3 5-4			8-1 8-2	9-1 9-2	10-1 10-2
Careers	1-2 1-4	2-1	3-2	4-1	5-3	6-2 6-3	7-2	8-2	9-1	10-1
Caregiving skills	1-1 1-2	2-2	3-1 3-2 3-3			6-3	7-1 7-2 7-3	8-2 8-3 8-4	9-1 9-2	10-2
Child observation	1-3		3-3				7-2		9-1 9-2	10-1 10-2
Consumer information		2-2	3-3		5-3 5-4	6-2 6-3	7-2			10-2
Developmental stages and influences	1-1 1-2	2-1	3-1 3-2	4-1	5-1 5-2 5-3 5-4	6-1 6-3	7-1 7-2 7-3	8-1 8-2	9-1 9-2	10-1
Effective parenting	1-1 1-2	2-2	3-1 3-2 3-3		5-1	6-1 6-2 6-3	7-1 7-2 7-3	8-1 8-2 8-3 8-4	9-1 9-2	10-1 10-2
Family and personal relationships	1-1 1-2	2-1 2-2	3-1 3-2	4-1 4-2	5-1 5-2 5-3	6-1 6-2 6-3	7-1 7-2 7-3	8-1 8-2 8-3 8-4	9-1 9-2	10-2
Health, safety, and nutrition	1-2	2-1		4-1 4-2	5-1 5-2 5-3 5-4	6-1 6-3	7-1 7-2 7-3	8-1 8-2 8-3 8-4	9-1 9-2	
Problem solving, decision making		2-1	3-2	4-1 4-2	5-4	6-2 6-3				
Responsibility and readiness	1-1	2-2	3-1 3-2	4-1 4-2	5-1 5-3 5-4	6-1 6-2 6-3	7-2 7-3	8-1 8-3 8-4	9-2	10-2
Society and community	1-2 1-3 1-4	2-1	3-3	4-1 4-2		6-3	7-2		9-1 9-2	10-2

	Ch 11	Ch 12	Ch 13	Ch 14	Ch 15	Ch 16	Ch 17	Ch 18	Ch 19	Ch 20
Brain development	11-2	12-1 12-2	13-1 13-2	14-1		16-1 16-2	17-1 17-4		19-1	20-2
Careers	11-1	12-2	13-1	14-2	15-1	16-2	17-2	18-1	19-1	20-1 20-2
Caregiving skills	11-1 11-2	12-1 12-2	13-1 13-2	14-1 14-2	15-1 15-2	16-1 16-2	17-1 17-2 17-3 17-4	18-1 18-2	19-1 19-2 19-3	20-1 20-2
Child observation	11-1 11-2	12-1 12-2	13-1 13-2	14-1 14-2	15-1 15-2	16-1 16-2	17-1 17-2 17-3 17-4	18-1 18-2	19-1 19-2 19-3	20-1 20-2
Consumer information	11-2		13-2	14-2			17-4	18-1 18-2	19-3	20-2
Developmental stages and influences	11-1 11-2	12-1 12-2	13-1 13-2	14-1 14-2	15-1 15-2	16-1 16-2	17-1 17-2 17-3 17-4		19-1 19-2	20-1 20-2
Effective parenting	11-1 11-2	12-1 12-2	13-1 13-2	14-1 14-2	15-1 15-2	16-1 16-2	17-1 17-2 17-3 17-4	18-1 18-2		20-1
Family and personal relationships	11-1 11-2	12-1 12-2	13-1 13-2	14-2	15-1 15-2	16-2	17-3 17-4	18-1 18-2	19-1 19-2 19-3	20-1
Health, safety, and nutrition	11-1 11-2	12-1 12-2	13-1	14-1 14-2	15-1		17-1	18-1 18-2	19-1 19-2 19-3	20-1 20-2
Problem solving, decision making			13-1	14-2			17-2 17-3 17-4	18-1 18-2	19-1 19-2 19-3	20-1 20-2
Responsibility and readiness	11-1 11-2	12-1 12-2	13-1 13-2	14-1 14-2	15-1 15-2	16-1 16-2	17-1 17-2 17-3 17-4	18-1 18-2	19-1 19-2 19-3	20-1 20-2
Society and community		12-1 12-2	13-1 13-2	14-1 14-2	15-2	16-2	17-1 17-2 17-3 17-4	18-1 18-2	19-1 19-2 19-3	20-1 20-2

Assessment Strategies

STRATEGIES	ADVANTAGES	DISADVANTAGES

Objective Measures
  Multiple choice
  Matching
  Item sets
  True/false
	Reliable
	Objective, if designed
	  effectively
	Low cost, efficient
	Automated administration
	Lends to equating
		Measures only cognitive
		  knowledge effectively; limit-
		  ed on other measures
		Not a good measure of overall
		  performance

Written Measures
  Essays
  Restricted response
  Written simulations
  Case analysis
  Problem-solving exercises
	Face validity (real life)
	In-depth assessment
	Measures writing skills and
	  higher level skills
	Reasonable developmental
	  costs and time
		Subjective scoring
		Time consuming and expen-
		  sive to score
		Limited breadth
		Difficult to equate
		Moderate reliability

Oral Measures
  Oral examinations
  Interviews
	Measures communications
	  and interpersonal skills
	In-depth assessment with var-
	  ied stimulus materials
	Learner involvement
		Costly and time consuming
		Limited reliability
		Narrow sample of content
		Scoring difficult, need multiple
		  raters

Simulated Activities
  In-basket
  Computer simulations
	Moderate reliability
	Performance-based measure
		Costly and time consuming
		Difficult to score, administer,
		  and develop

**Portfolio and Product
Analysis**
  Work samples
  Projects
  Work diaries and logs
  Achievement records
	Provides information not nor-
	  mally available
	Learner involvement
	Face validity (real life)
	Easy to collect information
		Costly to administer
		Labor and paper intensive
		Difficult to validate or equate
		Biased toward best samples
		  or outstanding qualities

Performance Measures
  Demonstrations
  Presentations
  Performances
  Production work
  Observation
	Job-related
	Relatively easy to administer
	In-depth assessment
	Face validity
		Rater training required
		Hard to equate
		Subjective scoring
		Time consuming if breadth is
		  needed

Performance Records
  References
  Performance rating forms
  Parental rating
	Efficient
	Low cost
	Easy to administer
		Low reliability
		Subjective
		Hard to equate
		Rater judgment

Self-Evaluation	Learner involvement and
	  empowerment
	Learner responsibility
	Measures dimensions not
	  available otherwise
		May be biased or unrealistic

Adapted from: *Business Education Forum*, April 1996

Internet Disclaimer

Some of the Resources listed include Websites as sources of extended information related to our text. We have made every effort to recommend sites that are informative and accurate. However, these sites are not under the control of Glencoe-McGraw-Hill, and therefore Glencoe/McGraw-Hill makes no representation concerning the content of these sites. We strongly encourage teachers to preview Internet sites before students use them. Many sites contain links to other sites, and following such links may eventually lead to exposure to inappropriate material. Internet sites are sometimes "under construction" and may not always be available. Sites may also move or have been discontinued completely by the time you or your students attempt to access them.

Al-Anon Family Headquarters, Inc.
1600 Corporate Landing Pkwy.
Virginia Beach, VA 12454
757-563-1600
http://www.al-anon.org

American Academy of Pediatrics
P.O.Box 927
141 Northwest Point Boulevard
Elk Grove Village, IL 60007-1098
847-228-5005
847-434-4000
http://www.aap.org

American Academy of Pediatric Dentistry
211 E. Chicago Avenue, Suite 700
Chicago, IL 60611-2663
312-337-2169
http://www.aapd.org

American Association of Family and Consumer Sciences (AAFCS)
1555 King Street
Alexandria, VA 22314-2738
http://www.aafcs.org

American Automobile Association
975 Meridium Lake Drive
Aurora, IL 60504
630-328-7000
http://www.aaa.com

American College of Obstetricians and Gynecologists, Resource Center
409 12th Street, SW
P.O.Box 96920
Washington, DC 20009-6920
202-638-5577
http://www.acog.org

American Dental Association
211 E. Chicago Ave.
Chicago, IL 60611
312-440-2500
http://www.ada.org

American Dietetic Association
216 W. Jackson Boulevard
Chicago, IL 60606-6995
312-899-0040
http://www.eatright.org

American Heart Association
7272 Greenville Avenue
Dallas, TX 75231
214-373-6300
http://www.amhrt.org

American Red Cross (contact the nearest local chapter)
http://www.redcross.org

American Society for Nutritional Services
9650 Rockville Pike
Bethesda, MD 20814
301-520-7050
http://www.nutrition.org/nutrition/

American Lung Association
61 Broadway, 6th Floor
New York, NY 10006
212-315-8700
http://www.lungusa.org

American Medical Association
515 North State Street
Chicago, IL 60610
312-464-5000
http://www.ama-assn.org

Association for Childhood Education International (ACEI)
17904 Georgia Avenue, Suite 215
Olney, MD 20832
301-570-2111
http://www.acei.org
http://www.udel.edu/bateman/acei

Asthma and Allergy Foundation of America
1233 20th Street, NW
Washington, DC 20036
202-466-7643
http://www.aafa.org

Autism Society of America
7910 Woodmont Avenue, Suite 650
Bethesda, MD 20814-3067
301-657-0881
http://www.autism-society.org

Birth Defects and Genetic Diseases
Branch Division of Birth Defects
and Developmental Disabilities
National Center for Environmental
Health
Centers for Disease Control and
Prevention
4770 Buford Highway NE,
Mail Stop F-45
Atlanta, GA 30341-3724
http://www.cdc.gov/nceh/
grograms/infants/brthdfct/
prevent/ntd_prev.htm

**Center for Career Development in
Early Care and Education,
Cooperative Extension System,
University of Connecticut**
1376 Storrs Rd., U-4036
Storrs, CT 60269-4036
860-486-1981
http://www.crc.uicu.edu/ccdece/
ccdece.htm

**Centers for Disease Control and
Prevention Office of
Communication Division of
Media Relations**
1600 Clifton Road Mail Stop D-25
Atlanta, GA 30333l
404-639-3286
http://www.cdc.gov/od/oc/media/
fact/fetal.htm

Children's Defense Fund
25 E. Street NW
Washington, DC 20001
202-528-8787
http://www.childrensdefence.org

**The Curriculum Center for Family
and Consumer Sciences Texas
Tech University**
Box 41161
Lubbock, TX 79409-1161
806-742-3029
http://www.edu/ccfcs

**Educational Resource Information
Center (ERIC)**
Early Childhood Education
University of Illinois
805 West Pennsylvania Avenue
Urbana, IL 61801
217-333-1386
http://www.ericir.sunsite.syr.edu/

Families and Work Institute
267 Fifth Ave., Floor 2
New York, NY 10016
212-465-2044
http://www.familiesandwork.org

**Family, Career, and Community
Leaders of America, Inc.**
1910 Association Drive
Reston, VA 22091-1584
http://www.fcclainc.org

Food and Drug Administration
5600 Fishers Lane
Rockville, MD 20857-0001
http://www.fda.gov

**Food and Nutrition Information
Center (FNIC), USDA**
10301 Baltimore Avenue
Beltsville, MD 20705-2351
301-504-5719
301-504-6409
http://www.nal.usda.gov/fnic
http://www.nutrition.gov

**Harvard Center for Children's
Health**
617-432-3222
http://www.hsph.harvard.edu/
children

I Am Your Child Campaign
335 North Maple Drive, Suite 135
Beverly Hills, CA 90210
310-285-2385
http://www.iamyourchild.org

**International Childbirth Education
Association**
P.O.Box 20048
Minneapolis, MN 55420
612-854-8660
http://www.icea c/o
metrix@notes.wordcom.com

**Juvenile Diabetes Foundation
International**
120 Walls Street
New York, NY 20005-4001
http://www.jdrf.org

**Juvenile Products Manufacturers
Association**
1700 Commerce Pkwy, Suite C
Mt.Laurel, NJ 08054
856-638-0420
http://www.jpma.org

kidsDoctor
http://www.kidsdoctor.com

Kids Health
http://www.kidshealth.org

La Leche International
9616 Minneapolis Avenue
Franklin Park, IL 60131
847-455-8317
http://www.lalecheleague.org

Lamaze International
2025 M Street, Suite 800
Washington, DC 20036-3309
http://www.lamaze.org

**Learning Disabilities Association
of America**
4156 Library Road
Pittsburgh, PA 15234
412-341-1515
http://www.ldanatl.org/index.shtml

**March of Dimes Birth Defects
Foundation**
1275 Mamaroneck Avenue
White Plains, NY 10605
914-428-7100
http://www.modimes.org

Maternal and Child Health Bureau
http://www.mchb.hrsa.gov

**Mayo's Pregnancy and Children's
Health Resource Center**
http://www.mayohealth.org/maho/
common/hmt/pregpg.htm

**National Association of
Childbearing Centers**
3123 Gottschall Road
Perkiomenville, PA 18074
215-234-8068
http://www.BirthCenters.org

**National Association for the
Education of Young Children**
1509 16th Street NW
Washington, DC 20036
http://www.naeyc.org

**National Center on Shaken Baby
Syndrome**
http://www.dontshake.com

National Child Care Association
1016 Rosser Street
Conyers, GA 30012
http://www.nccanet.org

**National Clearinghouse on Child
Abuse and Neglect**
330 C Street, SW
Washington, DC 20447
http://www.calib.com/nccanch

**National Committee to Prevent
Child Abuse**
2950 Tennyson St.
Denver, CO 80212
http://www.childabuse.org

**National Congress of Parents and
Toddlers, Alcohol Education
Program**
330 North Wabash Avenue,
Suite 2100
Chicago, IL 60611-3690
312-670-6782
http://www.pta.org

National Down Syndrome Society
666 Broadway
New York, NY 10012
212-460-9330
http://www.ndss.org

National Easter Seal Society
230 West Monroe, Suite 1800
Chicago, IL 60606
312-726-6200
http://www.easter-seal.org

**National Institute of Allergy and
Infectious Diseases, Information
Office**
DIAID
Building 31, Room 7A-50
31 Center Drive MSC 2520
Bethesda, MD 20892-2520
http://www.miad.nih.gov

**National Institute of Child Health
and Human Development**
Bldg 31, Room 2A-32
MSC 2425
31 Center Drive
Bethesda, MD 20892-2425
http://www.nichd.nih.gov

**National Maternal and Child
Health Clearinghouse**
2070 Chain Bridge Road, Suite 450
Vienna, VA 22182
703-821-8955
http://www.nmchc.org

**National Mental Health
Association**
2001 N. Beauregard Street,
12th Floor
Alexandria, VA 22311
703-684-7722
http://www.nmha.org

**Planned Parenthood Federation of
America, Inc.**
810 Seventh Avenue
New York, NY 10019
212-541-7800
http://www.plannedparenthood.org

U.S. Department of Education
200 Maryland Ave., SW
Washington, DC 20202-0498
http://www.ed.gov

U.S. Department of Health and Human Services
200 Independence Avenue, SW
Washington, DC 20201
877-696-6775
http://www.os.dhhs.gov

U.S. Department of Labor
Frances Perkings Bldg
200 Constitution Ave. NW
Washington, DC 20210
http://www.dol.gov

USDA Food and Nutrition Services,
National Agricultural Library,
Information Center 304
3101 Park Center Drive
Alexandria, VA 22302
703-305-2060
http://www.fns.usda.gov

Zero to Three
National Center for Infants, Toddlers and Families
200 M Street, NW, Suite 200
Washington, DC 20036
202-638-1144
http://www.zerotothree.org

Family Information Network (Supported by Clemson University)
Clemson University
Clemson, SC 29634
864-656-3311
http://www.clemson.edu/FIN

Parents Ask ERIC (located at University of Illinois at Urbana-Champaign)
University of Illinois at Urbana-Champaign
Children's Research Center
51 Gerty Drive
Champaign, IL 61820-7469
http://www.ericeece.org/askeric.html

American Library Association
50 E. Huron
Chicago, IL 60611
http://www.ala.org

National Organization of Adolescent Pregnancy, Parenting, and Prevention, Inc.
NOAPPP, Inc.
Suite 350
Washington, DC 20037
202-293-8370
http://www.noappp.org

American College of Nurse-Midwives
818 Connecticut Ave., NW, Suite 900
Washington, DC 20006
202-728-9860
http://www.midwife.org

US Consumer Product Safety Commission
4330 East-West Highway
Bethesda, MD 20814-4408
http://www.cpsc.gov

Postpartum Education for Parents
P.O. Box 6154
Santa Barbara, CA 93160
http://www.sbpep.org

Bright Horizons Family Solutions
200 Talcott Ave., South
Watertown, MA 02472
617-673-8000
http://www.brighthorizons.com/resources/othersites.html

The Developing Child

Ninth Edition

Holly E. Brisbane

 **Glencoe**

New York, New York   Columbus, Ohio   Chicago, Illinois   Peoria, Illinois   Woodland Hills, California

Teacher Reviewers

Carol Ann Flock
Family and Consumer Sciences
    Instructor
USD #389
Eureka, Kansas

Phil Goerner
Family and Consumer Sciences
    Instructor
St. Vrain Valley Schools
Longmont, Colorado

Janis Hewitt, M.Ed.
Family and Consumer Sciences
    Instructor
South Kitsap High School
Port Orchard, Washington

Linda J. Hupka
Early Childhood Teacher
Bremerton School District
Bremerton, Washington

Eleanor L. Keppler, M.S., CFCS
Family and Consumer Sciences
    Department Head
Lawrence Central High School
Indianapolis, Indiana

Georgia P. Lamirand, M.S.
Occupational Child Care Instructor
Francis Tuttle Tech Center
Oklahoma City, Oklahoma

Marlene S. Lobberecht, M.S., CFCS
Family and Consumer Sciences
    Teacher/Laboratory School
    Director
Cypress Creek High School
Houston, Texas

Technical Reviewers

Debra Anthony
Special Education Teacher
Highline School District
Burien, Washington

Glen W. Christen, M.D.
Physician, OB-GYN
Silverdale, Washington

John J. Corrales-Diaz, M.D., F.A.A.P.
Pediatrician
Port Orchard, Washington

Libby Correll
Reading Specialist
Central Kitsap Schools
Silverdale, Washington

Sherrie Ann Cowan
Director, Child Care Resource and
    Referral
Bremerton, Washington

Molly E. Evans, M.A.
Primary Gifted Teacher
Central Kitsap School District
Silverdale, Washington

Katie C. Ladner
Childbirth Educator/Nutrition
    Educator
WIC Program
Belfair, Washington

Ginger A. Lancasters
Elementary Teacher
Central Kitsap School District
Silverdale, Washington

Darlene Guderjan Montz, M.Ed.
Teacher/Parent Educator/Columnist
Yakima, Washington

Frances R. Murphy-Widmer, RN
OB-GYN Consultant
Oshkosh, Wisconsin

Lorraine Olsen, M.S., ECE
Head Start Director
Olympic Educational Service District
Bremerton, Washington

Diane T. Olson, M.S.
Educational Consultant
Gig Harbor, Washington

Rachel Thompson Perkins, M.S.
Child Development Technology
    Instructor
Hinds Community College
Utica, Mississippi

Patricia K.O. Rambo, M.S., CFCS
Tahoka High School
Tahoka, Texas

Harline R. Roberts, M.Ed., CFCS
Family Literacy Resource Teacher
Hillsborough County Schools
Tampa, Florida

Betty Millard Stout, M.A.
Pregnancy Support Coordinator
Tacoma, Washington

Kimberly White, Ed.D.
Teacher
North Kitsap School District
Poulsbo, Washington

 Glencoe

The McGraw·Hill Companies

Send all inquiries to:
Glencoe/McGraw-Hill
3008 W. Willow Knolls Drive
Peoria, IL 61615-1083

ISBN 0-07-846256-8 (Student Edition)
ISBN 0-07-846257-6 (Teacher Wraparound Edition)

Printed in the United States of America

2 3 4 5 6 7 8 9 10   071   08 07 06 05 04 03

CONTENTS IN BRIEF

CONTENTS

FEATURES

Parenting With Care

CAREER OPPORTUNITIES

Practicing Parenting

Ask the Experts

Meet the Experts

Pat Brodeen
Teen Parent Coordinator

Pat Brodeen received her bachelor and master of science degrees from Texas Tech University, where she specialized in child development and family studies. She has taught at Theodore Roosevelt High School in San Antonio, Texas, for more than 25 years. Twelve years ago, Ms. Brodeen began teaching a class for teen parents. She finds her greatest reward in watching a teen develop into a responsible parent. She advises teen parents to "stay in school if you want to provide a good life for yourself and your baby."

Dr. Van D. Stone
Pediatrician

Dr. Stone is practicing pediatrician in Tupelo, Mississippi. He received his medical degree at the University of Mississippi Medical Center at Jackson, Mississippi, and his pediatric training at Arkansas Children's Hospital. Over the last twenty years he has seen a substantial change in the area of children's nutrition and is pleased that "parents of all ages are open to new ideas and methods of quality care." Many of his patients' mothers are teens whose mothers participate in raising their grandchildren. He finds that these younger grandmothers are familiar with current trends in child care, and he values the wisdom of their experience.

Jacqueline Mault
Director of Special Services

Jacqueline Mault, who received her doctorate from the University of Oregon, has worked in early childhood education administration, in a state Department of Education, in a public school, and as a consultant. As Director of Special Services in Toppenish, Washington, she develops and manages programs for children from birth through high school. Dr. Mault urges people to "continue to meet the demands of changing families and work within communities for quality, comprehensive care and education."

Rachel Thompson Perkins
College Instructor of Child Development Technology

Rachel Thompson Perkins is a Child Development Technology Instructor at Hinds Community College in Utica, Mississippi. She received her master of science degree in Home Economics from Mississippi College, specializing in Child Development. She has worked in the public school system for more than 21 years teaching family and consumer sciences and occupational child care and guidance. She was very instrumental in beginning a school-to-work program and an after-school program for the lab school. Her main goal in teaching is to ensure that students "reach their potential while helping them develop a marketable skill."

Jean Illsley Clarke
Author and Parenting Workshop Facilitator

Jean Illsley Clarke is the director of J.I. Consultants in Minneapolis, where she designs and directs workshops in self-esteem, parenting, and group dynamics. She has written several books, magazine articles, and journal articles; appeared in videotapes and hosted a local television show; and received an honorary doctorate from Sierra University in Costa Mesa, California. Much of her background comes from teaching and conducting research abroad. These experiences have convinced her that "all human needs are the same, and children are best cared for by adults whose needs are met."

UNIT 1 OBJECTIVES

After completing Unit 1, students will be able to:

- Explain the benefits of studying child development.
- Describe the importance of families.
- Identify ways of guiding children's behavior and factors to consider in selecting child care.
- Explain how teens can avoid pregnancy.

UNIT 1 OVERVIEW

In **Chapter 1**, students consider the importance of childhood as a time for growth and development and evaluate career opportunities related to child development and care.

Chapter 2 explores the importance of family units and explains how couples can decide whether to become parents.

Chapter 3 teaches students effective techniques of guiding children and examines substitute child care.

In **Chapter 4**, students learn about the problem-solving process and making choices about sexual activity and pregnancy.

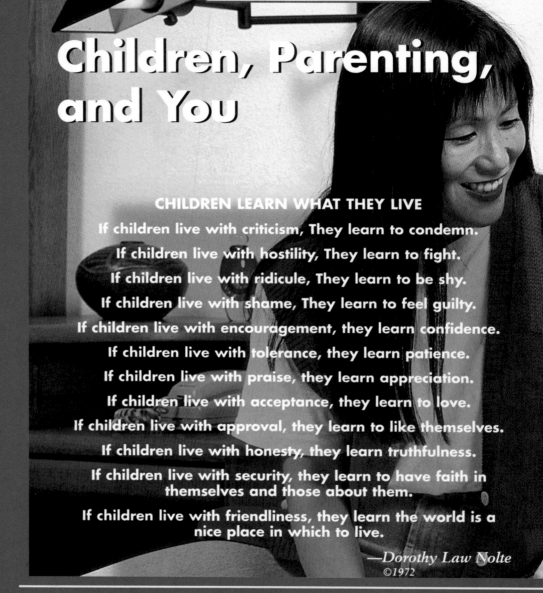

UNIT 1

Children, Parenting, and You

CHILDREN LEARN WHAT THEY LIVE

If children live with criticism, They learn to condemn.

If children live with hostility, They learn to fight.

If children live with ridicule, They learn to be shy.

If children live with shame, They learn to feel guilty.

If children live with encouragement, they learn confidence.

If children live with tolerance, they learn patience.

If children live with praise, they learn appreciation.

If children live with acceptance, they learn to love.

If children live with approval, they learn to like themselves.

If children live with honesty, they learn truthfulness.

If children live with security, they learn to have faith in themselves and those about them.

If children live with friendliness, they learn the world is a nice place in which to live.

—Dorothy Law Nolte
©1972

16 UNIT 1: Children, Parenting, and You

USING THE POEM	Dorothy Law Nolte's poem recognizes the important role that parents, caregivers, and family members play in shaping a child's self-esteem. Ask for a student volunteer to read aloud the poem; then have students create a	poem, story, or piece of art that reflects their individual thoughts and attitudes about children. Have the students share their creations in small groups or, if time allows, with the entire class.

INTRODUCING UNIT 1

- Display photographs of infants and children; if possible, include children from various cultures around the world. **Ask:** What do all these children have in common? What makes each child unique? How can learning how all children develop help you care for an individual child?
- **Ask:** What kind of feelings do the people in the photograph seem to share? What kind of relationship do you think they have? How will that relationship influence the child as she grows up?

COMPLETING UNIT 1

EXTENSION

Write on the board William Wordsworth's sentence, "The child is the father to the man." Have students create a work—an essay, a collage, or a multimedia presentation-that explores the meaning of this phrase.

EVALUATION

Use the Unit 1 Test on the Exam*View*® Test Generator or use the program to create your own test.

FCCLA Connection — Career Planning

Have students choose one general career area related to children that interest them. Based on this choice, have them plan a possible career—a series of related jobs—including at least three positions at different levels. Then have them identify what would be required to move to successively higher levels.

17

COMMUNITY AS CLASSROOM

Guest Speakers. The class could benefit by hearing from several professionals during the study of this unit. *For Chapter* 1: historian, child care center worker, career counselor. *For Chapter 2:* family counselor, social worker. *For Chapter 3:* parenting workshop leader, child psychologist. *For Chapter 4:* adoption agency counselor, welfare worker, teen mother and father.

Field Trips. The class could take field trips to a child care center or a career counseling service to enhance their study of this unit.

CHAPTER 1 RESOURCES

Teacher Resource Guide
• Chapter 1 Test, pp. 93-96
• Authentic Assessment,
  pp. 257-258
Student Motivation Kit
• Observations, pp. 27-28
Transparency Package
• CT-1 to CT-5
Effective Instruction CD-ROM

CHAPTER 1   OVERVIEW

In **Section 1-1**, students learn the benefits they gain by studying children. In **Section 1-2**, students explore child development and learn about the characteristics of development. In **Section 1-3**, students learn guidelines for observing children. In **Section 1-4**, students learn how to research jobs and analyze careers.

CHAPTER 1   OBJECTIVES

After completing Chapter 1, students will be able to:

• Identify the benefits of studying children.
• Explain the characteristics and leading theories of child development.
• Outline guidelines for observing children.
• Identify methods of researching jobs and factors to use to analyze careers.

CHAPTER 1

Learning About Children

RESOURCES TO EXPLORE

Child-Related Issues. Studying this chapter may motivate students to extend their awareness of children and child-related issues. You can get information such as the condition of children in your state and how elected officials vote on children's issues from the Children's Defense Fund (CDF). To request this information, write the group at 25 E Street NW, Washington, DC 20001, or access their web site at www.childrensdefense.org

Seven-month-old Chen is lucky, although he does not know it. Chen's parents talk to him constantly as they move about the house. They talk to him while they are changing his diaper and getting his food ready. They talk to him while they are bathing him and feeding him. His mother talks to him while running errands as Chen sits in his car seat. Everyone in the family talks to him when they go rollerblading after dinner while he rides in the stroller. His parents take turns singing to him when they put him to sleep at night. The next morning, when Chen wakes up, the talking starts all over again.

The constant talking is amazing because Chen—only seven months old—cannot answer back. Chen is lucky because all this talking is one of the best influences on his growing brain.

"Talking to a young child is one of the best influences on brain development."

- Tape record a young infant crying vigorously. As students enter the classroom, play the tape loudly and display a life-sized baby doll. Have volunteers use the doll to demonstrate what they would do for a crying baby. **Ask:** How confident do you feel caring for a crying infant—or an energetic four-year-old? How would having confidence help?
- **Ask:** What do you notice about how the father is talking to the baby? *(He's crouched to the baby's level; he's leaning close.)* Why is he doing that? *(So baby feels comfortable.)*

USING THE SCENARIO Have students read the story in the student text. Call on volunteers to share their own experiences talking to small children. Have them describe what kinds of things they talked about, what tone of voice they used, and how the children reacted.

KEY TO ABILITY LEVELS Each section gives skill-building activities. Each activity has been labeled for use with students of various learning styles and abilities.

L1 Level 1 activities are basic activities and should be within the range of all students.

L2 Level 2 activities are average activities and should be within the range of average and above average students.

L3 Level 3 activities are challenging activities designed for the ability range of above average students.

SECTION 1-1

Beginning Your Study of Children

(pages 20-25)

FOCUS

MOTIVATOR

Write the following statement on the board: "Studying children will help me understand myself by . . ." Ask for volunteers to complete the statement. After several students have answered, explain that as they read this section, they will learn more about how studying children can affect them.

VOCABULARY ACTIVITY

Ask for volunteers to define the terms. If necessary, help students by pointing out the relationship between *behavior* and *behave* and *development* and *develop*.

Beginning Your Study of Children

Have you ever seen a baby's delight as he plays peekaboo? Have you ever seen the look of triumph on a five-year-old's face as she ties her shoes? If so, you may have felt a surge of pleasure yourself. Children's mastery of new tasks reminds older people of just how far they themselves have come.

KEY TERMS

behaviors
caregivers
child development

OBJECTIVES:

• Explain why childhood is an important time of development.

• Identify ways that play benefits children.

• Describe reasons for studying children.

Why Is Childhood Crucial?

Childhood is a time of preparation. Scientists are finding that early childhood may be the most important stage of life for a person. They have learned that in the first few years of life, the brain develops connections between nerve cells that allow it to think and control the body in certain ways.

Observing & Participating

Have each student write a paragraph describing what they have observed in children they know. They could comment on the children's behavior, language, or personality. After writing their paragraphs, students should list any questions they have about children. What don't they understand about children? What puzzles them? Call on volunteers to read their paragraphs and questions to the class and discuss them.

These connections do not simply happen on their own. They can be encouraged when caregivers give a child lots of stimulation—especially by talking to him or her often. The links that develop in the child's brain promote mental and physical skills. They also have an impact on the social and emotional characteristics of that person as an adult.

Another way children form these links is through play. Researchers have learned a great deal about **child development**, the study of how children master new skills. They have found, for instance, that children benefit from play in many ways:

- **Physically.** Activities such as running, climbing, jumping rope, and riding a bicycle help the large muscles of the back, arms, and legs develop. Making jigsaw puzzles, finger painting, and stringing beads all help a child learn to control the small muscles of the hands.
- **Socially.** At first children play alone. Gradually, they learn to play together. From this play, they learn how to take turns, work together toward a common goal, lead, and follow.
- **Emotionally.** Play can help children work through life's challenges and problems. For example, acting out the role of a parent, firefighter, or jungle explorer can lessen the frustrations of being a small person in a big world.
- **Morally.** Play teaches valuable lessons about right and wrong. Through play, children learn to follow rules and act fairly toward others. They learn to share and to encourage the efforts of others.

Giving children a loving, caring environment does more than help them have a healthy childhood. It helps them prepare for the future. *What responsibilities do you think parents have toward children?*

COMPREHENSION CHECK

1. How can caregivers help in the development of a child's brain? (*With stimulation.*)
2. What is child development? (*The study of how children master new skills.*)

ACTIVITIES

Critical Thinking Activity

Analyzing. **Ask:** Why do some people get along very well with children? Is this due to a natural talent or is it a learned skill? **L2**

Teamwork Activity

Have students work in small groups. Have each group agree on a play activity that they enjoyed as children or that children they care for enjoy. Have them discuss how this play benefits children in at least three of the five areas described in the text. Have each group illustrate these benefits in a poster. Display posters on the bulletin board. **L2**

VISUAL LEARNING	Using the Photograph

Possible responses: Giving them food, clothing, shelter, making sure they are healthy; giving them love.

LEARNING STYLES	Interpersonal; Kinesthetic

Organize students into small groups and assign each group an area of development. Have the groups write a skit in which they illustrate activities they could do with children under their care to promote development in that area. After the groups present their skits, have the class evaluate the different activities. Would a child have benefited from them? Would a child have enjoyed them? What ages would the activity be appropriate for?

ACTIVITIES

Critical Thinking Activity

Drawing Conclusions. **Ask:** Why is it important to understand not just how children act, feel, and think, but also *why* they act, feel, and think in those ways? **L2**

VISUAL LEARNING	Using the Photograph

Possible responses: Stacking, colors, letters, numbers, balance.

DID *You* **Know?**

Studying Child Development. Child development is a fairly new discipline. Until the 1900s, society was relatively unconcerned with childhood. The study of child development had its beginnings early in this century, as specialists in anthropology, education, medicine, nutrition, nursing, physiology, psychology, social work, and sociology worked together at universities to educate themselves and each other in the common problems of the developing child.

Play makes an essential contribution to all five areas of child development. *How many different things can this child learn from playing with blocks?*

- **Intellectually.** A toy or game doesn't have to be "educational" to promote mental development. Simple activities such as singing nursery rhymes, stacking blocks, and sorting through a box of buttons help a child learn language, balance, and how to organize objects.

Why Study Children?

You can benefit from studying children in many ways. You can improve your understanding of how children grow and change. Studying children can also improve your understanding of yourself—and help you think about your future.

To Understand Children

In studying children, you will read about them, observe them, talk with them, play with them, and help them. In the process, your understanding of children will grow:

- **You will better understand why children act, feel, and think as they do.** It can be difficult to understand children, especially before they learn how to talk. Yet there is a set of typical **behaviors**—ways of acting or responding—for each stage of childhood. For example, Denise was puzzled that her two-year-old brother never played with a two-year-old neighbor boy, even when they were in the same room. Then Denise learned in her child development class that it's normal for two-year-olds to play alongside each other but not with each other.

- **You will understand the importance of caregivers.** Parents and others who take care of children are called **caregivers.** As you learn how children develop, you will see why they depend on others for such a long time. You will also learn why they need affection to grow emotionally and why they need the guidance and support of older people.

Finally, by learning about children, you'll come to see that children are fun. The more time you spend with children, the more you can appreciate how delightful they are. In their innocence, humor, generous affection, and curious minds, they are fascinating—and rewarding—to be with.

Management/Leadership Skills

Stress to students that there is a set of typical behaviors for each stage of childhood. Then have students work with partners to identify five situations in which a specific behavior is appropriate for a child of one age but not for a child of another age. Ask students to share their ideas with the rest of the class. Discuss how parents can use this information as they raise children.

To Gain Skills

As you learn about children, you will also gain many skills. You'll learn what children need at each stage of development and how to meet those needs.

You will have opportunities to apply your growing knowledge whether in a child care center, as a babysitter, or in your own family. The practice that you gain as a caregiver will make you a more effective one, too. Knowing how to bathe a baby, prepare a nutritious meal for a toddler, or encourage a three-year-old to settle down for a nap will give you confidence. Children feel more comfortable with people who care for them with confidence.

In studying child development, you can understand what foods are appropriate for children of different ages. *Why do you think this child might need to eat soft foods?*

To Understand Yourself

As you learn to understand children better, you will also come to know yourself better. You will learn more about what makes you the person you are.

You may think of yourself as a different person from the child you once were. It's true that you have grown and changed in many ways. No one changes completely, however. Who you are right now has developed from the child you once were and will continue to develop into your adult self. Experience, education, and life's situations help you mature. Still, the self you have already developed will always be part of you.

Ask family members or older friends what you were like as a young child. They may describe you as quiet, amazingly independent, or constantly active. Do those descriptions match how you are today?

To Build for the Future

Your increased understanding of children will be valuable not only now, but also throughout your life. Today, it may help you become a better babysitter, teacher's aide, or playground supervisor. In the future, your knowledge may help you as a parent or in a career related to children.

You will have opportunities to practice essential life skills. These include management, goal setting, problem solving, and decision making.

Studying children can also help you make career decisions. One student was planning on being a nurse until he took a child development course. By the end of the course, he wanted to be a teacher. "Now that I understand them better," he explained, "I like kids more than I used to."

Ask the E❓perts

Introducing the Feature

Ask students to brainstorm ways they can make a difference in a child's life. Record ideas on the board.

Answers to Thinking It Through
1. Children learn by modeling themselves on your behavior. *Possible example:* Children who see their parents show tolerance to others will show tolerance themselves.
2. *Answers will vary but should include specific points.*

Applying What You've Learned

Ask students to think about parents, teachers, and caregivers who stand out as role models. Have students choose one of these people (without identifying the person) and write a paragraph describing what qualities make the person a role model and how that person helps guide their own behavior with children. Ask volunteers to share what they wrote with the class. Have the class discuss the desirability of the different characteristics identified. **L1**

Ask the E❓perts

Rachel Perkins
Child Development Technology Instructor
Hinds Community College
Utica, Mississippi

MAKING *a Difference in a Child's Life*

 What can I do to make a difference in a child's life?

You're off to a good start in making a positive difference to children—you are interested, and you are concerned about learning to help children. Even your attitude in itself is a contribution to a child with whom you spend time.

I think what you need now is a chance to watch others work with children; you also need many comfortable experiences with children that will help you develop your own abilities and confidence.

Probably the best way to learn about interacting with children is to watch parents and teachers who work successfully with young children. Take time to observe these experienced people carefully. How do they talk to children? How do they listen? How do they use words, facial expressions, and physical contact to encourage and support children? How do they use positive reinforcement to guide children's behavior?

After your observation, think about how each teacher or parent approached the children. Which of these approaches will you feel comfortable using when you interact with children?

Remember when you observe successful parents and teachers, you are looking at models. As you learn more and more about children and about successful approaches and attitudes, you will develop your own personal style of interacting successfully with young children.

It's also important to remember that, just as teachers and parents serve as your models, you serve as a model for young children. Young children will observe—and try out for themselves—the words, attitudes, and actions that you demonstrate.

Thinking It Through

1. How do children learn from you when you are a caregiver? Give a specific example.
2. Think of someone whom you admire. How can you model your behavior on that person?

Management/Leadership Skills

Ask students to find out about the kinds of jobs that are related to children. Have students compile a list of these jobs in a bulletin-board display. Then have students look through their local newspaper to find want ads for jobs that are related to caring for children. Display these ads on the bulletin board as well. Discuss with the class how learning about children might benefit their career choices in the future.

Finally, learning about children can help you think about parenthood and prepare for its responsibilities. One student in a parenting course said, "I never realized that being a parent was so much work!"

Children and You

You are in an excellent position to study children—close to adulthood and able to think and reason but young enough that you can still remember what it was like to be a child. As you learn, you'll find some of your opinions reinforced and others challenged. You'll discover answers to questions that puzzled you—and find new questions that have no answers yet. Perhaps someday you will help answer them.

English poet William Wordsworth revealed a truth when he wrote, "The child is the father to the man." Childhood is a vital and significant time. In this period, the foundations are laid for the person who will be an adult. Knowing about childhood can help you help children build a strong foundation. It can also give you insight into the foundation you built for yourself.

SECTION 1-1 REVIEW

✔ Check Your Understanding

1. Why is childhood an important time of life?
2. What is one way parents and other caregivers stimulate the development of connections in a child's brain?
3. Name the five areas in which children benefit from play. Give an example of how children benefit from a particular kind of play.
4. Identify four reasons to study children.
5. Why is it helpful if caregivers are confident?
6. Would you assume two-year-olds and four-year-olds act the same when frustrated? Why or why not?

Putting Knowledge Into Practice

1. **Comparing.** Think of two younger children you know who are two different ages. Compare how they play. What kinds of play activities do they prefer? How do they act when they play?
2. **Applying.** Make a poster that expresses how you are a unique person.
3. **Observing and Participating.** Look at all the different people in your class. Write a paragraph explaining the range of different talents and abilities your classmates possess.

CHAPTER 1: Learning About Children **25**

ANSWERS TO SECTION 1-1 REVIEW

1. Connections in the brain are formed, affecting future development.
2. Talking to child frequently.
3. Physically, socially, emotionally, morally, and intellectually.
4. To understand children, to gain skills, to understand yourself, and to build for future.
5. Children are more comfortable with them.
6. No, they respond in different ways because they are at different developmental stages.

ASSESS

CHECKING COMPREHENSION

Have students answer the Check Your Understanding questions. Answers appear at the bottom of this page.

EVALUATION

Give students the Section 1-1 Quiz in the *Teacher Resource Guide*.

RETEACHING

1. Assign Reteaching Activities, page 7.
2. Ask students to write two paragraphs that relate their own experiences caring for children or explain how studying child development can help them in the future.

ENRICHMENT

Have students interview one or two parents about the rewards and responsibilities of being parents.

EXTENSION

Have graduates of the course speak to the class about how the course benefited them in parenthood or career. Allow students to ask questions.

CLOSE

Have students respond to the following statement: "Only students who already are parents or who want careers in child-related fields should study child development."

SECTION 1-2 RESOURCES

Teacher Resource Guide
- Lesson Plan Organizer, p. 34
- Section 1-2 Quiz, p. 90

Student Motivation Kit
- Reteaching Activity, p. 8
- Enrichment, p. 5

Student Workbook
- Study Guide, pp. 7-11
- Describing Development, pp. 14-15

Transparency Package
- CT-2 Child Development Theorists
- CT-3 Characteristics of Development

Effective Instruction CD-ROM

FOCUS

MOTIVATOR

Write the following on the board: "Taylor is like a child." **Ask:** What specific traits can you think of that would make this statement about an adult a criticism? A compliment? Have students generalize about the differences between childhood and adulthood on the basis of these responses.

VOCABULARY ACTIVITY

Help students read and discuss the vocabulary words. Ask them to share the science-related definition of environment, then relate it to child development.

Understanding Childhood

Think back to when you were a child. How did it feel when you could not do something that you wanted to do, such as tie your shoes? How did it feel when you *did* manage to tie them? What makes children different from adults?

KEY TERMS

adolescence
developmental tasks
environment
heredity
neurons
self-esteem
sequence

OBJECTIVES:
- Compare childhood in the past and present.
- Outline the leading ideas about how children develop.
- Describe five principles of development.
- Explain influences on development.
- Explain the role of self-esteem in development.

What Is Childhood?

Childhood is a period of life separate from adulthood. During this period, development occurs very rapidly. Babies are almost completely dependent on adults for every need. When childhood ends, people begin to prepare to be independent.

26 UNIT 1: Children, Parenting, and You

Observing & Participating

Have students observe children at play. Then read these quotations: "Childhood is a blissful time of play and fantasizing, of uninhibited sensual delight." (Clare Booth Luce) ". . . in all of our efforts to provide 'advantages' we have actually produced the busiest, most competitive, highly pressured and over-organized generation of youngsters in our history." (Eda J. LeShan)
Ask: Was the play they saw blissful or more structured? What impact will this type of play have on the children's lives?

People today see childhood as a special stage of life, but that was not always the case. **How has research into child development—like watching children at play—changed that?**

Many people have made a special study of this period. They have looked at how children develop, what their needs are, and how those needs can best be met. Perhaps their most important finding is that childhood has a profound influence on later life.

Childhood has not always been considered a separate, important stage of life, however. In fact, childhood—as we know it—is a fairly recent "discovery."

Childhood Past and Present

Until the twentieth century, few people in Western civilization believed that there was anything unusual or important about the early years of life. Adults knew little about the special needs of children. That has changed since 1900. Some of the differences between childhood in the past and today result from changing attitudes. Others grew out of advances in technology or social changes.

- **Work.** In the past, children were expected to work hard at an early age. Today, most children in our society are not part of the world of adult work. They may help around the house or have part-time jobs. Nowadays, though, the "job" of young children is simply to grow, learn, and play.
- **Play.** In the past, when children did play, they had fewer toys than today's children. Until the 1800s, toys were often homemade, carved out of wood or made from other natural materials. Even common games like baseball, football, and basketball didn't develop until the middle or late 1800s. Video games became available only in the 1970s.
- **Education.** Public education for all children did not become widespread in the United States until the early 1800s. Even then, schools were small and often included children of different ages and abilities. Today, schools are larger than the one-room schools of the past. Students now use modern technology such as computers to learn.

CHAPTER 1: Learning About Children **27**

COMPREHENSION CHECK

1. How were schools in the past different from today? *(Smaller; included children of different ages.)*
2. How has children's health improved? *(Fewer children die; better nutrition.)*

ACTIVITIES

Teamwork Activity

Organize students in small groups. Have each group list examples of parental love. Have the groups read their lists to the class. Discuss whether physical affection is the only way for parents to show love. What else can parents do to show their children their love? **L1**

VISUAL LEARNING | Using the Photograph

Answer. Answers will vary but may include buying them more things, more physical displays of affection.

INFOLINK

Brain Development

See Section 8-2, pp. 260-267, for more on the *brain*. Also look for the brain symbols throughout the book.

Do you think the ways parents show their children love today is different than in the past? If so, how?

- **Health.** Before the twentieth century, parents could not hope to raise every child born to them. Diseases caused the deaths of children in almost every family. In developed countries today, deadly diseases have been controlled. Better nutrition has helped children grow and thrive as never before.
- **Dress.** Until the seventeenth century, children were dressed as small adults. Around that time, children's clothing became more common, although these styles didn't permit much activity or play. Today, many boys and girls wear clothing that is similar in style and color. Practical, washable, lightweight clothing allows them comfort and freedom of movement.
- **Parental love.** Although childhood in the past was different in many ways from today, one thing hasn't changed— parents' love for their children. Parents have always worked hard to build lives for their children and to raise them as moral, responsible people.

28 UNIT 1: Children, Parenting, and You

DID You Know?

Childhood Diseases. Diphtheria, typhoid fever, and smallpox were dreaded diseases that killed many children, as well as adults, in the past. Cotton Mather, an early New England settler, saw eight of his fifteen children die before they even reached age two. By 1900, as many as two out of every five American families suffered the death of a child. Why is there new concern about such diseases today?

Ask if students have read or seen a film version of a novel by Charles Dickens. Point out that these works portray the lives of children during the nineteenth century. **Ask:** How do those children's lives compare with children's lives today? **L3**

Discussion Activity

Ask: Are parents today more or less likely to raise their children as they themselves were raised? Why or why not? **L2**

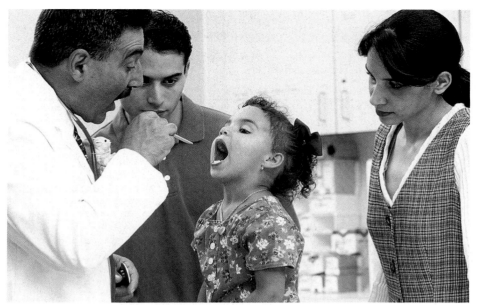

Children's lives have changed in many ways from the past to the present. They are less likely to work and spend more time in school. *How have advances in health care changed children's lives?*

The Study of Children

Many researchers have studied children closely. They have developed theories about development. Not everyone agrees on how parents and educators should apply their findings. Still, taken together, these scientists have made great strides in understanding how children develop. The chart on pages 30-31 summarizes the work of some major researchers. You will learn more about theories of child development throughout this book.

 **Brain Research**

One of the most important areas of recent research has been about the work-ings of the brain. What scientists have learned has great significance for caregivers.

At birth, the brain has billions of nerve cells called **neurons** (NER-ons). Babies immediately begin to develop pathways that link their neurons. These links "wire," or program, the brain so that it can control different body functions and thinking processes. The wiring of the brain takes place very quickly. Babies just four days old respond more to their parents' language than to another language. A two-year-old has almost as many of these pathways as an adult.

The areas of the brain that control different kinds of learning reach their peak at different times. The illustration on pages 32-33 shows the differences.

CHAPTER 1: Learning About Children **29**

The Developing Brain

 **Brain Development**

A baby's brain has about 100 billion nerve cells at birth. Starting shortly after birth, a baby's brain produces trillions of connections between the neurons. Most of the connections are made between birth and three years of age. This process is influenced by good nutrition and the kinds of stimulation the child's environment provides. Children who do not play much or are not touched much develop brains that are between 20 and 30 percent smaller than normal for their age. Students can read more about this process in Section 8-2.

Observing & Participating

Bring to class, or have students bring to class, reproductions of paintings in art or history books. Ask students to find examples of paintings showing children in earlier centuries. (An example of such a painting is Goya's The Family of Charles IV, which shows children dressed as adults in 1800.) Have students observe the kinds of clothing worn by these children. Then have them compare the styles worn by children in previous centuries to the styles worn by children today.

COMPREHENSION CHECK

1. Which researcher first suggested that the experiences of childhood influence adults? (Freud.)
2. Which researcher suggested that development follows a pattern? (Gesell or Piaget.)
3. Which researcher studied the psychological crises that each person went through? (Erikson)

ACTIVITIES

Critical Thinking Activity

Applying. Refer students to the ideas of Maria Montessori. Have them imagine that they are caring for a three-year-old. Based on Montessori's ideas, have students describe how they would play with the child to promote learning. Call on volunteers to share their ideas with the rest of the class. **L3**

VISUAL LEARNING

Using the Chart

Ask: How are the entries organized? (They are chronological by birthdate of the theorist.) Why are they placed in this order? (So students can more easily see how ideas of childhood changed over time.)

INFOLINK

Piaget

For more about *Piaget,* see pages 324-328 and 535-537.

> ## Major Theorists of Child Development

These are just a few of the researchers and thinkers who have added to our understanding of child development in the twentieth century.

Theorist	Findings or Ideas	Significance
Sigmund Freud (1856-1939)	Freud believed that personality develops through a series of stages. Emotional experiences in childhood have profound effects on a person as an adult.	The idea that early experiences affect adult life has profound importance for anyone caring for a child.
Maria Montessori (1870-1952)	Montessori stressed that children learn by using their senses and that they learn best by pursuing their interests.	Children need to be given objects to manipulate so they can exercise their sensory learning.
Arnold Gesell (1880-1961)	Gesell developed basic information about the order in which children master various skills and the typical rate of this development.	Parents and other caregivers need to be aware of the standard course of development.
Jean Piaget (1896-1980)	Piaget, the first to study children in a scientific way, focused on how children learned. He said that children go through four stages of thinking that shape how they see and learn about the world.	Children should be given learning tasks that are suitable for their stage of thinking.
Lev Vygotsky (1898-1934)	Vygotsky believed that both biological development and cultural experience influenced children's ability to think and learn. He said social contact was essential for intellectual development.	Children should have many opportunities for social interaction to develop intellectually.
Erik Erikson (1902-1994)	Erikson, like Freud, said personality develops through stages. He thought that each stage includes a unique psychological crisis. If that crisis is met in a positive way, the individual develops normally.	Parents and other caregivers must be aware of a child's needs at a particular stage and be sensitive to the child's needs at that stage.

30 UNIT 1: Children, Parenting, and You

Management/Leadership Skills

Read the following to students: "Marta took care of her little brother Ramon for two hours each day after school. Ramon liked to play with his toys and often had many of them strewn around the living room when he had finished playing."

Ask: How could Marta use Skinner's ideas to get Ramon to put away his toys when he finished playing? What positive reinforcement could Marta give Ramon to encourage him to put away his toys?

Major Theorists of Child Development Continued

Theorist	Findings or Ideas	Significance
B. F. Skinner (1904-1990)	Skinner argued that when a child's action repeatedly brings positive effects, it will be repeated and learned. When negative results repeatedly occur, the child will eventually stop the action.	Parents and other caregivers can use rewards and punishments to try to influence a child's behavior.
Abraham Maslow (1908-1970)	Maslow believed in a pyramid-shaped Hierarchy of Needs. He said that for personal growth, needs must be met in order: physiological, safety, love and belonging, and self-esteem. Self-actualization is the highest.	To reach their full potential in life, children's needs must be met sequentially, moving them up the pyramid.
Albert Bandura (1925-)	Bandura said that children learn by modeling. He disagreed with Skinner. He pointed out that although the environment shapes behavior, behavior also affects the environment.	Since children learn by modeling, parents and caregivers must provide good examples.
Robert Coles (1929-)	Coles has studied children's moral development. He stresses the important role that parents and other caregivers play by the examples they set.	For children to adopt moral learning, parents must show moral behavior.

What Researchers Have Found

None of these researchers has provided all the answers to questions about how children develop. Taken together, though, their findings and ideas have revealed much.

Characteristics of Development

As you have read, children develop through certain stages. Researchers have found that this development follows five patterns:

- **Development is similar for everyone.** Children go through the same stages in about the same order. For example, all babies lift their head before they lift their body and stand before they can walk.

1. Which researcher argued that positive results of an action will lead to the action being repeated? *(Skinner.)*
2. Which researchers are still active? *(Bandura, Coles.)*

ACTIVITIES

Critical Thinking Activity

Categorizing. Have students organize the theorists according to the area of child development that they studied. **Ask:** Which were involved in personality formation? (*Freud, Erikson, Maslow.*) Intellectual development? (*Montessori, Gesell, Piaget, Vygotsky, Skinner, Bandura.*) Social development? (*Vygotsky, Bandura, Coles.*) Point out that some researchers are involved in more than one area. Remind students that in human behavior, many different areas of activity overlap. **L2**

DID *You* **Know?**

Development. **Development refers to the changes over time in the structure, thought, or behavior of a person as a result of biological and environmental influences. Usually, these changes are cumulative and progressive—that is, they build on each other and move the person to more advanced skills. They generally produce increased size and complexity of behavior. Some types of development—such as prenatal growth—are primarily biological. Others—such as emotional growth—depends greatly on the environment. Most involves a mix of the two factors.**

When the brain is ready to learn

The brain is most ready to learn different tasks at different times. The area of the brain that controls vision is active by the second month of life. The part that relates to reasoning becomes active as early as six months. How can parents use these windows of opportunity?

32

Parenting in *Action*

Research has revealed that the kind of care a child receives has a great impact on brain development. Experts offer parents these guidelines:
• Be warm, loving, and responsive.
• Provide good nutrition.
• Talk, read, and sing to your child.

• Establish routines and rituals.
• Encourage safe exploration and play.
• Limit television watching.
• Use discipline as an opportunity to teach.
• Recognize that each child is unique.
• Choose quality child care and stay involved.

Math/logic: Starting at age one

Vision: Starting in the first year

Vocabulary: Starting in the first year

Acquiring a second language: Starting at age one

Emotional control: Starting in the first year

Motor development: Starting before birth

Music: Starting at age three

Social attachment: Starting in the first year

CHAPTER 1: Learning About Children **33**

Teamwork Activity

Have students work in groups to study the sequence of skills mastery in child development. Have each group select a skill, such as self-feeding or walking. Then have them write up a sequence of earlier skills on which that skill is based. **L2**

Critical Thinking Activity

Analyzing. Have students suggest skills and qualities that make a good caregiver. **Ask:** What could someone who doesn't have these skills or qualities do to obtain them? **L2**

ISSUES IN

CHILDREN'S HEALTH

The Pace of Development. Development takes place at an individual rate—each child proceeds at a unique pace. Discuss the relationship between the individual rate of development and the safety of a child. Some children at age three may be able to use playground equipment independently, while others may not be physically developed enough and may need assistance and careful watching. Ask students to give other examples of how knowing a child's individual rate of development is important to the safety of the child.

Parenting in *Action*

Have students brainstorm activities that they could undertake to promote a child's development at each of these peak periods of brain activity. You might form students into groups, assigning each group one of the eight types of learning that are highlighted. Or each group could take all eight areas and then, after meeting, compare their findings. In the class discussion, have students agree on what they think are the best suggestions for each area and write them in their notebooks.

COMPREHENSION CHECK

1. How does the development of different children compare? *(Follows the same sequence but at different rates.)*
2. When does development end? *(It continues throughout life.)*
3. How do heredity and environment interact? *(They affect each other.)*

ACTIVITIES

Discussion Activity

Point out to students that for young children, the family is the most important environmental influence. Ask students to give examples of how families influence children's development. **L1**

Teamwork Activity

Organize students into small groups. Have groups create a Venn diagram that includes three labels: "Heredity," "Environment," and "Both" and list under each label the characteristics that they believe are influenced by heredity, environment, or both. Discuss as a class the contents of the diagrams. **L2**

Nature or Nurture Debate

Hold a class debate in which students argue that either "nature" or "nurture" is stronger. **L3**

- **Development builds on earlier learning.** Development follows a step-by-step pattern, a **sequence**. The skills a child learns at one stage build directly on those mastered earlier. Before learning to run, a child must learn to walk. Before learning to speak in sentences, a child must learn to say single words.
- **Development proceeds at an individual rate.** Although all children follow a similar pattern of development, each child is an individual. The rate of growth differs from one child to another.
- **The different areas of development are interrelated.** Researchers find it easier to focus on one area of development at a time. In fact, however, changes in many areas are taking place at the same time.
- **Development is continuous throughout life.** The rate of development changes. Sometimes it is more rapid and sometimes less so. Still, development never stops.

Influences on Development

Each child develops as an individual because of the unique combination of factors that he or she experiences. Those factors can be placed in two categories:

- **Heredity.** One important influence is **heredity** (huh-RED-uht-ee), the passing on of certain characteristics from earlier generations. Blood type, eye color, and hair color are some characteristics set by heredity.
- **Environment.** Another major influence is the **environment,** the people, places, and things that surround and influence a

person. Your family, home, friends, and community are part of your environment.

Scientists and philosophers have debated for many decades about which factor has the stronger influence. Some have said heredity, often called *nature,* whereas others say environment, called *nurture.* Most now agree that the two work together. Psychiatrist Stanley Greenspan summarized this view: "Nature affects nurture affects nature and back and forth."

Consider how heredity and environment have worked together to make you you. From your parents and past generations, you inherited certain physical characteristics. From your family, you also learned certain attitudes and ways of doing things. You have also been influenced by the world around you. What you read, what you see on television, the type of community you live in—all these and countless other factors have shaped who you are as well.

Of course, you don't copy the attitudes and actions of others, either family or friends. Because you are an individual, you react to outside influences in your own way. Still, you are constantly shaped by the people around you and by your experiences.

The same is true for every child. During infancy and early childhood, outside forces have an especially strong influence on development. That is why caring for children is such an important responsibility—and such a challenging opportunity.

Lifelong Growth and Development

As you have read, development continues throughout life. Each person passes through

---

various stages *after* childhood. This is sometimes called the human life cycle. As with the stages of childhood, people follow typical patterns of development through these stages. Of course, people differ in how each individual experiences this pattern.

Development After Childhood

Each stage of life has particular challenges called **developmental tasks**. Meeting those challenges—mastering those tasks—prepares a person for the next stage.

You are now in the middle of **adolescence**, the stage of life between childhood and adulthood. In this important time of growth and change, you have three developmental tasks to achieve:

- Finding your identity.
- Becoming independent.
- Planning for your life's work.

After adolescence comes young adulthood, when a person is in his or her twenties. The young adult finishes preparing for a career and begins working in it. Many people marry in this period.

In middle life, from the thirties to the fifties, a person typically meets these tasks:

- Establishing roots, during the thirties, often means forming a family and settling down to live in a particular place.
- Reevaluating life leads many people in their forties to question the choices that they have made.
- Finding stability and peace, in the fifties, is a matter of readjusting. Very often the children who were born in earlier stages have moved out to make homes of their own. People in their fifties often have a new sense of freedom as a result. They may travel or spend time with friends.

The final stage of adulthood is late life, which covers the years from the sixties on. The main developmental task for a person in this period is to come to terms with life.

Development does not end in childhood—it continues throughout life. *What are the developmental tasks of adolescents?*

CHAPTER 1: Learning About Children **35**

ACTIVITIES

Language Arts Activity

Have students write the journal entry of a fictitious teen. The entry should describe experiences that affected the teen's self-esteem in both negative and positive ways. Ask volunteers to share their work with the class and discuss students' examples. **L2**

VISUAL LEARNING | **Using the Photograph**
Answer: Finding identity, becoming independent, planning life's work.

ISSUES IN CHILDREN'S HEALTH

Enhancing Self-Esteem. An important part of promoting healthy development in children is enhancing their self-esteem (see page 36). Caregivers can:
- genuinely accept the child.
- be interested in the child and concerned about him or her as a person.
- emphasize even the smallest successes.
- give sincere affection.
- praise the child with words.
- spend time with the child, doing something the child wants to do.
- listen intently to what a child has to say.

ISSUES IN TEEN PARENTING

Point out to students that the teen years are not the best time to have children. Have students write a paragraph explaining how the factors that influence development—heredity and environment—might be negative influences on the development of a child of teen parents. For example, a teen parent might be forced to provide an environment that is less positive for a child than the environment an adult could provide. Call on volunteers to share their paragraphs and discuss them with the rest of the class.

ASSESS

CHECKING COMPREHENSION

Have students answer the Check Your Understanding questions. Answers appear at the bottom of this page.

EVALUATION

Give students the Section 1-2 Quiz in the *Teacher Resource Guide*.

RETEACHING

1. Assign Reteaching Activities, page 8.
2. Have students show the influence of heredity and environment by creating a poster with the picture of a child in the center surrounded by images or words showing influences on his or her development.

ENRICHMENT

Have students read a magazine or newspaper article on recent research into development and summarize it for the class.

EXTENSION

Ask a pediatrician to talk to the class about the development of children from birth to age three. Have students prepare questions in advance.

CLOSE

Have students prepare a diagram that shows the five principles of child development.

The Role of Self-Esteem in Development

One resource that can help you meet these developmental tasks—both those of childhood and of adulthood—is something you carry within you. Your **self-esteem** is how you value yourself. If you think of yourself as a worthwhile person, your self-esteem is high. If you think you are not important, you have low self-esteem.

High self-esteem is more than just a good feeling about yourself. It is a tool that you can use to push yourself to achieve new goals. Look at the developmental tasks of adolescence. It may sound simple to say that one task is to plan your future. Making those plans isn't easy, though. You may feel confused trying to sort out what kind of a person you are and what kind of a job you want. Many people do. You may stumble on the road to a career. Many people do. High self-esteem can give you the energy to pick yourself up and the confidence to start moving down that road again.

Perhaps your self-esteem is low. It doesn't have to stay that way. Learning about child development will help you appreciate the tough challenges you have already met. Feel proud of what you have done, and remember that you have the resources within you to do even more.

SECTION 1-2 REVIEW

✔ Check Your Understanding

1. In what five areas does childhood today differ from childhood in the past?
2. Describe the importance of the work of Freud and Erikson in the understanding of young children.
3. What work do the pathways in the brain perform?
4. Identify the five principles of development and explain one.
5. What two factors influence development? Give an example of each.
6. What are the stages of life after childhood?
7. How can self-esteem affect development?

Putting Knowledge Into Practice

1. **Applying.** Give an example of how findings about brain development can be utilized by parents.
2. **Analyzing.** Suppose you heard someone say to a child "Do as I say, not as I do." In light of the ideas of Bandura and Coles, is this an effective way of guiding children's behavior? Why or why not?
3. **Observing and Participating.** Think of an activity that you are able to perform well—perhaps a hobby, a sport, or a subject in school. Create a chart showing how the skills you have or the facts you know now built on skills or facts that you learned earlier.

36   Unit 1: Children, Parenting, and You

ANSWERS TO SECTION 1-2 REVIEW

1. Work, play, education, health, dress.
2. *Freud:* how childhood experiences affect adult life. *Erikson:* how personality develops through stages.
3. Pathways allow brain to control different body functions or processes.
4. *The five principles are on pages 31 and 34.*

Explanations will vary.
5. *Heredity*—eye color, hair color. *Environment*—friends, traditions.
6. Adolescence, young adulthood, middle life, late life.
7. Can give confidence to meet challenges of developmental tasks.

CAREER OPPORTUNITIES

Parent

A CONVERSATON WITH CATHY REYNOLDS

How did you become interested in being a parent? I always wanted to have children. My husband and I simply waited until we were ready for the responsibility.

What are the tasks and responsibilities of being a parent? You name it! You have to teach children and encourage them. You have to help them learn right and wrong, how to tie their shoes, what foods are good for them, and what their name and address is.

What is the work environment like? The work environment is your home. I try to make ours as safe and comfortable and interesting as I can.

What are the working hours like? All day, every day. With the baby, I feed and change her, play with her, then start over again. Just when I have a moment to sit, she wakes up again! Older children need interaction and supervision, too.

What aptitudes are needed to be a parent? The first thing is patience. The second is cheerfulness. You can get very tired with children, but you can't let it show. You have to be curious about things because as they get older, children always ask "why?" Finally, you need to let go. Children have to learn to live their own lives. All you can do is give them the best start you can.

PARENT

Education and Training. Most parents learn on the job, although they can get help and information from classes and from books and other sources.

Career Outlook. Parents will always be in demand.

CONNECTING SCHOOL TO CAREER

1. **Basic Skills.** Write a letter to the editor explaining why you think parents should or should not be paid for their work.
2. **Information.** If you were creating a course for future parents, what information and skills would you teach?

CHAPTER 1: Learning About Children **37**

Building Career Skills

Personal Qualities. Have students write an individual profile of themselves that describes the personal qualities they have that would help them as parents. Once students complete their lists, compile a class list of the qualities that students think are useful for parents. Display the completed list in the classroom.

SECTION 1-3

SECTION 1-3

OBSERVING YOUNG CHILDREN

(pages 38-42)

SECTION 1-3 RESOURCES

Teacher Resource Guide
• Lesson Plan Organizer, p. 35
• Section 1-3 Quiz, p. 91

Student Motivation Kit
• Observ. & Case Studies (case study), p. 86
• Reteaching Activity, p. 9

Student Workbook
• Study Guide, pp. 7-11
• Developing Observation Skills, p. 16

Effective Instruction CD-ROM

FOCUS

MOTIVATOR

Write the following on the board: "When you begin observing, you may find it helpful to imagine yourself as a video camera." Have students respond to this statement.

VOCABULARY ACTIVITY

Have students pronounce all nine vocabulary terms. Let volunteers share their ideas about the definitions of the terms. Help students recognize the relationships between *anecdote* and *anecdotal*; *confidential* and *confidentiality*; *development* and *developmental*.

Observing Young Children

Child development comes to life when you can observe young children in action. Learning how to observe young children is an important skill for parents, teachers, and others who take care of children. With this skill, they constantly learn from what they see. In this course you will have the opportunity to observe children both formally and informally.

KEY TERMS

anecdotal record
baseline
confidentiality
developmental checklist
frequency count
interpret
objective
running record
subjective

OBJECTIVES:

• Explain the importance of observing young children.

• Evaluate four methods of observation.

• Discuss guidelines for observing young children.

• Explain why confidentiality is essential when observing and interpreting the behavior of children.

38   Unit 1: Children, Parenting, and You

Why Is Observing Children Important?

One of the most important reasons for observing children is to better understand their development. For instance, infants pass through a sequence of stages in learning to walk. Observing infants at various stages of this sequence makes it easy to see how each skill leads to the next. When you understand the sequence, you can provide experiences that will promote each skill.

Observing & Participating

Write the following questions on the board:
• Whom did you observe?
• What was the purpose for your observations?
• What did you learn from your observations?

Divide students into groups. Have each student determine a different purpose for observing. Then have all members observe the same child or children and answer the three questions. Have the groups discuss their observations.

Observation also helps you learn about individual children. Each child moves through developmental stages at his or her own rate. By observing a particular child's development, you can identify activities to meet his or her particular needs.

Observing children can also help you identify children who have special needs or disabilities. Once they have been identified, they can receive the special care and learning opportunities they need.

Finally, observing children gives you important feedback about your own approach to parenting or teaching. By observing how children respond to your attempts at guiding behavior, for instance, you can judge how effective your methods have been.

How to Observe Young Children

Observing children goes far beyond just watching what children do. Knowing how to observe effectively will make your observations more valuable.

Objective Versus Subjective Observations

One of the most difficult parts of becoming a good observer is learning to separate facts from opinions. Analyze these two observations of the same event:

- **Example 1.** Robbie is feeling selfish. He won't let anyone play with the toys in the sandbox. He gets mad at Eric a lot.
- **Example 2.** Robbie is sitting in the sandbox. He reaches out and takes a truck away from Eric. Eric grabs for the truck, but Robbie pulls it away. "It's my turn now," says Robbie, looking Eric straight in the face.

Example 1 is a <u>subjective</u> observation, one that uses personal opinions and feelings, rather than facts, to judge or describe things. Notice that, from reading this observation, you can't tell what really happened between Robbie and Eric. The observer in Example 1 is not recording facts, but recording opinions about Robbie's feelings.

Example 2 is an **objective** observation. It uses facts, not personal feelings or prejudices, to describe things. The observation describes what the observer saw and heard—and nothing more.

<u>Objective observations are much more valuable than subjective ones.</u> <u>Subjective</u> observations are based on the <u>false assumption</u> that the observer knows what is going on in the child's mind. They can also be misleading. Robbie might not have been acting selfishly. He might have had an earlier agreement with Eric about taking turns.

Finally, because subjective observations don't record facts, they are hard for others to use. A teacher who knew that Robbie was generally shy at school would want the full facts presented in Example 2. She might interpret Robbie's behavior as a sign of growing self-assertion.

It takes practice and discipline to write objective observations. <u>Remember to record only what you see and hear,</u> avoiding such words as *happy* or *sad*, *good* or *bad*. You can record that a child smiled or laughed, but avoid saying that the smiling or laughing child is happy. Such a comment is an interpretation, and interpretation takes place later. Stick to the facts.

Types of Observation Records

Four methods of recording observations are particularly useful. You will learn more about these later.

ACTIVITIES

Analyzing Children at Play

Show students a short video of one or more young children at play. Assign half the students to write a subjective observation of the video and the other half to write an objective observation. Then have students compare their descriptions. **Ask:** How are all the objective observations similar to one another? Are the subjective observations similar? Are subjective observations useful and reliable? Why or why not? **L2**

DID You Know?

Research and Observation. Most research on young children is based on observation because children cannot read a questionnaire or explain their feelings. Research can be longitudinal or cross-sectional. In longitudinal research, groups of children are observed over time. This type is good for trying to observe later effects of an event or action. Cross-sectional research observers study children of different ages. Researchers use this approach in studying language development, for example. Both methods are needed to understand human development.

LEARNING STYLES

Mathematical/Kinesthetic

Have students work in small groups. Students should choose one member of the group to be the observer. Have the other members take the roles of young children and act out a scene at a child care center. Have the observer report on the situation he or she observes by writing a subjective report. Have each group discuss the report. What assumptions did the report reveal? Did they match the intentions of the participants in the scene? If not, what does that reveal about subjective reports?

COMPREHENSION CHECK

1. What are the four types of observation records? (*Running record, anecdotal record, frequency count, developmental checklist.*)
2. Which method may need a baseline? (*Frequency count.*)
3. Where should you position yourself when observing? (*Where children won't notice you.*)

ACTIVITIES

Critical Thinking Activity

Analyzing. **Ask:** How might the behaviors of other people affect children being observed? How would those changes in the children's behavior affect the observations? **L2**

Teamwork Activity

Form students into groups and have each group brainstorm ideas for creating a developmental checklist aimed at their abilities as observers. What skills should an observer have? Once the groups have their checklists, compare their findings. Have the class agree on a list of qualities and then create a form. Students can use that form to rate their own abilities as observers during the course. **L2**

Discussion Activity

Ask: Are teachers and parents likely to interpret specific behavior the same way? Why or why not?

- **Running record.** The **running record** involves writing down for a set period of time everything observed about a particular child, group, or teacher. This method is useful if you are just getting to know a child or a group. A running record is also useful for analyzing a certain area of development, such as social interaction or motor skills.
- **Anecdotal record.** The **anecdotal** (AN-ek-DOE-tuhl) **record** is similar to a running record, but the behavior recorded all has to do with the same issue. (In a running record, *all* behaviors are recorded.) For example, suppose that you want to see how a child is adjusting to a new child care center. In that case, you could use an anecdotal record to write down how the child behaved at arrival time each day for several days.
- **Frequency count.** The **frequency count** is a tally of how often a certain behavior occurs. You can simply use a tally mark on a record sheet to note how often a particular child takes the action under study. This kind of record is useful when you are trying to change an undesirable behavior. First you find a **baseline,** which is a count taken before any methods are made to change the behavior. As you work with the child to change the behavior, you can make other frequency counts to see how well the efforts to change the behavior are succeeding.

- **Developmental checklist.** The **developmental checklist** identifies a series of specific skills or behaviors that a child of a certain age should master. To use the checklist as a record, simply check off the skills or behaviors you observe in a particular child.

When making observations, it is important to write down what you see as you see it. Otherwise, important information may be forgotten. Each record should include basic information: the date and time of the observation, the number of children present, their names and ages, and the number of adults working with them. The record should also mention the setting where you made the observation (school or home) and exactly where it occurred (for example, on the playground or in the science area).

How to Act While Observing

While observing young children, you don't want to be noticed. Your presence can affect their behavior and make it difficult for you to gather objective information. There is also the possibility that you might disrupt an adult who is with the child you are observing.

When observing, then, you should blend into the background. Choose a spot outside the area where the children are. Sit or stand off to one side with notepad and pen or pencil ready. Be sure to read the observation assignment completely before beginning to observe.

At first, the children may come over to ask who you are and what you are doing. Answer politely, but briefly. Avoid asking them any questions, which will only encourage more talking. If the children need to be persuaded to return to their

LEARNING STYLES

Auditory

Have students prepare an audiocassette to teach students who will be observing children. Have them first discuss ways that an individual should act to observe children most effectively. Then have group members organize their ideas into a checklist and record them. Tell them to use a different sound effect to symbolize each item on the checklist. Remind them to evaluate and edit their tape before creating a final copy. Ask them to share their final tape with the class, and have students evaluate the ideas and presentation.

Do you think this worker is positioned appropriately to make an observation? Why?

COMPREHENSION CHECK

1. What does interpret mean? *(To explain or make sense of something.)*
2. How do you practice confidentiality in your everyday life? *(When keeping a secret a friend tells you.)*

ACTIVITIES

Critical Thinking Activity

Interpreting. Have students watch a television program and observe a character. Have them write an objective report about him or her. Then have students exchange reports with a partner and write an interpretation based on the report written by the other student. Call on volunteers to read their interpretations to the class. Hold a class discussion to evaluate them. What evidence does someone making an interpretation need to support his or her conclusions? **L2**

VISUAL LEARNING	Using the Photograph

Answer: Yes; worker is close enough to observe. Some may say too close.

activities, you might say "I am writing a story about how children play. If you go back to playing, I can write about you in my story."

At times, you may need to stop being just an observer and take action. If, for instance, you see that a child is hurt and no adult knows about it, you should step in.

Sometimes an observer who is doing a developmental checklist does need to interact with the child. For instance, to find out how well a child can catch and throw a ball, you may take part in the activity.

Using Observations

Once you have the information, the next step is to use it. To **interpret** is to find meaning in, explain, or make sense of something. When recording, you made every effort to be objective. Now, however, it is time to express your ideas and opinions about what you observed. An hour's run-ning record of a child's behavior is of little use unless you analyze and interpret it.

Anyone who observes children and interprets information about them should follow the basic rule of **confidentiality** (CON-fuh-den-shee-AL-uht-ee), or privacy. This means sharing the information only with the child's main caregivers or your child development teacher.

Remember that you observe the child only for a brief time. How you interpret that child's behavior may not be accurate because you do not have all the relevant facts. For this reason, it's important to avoid saying things about a child to someone else. Comments such as "Devon is spoiled" or "Kendra's child is a slow learner" might lead to rumors that could hurt the child or family.

You may, of course, have questions or concerns about a child you observe or a child care setting that you visit. You can discuss these questions with your child development teacher—and no one else.

CHAPTER 1: Learning About Children **41**

Management/Leadership Skills

Read the following description to students: "At first, Erin seemed to wander around the room aimlessly. As she did, she knocked over Hashim's block tower, scattered the dishes Tonya and Kristi were using to play house, and knocked away crayons that Sonya was using."

Ask: What would you do if you worked in a child care center and saw this behavior?

CHECKING COMPREHENSION

Have students answer the Check Your Understanding questions. Answers appear at the bottom of this page.

EVALUATION

Give students the Section 1-3 Quiz in the *Teacher Resource Guide*.

RETEACHING

1. Assign Reteaching Activities, page 9.
2. Give students examples of objective and subjective observations. Ask them to identify the type of observation and to rewrite the subjective ones in objective form.

ENRICHMENT

Have students create a poster titled "Portrait of an Effective Observer."

EXTENSION

Obtain permission from a child care center to review old observation records. Have students analyze the types of observation records that were kept and what use was made of each type.

CLOSE

Ask each student to give one tip for effective observing.

Child care workers must be sure that they maintain confidentiality about their observations. **Why is this so important?**

SECTION 1-3 REVIEW

✔ Check Your Understanding

1. List four reasons for observing children.
2. What is the difference between a subjective and objective observation?
3. Describe the four types of observation records.
4. What basic facts should an observation record include?
5. List three things an observer can do to avoid disrupting children he or she is observing.
6. In what two situations is it acceptable to participate?
7. What does it mean to interpret an observation?

Putting Knowledge Into Practice

1. **Analyzing.** Why is confidentiality important in observations of children?
2. **Applying.** Clip a photo showing at least two children from a magazine or newspaper. Imagine you are viewing the scene. Write an observation of it. Share the photo and your observation with the class.
3. **Observing and Participating.** With a partner, observe a child for at least ten minutes. Each of you should write a running record. Then compare records with your partner to identify which notes are objective.

42 UNIT 1: Children, Parenting, and You

ANSWERS TO SECTION 1-3 REVIEW

1. To learn how children develop; see how a specific child is developing; identify children with special needs; get feedback about one's caregiving.
2. *Subjective*—Uses personal opinions and feelings; *Objective*—Uses facts.
3. *See the definitions on page 40.*
4. *See page 40.*
5. Be away from children; have materials ready; don't ask questions of children.
6. When safety is involved; when it's necessary for the observation.
7. To find meaning in, explain, or make sense of the facts recorded.

Working with Children

Juan wanted a career working with children, but he didn't know how to find out more about his options. You may also be gathering information so you can decide upon a career. A good place to start is with an understanding of the working world.

KEY TERMS

aptitude
entrepreneurs
entry-level jobs
job shadowing
lifelong learner
paraprofessional
professional
service learning
work environment
work-based learning

OBJECTIVES:

- Give examples of three different levels of jobs.
- Describe different methods of researching jobs.
- Identify factors that can be used to analyze careers.
- Describe skills needed to prepare for jobs of the future.

SECTION 1-4 RESOURCES

Teacher Resource Guide
- Lesson Plan Organizer, p. 36
- Section 1-4 Quiz, p. 92

Student Motivation Kit
- Reteaching Activity, p. 10
- Enrichment, p. 6

Student Workbook
- Study Guide, pp. 7-11
- Occupational Interests, pp. 17-18

Transparency Package
- CT-5 Analyzing Career Options

Effective Instruction CD-ROM

Your Career Options

Choosing a career may seem like a very difficult decision. Actually, most people begin by choosing a career area or career field—a group of similar careers. They later choose a specific career to prepare for. By taking this class, you have expressed an interest in children. While you may eventu-

FOCUS

MOTIVATOR

Write "Career" on the board. Have students suggest all the words that come to mind when they hear that word. Tell them that in this section, they will learn about careers.

VOCABULARY ACTIVITY

The prefix *para* often indicates a helping role. Ask students if they have heard of *paramedic* and *paralegal*. A *paraprofessional* is a trained aide who assists in a certain field. A degree from a two-year college is usually required.

Observing & Participating

Have students spend at least an hour at a child care center, observing the employees and how they carry out their responsibilities. Ask them to infer which employees have entry-level positions and which are professionals. Have them specify what the indicators are of each job level and how much contact employees at each job level have with the children. Have students report their findings in oral or written reports.

1. How could you use the knowledge and skills you gain from this class? *(As a parent or in a career. Other responses can be correct.)*
2. How do people move up from an entry-level job? *(Get more education and/or experience.)*

ACTIVITIES

Critical Thinking Activity

Classifying. Have students explain the differences among entry-level workers, paraprofessionals, and professionals, then list examples of jobs in each category.

Critical Thinking Activity

Analyzing. Point out to students that emotional health is important in building a satisfying adult life. Discuss the relationship between a career and emotional health. **Ask:** Do you know people whose entire lives have been affected by their job dissatisfaction? What prevents some people from obtaining satisfying careers? What are the emotional benefits of enjoyable, challenging work? **L1**

VISUAL LEARNING Using the Photograph *Answer:* Paraprofessional.

A dance teacher is a professional. Workers can also be classified as paraprofessionals and entry-level workers. *What level would a dental assistant be?*

ally use the knowledge and skills you gain from this class as a parent, there are also dozens of careers related to children that you might consider.

Opportunities Working with Children

Those interested in working directly with children often choose careers related to child development or child care. A pediatrician, for example, specializes in medical care for children. In-depth knowledge of child development, as well as medicine, is required. A lead teacher in a child care center depends on knowing about how children develop to plan appropriate activities and care. Look for the "Career Opportunities" features throughout this book for profiles of additional career options.

Levels of Jobs

Within a career area, there are usually jobs available at several levels. These levels correspond to the amount of education and training required and the degree of responsibility the job carries:

- **Entry-level jobs** are the kinds of jobs many people take when they first enter a career area. A sales clerk in a children's store has an entry-level job. Most people, however, don't stay at this level. With more experience, and perhaps more education, many move up to more responsible jobs. You might use an entry-level job to try out your interest in a career area.
- A **paraprofessional** has education beyond high school that trains him or her for a certain field. Many paraprofessional jobs require a related degree from a two-year college. An assistant teacher in a child care center, for instance, is a paraprofessional.
- A **professional** has a position that requires at least a degree from a four-year college or technical school in a particular area of study. Many professionals

44 UNIT 1: Children, Parenting, and You

ISSUES IN TEEN PARENTING Have students discuss the problems faced by teen parents who must manage their own lives and provide for a young child at the same time. **Ask:** What problems might teen parents have in planning a career? *(Possible responses: Caring for a child makes it difficult to get more education and move beyond entry-level jobs; having to juggle child and school or child and work makes it difficult to plan a career.)*

have more advanced degrees and years of experience. Professionals may be in charge of programs or supervise entry-level workers and paraprofessionals. Social workers are professionals.

Opportunities for Entrepreneurs

Most people work for someone else—an elementary teacher for a school district, a toy designer for a manufacturer. Others choose to be self-employed or own their own business, to be **entrepreneurs.** An entrepreneur's life is challenging. While you make the rules, set your own schedule, and make the decisions, you also assume all the risks of your businesses. Those who are self-employed need to be self-motivated, self-disciplined, good problem solvers, and willing to work hard. Entrepreneurial opportunities related to children include owning a child care business and writing children's books. What others can you identify?

Your Interests, Aptitudes, and Abilities

In order to make a good decision about a career to pursue, it's important to consider how well you would "fit" that career. Some careers may sound exciting, but when you look at them more closely, you see that they wouldn't be right for you. As you consider your career choices, be sure to evaluate your own interests and preferences, aptitudes, and abilities.

- **Interests and preferences.** Working toward a career that doesn't match your interests can set you up for a lifetime of unfulfilling work. Your interests can include areas of study you enjoy, such as psychology or science, or a hobby. In addition, consider which job characteristics you would prefer. Do you want a career that pays a high salary, or are you more concerned about the satisfaction of helping others? Are you willing to work weekends or long hours, or is time with family more important?

- **Aptitudes.** An **aptitude** is a natural talent or your potential for learning a skill. What kinds of learning come most easily to you? Perhaps you have a natural ability to talk with young children or an aptitude for learning new computer applications. Consider careers that match your strengths.

- **Abilities.** You have already developed many skills that will be useful in the working world. Identifying what these are can help you make career decisions. Now is also the time to expand and improve your abilities—both those specific to career areas that interest you and general skills, such as effective communication and reliability.

Finding Career Information

Another important component of career decision making is to research specific careers in your areas of interest. By doing so, you will be able to narrow your choices.

Gathering Information

The search for career information can lead you in many directions. On-line sources, libraries, and people can all be helpful.

The Internet can put you in touch with trade and professional organizations, government resources, job listings, and people working in various careers. One way to start a search is by entering key terms such as

Have students identify concrete examples of why entrepreneurs need the characteristics identified on this page. What other characteristics would be important? **L1**

Critical Thinking Activity

Analyzing. Using a chart format, have each student identify his or her own interests, preferences, aptitudes, and abilities. Have them keep this chart for reference as they complete this chapter. **L2**

Decision-Making Activity

Choosing a career to pursue is a major life decision. Review the steps in the decision-making process with students:
1. Identify the decision to be made.
2. Identify options.
3. Evaluate possible choices.
4. Make a choice.
5. Act on the decision.
6. Evaluate your choice.
Have students skim the headings in Section 1-4 and match the content to the steps in the process. **L2**

Management/Leadership Skills

Read the following aloud: "Nancy always wanted to be a teacher, but she was shy and had poor language skills. An aptitude test she took before entering college indicated that teaching would not be right for her. Nancy was determined, though. She took extra courses in speaking and writing and graduated from college with good grades. Now she is a happy teacher who is loved by students and respected by peers."

Ask: What can people do if they want a job or career for which they seem to have little aptitude?

COMPREHENSION CHECK

1. How could a job shadowing experience help you decide if a career might be right for you? (*See actual job setting and work that is done.*)
2. How can volunteering help a student learn about careers? (*Gives direct work experience; may lead to paying job.*)

ACTIVITIES

Discussion Activity

Ask students who have part-time or volunteer jobs to describe their work and discuss how they can use that job to prepare for a career. **L1**

Critical Thinking Activity

Analyzing. Give students information about two or three service learning programs at schools similar to yours. Include hours required, volunteer options, and reporting methods. Have students discuss what benefits such a program could bring to your school and community, as well as to the students themselves. What arguments might be made against such a program? **L2**

---

child care career or pediatric nursing to indicate what you are looking for.

Don't overlook libraries as a resource. The librarian can help you with your search. Most libraries have excellent resources on career information. These two government publications are also available on-line:

- *The Occupational Outlook Handbook,* which gives detailed information on hundreds of jobs.
- *The Occupational Outlook Quarterly,* that updates information on career trends every three months.

You can also talk to people about their work. Ask your school counselor, teachers, relatives, and friends about possible contacts. Most people are happy to share information about their career with others. Find a time to meet that is convenient for the person. Show up on time and with a list of questions. Be sure to express your thanks and also send a thank-you note.

When you volunteer, you usually get back more than you give. You can use volunteer activities to try out career areas that interest you.

Experiencing the World of Work

You can learn a great deal about a career—and yourself—by working. Summer work and part-time jobs are good ways to get started.

Another method of finding out more about what jobs are actually like is **job shadowing.** This process involves making contact with someone whose career interests you and making arrangements to spend time at work with that person. You can also ask the person questions about his or her job. Your guidance counselor may be able to help you make arrangements for one or more job shadowing experiences.

You can also learn a great deal by volunteering. Although volunteers don't get paid for their work, it offers great experience. Sometimes it even leads to a paying job. The added benefit of volunteering is the satisfaction of helping in your community.

Some school programs offer direct work experience. Schools with **service learning** programs have students volunteer in their community as a graduation requirement. Schools with **work-based learning** programs offer students the opportunity to combine in-school and on-the-job learning.

Work experience gives you another benefit besides a real taste for a job. You may meet people who know someone in the career area that interests you. Coworkers may also be willing to serve as a reference that a prospective employer can contact for information about your skills and character.

Getting College Credit. Some high schools have articulation agreements with community colleges that allow high school students to earn college credit for comparable courses taught in the high school. Often a two-semester high school course receives one semester of college credit because the material is presented at a slower pace. Some high school students may also be eligible to take regular college classes. For students who have specific career goals, these programs offer a head start.

Analyzing Careers

Now you know where to look for career information, but what should you try to find out? You can use eight factors to analyze careers:

- **Tasks and responsibilities.** What does a worker in this career do? Is the work the same every day or varied? Is the pace fast or slow? How much control does a worker have over the work?
- **Work with people, information, or technology.** Each career tends to emphasize one area over another. A reading teacher works mainly with people. An editor of children's books works mainly with information. A designer of children's clothing works mainly with technology.

- **Work environment.** The work environment is the physical and social surroundings at the workplace. Camp counselors work outdoors; nurses work indoors. Some people work alone, but others work in teams. Which kind of environment is most appealing to you?
- **Working hours.** Many people work from 9:00 in the morning to 5:00 at night, but many other workers have different hours. Some jobs require weekend and holiday work.
- **Aptitudes.** Compare the aptitudes needed for a career with your own. Assess how well they match.
- **Education and training.** Though many people gain experience on the job, they need the right education to land that job in the first place. What's required for the careers that interest you? Do your best in school. Check with your school counselor, libraries and the Internet for information about educational opportunities beyond high school and ways to pay for it.
- **Salary and benefits.** Income goes up with training and education. Income also tends to rise with experience—a first-year paraprofessional earns less than a coworker with five years in the same job.

CHAPTER 1: Learning About Children **47**

- **Career outlook.** What do experts think will happen to this career in the future? Will the demand for the career grow or shrink? Answers to these questions affect how easy it will be for you to find a job. Many sources estimate future trends for various jobs.

Preparing for Career Success

Some people just fall into any job that's available. While that occasionally works out, it's much smarter to think carefully about what career you would like and plan how to achieve it. What you do does make a real difference in how satisfied you will be with your life.

Setting and Achieving Goals

Career goals are like a roadmap to your desired destination. If you decide that you want a career as a kindergarten teacher, that's your long-term goal. However, getting there will take some years and many smaller achievements. To help you reach your long-term goal, it's important to set short-term goals for the next steps you need to take. By identifying specific actions you must achieve in the next month, year, or several years, you focus your attention and make progress. Without short-term goals, it's less likely that you will achieve your long-term goal.

Linette's long-term goal was to become a physical therapist. One of her short-term goals was to work with children on a daily basis to make certain she would like that aspect of the career. Through her job as a camp counselor, she met that goal. What other short-term goals do you think she might have had?

Developing Skills for a Lifetime

Preparing for your career involves more than learning about careers. You also have to prepare yourself for the working world of today—and the future. In the past, people often stayed with the same career all their lives. Now, people tend to change careers several times. To succeed in this working environment, you will need to remain flexible and commit to being a **lifelong learner.** By continuing to learn new information and skills throughout your working life, you are likely to be a more effective worker and a valued employee.

Now is the time to build the skills you will need for employment. Some of these require education related specifically to your area of career interest. Others are more universal skills that will make you a successful employee. You can put these universal skills to work immediately, improving your everyday life.

- **Personal qualities.** Employers look for employees who are enthusiastic, respectful, and willing to take initiative. Personal integrity and taking pride in one's work are also high on their list.
- **Interpersonal skills.** Employees need to be able to get along with coworkers and customers. They must have leadership skills and work well in teams made up of people from diverse backgrounds. Strong communication skills—verbal, nonverbal, written, and electronic—are keys to positive relationships.
- **Basic skills.** To succeed at work, employees need to be able to read, write, solve math problems, and speak and listen effectively.

Parenting in Action

Although many people consider job and family as two separate parts of life, they are intertwined. Have students work in small groups and brainstorm at least five ways work life can affect family life and vice versa. Discuss the similarities and differences in the lists. Have the class draw conclusions about the relationship between family life and work life. How do these responsibilities impact community involvement? How can management skills help families cope? You may refer to the feature on multiple roles on page 63.

- **Thinking skills.** Employers need workers who are able to learn, reason, think creatively, make decisions, and solve problems. How well do you handle these challenges?
- **Management skills.** Employees must be able to set goals and use available resources—information, time, materials, skills, and people—to get the work done efficiently. Being well organized is important to managing well.
- **Technology skills.** Today, most jobs require the ability to use computers and to communicate electronically. Many careers require highly specialized technology skills.

Focusing on your career interests and options now will put you on track for a ful-

filling life ahead. When you set and achieve short-term goals, you will move closer to your long-term career goals.

Perhaps you are already working or plan to get a job soon. Work experience can help you clarify what you want to do with your life and build the skills essential for a lifetime in the working world. The Career Success Handbook that starts on page 630 gives specific information on finding a job, achieving job success, and moving ahead in the world of work.

INFOLINK

Employment

To learn more about *finding, succeeding on, and leaving jobs,* see the Career Success Handbook that begins on page 630.

SECTION 1-4 REVIEW

✔ Check Your Understanding

1. Differentiate between the three levels of jobs.
2. What kinds of information about careers can you find in libraries?
3. What is the difference between service learning and cooperative education programs?
4. Where can you learn about the education you need so you can prepare for different jobs?
5. Which of the skills workers need in the future do you think is the hardest to gain? Why?
6. Why is lifelong learning important?

Putting Knowledge Into Practice

1. **Comparing.** Write a paragraph comparing the kind of information you can learn about a job from sources of published information, such as libraries, to what you can learn from interviewing someone who has the job.
2. **Prioritizing.** Write the list of factors you can use to analyze careers. Then rank them in order of most to least important, as you see them.
3. **Observing and Participating.** Choose one of the skills needed for a worker to be successful. If you have a job, explain how that job requires the skill. If you don't, explain how that skill is used by someone whose work you observed in your everyday life.

ASSESS

CHECKING COMPREHENSION

Have students answer the Check Your Understanding questions. Answers appear at the bottom of this page.

EVALUATION

Give students the Section 1-4 Quiz in the *Teacher Resource Guide*.

RETEACHING

1. Assign Reteaching Activities, page 10.
2. Have students choose a career. They should describe how they could learn about the career and what information they would try to find out.

ENRICHMENT

Ask students to identify specific ways lack of the employability skills mentioned can hinder life as a student.

EXTENSION

Using a catalog from a college or technical school, have students find programs that relate to children and list the courses required.

CLOSE

Have students describe the life they would like to live in ten years. What careers would help them reach that goal?

ANSWERS TO SECTION 1-4 REVIEW

1. Entry-level jobs require least training and are for people starting out; paraprofessional jobs require some training beyond high school; professional jobs require college or advanced degrees and experience.
2. Books, magazines, videos, computers, Internet access.
3. *Service learning*—Community service is part of school work; *cooperative education programs*— Businesses hire students, who work while studying.
4. Library, Internet.
5. *Answers will vary.*
6. Because it will help you stay in touch with changes in technology.

Write the following phrase on the board: "My favorite childhood toy was ...." Call on students to complete the phrase by naming their favorite childhood toy. **Ask:** How old were you when you played with the toy? What characteristics made it your favorite?

TEACH

COMPREHENSION CHECK

1. Denyse loves watching her mobile. What age is she likely to be? *(Less than a year.)*
2. Alexa is four. Her parents are thinking of getting her a bicycle. What would you advise? *(She's too young for a bicycle.)*

ACTIVITIES

Teamwork Activity

Have students work in small groups to create a toy that would be appropriate for one of the age groups. Students might make a sketch of the toy or they might create a model to present to the class. **L2**

Critical Thinking Activity

Using the lists of toys appropriate for various ages, have students identify the skills developed by these toys. **L2**

Parenting With Care

Helping Children Play

Play is children's most important activity.

It is how they learn and how they experience their world. Among the most important things that parents can do, then, are to encourage children to play and to provide them opportunities to play.

Psychologist Bruno Bettelheim added another important role. Parents, he says, need to take an interest in children's play. "All too often," he warned, "parents look on play as a 'childish' pastime." He reminded parents, though, that they must "give play not just respect and tolerance but also their personal interest" for the child to truly benefit. Children's play changes as they grow. Here's a brief look at typical kinds of play enjoyed by children of different ages:

- **From birth to age one.** Mobiles, rattles, mirrors, games with sounds, peekaboo, and hide-and-seek.
- **From ages one to two.** Blocks, stacking toys, music boxes, pail and shovel, shape sorters, play clay, pots and pans, push-and-pull toys.

- **From ages two to three.** Wheeled vehicles, clothes for dressing up, easy climbing games, crayons and fingerpaints, puzzles, large beads for stringing.
- **From ages three to four.** Balls, books, interlocking blocks, bubbles for blowing, climbing equipment, hand puppets, paper and scissors, sandbox, tricycle.
- **From ages four to five.** Simple board games, toy camera, magnets, musical instruments, paints and paintbrushes, playground equipment.
- **From ages five to seven.** Ball games, craft materials, dolls, bicycle, gardening tools, paints and paintbrushes.
- **From ages seven to twelve.** Board games, card games, models, complex imaginary play, magic, sports.

50 UNIT 1: Children, Parenting, and You

RESOURCES ON SAFETY

The Consumer Product Safety Commission (CPSC) has set safety regulations for toy manufacturers to meet. Some regulations include:
- Toys for children under 8 years of age should not have hazardous sharp edges.
- Electrical toys must be designed to prevent electric shock and burns.

- Toys for children under 3 years of age must not have small parts that could become stuck in their throats.

For information on toy safety, contact the U.S. Consumer Product Safety Commission at www.cpsc. gov

This is not a complete list, of course. Children at each stage enjoy a huge range of play, some involving running and jumping and others that call for sitting still. The important thing for parents is to give them a chance to play what they enjoy—and what they will learn from.

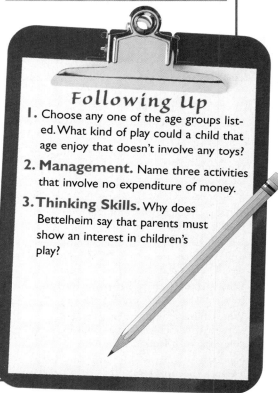

Following Up

1. Choose any one of the age groups listed. What kind of play could a child that age enjoy that doesn't involve any toys?

2. **Management.** Name three activities that involve no expenditure of money.

3. **Thinking Skills.** Why does Bettelheim say that parents must show an interest in children's play?

CHAPTER 1: Learning About Children **51**

Toys in the Past

Have students research the toys that children in earlier times played with. Students might investigate toys used in ancient Egypt or nineteenth century Europe. They could present their findings with illustrations or by making models of the toys. Have students comment on whether they think children today could enjoy the toys. Why or why not? **L3**

CLOSE

1. Tell students that they are going to babysit the four-year-old child of a neighbor in their own home. Have them list items in their home that would be appropriate as toys for a child that age.
2. **Extension.** Ask a preschool or kindergarten teacher to demonstrate to students the kinds of play that children they care for enjoy. Have students make inferences about the developmental tasks of an age based on the play that children enjoy.

CHECKING COMPREHENSION

Use the Summary and the Reviewing the Facts questions to help students review the most important ideas in Chapter 1. Encourage students to ask questions and add details.

CHAPTER 1 REVIEW

Answers to **Reviewing the Facts**

1. That is when vital connections in the brain develop, and these connections affect the person throughout life.
2. You can understand children, gain skills, understand yourself, and prepare for the future.
3. Bandura and Coles showed that children learn behavior by following the models of parents and other caregivers.
4. Recent brain research shows that how the brain works is shaped in childhood and continues throughout life.
5. Development is similar for everyone.
6. Objective observation uses facts; subjective observation uses personal opinions and feelings.
7. With your teacher only.
8. *Any three:* working in the career (including summer work, part-time work, volunteer work, job shadowing, service learning, and cooperative education programs); using the library; using Internet sites; interviewing someone in the field.
9. It teaches you about the job; provides you with experience; lets you meet people who might introduce you to other job possibilities or serve as references.

CHAPTER 1   REVIEW &

Summary

✔ Studying children helps you learn about children and yourself and prepare for the future. (Section 1-1)

✔ Research has revealed how children learn and develop. (Section 1-2)

✔ Development follows a predictable set of steps, but each person develops at his or her own rate. (Section 1-2)

✔ There are several methods used to record observations of children. (Section 1-3)

✔ Observations should be objective, private, and interpreted carefully. (Section 1-3)

✔ Some sources of career information involve direct experience. (Section 1-4)

✔ Workers need to develop key skills to prepare for a changing workplace. (Section 1-4)

Reviewing the Facts

1. Why is childhood an important time? (Section 1-1)
2. What four benefits do you get from studying children? (Section 1-1)
3. What is the significance of the work of Bandura and Coles? (Section 1-2)
4. What is the significance of recent research on the brain? (Section 1-2)
5. Babies in Florida and Sri Lanka both begin to speak at the same time. What principle of development does this reveal? (Section 1-2)
6. Why is an objective observation more useful than a subjective one? (Section 1-3)
7. With whom should you discuss any questions or concerns you have about a child you observe? (Section 1-3)
8. Name three sources of information about a career. (Section 1-4)

9. How does learning about careers through work experience benefit you? (Section 1-4)

Thinking Critically

1. **Synthesizing.** Think of a play activity you enjoyed when you were younger. Make a list of ways you benefited from that activity.
2. **Analyzing.** "Only students who are parents, who plan to become parents, or who want careers in a child-related field should learn about children." Do you agree or disagree? Why?
3. **Distinguishing Fact and Opinion.** Identify the facts and the opinions in this observation: "Sarah was happy when she arrived today. She was smiling and singing a song. When her mother left, she began to play. She did not like the way Ron played with the blocks, so she hit him."

Taking Action

1. **Looking at Theorists.** Research the work of one of the child development theorists profiled in the chapter. Make an oral presentation describing what you learned. *(Communication)*
2. **Writing Objectively.** Think of something that happened in one of your classes today. Write an observation, remembering to keep it objective. *(Communication)*

CONNECTIONS

Cross-Curricular Connections

1. **Language Arts.** Write a poem or story that reflects the idea that childhood is an important time of life.
2. **Health.** Research any of the following diseases: smallpox, measles, polio, diphtheria, malaria. What impact did the disease have on children in the past? What can health care workers do now prevent and treat the disease? Make a poster displaying your findings.

Workplace Connections

1. **Systems.** Compare and contrast the purpose, organization, and flexibility to change in a school system and a locally owned child care center.
2. **Basic Skills.** Suppose you learned that a certain job paid $400 per week. How much would a person in that job earn in a year? If the worker received a 3 percent salary increase the next year, what would be his or her new weekly and yearly income?

Family and Community Connections

1. **Making a Time Line.** Create a time line showing your own or someone else's personal growth. Identify at least six developmental stages that you want to chart—when you first spoke or walked or climbed the stairs. Talk to others in your family to find out when you reached the early stages. Use the information to create your time line.

2. **Childhood.** Interview two family members or friends who have a child. Ask what one topic or problem they wish they had known more about. Discuss your findings with the class.

3. **Schools.** Find out if there is a Montessori school in your community. If there is, talk to a teacher or administrator at the school. Ask him or her to describe the methods and materials used. Report your findings to the class.

Technology Connections

1. **Internet.** Conduct an Internet search to find the latest information about research on the brain. Report your findings to the class.
2. **Computer.** Use a computer program to create a table showing the factors you would want to analyze when considering a career for yourself. Expand on the factors listed in the textbook. Compare your table to those of classmates.

CHAPTER 1: Learning About Children **53**

EVALUATION

1. Use the reproducible Chapter 1 Test in the *Teacher Resource Guide,* or create your own test using the **Exam***View*® Test Generator.
2. For an alternative assessment, assign the Chapter 1 activity in the *Authentic Assessment* section of the *Teacher Resource Guide.*

ENRICHMENT

Assign students either of the two Chapter 1 activities in the *Enrichment Activities* booklet in the *Student Motivation Kit.*

EXTENSION

Invite parents to speak with the class. Have the students prepare questions for the parents. Possible questions: How has an understanding of child development helped you as a parent? How does observing your child help you understand your child and become a better parent?

CLOSE

Have students create a pamphlet that explains how a child studies class can benefit people interested in a career related to children. Have them incorporate what they know about characteristics of development, observing children, and the skills needed for future careers.

Answers to Connections

Workplace
2. Yearly wage: $20,800. Weekly wage after 3 percent raise: $412. Yearly wage after 3 percent raise: $21,424.

CHAPTER 2 RESOURCES

Teacher Resource Guide

• Chapter 2 Test, pp. 99-102

• Authentic Assessment, pp. 259-260

Student Motivation Kit

• Observations & Case Studies (observation), pp. 29-30

Transparency Package

• CT-6 to CT-7

Effective Instruction CD-ROM

CHAPTER 2 OVERVIEW

In **Section 2-1**, students learn about the functions of a family and then examine four kinds of family groups. They continue by examining the family life cycle and trends that affect families. Finally, students learn how families can be strengthened.

In **Section 2-2**, students focus on the many changes that parenthood brings. They also consider the rewards and benefits of parenthood. Students conclude by examining five considerations in decisions about parenthood.

CHAPTER 2 OBJECTIVES

After completing Chapter 2, students will be able to:

• Explain how families can be strengthened.

• Describe the changes that parenthood brings.

• Identify issues people should address before choosing to become parents.

CHAPTER 2

Learning About Families

RESOURCES TO EXPLORE

Parenting. Teens are generally less prepared than adults for the responsibilities of parenthood and need to realistically assess both the rewards and demands of parenting. Invite speakers (parents or from local organizations) to speak to the class. Possible topics include readiness for parenting, the realities of parenting, adoption, and sources of help for parents.

As far back as Michael can remember, his family was there to help him. He can recall when he was small, and his father would take him on walks and carry him on his shoulders. He can remember riding in the shopping cart while his mother was at the supermarket. He laughs whenever he thinks about the time he and his brother built the huge sand castle at the beach or when they used to shoot baskets at the playground.

All these memories are flooding over him now as he waits for the picture to be taken. Michael and Stephanie are about to have their first picture taken with Michael's parents and their baby. As he waits for the photographer, Michael makes a silent promise to the new baby—a promise that he'll do everything he can to give his daughter as many good memories as he has had.

"Parents build memories for their children."

- Have students think about an event in their lives that included family members. **Ask:** What was the reason for the gathering? (*Possible responses: holiday, birthday, religious observance, or family reunion.*) Have students write two paragraphs in which they describe the event and how it affected the family's bond.
- Have students look at the family photograph. **Ask:** What emotions might the grandparents feel? What might the granddaughter think ten years later if she sees this picture?

USING THE SCENARIO Have students read the story in the student text. **Ask:** Why might Michael and Stephanie wish to have the photograph taken? How does this wish reflect a value for family? How else might a parent show that family is important? How might a child show it?

KEY TO ABILITY LEVELS   Each section gives skill-building activities. Each activity has been labeled for use with students of various learning styles and abilities.

L1 Level 1 activities are basic activities and should be within the range of all students.

L2 Level 2 activities are average activities and should be within the range of average and above average students.

L3 Level 3 activities are challenging activities designed for the ability range of above average students.

SECTION 2-1

SECTION 2-1 RESOURCES

Teacher Resource Guide
- Lesson Plan Organizer, p. 37
- Section 2-1 Quiz, p. 97

Student Motivation Kit
- Observ. & Case Studies (case study), pp. 87-88
- Reteaching Activity, p. 11
- Enrichment, p. 7

Student Workbook
- Study Guide, pp. 19-21
- Identifying Characteristics of Families, pp. 22-23

Effective Instruction CD-ROM

FOCUS

MOTIVATOR

Have students raise their hands to show: (1) How many have a grandparent who lives in the same town? (2) How many have an aunt or uncle living in the same town? Tell students that the trend today is for people to move away from the community in which they were born, which weakens ties with extended families.

VOCABULARY ACTIVITY

Ask students to use the meaning of *to blend* (to mix) to infer what a blended family is. Next, have students explain how *extend* (to spread) suggests the meaning of extended family. Finally, ask what a *nucleus* is (an atom's center) and possible meanings for nuclear family.

Understanding Families

In every society, people gather into families. In some societies, family includes only parents and children. In others, aunts and uncles are important parts of the family. No matter how it is defined, though, the family is the foundation on which every human society is built.

KEY TERMS

adoption
blended family
extended family
family life cycle
foster children
guardians
nuclear family
single-parent family
values

OBJECTIVES:

- Explain the functions that families fulfill.

- Describe types of family structures and special issues related to each type.

- Identify stages that families with children go through.

- Analyze trends that affect families today.

The Functions of Family

Each day when she finishes school, Marisa picks up her little brother at the child care center. When they arrive home, she makes him a snack. Then they read, play, or watch television together until their mother gets home from work. Marisa's schedule sounds routine, but underlying these actions is the secret to the importance of family. The members of a family help meet each other's basic needs. Families also prepare children to live in society.

Observing & Participating

Have students discuss the families they see in movies or television shows. Have them think about the underlying dynamics of the families revealed in the scenes they have observed. Are the relationships realistic? If not, why not? How well do the families function? Are there lessons that could be learned from how family members interact? What are they?

Families take many different forms and include different numbers of people—even different generations. Still, all societies are built on families. *What do you think of when you think about the word family?*

Meeting Basic Needs

All people need food, clothing, and shelter. Families make sure that these basic needs are met.

Can you remember a time when an adult put a bandage on a cut or gave you some medicine when you were ill? Families also make sure that members' basic needs for safety and health are met.

Families meet their members' intellectual needs as well. The family is a child's first teacher, from whom he or she learns language, numbers, colors, and other concepts. In some families, children learn how to do the work they will perform as adults. Later, by encouraging children to do homework, parents contribute to a child's schooling.

Finally, families meet social and emotional needs. Each family member has the opportunity to love and to be loved, to care and to be cared for, to help others and to

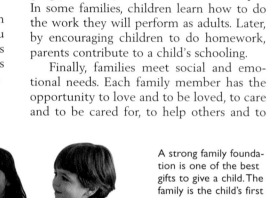

A strong family foundation is one of the best gifts to give a child. The family is the child's first connection to the world, and it provides each individual with the chance to love—and be loved. *How can simply spending time with children meet those emotional needs?*

57

TEACH

COMPREHENSION CHECK

1. What basic physical needs does every person have? *(Need for food, clothing, shelter, safety, health.)*
2. In what four areas do families meet the needs of members? *(Physical, social, intellectual, emotional.)*

ACTIVITIES

Teamwork Activity

Have students work in groups to prepare a manual for family members. Each student should create a page that explains how a parent can help meet a child's needs *and* how a child can help meet a parent's needs. Display the completed booklets. **L2**

VISUAL LEARNING | **Using the Photographs**
Top—Answers will vary, possibly focusing on family structure or what families do. Bottom—57: Possible response: By showing parents' love.

DID You Know?

Family Size **The size of the average American family is decreasing. Researchers cite the following reasons:**
• **Many women pursue a career and wait until later in life to marry and have children.**
• **The costs of raising a child are greater than in the past (about $200,000 per child).**
• **Parents have less help today from family members.**

LEARNING STYLES

Interpersonal

Have students act out a scene in which a teen and a parent discuss an issue that divides them, such as what time to return home after a night out with friends. Have the groups present their skits to the class. In the skits, students should address the issue of the family's values—what parents and children hold as important—and how those values are passed on. After presenting the skits, ask students to discuss the most effective ways that those values were communicated.

COMPREHENSION CHECK

1. The Richardsons include a parent and three children. What type of family is this? (*Single parent.*)
2. Bill and Natalie Jacobson are married with three children. What type of family is this? (*Nuclear.*)

ACTIVITIES

Discussion Activity

Ask: What are the advantages of living in a nuclear family? In a blended family? What might the disadvantages be?

Boys and Men **Recent research highlights the importance of boys having strong relationships with older men. Sons who interact regularly with fathers perform better in school than those who do not. Boys in single-parent homes where the father is absent who spent a significant amount of time with grandfathers, uncles, and older brothers ranked one-third higher in their classes than boys in single-parent, mother-led families who did not have these male relationships. Why might this be true?**

---

receive help. By living in families, we learn how to get along with others—how to share and take turns, how to work together toward a common goal.

The Developing Brain

Children need an environment with low stress. When a person feels stress, the body releases a chemical meant to prepare it for a physical response. If there is too much stress over time, though, that chemical can damage the brain's ability to learn and remember.

Preparing Children to Live in Society

Some years ago, Robert Fulghum wrote a book called *All I Really Need to Know I Learned in Kindergarten.* His point was that kindergarten teaches basic rules of life: "share everything," "play fair," "don't hit people," and several more. He might have said the same thing about family. By learning how to live with others in the family, we prepare to live with others in society.

Adults teach children what is important to people in their society. They pass on these **values** in three ways:

- **Through example.** In how they treat children and each other, adults show children how to behave.
- **Through talking.** When a parent tells a toddler not to hit or talks to a teen about respecting people's differences, he or she is passing on values by talking.
- **Through religious training.** In houses of worship, of whatever faith, children learn how to act in a moral way.

Each society has its own culture—its own way of life. Culture is revealed through art and music, through cooking and clothing styles, through how people greet one another and how they view work and play. The family introduces a child to the society's culture.

Adults also teach children about the traditions of society. Do you remember being told why people celebrate Thanksgiving? Adults also explain how to behave. What kind of language is appropriate? How should a child speak to adults? These and similar questions are first answered in the family.

Family Structure

Families come in many shapes and sizes. These variations can be grouped into a few common types.

Nuclear Families

A **nuclear family** includes a mother and father and at least one child. An advantage of the nuclear family is that there are two parents who can both help with raising the children. These families differ depending on how many children there are and how many parents work outside the home.

The Wongs have three children and both parents work outside the home. The Hendersons have one child, who the mother cares for while the father works outside the home. In the Martinez family, both parents work, but at different times so there is always one parent home with their toddler. With the Kojoyians, the mother works outside the home while the father works in a home office and looks after the twins.

Single-Parent Families

A **single-parent family** includes either a mother or father and at least one child. The parent may be unmarried, or the other parent might be gone due to divorce or death.

Raising a child alone puts many demands on the parent. He or she has little free time and has no spouse who can share the work or help solve problems. Single parents often have less income than two-parent families, which makes the burdens of parenting harder.

Many single parents receive help from friends or relatives. They may provide child care while the single parent works. They may help simply by giving the parent a sounding board—someone he or she can talk to in the search for solutions to problems.

Blended Families

A **blended family** is formed when a single parent marries another person, who may or may not be a parent as well. To the child, the parent's new spouse is a stepparent. To the new spouse, each child of the husband or wife is a stepchild. If both spouses have children when they marry, the children become stepbrothers or stepsisters.

At first, the members of a blended family may have problems in establishing the new family unit. Parents and children need time to adjust to one another. Each has to learn about and adapt to a new person's habits, likes, and dislikes. Being in a blended family creates challenges.

Extended Families

An **extended family** includes relatives other than a parent or child who live with them. A grandparent may live with a nuclear family or an aunt or uncle with a single-parent family. Another example is an adult child who lives in his or her parent's house.

Sometimes, the term *extended family* is used to refer to people who do not live with the core family but play important roles in the child's life. Among some Native American people, for instance, uncles help instruct boys in the group's traditional religion.

Entering a Family

Most families include the parents' biological children. Some include children who have joined the family in other ways, though. If both parents die, other relatives may take the children into their homes. These **guardians** take all financial and legal responsibility for raising the children.

Adoption is a legal process in which children enter a family they were not born into. The adopted child has the same rights as any biological children those parents have.

Many adults now are caring not only for their own children but for their elderly parents. *What factors have contributed to this trend?*

Parenting in Action

Today's blended families are often dealing with the issue of joint custody when divorced parents share equally in raising their children. Experts suggest that the arrangement works best if the former spouses:
- Have a primary residence for the child with one parent while including frequent visits to the other's house.
- Communicate on matters of discipline and daily routines.
- Give the child some transition time when switching between homes.
- Live near one another.

Ask the Eperts

Introducing the Feature

Ask students to imagine that two children in a new blended family are moving into their new home. The two haven't lived together before. Now they will have to share their bedroom and will have to learn to get along with the new children. What problems do students predict?

Answers to Thinking It Through

1. *Possible response:* It is easier when children are of widely different ages because they will have fewer rivalries or jealousies.
2. *Possible response:* Become involved in their after-school activities, for example, visiting their sports games or taking interest in hobbies.

Applying What You've Learned

Have students perform a radio talk show on which the host is an expert on blended families. Students can take turns being the expert while the rest of the class "calls in" with questions.

Ask the Eperts

Pat Brodeen
Teacher and Teen Parent Coordinator at Theodore Roosevelt High School in San Antonio, Texas

ADJUSTING *to a Blended Family*

Q What special adjustments are needed to live in a blended family?

A You're right to think that blended families provide special challenges to people. Many factors are at work to create problems. Blended families bring together two different sets of habits, customs, or ways of thinking. Often, too, one family moves into the other family's home. The members of one family may still feel pain or regret over the breakup of that family unit.

All these factors can produce friction. Problems can be met, however. It simply requires patience, understanding, hard work, and desire for the new family to succeed.

Here are some tips for building a healthy blended family:

* *Recognize that a new family is being created and that each member can—and should—contribute to it. Be open to new ideas.*
* *Communicate openly, honestly, and with respect and consideration.*
* *Help the new parents build their relationship. A successful marriage will be the foundation for the new family.*
* *Give a chance to stepparents and their children.*

* *Respect relationships with parents outside the household.*
* *Incorporate traditions from both of the former families.*
* *If the new family moves into your home, help them feel at home. If you are moving into theirs, show respect for their things.*

Forming a blended family is like starting in a new school. There are new rules, routines, and people to adapt to. Over time, they will all become familiar. Just be willing to give it time—and to do your part to help.

Thinking It Through

1. Do you think it is easier to form a blended family when children are of similar ages or widely different ages? Explain your answer.
2. Suppose you were a man who married a woman with two children aged six and eight. What would you do to establish a relationship with the children?

60 UNIT 1: Children, Parenting, and You

Parenting in *Action*

Read the following to students: "Ken's mother just remarried, and his new stepfather has two children, who now live with Ken. Ken feels angry when his new stepsister wants to play with his toys. His mother says: 'I can't believe you are making this hard for me. Share your toys and stop making a fuss over nothing!'"

Ask: If you were Ken's mother, how would you have handled the situation? What would you have done if you were Ken's stepfather and had seen the incident and Ken's mother wasn't around?

In the past, children were always matched closely with the families adopting them. Adoption agencies looked carefully at the child's and parents' race, ethnic and religious background, and physical characteristics. The emphasis now is more on finding a good home rather than a home with parents who match the child in some outward ways.

At some time or other, adopted children will probably ask why their biological parents "gave me away." They may feel rejected—and they need reassurance. Parents should avoid saying that the biological parents did not want their baby. A hug and the comment "I don't know, but I'm glad it worked out this way" can help give the child the comfort he or she needs. Showing adopted children that they are loved and wanted helps them realize that they truly belong in the family—and will not be given up again.

Parents also should avoid saying anything against the child's biological parents. Children need to know that putting a child up for adoption is difficult but can be necessary or in the best interests of the child.

Sometimes older children feel a need to seek out their biological parents. This may be from a need for medical information or simply a desire to know their past. In the past, adoption records were always sealed. However, it is more common today for biological parents who wish to contact the child they gave up for adoption to leave contact information with the adoption agency. In "open adoptions," the biological parent or parents choose or meet with the adoptive parents. How could this be helpful? Could it ever be a problem?

Some children enter a family as **foster children.** Usually, foster children come from troubled families. They need a temporary home until their parents can solve their problems or until the children can find a

permanent adoptive home. Foster parents care for the child until then. Adults must apply to the state government to become foster parents. They receive training and a license. They also get some money to help meet the expenses of caring for the child.

The Family Life Cycle

There are many differences between families, but there are many similarities, too. Families go through a series of stages called the **family life cycle.** The chart on pages 64-65 shows these different stages.

Of course, families differ in how they experience this pattern. Families spend different amounts of time in the same stage. Some may return to a stage after they had left it. The Desais, for instance, adopted a baby after their last child moved out of the home. This started them in the expanding stage all over again. Changes like divorce or remarriage have an effect on the pattern too.

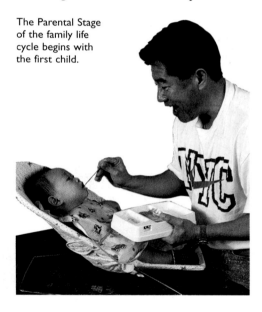

The Parental Stage of the family life cycle begins with the first child.

CHAPTER 2: Learning About Families **61**

COMPREHENSION CHECK

1. Which arrangement provides a permanent home—adoption or foster care? (*Adoption.*)
2. How might adoptive children feel about being adopted? (*May feel rejected or want to find their biological parents. Allow other answers.*)

ACTIVITIES

Teamwork Activity

Have students work in groups to create a board game based on the trends affecting families today. Students should design their games so that players advance or fall behind depending on the impact of various events on their lives. For example, a player may move ahead when an elderly parent moves in and helps with the children, but then may have to take a detour because they have to work longer hours to absorb the added financial burden. **L2**

Management/Leadership Skills

Locate someone in the community who has taken in a foster child or a professional who arranges for foster children. Have students prepare interview questions beforehand. You may wish to review the questions before the person arrives to meet with the class. Have the students take turns asking their questions. After the question-and-answer session is completed, have students write two or three paragraphs explaining their thoughts about being a foster parent.

COMPREHENSION CHECK

1. How has mobility affected families? (*May not be extended family members close by to help.*)
2. How can the national economy impact families? (*May result in fewer jobs, lower salaries, etc.*)

ACTIVITIES

Discussion Activity

One result of the growing number of two-income families is decreased time for parents to devote to child care and housework. As a result, more and more married couples share these responsibilities. **Ask:** Do you think most people find it easier to accept men's moving into women's traditional roles or vice versa? Why? **L1**

Discussion Activity

What parenting problems related to their children's health and welfare may parents new to this country experience? Where might they find help? What obstacles might they find? **L2**

Critical Thinking Activity

Making Inferences. Many parents work more than one job. Why might they do so? What are the implications for family life and the welfare of children? Have students calculate the weekly and monthly income of a full-time (40 hrs. per week) minimum-wage worker at $5.15 per hour. What problems would such an income level pose for a parent? **L3**

Trends Affecting Families

Families of all types are affected by trends in the society around them. These trends may put pressure on families.

Mobility

A hundred years ago, it wasn't unusual for an adult to die in the same home where he or she had been born. Today, most adults don't even live in the same community.

As a result, families often lack close, supportive connections with relatives. Families rely more on themselves and close friends. Extended family relationships take effort.

Cultural Diversity

The United States has always been a country whose citizens' heritage could be traced to countries around the world. U.S. Census Bureau figures indicate that it is still true. Each group has contributed to America. Immigrants from other countries value the freedom citizenship guarantees and continue the tradition of strengthening their new country.

The transition to a new society is not always an easy one for families and children. Language and societal differences can be barriers. A family's support system may have been left behind. Cultural traditions may not always be understood in a new country.

Aging Population

People now live longer than in the past. Advances in medicine and nutrition are two factors. As a result, more people find themselves caring not only for children, but also for aging parents. This can create both stress and opportunities for intergenerational interaction. Sometimes grandparents also end up raising grandchildren if their own parents are not able to.

Economic Changes

Many families struggle to make ends meet. This is particularly true in times of economic downturn. Economics is one reason many mothers work outside the home. When both parents work, there is an impact on the children. Families are generally smaller than they used to be. Couples sometimes delay having children. The rise in two-worker families has also added to the demand for child care, including for school-age children.

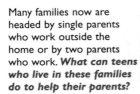

Many families now are headed by single parents who work outside the home or by two parents who work. *What can teens who live in these families do to help their parents?*

62 UNIT 1: Children, Parenting, and You

Practicing Parenting

Managing Multiple Roles

*T*he term "parent" sounds deceptively simple. However, parents typically juggle many diverse roles related to family life, work, and community involvement. Each carries its own responsibilities, but also rewards. In addition, what happens in one part of life can affect other aspects. If a baby is sick, a parent may need to stay home to provide care.

Do you already feel that there's just not enough time to do everything and do it well? This time squeeze will increase as your roles and responsibilities do. However, these strategies can help you and your family better juggle roles.

- ❤ **Consider the relative importance of roles.** If your role as a student is more important than as a sports fan, you can make appropriate choices when priorities conflict.
- ❤ **Set your goals and base your decisions on them.** Parents who want to provide their child with the best possible education can base related decisions on that goal.
- ❤ **Realize that there are always trade-offs.** A parent who volunteers at school gives up something else to better the school and community.
- ❤ **Improve your leadership and teamwork skills.** Both require excellent communication skills and the ability to work cooperatively and to negotiate different points of view.
- ❤ **Treat time as a valuable resource.** Keep a time log to check your time use. Weed out the time-wasters. A daily planner, calendar, and "to do" list can help.

- ❤ **Stay organized.** Build routines for everyday tasks. Keep your surroundings neat. Your life will work more smoothly.
- ❤ **Find ways to cope with stress.** Flexibility and a "go with the flow" attitude help. As things change, concentrate on adapting, rather than reacting with anger or fear. Spend some time in an activity you enjoy.
- ❤ **Share responsibilities.** Are responsibilities shared appropriately in your family? Does everyone help out? No one can—or should—do it all.

APPLY YOUR KNOWLEDGE

1. For five of your parent's roles, indicate key responsibilities and rewards of each.
2. What would happen if no one made community service a priority? What specific benefits and opportunities would your community lose?

COMPREHENSION CHECK

1. What event begins the family life cycle? (*Marriage.*)
2. Do all families pass through all these stages? Why or why not? (*No; they make different choices such as not having children or having them late in life.*)

ACTIVITIES

Critical Thinking Activity

Analyzing. Why are there three different "parental" stages? Why not just have one? (*Each has distinct challenges and rewards. The birth of a baby doesn't put the same demands on parents as readying for the child's leaving to set up own household.*) **L2**

Discussion Activity

Ask: How does the family life cycle help you understand family life from the point of view of parents? **L2**

VISUAL LEARNING

Using the Chart Have students compile photo albums for one stage in the family life cycle. Pictures can be taken from available sources or drawn. Students should write captions describing how the images reflect the challenges and rewards of the stage. **L2**

The Family Life Cycle

As you study the chart, think about the special challenges and rewards that may be associated with each stage in this life cycle.

BEGINNING STAGE:
A couple works to establish a home and a marriage relationship.

PARENTAL STAGE 1:
Expanding: The couple prepares for and adjusts to parenthood.

PARENTAL STAGE 2:
Developing: As children grow, parents work to meet children's changing needs and help them develop independence.

64 UNIT 1: Children, Parenting, and You

ISSUES IN TEEN PARENTING Teen parents face a special challenge because they skip the beginning stage of the family life cycle completely and move directly into Parental Stage 1. Because they have not had time to establish their marriage relationship, problems that would have been resolved during the beginning stage are carried over into the childbearing stage. This places added stress on young people who are also trying to adjust to the demands of parenthood. Outside support is crucial to the resolution of these issues: parents need to have time alone while a caregiver tends to the baby, so that they can work on their relationship.

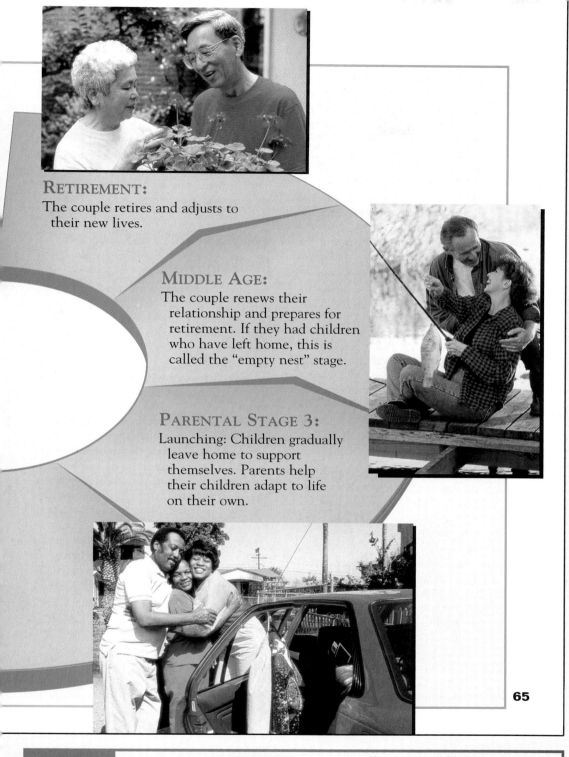

RETIREMENT:
The couple retires and adjusts to their new lives.

MIDDLE AGE:
The couple renews their relationship and prepares for retirement. If they had children who have left home, this is called the "empty nest" stage.

PARENTAL STAGE 3:
Launching: Children gradually leave home to support themselves. Parents help their children adapt to life on their own.

ACTIVITIES

Critical Thinking Activity

Comparing and Contrasting. Have students compare how people stayed in touch over distances one hundred years ago with how they do so today. How long did it take for news to travel from town to town at the beginning of the twentieth century? How long does it take today? Encourage students to use charts and diagrams in making their comparisons. **L2**

Discussion Activity

Ask: What changes arise in the home when parents work at home? How would that be easier or harder depending on the age and number of children in the family? **L1**

ISSUES IN

CHILDREN'S HEALTH

Computers. Long hours spent on the computer can have a negative impact on your health. Follow some basic precautions to reduce the risk of injury:

- Take frequent breaks—every half hour or so—to rest your eyes and your body.
- Use a wrist pad to support your wrists.
- Be sure your chair is comfortable: your feet should rest easily on the floor and your back should be supported.
- Elevate your feet under your desk if possible.

Workplace Changes

The working world is changing rapidly. Old manufacturing industries are declining. Many companies decide to employ fewer workers. As a result of these changes, people have lost their jobs. Many accept replacement jobs with lower pay and fewer benefits. It's not uncommon for full-time workers to lack health-care benefits.

Another change is the growing demand for more education and new skills. This has convinced many workers to invest time and money on additional education. These workers are building for the future, but the decision has an impact today. Markeeta's mother decided to take a course in computer programming. Markeeta was happy for her mother, but missed her at home.

Another trend is the growing number of people who work at home. Whether working in the house for an employer or running their own business, more and more people are making the home a place of business. Such an arrangement puts new demands on children, who have to be quiet during work hours and who might be asked to help out.

Technology

The spread of computers, scanners, and fax machines has contributed to the rise in home offices. Other changes in technology are affecting the family as well. DVDs, satellite television, and computer games offer people many ways to entertain themselves. The popularity of the Internet allows people to obtain information from all over the world. Some critics say that these forms of entertainment tend to isolate people from one another. They say that people are losing the ability to talk to one another.

Some of the new technology also helps family members stay in touch. When Joe Silvestri was caught on an empty road with car trouble, he used his cell phone to call for help. E-mail helps his family members living far apart to communicate.

Coping with Pressures on the Family

All these trends have made profound changes in how people live. Some experts talk about the growing problem of the "frantic family." Parents have to juggle their time to do their work, run the household, and help children with school and after-school activities. As adults and children rush around, they have too little time for each other.

There are some steps you can take to avoid the "frantic family syndrome":

- **Avoid scheduling too many activities.** Allow some free time in every week. This will give each family member a chance to do something for himself or herself—and for the whole family to be together.
- **Watch for clues that family members need a break.** If people are always tired or grumpy, they may need some rest.

Management/Leadership Skills

Have students analyze their own families to determine whether they are suffering from "frantic family syndrome." Suggest they use the list of steps to avoid the syndrome as a checklist to gauge their family's health. Do family members have too many activities scheduled? Are family members consistently grumpy? Tell students to be sure to include specific examples to back up their conclusions. Have students write up a "diagnosis" of their family's condition to share with other family members if they wish.

- **Focus on responsibilities and on activities that people enjoy.** There isn't enough time to do everything, so concentrate on activities that people must do and those they really like.
- **Schedule family meals.** Meals are excellent opportunities for family members to gather together and share their thoughts and feelings.

- **Plan ahead.** Take time each night to prepare school lunches or take out the next day's clothes. Plan trips to consolidate errands. By thinking ahead, you can cut down on trips rushing around and on wasted effort.
- **Maintain your sense of humor.** Having a good laugh—even at yourself—can help relieve the pressure.

SECTION 2-1 REVIEW

✔ Check Your Understanding

1. Give an example of each of the basic needs—physical, intellectual, social, and emotional—that families meet.
2. How do parents pass along values?
3. Describe four different family structures.
4. What is the difference between an adopted child and a foster child?
5. What stage of the life cycle do you think causes the greatest adjustment for a couple: the beginning stage, the first parental stage, or the retirement stage. Explain your answer.
6. How does increased mobility affect families?
7. How have workplace changes affected the family?

Putting Knowledge Into Practice

1. **Applying.** Think about what your culture has to offer and what you have learned from others about your culture. What unique qualities would you like to pass on to future generations?
2. **Predicting Consequences.** In groups, research one of the trends affecting families and identify positive and negative implications for children's health and welfare.
3. **Observing and Participating.** Watch a young child and an adult in a public place. How does the child imitate the adult's behavior? What implications does this have for setting an example?

CHAPTER 2: Learning About Families **67**

ASSESS

CHECKING COMPREHENSION

Have students answer the Check Your Understanding questions. Answers appear at the bottom of this page.

EVALUATION

Give students the Section 2-1 Quiz in the *Teacher Resource Guide.*

RETEACHING

1. Assign Reteaching Activities, page 11.
2. Have students describe what makes a family different from other groups, such as a class of students or a team.

ENRICHMENT

Have students identify one thing about their families of which they are proud and one thing they want to change. Ask them to write a short essay explaining both.

EXTENSION

Invite a parent, preferably a fairly new parent, to class to discuss the challenges and rewards of their new roles. Have students make a list headed "Challenges" and "Rewards" after the talk.

CLOSE

Have students complete this sentence: "In a healthy family, family members . . ."

ANSWERS TO SECTION 2-1 REVIEW

1. *Examples will vary.*
2. Example, talking, religious training.
3. *See the definitions on pages 58-61.*
4. *Adopted*—permanently enter family. *Foster*—lives with family temporarily.
5. *Answers will vary.*
6. Mobility makes it harder for relatives to maintain their relationships.
7. Loss of jobs or income puts pressure on family finances; time spent training or learning about new jobs cuts into family time; working at home puts new demands on family.

CAREER OPPORTUNITIES

Introducing the Feature

Ask students if they ever wish they had someone to talk to about a problem other than their family or friends. Explain that family counselors are neutral parties and can provide the empathy that people need at times.

Answers to CONNECTING SCHOOL TO CAREER

1. **Possible response:** Conflict resolution; effectively communicating needs; coping skills after divorce.
2. *Answers will vary.*

Applying What You've Learned

Have students write a paragraph comparing and contrasting the career of family counselor to that of teacher.

CAREER OPPORTUNITIES

Family Counselor

A CONVERSATION WITH PAT WILKINS

How did you become interested in becoming a family counselor? My parents had a great marriage, but many of my friends were not so fortunate. When the parents of my closest friend divorced, he took the blow very hard. I tried to listen and help him. Later, I thought about a career in counseling.

What are the tasks and responsibilities of a family counselor? My main job is to meet and talk with married couples or with parents and children. At these sessions, I try to help them find solutions to their problems.

What is the work environment like? I work in an office in a busy clinic. Some colleagues have their own practices as counselors. They work out of small offices or their homes.

What are the working hours like? I work weekdays plus two nights a week and one Saturday a month. The extra hours make time for clients' work schedules.

What aptitudes are needed to be a family counselor? You have to be a good listener first of all. You also have to be able to hear more than what people say. Sometimes words don't convey people's full meaning. You have to be patient with people who aren't ready to open up, and you have to build up their confidence and trust so that they will. Most of all, you have to treat what people tell you in strictest confidence.

Career Facts

FAMILY COUNSELOR

Education and Training. Family counselors must have a bachelor's degree (sociology, psychology, or social work). Some have master's degrees or doctorate degrees.

Career Outlook. The demand for family counselors is expected to grow moderately.

CONNECTING SCHOOL TO CAREER

1. **Thinking Skills.** What kinds of problems do you think a family counselor would help people with?
2. **Interpersonal Skills.** How would you rate your ability to listen, your patience, your ability to build trust, and your ability to hold information in confidence? In which of these areas do you think you need to improve? Why?

68 UNIT 1: Children, Parenting, and You

Building Career Skills

Technology. Ask students whether they they think family counselors are likely to make use of current technology, such as computers, the Internet, fax machines, and so on. Have them discuss in what ways they think such technology would or would not be helpful in a family counseling practice.

What Parenthood Means

When a baby is born, parents can feel great joy. Some also feel that a great burden has been placed on their shoulders. The decision to become a parent is a serious one. Being a parent radically changes a person's life and creates new responsibilities.

KEY TERMS

emotional maturity
parenthood

OBJECTIVES:

- Describe the changes that parenthood brings.
- List considerations couples should look at before deciding to become parents.
- Use a process to build management skills.

Parenthood Brings Changes

When April was born, Dominique and Ross were more excited than they had ever been. Life with April seemed easy at first. Dominique's parents stayed with them for a week to help. Everyone was smiling all the time, and they were happy.

CHAPTER 2: Learning About Families **69**

Observing & Participating

Have students write down their daily schedules for three days, including one weekend. They should include all of their activities on the schedule. Then have them examine that schedule while imagining that they are now parents. How would their daily lives change? What new activities would be added? What would they have to drop?

SECTION 2-2 RESOURCES

Teacher Resource Guide
- Lesson Plan Organizer, p. 38
- Section 2-2 Quiz, p. 98

Student Motivation Kit
- Observations & Case Studies (case study), pp. 89-90
- Reteaching Activity, p. 12
- Enrichment, p. 8
- Teen Parenting Skills, pp. 120-121

Student Workbook
- Study Guide, pp. 19-21
- Management Skills, pp. 24-25

Transparency Package
- CT-6 Ready for Parenthood?
- CT-7 Parents Manage Many Roles

Effective Instruction CD-ROM

FOCUS

MOTIVATOR

Point out to students that parenthood is often romanticized, or talked about in a way that focuses on only the positive aspects of parenting. Encourage students to share their romantic images of parenthood. Does there seem to be a difference between boys' and girls' ideas of parenthood?

VOCABULARY ACTIVITY

Ask students to define the word *childhood*. Then have them use their knowledge of the suffix *-hood* to define *parenthood*.

1. Whose needs must parents consider first? (*The child's.*)
2. Give an example of how lifestyle changes with parenthood. (*Possible response: Parents may not be able to go out with friends.*)

ACTIVITIES

Math Activity

Have students calculate how much time a new parent might spend feeding an infant assuming that the baby is fed every three hours, and each feeding lasts 45 minutes. How much time is spent feeding the baby each day? Each week? (*6 hours/day; 42 hours/week.*) **L1**

VISUAL LEARNING | Using the Photograph

Left— Possible responses: May have less time for work or miss work to care for sick child.

Page 71: *Possible responses:* Sharing problems helps you feel better; talking together may help people see a solution.

A big part of being a parent is accepting responsibility for a child's welfare—not just for days or weeks, but for many years. *How might this responsibility affect this parent's career?*

After her parents left, though, things changed. The baby cried every night and hardly slept. Dominique and Ross didn't get much sleep, either. Ross dragged himself off to work each day feeling exhausted. Meanwhile, Dominique was alone with the baby—feeling abandoned. Having a baby didn't seem like much fun anymore.

Parenthood begins with having a child by birth or adoption. It doesn't end there,

however. Having a child brings dramatic and long-lasting changes. Some involve great joy, but others can be difficult to deal with.

New Responsibilities

Raising a child is more than just a day-to-day assignment. It is a lifelong commitment. A child needs physical care, financial support, love, and guidance into adulthood. Once they become parents, people can no longer think of their own needs first. They first have to consider what their child needs.

First-time parents can feel overwhelmed by these new responsibilities. They need to remember that they are not alone. Family and friends can help in many ways, from watching a child while the parent goes shopping to just listening. The community has many resources as well, from religious leaders to government agencies to private groups.

Changes in Lifestyle

New parents have to adjust to major changes in their daily lives. Caring for a child—especially a newborn—takes a huge amount of time and energy. A newborn needs to be fed every few hours, both day and night. In addition, babies must be diapered, played with, and comforted.

With children of any age, parents have limits placed on their personal freedom. They may not be able to go out with friends because they have to stay home to watch the children. Instead of relaxing right after a hard day's work, they have to fix dinner.

Couples are better able to adjust to these changes in life if they prepare for them. They can read books and articles on parenting and child development, talk to

---

ISSUES IN TEEN PARENTING

Being a teen parent can be a difficult experience. In addition, teens who have become parents often face unique conflicts that arise from living in a three-generation household. Trying to satisfy two roles—as parent and as child—can be confusing. Another complicating factor is that the teens' parents may play a major role in caring for her child. On the other hand, teen parents who live at home enjoy certain advantages too. Ask students to discuss how problems arise, how they can be resolved, and what advantages live-at-home teen parents may have.

Practicing Parenting

What Every Child Needs

*P*arents are responsible for meeting ten key needs that each child has:

- 💜 The loving reassurance that comes in hugs.
- 💜 An environment that is safe and healthy.
- 💜 A relationship with caregivers that lasts.
- 💜 Communication by talking and gestures.
- 💜 A chance to see and hear other people.
- 💜 A place where they are safe to explore and learn.
- 💜 Praise, to build their self-esteem.
- 💜 Opportunities to play so they can learn.
- 💜 Music and rhythm.
- 💜 Being read to.

APPLY YOUR KNOWLEDGE

1. Why is it important for children to have lasting relationships with caregivers?
2. Why do you think reading is more important for children than watching television?

Some new mothers, who care for their babies full time, feel that they never have a break. Some new fathers, who work outside the home, may feel that they miss their baby's growth. *How can talking help couples handle these feelings?*

family members or friends who are parents, and take parenting classes. These steps can make the demands of parenthood less surprising and unsettling.

Emotional Adjustments

Parenthood requires many emotional adjustments. Going through so many changes is stressful in itself. On top of that, many parents feel conflicting—and sometimes difficult—emotions, such as:

Defining a Problem. Have students write a list of questions they would want to ask a spouse before deciding to have a child. Then have them consider what responses they would find acceptable. **L1**

Discussion Activity

Read the following scenario to students: "Lisa is at home with her three-week-old son while her husband is away at work. She feels lonely and worries about how the loss of her income will affect family finances. On top of this, the baby is fussy. Nothing Lisa does seems to prevent it from crying and being uncomfortable."

Ask: What suggestions can students give Lisa to cope with these stresses? **L1**

Practicing Parenting

Ask students what they think would be the most important thing for a parent to give a child. Why do they place such value on this?

Answers to Apply Your Knowledge

1. *Possible response:* Children need stability to build trust.
2. *Possible response*: Reading calls for interaction, which isn't true of television.

Parenting in *Action*

In addition to learning what to expect from parenthood, what can a couple do to avoid problems in the relationship? Here are some suggestions:

- Talk issues over ahead of time to prevent problems from arising later.
- Decide how to share parenting and household tasks.
- Make time for each other.
- Relax, keep a sense of humor, and remember, no new parents feel confident. This perspective can keep minor tensions from becoming major sources of conflict.

COMPREHENSION CHECK

1. Why do new parents sometimes feel conflict when their own parents give advice? (*They may see it as criticism.*)
2. What positive feelings does parenthood bring? (*Happiness, pride, love.*)
3. Why should prospective parents have a health checkup? (*Any medical problem they have could affect the baby.*)

ACTIVITIES

Discussion Activity

Ask: When thinking about parenthood, do you think people look beyond the first few years of the child's life? Why or why not?

DID *You* **Know?**

Managing Stress For the parent already overwhelmed with the emotional adjustments of parenthood, a late night (or early morning) with a crying infant can seem like the last straw. Parents can use various coping techniques:
- Get a temporary caregiver at least once a week.
- Exercise to release tension. Take the baby for a walk, or take a walk alone while someone else watches the baby.
- Share your feelings with a spouse, friend, or other adult.

Raising a child brings a parent carries heavy responsibilities—but it also brings many rewards. Seeing a happy, growing child gives a parent a deep sense of accomplishment.

- Fear of not being a good parent.
- Frustration at the loss of personal freedom and the addition of new responsibilities.
- Worry over money matters.
- Jealousy of the baby and the attention he or she gets.
- Depression due to exhaustion or to the physical changes of pregnancy and birth.

Parents can feel confused and troubled by these negative emotions, but these feelings are normal. With time, most parents get over these rough spots. They learn to accept that they will have negative feelings from time to time, and they learn how to handle them.

Changes in Relationships

When people have a child, they are likely to notice changes in how they interact with each other and with other family members. This is especially true for first-time parents.

The birth of a baby is a wonderful time. Some parents, though, feel overwhelmed by negative emotions and begin to bicker or fight with one another. Having patience and being understanding can reduce the danger of frustration boiling over into anger. The key to getting past trouble spots is for the couple to have good communication.

A birth changes the relationship between the child's parents and their parents. Grandparents feel love and joy of their own and want to spend time with the baby.

Many want to help with the baby or with chores around the house. Sometimes, offers of help cause friction. New parents may feel that the grandparents' advice is really a criticism and resent it. At the same time, the grandparents feel hurt if their suggestions are rejected.

Many new parents feel that having a baby brings them closer to their own parents. Understanding what it is to be a parent, they now appreciate their own parents more.

72 UNIT 1: Children, Parenting, and You

LEARNING STYLES

Kinesthetic

Have students create short public service videos for new parents on how to cope with the challenges of their new role. Students can use dolls as babies and feature new parents caring for a child while a narrator describes challenges and tips in the background.

Changes at Work

Having children has an impact on careers. Working women may quit work or cut back on their hours to care for their child. Workers who often worked overtime or weekends before a child may be less willing to put in extra hours once they become parents.

At the same time, a growing number of companies have policies to help working parents. Some have child care facilities at the workplace. Others offer flexible hours or part-time work, which allows a parent to be there when children arrive home from school.

The Rewards of Parenthood

Parenthood brings many joys as well. Nothing is quite like a baby's first smile or hearing a three-year-old say "I love you, Mommy." Parents feel happiness, pride, and love that they never felt before.

By helping children discover the world, parents can see it with new eyes themselves. Having children can enrich an already strong marriage. Finally, raising children can give parents a great sense of accomplishment.

Making Decisions About Parenthood

People who are thinking about parenthood should have a clear picture of what parenthood is. They also need to take a realistic look at themselves to see if they are ready for parenthood.

Emotional Maturity

To handle the changes that parenthood brings, a person needs **emotional maturity.** That means being responsible enough to consistently put someone else's needs before your own. It means being secure enough to devote your full attention to an infant without receiving any attention in return. It means being able to hold your temper when a toddler breaks something.

Prospective parents should take an honest look at their maturity. Are they equipped to handle the challenges of parenthood? If they have any doubts, it may be best to postpone becoming a parent.

Desire for Parenthood

Some prospective parents hope that having a child will solve some other problem. Not all the reasons for wanting children indicate real readiness for parenthood. Think about the reasons shown on the chart on page 74.

Health Considerations

The best gift a woman can give a baby is good health. That starts with good nutrition before prgnancy begins. Following the Food Guide Pyramid can help. Most teens and young women don't get enough calcium, iron, and folic acid—key nutrients—from what they eat. A doctor may recommend a prenatal vitamin.

It is best for both prospective parents to see a doctor for a checkup. If either has a medical problem, it could affect the health of the baby or the person's ability to care for the child. The age of the prospective mother should also be considered. If she is under seventeen or over thirty-five, pregnancy is riskier for both her and the baby.

CHAPTER 2: Learning About Families **73**

COMPREHENSION CHECK

1. What is the financial impact if one spouse in a two-worker family quits his or her job? (*Loss of income.*) What is the financial impact if both spouses continue to work after the child is born? (*Cost of child care.*)

2. Why evaluate an attempt to solve a problem? (*To see if new steps are needed; to improve problem solving.*)

ACTIVITIES

Health Activity

Suggest that students research the risks involved in having a baby when the mother is under seventeen or over thirty-five. Students should learn what steps are taken during pregnancy to lessen these risks and what things the prospective mother can do herself. Have students report on their findings in a brief report. **L2**

▶ Reasons for Parenthood

UNSOUND REASONS	SOUND REASONS
• Our marriage is in trouble. Maybe having a baby will solve our problems.	• Having children will add depth to our relationship, which is already strong.
• A baby is someone who will love me and belong to me.	• I want to give a baby my care and love.
• I feel like I'm nobody. Being a parent will make me somebody.	• I feel good about myself and believe that parenthood will be a rewarding experience.
• I want someone who will take care of me when I'm old.	• I want to experience the special bond between parent and child, which lasts a lifetime.
• Our parents want grandchildren.	• I love children, and I want to be a parent.

To raise a child, a parent needs to juggle many demands. *What resources do parents have to manage when they raise children?*

Financial Concerns

Raising a child is expensive. Before deciding on parenthood, couples should take a careful look at the costs involved over the years ahead. They may need to change their way of life to prepare for these expenses.

If both prospective parents work, they need to think about what they will do after the baby arrives. Will one leave his or her job to care for the baby? If so, the family's income will drop. Will they both continue working? If so, they will need additional money to pay for child care for the baby.

LEARNING STYLES	**Auditory**

Auditory

In small groups, have students create a self-help audiotape for parents planning to have a child. The tape might cover such issues as: making sure parenthood is right for them; getting a health check; getting finances in order; and applying management skills to their new lives as parents. Have students write an outline of their main points before making the tape, and listen to their tape and revise it before presenting it to the rest of the class.

Management Skills

Whatever the decision, parents will need good money management skills. In fact, they will need to effectively manage their other resources—such as time, skills, money, and energy—as well. There are five key steps to good management:

- **Set goals.** Decide what is important to you and then make them into objectives for you to achieve.
- **Identify resources.** Figure out your resources for achieving your goal.

- **Make a plan.** Decide how you will use your resources to meet that goal.
- **Put the plan in action.** Once you have a plan, start working toward your goals. Base decisions on your goals.
- **Reevaluate from time to time.** Step back and take stock of your progress. Do you need more resources or different ones? Did you achieve your goal more easily than you expected? What new goals do you now have?

SECTION 2-2 REVIEW

✔ Check Your Understanding

1. Which of the changes caused by parenting do you think is the biggest? Explain your answer.
2. How can parents-to-be prepare for the changes brought on by parenthood?
3. Why are the negative emotions of parenthood hard to accept?
4. What impact can having a child have on a working parent?
5. Use your own words to define *emotional maturity*.
6. Why is "Our parents want grandchildren" an *unsound* reason for having a baby?
7. List the five steps of being a good manager.

Putting Knowledge Into Practice

1. **Drawing Conclusions.** Suppose people had to earn a license before becoming parents. What skills do you think they would need to qualify for the license?
2. **Applying.** With a group of classmates, take turns acting out various situations in which people express their feelings about having a new child. Identify the specific emotions being expressed, and discuss the probable reasons for those emotions.
3. **Observing and Participating.** Observe a new parent caring for a young baby for a period of two hours or more. Briefly describe the demands made by the baby and explain how the parent responded. Did the parent try to accomplish anything else while with the baby? If so, was he or she successful? If not, why do you think he or she didn't try to do anything else?
4. **Applying.** Write a scenario about a couple's use of the management process to decide on care of an expected baby.

ANSWERS TO SECTION 2-2 REVIEW

ANSWERS TO SECTION 2-2 REVIEW

1. *Answers and reasons will vary.*
2. Read books and articles; talk to family and friends; take classes in parenting.
3. *Possible response:* People expect to feel joy; negative feelings surprise.
4. *Possible response:* A working parent may be less willing to work

extra hours.
5. *Possible response:* Putting others' needs before your own needs.
6. *Possible response:* Because the parents—not the grandparents—are taking on the responsibility of caring for the child.
7. *See the list on this page.*

ASSESS

CHECKING COMPREHENSION

Have students answer the Check Your Understanding. Answers appear at the bottom of the page.

EVALUATION

Give students the Section 2-2 Quiz in the *Teacher Resource Guide.*

RETEACHING

1. Assign Reteaching Activities, page 12.
2. Have students make two lists, one on ways parenthood changes your life and one on factors to be considered before becoming a parent.

ENRICHMENT

Have students create posters that illustrate the rewards and responsibilities of parenthood.

EXTENSION

Invite a teen parent and a parent who waited until the thirties to have a child. Have them share the special challenges they face as the result of their age. Have students write an essay on which choice they think is more difficult and why.

CLOSE

Have students sum up in a paragraph what being a parent means to the parent and to the child.

Have students draw a pie chart in which the wedges represent the necessary ingredients for a healthy family. Student should vary the size of the wedges to show which elements they think have greater and lesser value.

TEACH

COMPREHENSION CHECK

1. Who is responsible for helping create a healthy family? (*Every member.*)
2. What effect does spending time together have? (*Helps build strong bonds.*)

ACTIVITIES

Critical Thinking Activity

Analyzing Primary Sources. Read students the following from child advocate Tipper Gore: "Hugging, kissing, smiling, laughing—all are crucial to the healthy development of a baby and young child. It's a big, complicated, not-always-friendly world they'll be growing up in. Your love can serve as a powerful immunization, sheltering them from self-doubt, giving them the strength they'll need to blossom and thrive."
Have students write a paragraph that explains how this statement relates to the feature. **L1**

Parenting With Care

Building a Healthy Family

A strong family requires everyone working together.

Because families serve such important functions, they should be supported and encouraged.

What does it take for a family to function well? Every member must take responsibility for making the family work. Here are some ways:

- **Feeling Committed.** In a healthy family, each member feels committed to the family as a whole and to each other member. Each person can show this commitment through respect, support, and consideration.
- **Making Time Together.** By spending time together, family members build strong bonds. A family with young children might go to the park. A family with teens might take a hike or biking trip. Even shopping for clothes, cooking meals, or cleaning the home can help build bonds if people share the work together.

- **Communicating.** Families need open and honest communication. Members need to tell each other what they think and feel—and they need to be considerate of other members' thoughts and feelings. Of course, family members will not always agree with each other. If they respect each other, though, they can disagree without hurting feelings.
- **Appreciation.** People in healthy families like each other—and say so. They speak and act affectionately and in a caring way.
- **Shared Beliefs.** Healthy families build their strong relations on a foundation of shared beliefs. These beliefs form a basis for making decisions—they reflect what is important to family members.

76 UNIT 1: Children, Parenting, and You

RESOURCES ON SINGLE-PARENT FAMILIES

The challenge of building a healthy family is even harder for single parents. Although they must provide for the family financially, they also must make sure they spend enough time with their children. They also have to handle the entire burden when problems arise. Students might find it interesting to contact Parents Without Partners, which has local branches in all fifty states. For more information, contact the organization at 1650 South Dixie Highway, Suite 510, Boca Raton, FL 33432 or through its Website: www. parentswithoutpartners.org

• **Coping Skills.** Every family has to deal with problems. Having good coping skills helps them get past these problems. Two important coping skills are the ability to recognize a problem and the willingness to admit to it. Admitting to a problem is not a sign of weakness but of strength.

Following Up

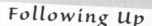

1. Make a list of local sites, events, or outings that would be appropriate for a family with children aged one to three, with children aged four to six, with children aged seven to twelve, or with teens.

2. **Communication.** Why does open and honest communication help build strong families?

3. **Thinking Skills.** How is admitting to a problem a sign of strength?

CHAPTER 2: Learning About Families **77**

CLOSE

1. Have students create a schedule for a week in which they block out "family time." The schedule should show required events in the lives of students and other family members. After seeing which times are already filled, students can then determine what time is available for the family to make time to spend together.

2. **Extension.** Have students get permission from a local pediatrician to spend time in their waiting room observing the parents and children there. Students should note how the parents interact with their children and the differing parenting styles exhibited.

Answers to Following Up

1. *Answers will vary but should show some recognition of the differences among different ages.*
2. *Possible response:* Because it helps build trust.
3. *Possible response:* Because it takes strength and confidence to be willing to admit that there is room for improvement.

CHECKING COMPREHENSION

Use the Summary and the Reviewing the Facts questions to help students go over the most important ideas in Chapter 2. Encourage students to ask questions and add details.

CHAPTER 2 REVIEW

Answers to Reviewing the Facts

1. Physical, intellectual, social, and emotional needs.
2. Don't have another person to share parenting responsibilities with; don't have someone who can add to family income.
3. Listening; empathy; compromise. *Possible response*: Because they help people get along with one another and solve interpersonal problems.
4. *Possible responses*: When a blended family forms and new children are born, starting the parental stages again; when a couple marries but does not have children.
5. *Possible response*: Economic changes, specifically the increase in two-income families.
6. *Possible response*: Limits on freedom.
7. They have to adjust to new relationships, for instance, over the issue of giving help or advice.
8. *Possible response*: Parent wants to watch a favorite television show, but child is sick and needs comforting.
9. Because it is expensive to raise a child.
10. Helps them use resources effectively.

CHAPTER 2   REVIEW &

Summary

✔ Families meet members' basic needs and prepare them to live in society. (Section 2-1)

✔ Family structure, stages of life, and changes in society all have an impact on families. (Section 2-1)

✔ Parenthood causes many changes, especially for first-time parents. (Section 2-2)

✔ Before deciding to become parents, couples should seriously consider their readiness for parenthood. (Section 2-2)

✔ Learning management skills helps parents cope with the demands on their time, energy, and money. (Section 2-2)

Reviewing the Facts

1. What kinds of basic needs do families meet? (Section 2-1)
2. What two difficulties do single parents face that are not present in two-parent families? (Section 2-1)
3. What skills are especially useful in blended families? Why? (Section 2-1)
4. Give examples of two different variations on the family life cycle. (Section 2-1)
5. Families eat more and more meals outside the home. Which social trends described in the chapter do you think this is related to? Explain why. (Section 2-1)
6. Give an example of a change in lifestyle caused by parenthood. (Section 2-2)
7. How do parents and grandparents of a new baby have to adjust? (Section 2-2)

8. Describe a situation in which a parent shows emotional maturity. (Section 2-2)
9. Why are financial issues significant for parents? (Section 2-2)
10. How can management skills help a parent? (Section 2-2)

Thinking Critically

1. **Analyzing.** Marty's father died. Two years later, his mother married a man who had a daughter. Because there were only two bedrooms available for children, Marty was asked to give up his room for his stepsister and share a room with his brother. Do you think that was fair? Why or why not?
2. **Synthesizing.** Adults who care for both their own children and their aged parents are sometimes called members of the "sandwich generation." Why is that an appropriate name?
3. **Ranking.** Which of the issues about parenthood do you think is the most important? Why?

Taking Action

1. **Sending a Message.** Write a public-service announcement that informs young couples about the responsibilities of having children. *(Leadership)*

CONNECTIONS

2. **In the News.** Scan the newspaper or a magazine for articles that you think describe a social trend that has an impact on the family. Bring one article to class and explain how the trend affects the family. *(Communication)*

3. **Making a List.** Write down a list of ten questions that you think a person should ask himself or herself before deciding to become a parent. Share your list with the class. *(Thinking Skills)*

 ## Cross-Curricular Connections

1. **Math.** Searching in the library or online, find the number of households headed by two parents and one parent in both of the last two censuses. Calculate the percentage of change for both types of family structures.

2. **Language Arts.** Write a scene in which a young couple discusses whether or not to have children. You can end the scene with either decision, but be sure to have both characters show good communication skills as they talk about the issue.

 ## Workplace Connections

1. **Personal Qualities.** List the personal qualities you think would be needed by someone who worked with families wanting to adopt a child.

2. **Thinking Skills.** Suppose you were a business owner. What policies could you devise for your business that would be helpful for your employees who had children?

 ## Family and Community Connections

1. **Foster Children.** Find out from local agencies what a person needs to do to qualify as a foster parent. Present your findings to the class and discuss them.

2. **Community Resources.** Identify a local agency or group that offers child care classes to prospective or new parents. Prepare a fact sheet that tells where and when the class are held, how many sessions are included, how long each session lasts, and what material is covered.

Technology Connections

1. **Internet.** Search for Web sites that offer help for people in single-parent or blended families.

2. **Video or Audiotape.** Tape an interview with an adult who describes the changes experienced when he or she had a first child. If tape equipment is not available, write down the interviewee's comments and share them with the class.

EVALUATION

1. Use the reproducible Chapter 2 Test in the *Teacher Resource Guide*, or construct your own test using the **Exam**View® Test Generator.

2. For an alternative assessment, assign the Chapter 2 activity in the *Authentic Assessment* section of the *Teacher Resource Guide*.

ENRICHMENT

Assign students either of the two enrichment activities in the *Enrichment Activities* booklet in the *Student Motivation Kit*.

EXTENSION

Have students prepare a lesson plan for a parenting class addressing the issue of the decision to become parents.

CLOSE

Have students create a new type of family "tree" by drawing a tree and then labeling the branches with the various types of family structures. This same exercise can be used to show the trends affecting families or the issues to consider when deciding whether or not to become a parent.

CHAPTER 3 RESOURCES

Teacher Resource Guide
• Chapter 3 Test, pp. 106-109
• Authentic Assessment,
  pp. 261-262
Student Motivation Kit
• Case Studies & Observations,
  pp. 31-32
Transparency Package
• CT-8 to CT-9
Effective Instruction CD-ROM

CHAPTER 3   **OVERVIEW**

In **Section 3-1**, students are introduced to a variety of parenting styles and skills.

In **Section 3-2**, students learn why guiding children's behavior is so important, why consistency is crucial, and how to deal with inappropriate behavior.

In **Section 3-3**, students explore the various child care options available and learn how to evaluate a care provider.

CHAPTER 3   **OBJECTIVES**

After completing Chapter 3, students will be able to:

• Discuss the skills needed for parenting skills and how they can be acquired.
• Describe effective methods for guiding the behavior of young children.
• Discuss the need for substitute care and evaluate substitute care options.

CHAPTER 3

Effective Parenting Skills

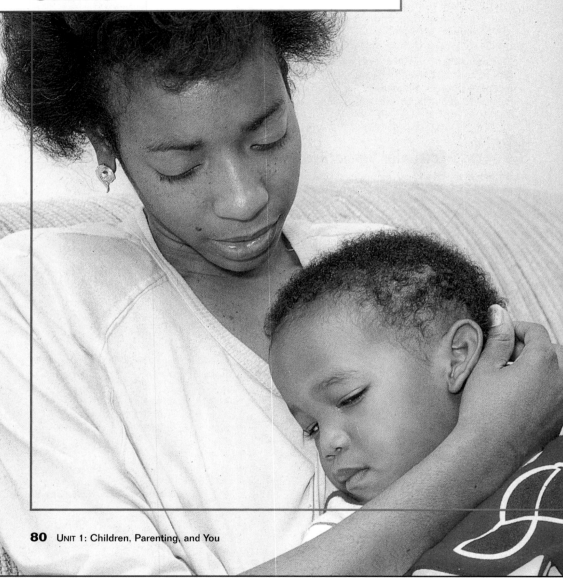

80   UNIT 1: Children, Parenting, and You

RESOURCES TO EXPLORE

Child Care. It is often difficult for teen parents to remain in school, pressured by the demands of school, child care, and finances. Because of the critical importance of a complete education for the family's long-term success, teen parents need to make informed choices about substitute care. Furthermore, they need to feel reassured about the quality of the care they have chosen. For local referrals of accredited child care programs, teen parents can contact the Child Care Information Service/National Association for the Education of Young Children. The Website is www.naeyc.org

As the thunder rolled and the lightning cracked during the night, two-year-old Ian cried out. His mother awoke from her own sleep with a start and quickly ran to his room. She took Ian out of the crib. Holding him close, she carried him to the rocking chair. She sat down and began rocking, singing softly to comfort him. The storm passed and so did his fears. Soon Ian was asleep again. Once his mother was sure he was sound asleep, she put him back in his crib.

The next morning, Ian awoke as though nothing had happened. He was cheerful and ready to take on the world. His mother gave him a reassuring hug, and he ran off to play.

> "She sat down and began rocking, singing softly to comfort him. The storm passed and so did his fears."

INTRODUCING CHAPTER 3

- Write the following on the board: "Wanted—Perfect Parents." **Ask:** What are the qualities and characteristics of perfect parents? Record students' suggestions on the board.
- Have students examine the photograph on the opening page. **Ask:** What would you say to a two-year-old who was frightened of thunder and lightning? What about a four-year-old? What about a six-year-old? After they have made suggestions for each age, have them discuss why the responses differ.

USING THE SCENARIO Have students read the story in the student text. Explain that the scenario depicts a typical situation in which a parent has to respond to a child's needs. Have them create another example.

CHAPTER 3: Effective Parenting Skills **81**

KEY TO ABILITY LEVELS Each section gives skill-building activities. Each activity has been labeled for use with students of various learning styles and abilities.

L1 Level 1 activities are basic activities and should be within the range of all students.

L2 Level 2 activities are average activities and should be within the range of average and above average students.

L3 Level 3 activities are challenging activities designed for the ability range of above average students.

SECTION 3-1 RESOURCES

Teacher Resource Guide
- Lesson Plan Organizer, p. 39
- Section 3-1 Quiz, p. 103

Student Motivation Kit
- Reteaching Activity, p. 13

Student Workbook
- Study Guide, pp. 26-30
- Parenting and You, pp. 31-32

Transparency Package
- CT-8 Positive Parenting Techniques

Effective Instruction CD-ROM

FOCUS

MOTIVATOR

Ask students whether they think being a good parent comes naturally or is a skill that can be learned. After a short discussion, explain to the class that it is a learned skill—one which anyone can master.

VOCABULARY ACTIVITY

Ask: What does it mean when a person has authority? What is a democracy? What does it mean to permit something? Based on these definitions, have students hypothesize about the meanings of the authoritarian, democratic, and permissive styles of parenting.

What Is Parenting?

Parenting is a strange kind of job. If you do the job right, you work yourself out of it! By the time you are done parenting, the child has grown to adulthood and is ready to start an independent life.

KEY TERMS

authoritarian style
democratic style
deprivation
nurturing
parenting
permissive style

OBJECTIVES:

- Explain how knowledge of child development is linked to reasonable expectations.
- Distinguish among different parenting styles.
- Identify ways to improve parenting skills.
- Describe how to nurture children.

82

Parenting: A Learning Process

Parenting—caring for children and helping them develop—is complicated. It requires understanding a child's needs and meeting those needs. It also demands good judgment in three ways:
- Parenting requires knowing when to help and when to back off so that a child can do a task himself or herself.

Observing & Participating

To help students better understand the three main styles of parenting, have them think of a parent in a movie or television show. Ask them to explain how the parent guides behavior, handles conflicts with children, and generally interacts with children. Have them address such issues as: What kind of home atmosphere do these practices create? How do the children interact with the parent? How effective is this parent's approach to parenting? After students have read about the different parenting styles, have them identify which style this parent uses.

- Parents need to avoid pushing children to try activities they are not yet ready for. On the other hand, they have to avoid holding children back out of fear that they might fail. Children have to learn how to bounce back and try again.
- The skills that parents need change as children grow up. Parents must adapt their parenting skills at each stage of a child's development.

It's not just parents who need parenting skills. They are essential for anyone who works with children.

Having Reasonable Expectations

Have you ever heard an adult tell a child, "Act your age." Children usually *do* act their age, but adults don't always know what to expect. That's why understanding child development is so important. Having reasonable expectations for children is an essential first step in effective parenting. Kristin grew increasingly frustrated when two-year-old Adam said "no" to everything. Then her mother told her that children usually go through a negative stage at that age. Relieved that Adam would outgrow the behavior, she was better able to handle it.

Caregivers need to be sure to match their expectations to the particular child. Some children learn to walk earlier than others. Some need more encouragement making friends. Caregivers need to respect the differences between children.

Finding a Comfortable Parenting Style

Caregivers look for a parenting style they feel comfortable with—one that matches their personality and values. There are three main styles of parenting:

- **Authoritarian style.** The **authoritarian style** is based on the idea that children should obey their parents without question. In this style, a parent tells a child what to do, and the child's responsibility is to do it. When rules are broken, the authoritarian parent usually acts quickly and firmly.
- **Democratic style.** In the **democratic style,** children have more input into rules and limits. Children are given a certain amount of independence and freedom of choice within those rules.
- **Permissive style.** In the **permissive style,** parents give children a wide range of freedom. In this style, children may set their own rules.

Of course, few parents follow any one style exclusively. A parent may use a more authoritarian style on some issues—say, where health or safety are involved—and be more democratic on, say, clothing. Parents may change their style as children age, too. They may feel that before, say, age eight, children need firm rules, but after that age they can have more freedom.

Getting Help

How do people learn parenting? High school classes in child development and parenting are good sources of information and help. Hospitals, schools, community groups, and private instructors also offer courses or workshops in parenting. These courses can be very helpful. Instructors know the subject and have experience in how to pass their information to others.

Even if you don't take a course, there are many ways to build parenting skills:
- Reading books and magazine articles about parenting.

CHAPTER 3: Effective Parenting Skills **83**

COMPREHENSION CHECK

1. Why do the skills that parents need change? (*Meet children's changing needs.*)
2. How do a parent's expectations affect parenting? (*Influence how parent responds to child.*)

ACTIVITIES

Discussion Activity

Have students name jobs they could have without training or experience. **Ask:** How much responsibility do these jobs involve? How much does parenting involve? Should a person be required to have training before becoming a parent? Why or why not? **L1**

Critical Thinking Activity

Comparing Points of View. Have students identify how a parent might react to this situation, depending on parenting style: It is 10:00 p.m. and two brothers are still playing in their bedroom. Bedtime is supposed to be at 9:00 p.m. **L1**

DID *You* **Know?**

The Importance of Parenting. Judith Harris' book The Nurture Assumption casts doubt on the importance of parenting. Harris argues that peers, not parents, are the most important influence on a child's behavior— even at an early age. Harris points out that many studies fail to find clear effects of parental action on children's personality and development. The reason, she says, is that researchers have focused on family and not peer groups. Children's dress, speech, and habits are influenced by their peers.

COMPREHENSION CHECK

1. Where can people take courses in parenting? (*High school, hospitals, schools, community groups, private instructors.*)
2. What are the three tasks of parenting? (*Meeting child's basic needs; nurturing children; guiding behavior.*)
3. In what areas of development do children have needs to be met? (*Physical, emotional, social, intellectual, moral.*)

ACTIVITIES

Critical Thinking Activity

Formulating Questions. Have students imagine that they are parents of a two-year-old. Have them jot down a list of questions they might ask family members or doctors about children and parenting.

Child Advocacy Activity

Have students write a speech that might be given by a spokesperson for a child advocacy group such as the Children's Defense Fund. The speech should explain the responsibility of parents to meet a child's basic needs and nurture children.
L3

| **VISUAL LEARNING** | Using the Photograph |

Possible response: The child will be very messy at first.

Alex is just learning to feed himself. *What expectations should his parents have about neatness?*

- Gaining experience with children.
- Asking the advice of family members and friends.
- Observing other parents and children.

Whatever the method used, try to give yourself as many options as possible. Each child is different, and ideas or techniques that work with some children do not work with others. By learning many different strategies, you are more likely to find one that will work with a particular child.

The Tasks of Parenting

Parenting has three basic tasks. The first is to meet the child's basic needs. The second is to nurture children. The third task of parenting is to guide children to show appropriate behavior. That complex task is discussed in Section 3-2.

Meeting Children's Needs

As you read in Chapter 2, families meet the basic needs of their members. It is the responsibility of parents to meet these needs for children:

- Provide them with food, clothing, and shelter.
- Watch over their safety and health.
- Begin teaching them language.
- Foster intellectual growth by taking an active role in their schooling.
- Teach them to get along with others.
- Provide opportunities for them to love and be loved.

Nurturing

Nurturing means giving a child opportunities for encouragement and enrichment. It also involves showing love, support, and concern.

Parents are children's first teachers. Children naturally learn by exploring their world, trying new things, and imitating others. Nurturing parents give children the freedom they need in order to learn.

Adults should remove as many barriers as possible that prevent children from exploring the world on their own. For an infant, this means a safe environment to explore. For a preschooler, this might mean letting the child play in the sandbox without worrying about dirty hands and clothes.

Parenting in *Action*

Help teens turn the abstract list of children's needs into concrete ideas for their implementation. Suggest that for every item on the list, students supply at least two specific ideas for how to meet that need. For example, for "Begin teaching them language," students might list "Talk to a baby often" and "Read to a child every night." After students have completed their lists, have them exchange them. In this way, students can benefit from the ideas of others and share their own ideas.

Unfortunately, some parents don't encourage their children. These children then lag behind others in their development. They suffer from **deprivation,** or the lack of an enriching environment.

Some people confuse deprivation with poverty. They are not the same. The families of deprived children may be wealthy or poor—or anywhere in between. It is not a matter of money, but of what kind of environment the child has.

As you learned in Section 1-2, a child's brain is ready for certain types of learning at specific ages. A deprived child may have missed the "window of opportunity" for a certain type of development. After this "window", the learning process is more difficult.

Children don't really need lots of fancy toys. Everyday objects and experiences can provide great opportunities for learning.

INFOLINK

Windows of Brain Development

To learn more about *windows of brain development,* see Chapter 1, pages 29-33.

The other part of nurturing is providing love and support. Children need love just as much as they need food to eat and a bed to sleep in.

Teaching a child to ride shows parenting in action. Parents give help and guidance, but then must back off to allow children to master skills on their own. *How can failing help children learn?*

CHAPTER 3: Effective Parenting Skills **85**

Discussion Activity

Present the following family situation to the class: Dana's father has been ill and unable to work for over a year. Her mother was laid off from her job and cannot find another. The family has very little money and cannot make ends meet. Dana's family has pulled together during these trying times, and Dana feels loved and secure, despite her parents' problems. **Ask:** Is Dana deprived? If so, in what way? If not, why not? **L1**

The Developing Brain

Thinking Skills

Experts suggest certain steps parents can take to develop children's thinking skills:
• Let the child do a task rather than doing it for the child.
• Give hints toward solving a problem if the child needs it, but don't specifically tell a child what to do.
• Word advice as questions.
• Praise the child's successes.
• Elaborate on the child's language—answer short statements with more details.

VISUAL LEARNING Using the Photograph *Possible response:* They learn from mistakes.

Management/Leadership Skills

Suggest that students volunteer to work with a young child in order to practice nurturing behavior. Either you or they can contact a teacher in the elementary school who might identify a student who would benefit from one-on-one interaction with an older child for a limited time. Suggest that students follow up their experience with a report in which they outline the techniques they tried, the difficulties they faced, and the successes they felt they achieved.

ACTIVITIES

Discussion Activity

Read this statement from the text: "Children need love just as much as they need food to eat and a bed to sleep in." **Ask:** Do you agree or disagree with this statement? Why? Is it difficult or easy to measure the effects of a nurturing versus a deprived environment? Why? **L1**

DID *You* **Know?**

Nurturing. The following guidelines will help boost a child's self-confidence:

- Help a child set reasonable goals that will not result in frustration.
- Identify good role models.
- Maintain an atmosphere of respect and love.
- Encourage a child to complete goals and follow through with plans.
- Teach that mistakes are an opportunity to learn.

VISUAL LEARNING Using the Photographs

Left—Possible response: They learn form mistakes. Answers will vary; have students discuss the reasons for their responses.
Right—Possible response: Hand-eye coordination.

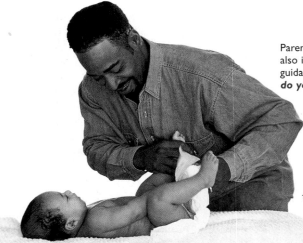

Parenting involves providing physical care but also includes giving love, encouragement, and guidance. *Which of these tasks of parenting do you think is the most important?*

The Developing Brain

Hugs do more than give a child emotional reassurance. Touching through daily massage helps premature babies gain weight faster. Massage is also linked to lower levels of stress and better motor skills.

Parents can show children love in many different ways, including hugs, kisses, and smiles. Patient listening and giving time and attention also show love and support. It can be discussing ways to get along better with a playmate or helping fix a broken toy.

Some parents have difficulty showing affection for their children. They may be embarrassed or feel that affection will make their children "too soft." Without a loving parent's recognition of their accomplishments, however, children may feel insecure and worthless. They may have a difficult time forming healthy relationships because they never learned how to give and receive love.

Some parents become overprotective and overattentive. They shower a child with too much attention, too many toys, too many treats. They may try to shield the child from unpleasant experiences. These practices harm children, too. Children learn from trial and error. They need to make mistakes so they can learn from them.

Communicating Positively

Good communication is an important part of good parenting. Being a good listener is one way of showing children that you respect them. The way you talk to children is equally important.

Techniques for good communication include the following:
- Use words the child can understand, but avoid talking down to the child.
- Be clear. Think in terms of the child's point of view.
- Be positive and polite. Hearing a constant series of "don'ts" is discouraging. Try saying, "Please shut the door quietly."
- Give praise and love. Everyone needs to hear good things about themselves—especially young children.

86 UNIT 1: Children, Parenting, and You

LEARNING STYLES

Interpersonal

Have students answer the following question: Are you a good nurturer? Why or why not? To answer the question, assign the following activity. For one day, have students monitor their own interactions with others. Have them identify the opportunities they can to nurture the people they come in contact with. Have them make a note of these occasions and how they responded. When they are done, they should write a paragraph describing whether they are a good nurturer or not. If not, what could they do to improve?

- Children often tune out adults who only give commands or directions. Limit the directions to those that are essential.
- Talk about what's meaningful to the child. Comments about the picture he drew or the tower she built says you care about what he or she does.

Everyday objects like these wooden spoons and plastic containers can become opportunities for young children to explore, learn, and have fun. *What skills can children develop by playing with these things?*

SECTION 3-1 REVIEW

✔ Check Your Understanding

1. Why must parents learn to adapt their parenting skills over time?
2. Why is it important to understand child development?
3. Describe the three styles of parenting.
4. What do you think is an advantage of taking a course in parenting?
5. Why is providing enrichment part of nurturing?
6. Why should caregivers avoid talking down to a child?

Putting Knowledge Into Practice

1. **Predicting Consequences.** What will probably happen to a child if parents consistently give him or her tasks for which he or she is not developmentally ready?
2. **Drawing Conclusions.** Thirteen-year-old Danette wants a bicycle, but her parents can't afford a new one. They say that if she uses some of her money from babysitting they will match the sum to buy her a used bike. Is this an example of deprivation? Why or why not?
3. **Observing and Participating.** Observe the teachers in your classes. Without naming names, describe an incident you saw in which a teacher encouraged a student to try something new or to recover from a mistake.

CHAPTER 3: Effective Parenting Skills **87**

ANSWERS TO SECTION 3-1 REVIEW

1. Because skills they need change as children grow and develop and have different needs.
2. So you can have reasonable expectations.
3. *See the definitions on page 83.*
4. *Possible responses*: It is an opportunity to learn from a knowledgeable person; you can gain exposure to varied parenting techniques.
5. Gives a child a chance to grow and develop.
6. *Possible response:* If you talk down to the child, he or she may not listen, feeling a lack of respect.

SECTION 3-2 RESOURCES

Teacher Resource Guide
- Lesson Plan Organizer, p. 40
- Section 3-2 Quiz, p. 104

Student Motivation Kit
- Observ. & Case Studies (case study), pp. 91-92
- Reteaching Activity, p. 14
- Enrichment, pp. 9-10

Student Workbook
- Study Guide, pp. 26-30
- Being Positive, pp. 33-34

Effective Instruction CD-ROM

FOCUS

MOTIVATOR

Have students think back to a time when they did not behave appropriately. How did their parents or guardians handle the situation? What type of disciplinary measures, if any, were taken? How effective were those measures? Discuss students' responses briefly.

VOCABULARY ACTIVITY

Have students use dictionaries to learn the derivation of *discipline* (from the Latin for "teaching"). How does this help clarify the meaning of *self-discipline*? **Ask:** What is a time-out during a sports game? Can students guess the meaning of *time-out* in relation to child guidance?

Guiding Children's Behavior

Amy was frustrated because four-year-old Jenny never put her toys away. She tried reminding Jenny, scolding her, and even banning television until the toys were picked up. Nothing seemed to work. She didn't know what to do.

KEY TERMS
- conscience
- guidance
- negative reinforcement
- positive reinforcement
- self-discipline
- time-out

OBJECTIVES:
- Explain the importance of consistency in guiding children.
- Apply effective techniques for encouraging appropriate behavior.
- Explain how and why to set limits.
- Identify effective ways of dealing with misbehavior.

Understanding Guidance

Some people think of guiding behavior as disciplining children when they do something wrong. Punishment *is* part of guidance, but just a small part. It should be used only when necessary and only in specific

---

Observing & Participating

Have students go to a shopping mall or supermarket to observe children and their parents. Students should list each type of guidance and disciplinary techniques they observe. Which techniques are used most often? Ask students to note any general observations. For example, do parents tend to use more physical forms of punishment when a child acts in an unsafe manner?

Being positive and encouraging is an important principle of good communication. **Does it only apply to communication between parents and children? Why or why not?**

COMPREHENSION CHECK

1. What is the purpose of guidance? (*For children to control their own behavior.*)
2. How could the parents of a child be consistent in their guidance? (*Possible answer: By agreeing on rules.*)

ACTIVITIES

Critical Thinking Activity

Analyzing Primary Sources. Read the following quotation from child psychologist Penelope Leach to students: "Be consistent in your principles. It's very hard to teach a child to behave if you yourself don't know how to behave. You must be a good role model." Have students discuss the meaning of this comment. **L1**

VISUAL LEARNING | **Using the Photograph**

Answers will vary. In discussion, lead students to see that these principles are appropriate in all relationships.

ways, as you will learn. Guidance doesn't mean "making children behave" either. **Guidance** means using firmness and understanding to help children learn to control their own behavior. The result of effective guidance is **self-discipline**—children's ability to control their own behavior.

Effective guidance is linked to a child's age and emotional and social development. Effective guidance helps children learn to get along with others and to handle their own feelings in acceptable ways. It promotes security and a positive feeling about self.

Guidance also helps children in their moral development. Very young children understand right and wrong only in terms of being praised or scolded. Gradually, children develop a **conscience** (KON-shuns), or an inner sense of what is right. As they mature, they use this conscience to act morally when facing new situations.

Consistency

Being consistent is the key to guiding children's behavior. Consistency is a matter of clearly making rules and applying them in the same way in all situations. Consistency helps children know what is expected of them and what responses they can expect from parents.

Children lose trust and confidence in a caregiver who constantly changes rules or fails to enforce them in a consistent way. If a parent permits a behavior one day and punishes the child for the same behavior the next, the child will feel confused and insecure. He or she will pay little attention to the next limits that are set.

Consistency becomes an important issue when more than one person cares for a child. These people need to agree in advance on rules and ways to enforce them. Each one also needs to be careful not to

CHAPTER 3: Effective Parenting Skills **89**

ISSUES IN TEEN PARENTING

It may be especially challenging for teen parents to guide their child's behavior. This is because they are fairly new at practicing self-discipline themselves. Being inconsistent is detrimental to child guidance, but a normal part of the teen years, when young adults try on many roles before finding their true identities. Conversely, teen parents may sometimes achieve greater success with discipline than an older parent, for the simple reason that they can empathize with the child in a unique way, having just emerged from the confusing challenges of childhood themselves.

COMPREHENSION CHECK

1. Would it be good for a parent to give food as a reward for appropriate behavior? Why or why not? (*Answers will vary.*)

ACTIVITIES

Discussion Activity

Read the following scenario to students: "Ricki has told his three-year-old son four times not to throw a ball in the house. When he starts to do so a fifth time, Ricki grabs the ball, throws it into the playpen, and yells."
Have students suggest other steps Ricki could have taken. **L1**

Critical Thinking Activity

Recognizing Point of View. Read students the direction "Express your anger using words, not by hitting people." Have them describe how they would express this guidance to a two-year-old, a five-year-old, and a ten-year-old. Would this direction be successful for all age groups? **L1**

VISUAL LEARNING Using the Photograph
Possible response: No, an infant doesn't have the language skills to understand the reason for time-out.

---

undercut the other's decisions. If caregivers don't agree, children can use the inconsistency to their advantage, playing one adult against the other.

There are three ways that adults can guide children to behave appropriately:
- Encouraging appropriate behavior.
- Setting and enforcing limits.
- Dealing with inappropriate behavior in effective ways.

"Time-out" is an effective way of giving a child a chance to calm down. *Do you think this method would work with an infant? Why or why not?*

Encouraging Appropriate Behavior

Suppose you are a young child. No one ever explains to you what kind of behavior is expected or praises you for doing the right thing. Every so often, you are punished for something. Perhaps it is for spilling juice or pulling someone's hair. In this situation, you can't understand how you are supposed to behave. Guidance that is applied only after a child has done something wrong has little chance of success.

You can encourage appropriate behavior by setting a good example, explaining what is desired, praising correct behavior, and offering choices.

Setting a Good Example

Children are great imitators. Children learn best by being shown what to do rather than by just being told. For instance, parents who want their child to talk politely to others get good results when they themselves consistently are polite.

The desire to imitate applies to all the examples—not just good ones. Five-year-old Mark sees his older brothers yell at each other when they disagree. It's little wonder, then, that Mark yells at his friends when he is upset with them.

Telling What Is Expected

Children need to be told what is expected of them in ways they can understand. At first, it isn't necessary to explain the reasons for expected behavior. For a one-year-old, the instruction "Pat the doggy" combined with a demonstration of gentle handling is enough.

Management/Leadership Skills

Remind students that, as members of society, it is their responsibility to set a good example for others. In school, for example, they should set a good example for younger students. Have students create lists identifying ways they can provide positive role models for younger students. Examples include acting with good sportsmanship at sporting events, participating in school government, etc.

When a child is in danger, the appropriate response is to act immediately to protect the child. *In other situations, how can a parent respond to a child's inappropriate behavior?*

Around age three, children begin to understand simple reasoning. Then they can understand a direction that includes the reason for it: "It hurts the dog when you pull his tail. If you want to play with him, you will have to be gentle."

Praising Appropriate Behavior

Giving a child attention when his or her actions are appropriate is an example of **positive reinforcement,** a response that encourages a particular behavior. When children learn that an action wins attention and approval from adults, they are likely to repeat that action.

Learning to put toys away after playing with them is just one example of how children learn self-discipline. *Can you name another?*

CHAPTER 3: Effective Parenting Skills **91**

Parenting in *Action*

Guidelines to use when praising a child include the following:
- Vary the nice things you say to the child. Doing so shows that your words are meaningful.
- Praise behavior, not the child; praise the child for what he or she has done, not what he or she is.
- Be physically affectionate. Touch the child on the shoulder or give a big hug along with your words of praise.

COMPREHENSION CHECK

1. Why give a child choices? (*They learn responsibility for own actions.*)
2. Give an example of a limit. (*Answers will vary.*)

Practicing Parenting

Have students write down either "positively" or "negatively" to each of the following questions: How do you respond when someone yells at you? How do you respond when someone praises your work and then makes a suggestion for improvement? How do you respond when someone issues three or four directives in a row?

Answers to Apply Your Knowledge

1. It is not effective because it is negative and does not tell the child what he *can* do. More effective would be: "Take your muddy shoes off before entering the house."
2. *Possible responses:* Keep all modeling dough on your table; put plastic on the floor below the table where the child is working.
3. *Possible response:* Give one direction at a time. Let the child complete the activity before giving other directions.

Practicing Parenting

How to Talk to Children

*P*arents and other caregivers are often called on to tell children what to do. These suggestions can help you give those directions in a way that makes it easier for children to follow them:

- ♥ **First, be sure that you have the child's attention.** Try to make eye contact—you may need to stoop down or sit beside the child to do so.
- ♥ **Use a pleasant voice.** Speak normally, not in a harsh way.
- ♥ **Use positive statements.** A child will respond better if told "Dry the dishes thoroughly" rather than "Don't put wet dishes in the cabinet."
- ♥ **Use specific words.** Say "Be sure to paint on the paper," not "Don't paint sloppily."
- ♥ **Begin with an action verb.** Beginning this way helps keep directions simple.

- ♥ **Give only one direction at a time.** Limit directions to make them easier to understand, remember, and follow.

APPLY YOUR KNOWLEDGE

1. Read the following direction: "Don't track mud into the house." Why is it an ineffective one? How would you word it to be effective?
2. How would you tell a four-year-old playing with modeling dough to be sure not to get any dough on the floor?
3. What would you do if you wanted to give a child several directions?

The following guidelines will help you encourage appropriate behavior:

- **Be specific.** Clearly comment on the behavior you are acknowledging: "You did a good job brushing your teeth."
- **Notice the behavior as soon as possible.** Recognize the behavior right away to help the child link the action and the praise.

- **Recognize small steps.** Encourage steps in the right direction—don't wait for perfect behavior. If a child usually spends story time trying to distract others, acknowledge even a short moment of "being a good listener."
- **Help the child take pride in his or her actions.** Saying "That was hard work to pick up your toys, but you did it!" helps

92 UNIT 1: Children, Parenting, and You

Management/Leadership Skills

Give students the following situations and have them suggest choices that a caregiver might offer to encourage appropriate behavior:
- A two-year-old refuses to get into the bathtub.
- A three-year-old refuses to leave the park.
- A three-year-old is throwing food onto the floor.
- A five-year-old does not want to help set the table.
- A six-year-old wants to splash through deep puddles.

a child feel competent. Saying "I'm so happy you picked up your toys!" encourages a child to behave only to gain your approval.

- **Tailor the encouragement to the needs of the child.** Praise behaviors that are difficult for that child. The child who usually forgets to put away toys should be rewarded with approval for remembering to do so.

Offering Choices

As children become more mature, they can be allowed to make some decisions for themselves. This helps them learn that they are responsible for their actions.

For example, three-year-old Gavin sometimes hits his younger sister. To encourage appropriate behavior, his parents might say, "Sonya looks up to you. That's why she wants to play with the same toy you do. I know that it makes you angry when she grabs your toy, but I can't allow you to hurt her. Either choose one of your toys that she can play with, or play in your room alone for a little while so you have privacy."

Of course, the choices offered have to reflect acceptable behavior. Gavin is given choices that respect his right to have some control over his toys and his play. At the same time, he must respect Sonya's right not to be hurt.

Setting Limits

Setting limits is another way to guide children toward appropriate, safe behavior. Limits include physical restrictions, such as preventing a child from crossing the street.

Enforcing rules in a consistent way helps children feel more comfortable and secure. **Why?**

Critical Thinking Activity

Analyzing. Have students recall a situation in which limits were not set for a child—or were set but not enforced. What were the results for the parent? For the child? If the results were negative, how could they have been avoided? **L1**

Teamwork Activity

Have students work in groups to create and play a game testing parenting skills. Each group should identify difficult situations that might arise between a child and parent, writing each situation on an index card. Groups then exchange cards. Then have students choose a card and explain how they would respond. Have the group discuss these responses. **L1**

VISUAL LEARNING	Using the Photograph

Answer: They know what to expect and what is expected of them. It removes uncertainty.

Moral Conscience. **Dr. Robert Coles of Harvard University has extensively researched the development of morals in children.** He worries that too many parents do not reprimand their children as often as they should, for fear of making them feel badly. In fact, Coles argues, children should feel bad when they have done something wrong. Therein lies the essence of a conscience.

Parenting in Action

Let students consider the following situations, each involving a four-year-old child. What limits should be set? How should the child be told of those limits?
- Rob will be attending his friend's birthday party at the zoo.
- Michelle is going to a public swimming pool with her older sister.
- Jarrod is going to fingerpaint at the kitchen table.
- Zoe is going with a friend and the friend's babysitter to play in a park.

COMPREHENSION CHECK

1. Why do limits need to be repeated? (*Children don't always remember them.*)
2. Reword the following limit so that it's clear: "You can read for a little while, but then you must go to sleep." ("*You can read for 15 minutes before turning out the light.*")
3. Why does a caregiver have to ask certain questions before handling a situation involving misbehavior? (*Must identify whether the misbehavior merits punishment.*)

ACTIVITIES

Critical Thinking Activity

Making Inferences. How do you think explanations of limits should be affected by the child's age? **L1**

Discussion Activity

Ask: What happens when two parents set different limits? Could divorce make this more likely to happen? How? How can communication help people in all these situations? **L1**

VISUAL LEARNING	Using the Photograph

Possible responses: Explaining what is desired, giving praise, offering choices.

Another kind of limit is a rule of behavior: "We don't hit other people."

What Should Limits Be?

In setting limits, parents and other caregivers often follow this general guideline: Limits should keep children from hurting themselves, other people, or property. Children will respect and follow limits if they are few and reasonable.

When setting limits, keep these questions in mind:

- Does the limit allow the child to learn, explore, and grow? Too much restriction hinders development.
- Is the limit fair and appropriate for the child's age? A toddler might be restricted to a fenced-in yard. A school-age child might be permitted to visit a friend living down the street.
- Does the limit benefit the child, or is it merely for the adult's convenience? Restrictions should be for the child's good, not because they fit a routine.

Making Limits Clear

State limits simply and briefly—for example, "We walk inside the house. Running is done outside." You will probably need to restate the limit each time the situation arises. Children, especially young ones, don't always remember limits from one day to the next. They may not realize that limits stated one day still apply another day.

If you think the child remembers the limit, ask. Doing so gives the child a chance to show that he or she is learning—and gives the parent an occasion to praise the child. Keith's mother asks, "What do we do before rollerblading?" Keith quickly answers, "Put a helmet and pads on!" His mother then says, "That's right! That's the way to take care of yourself!"

Limits must be clear. Telling three-year-old Julie that she can have "a small snack" is not a useful limit. She can't know what makes a snack "small." A better limit would be "You can have an apple or a banana and a glass of milk."

Use a calm, direct tone of voice when setting limits. This indicates the limit is real and should be respected.

Setting a good example is one way of encouraging appropriate behavior. **What are three other ways?**

DID *You* **Know?**

Setting Limits. An early researcher in child behavior was interested in exploring the concept of whether or not children needed limits. A group of children was accustomed to playing in a yard surrounded by a chain link fence. The researcher removed the fence, thinking that the children would experience more freedom in their play. However, the children huddled together in the center of the yard. Few ventured to the edge of the yard, and none tried to wander away. On the basis of such experiments, researchers have concluded that children find security within defined limits.

Children can be given praise for many different activities, such as helping around the house.

Have students work in groups to consider the following situation: "Your child has gotten into the bathroom cabinet and is drawing on the mirror with a tube of lipstick." Have groups agree on a response to the situation and then present their idea to the class. After all the groups have finished, discuss the various options. **L1**

Critical Thinking Activity

While, in general, guidance should be appropriate for a child's age, it really must be linked to the child's level of understanding. Have students discuss how guidance techniques may need to be modified for children with disabilities. **L3**

Setting limits includes four steps:
- **Show understanding of the child's desires.** "I know you think it is fun to draw on the wall."
- **Set the limit and explain it.** "You may not draw on the wall. It is hard to clean crayon marks off the wall."
- **Acknowledge the child's feelings.** "I know you may not be happy with this, but some things are not acceptable."
- **Give alternatives.** If possible, give the child a chance to continue the same activity but in an acceptable way. "If you want to draw, you may draw on this paper. Or, you can do something else, like playing with your blocks. Which would you like?"

Once established and explained, limits should be firmly and consistently enforced. Parents who give in teach their children that they don't mean what they say. Children take rules more seriously if they remain in force at all times.

Dealing with Inappropriate Behavior

No matter how much adults do to encourage appropriate behavior, children—*all* children—misbehave from time to time. When this happens, adults must deal with the situation appropriately and effectively.

The child's age should shape the response. A one-year-old who bites another child can be told, "No! Don't bite," but the child can't be expected to understand the meaning of his or her action. A four-year-old can understand that biting is unacceptable. With a child this age, a punishment may be in order.

A caregiver should ask these questions when responding to a child's misbehavior:
- Is the expected behavior appropriate, given the child's development?
- Does the child understand that the behavior is wrong?

CHAPTER 3: Effective Parenting Skills **95**

MULTIPLE INTELLIGENCES

Caregivers should try to set limits in a way that matches a child's kind of intelligence. Suppose a parent wants to establish the boundaries for a child's playing outside. A verbal child can be told in words. With a child high in mathematical-spatial intelligence, a map might be better. For a kinesthetic child, the parent may wish to take the child walking around those boundaries.

Discipline. Pediatrician Marianne Neifert (a.k.a. "Dr. Mom") gives this advice:
- Change the scene to distract the child.
- Ignore minor misbehavior when you think the child is doing it to get attention.
- Ensure that a child makes amends for harm caused to another person.
- If a child is ignoring a command to do something, take him by the hand and guide him through the task to show that you expect cooperation right away.
- Get your child's input on how to solve a recurring disciplinary problem.

COMPREHENSION CHECK

1. What is negative reinforcement? (*A response aimed at discouraging a child from repeating a behavior.*)
2. How can warnings be useful? (*Reminds a child of a rule and gives child a chance to correct the behavior.*)
3. Name a situation in which loss of privileges is better than natural consequences. (*Answers will vary.*)

ACTIVITIES

Art Activity

Have students create a comic strip that addresses the questions a caregiver should ask before responding to misbehavior. Students should create specific examples that deal with each question. The comic strip does not have to be humorous, but it can be. Students can use simple line drawings and create one or several comic strips. **L2**

Discussion Activity

Read the following to the class: "Four-year-old Ross accidentally knocked over a glass of juice. His father quickly reprimanded him for it." How would Ross feel? What if his father usually responded that way? **L1**

VISUAL LEARNING	Using the Photograph *Answers will vary.*

- Was the behavior done knowingly and deliberately, or was it beyond the child's control?

Unintentional Misbehavior

With children of any age, misbehavior is sometimes unintentional. A young child may drop a glass of milk that is too heavy or accidentally break something that should have been out of reach. These unintentional actions shouldn't be punished.

Misbehavior is also unintentional if the child had no way of knowing it was wrong. For example, Brittany picked a flower in the park and brought it to her father. People shouldn't pick the flowers in parks, but Brittany had never been told that. Rather than scolding, Brittany's father simply explained that she shouldn't have done it.

Parents need to tailor their explanations of limits to the age of the child. A very young child will not be able to pay attention to a long explanation. *How can this father tell this young child that it's time for a nap?*

96 UNIT 1: Children, Parenting, and You

Using Punishment Effectively

When children deliberately do something that they know is wrong, some form of punishment may be necessary. Punishment is **negative reinforcement**, a response aimed at discouraging a child from repeating a behavior. By encouraging the desired behavior and setting limits, you are more likely to teach a child to act as you wish. Still, there are times when punishment—used with good judgment—is effective. In punishing, the parent should make clear that he or she disapproves of the *behavior* but still loves the child.

The first time a child breaks a rule, many caregivers give a warning rather than a punishment. Even a child with good self-control makes an occasional mistake. A warning reminds the child of the rule and its importance. It also gives him or her a chance to regain self-control.

Parenting in *Action*

Have students organize a round table discussion about the merits and drawbacks of using time-out as a disciplinary measure. Have them invite parents, as well as child care providers, pediatricians, and counselors or child psychologists, to participate. They should develop three or four discussion points beforehand and invite each guest to speak for two minutes on each topic. Then open the discussion to the general audience. Students can act as moderators as well as members of the audience.

What kind of limits can parents set for a child who wishes to in-line skate?

After a rule has been broken another time, punishment is in order. The punishment given should be in proportion to the misbehavior. Forgetting to put away one set of toys before taking out another doesn't deserve severe punishment.

Here are some useful techniques for dealing with inappropriate behavior:

- **Natural consequences.** Sometimes it is punishment enough for the child to suffer the results of his or her behavior. Suppose Kwan bangs a toy on the floor and breaks it. Losing the chance to play with the toy should be enough to remind Kwan to be careful in the future.
- **Loss of privileges.** Sometimes allowing the natural consequences isn't appropriate. If a child runs into the street, the natural consequences—being hit by a car—are far too dangerous. A parent might then take away a privilege, such as playing outside, instead. This type of punishment is most effective for children five and older. It works best if the privilege taken away is related to the misbehavior. That way, the child is more likely to associate the two.
- **Giving time-out.** Another way to respond to misbehavior is to use **time-out.** This is a short period of time in which a child sits away from other peo-

ple and the center of activity. The purpose is to give the child a chance to calm down and regain self-control. One minute of time-out for each year of a child's age is a good length of time.

Poor Disciplinary Measures

Well-meaning caregivers sometimes use disciplinary methods that are less effective than others—and sometimes even harmful. Parents and caregivers who follow the positive discipline techniques already described in this chapter should find they don't need to use the following measures:

CHAPTER 3: Effective Parenting Skills **97**

Teamwork Activity

Have students work in groups to design a new product for parents that can help them deal with the issue of discipline. For example, students might design a colorful, silly-looking timer that parents can set during a time-out. Students should write a description of the product that includes how it would help both caregiver and child. They could also make a sketch or model of the product. **L3**

VISUAL LEARNING **Using the Photograph**
Possible responses: To always wear safety gear; limits on where the child can skate; limits on hours of day that the child can skate.

Time-Outs. Discuss these guidelines for using time-outs:

- **Use them for very poor behavior; if overused, they lose effectiveness.**
- **Identify the behavior, not the child, as the problem.**
- **Keep time-outs short; most children forget things after ten minutes.**
- **After time-out is over, give the child another chance.**
- **If a child resists or has a temper tantrum, wait until it stops; then continue the time-out, but don't mention the tantrum.**

LEARNING STYLES

Auditory

Have students play a quiz game in which teams ask each other questions about the Section and points are awarded for correct answers. Before beginning the game, each student should write three questions related to Section content, putting each question on a separate index card. Students should rate their questions as being worth three, five, or ten points, depending on the level of difficulty. All questions should all be placed in a box, with cards drawn randomly for the game.

CHECKING COMPREHENSION

1. Give examples of ways parenets bribe children. (*Answers will vary.*)
2. Why do children need to learn to handle their anger? (*They don't do so naturally.*)

ACTIVITIES

Critical Thinking Activity

Predicting Outcomes. Review the following list of additional poor disciplinary measures. Then ask students to predict why each is considered ineffective:

• Invoking guilt ("If you loved me, you wouldn't do that.")
• Comparing to a sibling ("Why can't you be more like your brother?") **L1**

Discussion Activity

Have students review the guidelines for good communication on pages 86-87. **Ask:** How can these suggestions be useful in handling the anger and conflict that may arise when a child is disciplined? **L1**

Art Activity

Have students design a magazine advertisement that promotes handling conflict in a healthy manner. Post students' ads in the classroom and encourage other students to discuss and evaluate them. **L1**

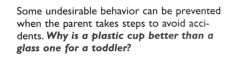

Some undesirable behavior can be prevented when the parent takes steps to avoid accidents. **Why is a plastic cup better than a glass one for a toddler?**

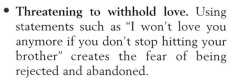

• **Bribing.** Bribing a child with a treat if he or she stops misbehaving can backfire. Instead of learning self-control, the child learns to expect rewards for ending incorrect behavior. The child may even misbehave on purpose, knowing that by stopping he or she can earn the treat again. Don't confuse bribing with rewarding desirable behavior. Giving positive reinforcement for the behavior you want is fine.

• **Making children promise to behave.** In the process of learning to control their behavior, children naturally make mistakes. When a promise has been made, the child may feel forced to lie about misbehavior rather than disappoint someone he or she loves.

• **Shouting or yelling.** When a child misbehaves, a caregiver's anger and disappointment should be expressed in a calm, reasonable voice. A loud, harsh voice can frighten a young child. Older children may learn to "tune out" yelling.

• **Shaming or belittling.** Parents and caregivers shouldn't ridicule a child's mistakes or use responses such as "If this keeps up, you'll never amount to anything." Doing so can harm the child's self-confidence.

98 Unit 1: Children, Parenting, and You

• **Threatening to withhold love.** Using statements such as "I won't love you anymore if you don't stop hitting your brother" creates the fear of being rejected and abandoned.

Of course, there should be a clear distinction between appropriate punishment and abusing a child. A parent or other caregiver should always be in control of his or her own feelings when punishing a child.

Handling Conflict

Children may feel angry when they can't get their way. Caregivers must be prepared to deal with this anger. Avoid making the child feel guilty about his or her anger—it's a normal emotion.

INFOLINK

Child Abuse.

To read more about *child abuse*, see Chapter 19, Section 2.

DID You Know?

Bribery. **The flip side of bribery is the use of incentives, which encourage a child to change behavior over the long term. Incentives include having children earn stars on a chart each time they pick up their toys or make their bed. Before beginning** such a program, parents should sit down with the child and explain what behavior the incentives are meant to promote and why. Then they should keep track of progress by putting stars on the chart together because a parent's idea of progress may differ from a child's.

By the same token, caregivers can help the child learn that there are acceptable ways of handling that anger:

- **Using words.** Rather than hitting or lashing out, children—and adults—should express feelings with words.
- **Speaking calmly.** Even when angry, people should speak calmly, not scream or yell.

- **Counting to ten.** Help the child control his or her emotions by counting to ten and taking a few deep breaths.

It may help to discuss the misbehavior and the punishment some time after the child has calmed down. Then the parent can help the child see how he or she misbehaved. The parent can also explain what the child should have done instead.

ASSESS

CHECKING COMPREHENSION

Have students answer the Check Your Understanding questions. Answers appear at the bottom of this page.

EVALUATION

Give students the Section 3-2 Quiz in the *Teacher Resource Guide*.

RETEACHING

1. Assign Reteaching Activities, page 14.
2. Have students design a questionnaire that could be used to ask parents about their strategies for guiding children.

ENRICHMENT

Have students study the principles of positive and negative reinforcement. Have them report their findings to the class.

EXTENSION

Have students design a brochure that gives parents advice on guiding behavior or using discipline.

CLOSE

Have students write a list of five positive behaviors a child might do. Then have them exchange papers and write ways parents could praise those behaviors.

SECTION 3-2 REVIEW

✔ Check Your Understanding

1. How is guidance connected to conscience?
2. Why is consistency in guiding a child's behavior important?
3. What are the four ways of encouraging appropriate behavior?
4. What four steps are involved in setting limits?
5. When should punishment be used?
6. What is a good rule of thumb in determining how much time to give for time-out?
7. Why is bribing an ineffective form of discipline
8. What are acceptable ways of handling anger?

Putting Knowledge Into Practice

1. **Applying.** When Mike gives time-out to his five-year-old, he says "You have time-out until you can tell me why what you did was wrong and that you are ready to behave differently." Do you think this is a good idea or not? Why?
2. **Synthesizing.** Maria taught her daughter to say "please" and "thank you" whenever she asked for anything. Ever since Cristina began spending time at a child care center, she has lost this habit. What can Maria do?
3. **Observing and Participating.** Visit a child care center and watch how the workers interact with the children. What techniques described in this chapter did they use? How effective were they? Report to the class.

CHAPTER 3: Effective Parenting Skills **99**

ANSWERS TO SECTION 3-2 REVIEW

1. Guidance helps children develop conscience.
2. Shows that limits are real; maintains trust in the caregiver.
3. *See the list on page 90.*
4. *See the list on page 95.*
5. When behavior is wrong and intentional. After a warning has been given.
6. One minute for each year of child's age.
7. Because it can lead children to misbehave on purpose.
8. Using words; speaking calmly; counting to ten.

Introducing the Feature

Have students try to predict what sort of issues they think a child psychologist would handle in a day. Ask students to try to list three and then discuss their ideas briefly.

Answers to CONNECTING SCHOOL TO CAREER

1. Computers for reading material over the Internet, sending e-mail, and for writing; video cameras for recording children at play.

2. *Possible response:* Because they have to interact with children, interpret the information they read, write reports and papers, and talk to parents.

Applying What You've Learned

Have students draw a graphic organizer in which they outline the information given in the feature. Suggest that students focus on these main headings: "Tasks and Responsibilities," "Aptitudes," "Education and Training," "Salary and Benefits."

CAREER OPPORTUNITIES

Child Psychologist

A CONVERSATION WITH LUIS ALVAREZ

How did you become interested in becoming a child psychologist? I was always interested in psychology—how people behave and why. What brought me into child psychology was the realization that what we're like as adults is influenced by our experiences as children.

What are the tasks and responsibilities of a child psychologist? They vary. Some work in clinics and help children who have problems. Some work in schools, testing children who may have a learning disorder or some other problem. I teach at a university. My most enjoyable time, though, is when I'm at the university's child care center. My job also requires a lot of reading to keep up with new information.

What is the work environment like? I'm alone in my office at home when I do my reading and writing, and that's fairly quiet. When I'm teaching or at the child care center, I am with people constantly and the pace is quite hectic.

What are the working hours like? Teaching and work at the center occupy most of the day every day. I do my reading and writing at night, often at home.

What aptitudes are needed to be a child psychologist? You have to be a good observer with attention to detail. You need to be able to notice the subtle changes in children's behavior. You need to have an open mind so you can question your assumptions. You need empathy and good communication skills.

CHILD PSYCHOLOGIST

Education and Training. To be a counselor, people need at least a master's degree. Those who want to be a full psychologist need a doctoral degree (Ph.D.) and perhaps training in a clinic.

Career Outlook. The outlook for child psychologists is very good in the near future.

CONNECTING SCHOOL TO CAREER

1. **Technology.** What kinds of technology do you think a psychologist could use?
2. **Basic Skills.** Why do you think psychologists need good communications skills?

100 UNIT 1: Children, Parenting, and You

Building Career Skills

Personal Qualities. Have students consider their own personalities in light of the career of child psychologist. What traits do students have that they think would benefit them in such a career? What traits might pose a challenge to them or need work if they were a child psychologist?

Child Care Options

On the way to work each day, Andy leaves his son Chris at a child care center. At the end of her workday, Chris's mother, Liz, comes to get him and brings him home. Liz and Andy, like millions of parents, rely on substitute child care.

KEY TERMS

accreditation
child care center
family child care
Head Start
license
Montessori preschool
nanny
parent cooperative
play group
preschool
subsidized child care

OBJECTIVES:

- Explain why people need substitute child care.
- Analyze the advantages and disadvantages of the types of substitute care that are available.

The Need for Substitute Care

In recent years, more and more parents have come to rely on other people to care for their children at least some of the time. There are several reasons for this trend:

- Many children live in two-parent families where both parents work away from home. These children usually need substitute care.

CHAPTER 3: Effective Parenting Skills **101**

Observing & Participating

Bring to class schedules of activities for one day from various child care centers in your area. Have students examine the schedules and answer these questions: What types of activities do most centers include? How does the age of the children affect the types and numbers of activities? Do some centers include more scheduled activities than others? Do you think scheduled activities are important? Why or why not?

SECTION 3-3 RESOURCES

Teacher Resource Guide
- Lesson Plan Organizer, p. 41
- Section 3-3 Quiz, p. 105

Student Motivation Kit
- Observ. & Case Study (case study), pp. 93-94
- Reteaching Activity, p. 15
- Enrichment, pp. 11-12
- Teen Parenting Skills, pp. 98-99

Transparency Package
- CT-9 Characteristics of Quality Child Care

Student Workbook
- Study Guide, pp. 26-30
- Evaluating Child Care Choices, p. 35

Effective Instruction CD-ROM

FOCUS

MOTIVATOR

Ask: How many experienced child care when younger? What types of child care situations did they have? Ask volunteers to summarize their experiences in a few words. Tell students that in this section they will learn what factors contribute to a good substitute care experience for children.

VOCABULARY ACTIVITY

Ask students to define the word *cooperate*. Can they predict the meaning of the term *parent cooperative*? Based on what *school* means, what do they think a *preschool* is?

COMPREHENSION CHECK

1. What are the two general categories of substitute care? (*Home-based and center-based.*)
2. Why should children not simply sit in front of the television? (*Need more stimulating experiences.*)

ACTIVITIES

Discussion Activity

Ask: Why do some people believe that substitute care should not be used on a regular basis? What disadvantages do these people identify? Why do others support regular use of substitute care for children? What advantages do they consider important? **L1**

Trends in Families

Have students find statistics for the past ten years on working women, single parents, dual-career families, and on the numbers of children now living in each kind of family. Ask students to compile their findings in graph form to show what changes have occurred over the past ten years. **L3**

VISUAL LEARNING	Using the Photograph

Answer: If both parents work, usually neither can stay home with a child.

- Many more children live with a single parent who has a full-time job. Such a parent needs full-time or part-time child care.
- Some parents who care for their children at home feel that their children can benefit by being with other children. They place their child in a center for some time each week.

Types of Substitute Care

Parents who need substitute care can choose from many different types. All provide the child with physical care and a place to play. Substitute care is provided in two general settings. Some services are offered in a home. Others are provided in a child care center.

>
> **The Developing Brain**
> Studies show that child care outside the home <u>can</u> promote a child's brain development. What children need is a child care setting in which they get lots of verbal attention, plus nurturing.

Home-Based Care

Many young children receive care in their own or another family's home. A home setting may be easier for a child to get used to because the surroundings are familiar. Home-based care may also be more available and convenient for parents. Some parents like this arrangement because the caregiver is a friend, relative, or neighbor—someone they know and trust.

Home-based care usually involves a smaller group of children than center-based

102   UNIT 1: Children, Parenting, and You

---

care. This makes it a good choice for infants or other children who need individual attention.

There are three main types of home-based care:

- **Care in the child's own home.** Many parents have their child cared for by someone who comes to their home. In-home care is convenient, but it can be costly. Also, the child may not have a chance to play with other children.

  Some families **nannies**—trained workers hired by a family to provide live-in child care. Although this arrangement is fairly expensive—including the cost of living space for the nanny—it offers reliable care at almost any time of day. Of course, a nanny's credentials and references should be checked before the person is hired.

More and more parents today use substitute care for their children. *Why does the rise in two-career families contribute to this trend?*

Management/Leadership Skills

Have students work in teams to investigate the requirements for becoming a nanny. Have each team contact an agency that provides professional training to obtain information on the course curriculum, supervised work experiences, length of training, costs involved, and placement service. Ask each team to evaluate this program and then compare their findings to those of other teams.

Some families—especially those with children with special needs—use respite care. A respite-care provider gives the family a break—a respite—during the day. Such a worker might come to the family home for a few hours, allowing the parent to do errands or other chores outside the house that may not be possible otherwise.

- **Family child care.** Some parents put their children in **family child care.** In this situation, a small number of children are cared for by someone in his or her own home. The group may include the caregiver's own children.

Family child care provides the comfort of a home setting with opportunities for social play. Since the group size is small, there can be plenty of individual attention. Family child care usually costs less than care in the child's own home but has less extensive facilities than a child care center.

Some states require caregivers to have **licenses,** which show that they meet health and safety standards. These licenses do not give an indication of the quality of the care provided, however.

- **Play groups.** Some parents take part in a **play group.** In this arrangement, parents take turns caring for each other's children in their own homes. A play group is similar to family child care, but it involves a number of different homes and caregivers. Most play groups involve no fees since the work is shared by many. This type of care is a good idea for parents who don't work full-time.

Quality home-based care includes both quiet and active times. Look for a good mix of planned activities and informal play. In no care setting should children be allowed to simply sit in front of the television set or be left without supervision.

One disadvantage of home-based care is the issue of backup options. If the person who runs family care becomes ill, he or she can't care for children in the usual way. Parents need to find a replacement.

The growing need for child care has revived the tradition of the nanny, a person who lives with the family and cares for its children. *What kind of training would a nanny need?*

ISSUES IN TEEN PARENTING

Teen parents who are trying to finish high school have a critical need for substitute, and affordable, child care. These parents often find themselves in a Catch-22 situation in which they must work to pay for child care, which interferes with their goal of getting a diploma. It is most beneficial for teen parents—at least financially—when a family member can donate time to care for a child while the parent attends school.

Ask the Experts

Introducing the Feature

One poll shows that what parents worry about the most when placing their child in a child center is that the child gains important skills. Their next weightiest concerns are whether their child is getting enough attention and adjusting well to the arrangement. These are closely followed by concerns about how well their child is eating and whether the child might pick up germs.

Answers to Thinking It Through

1. They have the opportunity to interact with more children than they would at home.
2. *Possible response*: Yes, because the study covered many children and followed them for several years.

Applying What You've Learned

Ask students to suppose they are married and have a child. They must decide whether to scrape by on one income so that one parent can stay home with the child or to use substitute care while both parents work. Have students write a paragraph explaining which choice they would make and why.

Ask the Experts

Pat Brodeen
Teacher and Teen Parent Coordinator at Theodore Roosevelt High School in San Antonio, Texas

WHAT *About Center-Based Care?*

 Does it hurt children to put them in child care?

This is one of the most troubling questions for many parents. They read that child development specialists consider parents a child's best source of love and learning, and that they advise parents to stay home to provide child care for as long as possible.

Yet often parents' lives do not permit them to stay home with their children. So, when they hear experts praise the benefits of home care, many parents wonder whether their child suffers by being placed in substitute care.

A recent study suggests that they need not worry so much. The study followed over 1,300 children from birth to age three. About 20 percent were cared for in the home; the rest received some form of substitute care. Researchers found that overall children with quality substitute care actually did better in some language and learning abilities than children who were cared for by a parent.

The study echoed what brain researchers have found. Children develop best in these areas when they have caregivers who provide lots of talk and interaction. Those caregivers can be parents or other people providing substitute care. The key is quality interaction between baby and caregiver.

The researchers reached one other conclusion, which should help parents set aside their worries. The most important factor to children's mental and emotional growth is not the child care arrangement but the home environment. A mother's and father's loving care still counts the most.

Thinking It Through

1. How can children benefit mentally by being in substitute care?
2. Do the results of the study convince you that children will not suffer if placed in substitute care? Why or why not?

The Developing Brain

 The Effect of Child Care. New brain research raises the question, What is the effect of child care on the child's developing brain? The answer seems to be "not much." The home environment is more important. Parents who give their child a stimulating, nurturing environment can counteract the effects of poor quality child care, even if it is full-day care. The children who suffered the most had both poor quality child care and lacked rich experiences at home.

Some parents use child care given by an adult they know—sometimes even a friend or neighbor. *What might be the advantages of this choice?*

Center-Based Care

In child care centers, several adults care for one or more groups of children. Centers vary widely in their hours, their fees, and the ages of children they accept. They also differ in the activities, equipment, and play areas provided and in the training and experience of the staff.

Some child care centers are businesses run for profit, while others charge fees that just cover expenses. Still others are funded by the city, state, or federal government. Care at these centers may be offered for free or at a reduced cost to those who qualify. Finally, some centers are run by businesses who offer child care as a benefit to their workers.

Each state has an agency that licenses child care centers. A center must meet minimum health and safety requirements in order to be licensed. The license also limits the number of children a center may accept, depending on space, facilities, and size of the staff.

Professionals in the field have created a system to recognize centers that meet strict standards. Centers and preschools can choose to join the National Association for the Education of Young Children (NAEYC). Members apply to the group for **accreditation**. This involves a review of the facility's staff, programs, and environment to see if they meet the association's strict standards.

These are the most common types of center-based child care:

- **Child care centers.** A **child care center** provides care for children whose parents are not available during working hours. The typical center offers children a variety of activities. Some centers emphasize specific learning activities, but others allow more time for informal play. Usually, there is a daily routine with time set aside for indoor and outdoor play, meals, and naps.

    Child care centers may offer half-day or full-day programs. Most child care centers are designed for children two years old and older. Some provide care for infants.

ACTIVITIES

Critical Thinking Activity

Drawing Conclusions. Have students investigate preschool programs that are linked to retirement homes or senior citizen programs. How does this kind of arrangement benefit the children? the seniors? Who else might benefit? How? Have students outline their findings in a brief report. **L3**

Licensing Child Care

Research licensing requirements in your state. Which agency is responsible? What standards must be met? How often are centers inspected? **L2**

VISUAL LEARNING | **Using the Photograph**
Possible response: If a friend or neighbor, caregiver is someone the parent knows and trusts.

ISSUES IN
CHILDREN'S HEALTH

Care for Sick Children. Many substitute care facilities will not take sick children, and often parents have no relatives available to help. It is usually difficult for parents to stay home from work to care for their children. In the last few years, however, a growing number of hospitals have begun to offer sick-child care in the pediatric ward. The programs use vacant pediatric beds, provide work for hospital employees, and create goodwill that hospitals hope will lead to later use of their facilities by families.

Practicing Parenting

Ask students to consider how many children they think one person can care for effectively. How might the children's ages affect their answers? How about the experience of the caregiver? Is there an upper limit, beyond which even a highly trained caregiver could not handle more children?

Answers to Apply Your Knowledge

1. Yes.

2. *Possible responses:* To allow children of separate ages to have different spaces; to allow a quiet place for nap time.

Practicing Parenting

NAEYC Recommendations for Child Care Centers

*N*AEYC—*the National Association for the Education of Young Children—recommends that a child care center meet certain minimum standards:*

♥ **Number of infant caregivers.** At least one caregiver for every three or four infants.

♥ **Number of toddler caregivers.** At least one caregiver for every four to six toddlers.

♥ **Number of preschooler caregivers.** At least one caregiver for every seven to ten children aged three to five.

♥ **Group size.** The total number of children in a group should be no larger than two times the ratio of staff to children. That is, there should be no more than eight infants, twelve toddlers, or twenty children aged three to five.

♥ **Indoor play space.** The center should have at least 35 square feet of play space indoors per child. This does not include space for other purposes.

♥ **Outdoor play space.** The center should have at least 75 square feet of outdoor play space per child.

♥ **Separating space.** The center should have indoor space divided into separate rooms, rather than being one large shared space.

APPLY YOUR KNOWLEDGE

1. A center with twenty children has 1000 square feet of indoor play space and 2000 square feet of outdoor play space. Does it meet NAEYC standards?

2. Why do you think NAEYC recommends that the indoor space be divided into separate rooms?

Some employers offer child care centers for their workers' children at the workplace. *Why would that be convenient for parents?*

106

- **Parent cooperatives.** In a **parent cooperative,** child care is provided by the children's parents who take turns staffing the co-op. A preschool teacher or another qualified caregiver may organize the program and guide parents. Working at the co-op helps parents understand their child's development. Such a program costs considerably less than a child care center. It is probably not an option for families with both parents working full-time, however.

- **Head Start centers.** In the 1960s, the federal government began **Head Start.** This program set up locally run child care facilities designed to help lower-income and disadvantaged children become ready for school. Most Head Start centers have half-day sessions for four-year-olds.

  Head Start offers a variety of activities. It also provides children with meals, health care, and social services. Parents are expected to be active in the Head Start program.

  Critics of Head Start say that whatever benefits children enjoy from Head Start vanish after their first few years in school. Supporters point to several studies, which show that children who attend well-planned Head Start programs score better on tests and have better school readiness skills.

- **Preschools.** A **preschool** provides education programs for children aged three to five. A preschool typically offers activities that help children develop in all areas. The staff usually includes one or more teachers and a number of aides. Aides assist the person in charge. They usually have some training in child care, but not as much as a lead teacher.

  Preschools usually offer half-day sessions from two to five days a week. Some centers offer both child care for younger children and preschool programs for three- to five-year-olds. A

The purpose of all center-based programs should be to provide children with learning opportunities, not just care.

1. What cost benefit does a parent cooperative supply? (*Less expensive than child care center.*)
2. Why couldn't full-time workers join in a parent cooperative? (*Because they are at work and unavailable to share in caregiving.*)
3. What age are most children who attend Head Start? (*Four years old.*)

ACTIVITIES

Critical Thinking Activity

Making Inferences. Ask students what they would do if they were the parents of these children:

- Four-year-old Bobby has been in the same care facility for two years. Suddenly, however, his behavior at home is aggressive and violent.
- Eighteen-month-old Tasha has a new in-home nanny. At first, the two did very well, but after a week, Tasha began clinging to her mother and refusing to go to the nanny. **L1**

DID *You* **Know?**

High/Scope. The High/Scope Foundation is an independent nonprofit group that conducts research into children's learning and development. High/Scope also offers training to caregivers—and to parents. Training workshops, which last two days, are held throughout the country. For more about the program, students can visit the High/Scope Website at http://highscope.org

COMPREHENSION CHECK

1. A working parent needs substitute care for more than just the hours worked. Why? (*Also needed for travel time to and from care center.*)

ACTIVITIES

Teamwork Activity

Have students work in small groups to prepare a report or documentary on substitute care in the United States today. Groups should use current news articles and books to gather data about the availability of substitute care and the general satisfaction of parents with the options available. **L3**

ISSUES IN
CHILDREN'S HEALTH

Latchkey Children. Latchkey children—those who are unsupervised from the time they come home from school until their parents return from work—are common in our society. For these children, it is imperative that parents set up emergency procedures, safety rules, and a daily schedule to be followed. In addition, parents should arrange for children to check-in with a telephone call when they arrive home. Children should follow the same route home from school each day, walking with friends or siblings when possible. Does your community have any special programs for these children?

---

growing trend is for children to attend a prekindergarten (pre-K) program the year before kindergarten.

- **Specialized preschools.** Some preschools provide a specialized program that differs from the traditional approach. **Montessori** (mon-tuh-SORE-ee) **preschools** are one example. They use special learning materials and follow the ideas of Dr. Maria Montessori, an Italian educator. Children are encouraged to learn by exploring and experimenting with the materials provided. They are given the freedom to move from one activity to another as they wish. Another example is called Highscope. This program encourages children to be in charge of their learning.

Care for Older Children

Because of parents' work schedules, many school-age children need child care before or after school. Child care experts advise against leaving children through age twelve without adult supervision.

Some parents make arrangements for children to go to the home of a neighbor or relative. Others depend on latchkey programs run by schools or religious or community groups. Such programs offer a safe place where children can have a snack, do their homework, and enjoy supervised recreation and crafts.

Choosing the best possible care for infants and toddlers is especially important. Their growth and development depend on nurturing and stimulation.

Choosing Substitute Child Care

Which type of child care is best for an individual child? There are no easy answers. Parents must consider many factors. Besides quality, the types of care available in the area, the cost, the convenience, and the age and particular needs of the child all influence the decision. Whatever the type of substitute care, parents need a caregiver who enjoys the child, spends time playing with him or her, and communicates well with the parents.

Being involved in their child's care is very important for parents as well. By talking often with the caregiver, they can both discover and pass on information about the child's development. This way, too, they can keep watch on the quality of the care the child is receiving.

The Cost of Substitute Care

The cost of child care can vary significantly depending on type and location. In

MULTIPLE INTELLIGENCES

Children have different kinds of intelligence, meaning that they have skills in different areas. High-quality substitute care provides a variety of learning activities to cultivate these different strengths. Play with crayons, finger paints, or modeling dough appeals to children with kinesthetic and spatial intelligences. Units addressing the changing seasons will be enjoyed by a child with naturalistic intelligence. Parents should look for this variety of experiences—especially with home-based care, where the caregiver may not have as many materials as in center-based care.

major cities, families may pay $1,000 per month for a single toddler at a child care center.

In general, the least expensive child care option is care provided by family and friends. Nannies are the most costly choice. Child care centers are typically more expensive then family day care.

The age of the child is also a factor. Care of infants and school-age children is typically higher than for preschoolers.

The cost of substitute care adds up. Children may need outside care for nine or ten hours a day, five days a week. In two-parent families, when earnings are compared to child care and other job-related costs, it's sometimes less expensive for one parent to stay at home.

Parents with outside jobs deal with the costs in various ways. Some families qualify for **subsidized child care**—an option in which a government or social service program pays a portion of the actual cost of care. Availability usually depends on income. In other families, parents may work different schedules so a parent is always home with a child.

Sources of Information

Community groups can supply listings of sources of substitute care. Groups such as Child Care Aware and the National Association for the Education of Young Children may also have listings for your area. Many parents find substitute care by asking friends what they use—and finding out if those friends are satisfied.

It is essential that the parents visit each home or child care center they are considering before choosing one. This takes time, but it allows parents to see the facility and

Parents need to pay close attention to children's feedback to identify any problems that arise.

the caregivers firsthand. In fact, taking the child to visit the site helps see how he or she responds to the place and the people.

When considering any substitute care option, ask for references. Any child care service—whether a center or a home-based one—should be willing to give the names and phone numbers of parents whose children attend. Ask these parents how long they have been using the service, and what strengths and weaknesses they have seen.

CHAPTER 3: Effective Parenting Skills **109**

Critical Thinking Activity

Understanding Point of View. Make a list of what a child would look for in child care. What facilities would the child want? What qualities and skills would be desirable in a caregiver. What activities would the child enjoy? **L1**

Critical Thinking Activity

The costs of child care must be considered in the decision to work outside the home. What are some other "costs" of working? How might these impact parents' employment decisions? **L2**

Parenting in Action

Before hiring a caregiver, parents should interview several. The Parenting Resource Center on the Internet offers tips for interviewing candidates:

• Begin with small talk to get acquainted.
• Have your child present at the interview to see whether he or she is comfortable with the caregiver.
• Pose open-ended questions to learn more about the caregiver's methods and perspectives. For example, ask: "How would you handle a tantrum?"
• Outline the terms of employment—hours, wages, provisions for sickness, and so on.

ACTIVITIES

Writing Activity

Have students create newspaper advertisements for child care services. Let them decide on the type of program they will advertise and the special features their program will provide. Then allow time for students to share and discuss their completed ads. Which are parents most likely to respond to? Why?
L2

VISUAL LEARNING

Using the Chart
Ask: Why should parents be concerned about each question? What efforts might parents have to make to find answers to these questions? What problems could arise if parents fail to ask or get accurate answers to the questions? **L1**

DID *You* **Know?**

Attitudes to Child Care. **A recent study asked mothers how they needed to improve as parents. Answers differed depending on child care arrangements. Mothers with children enrolled in a university preschool lab felt they needed to improve in discipline. Mothers who cared for their own children felt they needed to work on patience. Mothers with children in child care centers felt they needed to improve in both discipline and patience.**

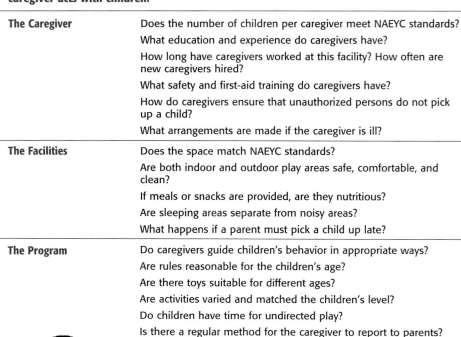

Child Care: Questions to Ask

These are just a few of the areas parent should look at when checking a substitute care facility. Some are questions to ask the caregiver. Others are points that the parent needs to learn by observing how the caregiver acts with children.

The Caregiver	Does the number of children per caregiver meet NAEYC standards?
	What education and experience do caregivers have?
	How long have caregivers worked at this facility? How often are new caregivers hired?
	What safety and first-aid training do caregivers have?
	How do caregivers ensure that unauthorized persons do not pick up a child?
	What arrangements are made if the caregiver is ill?
The Facilities	Does the space match NAEYC standards?
	Are both indoor and outdoor play areas safe, comfortable, and clean?
	If meals or snacks are provided, are they nutritious?
	Are sleeping areas separate from noisy areas?
	What happens if a parent must pick a child up late?
The Program	Do caregivers guide children's behavior in appropriate ways?
	Are rules reasonable for the children's age?
	Are there toys suitable for different ages?
	Are activities varied and matched the children's level?
	Do children have time for undirected play?
	Is there a regular method for the caregiver to report to parents?
	Do the children seem involved and happy?
	If you were a child, would you like to spend time there?

110 UNIT 1: Children, Parenting, and You

ISSUES IN TEEN PARENTING

A teen mother who lives at home and depends on the support of her family can benefit by designing a contract that outlines her responsibilities. Some issues to address are:

• Housecleaning. Who takes care of the baby's clutter?

• Meals. What is the feeding schedule, who prepares the food and cleans up?

• Guidance. Who has primary responsibility for child guidance?

• Social activities. Is a curfew for the baby's mother in effect? What arrangements are acceptable for visits from the baby's father?

What to Look For

The chart on page 110 gives a checklist of questions to ask when evaluating a child care setting. It is tailored to a child care center, but the questions can be adapted to other situations as well.

Once parents have chosen a service, they should drop by unexpectedly from time to time. These visits can help confirm that the care is as promised. After two or three weeks, the parent should ask what the child thinks. The child's happiness is a good signal of the quality of the child care.

As a child grows, it may be necessary to have a new arrangement. Mary put two-year-old Todd in family child care. At four years old, she put him in a preschool. The child's behavior could signal a need to change, too. If a child suddenly begins to cause trouble at child care, it may be because he or she is bored. Perhaps the activities are no longer interesting or challenging. If the care being given a child seems to have declined in quality, it may be time to move to another setting.

SECTION 3-3 REVIEW

✔ Check Your Understanding

1. What are two reasons why people use substitute care?
2. What are the advantages of home care? Of family child care?
3. Define *license* and *accreditation*.
4. What is the difference between a play group and a parent cooperative?
5. Explain the difference between a child care center and a preschool.
6. Where can parents find after-school programs for school-age children?
7. Why should parents ask for references before deciding on substitute care?

Putting Knowledge Into Practice

1. **Drawing Conclusions.** Why aren't play groups or parent cooperatives usually suitable for parents who work full-time?
2. **Synthesizing.** The NAEYC suggests different ratios of staff to children depending on the age of the children. (See the *Practicing Parenting* feature.) Why?
3. **Observing and Participating.** Working with a partner, adapt the checklist in the chart on page 110 to be useful for evaluating family child care.

ANSWERS TO SECTION 3-3 REVIEW

1. Working single parent; two working parents.
2. *Home care:* Easier for child to adapt; more convenient; fewer children. *Family:* Home setting with social play.
3. *License:* State says that caregiver meets standards. *Accreditation:* NAEYC says that facility meets its standards.
4. *Play group:* Parents provide care in turns. *Cooperative:* Parents provide care under professional's guidance.
5. *Center:* Care for infants to three- or four-year olds. *Preschool:* Educational programs for three- to five-year-olds.
6. Schools, religious groups, community groups.
7. *Possible response:* To hear feedback from parents who know the caregiver.

MOTIVATOR

Have students write a brief description of how they would like to act if they were a father.

TEACH

ACTIVITIES

Discussion Activity

Discuss with students the benefits to be gained by both children and adults when fathers take an active role in parenting. What do fathers lose by not being involved? **L1**

Teamwork Activity

Have students design a poster that encourages fathers to be active in their children's lives. Display students' work around the classroom. **L2**

Parenting With Care

Fathers Are Caregivers, Too

Mothers and fathers bring different qualities to parenting.

There are endless opportunities for dads to get involved and stay involved with their children. The payoff is great!

Mothers often receive the most attention when parenting is being discussed because they usually take primary responsibility for children. What about fathers? They bring many skills to parenting.

Researchers have found that fathers act differently with children than do mothers. When infants begin to crawl, fathers tend to let them crawl farther than do mothers before bringing them back. Fathers usually play more physically with children—games such as wrestling or tag. When children discover something new, mothers are likely to stay nearby, offering reassurance. Fathers tend to stay back and let the children explore it. These approaches give children new chances to learn about the world. They help build independence.

Researchers have also found that when fathers take an active part in caring for infants, children are less likely to cry when a stranger nears.

Most families share care responsibilities. Some fathers raise their children alone. Here are some ideas for active involvement:

- **Mealtime.** Meals provide opportunities for talking, teaching, and showing love. Father and child can talk about many subjects: for infants, shape and color; for preschoolers, basic nutrition; for school-age children, what happened that day.
- **Baths.** Fathers can bathe babies and toddlers. In doing so, they get a chance to enjoy some close time with their child.
- **Dressing.** After a nice bath, fathers can help their children by picking out clothes and dressing them. As children get

112   UNIT 1: Children, Parenting and You

RESOURCES ON CHILD CARE

Many child care providers belong to the National Child Care Association (NCCA). Only private (for-profit) licensed child care providers can belong. While the NCCA provides services to members, it can also be a resource for parents looking for child care. They can contact the group to find members in their areas. If interested, write the organization at 1016 Rosser Street, Conyers, GA 20012. Visit their Web site at www.nccanet.org.

older, fathers can teach them how to dress themselves.

- **Doctor visits.** Fathers can take a child to routine checkups and emergency care.
- **Being a role model.** Fathers can set examples for their children in many areas of life. Solving problems, calming down when angry, and caring for possessions are just a few examples.
- **Taking a walk.** A walk at the end of the day—even a short walk—can help relieve stress. In the company of a child who constantly finds new things to learn, the walk becomes a voyage of discovery.
- **Active play.** Sometimes a child needs physical activity. Then a trip to the park and an exciting ride on the swing or down the slide fits the bill.
- **Reading.** Children of all ages enjoy being read to. Sharing a book is a perfect way to end a day. All that's needed is the patience to read the same story many times— always the same way!

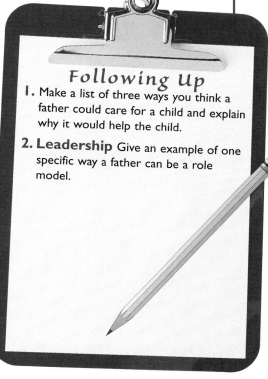

Following Up

1. Make a list of three ways you think a father could care for a child and explain why it would help the child.

2. **Leadership** Give an example of one specific way a father can be a role model.

CHAPTER 3: Effective Parenting Skills **113**

CLOSE

1. Create a book with the same title as the feature—"Fathers Are Caregivers, Too." Students' books should include quotations from fathers and children, photographs from magazines, drawings, and text that describes the benefits of active fathering.

2. **Extension.** Arrange for students to spend time on a Saturday at pediatricians' offices, local parks, malls, restaurants, and grocery stores. Have them count how many children are with their mothers, how many are with their fathers, and how many are with both mothers and fathers. What does their research suggest about fathers as caregivers?

Answers to Following Up

1. Answers will vary but should include different examples from those in the feature.
2. Possible response: Helping a child learn how to express anger in acceptable ways.

CHECKING COMPREHENSION

Use the Summary and the Reviewing the Facts questions to help students go over the most important ideas in Chapter 3. Encourage students to ask questions and add details.

CHAPTER 3 REVIEW

Answers to Reviewing the Facts

1. Having reasonable expectations. *Possible response*: So parents can understand children's needs.
2. *Possible response*: May change styles as children grow.
3. *Possible response*: Taking a course; to get exposure to different strategies.
4. Giving child opportunities for encouragement and enrichment; showing love, support, and concern.
5. Children lose trust and confidence, become confused.
6. *Possible response*: Setting a good example is effective because children learn by imitation.
7. Understand the child's desires; set the limit and explain it; acknowledge the child's feelings; give alternatives.
8. *Possible response*: They recognize that all people make mistakes; to remind the child of the limit.
9. Parents work or want the children to have social opportunities.
10. Both take place in a home setting. Home care is in the child's own home and is more expensive. Family care may include other children.

CHAPTER 3   REVIEW &

Summary

✔ Parents must meet children's basic needs, nurture them, and guide their behavior. (Section 3-1)

✔ Guidance includes encouraging appropriate behavior, setting limits, and dealing with inappropriate behavior. Parents should be consistent. (Section 3-2)

✔ Home-based care options provide comfortable surroundings but caregivers may not be trained. Center-based care may have better facilities but may be inflexible in hours. (Section 3-3)

✔ Parents and children should visit a substitute care facility and ask questions before choosing it. (Section 3-3)

Reviewing the Facts

1. What is the first step in effective parenting? Why? (Section 3-1)
2. Why do parents sometimes change the same parenting style they use? (Section 3-1)
3. What do you think is the best way of gaining parenting skills? Why? (Section 3-1)
4. What is *nurturing*? (Section 3-1)
5. What problems are caused by inconsistent guidance? (Section 3-2)
6. Choose one technique for encouraging appropriate behavior and describe why it is an effective technique. (Section 3-2)
7. Why is giving alternatives an important part of setting limits? (Section 3-2)
8. Why do some parents give a warning when a child first does something wrong? (Section 3-2)
9. Why do people use substitute care on a regular basis? (Section 3-3)
10. Compare home care to family child care. (Section 3-3)

Thinking Critically

1. **Comparing.** What do you think is more damaging to a child, deprivation or over-parenting? Why?
2. **Applying.** Nadine told Justin, age three, "Your room is messy. Take care of it!" How would you reword Nadine's direction?
3. **Ranking.** Which do you think are the five most important factors in evaluating a child care center? Why?

Taking Action

1. **Enriching Life.** Give an example of something parents on a tight budget could do to provide enriching experiences for a child. *(Management)*
2. **Modeling.** Write a script showing what a child will think if a caregiver tells him or her to act one way but gives examples of different ways of behaving. *(Leadership)*

CONNECTIONS CHAPTER 3

Cross-Curricular Connections

1. **Language Arts.** Write a brochure describing a parenting class intended for first-time parents. In the brochure, list the topics that would be covered in the course.

2. **Math.** If a child care center costs $3.50 an hour, how much would it cost *per week* to have a child in the program for five half-day sessions of four hours each? How about five full-day sessions of nine hours each?

Workplace Connections

1. **Interpersonal Skills.** Whenever two-year-old Addie becomes frustrated, she begins to hit other children. As a child care teacher, how would you talk to her parents about this problem?

2. **Information Systems.** Suppose you were providing family child care for four children. What basic information would you want to keep on each child? How would you keep these records?

Family and Community Connections

1. **Evaluating Resources.** Visit a library or bookstore and make a list of all the magazines that offer advice to parents. Choose one and read two or three articles. Report to the class about how valuable you think the advice is.

2. **Community Child Care.** As a class, create a fact sheet with the basic information you think is important about a child care center. Use one of those sheets to gather information about a child care center in your area. Add your sheet to a class booklet called "Community Child Care Services."

 Technology Connections

1. **Internet.** Use the Internet to find out more about Head Start, Montessori preschools, or Highscope preschools. What are the programs like? Who qualifies to enter each program? What role do parents play? Write a one-page summary of your findings.

2. **Entertainment.** Experts say that the amount of time spent watching television or playing with computer games should be limited for children in substitute care settings. Why do you think they make that recommendation? Do you agree?

EVALUATION

1. Use the reproducible Chapter 3 Test in the *Teacher Resource Guide,* or construct your own test using the **Exam***View*® Test Generator.

2. For an alternative assessment, assign the Chapter 3 activity in the *Authentic Assessment* section of the *Teacher Resource Guide.*

ENRICHMENT

Assign students either of the two enrichment activities in the *Enrichment Activities* booklet in the *Student Motivation Kit.*

EXTENSION

Have students create a cross-word puzzle that gives clues to important concepts in the chapter. Have them trade puzzles with another student and then complete the puzzle.

CLOSE

Have students plan a theme for a booth they could create for a Parenting Fair. Possible themes include parenting in general, child guidance, and substitute care. Students should make lists of what activities, guest speakers, demonstrations, and reading materials will be available at their booth.

CHAPTER 4 RESOURCES

Teacher Resource Guide
- Chapter 4 Test, pp. 112-116
- Authentic Assessment,
  pp. 263-264

Student Motivation Kit
- Observations & Case Studies
  (observation), pp. 33-34

Transparency Package
- CT-10 to CT-11

Effective Instruction CD-ROM

CHAPTER 4   OVERVIEW

Section 4-1 introduces the subject of teen sexuality and outlines factors that have an impact on a teen's decision making.

Section 4-2 provides students with a six-step process for solving problems. It also explores the consequences of teen parenthood and the options pregnant teens have.

CHAPTER 4   OBJECTIVES

After completing Chapter 4, students will be able to:

- Explain the relationship between values and sexuality.
- List the consequences of teen sexual activity.
- Explain how to apply the problem-solving process in making decisions related to sexuality.
- Describe the options pregnant teens have.

CHAPTER 4

Teen Pregnancy and Parenthood

116   UNIT 1: Children, Parenting, and You

RESOURCES TO EXPLORE

Teen Pregnancy. Teenagers who are or soon will be parents need to fully acquaint themselves with the realities of teen parenting in order to be successful. Teen parents face difficulties unique to them and which complicate an already demanding role. For more information on the particular burdens of teen parenting as well as referrals to local support groups (or how to begin one), contact: National Organization of Adolescent Pregnancy, Parenting, and Prevention, Inc. (202) 293-8370, www.noappp.org, P.O. Box 2365, Reston, VA 22090.

The classroom was quiet. The students didn't stir. Finally, Adrienne spoke again. "You see, I was so innocent, so naïve. "It will never happen to me," I told myself. "Doug will take care of me," I thought. But I was wrong. It did happen to me, even though we only did it once. I did get pregnant, and Doug dropped me as soon as I told him. I felt so alone. I was only fifteen. I couldn't take care of the baby, but I wanted him to have a good home. I got some help from some wonderful people, and we found a great family for my baby. Every year, on his birthday, they send me a card and a picture. He's so cute, and I'm so happy for him."

Then she looked in the eyes of each student before she spoke again. "It's taken me six years to put my life back together. I'm happy now, but it was a long, hard road. Spare yourself the pain. Wait until you're married."

"'It will never happen to me,' I told myself."

CHAPTER 4: Teen Pregnancy and Parenthood **117**

INTRODUCING CHAPTER 4

- Have three students role-play a situation in which a teen tells her parents that she is pregnant. After the role play, have students list words describing the reactions and emotions they observed in each character. Explain that in this chapter students will learn about the realities of pregnancy and parenting.
- Have students look at the photograph on page 116. **Ask:** What might Adrienne be feeling as she told her story to the high school class?

USING THE SCENARIO Have students read the story on this page of the student text. Ask why Adrienne put the baby up for adoption and the feelings she might have had about doing so. Discuss Doug's role—what should he have done to help Adrienne?

KEY TO ABILITY LEVELS   Each section gives skill-building activities. Each activity has been labeled for use with students of various learning styles and abilities.

L1 Level 1 activities are basic activities and should be within the range of all students.

L2 Level 2 activities are average activities and should be within the range of average and above average students.

L3 Level 3 activities are challenging activities designed for the ability range of above average students.

The Realities of Teen Pregnancy

(pages 118-124)

SECTION 4-1 RESOURCES
Teacher Resource Guide
- Lesson Plan Organizer, p. 42
- Section 4-1 Quiz, p. 110

Student Motivation Kit
- Observ. & Case Study (case study), pp. 95-96
- Reteaching Activity, p. 16
- Enrichment, pp. 13-14
- Nurturing Brain Development, pp. 49-50
- Teen Parenting Skills, p. 28

Student Workbook
- Study Guide, pp. 36-38
- Pledging Abstinence, p. 39

Transparency Package
- CT-10 How Would Parenthood Change Your Life?

Effective Instruction CD-ROM

FOCUS

MOTIVATOR

Write the following on the chalkboard and ask students to complete the sentence: "The negatives of becoming sexually active as a teen include ..." Discuss students' responses.

VOCABULARY ACTIVITY

Ask students to define the verb *abstain*. Ask them to identify the term that derives from that verb. Based on the meaning of the verb, what do they think that word means?

The Realities of Teen Pregnancy

As you know, the teen years are filled with growth and change, new issues, new decisions. Among the most important are those related to sexual activity. What are the consequences of sexual activity? How can those results change plans for the future, and how can that be prevented? Teens are better prepared to answer these questions if they understand the meaning of sexuality and the effects of sexual activity.

KEY TERMS

abstinence
hormones
paternity
peer pressure
sexuality
sexually transmitted
  diseases (STDs)

OBJECTIVES:
- Distinguish between sexuality and sexual activity.
- Explain how values can help teens face issues of sexuality.
- Describe the negative consequences of sexual activity.

Teen Sexuality

Sexuality and sexual activity aren't the same thing. **Sexuality** refers to a person's view of himself or herself as a male or female. Sexuality involves much more than physical maturity or the ability to be sexually active. It includes a person's regard for himself or herself and that person's sense of responsibility for and understanding of other people. Thus sexuality has physical, intellectual, emotional, and social aspects.

118

Observing & Participating

Ask students to discuss a television show they have seen in which one of the characters has to deal with a situation that involves conflicting values. Call on students to describe the situations to the class and to indicate how the conflict were resolved.

Discuss with the class what values the characters felt most strongly about. Then discuss with the class why it is important for individuals to have a well-defined set of values.

Individuals show their sexuality in various ways. They show their maleness or femaleness in the way they walk, talk, move, dress, and laugh.

In the teen years, you develop a sense of your own sexuality. This process is influenced by a number of powerful factors. Dramatic physical changes occur as part of achieving sexual maturity. Changing **hormones,** chemicals in the body, shape these changes. They often have emotional impact as well, causing mood swings and emotional ups and downs.

Teen years are a time of growth and change. *How can keeping a journal help you adjust to these changes?*

Social development shifts into high gear. There are attractions to new friends. Relationships with other family members often change as you take on more personal responsibility.

In the midst of these changes, messages about sexual activity seem to be everywhere. The media—television, radio, movies, commercials, and music—often imply that sexual activity is a necessary part of sexuality. **Peer pressure,** the influence of other teens, comes with remarks like "Everyone is doing it—what's wrong with you?"

With such pressures, it's easy to lose sight of what's important. Dating—as couples or in groups—helps in learning what qualities or characteristics in another person you find attractive. You learn more about building relationships. You can have plenty of fun without the hazards of becoming sexually active.

Values and Sexuality

Who am I as a male or female? How should I treat people of the opposite sex? How can I balance old friendships and new relationships with someone of the other sex? Values help shape how each person answers those questions.

As you read in Chapter 2, one role of families is to pass on the family's and society's values. These are the principles they consider important—the rules they use to guide their lives.

CHAPTER 4: Teen Pregnancy and Parenthood **119**

COMPREHENSION CHECK

1. What is the single best way to prevent getting an STD? (*Abstinence.*)
2. What is the difference between HIV and AIDS? (*HIV is the infection; AIDS is the disease that can result.*)
3. For which STDs is there no cure? (*Genital herpes; genital warts; hepatitis B; AIDS.*)

ACTIVITIES

Charting Activity

Have students do research to find statistics such as the number of teen pregnancies each year or trends in the spread of STDs among teens. Have them present their information in a chart or a graph. **L3**

Critical Thinking Activity

Analyzing. Point out to students that individuals infected with HIV or AIDS often face discrimination. Ask student how they think the rights of someone with HIV or AIDS could be protected. **L1**

VISUAL LEARNING | Using the Photograph
Possible response: Gives them a chance to spend time with and learn about people of the opposite sex without being sexually active.

Group activities that involve both males and females give teens a chance to get to know others of the opposite sex. *How can these activities help them develop?*

Familiar examples include trust, self-respect, respect for others, commitment, and loyalty.

By drawing on your values, you can choose to build a sense of your own sexuality *without* becoming sexually active. A look at the consequences of sexual activity shows that this is a wise decision.

The Consequences of Sexual Activity

Teens who do become sexually active often regret that decision. Sexual activity can cause serious problems.

Sexually Transmitted Diseases

A **sexually transmitted disease (STD)** is an illness spread from one person to another by sexual contact. There are about 12 million cases of STDs in the United States each year. About 3 million of those cases affect teens.

All these STDs are preventable. The best way to prevent them is **abstinence**—avoiding sexual activity.

Some STDs can be treated. Others last a person's entire life. The chart on page 121 discusses the most common STDs.

AIDS

One STD has deadly results. Acquired immune deficiency syndrome (AIDS) is caused by the human immunodeficiency virus (HIV). HIV can remain in a person's blood for many years before it develops into AIDS. Although AIDS does not kill its victims, it allows other diseases to invade the body. Eventually, the AIDS patient dies. There is no known cure for AIDS at this time, although research is continuing.

120 UNIT 1: Children, Parenting, and You

LEARNING STYLES | Kinesthetic

Ask students to imagine that their younger brother or sister wants to know about sexually transmitted diseases. Have students work with partners and create skits that illustrate the advice they would give a younger sibling about STDs. Each pair of students should include at least three facts in their skits. Call on partners to present their skits to the class.

▶ Common Sexually Transmitted Diseases

Some of these symptoms may indicate other diseases or conditions as well. Anyone who experiences any of these symptoms should be tested so that his or her exact condition can be determined and treatment begun.

Disease	Symptoms	Treatment	Effects
Chlamydia (kluh-MIH-dee-uh)	Pain when urinating. Women may feel abdominal pain, nausea, low fever. *Note:* Some people show *no* symptoms.	Can be cured with antibiotics.	Can cause sterility—the inability to have children.
Genital herpes (JEN-uh-tuhl HER-pees)	Open sores on sex organs, which go away in a few weeks. Painful urination, fever.	There is no cure. Symptoms can be treated.	Can cause brain damage or death if passed by pregnant women to infants.
Genital warts	Small growths on the sex organs, which cause discomfort and itching.	There is no cure, but a doctor can remove them.	If left alone, they may become cancerous.
Hepatitis B (hep-uh-TY-tuhs)	Causes flulike symptoms.	There is no cure, but a vaccine is available. It can prevent the disease.	Can lead to liver disease or cancer
Gonorrhea (gon-uh-REE-uh)	Burning, itching, and the discharge of liquids from infected areas.	Can be treated with antibiotics.	Can cause sterility in females. A baby born to an infected mother can suffer eye damage.
Syphilis (SIF-uh-luhs)	In early stages: sores on the sex organs, fevers, rashes, and hair loss.	Can be cured with antibiotics.	Can cause insanity and death.
AIDS	Caused by the human immunodeficiency virus (HIV), which can remain unknown in the bloodstream for many years.	Once HIV develops into AIDS, there is no cure. Some medicines can delay the development of AIDS.	AIDS opens the door to other illnesses, which cause death.

Teamwork Activity

Organize students into small groups. Have group members create public service announcements about preventing STDs. The announcements should include information about the diseases themselves, statistics about the effects of the diseases on teens, and suggestions for prevention. **L1**

DID You Know?

STDs. **Every year about one in four sexually active teens contracts a sexually transmitted disease. In a single act of unprotected sex with an infected partner, a teenage girl has a 1 percent risk of getting HIV, a 30 percent risk of getting genital herpes, and a 50 percent chance of getting gonorrhea. Chlamydia and gonorrhea are more common among sexually active teens than among older men and women. The human papilloma virus (HPV) grows aggressively during pregnancy and often becomes cancerous.**

Management/Leadership Skills

Ask students to find out how teens in their community can find accurate medical information about sexual activity, contraceptives, and the prevention of STDs. Ask them to work with a group to compile a list of classes, hot lines, clinics, and other sources of information and assistance. Have students present their findings in a brochure or a poster.

COMPREHENSION CHECK

1. Why do health concerns arise when teens become pregnant? (*Their bodies may be too young for the extra demands of pregnancy.*)
2. What proportion of teen mothers never finishes school? (*About half.*)
3. What impact can financial problems have? (*Can lead to arguments.*)

ACTIVITIES

Discussion Activity

Have students discuss the factors that lead some teenagers to become sexually active, including physical and emotional desires. Ask students to identify techniques that help teens abstain from sexual activity.
L1

Consumer Activity

Have students list items a person would have to get for a new baby—both for the baby and for equipment for the home. Ask them to look through store ads or go to stores to find the prices of these items. **L1**

DID *You* **Know?**

Infant Survival. Healthy babies born to mothers age 15 or younger are twice as likely to die during their first year.

Pregnancy

Another possible consequence of sexual activity, of course, is pregnancy. Pregnancy raises many problems—and they affect the teen father as well as the mother. When Tonya became pregnant, she and Parker married. Parker took a job, planning to finish high school after a year. Just before the year ended, the car broke down, and he needed to work extra to afford repairs. Soon after, Tonya became pregnant again. By the time their second child was a year old, Parker had been out of high school almost three years. He didn't feel like going back—although he knew if he did he could earn more money.

Teen pregnancy creates four types of problems:

- **Health risks.** Pregnancy presents special health risks for both a teen mother and her baby. A teen's body may not be ready for the extra demands pregnancy places on it. Teen mothers are more likely to suffer from iron deficiency and very high blood pressure.

  Because her own nutritional needs are high, without extra emphasis on nutrition, a teen may not be able to provide the nutrients her baby needs. A critical period of development also occurs before mothers usually know they are pregnant. Babies of teen mothers are more likely to be premature and have low birth weight. These conditions are linked to other problems, including learning difficulties. Babies of teens are more likely to die before their first birthday.

- **Education.** The best thing pregnant teens can do is to complete their schooling. Yet many teens drop of out school after they become pregnant or after the baby is born. Nearly half of the teen mothers who leave school—even those who planned to return—never complete their education. Without a high school diploma, these teens have a hard time finding a job and often can't support themselves and their babies.

  Pregnant teens can work with school counselors and social service agencies that help teens. Some schools have special classes for teen parents. Some provide care in school for the babies while the mothers take classes. Staying in school can help avoid life-long problems.

- **Financial problems.** Money problems begin with the pregnancy. To avoid the health risks of pregnancy, teen mothers need good medical care. That care costs money, as does childbirth. After the birth, teen parents who keep their child must bear the responsibility for providing the child with food, clothing, housing, and health care. This continues for at least eighteen years.

  Even if teen parents who keep their baby don't marry, they are legally responsible for providing financially for their child. If the father chooses not to stay involved with the child, it's especially important to establish **paternity**. This legally identifies the man as the father and his responsibilities toward the child. A medical test can prove paternity.

  For many teen couples, the financial burden becomes overwhelming. It blights hopes and often leads to bitter arguments. This tension can spill over to their relationship with other family members and even with the baby.

Parenting in *Action*

Have students try the following experiment at home (it requires the cooperation of an adult). For three days, students imagine that they are the parents of a newborn. To help students, the adult is to set off an alarm clock at random intervals, but no more than 90 minutes apart. The students—at the sound of the alarm— drop what they are doing and spend the next ten minutes on housework to simulate needing to care for the baby. Have students who try the experiment talk to the class about how "parenthood" affected their daily lives.

Ask the E**X**perts

Pat Brodeen
Teacher and Teen Parent Coordinator at Theodore Roosevelt High School in San Antonio, Texas

MANAGING *the Stress of Teen Parenting*

I am a teen mom with a four-month-old son. Sometimes I just feel completely overwhelmed— can you help me help myself?

Of course you feel over-whelmed—having a child has added a lot of stress to your life. You can make your life—and your baby's life—easier by learning techniques for managing stress.

I know you feel you already have too much to do, but you'll handle stress better when you find time to take good care of yourself:

- **Exercise every day even if you are tired. *This will help keep you physically and emotionally healthy.***
- ***Eat a balanced diet. When you grab a cola and chips instead of a sandwich and fruit, you're undermining your health and making yourself more vulnerable to stress.***
- **Take time to relax. *Learn some relaxation techniques, listen to music, take a warm bath.***
- ***Develop a network of supportive friends, including other young mothers, adults, and other teens. When you feel tense, angry, or in need of support, contact someone you can count on.***

- ***Keep a positive attitude to reduce stress. Ask your friends for help with this.***

- ***Make plans for the future. Ask a counselor or teacher to help you explore your employment options. Find out about educational and training opportunities.***

Thinking It Through

1. How can teen fathers help teen mothers follow Pat Brodeen's suggestions?
2. Why is it important to make friends with other teen parents?
3. Why would it be helpful for a teen mother to be sure to finish high school?

CHAPTER 4: Teen Pregnancy and Parenthood **123**

Ask the E**X**perts

Introducing the Feature
Ask students to brainstorm ways that a teen mother can take care of herself.

Answers to Thinking It Through
1. *Possible response:* By caring for the child every day; by allowing the mother some time to relax or exercise.
2. *Possible responses:* Because they can share experiences, frustrations, and solutions to problems; because they share the same concerns.
3. *Possible response:* It's the first step toward planning for the future.

Applying What You've Learned

Have students research one of the three suggestions described in the feature for controlling stress. They could also look into other stress management techniques. Have them share their findings with the class.

VISUAL LEARNING Using the Photograph
Next page—Possible response: They can't join others in activities because of their responsibilities as parents.

ISSUES IN TEEN PARENTING Building a strong support system is perhaps one of the most important strategies for managing stress. The supportive people may include family, friends, a religious leader, teachers, or employers. A strong support system might include several of these people. A community group can give teen parents a chance to socialize with others who are going through the same experiences. Ask students to research support groups for teen parents. If none exist, discuss the possibility of starting one.

CHECKING COMPREHENSION

Have students answer the Check Your Understanding questions. Answers appear at the bottom of this page.

EVALUATION

Give students the Section 4-1 Quiz in the *Teacher Resource Guide*.

RETEACHING

1. Assign Reteaching Activities, page 16.
2. Have students create a graphic organizer showing the effects of sexuality on a teen's life.

ENRICHMENT

Have students find out how many people are infected with HIV each year. Compare U.S. and world figures.

EXTENSION

Have students find out sources of help in their community for people with HIV and AIDS.

CLOSE

Have students review the way they completed the Motivator activity at the beginning of the lesson (page 118). After reading and thinking about the text, would they now answer differently?

• **Emotional and social stress.** Adjusting to new relationships can cause great stress. So, too, can changes to old relationships. Teen parents may miss their old friends. When they see those friends, however, they may feel that they no longer have much in common with them. Teens who enjoyed sports or other after-school activities must give them up. Teen parents realize quickly that their lives have changed in profound ways.

Why do teen parents sometimes feel isolated from their peers?

SECTION 4-1 REVIEW

✔ Check Your Understanding

1. Define *sexuality*.
2. What forces seem to push teens to choosing sexual activity?
3. What are values?
4. Why are teen mothers and their babies more likely to suffer physical problems?
5. Which sexually transmitted diseases can be fatal?
6. What four kinds of problems are associated with teen pregnancy?
7. Why do teens find that their relationships with old friends change after they become parents?

Putting Knowledge Into Practice

1. **Making Inferences.** Why are group dates a good way to reduce the pressure to become sexually active?
2. **Synthesizing.** Health care experts say that someone who becomes sexually active becomes involved not just with one partner but with all that partner's past partners. What do they mean by that?
3. **Observing and Participating.** Write down three goals you have for your future. Which of your values can help you achieve those goals?

124 UNIT 1: Children, Parenting, and You

ANSWERS TO SECTION 4-1 REVIEW

1. A person's sense of his or her own maleness or femaleness.
2. Media; peer pressure.
3. The principles that one lives by.
4. Bodies are growing; not ready for the extra physical demands of pregnancy.
5. Syphilis, AIDS.
6. Health risks, education problems, financial problems, social and emotional stress.
7. *Possible response:* Because the teen parent has different issues and responsibilities.

CAREER OPPORTUNITIES

Social Worker

A CONVERSATION WITH DEANA STOLTZ

How did you become interested in becoming a social worker? My family had some problems when I was younger. A social worker helped us get through them. She really inspired me!

What are the tasks and responsibilities of a social worker? It varies. I work for a human services agency, handling many cases. Some of my families need help with substance, spouse, or child abuse, and others with job issues. I find it rewarding to help teen parents—I feel like I'm helping a family get off to a good start.

What is the work environment like? We use our office for paperwork and writing reports. We meet with individuals and families, often in their homes. We also teach classes—like a class in parenting skills I teach.

What are the working hours like? Our work with clients—the people we help—is usually during the day. At night, I catch up on my reading or paperwork.

What aptitudes are needed to be a social worker? You certainly need to be a good listener. In fact, you need good communications skills of all sorts. You also need to be a problem solver. You need to be sympathetic to people who have problems—but you have to be tough, too, to help them see how to solve their own problems. You also need a positive attitude.

SOCIAL WORKER

Education and Training. Social workers need a bachelor's degree (psychology, sociology, social work). They also receive practical training. To practice, they must pass a licensing exam.

Career Outlook. The demand for social workers is expected to remain strong.

---CONNECTING SCHOOL TO CAREER---

1. **Personal Qualities.** Why would a social worker need to be well organized?
2. **Basic Skills.** Would a social worker need stronger math or language skills? Why?
3. **Interpersonal Skills.** What relationship skills would be important to success as a social worker?

CHAPTER 4: Teen Pregnancy and Parenthood **125**

SECTION 4-2

SECTION 4-2 RESOURCES

Teacher Resource Guide
- Lesson Plan Organizer, p. 43
- Section 4-2 Quiz, p. 111

Student Motivation Kit
- Observ. & Case Study (case study), pp. 97-98
- Reteaching Activity, p. 17
- Enrichment, p. 15

Student Workbook
- Study Guide, pp. 36-38
- Applying the Problem-Solving Process, pp. 40-41

Transparency Package
- CT-11 The Problem-Solving Process

Effective Instruction CD-ROM

FOCUS

MOTIVATOR

Have students list three recent decisions they have made. Next to each decision, ask them to indicate how they made the decision and whether they now think the decision was a good one.

VOCABULARY ACTIVITY

Have students find the definition of *adoption*. Have them speculate about what closed and open adoptions are.

Solving Problems

Think about all the choices you make. Some, such as what to eat for lunch, are quick decisions. Others, like which movie the group should see, take more time, but still don't have much effect on future life. Issues related to sexuality, though, are among the most profound ones you may face. They impact life in deep and lasting ways. For that reason, they deserve careful thought.

KEY TERMS

closed adoption
miscarriage
open adoption

OBJECTIVES:
- Apply the six-part process to solving problems.
- Analyze the various options a pregnant teen has.

Using the Problem-Solving Process

When faced with important issues, it helps to follow the problem-solving process shown on the next page. Before you begin, review your major goals that may be related to the issue. Here are some tips to help you use the process effectively:

126 Unit 1: Children, Parenting, and You

Observing & Participating

Ask students to identify one minor decision and one more complex problem they're currently facing. Then have students assess why each deserves a different amount of effort. Have students rough out a plan for solving the complex problem using the six steps of the problem-solving process. How could the problem-solving process help them think more clearly and rationally about the situation.

- The process doesn't need to be followed in sequential order. You may need to move back and forth among the various parts.
- As you gather information, carefully evaluate the reliability of your sources.
- In identifying the consequences, or results, of an action, think not only of those that will happen right away, but also of those that will take place later.
- Remember to think about the consequences for people other than yourself. Trying out for a sports team affects more people than just you. If you make the team, and have to stay after school for practices, that will impact your family's life. If you have a job, playing on the team will affect the work schedules of other people.

- Choosing an alternative is not always a matter of choosing the one with the most good results or the fewest bad results. Use your values to look at *how important* those results are to you.
- To evaluate how you solved the problem, ask yourself some basic questions. Did the action have the results you expected? Did it have better or worse ones? Do you need to go back and reconsider other alternatives?
- Another reason to evaluate the results of the action is to improve your problem-solving skills. How did you do in identifying alternatives and weighing pros and cons? Is there something you wish you could do better next time? If so, how can you improve your performance?

THE PROBLEM-SOLVING PROCESS

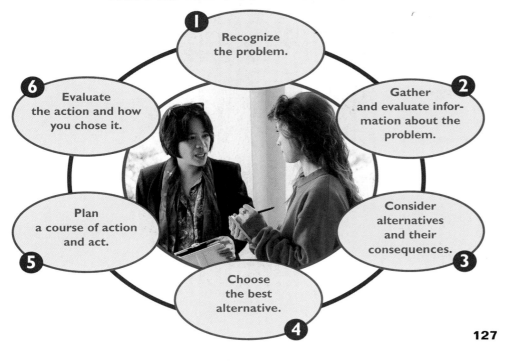

1. Recognize the problem.
2. Gather and evaluate information about the problem.
3. Consider alternatives and their consequences.
4. Choose the best alternative.
5. Plan a course of action and act.
6. Evaluate the action and how you chose it.

127

COMPREHENSION CHECK

1. What is the only 100 percent certain way of making sure that a pregnancy doesn't occur? (*Abstinence.*)
2. In what kind of setting should teens talk about the decision not to be sexually active? (*Where they can talk calmly and without emotion.*)

ACTIVITIES

Discussion Activity

Discuss the idea that the decision to be sexually active affects more than just the two teens. Ask students to describe how that decision could affect a teen's parents and siblings. **L1**

Health Activity

Ask students to review the consequences of sexual activity for teens—both physically and emotionally. **L1**

VISUAL LEARNING Using the Photograph
Possible responses: Parents; friends; child, if pregnancy results.

DID *You* **Know?**

Teens and Abstinence. In a recent national study, the main reason that teenage girls who have never had sexual relations give for abstinence is that having sex would be against their religion or moral values.

The problem-solving process may seem awkward or complicated at first. With everyday practice, though, you'll find it comes to you naturally. Making this process a part of your life can bring great benefits.

Making Responsible Decisions About Sexuality

The problem-solving process can help you face the difficult questions related to sexuality. These choices are too important to be made casually. They deserve careful consideration because they have serious consequences. The effects can last throughout the teen's life.

Bear in mind that choosing to be sexually active affects more than just the two teens involved. Their parents can be touched by it as well. So can their brothers and sisters. If the decision results in a pregnancy, another person—the child who will be born—has to be taken into account, too.

It can be helpful to discuss this decision with other people. Trusted adults—a parent or older family member, teacher, doctor, religious leader, or an adult friend—can be valuable resources. Peers can be good listeners who can share their own experiences.

Decisions about sexuality affect people other than the teen couple. *Who else is affected?*

Predicting Consequences

When you consider the consequences of sexual activity, think about the information in the previous section. The dangers of sexually transmitted diseases are real. The burdens of pregnancy are heavy. Either of these results will change your life in painful and difficult ways. These consequences can be avoided simply by abstaining from sexual activity.

You also need to think about other consequences. Sexual activity has emotional impact as well. Look inside yourself. How will you feel about yourself—and your partner—if you become sexually active? How will your partner feel about you? How will you face your parents and others?

These are difficult questions to answer. The truth lies hidden in the future. Strong emotions can cloud judgment. Still, with careful thought, you may be able to make some good predictions.

Management/Leadership Skills

Present students with the following situation: Zach and Alyssa have been dating for two years. Neither wants to be sexually active, but each is concerned that the other may want to be. Have students write a scene in which Zach and Alyssa talk about the situation.

Reasons for Saying "No"

Sexual activity can have terrible conse-quences on a teen's physical and emotional health. There are many good reasons to say "no" to sexual activity:

- You don't want to be pregnant or cause someone else to be pregnant.
- You don't want to be infected by an STD.
- You would lose respect for yourself.
- Your parents would lose respect for you and trust in you.
- It goes against your values.
- It would hurt your reputation.
- You don't want a sexual relationship.
- You have big plans for your future, and being sexu-ally active would interfere.
- You think there are better ways of showing affection.
- You want to set a good example for your younger brother or sister.
- You want to wait until marriage.

FOLLOWING UP

1. Which reason to abstain do you think is best? Why?
2. Write down a reason of your own.

It is important to be hard-headed and clear-eyed when thinking about conse-quences. Some teens find themselves in a troubled relationship. Some want the other person in the relationship to care for them as much as they care for him or her. These teens may feel that by becoming sexually active, they can make these wishes come true. Such thinking is giving in to wild hopes. Usually such relationships end, and the teen is left feeling hurt and alone. Hopes and wishes are not the foundation for a strong relationship. Common values, real caring, and effective communication are.

Deciding to Abstain

"It can't happen to me." Thousands of teens have thought that—and thousands were wrong. The threat of sexually trans-mitted diseases is very real, as is the threat of pregnancy. There is only one guaranteed way of avoiding these problems—abstaining from sexual activity.

Using the problem-solving process takes time and rational consideration. It's not rea-sonable to expect to reach the decision to abstain in a moment of passion. You need to take time to really think it through.

Synthesizing. Ask students to write an imaginary letter to a friend in which they explain why they've decided not to become sexually active. In the letters, students should share career goals and other ambitions in life and explain how becoming a parent or contracting an STD would affect such plans.
L1

Call on volunteers to give examples of situations in which one person had to say no to something another person want-ed them to do. For example, stu-dents might choose a situation in which one person tried to get another to smoke. Call on stu-dents to give examples of ways that a person can effectively say no to something that conflicts with personal values.

Answers to
FOLLOWING UP

1. Answers will vary but should be supported by a reason.
2. Accept any valid reason.

Auditory

Tell students to imagine that they have been asked by the school adminis-tration to prepare a public service announcement that discourages teens from becoming sexually active. Have students work in small groups to create their announcements. Call on students to present their announcements to the rest of the class and discuss the effec-tiveness of each announcement.

COMPREHENSION CHECK

1. What options do pregnant teens have? (*If the pregnancy goes to full term, being a single parent; marrying; putting the baby up for adoption.*)
2. Why is it a mistake for a teen who thinks she's pregnant to not talk to anyone? (*Possible responses: Needs medical care for a healthy pregnancy; needs advice; needs someone simply to listen.*)

ACTIVITIES

Critical Thinking Activity

Recognizing Point of View. Ask students to review the early signs of pregnancy discussed in Chapter 6. Have them brainstorm what emotional responses a teen who experiences one of these signs might have. **L1**

Readiness for Children

Have students write brief paragraphs about how they feel about having children, their readiness to be parents, and what kinds of parents they think they might be someday. Call on volunteers to share their ideas. **L1**

Once you have decided to abstain, stick to your decision. Talk to your partner in a setting where you can both discuss the situation calmly and without emotion. If two people cannot discuss the consequences of sexual activity in a serious way, they are not ready for that level of involvement.

Explain why you have chosen abstinence. Discuss all the negative consequences of sexual activity. Make clear to your partner that you expect him or her to respect your decision. Someone who really cares for you would show that respect and never put pressure on you to begin sexual activity.

When Pregnancy Occurs

Sometimes teens do get pregnant. Often, teens have trouble believing and acknowledging the symptoms of pregnancy. A girl who fears she might be pregnant may try to ignore the symptoms. This kind of avoidance makes it impossible for her to begin dealing with the pregnancy. It is essential for the mother's and baby's health to get good prenatal care as soon as possible.

Teens who are sexually active should be aware of the early signs of pregnancy. As difficult as this may be, a teen who suspects she might be pregnant needs to discuss her concerns with someone close—her boyfriend, a parent or other family member, a trusted friend, or a special teacher or counselor. She should also

INFOLINK

Signs of Pregnancy

For more information on *signs of pregnancy*, see Chapter 6, pages 180-181.

Why is abstinence the best choice for teens?

see a physician, who can tell her definitely whether or not she is pregnant.

Once her pregnancy has been confirmed, a teen can begin to decide what to do. In order to make a responsible decision, she will have to consider her alternatives and their consequences.

The partner of a pregnant teen should take part in the decision. The father has rights and responsibilities, too. No matter what the decision is, the pregnancy will have a long-lasting effect on his life. Even if the couple does not marry, he has a responsibility to help provide for the care of the child.

Teen fathers have rights and responsibilities toward the baby. *How can they help meet those responsibilities by working?*

Weighing Options

When a teen becomes pregnant, decisions must be made and plans developed. The pros and cons of several common options follow.

Single Parenthood. Having a tiny baby to cuddle and love can seem very attractive. It can be rewarding to care for someone who is helpless and dependent. However, caring for a newborn is a huge responsibility, and becoming a parent is a lifetime commitment.

Single parents face special challenges because they take on—alone—complete responsibility for their child. They also have to do all household chores and meet financial obligations. All these responsibilities can be draining—especially for a teen. Not surprisingly, many teen parents suffer from burnout or depression.

Why is single parenthood so difficult for teens?

CHAPTER 4: Teen Pregnancy and Parenthood **131**

Discussion Activity

Discuss with students the rights and responsibilities that they believe teen males have when their sexual partner becomes pregnant. Ask them if they think the role of the father-to-be is different from that of the mother-to-be and to give reasons for their opinions. **L1**

Teamwork Activity

Organize the class into groups of only male or only female students. Ask each group to list reasons for getting married. Ask a spokesperson from each group to read the results. Have students compare the results and discuss the differences and similarities between the two groups. **L1**

VISUAL LEARNING	Using the Photograph

Top—Possible response: Generates money, which teen father can use to help meet financial obligation of child.

Bottom—Possible responses: Having no partner to help; lack of money; loss of freedom.

Observing & Participating

Tell students to form small groups, and have each group prepare a television talk show that includes teens who are raising the child alone and teens who decided to get married and raise the child. The "host" could ask questions such as: What factors should pregnant teens consider in deciding whether to marry? What are the advantages and disadvantages of marriage? What happens to a mother who doesn't have the father's support? How do fathers feel when excluded from parenting? Are teen single parents at a greater disadvantage than older single parents? Why?

COMPREHENSION CHECK

1. What dual adjustments are faced by teens who marry because of pregnancy? (*To marriage and to parenthood.*)
2. Why do some people choose adoption? (*They feel they are giving the child an opportunity for more parental care than they can manage at the time.*)
3. When does a miscarriage usually occur? (*In the first 20 weeks of pregnancy.*)

ACTIVITIES

Critical Thinking Activity

Analyzing. Have students hold a panel discussion on pros and cons of closed and open adoptions. **L2**

VISUAL LEARNING	Using the Photograph

Possible responses: Helps teen continue with normal development; helps child by providing secure, loving home.

Teens who are considering single parenthood should be as realistic as possible. How much help—emotional and financial—can the teen mother expect from the baby's father? From her own parents and other family members? A teen who is considering single parenthood must be especially careful to avoid romanticizing the situation. A teen partner who was not interested in marriage during the pregnancy is unlikely to change his or her mind once the baby is born, for example. Parents, counselors, and other adults can help teens develop realistic expectations for their own situations as single parents.

Marriage. The prospect of getting married seems exciting, but married teens face many problems. As the early excitement wears off, the strains of responsibility set in. Also, many married teens feel socially isolated. They no longer fit in with their single friends, but their interests and activities are not the same as those of older married couples. Teens who marry because of a pregnancy face an additional problem. They have to adjust to parenthood at the same time they're adjusting to being married.

At the same time, getting married has benefits. Married teens who meet these challenges can find themselves with a strong and rewarding relationship. Having two people share the load of child care lessens the work of each. Finally, married teens can build a caring home for a child—and provide the child with role models of both sexes.

Adoption. Another alternative for pregnant teens is adoption. In an adoption, the birth mother and father give up their rights and responsibilities for raising the child, which another family legally takes on.

Why do birth parents choose adoption? Many make this choice because they feel they are giving their child an opportunity for more care, guidance, and love than they can provide at this stage of their lives.

Birth parents who choose adoption should find a reputable adoption agency or program—one that will treat them fairly and try to find a good home for their child. The county department of human services or the local health department will have lists of such agencies. Birth parents can also ask a religious leader or counselor.

About 20,000 unwed teens give their babies up for adoption each year. *How does this choice help both the teen and the child?*

ISSUES IN TEEN PARENTING In the past, adoption was a much more common alternative for pregnant teens than it is today. Have students explore the issues surrounding this situation. Ask them why teens today often keep their babies to raise themselves. What social changes support and discourage this trend? What are the pros and cons for both mother and baby of doing this? Ask students why the lists of couples who are waiting to adopt are very long today. Should this be a factor in a teen's decision of whether or not to keep the baby?

Adoption should be carried out by professionals who carefully screen prospective parents and prepare them for a new baby. Many agencies also give counseling and health care to the pregnant teen and her partner. It is important for the pregnant mother, for instance, to make sure that she and the baby are healthy during her pregnancy.

In a **closed adoption,** the birth parents don't know the names of the adoptive parents. Some adoptive parents feel more comfortable with this situation. More and more adoptions are what are called **open adoptions.** In this arrangement, birth parents are told about the adopting parents and may even get to meet them. Some agencies even let the birth parents read through the files of several possible adoptive parents and choose one for their child.

Decisions linked to unplanned pregnancies can be deeply disturbing emotionally to the couple and their families. This turmoil can be avoided by practicing abstinence. That prevents pregnancy from occurring.

When a Pregnancy Ends

Sometimes difficulties develop in a pregnancy. Growth stops, the baby dies, and the mother's body expels it from the uterus. This usually happens within the first 20 weeks of pregnancy and is called a **miscarriage.** Anyone who suspects she has had a miscarriage should contact a doctor immediately.

SECTION 4-2 REVIEW

✔ Check Your Understanding

1. What are the six parts in the problem-solving process?
2. Why do you need to evaluate information you gather?
3. Name two things to remember when looking at consequences.
4. What are the drawbacks of single parenthood?
5. What pressures can affect a teen marriage?
6. Distinguish between closed and open adoption.

Putting Knowledge Into Practice

1. **Analyzing.** The text says: "If two people cannot discuss the possible consequences of sexual activity in a serious way, they are not ready for that level of involvement." Do you agree or disagree? Why?
2. **Applying.** Suppose a seventeen-year-old friend told you she was pregnant. How would you respond? What advice would you give her?
3. **Observing and Participating.** Think of an example of a serious problem that teens commonly face, such as what career to choose. Make a chart showing how the problem-solving process can be used to make this decision.

CHAPTER 4: Teen Pregnancy and Parenthood **133**

ASSESS

CHECKING COMPREHENSION

Have students answer the Check Your Understanding questions. Answers appear at the bottom of this page.

EVALUATION

Give students the Section 4-2 Quiz in the *Teacher Resource Guide.*

RETEACHING

1. Assign Reteaching Activities, page 17.
2. Have students write a letter responding to a 15-year old girl who writes to an advice column saying she is pregnant.

ENRICHMENT

Have students find out about classes for expectant parents for childbirth and parenthood. What information do they include?

EXTENSION

Invite a visiting nurse to discuss local services available to teens who want to avoid pregnancy or have a pregnancy test.

CLOSE

Have students compile their own list of reasons to avoid sexual activity.

Ask students to list sources of help they would recommend to another teen who confided in them that she was pregnant. List students' responses on the board. After students have read the feature, have them compare their responses with the information in the feature.

TEACH

Teamwork Activity

Have pairs of students take turns role-playing a conversation between a teen father-to-be and one of the people discussed in the feature. In preparing their dramatizations, pairs should agree on specific details of the scenario. Call on pairs to present their skits to the class.

L1

Parenting With Care

Finding Help

What happens when you're a teen and the pregnancy test is positive?

Pregnancy is a life-changing event. When you are a teen, it can be hard to know where to turn.

Teens who are pregnant need help. Fortunately, that help is available from many different people:

- **The father-to-be.** The teen should certainly talk to the father. He should be involved in making decisions.
- **Parents.** Most pregnant teens are reluctant to discuss their situation with their parents. Parents are often hurt or angry when they first learn of the pregnancy. However, parents are often in the best position to help teens think through the meaning and implications of pregnancy and parenthood. The emotional support that parents offer can be valuable in helping teens deal with the problem and live with the consequences of their decisions.

- **Religious leaders.** Teens who feel uncomfortable talking with their parents right away may be able to discuss the pregnancy with a religious leader. In many cases, they can help teens discuss the matter with their own parents.
- **School personnel.** Teachers, counselors, or the school nurse can offer advice and assistance when teens feel frightened or confused. Although rules vary, discussions with these workers can usually be confidential unless a teen's life or health is in danger.
- **Family counselors.** Nonprofit and privately funded agencies have trained counselors who can help. So do many public agencies such as county departments of social services. These professionals can help teens consider their options.

They can also help teens make contact with agencies that give financial and medical help during the pregnancy. Such groups may also provide baby clothes, food supplies, and furniture when the baby arrives.

- **National organizations.** National groups such as the National Adoption Information Clearinghouse can put teens in touch with local groups that can help.

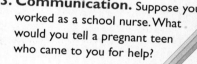

Following Up

1. Why are religious leaders and school personnel good resources?

2. **Leadership.** Write a help-wanted ad for a family counselor. What skills and qualities would such a worker need?

3. **Communication.** Suppose you worked as a school nurse. What would you tell a pregnant teen who came to you for help?

Have students prepare a questionnaire that could be used to interview representatives of family planning agencies. The questions should be used to determine the training of these professionals and other requirements of the job. Have students share and discuss the questionnaires. Interested students might use their questionnaires to actually interview a representative of a local family planning agency. **L2**

CLOSE

1. Have students complete the following phrase: "the best source of help for a pregnant teen is ...." Discuss the choices.

2. **Extension.** Ask students to contact a community organization that helps pregnant teens. Have them find out the kind of help the organization provides. Ask students to report their findings to the class.

Answers to Following Up

1. *Possible response:* They often have experience with such situations and can offer good advice.

2. *Student materials should meet the requirements of the assignment.*

CHECKING COMPREHENSION

Use the Summary and the Reviewing the Facts questions to help students go over the most important ideas in Chapter 4. Encourage students to ask questions and add details.

CHAPTER 4 **REVIEW**

Answers to Reviewing the Facts

1. *Sexuality:* a person's sense of maleness and femaleness. *Sexual activity:* one particular behavior, but not the only way that people of the different sexes relate to one another.
2. *Possible responses:* self-respect, respect for others, desire to build a future.
3. Possibility of becoming infected with an STD and becoming pregnant.
4. *Possible response:* Financial problems: A teen father has to contribute to his child's upbringing but doesn't earn enough money.
5. Short-term and long-term consequences; those that affect you and those that affect others.
6. To evaluate the decision itself and see if anything needs to change; to improve in how you use the process.
7. *Possible response:* Freedom from worry.
8. Alone with all the responsibilities of parenthood; face financial problems.
9. An adoption in which the birth parents know who the adoptive parents are.

CHAPTER 4 | REVIEW &

Summary

✔ Teens can use dating and other relationships with people of the opposite sex to build a sense of their sexuality. (Section 4-1)

✔ The negative consequences of sexual activity can greatly affect teens. (Section 4-1)

✔ Teen pregnancy leads to many physical, emotional, and social problems. (Section 4-1)

✔ Using the problem-solving process can help you think through important issues. (Section 4-2)

✔ The only certain way of avoiding sexually transmitted diseases and pregnancy is to abstain from sexual activity. (Section 4-2)

✔ A teen who becomes pregnant can choose to be a single parent, marry, or put the child up for adoption. (Section 4-2)

Reviewing the Facts

1. What is the difference between *sexuality* and *sexual activity?* (Section 4-1)
2. What values might a teen rely on to choose to avoid sexual activity? (Section 4-1)
3. What negative consequences result from sexual activity? (Section 4-1)
4. Choose one problem of teen pregnancy and explain how it affects both the father-to-be and the mother-to-be. (Section 4-1)
5. What are two kinds of consequences to consider when making choices? (Section 4-2)
6. What are two benefits you can gain from evaluating decisions? (Section 4-2)
7. What do you gain by abstaining from sexual activity? (Section 4-2)

8. Why is life so hard for single teen parents? (Section 4-2)
9. What is open adoption? (Section 4-2)

Thinking Critically

1. **Analyzing.** What rights and responsibilities do you think a teen male has when his sexual partner becomes pregnant? How—if at all—does his role differ from that of the mother-to-be?
2. **Comparing.** Write a paragraph explaining why an adult would be more helpful than a peer when a teen wishes to discuss becoming sexually active.
3. **Synthesizing.** Why might having a child weaken an already weak relationship between a couple?

Taking Action

1. **Identifying Alternatives.** Generate a list of activities that teens who have chosen to abstain from sexual activity can do in your community while on a date. *(Leadership)*
2. **Researching.** Investigate the legal rights and responsibilities of a father. What are the advantages of establishing paternity? *(Management)*

CONNECTIONS

Cross-Curricular Connections

1. **Art.** Create a poster that warns teens of the dangers of sexually transmitted diseases.
2. **Language Arts.** With a partner, plan and write a skit showing a teen boy and girl discussing becoming sexually active. Have them use the problem-solving process to decide in favor of abstaining from sexual activity.

Workplace Connections

1. **Personal Qualities.** Why is keeping information confidential important for people who work as counselors?
2. **Interpersonal Skills.** What interpersonal skills would be needed by someone who advises pregnant teens?

Family and Community Connections

1. **Media Watch.** Some people criticize the media for showing material that promotes sexual activity. Have a class debate on whether or not television shows should be censored.
2. **Abstinence Pledge.** Students in some places write a formal pledge in which they promise not to become sexually active. Then they sign the pledge, promising to uphold it. As a class, write a pledge that

contains a promise of abstinence. Discuss how you could persuade other students to sign it.

3. **First-Person Accounts.** In the library or a bookstore, find a magazine article that contains the true story of a pregnant teen who became a single parent, married and raised the child, or put the child up for adoption. Remember that the account could be written by a boy or a girl. Read the person's story and then relate it to the class.

Technology Connections

1. **Video or Audiotape.** Create a radio or television public service announcement that calls attention to the responsibilities and realities of teen parenthood and urges teens not to become sexually active.
2. **Computer.** Using a spreadsheet program, develop a budget for a single parent or a young married couple with a child.

EVALUATION

1. Use the reproducible Chapter 4 Test in the *Teacher Resource Guide*, or construct your own test using the **Exam***View*® Test Generator.
2. For an alternative, assign the Chapter 4 activity in the *Authentic Assessment* section of the *Teacher Resource Guide*.

ENRICHMENT

Assign students either of the two enrichment activities in the *Enrichment Activities* booklet in the *Student Motivation Kit*.

EXTENSION

Invite teen parents (including some still in school and some who dropped out) to speak to the class about being a parent. Ask them to discuss how being a parent has affected their schooling, family relationships, and social life. Ask if they were ready to face the responsibilities of parenthood.

CLOSE

Have students work in pairs to create a poster titled "The Ten Most Important Things a Teen Should Know About Pregnancy and Parenting."

UNIT 2 OBJECTIVES

After completing Unit 2, students will be able to:

- Describe the normal development of babies before birth and identify hazards that can interfere with normal development.
- Discuss preparations prospective parents should make before birth.
- Describe the process by which a baby is born and discuss the care a newborn requires.

UNIT 2 OVERVIEW

Chapter 5 discusses the stages of pregnancy and examines genetics and some important birth defects.

Chapter 6 describes how parents prepare for the birth of a baby, including prenatal care, financial planning, and options for delivery.

Chapter 7 outlines the three stages of labor and the care that newborn babies require.

UNIT 2

Pregnancy and Childbirth

138 UNIT 2: Pregnancy and Childbirth

USING THE POEM When a new baby is born, older children in the family might feel confused, even rejected. Have students point out the words of affection used by "mom" to describe the speaker in the poem. **Ask:** How would a child feel hearing such words also used to describe a new baby? How does the baby's arrival change his or her relationship with his parents? grandparents and other relatives? What can parents do to minimize hurt feelings?

"SOME THINGS DON'T MAKE ANY SENSE AT ALL"

My mom says I'm her sugarplum.

My mom says I'm her lamb.

My mom says I'm completely perfect

Just the way I am.

My mom says I'm a super-special terrific little guy.

My mom just had another baby.

Why?

—*Judith Viorst*

139

- Show students a photo of a healthy newborn taken soon after birth. **Ask:** How does the picture match your image of a newborn? How is it different? How did the baby develop before birth? Who cared for the baby then?
- Have students write a diary entry reflecting the thoughts of either the father or mother in the picture. What feelings do they have about the birth of their new child?

COMPLETING | **UNIT 2**

EXTENSION

Invite a panel of pregnant women to discuss their pregnancy. How have they felt physically? Emotionally? What preparations are they making for delivery?

EVALUATION

Use the Unit 2 Test on the **Exam**View® Test Generator or use the program to create your own test.

FCCLA Connection | **Car Seat Safety**

Have the chapter work with a local car dealer, health agency, or other group to plan and carry out a car seat safety inspection day. Students can learn about safe and unsafe installation, develop publicity, and provide organization, child care, and literature.

Guest Speakers. The class could benefit by hearing from several professionals during the study of this unit. For *Chapter 5:* geneticist, parent of child with a birth defect. For *Chapter 6:* dietitian. For *Chapter 7:* obstetrician, visiting nurse.

Field Trips. The class could take field trips to a birthing center or hospital maternity area to enhance their study of this unit.

CHAPTER 5 RESOURCES

Teacher Resource Guide
• Chapter 5 Test, p. 120
• Authentic Assessment, p. 265
Student Motivation Kit
• Observ. & Case Studies
  (observation), pp. 35-36
Transparency Package
• CT-12 to CT-18
Effective Instruction CD-ROM

CHAPTER 5 OVERVIEW

Section 5-1 looks at conception and changes in the developing baby and pregnant woman. **Section 5-2** explores genetics, multiple births, and infertility. **Section 5-3** covers birth defects. **Section 5-4** examines dangers to prenatal development.

CHAPTER 5 OBJECTIVES

After completing Chapter 5, students will be able to:

• Describe development during each stage of pregnancy.
• Explain how genetics influence development and identify options for infertile couples.
• Explain the causes, diagnosis, and prevention of birth defects.
• Summarize the dangers posed by exposure to certain hazards during pregnancy.

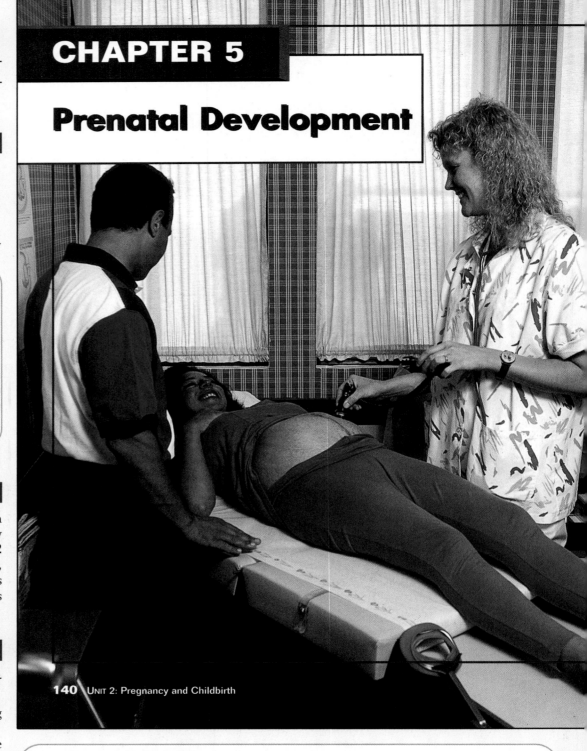

CHAPTER 5

Prenatal Development

140 | Unit 2: Pregnancy and Childbirth

RESOURCES TO EXPLORE

Birth Defects. The March of Dimes supports health service programs, education about birth defects, and research into their causes and prevention. The group funds basic research into the causes of birth defects; studies of the means of preventing and treating birth defects; and investigations into the social and behavioral effects of low birth weight. For more information, contact your local chapter or: The March of Dimes, 1275 Mamaroneck Avenue, White Plains, NY 10605, www.modimes.org

Stefan and Julia exchanged excited glances. Julia was about 20 weeks pregnant and had come to see her doctor for her monthly visit. As always, Stefan came along. This was their first child, and he wanted to know how the baby—and Julia—were doing. Besides, today was a special day. Last month, the doctor had said that they would try to hear the baby's heartbeat today.

The doctor had been asking Julia questions about how she felt in the past month. As she finished writing down Julia's answers, the mother- and father-to-be could hardly contain themselves. Then Dr. Aditya looked up from her paper with a broad smile. "Are you ready?" she asked. Stefan and Julia both nodded quickly.

Dr. Aditya listened first and said "Oh, we've got a good, strong heartbeat here." Then the nurse positioned the special stethoscope so Julia and Stefan could hear. There it was—the rapid thump, thump of their baby's heart! Smiles broke out on their faces, but they also felt a sense of awe. The reality of the new life they had created began to sink in.

"There it was—the rapid thump, thump of their baby's heart!"

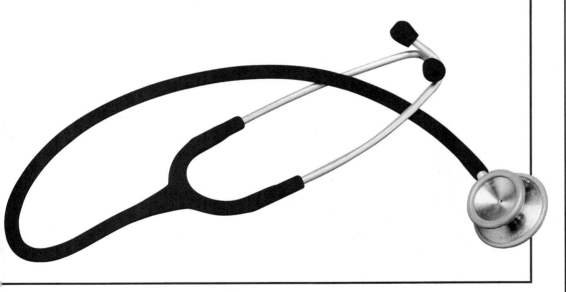

CHAPTER 5: Prenatal Development **141**

- Show pictures of people from different stages of life, from childhood to old age. **Ask:** What happened to each of these people before birth? How might those developments have affected the person in later life?
- Have students take the role of the physician. Ask them to assume that this is a couple's first visit for a prenatal exam. Have students write a paragraph explaining what they would say to the couple on this visit.

USING THE SCENARIO Have small groups discuss the following questions and then share their answers with the class: Why would hearing the baby's heartbeat be significant for expectant parents? What other experience of the baby would be exciting them? Why might hearing the heartbeat be especially moving for the father?

KEY TO ABILITY LEVELS Each section gives skill-building activities. Each activity has been labeled for use with students of various learning styles and abilities.

L1 Level 1 activities are basic activities and should be within the range of all students.

L2 Level 2 activities are average activities and should be within the range of average and above average students.

L3 Level 3 activities are challenging activities designed for the ability range of above average students.

The Developing Baby

(pages 142-149)

FOCUS

MOTIVATOR

Tell students to imagine that a cousin tells them she is going to have a baby. **Ask:** How do they picture their cousin: with a big belly or holding a newborn? Tell students that even before the big belly appears, the mother's body undergoes many changes.

VOCABULARY ACTIVITY

Write prenatal on the chalkboard and ask students to identify the parts of the word—the prefix *pre* ("before") and the root natal ("relating to birth"). What other words do they know that begin with the prefix *pre*?

The Developing Baby

During pregnancy, a single cell grows and develops into a human being capable of independent life. This amazing process, which takes about nine months, is called **prenatal development**.

KEY TERMS

amniotic fluid
conception
embryo
fetus
ovum
placenta
prenatal development
sperm
umbilical cord
uterus
zygote

OBJECTIVES:

• Distinguish among the three stages of pregnancy.

• Describe prenatal development during each stage of pregnancy.

• Explain what changes affect a woman during each stage of pregnancy.

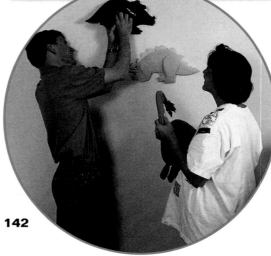

142

Conception

About once each month, an **ovum** (OH-vum)—a female cell or egg—is released by one of a woman's ovaries. The egg moves through the Fallopian tube to the **uterus** (UTE-uh-rus), the organ in a woman's body in which a baby develops during pregnancy. The journey takes about two or three days.

Observing & Participating

Invite a local obstetrician or midwife to speak to the class. Before the visit, have students draw up a list of questions and encourage them to take notes during the talk. Ask your guest to discuss how closely his or her patients' symptoms resemble those described on the Pregnancy by Month chart on page 145. Ask: What happens during a checkup? How frequent are they? How are the mother's and baby's health linked to each other?

CONCEPTION

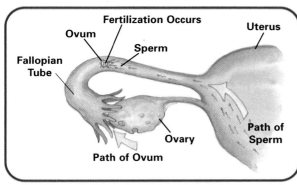

When the egg reaches the uterus, it usually disintegrates and is flushed out of the body with the menstrual flow. Sometimes, however, the egg meets and is fertilized by a **sperm**, or male cell. When the ovum and a sperm unite, **conception** takes place, and pregnancy begins.

An ovum lives 12 to 24 hours, while sperm is capable of fertilizing an ovum for 48 to 72 hours. There are three to four days in each woman's cycle during which intercourse could lead to conception.

Period of the Zygote

The baby's development is often grouped into three stages, called the periods of the zygote, the embryo, and the fetus. The charts on pages 145 to 147 show how the unborn baby and mother change during these months.

In looking at this chart, remember that growth patterns and reactions are individual. Not all babies develop at exactly the same rate. Every woman does not experience all of the effects described here.

The first stage in development is the period of the **zygote** (ZY-goat), or fertilized egg. It lasts about two weeks.

In this period, the zygote travels down the Fallopian tube and attaches itself to the thickened lining of the uterus. This lining provides a soft, warm bed. From the uterus, the zygote draws nourishment from the mother's body.

The zygote grows by cell division. The single, complete cell divides and becomes two. Then these two cells become four and so on, until there is a mass of cells. Despite this remarkable growth, after two weeks, the zygote is only the size of a pinhead.

Period of the Embryo

The second stage of pregnancy is the period of the **embryo**. The embryo is the developing baby from about the third through eighth weeks of pregnancy. During this time, the embryo grows rapidly. It is also in this period that several important and amazing changes occur.

EMBRYO ATTACHES TO UTERUS

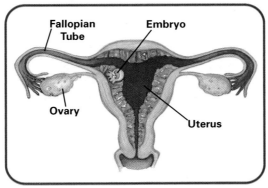

CHAPTER 5: Prenatal Development **143**

COMPREHENSION CHECK

1. How long is the time each month in which a female can become pregnant? (*Three to four days.*)
2. When is the period of the embryo? (*Third to eighth weeks of pregnancy.*)

ACTIVITIES

Critical Thinking Activity

Analyzing. Give pairs of students a few minutes to jot down notes about why it is important to understand how conception takes place. Then have pairs discuss their ideas and reach agreement on two to three reasons. Allow the entire class to share views. **L1**

VISUAL LEARNING	Using the Drawings

Have students describe the process of conception using the drawings on this page. Where does fertilization take place? (*Fallopian tube.*) Where does implantation occur? (*Uterus.*)

Small Size of the Zygote and Embryo. At conception, the fertilized egg is no larger than the dot over a printed letter i. Even when it attaches to the uterus, it is no larger than a grain of rice.

Parenting in *Action*

Ask students what prospective parents can do to keep mentally, emotionally, and physically healthy and prepare for birth and their baby. Where could the parents find reliable information? Bring in copies of magazines that advise new and prospective parents. Have students judge the usefulness and reliability of the various magazines.

ACTIVITIES

Critical Thinking Activity

Comparing and Contrasting. Ask students to compare the sensation of being underwater, as in a swimming pool, to the protection amniotic fluid provides the embryo and fetus. What other comparisons might help clarify the role of the amniotic fluid? **L1**

VISUAL LEARNING	Using the Illustration

Have students identify the umbilical cord in the drawing.

Tell students that after fertilization, it takes about three to five days for the zygote to reach the uterus. Another five-day period is needed for the egg to become implanted on the uterine wall. When implantation is complete, the egg produces hormones that give the signal to stop the menstrual period.

Answers to FOLLOWING UP

1. The shedding of the inner lining of the uterus because an egg has not been fertilized.

2. She may be pregnant. She should see a doctor.

Menstruation

At the same time that an egg is released by the ovary, the woman's body releases specific hormones. These prepare the uterus in case the egg is fertilized. The inner lining of the uterus begins to grow and thicken. If the egg is not fertilized, this inner lining breaks down and passes out of the body. This is the bleeding that women experience every month as a menstrual period. Periods usually are about 28 days apart.

When fertilization takes place, though, the zygote attaches itself to this lining. In that case, the lining of the uterus cannot be shed. When fertilization takes place, then, the woman's menstrual periods stop. They will not begin again until after the baby is born.

For some women, periods may be delayed even longer. The menstrual period may not begin again while a woman is breast-feeding her baby.

FOLLOWING UP

1. What causes a woman to menstruate?

2. If a woman does not have a menstrual period, what may have taken place? What should she do?

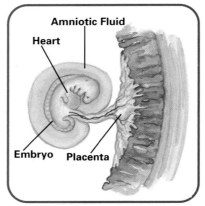

EMBRYO AT 3 WEEKS

Amniotic Fluid

Heart

Embryo   Placenta

First, the mass of cells develops into all the major systems of the human body—heart and lungs, bones and muscle. These internal organs are not ready to function yet, however. They continue to develop in the rest of the pregnancy. Even this early, though, the brain begins to take control of these body systems. Because brain development can be harmed by drugs or alcohol, it is important that a pregnant woman avoid these substances.

Second, a sac filled with fluid forms around the embryo. This **amniotic** (AM-knee-AH-tik) **fluid** protects the developing baby. It cushions the embryo from any bumps or falls that the mother might have.

Third, a tissue called the **placenta** (pluh-SEN-tuh) develops. The placenta is very rich in blood vessels. The mother's bloodstream carries food and oxygen to the placenta. From there, it reaches the baby through the **umbilical** (um-BILL-uh-cuhl) **cord**—the fourth important change of this period.

144 UNIT 2: Pregnancy and Childbirth

LEARNING STYLES	Visual

Form students into groups of three and give them encyclopedias, health, or physiology reference books. Have each group investigate one body system, learning its components and what functions it performs. Each group should draw or develop a simple visual to accompany the report of their findings.

Pregnancy Development
Month by Month

Month 1
- Missed menstrual period.
- Other signs of pregnancy may not yet be noticeable.

Month 2
- Breasts begin to swell.
- Pressure on bladder from enlarging uterus results in need to urinate more frequently.
- Possible nausea ("morning sickness").
- Fatigue is common.

Month 3
- Breasts become firmer and fuller, may ache.
- Nausea, fatigue, and frequent urination may continue.
- Abdomen becomes slightly larger. The uterus is about the size of an orange.
- Weight gain may total 2-4 pounds (0.9-1.8 kg).

Month 4
- Abdomen continues to grow slowly.
- Most discomforts of early pregnancy, such as morning sickness, usually gone.
- Appetite increases.

Month 5
- Enlarged abdomen becomes apparent.
- Slight fetal movements felt.
- Increased size may begin to affect posture.

Month 6
- Fetal movements sensed as strong kicks, thumps, and bumps. Some may be visible.
- Weight gain by the beginning of this month may total 10-12 pounds (4.5-5.4 kg).

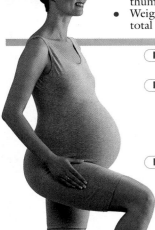

Month 7
- Increased size may affect posture.

Month 8
- Discomfort may result from increased size. Backache, leg cramps, shortness of breath, and fatigue are common.
- Fetal kicks may disturb the mother's rest.
- At the beginning of this month, weight gain totals about 18-20 pounds (8.2-9.1 kg).

Month 9
- "Lightening" felt as the fetus drops into the pelvis. Breathing becomes easier.
- Other discomforts may continue.
- A total weight gain of 25-35 pounds (11.3-15.9 kg) is typical.
- False labor pains may be experienced.

CHAPTER 5: Prenatal Development **145**

COMPREHENSION CHECK

1. In what month might a woman begin to feel "morning sickness"? (*Second.*)
2. When does a pregnant woman begin to feel some fetal movement? (*Fifth month.*)

ACTIVITIES

Critical Thinking Activity

Evaluating. After they have studied the chart, ask students to write a paragraph explaining which period of the pregnancy they think would be the most comfortable for the mother and why. **L1**

VISUAL LEARNING | **Using the Chart**
Have students create a double line graph showing the average weight gain of the mother and baby (see pages 146-147) month by month. Suggest that they record weight gain on the vertical axis and month on the horizontal. **Ask:** Why does the mother gain 25 to 35 pounds when the baby at birth weighs only 7 to 9 pounds? What might be some sources of the additional weight? (*The enlarged uterus, amniotic fluid, placenta.*)

Management/Leadership Skills

Have students brainstorm physical and emotional adjustments they think new parents might have to make with the arrival of a new baby. Students may mention concerns such as making space for the baby and equipment; having to get up in the middle of the night to feed and change the baby; managing finances; and finding a caregiver if both parents will work.

COMPREHENSION CHECK

1. When are all internal organs present? (*Third month.*)
2. When does fat begin to form under the skin? (*Sixth month.*)
3. What changes take place in the baby during the last two months of prenatal development? (*Weight gain, adding fat, moving into position for birth.*)

ACTIVITIES

Discussion Activity

Remind students that some infants are born before prenatal development is complete. Have them predict what development must take place before an infant can survive outside the uterus. Have students verify or correct these predictions as they continue reading. **L1**

| **VISUAL LEARNING** | Using the Illustration |

Divide the class into nine small groups. Assign one month of prenatal development to each group. Give each group a large piece of drawing or construction paper. Ask groups to create a drawing of the baby at that stage of development and use labels to highlight the changes that took place that month. Remind students to title their drawings with the month represented. Then display the drawings on the bulletin board.

Fetal Development
Month by Month

Month 1

- Size: At two weeks, the size of a pinhead.
- Egg attaches to lining of uterus.
- Critical stage for brain and spinal cord development.
- Internal organs and circulatory system begin to form. The heart begins to beat.

Month 2

- Size: About ¼ inch (6 mm) long as month begins.
- Face, eyes, ears, and limbs take shape.
- Bones begin to form.

Month 3

- Size: About 1 inch (25 mm) long as month begins.
- Nostrils, mouth, lips, teeth buds, and eyelids form.
- Fingers and toes almost complete.
- All organs present, although immature.

Month 4

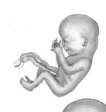

- Size: About 3 inches (76 mm) long, 1 ounce (28 g) as month begins.
- Can suck its thumb, swallow, hiccup, and move around.
- Facial features become clearer.

Month 5

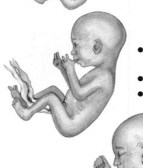

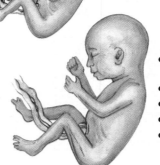

- Size: About 6½-7 inches (16-18 cm) long, about 4-5 ounces (113-142 g) as month begins.
- Hair, eyelashes, and eyebrows appear.
- Teeth continue to develop.
- Organs are maturing.
- Becomes more active.

146 UNIT 2: Pregnancy and Childbirth

| **LEARNING STYLES** | **Auditory** |

Have students put the information in the illustration into verse form, using one stanza for each month. Encourage students to use a regular rhythm and rhyme pattern to make the information easier to remember. Students can rephrase the information to fit the verses, but they must use correct terms. Then use popcorn reading to review the material: Have one student read one stanza aloud and then call out the name of another student to read the next stanza.

Month 6

- Size: About 8-10 inches (21-25 cm) long, about 8-12 ounces (227-340 g) as month begins.
- Fat deposits under skin, but fetus appears wrinkled.
- Breathing movements begin.

Month 7

- Size: About 10-12 inches long , about 1½-2 pounds (680-907 g) as month begins.
- Periods of activity followed by periods of rest and quiet.

Month 8

- Size: About 14-16 inches (36-41 cm) long, about 2½-3 pounds (1.0-1.4 kg) as month begins.
- Weight gain continues rapidly.
- May react to loud noises with a reflex jerking action.
- Moves into a head down position.

Month 9

- Size: About 17-18 inches (43-46 cm) long, 5-6 pounds (2.3-2.7 kg) as month begins.
- Weight gain continues until the week before birth.
- Skin becomes smooth as fat deposits continue.
- Movements decrease as the fetus has less room to move around.
- Acquires disease-fighting antibodies from the mother's blood.
- Descends into pelvis, ready for birth.

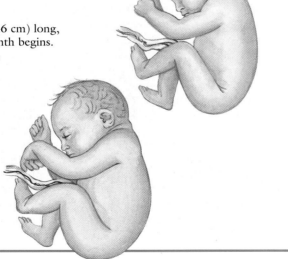

CHAPTER 5: Prenatal Development **147**

Discussion Activity

Ask students to consider the role played by the umbilical cord in nurturing the embryo and fetus. If the umbilical cord were pinched or the free flow of fluid obstructed in some way, how might the developing fetus be affected? **L1**

Critical Thinking Activity

Comparing and Contrasting. Ask students to compare the sensation of being underwater, as in a swimming pool, to the protection amniotic fluid provides the embryo and fetus. What other comparisons might help clarify the role of the amniotic fluid? **L2**

Critical Thinking Activity

Identifying Causes and Effects. Ask: Why do you think a baby does not build immunities until the end of the pregnancy? (*Until then it is protected by the mother's immunities; afterwards, the baby's body needs its own protection.*) **L2**

DID You Know?

Fetal Development. **About the fifth month, the fetus weighs only 8 ounces (227 g). At full term, it weighs 7 to 9 pounds (3-4 kg). At five months, the fetus is covered with fine, downy hair, called lanugo. By the ninth month, lanugo remains only on the shoulders and arms. During the ninth month, hundreds of pints of blood are pumped through the fetus each day, but it has only about 1 cup (240 mL) in its system.**

COMPREHENSION CHECK

1. When does the period of the fetus take place? (*Eighth or ninth week until birth.*)
2. When does "quickening" occur? (*Fourth or fifth month.*)

ACTIVITIES

Teamwork Activity

Divide the class into small groups and give each group four large pieces of writing paper. Have the groups label each paper with one of four headings: "Conception," "Period of the Zygote," "Period of the Embryo," "Period of the Fetus." Have each student write one fact on the paper and pass it to the student to the left. They should repeat the procedure until all students have contributed to every category and no one can think of any more information. Then, together, have all members agree on the accuracy or the facts, checking in their books to clear up any doubts, and making any necessary corrections. **L2**

VISUAL LEARNING | **Using the Drawings**

Have students compare the drawings on pages 148-149. How do the four-month-old and nine-month-old fetuses compare?

The umbilical cord brings nourishment to the baby and takes waste products away. It is usually stiff and firm, like a garden hose filled with water. It is generally not flexible enough to loop around the fetus, although this may occur in rare cases. Only after the baby is born does the umbilical cord become limp.

Period of the Fetus

The third and last stage of pregnancy begins about the eight or ninth week and lasts until birth. This is the period of the **fetus** (FEE-tuhs), the name for the unborn baby from about the eighth or ninth week of pregnancy until birth.

The Developing Brain

Studies show that the fetus already learns and responds to its environment. When light is shined on the fetus, it turns away. When loud music is played, its heart rate increases, and it moves.

Sometime during the fourth or fifth month, the kicks and other movements of the fetus touch the wall of the uterus. These movements are faint and infrequent at first. Gloria felt her baby's movement as a kind of fluttering. Gradually, they become stronger and more frequent. These sensations, sometimes called "quickening," tell the mother that she does, indeed, carry a live child within her. Actually, the baby has been very active long before this time.

A pregnant woman's doctor usually asks her when she first felt these movements. Knowing this helps the doctor estimate the baby's age. That can be used to project a more accurate delivery date.

FETUS AT 4 MONTHS

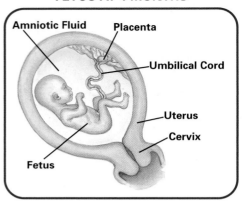

Amniotic Fluid · Placenta · Umbilical Cord · Uterus · Cervix · Fetus

As the fetus grows, so does the amount of the surrounding fluid. The uterus expands, too, and the woman's abdomen grows. Just before delivery, the amount of amniotic fluid decreases. The baby is swallowing it. When the fetus grows large, it no longer has the room to stretch out. It curls up inside the uterus in what is called the fetal position.

By the seventh month, the fetus is capable of living outside the uterus, but not without a great deal of medical help. In the next few months, the fetus becomes ready to live independently. The body's major organs become ready to function without help from the mother's body. The fetus also gains weight rapidly. Fat deposits, which will help the baby maintain body heat after birth, are added under the skin. The fetus, which had been thin and wrinkled, takes on the smoother, rounder appearance of a baby. During these final weeks, the fetus also stores nutrients and builds immunity to diseases and infections.

The fetus can do a surprising number of things—suck its thumb, cough, sneeze, yawn, kick, and hiccup. A baby can even cry before birth.

ISSUES IN TEEN PARENTING

Teen parents have many special needs: (1) to feel accepted and worthwhile; (2) support to build self-esteem; (3) guidance in making good decisions for themselves and their babies; (4) help finding good medical care, proper food, and housing; (5) to learn parenting and employability skills. Ask the school librarian to put together a presentation showing students how to find the names, addresses, phone numbers, and basic information about local agencies that provide these services.

Preparing for Birth

Sometime during the ninth month of pregnancy, the baby's weight seems to shift down and the mother feels more comfortable in her upper abdomen. This shift is called "lightening." It means that the baby has dropped into the birth canal. With a first baby, lightening may take place several days—or even weeks—before labor begins. If the mother has given birth before, lightening may not occur until just before labor begins.

At this point, the fetus is usually upside down, with the head nestled in the mother's pelvis. This is the easiest and safest position for birth. The baby is less active than in previous weeks, because there is little space in which to move!

The skin of the mother's abdomen appears stretched to capacity. The abdominal muscles are stretched, too. They are

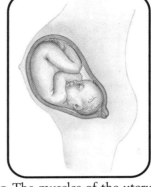

FETUS AT 9 MONTHS

both capable of remarkable stretching— and contracting. The muscles of the uterus and abdomen can be stretched up to 60 times their original size during pregnancy, yet they return to nearly their original size within six weeks or so after the birth. Pregnancy brings many changes, both in the pregnant woman and the developing baby. After 37 to 42 weeks of preparation, the baby is ready to be born.

SECTION 5-1 REVIEW

✔ Check Your Understanding

1. What cells join together to cause conception?
2. What happens during the period of the zygote? How long does it last?
3. What changes might a pregnant woman feel in the period of the zygote and embryo?
4. What four changes take place in the period of the embryo?
5. What are the most important changes that take place in a fetus during the last two months of pregnancy?
6. How does a pregnant woman feel when "lightening" occurs? Why?

Putting Knowledge Into Practice

1. **Diagramming.** Draw a diagram showing the uterus, amniotic sac, placenta, umbilical cord, and fetus. Label these parts.
2. **Comparing.** In a few paragraphs, compare the three stages of prenatal development in terms of the changes that the developing baby undergoes.
3. **Observing and Participating.** Talk to a pregnant female about the physical and emotional changes she has experienced. Record her answers and share them with the class.

CHAPTER 5: Prenatal Development **149**

ANSWERS TO SECTION 5-1 REVIEW

1. Sperm and ovum.
2. Zygote attaches to inner lining of uterus; cell mass grows. Lasts 2 weeks.
3. *See months 1 and 2 on page 145.*
4. Embryo develops major body systems; sac holding amniotic fluid, placenta, and umbilical cord form.
5. *Possible responses:* Organs can work outside mother's body; fat is stored; fetus drops into birth canal.
6. *Possible response:* More comfortable because the pressure on her upper abdomen has been relieved.

SECTION 5-2 RESOURCES
Teacher Resource Guide
• Lesson Plan Organizer, p. 45
• Section 5-2 Quiz, p. 117
Student Motivation Kit
• Reteaching Activity, p. 19
Student Workbook
• Study Guide, pp. 42-46
• Heredity in the Works, p. 49
Effective Instruction CD-ROM

FOCUS

MOTIVATOR

Ask for volunteers to share photographs of their families. Tell students to look closely at the pictures. What physical characteristics do family members have in common? What are the most striking differences between them? How do students account for these similarities and differences?

VOCABULARY ACTIVITY

Show students how to pronounce each term and explain what it means. After discussing the material, ask them to use each word in a sentence.

SECTION 5-2

A Closer Look at Conception

Have you ever been at a family gathering when someone said that you looked just like a relative? Your uncle may have said "You have your mother's eyes." Perhaps your grandmother said, "Your hair is just like your father's." Why do people look like their parents?

KEY TERMS
chromosomes
dominant
genes
infertility
recessive
surrogate

OBJECTIVES:
• Describe how personal characteristics are inherited.
• Explain the causes of multiple births.
• Evaluate different possible solutions for infertility.

The Genetic Package

Each person inherits many characteristics from his or her parents. They include physical build; skin color; hair texture and color; the color and shape of the eyes; the shape and size of the ears, hands, and feet; and blood type. Musical ability may be passed on from parents to children. So, too, are some medical conditions. How does this happen? Scientists have learned a

Observing & Participating

Have students volunteer their observations about physical characteristics in their own families that have been passed down from one generation to another. Ask students to think about people who have the same talent as a parent or grandparent. How might genetics explain how those people got their talents? To what degree are talents the result of environment and not genetics? How do opportunities to practice a talent or pursue an interest affect a person?

great deal about how heredity—the passing on of characteristics—works.

At conception, every human baby receives 46 **chromosomes** (CROW-muh-soams), tiny threadlike particles in the nucleus of every cell. These chromosomes come in 23 pairs. The father's sperm and the mother's ovum both contribute a chromosome to each pair. Each chromosome has thousands of **genes,** the units that determine the child's inherited characteristics. Genes make up chromosomes as beads make up a necklace.

For every inherited characteristic, a person receives two copies of a gene—one from the mother and one from the father. When both are the same, the child has that characteristic. Thus, two genes for blue eyes give the child blue eyes.

What happens if a person receives two different genes, such as one gene for blue eyes and one gene for brown eyes? The way the characteristic is expressed will be controlled by the **dominant,** or stronger, gene.

The **recessive,** or weaker, gene will not be expressed. In this example, they will have brown eyes because the brown eye gene is the dominant one.

Of course, the terms *dominant* and *recessive* refer only to the relationship of genes to each other. Blue eyes are not weaker than brown eyes.

Making a Unique Person

Heredity explains why brothers and sisters often resemble each other—and why they can look quite different. Each sperm or egg cell contains a different combination of genes. When they combine in a fertilized egg, they produce a unique individual. That person may have a father's brown eyes; a mother's dimples; a grandfather's tall, lean build; and a grandmother's clear, sweet singing voice. These traits—and many, many others—are determined by the particular combinations of genes brought together at conception.

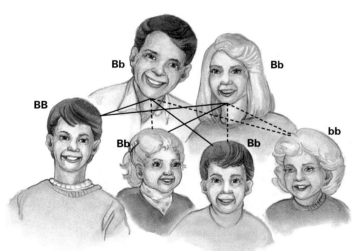

Bb Bb BB Bb Bb bb

The dominant gene, for brown eyes, is shown with a capital **B.** The recessive gene, for blue eyes, is shown with a lowercase **b.** Only a child who receives the recessive gene from both parents will have blue eyes. If both parents carry the recessive gene, each child has a one in four chance of having blue eyes. *Could these parents have more than one child with blue eyes? Why do more people around the world have brown eyes than blue?*

CHAPTER 5: Prenatal Development **151**

ACTIVITIES

Science Activity

Tell students that how Brussels sprouts taste to each person is shaped by genetics. Brussels sprouts contain phenylthiocarbamide (PTC), a substance that some people can taste and others cannot. People who have two "tasting" genes find Brussels sprouts bitter; people who have two "nontasting" genes find them sweet. The "tasting" gene is dominant, however, so people who have one of each gene may find them bitter. Have students create a diagram similar to the illustration about eye color to show all the possible genetic combinations for children of a couple that is Tt and Tt. Ask students to label which genetic combinations would taste PTC and which would not. **L3**

VISUAL LEARNING	Using the Illustration

Answer to caption: (a) The parents could have more than one child with blue eyes since *every* child has a one in four chance of having blue eyes. (b) Most people have brown eyes because both the people with two brown genes and one brown gene and one blue gene have brown eyes.

COMPREHENSION CHECK

1. Which are more frequent—identical or fraternal twins? (*Fraternal.*)
2. Why do you think multiple-birth newborns typically have lower birth weights than single birth infants? (*Food from the mother's body must be shared.*)

ACTIVITIES

Math Activity

Have students gather information within the class about the following recessive traits: blue eyes, green or hazel eyes, straight hair, blond or red hair, second toes that are longer than big toes. Have them tally the number of students having each recessive trait and calculate the percentage of those with each recessive trait. **L2**

Children inherit their physical characteristics in different combinations from their parents. While they share some traits, each child has a unique genetic makeup.

The sex of a child is also set at conception. It is determined by the sex chromosomes, which come in two types, X and Y. Every egg cell contains an X chromosome. Each sperm cell contains either an X or a Y chromosome. If the sperm that fertilizes the egg carries an X chromosome, an XX combination results, and the child is a girl. If the sperm carries a Y chromosome, an XY combination results, and the child is a boy.

Multiple Births

Sometimes a pregnant woman gives birth to more than one baby. This, too, is set at conception or soon after.

As you know, a fertilized egg starts growing by dividing into two cells. These cells continue to divide. Sometimes the mass of cells splits in half soon after fertilization. Then each clump of cells continues to divide and grow into a separate embryo. The result is identical twins. Identical twins are always the same sex and have very similar characteristics because both began as one zygote.

Fraternal twins form when two eggs are released at the same time and each is fertilized. They grow side by side in the uterus. Because they result from the union of different eggs and sperm, fraternal twins are no more alike in terms of heredity than any other siblings. Unlike identical twins, they may even be of opposite sexes.

When more than two babies are born, they may be identical or fraternal—or a combination. As with twins, it depends on whether one fertilized egg splits or more than one egg is fertilized at the same time.

In the United States, about 2.5 percent of births are twin births. (Fraternal twins occur three times more often than identical twins.) Multiple births of more than two are rare, but are happening at a growing rate. A major reason for this increase is the treatment people receive to overcome **infertility,** or the inability to become pregnant.

Infertility

Not all couples who want to have children are able to become pregnant. Infertility may have many causes.

People who have problems with fertility often feel that they aren't normal. Many feel that they are alone in facing this situation. Medical and counseling support can help them overcome these feelings.

152 Unit 2: Pregnancy and Childbirth

ISSUES IN TEEN PARENTING

Multiple births are a serious challenge for teen mothers. During the pregnancy, teens need to pay special attention to their health and follow their doctor's instructions carefully. They also need to prepare for the emotional demands of caring for two or more children. Experienced parents and pediatricians say parents should get help at least for the first few months.

Multiple births may be identical or fraternal. *What is the difference?*

Medical advances have helped many of these couples overcome infertility. When these couples seek medical advice, a doctor makes a detailed study of both the man's and woman's health. Often, this reveals that one or both have physical problems that prevent pregnancy. Surgery or medication may solve the problem.

If the woman's ovaries are not releasing an egg each month, the doctor may prescribe fertility drugs. These substances stimulate a woman's ovaries to release eggs. Fertility drugs have several drawbacks. Some women who take them have serious side effects, such as lung problems, abdominal pain, nausea, diarrhea, or dizziness. Also, fertility drugs increase the chances of multiple babies. The more children a pregnant woman carries, the more difficult it is for them all to survive.

Options for Infertile Couples

Some couples can't conceive a child even after treatment for infertility. They may consider several other options.

- **Adoption.** By adopting, the couple legally takes all responsibilities and rights for raising a child already born.
- **Artificial insemination.** In this process, a doctor injects sperm into a woman's uterus with a special needle. The sperm may be the husband's. If he has a history of genetic disorders, the sperm may come from another male, who is called a donor.
- **In vitro fertilization.** This process is used when a woman has damaged Fallopian tubes that prevent pregnancy. In a small glass dish, a doctor combines a mature egg from the woman

People who have problems with fertility may feel alone with their problems. *How can a counselor help them?*

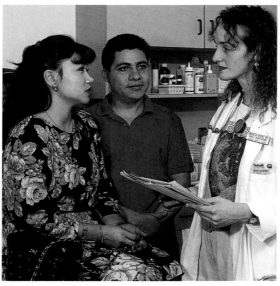

CHAPTER 5: Prenatal Development **153**

CHECKING COMPREHENSION

Have students answer the Check Your Understanding questions. Answers appear at the bottom of this page.

EVALUATION

Give students the Section 5-2 Quiz in the *Teacher Resource Guide*.

RETEACHING

1. Assign Reteaching Activities, page 19.
2. Work with small groups of students to identify and discuss examples of inherited traits.

ENRICHMENT

Draw a poster illustrating the cell division of identical, fraternal, and conjoined twins.

EXTENSION

Invite to class a social worker or a representative from an adoption agency to discuss adoption. How have attitudes toward adoption changed in recent years?

CLOSE

Have students design a graphic organizer listing the advantages and disadvantages of the different options available to infertile couples.

and sperm from her husband. If fertilization takes place, the doctor places the zygote in the woman's uterus. If the zygote attaches itself to the uterus, a normal pregnancy takes place.

- **Ovum transfer.** This procedure uses an egg taken from a female donor and in vitro fertilization. It may be used by women who lack working ovaries or who have inherited disorders.
- **Surrogate mother.** A **surrogate** (SIR-uh-get) or substitute, mother is a woman who becomes pregnant for another couple. She may carry a couple's fertilized egg, removed from the biological mother because she is unable to carry a pregnancy to completion. Other surrogates are artificially inseminated with sperm from the husband of an infertile woman. This process usually includes legal arrangements and must meet state laws.

Questions Raised

As technology continues to advance, other options may be available. However, not everyone thinks these alternatives are acceptable. The use of ovum transfers or surrogate mothers is especially controversial. These practices raise many ethical questions.

SECTION 5-2 REVIEW

✔ Check Your Understanding

1. List some traits that are inherited.
2. Explain how dominant and recessive genes work.
3. Why is each person unique?
4. How is the sex of a baby determined?
5. What is the difference between identical twins and fraternal twins?
6. Name some disadvantages of fertility drugs.
7. What options does an infertile couple have if fertility treatment does not work?

Putting Knowledge Into Practice

1. **Making Inferences.** Scientists are trying to identify each of the genes—up to 100,000 of them—found on human chromosomes. Why do you think they are making this effort? What benefits could this research provide?
2. **Synthesizing.** Why would having damaged Fallopian tubes prevent a woman from becoming pregnant?
3. **Observing and Participating.** Make a chart showing the generations of your family or a family you know from grandparents through parents and their brothers and sisters to the present generation—including brothers, sisters, and cousins. On the chart, show the hair color and eye color of each person. Write a paragraph describing any patterns you see.

154 UNIT 2: Pregnancy and Childbirth

ANSWERS TO SECTION 5-2 REVIEW

1. Physical build; skin and eye color; some abilities and medical conditions.
2. Person with two dominant genes or dominant and a recessive shows dominant trait. Person with two recessives shows recessive trait.
3. Each person has unique mix of genes.
4. *Females:* two X; *males:* X and a Y.
5. Identical twins come from same egg. Fraternal twins come from different eggs.
6. Side effects; may lead to multiple births.
7. Adoption; artificial insemination, in vitro fertilization, ovum transfer, or a surrogate mother.

Problems in Prenatal Development

Will the baby be all right? This is a major concern for all parents-to-be. Fortunately, most babies develop normally and are born healthy. For a variety of reasons, however, prenatal development does not always proceed normally.

KEY TERMS

amniocentesis
birth defect
chorionic villi sampling
miscarriage
stillbirth
ultrasound

OBJECTIVES:

- Contrast miscarriage and stillbirth.
- Identify some major birth defects.
- Explain the four causes of birth defects.
- Describe how birth defects can be diagnosed and prevented.

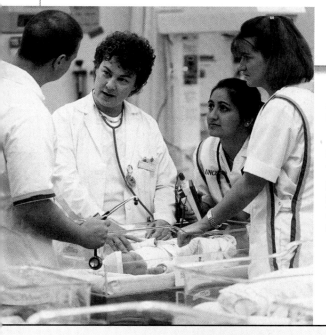

Losing a Baby

Sometimes a baby does not develop normally. In some of those cases, the developing baby dies. If this happens before 20 weeks of pregnancy, it is called a **miscarriage** (MISS-care-uj). If it occurs after 20 weeks, it is called a **stillbirth**.

CHAPTER 5: Prenatal Development   **155**

Observing & Participating

Have small groups compose letters to organizations that provide services and fund work with birth defects. Tell students to ask for information about causes, current research, diagnosis, and prevention. If possible, you or the librarian could show students how to find information through the Internet. Some sites students could start with are the March of Dimes and the Department of Health and Human Services.

SECTION 5-3 RESOURCES
Teacher Resource Guide
- Lesson Plan Organizer, p. 46
- Section 5-3 Quiz, p. 118
Student Motivation Kit
- Reteaching Activity, p. 20
Student Workbook
- Study Guide, pp. 42-46
- Understanding Birth Defects, p. 50
Effective Instruction CD-ROM

FOCUS

MOTIVATOR

Read aloud to the class a brief selection from a book such as Helen Keller's *The Story of My Life*, which addresses birth defects. Encourage students to discuss what they think it would be like to live with a birth defect.

VOCABULARY ACTIVITY

Explain to students that some nouns are made up of two or three words. (*Examples: Peanut butter, earthquake, sister-in-law.*) Compound nouns are spelled as one word, as separate words, or hyphenated. Ask students to find two compound nouns among the terms. (*Birth defect, stillbirth*)

A miscarriage can be difficult to accept. *How can a couple who suffered a miscarriage help each other?*

These losses can be severe shocks and bring great pain. Most couples look forward to their baby's birth. When a miscarriage or stillbirth takes place, they feel as though they lost a child who had been born. They go through the same stages of grief as does anyone who has had a family member die.

Sometimes, these parents feel terribly alone. They may blame themselves for the death. Usually, these losses happen naturally and are not the fault of either the father or the mother. Nor are these parents alone. In fact, as many as 20 percent of all pregnancies end in miscarriage.

Special services and support groups can help these couples. Most couples who suffer the death of a fetus are able to have a successful pregnancy later.

Types of Birth Defects

Some babies are born with serious problems that threaten their health or ability to live. These problems are called **birth defects**. There are hundreds of birth defects, and they vary widely in their effects. Some are mild or can be readily corrected. Others result in severe lifelong disabilities or even death. About 3 out of every 100 children born in the United States have a birth defect. Scientists and health professionals are working to decrease that rate.

Miscarriage. **Possible causes include abnormal implantation of the placenta; chromosomal abnormalities; abnormalities in fetal development; and maternal factors, such as** infections or nutritional deficiencies. Some women feel that they miscarry because they are physically active. No evidence supports this supposition. Doctors do recommend that once a woman miscarries, she should get adequate rest and exercise moderately during subsequent pregnancies.

Some birth defects affect the shape or size of the body or of certain parts of the body. For instance, a child may be born with a misshapen foot or an extra or a missing finger. With others, a part or system of the body does not function properly. Blindness, deafness, and mental retardation are examples.

Not all birth defects are apparent at birth. Sometimes the abnormality does not cause problems until months—or even years—have passed.

Many children with birth defects can still lead full, rich lives.

Causes of Birth Defects

Scientists don't yet understand the cause of about 60 percent of all birth defects. They are constantly researching to find the answers, though. They have found four main causes for birth defects. Some are caused by factors in the environment of the developing baby. Some result from abnormal genes or errors in chromosomes. Many result from a combination of environment and heredity.

Environmental Causes

During the first few weeks of pregnancy, a baby develops all the bodily systems needed for survival and a normal life. During this time, the developing baby depends completely on the mother's body for nourishment and oxygen.

Many choices the mother makes—as well as many conditions of which the mother may be unaware—can affect the development of her baby. They include:
- The nutritional balance of her diet.
- Any diseases or infections the mother has during pregnancy.
- Harmful substances the mother takes in, including alcohol, tobacco, and drugs.
- Some medicines that benefit the mother, but which can hurt the baby.
- Exposure to outside hazards such as radiation, especially early in pregnancy.

CHAPTER 5: Prenatal Development **157**

Connecting to History

Have students read about birth defects within royal families or other historical figures. One example that proved to be historically significant was that of the son of Czar Nicholas II, who suffered from hemophilia. Another example is the Hapsburg jaw. Have students create a family tree, with portraits and a paragraph about the members of the family. **L2**

Many women pay more attention to their nutrition when pregnant than at any other time. How can they use pregnancy to establish good eating habits and use motherhood to keep them up?

Answers to
FOLLOWING UP

1. Because most substances in the mother's bloodstream pass to the baby.

2. *Possible response:* Immediately, since no one knows how early smoking begins having ill effects on the developing baby.

Taking Care of Two

*E*verything a pregnant woman takes into her body—pills, injections, tobacco smoke, and alcohol—may affect her unborn child. The placenta may act as a partial barrier, and certain substances may have difficulty crossing to the child. Most substances, however, do reach the embryo or fetus. If the concentration of any substance in the mother's blood is high enough, some of these substances can damage the baby.

Researchers have not been able to find a "safe level" for the substances that can harm a developing baby. The best course is a simple one: avoid all suspect substances during pregnancy. This step helps more than the baby. It helps the mother be healthy, too.

Most women don't realize they are pregnant right away. If they are not careful, they could take harmful substances into their body in the crucial early weeks of the baby's development. They can avoid this problem by planning a pregnancy and by avoiding all harmful substances before they become pregnant.

FOLLOWING UP

1. Why is the developing baby affected by substances that the pregnant woman takes into her body?

2. Amira and Doug have been married two years and now want to have a baby. When should Amira stop smoking?

Hereditary Causes

Thousands of genes make up a genetic blueprint. For each person, about five or six of the recessive genes are imperfect. A single copy of these genes will have no effect on the development of that person—or the baby who inherits the gene. Sometimes, though, each parent passes on the same recessive defective gene. Sometimes, too, a defective gene is dominant. In these cases, the baby may develop a birth defect.

Some inherited conditions affect only one sex. Hemophilia, a condition that prevents the blood from clotting, and color blindness are two examples of birth defects that affect only males.

Errors in Chromosomes

A few types of birth defects are linked to a problem with the baby's chromosomes. For example, there may be too many—or too few—chromosomes in each of the

158 UNIT 2: Pregnancy and Childbirth

LEARNING STYLES

Visual

Have students prepare posters showing how birth defects can be inherited. Have them diagram how genes are passed from one generation to the next. Graphs could show the frequency with which selected birth defects occur. How must families adapt to compensate for them? Instruct them to include labels. Display the posters in class and then have a "gallery walk" in which students look at the posters and ask one or two questions of the designer.

Selected Birth Defects

Cerebral Palsy
- **Description:** Cerebral palsy is a general term for a variety of problems of the motor system. The symptoms can include lack of coordination, stiffness, jerkiness, difficulty with speech, and paralysis.
- **Causes:** Cerebral palsy results from damage to the brain before, during, or shortly after birth. The causes of this damage vary.
- **Detection:** The symptoms usually appear during the first year of life.
- **Treatment:** The damage caused to the brain is irreversible. However, physical therapy, speech therapy, surgery, and medication can lessen the effects of this damage in many cases.

Cleft Lip and/or Cleft Palate
- **Description:** A gap in the upper lip or palate (the roof of the mouth) causes problems with eating, swallowing, speech, and appearance.
- **Causes:** Condition may be caused by hereditary or environmental factors or both.
- **Detection:** Both cleft lip and cleft palate are apparent at birth.
- **Treatment:** Surgery can correct the gap and eliminate the problems associated with it.

Cystic Fibrosis
- **Description:** Cystic fibrosis (CF) affects the respiratory and digestive systems. Many with CF die before reaching adulthood, although treatment now allows people with the condition to live longer than in the past.
- **Cause:** It is far more likely to affect whites than African or Asian Americans. CF is caused by inheriting defective recessive genes from both parents.
- **Detection:** Symptoms include very salty sweat and a cough that doesn't go away. Tests can identify carriers of the gene and can diagnose an affected child or fetus.
- **Treatment:** There is no known cure. Those with CF can be helped by special diets, lung exercises, and treatment.

Down Syndrome
- **Description:** A group of problems that may include, among other conditions, mental retardation; problems of the heart, blood, and digestive system; and poor muscle tone.
- **Cause:** Down syndrome is caused by the presence of an extra chromosome 21.
- **Detection:** It can be detected in a fetus by amniocentesis or chorionic villi sampling; can be found in a child by a blood test.
- **Treatment:** Treatment includes therapy, special schooling, and, in some cases, corrective surgery. The earlier it begins, the better for the child.

(Continued on next page)

ACTIVITIES

Critical Thinking Activity

Classifying Information. Ask students to create a graphic organizer showing these birth defects and their causes. Have them group the birth defects according to the types of causes. **L2**

Teamwork Activity

Bring health reference books to class or have students work in groups to research one of the birth defects presented on the chart. Have each group prepare an illustrated booklet, including information on the causes, diagnosis, and treatment of the defect. **L2**

VISUAL LEARNING **Using the Chart** Divide the class into groups of three and give each member a number. Each number is assigned three of the birth defects on the chart. Have students regroup by number and study and quiz one another until they become "experts" on their assigned topics. Then tell them to reassemble into their original groups. Each student is responsible for teaching the other two students the material about which he or she is expert.

ISSUES IN CHILDREN'S HEALTH **Hemophilia.** Do only males have hemophilia? The gene for hemophilia is carried on the X chromosome. Because females have XX sex chromosomes and the hemophilia gene is recessive, a woman who has one normal sex chromosome and one carrying the hemophilia gene does not suffer from the condition. However, if a man with hemophilia marries a woman who carries the gene, they could have a daughter who inherits two recessive genes and therefore have the disease. This is very rare, however.

ACTIVITIES

Critical Thinking Activity

Applying Concepts. Review the options for infertile couples in Section 5-2. Ask students to consider the relevance of these options to couples with a family history of hereditary birth defects. **L2**

Discussion Activity

Ask: What emotional and financial strains affect a family that has a child with a birth defect? Are there any benefits to a family that has a child with a birth defect? What are they? How can families be encouraged to recognize them? **L1**

Critical Thinking Activity

Recognizing Points of View. Have students consider how parents might respond to the news that a child has a birth defect. Would their reaction differ according to the cause of the defect? **L2**

▶ **Selected Birth Defects** Continued

Muscular Dystrophy
- **Description:** There are many different types of muscular dystrophy; all involve a progressive weakness and shrinking of the muscles. The most common form begins between the ages of two and six.
- **Causes:** Most types of muscular dystrophy are hereditary. The most common form is transmitted by female carriers of the gene but affects only males.
- **Detection:** The disease is recognized once symptoms appear. Genetic counseling can identify carriers.
- **Treatment:** There is no known cure. Physical therapy can minimize the disabilities.

PKU
- **Description:** PKU is a condition in which the body is unable to process and use a specific protein. Mental retardation can result.
- **Cause:** A child with PKU inherits defective recessive genes from both parents.
- **Detection:** Newborns are tested for PKU, as required by law in all states.
- **Treatment:** There is no known cure for PKU. If it is diagnosed early, a special diet can reduce or prevent brain damage.

Sickle Cell Anemia
- **Description:** Malformed red blood cells interfere with the supply of oxygen to all parts of the body. The symptoms include tiredness, lack of appetite, and pain. Sickle cell anemia can lead to early death.
- **Cause:** Sickle cell anemia is caused by inheriting defective recessive genes from both parents. African Americans are more likely to have this condition than any other group.
- **Detection:** Amniocentesis or chorionic villi sampling can identify anemia in a fetus. Genetic counseling can identify parents who carry the gene. Blood tests can show the presence of the condition after birth.
- **Treatment:** There is no known cure for sickle cell anemia. Medication can treat the symptoms.

Spina Bifida and Hydrocephalus
- **Description:** In spina bifida, an incompletely formed spinal cord may lead to stiff joints, difficulty moving the legs, partial paralysis, and problems with the kidneys and urinary tract. Seventy of every 100 children with spina bifida also have hydrocephalus, in which an excess of fluid surrounds the brain, causing brain damage.
- **Causes:** The problem seems to be caused by a combination of hereditary and environmental factors. Taking folic acid during pregnancy helps reduce incidence.

(Continued on next page)

160 UNIT 2: Pregnancy and Childbirth

LEARNING STYLES

Interpersonal
Tell students to prepare a panel discussion based on either of the two situations below. Each student should take one of the following roles: moderator, financial/employment specialist, psychological/emotional counselor, health professional, social worker.

- A couple's first child is diagnosed with cerebral palsy. The couple had wanted a large family.
- A single mother with a low-paying job gives birth to a daughter with cystic fibrosis.

Selected Birth Defects Continued

Spina Bifida and Hydrocephalus (continued)
- **Detection:** Spina bifida is apparent at birth. Hydrocephalus is indicated by overly rapid growth of the head. Tests of the mother's blood, amniocentesis, and ultrasound can reveal suspected cases in a fetus.
- **Treatment:** Corrective surgery, physical therapy, and special schooling can minimize disabilities caused by spina bifida. Hydrocephalus can be helped by an operation that relieves the fluid that has built up.

Tay-Sachs Disease
- **Description:** Babies born with Tay-Sachs disease lack a certain chemical in their blood that makes their bodies unable to process and use fats. The condition leads to severe brain damage and to death, usually by the age of four.
- **Cause:** Tay-Sachs disease is caused by inheriting defective recessive genes from both parents. It is most common in families descended from eastern European Jews.
- **Detection:** Amniocentesis or chorionic villi sampling can identify Tay-Sachs disease in a fetus. Blood tests can identify those who carry the defective gene and can test for the condition after birth.
- **Treatment:** There is no known cure or treatment for this disease.

Critical Thinking Activity

Formulating a Plan. Present the following scenario to students: Todd, who is thirteen, sometimes goes to a friend's house but never invites anyone to his home. He has a six-year-old brother, Jimmy, who has Down syndrome. Ask students why Todd might act the way he does. Is he helping or hurting himself? What about Jimmy? What would you advise Todd to do? **L2**

VISUAL LEARNING Using the Photograph
Answer: There's an extra chromosome 21.

baby's cells. This is not a hereditary defect because the child does not inherit the condition from a parent.

The most common birth defect of this type is Down syndrome. One child in every 800 births has this condition. The risk increases if the mother is thirty-five or older. A child with Down syndrome has an extra chromosome 21. Because each chromosome carries hundreds of genes, the defect can interfere with development in many ways.

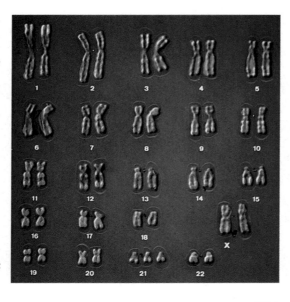

Images of chromosomes can reveal damage. In this case, Down syndrome is shown by what unusual circumstance in chromosome 21?

CHAPTER 5: Prenatal Development **161**

ISSUES IN CHILDREN'S HEALTH

Folic Acid. The Centers for Disease Control and Prevention recommends that all women between the ages of 15 and 45 take 0.4 mg of folic acid daily. Because spine and brain damage occurs very early in the pregnancy, birth defects could occur before a woman realizes that she is pregnant. Moreover, the fact that half of U.S. pregnancies are unplanned signifies that many pregnant women are not thinking about prenatal care. As a result, the Food and Drug Administration approved the enriching of grain products with folic acid to help avoid preventable birth defects.

ISSUES IN TEEN PARENTING

Stress felt by the mother is a potential source of health problems for an unborn child, and conflict with male partners is a principal source of stress for pregnant women. Teen fathers may contribute to this stress—but teen fathers can take positive action to help partners have a healthy pregnancy and minimize stress. A father can help the mother eat a nutritious diet by avoiding junk foods himself. He can go on walks with her to help her get her exercise. He can learn about the changes that a woman undergoes during pregnancy and offer support.

COMPREHENSION CHECK

1. Can all birth defects be prevented? (*No, but some can.*)

ACTIVITIES

Discussion Activity

Present the following scenario to the class: Tess and Jake have learned from a genetic counselor that any child born to them might have Tay-Sachs disease, meaning the child will probably die within the first five years of life. What decision do Tess and Jake have to make? What would you do? Why? **L2**

Critical Thinking Activity

Drawing Conclusions. Who might choose to seek advice from a genetic counselor? How might they benefit from the advice? Why? **L2**

VISUAL LEARNING | Using the Photograph
Possible responses: Emotional strain; financial drain.

Interaction of Heredity and Environment

Some birth defects result from heredity and environment working together. For example, a baby may inherit the tendency for a heart defect. This defect appears only if some factor—such as a drug or a virus—affects the baby during his or her development. If only one of these conditions had been met, the heart would probably have been normal.

Researchers think that the interaction of heredity and the environment is probably the cause for cleft lip, cleft palate, and spina bifida. With good care, though, some of these problems may be preventable. The Public Health Service says that if pregnant women took the recommended amount of the vitamin folic acid, more than 1,000 cases of spina bifida could be prevented each year.

Parents of children born with birth defects face many challenges. One of them is to make sure that other children receive attention. **Name another.**

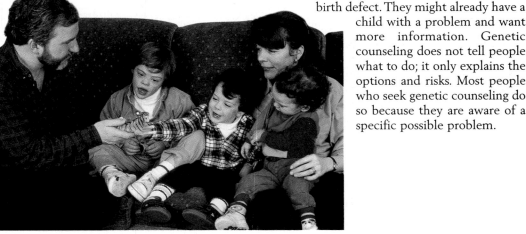

162 UNIT 2: Pregnancy and Childbirth

Prevention and Diagnosis of Birth Defects

It is difficult for a child born with a serious medical problem to lead a normal life. The rest of the child's family is affected by the emotional and financial strain the defect causes. Responsible couples do everything they can to minimize the possibility of birth defects.

Some causes of birth defects, such as infections, drugs, and alcohol, can be controlled. Parents simply need to make healthy choices to prevent a baby from being harmed by these substances. Although most birth defects cannot yet be prevented, tests can sometimes determine how probable it is that a child will develop specific defects. This can make early treatment possible.

Genetic Counseling

Some people seek genetic counseling. The patients could be a couple who wish to have a child but are concerned about their chances of having a baby with a serious birth defect. They might already have a child with a problem and want more information. Genetic counseling does not tell people what to do; it only explains the options and risks. Most people who seek genetic counseling do so because they are aware of a specific possible problem.

LEARNING STYLES | **Mathematical**

Have students create a "Parenting Possibilities" web. In the center of a large piece of paper, tell them to write "Couple Wants to Have Children" and enclose it in a circle. Then from different spokes have them trace different courses that their lives could take, such as "get pregnant," "cannot get pregnant," "adopt," and so on.

Ask the Eperts

Jacqueline Mault
Director of Special Services for the Toppenish School District in Toppenish, Washington

Sources *of Support for Special Needs Children*

 Q Where can the parents of young children with special needs go for help and support?

A Children with special needs, such as those who have problems related to birth defects, require extra medical attention. Most also require other kinds of professional help in dealing with particular physical, social, or educational problems. In addition, parents and other family members usually benefit from support in coping with their added responsibilities in caring for a special needs child.

The first source of help usually is the child's pediatrician or the family's primary physician. Physicians are able to refer babies and young children to medical specialists. More and more, physicians are also able to refer families to other helpful resources within the community.

In many communities across the country, public schools have become an important source of assistance. Services may include center- or school-based preschool classes and home-based instruction. Speech/language therapy, physical therapy, occupational therapy, counseling, and transportation may be available as well. Many programs emphasize providing parents with the skills to help their developing child. Some public schools also provide assessment and support for children from birth to age three.

For emotional support, many parents turn to their own extended families or specific support programs, often affiliated with a local hospital; the department of social services; or the local, county, or state health department. Some parents find help on the Internet, either by using it as a source of information or by joining chat groups for support.

Thinking It Through

1. Why would transportation services help parents of children with special needs?
2. How could parents of special needs children find an Internet chat group that could provide support?

CHAPTER 5: Prenatal Development **163**

Ask the Eperts

Introducing the Feature

Explore how the family of a child with birth defects is affected. Have students take notes on a chart with two columns labeled "Parents" and "Siblings" and with rows labeled "Emotionally," "Financially," "Educationally," "Socially," and "Physically."

Answers to Thinking It Through
1. *Possible response:* Because the children might need to be taken to different places for treatment and therapy.
2. *Possible response:* By using Internet search engines.

Applying What You've Learned

Have students share their ideas about the usefulness of support groups for families with members who have birth defects. Who could benefit from such support groups? How? Are there people for whom such groups might be inappropriate? If so, who and why?

Management/Leadership Skills

Employers are beginning to take an interest in the health of employees who are or plan to be pregnant. It is economical for them to have healthy employees who are mothers of healthy babies. Some provide prepregnancy classes or health screening for workers planning to have a baby. **Ask:** Is it a good or bad idea for employers to take such an interest in their workers? Is there a potential for an invasion of privacy? If you were to set up some program involved in prenatal health, how would you do it?

COMPREHENSION CHECK

1. List the steps taken by a genetic counselor in order to advise a couple. (*Obtain a family medical history; have couple get physical examinations; order laboratory tests.*)
2. Which of the tests discussed is the safest? Why? (*Ultrasound: there are no known risks to mother or developing baby.*)
3. What is the most frequent cause for doing an amniocentesis? (*Checking if there is Down syndrome.*)
4. How are amniocentesis and chorionic villi sampling tests similar? (*Both test the fetus's environment.*)

ACTIVITIES

Critical Thinking Activity

Analyzing and Classifying. Have students take notes on the different prenatal tests in outline form. Remind them that outlines organize ideas by levels of importance. Discuss the type of information given for all of the prenatal tests covered. (*Description, purpose, risks.*) You may wish to outline the first test on the chalkboard to show students how to proceed. **L1**

VISUAL LEARNING	Using the Photograph

Possible response: Because they pose some risks to the mother and developing baby.

Family doctors can perform genetic counseling, but it is best provided by a specialist. Genetic counselors are trained to understand genetic disorders. They have good communication skills, so they can explain the situation to the family and help family members deal with the impact of their situation.

A genetic counselor begins by obtaining complete family medical histories from the couple. This includes information relating to diseases and causes of death of all their close relatives. If they are concerned about a baby who is already born, they are also asked about events during this pregnancy and any previous pregnancies.

The patients—and, in some cases, other family members—may be given thorough physical examinations. If necessary, special laboratory tests are also performed. The most specialized testing is done at major medical centers in large cities, but most states have regional services.

When all the questionnaires and tests are completed, the counselor can usually tell the couple whether genetic problems are present. The couple may also be told the probability that they will have a child with a serious birth defect.

Prenatal Tests

More than 100 kinds of birth defects can now be diagnosed before a baby is born. Of course, no tests will tell whether a baby will be normal. Some tests, though, can alert the physician to a condition in the baby that must be treated before or immediately after birth.

For example, the first child of a Boston woman died three months after birth. The cause of death was a hereditary problem. When she was pregnant a second time, the woman had an amniocentesis, one of the tests described here. The results showed that this child had the same condition. The sad

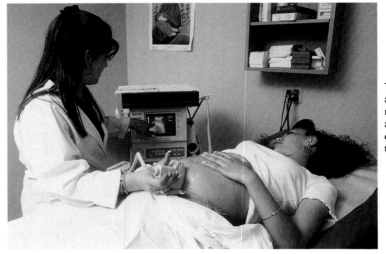

Tests like ultrasound (left) and amniocentesis (top of next page) provide valuable information. *Why aren't these tests given to all pregnant women?*

164 UNIT 2: Pregnancy and Childbirth

Parenting in *Action*

Tell students that at the beginning of and throughout a pregnancy routine tests are performed to track the mother's and baby's health. These include blood and urine tests that are not invasive to the baby. Discuss the importance of taking these tests faithfully. How should the expectant parents monitor the results? What kinds of questions should they ask their doctor about the tests? Why? Should they keep records or take notes of the results themselves? Why or why not?

fate of the first child could be prevented, though. By giving the mother vitamins—which then reached the developing baby—doctors were able to correct the problem. The second baby was normal at birth.

Sometimes a pregnant woman or her doctor suspect that a birth defect may be likely. If so, special prenatal tests can be given to see whether specific birth defects are present.

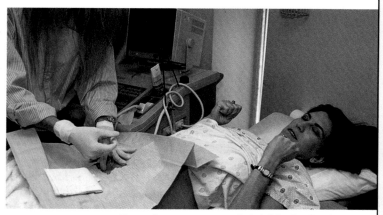
Prenatal testing can provide helpful informatioln.

Sometimes this information can be supplied through blood tests. In other cases, doctors and parents-to-be choose other methods. These tests can be risky. Although they provide valuable information, they may harm the developing baby. The doctor and the parents can use the information from blood tests to decide whether there is a good medical reason to perform one of the tests described below. The pregnant woman and her partner have the right to decide whether or not to have the tests done.

Today, doctors mainly use three procedures to make a prenatal diagnosis:

- **Ultrasound** uses sound waves to make a video image of an unborn baby to check for specific health problems. It can show whether the fetus is developing on schedule. Certain defects, such as those that involve the skeleton and other organs, can also be detected. The test can also be used to confirm the due date or that twins are present.

  This test has become common. To date, researchers have not found any risk to either the mother or the developing baby from an ultrasound.

- **Amniocentesis** (AM-knee-oh-sen-TEE-sis) is the process of withdrawing a sample of the amniotic fluid surrounding an unborn baby and testing that fluid for indications of specific birth defects or other health problems. The doctor withdraws the fluid by using a needle. An ultrasound image is used as a guide when inserting the needle. Some cells from the fetus are contained within the fluid sample. These are the cells tested for evidence of birth defects.

  Amniocentesis is most often used as a test for Down syndrome when the expectant mother is over age thirty-five. At thirty-five or older, a woman is more likely to have a baby with that condition. The procedure does involve some risks. About 1 in every 200 women who have had amniocentesis have a miscarriage. As a result of these risks, it is performed only when there is a strong medical reason.

- **Chorionic villi** (CORE-ee-ON-ik VI-lie) **sampling** tests for specific birth

ACTIVITIES

Discussion Activity

If available, show the class an ultrasound picture of a fetus. Let them identify the features of the developing baby. **L2**

Critical Thinking Activity

Evaluating Options. Ask students under what circumstances they think doctors would be likely to recommend chorionic villi sampling over amniocentesis? Amniocentesis over chorionic villi sampling? Why? **L2**

ISSUES IN CHILDREN'S HEALTH

Prenatal Testing. Although prenatal tests can reveal abnormalities, many genetic counselors feel that these should be administered with caution. Some reports have shown that 90 percent of tests reveal no abnormalities. In addition, inconclusive or unreliable results cause parents needless anxiety.

DID You Know?

In utero surgery. Fetal medicine is said to have had its beginnings in the early 1960s when medical researchers developed a way to treat Rh incompatibility with an intrauterine blood transfusion. Today doctors are specially trained to detect and treat a variety of fetal conditions. Although the risks of fetal surgery remain high, doctors hope that with technological advances and drug research, more tiny patients will be cured before birth.

Have students answer the Check Your Understanding questions. Answers appear at the bottom of this page.

EVALUATION

Give students the Section 5-3 Quiz in the *Teacher Resource Guide*.

RETEACHING

1. Assign Reteaching Activities, page 20.
2. Have students complete their K-W-L chart from p. 156. Review the information they included and ask what they can add to it after class discussion.

ENRICHMENT

Have small groups look up the benefits and risks of specific prenatal tests. What new tests are being developed? What advantages might they have over existing tests?

EXTENSION

Ask students to research and write a brief report on how blood types (A, B, AB, and O) work. Explain how blood types are inherited and why some are incompatible with others.

CLOSE

Have each student complete the following sentence: "Birth defects affect . . ." Discuss the responses.

defects by sampling small amounts of the tissue from the membrane that encases the fetus. Guided by an ultrasound image, a doctor inserts a small tube through the vagina into the uterus. There, samples of the tissue are snipped or suctioned off for analysis.

Chorionic villi sampling is used to test for the same disorders as amniocentesis. An advantage is that this testing can be done earlier in a pregnancy than amniocentesis can. However, the risks that chorionic villi sampling will cause miscarriage or birth defects are much greater than the risks involved in amniocentesis. It is done only after careful consideration of the medical reasons and risks.

Several other methods of prenatal diagnosis are now in the experimental stages. These may someday provide more accurate information at earlier stages of development. For example, it has become possible to view the fetus directly through a special instrument, obtain samples of fetal blood and tissue, and even perform surgery on an unborn child. As yet, these tests are quite dangerous for the developing baby. Further breakthroughs may make them safe enough for widespread use.

SECTION 5-3 REVIEW

✔ Check Your Understanding

1. What is the difference between a miscarriage and a stillbirth?
2. What is the cause of Down syndrome? What is one factor that increases the risk of Down syndrome?
3. What group is most likely to have sickle cell anemia?
4. What are the four causes of birth defects?
5. How does genetic counseling help parents?
6. What are two parts of genetic counseling?
7. What can be learned from ultrasound, amniocentesis, and chorionic villi sampling? What risks are involved in each procedure?

Putting Knowledge Into Practice

1. **Analyzing Arguments.** "Genetic counseling isn't helpful because all it does is identify problems." Do you agree or disagree with this statement? Explain your answer.
2. **Making Inferences.** Why do you think some couples might wish to seek genetic counseling?
3. **Observing and Participating.** Contact a group that works to help children with birth defects such as the National Foundation/March of Dimes. Find out how they raise money for their work. Plan a fund-raising project you and your class could do.

166 UNIT 2: Pregnancy and Childbirth

ANSWERS TO SECTION 5-3 REVIEW

1. *Miscarriage:* death before 20 weeks; *stillbirth:* after 20 weeks.
2. Cause: an extra chromosome 21. Risk increases if mother is 35 or older.
3. African Americans.
4. Environment, heredity, their interaction, errors in chromosomes.
5. Identify odds of birth defects.
6. *Any two:* Medical histories; physical examinations; lab tests.
7. *See the information on pages 165-166.*

CAREER OPPORTUNITIES

Genetic Counselor

A CONVERSATION WITH
KAY TANNER

How did you become interested in becoming a genetic counselor?
When I took a biology course in high school, I became fascinated by genetics. But I really like people, too. I didn't want to spend my whole life in a lab. This career is perfect for me—it combines my interest in the science with a chance to work with people.

What are the tasks and responsibilities of a genetic counselor? We meet with couples who are concerned. First we just talk to them, then we take a family medical history and order some tests. We use statistical analysis to figure out the probability that the couple could have a baby with a problem caused by genetics.

What is the work environment like?
Well, we work in offices and labs. Sometimes meetings with parents can become very emotional especially when a couple has a high likelihood of having a baby with a birth defect. We try to comfort them and point out the options, but they face hard choices.

What are the working hours like? Our office is open 9:00 to 5:00 during the week. Some offices have evening hours.

What aptitudes are needed to be a genetic counselor? Well, like any scientist, you have to have great attention for detail. You need strong math and science skills. Because you're dealing with people so much—and in very emotional situations—you need strong people and counseling skills, too.

GENETIC COUNSELOR

Education and Training. Genetic counselors must have at least a bachelor's degree with emphasis on genetics, psychology, and counseling. Special training is needed.

Career Outlook. Job openings for genetic scientists are expected to grow faster than the average

CONNECTING SCHOOL TO CAREER

1. **Interpersonal Skills.** Suppose you were a genetic counselor. How would you tell a couple that they had a fairly high probability of having a child with a birth defect caused by a genetic problem?
2. **Technology.** In what ways would genetic counselors be likely to use computers in their work?

CAREER OPPORTUNITIES

Introducing the Feature
Tell students to visualize themselves in a doctor's office waiting to get a pain in their side evaluated. How would they want to be treated What would they expect of a doctor and nurses? Introduce the term "people skills." Define it as a class before discussing the work of a genetic counselor.

Answers to
CONNECTING SCHOOL TO CAREER

1. Answers will vary but should reflect the need for sensitivity to couple's feelings.
2. **Possible response:** To perform statistical analysis; to write reports; to keep track of clients' records.

Applying What You've Learned
How might a genetic counselor use math and science? What kinds of math and science courses do students think such a worker would need? Have students explore the probable need for courses in biology, genetics, physiology, chemistry, statistics, and others that they may be familiar with.

Building Career Skills

Basic Skills. A genetic counselor cannot help a couple without first *listening* to their concerns. It is difficult to solve problems without paying attention to other people's words and feelings. Have five or six volunteers complete the following exercise by turns while the rest of the class listens. Give the first student an exciting five sentence beginning to a story to read from a card. Each other student in the group will add, in turn, five more sentences that are logical and probable. Discuss the results.

SECTION 5-4

Avoiding Dangers to the Baby
(pages 168-173)

SECTION 5-4 RESOURCES
Teacher Resource Guide
- Lesson Plan Organizer, p. 47
- Section 5-4 Quiz, p. 119

Student Motivation Kit
- Observations & Case Studies (case study), p. 101
- Reteaching Activity, p. 21
- Enrichment, p. 17
- Nurturing Brain Development, p. 46
- Teen Parenting Skills, pp. 26-27

Student Workbook
- Study Guide, pp. 42-46
- Help this Unborn Child, pp. 51-52

Effective Instruction CD-ROM

FOCUS

MOTIVATOR

Present this scenario to the class: A 24-year-old married woman is in generally good health. She smokes a pack of cigarettes a day and has a glass or two of wine with dinner three times a week. Today she learned that she is six weeks pregnant. Does the woman's behavior pose any dangers to her unborn baby? Should she change her behavior?

VOCABULARY ACTIVITY

Have volunteers offer definitions of *effects* and *syndrome*. Then let one student check the definitions in a dictionary. Which of the two is likely to indicate a more serious condition?

168

Avoiding Dangers to the Baby

In *every* pregnancy, the mother-to-be is responsible for taking the most important step in increasing the chances of having a healthy baby. She must take care of herself and keep herself safe and healthy. An essential part of good prenatal care is avoiding the harmful effects of such hazards as alcohol and other drugs, smoking, X rays, and infections.

KEY TERMS

fetal alcohol effects
fetal alcohol syndrome (FAS)

OBJECTIVES:
- Identify the hazards that alcohol and other drugs pose to prenatal development.
- Discuss other environmental hazards that pregnant women should avoid.

Alcohol

Alcohol is a drug—a dangerous one. The dangers of alcohol can touch a developing baby. A woman who drinks during pregnancy risks having a child with **fetal alcohol syndrome.** This condition, also called FAS, includes physical and mental problems that result from a mother drinking alcohol while she is pregnant.

168 UNIT 2: Pregnancy and Childbirth

Observing & Participating

A study by the Centers for Disease Control and Prevention has found that frequent drinking (5 drinks on one occasion per month or 7 drinks per week) during pregnancy has been increasing. To bring home the consequences of birth defects for babies and their families, you may wish to show students illustrations from medical or nursing books of children suffering from them.

One in five of the babies born with FAS dies soon after birth. Those who survive suffer from a host of problems. Some are mentally retarded. This is because alcohol interferes with tissue growth and development, and brain tissue is most easily injured by this drug. Many children born with FAS also have other problems, such as slow growth, poor coordination, heart defects, and facial disfigurement. Many also suffer from learning problems and hyperactivity. They also have difficulty controlling their behavior.

Some children suffer from **fetal alcohol effects**. This condition is less severe than FAS. Still, the baby suffers some of the damage caused by alcohol.

The degree of damage to the child is usually directly related to the amount of alcohol the mother consumed during pregnancy. It may also be affected by the stage of the pregnancy during which she drank and by the presence of other drugs in her system. There is no cure for fetal alcohol syndrome or fetal alcohol effects.

Still, both conditions can be prevented—by not drinking alcohol. Doctors don't know just how much alcohol presents a danger to the developing baby. There is no known amount of alcohol that a pregnant woman can safely drink without risking harm to her unborn child. For this reason, doctors recommend that women avoid alcohol completely when they are pregnant—and even when they plan to become pregnant.

Other Drugs

Many doctors believe that drugs taken during pregnancy are among the major causes of birth defects linked to environmental factors. Alcohol is one of those drugs. Others include:

- Medicines, including both those that doctors prescribe and over-the-counter types.
- Caffeine, found in some foods and beverages.
- Nicotine, found in tobacco.
- Illegal drugs such as heroin, LSD, ecstasy, marijuana, and all forms of cocaine.
- Inhalants—fumes that are inhaled into the lungs.

Eating well and staying healthy are a mother's best gift to her unborn baby. *What substances should pregnant women avoid?*

CHAPTER 5: Prenatal Development **169**

Management/Leadership Skills

Expectant mothers and fathers sometimes work in places where they handle materials that are highly toxic to an unborn child. Workers in plants that use heavy metals, chemical solvents, or pesticides face risks like birth defects and miscarriage or stillbirth. Substances like lead dust can get tracked home on clothing and shoes. Discuss what men and women in these kinds of jobs can do to protect their children from risk. How could they work with their employers to reduce the risks?

COMPREHENSION CHECK

1. At what stage of a pregnancy do medicines have the most devastating effect? (*The first three months.*)
2. How can pregnant women who wish or need to take medicine ensure their baby's safety? (*By checking with a doctor about the medicine.*)

ACTIVITIES

Teamwork Activity

Present students with this scenario: On a Saturday night, a pregnant woman finds that she has developed a cold. Although she is tired, she is having trouble breathing and cannot get to sleep. Divide the class into small groups, giving each student an index card. Ask each student to write three suggestions to help her until she can see her doctor. Tell groups to discuss all of the suggestions and agree on three to five to share their ideas with the class. **L2**

VISUAL LEARNING | Using the Photograph
Possible response: By checking with her doctor..

Even common medicines that are sold in pharmacies and supermarkets may be unsafe for an unborn baby. **How can a pregnant woman be sure that a medicine is safe?**

Prescription and Over-the-Counter Drugs

For a pregnant woman and her baby, there is no such thing as a completely safe drug. Even aspirin, cold remedies, and antihistamines can harm an unborn child. An extreme example is thalidomide, used to relieve morning sickness during the late 1950s. Before its effects were discovered, thalidomide caused more than 5,000 babies to be born with severe birth defects—including missing arms and legs.

Medicines or infections that reach the developing baby in the first three months of pregnancy have the most devastating effect. During these months, the baby's body systems are being formed. This is also a critical period of brain development, so drugs can cause mental retardation.

In the last six months of pregnancy, harmful substances that reach the fetus may cause slow growth, infections, or bleeding at birth. Drugs taken just before delivery will still be in the baby's body at birth.

Doctors say that a woman shouldn't take any medicines unless they are specifically prescribed by her physician for use while she is pregnant. Drugs needed for serious conditions, such as diabetes and high blood pressure, can be taken—but under a doctor's direction.

Caffeine

Caffeine is widely found in beverages such as coffee, tea, cocoa, and many soft drinks. It is also present in some foods and many medications. Because it is so common, caffeine is often not considered a drug—but it is.

Small amounts of caffeine, such as two cups of coffee or three caffeinated soft drinks per day, don't seem to pose pregnancy risks. However, larger quantities have been associated with a variety of problems. These include an increased risk of miscarriage and low birth weight, and higher rates of infant death.

170 UNIT 2: Pregnancy and Childbirth

ISSUES IN CHILDREN'S HEALTH Even commonly used dietary supplements and over-the-counter medications can be dangerous to an unborn baby. Although doctors generally give pregnant women vitamin and mineral supplements, doses in excess of what is prescribed can harm rather than help the baby. Too much vitamin A is believed to lead to birth defects. Aspirin taken frequently late in the pregnancy can interfere with the baby's blood clotting mechanism and, at delivery, even with the mother's ability to clot. Heavy use could delay labor and cause excessive bleeding.

Tobacco

The nicotine in cigarettes is also a dangerous drug. The more a mother smokes, the smaller her baby is likely to be. A newborn's weight is a critical factor in survival. Heavy smoking is believed to cause premature birth as well. Finally, smoking is linked to respiratory infections and allergies among children after birth.

Smoke from others can also be harmful. Its dangerous nicotine reaches the baby just the same as if the mother had smoked herself.

Illegal Drugs

Increases in the use of cocaine, marijuana, and other illegal drugs have given doctors new problems. A mother who is addicted to a drug when pregnant usually passes her addiction on to her baby. These children suffer all their lives.

Right after birth, these addicted infants must go through a period of withdrawal. This painful condition results from the body no longer receiving the drug that it depends on. For some addicted babies, withdrawal is so severe that they die.

For the babies who survive withdrawal, the future is uncertain. Experts worry that the long-range effects of prenatal addiction may be serious. Many of these children are able to follow only very simple directions and often cannot understand school classes.

Cocaine is known to cause miscarriage, stillbirth, premature birth, and birth defects. Similar results are suggested in studies on marijuana. Other effects of drugs are still being studied. While research continues, the best advice is to avoid taking *any* drugs before or during pregnancy.

Pregnant women can enjoy many healthy alternatives to beverages with caffeine.

DID You Know?

Smoking During Pregnancy. A baby's birth weight is reduced by about ¼ pound (115 g) for every pack of cigarettes that a pregnant woman regularly smokes each day. Passive smoking has a similar effect. Normal birthweight is considered to be at least 5½ pounds. When babies weigh less than 4 pounds, 6 ounces, they run the risk of complications with breathing, heart function, body temperature, and blood sugar.

ISSUES IN TEEN PARENTING Passive, or sidestream, smoke can harm a baby. How can pregnant teens deal with older smokers with whom they live or work? These smokers may have had their own children at a time when no one worried about cigarette smoke, and not be convinced of the dangers. Have students draw up a set of strategies a teen mother can use to protect herself and her baby. Remind students that the strategies should not alienate her from her family or create a difficult work environment for her.

COMPREHENSION CHECK

1. What dangers are linked to prenatal use of cocaine? (*Miscarriage and stillbirth; premature birth, birth defects.*)
2. What is another name for rubella? (*German measles.*)

ACTIVITIES

Discussion Activity

Ask students to review the dangers posed by X rays. Do these dangers justify disqualifying women of child-bearing age from jobs that involve the use of X rays? Why or why not? **L2**

Discussion Activity

Tell students that half the babies whose mothers have rubella in the first four weeks of pregnancy have at least one major birth defect. Ask: How might a pregnant woman contract rubella? How can she protect herself? **L1**

Teamwork Activity

Divide the class into seven groups, and assign an STD to each group. Have the group create a web about the disease, showing its causes, detection, physical complications, and treatment. Then have each group report the information to the rest of the class. Display the webs after the reports are given. **L2**

VISUAL LEARNING	Using the Photograph

The child may be born with the virus that causes AIDS.

X Rays

X rays present another potential danger to the unborn baby. Radiation from X rays—or from other sources—can cause birth defects. A pregnant woman who is in an accident, is sick, or has dental work should inform medical personnel of her pregnancy. They can then take special precautions if X rays are necessary.

X rays are useful tools for health care workers. Still, they are also powerful and can be dangerous. It is important to avoid unneeded X rays before pregnancy. In fact, both men and women should request abdominal shields during routine X rays.

Rubella

The terrible effect of certain infections on unborn children was highlighted by the epidemic of rubella (sometimes called German measles) that swept the country several decades ago. Thousands of unborn babies were affected when their mothers came down with German measles during pregnancy. Although most of the women had few or even no symptoms of illness, the developing babies suffered. Some of these babies were born with deafness, blindness, heart disease, or mental retardation.

A vaccine for rubella is now available, and millions of children have been vaccinated. The vaccine may be dangerous, however, for women who are pregnant or who become pregnant shortly after receiving it. A woman who is unsure whether she has been vaccinated can check her health records or ask her doctor to test her. Every woman should be sure she is immune to rubella before she considers becoming pregnant.

Sexually Transmitted Diseases (STDs)

Like rubella, sexually transmitted diseases, or STDs, can do great harm to unborn babies. They include all the following:

- Syphilis
- Gonorrhea
- Hepatitis B
- Genital herpes
- AIDS
- Group B streptococcus
- Chlamydia

Many of these diseases can be passed on from the pregnant woman to the unborn baby. They can result in serious illness, deformity, or even death.

Health organizations provide a great deal of important and useful information about AIDS. *How is an unborn child affected if a pregnant woman has AIDS?*

The Developing Brain

Toxoplasmosis

Toxoplasmosis is a disease that is caused by parasites in the feces of some animals—notably cats. Although not a serious threat to adults, it can cause brain and eye damage in a fetus. Pregnant women should not clean a cat's box or do yardwork in areas that might have been used by a cat. If the pregnant woman has no alternative but to do these jobs herself, she should wear rubber gloves.

A person can be infected with a sexually transmitted disease without realizing it. For this reason, special measures are often taken to protect babies against the effects of STDs. Most doctors routinely test pregnant women for syphilis—in fact, such tests are required by law in many states. In addition, doctors usually treat the eyes of newborns with a solution to kill gonorrhea germs that could otherwise cause blindness.

Treatment can cure syphilis and gonorrhea and can relieve the symptoms of herpes in adults. No drug can cure the damage to the newborn that results from a delay in diagnosis and treatment. Any pregnant woman who suspects she could have a sexually transmitted disease should discuss the condition frankly with her doctor.

AIDS

A developing baby can be infected with AIDS by the mother. The virus that causes AIDS may lie hidden in a person for many years before causing symptoms, so testing is essential. If a woman who has AIDS gives birth to a child, her baby also is at risk to develop AIDS and die. If a doctor knows that a pregnant woman has the virus that causes AIDS, she can be given treatment that can reduce the chances that her baby will develop AIDS. The baby can be given treatment as well. For these reasons, early testing for AIDS is very important.

SECTION 5-4 REVIEW

✔ Check Your Understanding

1. Why does alcohol harm a developing baby?
2. What kinds of drugs, other than alcohol, can harm a developing baby?
3. How much caffeine is safe for a pregnant woman to have?
4. How can smoke affect an unborn baby?
5. Why should a woman tell a dentist or orthodontist if she is pregnant?
6. Why is it a good idea for a woman to be vaccinated against rubella before becoming pregnant?
7. Why do many states require doctors to test pregnant women for syphilis?
8. How can a developing baby benefit from having the pregnant mother receive an early test for the AIDS virus?

Putting Knowledge Into Practice

1. **Applying.** Suppose a pregnant woman has a headache or a cold. What should she do to treat it?
2. **Applying.** If a pregnant woman inhales smoke from another person's cigarette, the developing baby can suffer damage. Suppose you were a pregnant woman who worked as a waitress. You often worked in the smoking section. What would you do?
3. **Observing and Participating.** Read the label on an over-the-counter medicine. Write down the type of medicine and the directions given for use by pregnant women. Bring your results to class and compare them to your classmates' findings.

CHAPTER 5: Prenatal Development **173**

CHECKING COMPREHENSION

Have students answer the Check Your Understanding questions. Answers appear at the bottom of this page.

EVALUATION

Give students the Section 5-4 Quiz in the Teacher's Classroom Resources box.

RETEACHING

1. Assign Reteaching Activities, page 21.
2. Write different health hazards at the top of different pieces of construction paper. Have students add information about a hazard to the appropriate piece of construction paper.

ENRICHMENT

Tell students to plan, write, and illustrate a pamphlet discussing the hazards of drug use during pregnancy.

EXTENSION

Invite a representative from Alcoholics Anonymous to speak to the class about the services available to addicts and their families, the techniques used to overcome addiction, and the advantages of support groups.

CLOSE

Have students discuss the role of the expectant father in ensuring a healthy prenatal environment.

FOCUS

MOTIVATOR

Ask students to name "positive" feelings (e.g. happiness, satisfaction, love). Ask them how these feelings are related to a person's health.

TEACH

ACTIVITIES

Discussion Activity

Have students define physical, emotional, and social health. Engage students in a discussion of the importance of each. **L1**

Critical Thinking Activity

Classifying Ideas. Have students organize the information about the three types of health in a graphic organizer. Tell them to create a wide box at the top of a sheet of paper and write "Good Health" in it. Then draw three lines descending from it with boxes labeled "Physical," "Emotional, and "Social." From each of these, students should draw a string of boxes adding supporting details from the reading and class discussion. **L1**

Parenting With Care

Developing Healthy Habits for a Lifetime

A woman who is pregnant has a great responsibility.

How she acts can have a tremendous lifelong impact on the health of her developing baby. Expectant fathers have this impact, too. For example, a father-to-be who smokes cigarettes can be damaging his child every time the mother breathes in the smoke.

The best way to prepare for parenthood is to develop healthy habits now. Your present health and that of any future children will benefit.

Good health has three aspects:

Physical Health

An essential part of good health is taking care of yourself physically. Here are some tips:

- **Have regular check-ups.** Any health problems can be caught and dealt with early. Tell your doctor if you plan to become pregnant.
- **Eat a balanced diet.** Include a variety of nutritious foods in your meals and snacks.
- **Get regular exercise.** Choose sports and other activities that you enjoy.
- **Get plenty of sleep.** Remember that eight hours per night is a minimum requirement for most teens.
- **Learn safety rules.** Once you know them, be sure to follow them.
- **Avoid harmful substances.** Stay away from alcohol, other drugs, and tobacco.

Emotional Health

You can build your emotional health in various ways:

- **List your accomplishments.** Your sense of worth grows from a positive feeling about yourself. You can reinforce that feeling by accomplishing things you're proud of. Make a list and look at it when you need a boost.
- **Use positive "self-talk."** Send yourself positive messages. When you think about yourself, focus on your good points. Decide how to improve the others.

174 UNIT 2: Pregnancy and Childbirth

RESOURCES ON AIDS EDUCATION

In the United States, AIDS is the leading killer among people between 25 and 44 years of age. An excellent resource about the dangers of AIDS is the American Red Cross, which has designed HIV/AIDS education programs aimed at different segments of the population, including one for African American and one for Hispanic youths and their families. Contact your local chapter of the American Red Cross for more information.

- **Handle your emotions.** Learn to manage your negative emotions. Find safe ways of expressing those emotions so you can stay in control.

Social Health

The other part of your health is your social well-being. Some habits can help you build good social health:

- **Spend time with your family.** The bonds between family members are strengthened the more time the people spend together.
- **Be a good friend.** If you act as a good friend, you will have good friends.
- **Play an active part in your community.** There are many things you can do to make a difference in your community, from tutoring to cleaning up a park to spending time with older people.

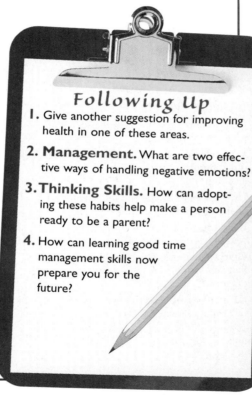

Following Up

1. Give another suggestion for improving health in one of these areas.

2. **Management.** What are two effective ways of handling negative emotions?

3. **Thinking Skills.** How can adopting these habits help make a person ready to be a parent?

4. How can learning good time management skills now prepare you for the future?

CHAPTER 5: Prenatal Development **175**

CHECKING COMPREHENSION

Use the Summary and the Reviewing the Facts questions to help students go over the most important ideas in Chapter 5. Encourage students to ask questions and add details.

CHAPTER 5 REVIEW

Answers to Reviewing the Facts

1. *Zygote:* about two weeks. *Embryo:* three to eight weeks. *Fetus:* eight to birth.
2. Lightening (*fetus moves down toward the birth canal*); fetus turns head down.
3. If two corresponding genes are the same, a characteristic is expressed. If the genes are different, the dominant one controls how the characteristic is expressed.
4. Infertile couples can try to get treatment through surgery or infertility drugs. If these do not work, they can adopt or use artificial insemination, in vitro fertilization, ovum transfer, or a surrogate mother.
5. *Possible response: Environmental* —problems caused by alcohol, drugs, or tobacco smoke; *hereditary*—hemophilia; *chromosome error*—Down syndrome; *combination of heredity and environment*—spina bifida.
6. *Possible response*: Amniocentesis identified a condition that could lead to retardation in the child. With vitamin therapy, the child was normal.
7. Stay away from alcohol, caffeine, tobacco, and other drugs.
8. The earlier the treatment, the better for the child.

CHAPTER 5 | REVIEW &

Summary

✔ Prenatal development begins with conception and moves through three stages. (Section 5-1)
✔ Chromosomes carry the genes that determine all the traits we inherit. (Section 5-2)
✔ Infertility problems may be treated with surgery or medication, or infertile couples can choose among other options. (Section 5-2)
✔ Birth defects have a variety of causes. Some can be predicted by tests. (Section 5-3)
✔ A pregnant woman should avoid alcohol, other drugs, and tobacco to have a healthy baby. (Section 5-4)

Reviewing the Facts

1. How long is each of the three stages of pregnancy? (Section 5-1)
2. What changes occur in the fetus in the ninth month of prenatal development? (Section 5-1)
3. How do genes shape the inheritance of characteristics? (Section 5-2)
4. If an infertile couple wants children, what options do they have? (Section 5-2)
5. Give an example of a birth defect caused by each of the four factors that cause birth defects. (Section 5-3)
6. Give an example of the benefits of prenatal testing. (Section 5-3)
7. What is the best advice for pregnant women regarding the use of any drugs? (Section 5-4)

8. Why is it important for pregnant women to talk to the doctor as early as possible about the possibility of an STD? (Section 5-4)

Thinking Critically

1. **Analyzing.** A baby can usually survive if born in the seventh month. Why does the baby need to continue developing for two more months?
2. **Synthesizing.** If identical twins have the exact same genetic blueprint, will they have the exact same personalities? Why or why not?
3. **Evaluating.** What do you consider good reasons for having prenatal tests done? Why?

Taking Action

1. **Gathering Resources.** Gather pamphlets and other resource materials on one birth defect. Use the information to create a poster to be displayed in the classroom. (*Communication*)
2. **Identifying Alternatives.** As a group, brainstorm a list of healthy cold drinks that a pregnant woman could enjoy in place of soda with caffeine. As a class, vote on the choice that is the most nutritious. (*Management*)

CONNECTIONS

Cross-Curricular Connections

1. **Language Arts.** With a partner or group, write and perform a skit showing a teen being offered alcohol. In the skit, show effective ways of saying "no" to drugs. Discuss how young adults might also feel pressured.

2. **Math.** Using the diagram in Section 5-2 on eye color, figure the odds of each child having blue eyes.

Workplace Connections

1. **Information.** Suppose you were a public health nurse. Write the text of a talk you would give mothers-to-be outlining the changes they will feel during a pregnancy.

2. **Technology.** If you ran a genetic counseling office, how could you use technology to keep genetic records private?

Family and Community Connections

1. **Multiple Births.** Search on the Internet for information from the Public Health Service on multiple births. Report to the class on the trends in the past five, ten, or twenty years in the nation as a whole and in your state. Explain why the rate is changing.

2. **Helping Others.** Search on the Internet for a group involved in helping children born with a particular birth defect. Find out what information and support the group gives to children with that birth defect and to their parents. Bring your information to class to put in a class binder called "Helping Children with Special Needs."

Technology Connections

1. **Fertility Treatments.** Research recent developments in the use of fertility drugs. How safe are they? What are the pros and cons of their use? Report your findings to the class.

2. **X Rays.** Conduct research into the discovery, use, or possible dangers of X rays. Report your findings to the class.

EVALUATION

1. Use the reproducible Chapter 5 Test in the *Teacher Resource Guide,* or construct your own test using the **Exam***View*® Test Generator.

2. For an alternative assessment, assign the Chapter 5 activity in the *Authentic Assessment* section of the *Teacher Resource Guide.*

ENRICHMENT

Assign students either of the two enrichment activities in the *Enrichment Activities* booklet in the *Student Motivation Kit.*

EXTENSION

Have students create a "Prenatal Development" scrapbook that includes illustrations (magazine pictures, drawings) and their own notes and comments.

CLOSE

Give students the following writing prompt, and ask them to complete the sentence and write a brief essay explaining their ideas. Remind them to provide evidence to support their opinions: "I think every expectant parent should . . ."

CHAPTER 6 RESOURCES

Teacher Resource Guide
• Chapter 6 Test, p. 127
• Authentic Assessment, p. 267
Student Motivation Kit
• Observ. & Case Studies
  (observation), pp. 37-38
Transparency Package
• CT-19 to CT-20
Effective Instruction CD-ROM

CHAPTER 6 | OVERVIEW

Section 6-1 covers the physical and emotional health of the mother. It discusses the first signs of pregnancy, seeing a doctor, discomforts, and complications.

Section 6-2 explores parental decisions about child care, feeding a baby, and preparing for a new arrival, including the costs of raising a child.

Section 6-3 discusses choices for childbirth.

CHAPTER 6 | OBJECTIVES

After completing Chapter 6, students will be able to:

• Explain how pregnant women can care for their own health and that of their developing baby.
• Identify the preparations parents need to make for the arrival of a baby.
• Describe childbirth options.

CHAPTER 6

Preparing for Birth

178 UNIT 2: Pregnancy and Childbirth

RESOURCES TO EXPLORE

Alternative Birth Centers. One attraction of birth centers is that they are less expensive than traditional births. Another attraction is the continuous support of the midwife, who stays with the mother through the entire labor and birth. Some birth centers have special programs for pregnant teens. For more information and referrals to local birth centers, contact The National Association of Childbearing Centers at 3123 Gottschall Road, Perkiomenville, PA 18074, 215-234-8068 or check their web site at http://www.BirthCenters.org

Elissa held her friend's hand. "Don't worry," she said. "You'll be fine. I had the same problem you did—I felt sick every morning. After the first three months, though, it went away. For the rest of the time I was pregnant, I felt great. Until the last month, of course! Then I couldn't wait for the baby to be born."

Shanta smiled weakly. "That's what my mother said, too—and so did the obstetrician. I just worry that I won't be able to eat anything until I get my appetite back. If I don't eat, then how will the baby grow?"

Elissa laughed. "Oh, you'll eat. And the baby will grow just fine. In the meantime, you can do something to help yourself feel better. Whenever you feel queasy, munch on a couple of crackers. They help settle your stomach. Now, how about doing what we said? Let me show you that crib you can use."

"I had morning sickness, too, but for the rest of my pregnancy, I felt great."

- Read the following opinions aloud and ask students to discuss the arguments in favor or against: "During pregnancy, it is best to avoid activities like tennis, bicycling, and swimming." "Parents should discuss child rearing away from grandparents and relatives."

- Have students discuss how pregnant women can benefit from discussing their experiences with women who have been through pregnancy and childbirth. Are there any negatives to such conversations? What can be learned? How might the words of a friend conflict with what doctors say?

USING THE SCENARIO Ask students if they have any close family members or friends who are pregnant or had a baby recently. Did they experience nausea? What did they do about it? Did they have other symptoms, such as feeling sleepy? How did they handle those symptoms? What can a woman who is feeling nauseous or sleepy at work do?

KEY TO ABILITY LEVELS Each section gives skill-building activities. Each activity has been labeled for use with students of various learning styles and abilities.

L1 Level 1 activities are basic activities and should be within the range of all students.

L2 Level 2 activities are average activities and should be within the range of average and above average students.

L3 Level 3 activities are challenging activities designed for the ability range of above average students.

A Healthy Pregnancy

(pages 180-191)

FOCUS

MOTIVATOR

Show students photographs of two pregnant women, one who does not yet look very pregnant and the other who is nearing delivery. Ask students what they imagine the two women might be doing to prepare for the birth of their babies. How would their preparations be similar? different?

VOCABULARY ACTIVITY

After students have read the section, ask them to group each of the following words with two other words that are related in meaning. (*For example: anemia, iron, tiredness; obstetrician, checkups, delivery; Rh factor, blood, injection.*)

180

A Healthy Pregnancy

A pregnant woman carries inside her a new life. She has a huge responsibility: to get that life off to a good start. That means she has to take care of the developing baby—and of herself.

KEY TERMS

anemia
obstetrician
Rh factor

OBJECTIVES:

- List the early signs of pregnancy.
- Assess the importance of early and regular medical care during pregnancy.
- Plan a nutritious diet during pregnancy.
- Give recommendations about personal care for a pregnant woman.

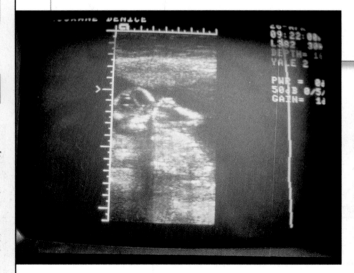

Early Signs of Pregnancy

How does a woman know that she is pregnant? Within several weeks of conception, a woman will probably feel one or more of these early signs of pregnancy:

180   UNIT 2: Pregnancy and Childbirth

Observing & Participating

Pregnant women should avoid too much sugar. Since ingredients are listed on food labels in order of greatest to least quantity, it is possible to determine which foods have a high proportion of sugar. Ask the class to bring in labels and empty food boxes.

Explain that sugar may be found under different names, for example fructose, sucrose, maltose, dextrose, honey, corn syrup, and corn sweetener. Have students examine the labels and boxes and determine which foods are high in sugar.

- A missed period (usually the first indication).
- A fullness or mild ache in her lower abdomen.
- Feeling tired, drowsy, or faint.
- The need to urinate more often than usual.
- Discomfort or tenderness in her breasts.
- Periods of nausea, especially early in the day.

These symptoms may be caused by something other than pregnancy. To be sure, the woman can take a pregnancy test.

Medical Care During Pregnancy

As soon as a woman suspects she is pregnant, she should see a doctor. Some women see a general doctor. Many prefer to see an **obstetrician** (AHB-stuh-TRISH-un), a doctor who specializes in pregnancy and birth.

The pregnant woman and her doctor will have an important relationship over the next nine months. She will see the doctor many times for checkups, and the doctor will also assist when the baby is born. For these reasons, an expectant mother should choose a doctor she likes and trusts.

Many obstetricians work as part of a group. They take turns covering for each other during the night and on weekends. When the baby is born, then, one of the other doctors in the group may be present. Usually the woman sees each of the other doctors on one office visit during the pregnancy. That way, she can get to know them. Most checkups, though, are done by the woman's primary doctor.

Most obstetricians charge one lump sum for their care of a pregnant woman. This amount covers all prenatal exams, a normal birth, and a checkup after the birth. Some women think they can save money by only seeing the doctor at the end of the pregnancy. However, the doctor will charge as much then as if the woman had started care in her first month. It pays to get good prenatal care right from the start.

Women can purchase kits to test themselves for pregnancy. **Why should a follow-up visit be scheduled with a doctor?**

COMPREHENSION CHECK

1. Name two early signs of pregnancy. (*See the text list.*)
2. Why does a pregnant woman meet all the doctors in a group practice? (*In case the baby is born when her doctor is not on call.*)

ACTIVITIES

Discussion Activity

Ask: Why should a woman consult a doctor when she suspects she is pregnant? What risks does a woman run if she doesn't? **L1**

Reading Skills

Remind students to vary reading strategy according to their purpose. Tell them to *skim* when they are first assigned a section to get a general idea; to *read slowly* to learn material or study for a test; and to *scan* or look for key words when looking for specific information, such as the answer to a question. When you first assign Section 6-1, give students time to skim it and ask them to name the subject and several subtopics. **L1**

VISUAL LEARNING	Using the Photograph

Possible response: So doctor can continue to watch mother's and developing baby's health.

Ask the Eperts

Introducing the Feature

Before discussing this feature, ask students to conduct a survey of mothers and fathers of their acquaintance, asking them if they were aware of any myths about pregnancy, childbirth, or child rearing. Were they influenced by these myths?

Answers to Thinking It Through

1. *Answers will vary but should include reasoned support for students' conclusions.*
2. *Possible response:* By pointing her to reliable sources of information.

Applying What You've Learned

Ask students to speculate about the possible sources of the myths. Why might a pregnant woman be inclined to believe a myth without verifying its truth? What dangers do myths present? How do doctors and health professionals counteract their influence?

Myths. One commonly believed myth about breast-feeding is that some women are unable to produce enough milk for their babies. The amount of milk produced is based on the amount demanded by an infant. If a woman feeds her baby regularly until the baby is satisfied, the body will seldom be unable to furnish enough.

Ask the Eperts

Pat Brodeen
Teacher and Teen Parent Coordinator at Theodore Roosevelt High School in San Antonio, Texas

THE *Myths of Pregnancy*

Q How can I unravel the myths associated with pregnancy?

A I'm glad you realize that not everything you hear about pregnancy is true. Some of the stories you hear reflect individual experiences. Others pass down cultural beliefs. Still other stories actually do give information or reliable advice. Have you ever heard these tales?

- *If a pregnant woman is carrying high, she'll have a boy. If she's carrying low, she'll have a girl.*
- *Eating lots of hot sauce will cause the baby to have a lot of hair.*
- *A pregnant woman who sees something frightening, or rubs her belly during a full moon will have a baby with an ugly birthmark.*

All these stories are completely false. Where the baby is positioned has nothing to do with gender—only with the muscle tone of the mother's abdomen. Normal activities cannot affect the baby's safety. Nor will what the mother sees or eats affect the baby's safety or appearance—as long as the mother has a nutritious balanced diet.

Some age-old adages are at least partially true. Maybe you've heard people say this: A woman loses a tooth for every baby she has. Although this story is untrue, it does have a sound basis. A pregnant woman may lose some calcium from her teeth and bones if her diet doesn't provide enough calcium for the baby's development. Hormonal changes sometimes cause inflammation of the gums. It is especially important for a pregnant woman to keep her teeth and gums clean, and have a dental check-up regularly.

A pregnant woman has an excellent source of information—her physician. During her regular checkups, she should discuss her questions and concerns openly. Books written by doctors, dietitians, or other health professionals are also good sources of information.

Thinking It Through

1. What stories about pregnancy have you heard? Do you think they are true or a myth? Why or why not?
2. How might a librarian help a pregnant woman?

Parenting in *Action*

When should expectant parents reveal that they are expecting? Couples often hesitate before telling others. Some may fear miscarriage and not want to speak too soon. Others may want to savor the knowledge for a while. Aware that their lives will change without being sure how, others need time to absorb the news. Have students discuss the nature of the decision—not just when the news should be spread but to whom. Should future grandparents be informed at the same time as employers? What other factors go into the decision? (*For example, the woman's ability to hide her discomforts.*)

As long as no problems develop, a pregnant woman can follow her normal routine. At the initial exam—or at any of the other follow-up exams—she can ask her doctor if an activity is safe.

The Initial Exam

When pregnancy has been confirmed, the woman has a thorough examination:

- The doctor checks her blood pressure, pulse, respiration, and initial weight.
- The doctor asks about and records her medical history. This history may reveal conditions that require special treatment or observation.
- The doctor measures her pelvis to determine whether the birth passageway is wide enough to allow a normal-sized baby to be born.

- The doctor analyzes her urine for the presence of infection, diabetes, or a condition called preeclampsia (high blood pressure).
- The doctor takes a blood test to see if she has **anemia** (ah-KNEE-mee-ah). This condition, caused by lack of iron, results in poor appetite, tiredness, and weakness.

  The blood test is also used to check the **Rh factor** in the blood. A person's blood is either Rh positive—having a certain protein—or negative—not having that protein. Problems can arise if the mother's blood lacks that protein and the fetus's blood has it. (The fetus may inherit this blood factor from the father.) In this case, the mother's blood will produce antibodies that attack the protein in the fetus's blood, as though it were a germ invading the mother's body. By injecting a certain chemical into the mother, doctors can prevent this problem from arising.
- The doctor checks her for immunity to rubella, or German measles. This disease can seriously harm a developing baby. If the mother has not had the disease or been vaccinated for it, she has no immunity. She must then be careful to avoid coming into contact with anyone who has rubella or the baby could be in danger.

CHAPTER 6: Preparing for Birth **183**

COMPREHENSION CHECK

1. What are varicose veins? (*Swollen veins in the legs.*)
2. How can a pregnant woman relieve lower back pain? (*By wearing low heeled shows, bending when lifting, and exercising.*)
3. Name three symptoms of serious complications. (*See "Possible Complications."*)

ACTIVITIES

Discussion Activity

Ask: How many babies are delivered exactly on their due date? What attitude should expectant parents have toward that date? What might expectant parents say when others ask "When will your baby be born?" **L2**

Teamwork Activity.

Ask: How can a woman's family help her deal with the discomforts of pregnancy and share in the responsibilities? Then have students gather in small groups to discuss their views and compile a list of suggestions to share with the class. Remind students to include suggestions for the baby's father. **L1**

When will the baby be born? This is one of the first questions a pregnant woman asks. The due date is nine months plus one week after the woman's last menstrual period began. Doctors usually advise that the birth could well take place any time from two weeks before or after that date.

Later Checkups

Typically, an expectant mother has a checkup once a month until the sixth or seventh month of pregnancy. Then most doctors schedule two visits a month. In the ninth month, she sees the doctor once a week. These checkups are important in monitoring the development of the baby and making sure that the woman is healthy.

Most doctors welcome an expectant father at these checkups. This gives the man a chance to meet the doctor and to be aware of the baby's growth. Both parents can use the checkups to ask any questions they might have.

Discomforts of Pregnancy

Many women go through pregnancy without any problems or complications. In fact, some women find pregnancy a time in which they feel particularly healthy.

Other women do feel some discomfort. These feelings usually do not indicate serious problems, but a woman who feels any of the following symptoms should tell her doctor:

Some women feel nausea early in the pregnancy. They can gain some relief by eating smaller, more frequent meals. Name other discomforts associated with pregnancy.

184 UNIT 2: Pregnancy and Childbirth

- Nausea is the most common complaint among pregnant women. It is often called morning sickness, although it doesn't only happen in the morning. Nausea rarely lasts beyond the fourth month of pregnancy. If a woman suffers severe and prolonged nausea, she should tell her doctor.
- Sleepiness—due to hormonal changes—is fairly common early in a pregnancy. Many women feel less tired in the middle months of the pregnancy, but for some, tiredness returns in the last months.
- Pregnant women often suffer from heartburn, a burning feeling in the upper stomach. (Despite the name, it has nothing to do with the heart.) A woman with heartburn should ask her doctor about the safest source of relief.

Observing & Participating

Invite an obstetrician/gynecologist to speak to the class. Have students prepare questions about pregnancy, childbearing, and related health concerns. Students could ask about the difference between obstetrics and gynecology. How prenatal checkups differ from other checkups. Why should pregnant women—even those who are careful about their diets—take vitamins? Why does the mother's body gain more weight than the weight of the baby, placenta, etc.? What purpose does the additional weight serve?

- Late in the pregnancy, a woman may feel short of breath because of pressure on the lungs from the growing baby.
- Some pregnant women develop varicose (swollen) veins in the legs from pressure on the blood vessels there. Getting regular exercise, resting with the legs and feet elevated, and using support stockings can help.
- Many pregnant women suffer muscle cramps in their legs. These cramps can be relieved by gentle stretching and rest. A diet rich in calcium may prevent these cramps.
- During the last months of pregnancy, many women feel lower back pain. Back problems can be minimized by wearing low-heeled shoes and bending the knees when lifting. Exercises can help relieve backache.

Possible Complications

A few women experience more serious complications during pregnancy. A pregnant woman who has any of the following symptoms should report them to her doctor immediately:
- Vaginal bleeding.
- Unusual weight gain.
- Excessive thirst.
- Reduced or painful urination.
- Severe abdominal pain.
- Persistent headaches.
- Severe vomiting.
- Fever.
- Swelling of the face, hands, or ankles.
- Blurred vision or dizziness.
- Prolonged backache.
- Increased vaginal mucus.

Nutrition During Pregnancy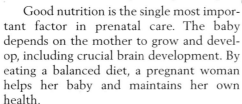

Good nutrition is the single most important factor in prenatal care. The baby depends on the mother to grow and develop, including crucial brain development. By eating a balanced diet, a pregnant woman helps her baby and maintains her own health.

The Role of Nutrients

A healthy diet contains the five types of nutrients a body needs. Each nutrient plays a special role in promoting health:
- **Protein.** Meat, fish, poultry, eggs, milk, cheese, beans, and nuts provide this nutrient. Protein is vital for the growth of the baby and helps keep the mother's body in good repair. Because of the growing fetus, a pregnant woman needs extra protein.

Pregnant women who experience certain symptoms should call their doctor immediately.

Building Reading Skills

Have students create two large webs, one for discomforts of pregnancy and one for its possible complications, leaving plenty of space to add information. **L1**

Discussion Activity

Because monthly checkups during pregnancy may seem routine, some women may think they are not important. Why are checkups important? How can they help a woman who is suffering from discomfort? Are they of equal importance to women who aren't experiencing discomforts? **L1**

Teamwork Activity

Have students work in groups to review the discomforts of a normal pregnancy and the symptoms that may indicate serious complications. Ask groups to write each discomfort or symptom on a separate index card. Then have them place all the index cards face down on a table and take turns selecting a card and telling whether the item on the card is a normal discomfort or a possible symptom of a serious problem. **L1**

VISUAL LEARNING | **Using the Photograph**
Discuss the difference between the minor symptoms of discomfort and possible signs of major complications.

Parenting in *Action*

Ask small groups to discuss the kinds of information expectant parents can benefit from. Examples include:
- About prenatal development.
- About prenatal tests.
- About their own state of health and how it can affect the baby.
- About maternity leave at work.
- What their health insurance covers.

Have groups report their lists to the class and discuss.

ACTIVITIES

Critical Thinking Activity

Synthesizing. Have students summarize in a few sentences the importance of each nutrient. Ask for volunteers to read theirs to the class and have the class choose the most precise summary. **L2**

Promoting Health Activity

Have students research artificial sweeteners and colors. What foods are they used in? Do they have any known or suspected side effects? Have they been studied in relation to prenatal development? **L3**

Teamwork Activity

Have groups create a poster called "Nutrients for a Healthy Pregnancy." Tell them to include nutritious snacks for a pregnant woman. **L1**

VISUAL LEARNING Using the Photograph
Because it supplies calcium.

Salt Intake. For years, pregnant women were told to avoid salt. Salt was assumed to promote fluid retention and swelling, which were considered problems. Moderate fluid retention is now known to be necessary for an adequate volume of blood and amniotic fluid. Abnormal fluid retention during pregnancy is caused by kidney and liver impairment.

- **Vitamins.** A woman needs higher levels of vitamins during pregnancy. For instance, pregnancy doubles a woman's need for folic acid. A diet lacking in vitamins increases the risk that a baby will have spine or brain defects. To make sure that a pregnant woman gets enough vitamins, her doctor may recommend that she take a prenatal multiple vitamin every day. Some advise this before pregnancy.

  Vitamin A ensures proper eye development. B vitamins assist in the overall development of the fetus. Vitamin C helps build healthy teeth and gums and helps make the material that holds body cells together. Vitamin D aids in making bones and teeth.

  Fresh fruits and vegetables, whole-grain breads and cereal products, and fortified milk are especially rich sources of vitamins. Fortified milk will say "vitamins A and D" on the label.

- **Minerals.** These nutrients are needed for sturdy bones and teeth, healthy blood, and regular elimination of waste products. The doctor may tell the woman take a mineral supplement.

  Pregnant women have a particular need for iron, which helps prevent anemia and helps the fetus build its own blood supply. Extra iron is stored in the baby's liver to be used for several months after birth, when the baby's diet lacks iron. Meat is a good source of iron. Other sources include beans, peas, spinach, raisins, and dates.

  Calcium and phosphorous are also especially important during pregnancy. They are needed by both mother and baby to have healthy bones and teeth. Milk supplies much of the calcium and phosphorous a pregnant woman needs.

- **Carbohydrates and fats.** These nutrients are necessary for heat and energy. Good sources of carbohydrates are fruits, vegetables, whole-grain breads, and cereals. Most people get more than enough fat in their diet, so fatty foods should be avoided.

Why is milk important for pregnant women?

LEARNING STYLES

Visual

Have students create a comic book that shows the role each nutrient plays in maintaining the health of a pregnant woman and her developing baby. Suggest that students create a character for each nutrient who could be performing a job or in some other way illustrating its function. The student could narrate a story by means of the characters or use a succession of discrete scenes to illustrate his or her points.

The Food Guide Pyramid

A Guide for Pregnant and Nursing Women

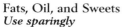

Fats, Oil, and Sweets
Use sparingly
The foods in this group, such as margarine and sugar, are generally high in calories and low in nutrition. They are not considered part of a healthy diet. Foods from other groups also include some fats and sugars.

Milk, Yogurt, and Cheese Group
3 *servings* (Teens 4)
The milk a pregnant woman drinks should be fortified with vitamin D and have 1 percent fat. If a woman has diffculty maintaining or gaining weight, she may drink milk with higher fat content. Cheese, yogurt, and ice cream can be substituted for some of the milk.

Vegetable Group
3-5 *servings*
At least one of the servings from this group should be a deep yellow or dark green, leafy vegetable. A pregnant woman should also try to include vegetables high in vitamin C, such as cabbage, in her diet.

Meat, Poultry, Fish, Dry Beans, Eggs, and Nuts Group
2-3 *servings*
The foods in this group, include all types of meat, poultry, and fish and seafood, as well as eggs, nuts, dry beans and peas, and lentils.

Fruit Group
2-4 *servings*
One or more of the servings from this group should be a fruit high in vitamin C, such as citrus fruit, berries, or melons.

Bread, Cereal, Rice, and Pasta Group
6-11 *servings*
Foods in this group include whole-grain or enriched breads, cereals and other grain products, such as rice, macaroni, and noodles.

These are the recommended number of servings that a pregnant or a nursing woman should eat *each day* from each of the food groups.

Critical Thinking Activity

Analyzing. **Ask:** Does eating nutritiously cost more than not eating well? How can a pregnant woman on a limited budget make the best choices for her diet? **L1**

Critical Thinking Activity

Estimating. Have students estimate serving sizes for the foods in the various sections of the Food Guide Pyramid. Then give them a list of actual adult serving sizes. For which foods did they estimate incorrectly? Why? **L1**

Critical Thinking Activity

Researching. Have students research and report on foods that may be hazardous during pregnancy. Examples include fish contaminated with mercury, raw meat, unpasteurized milk, and some soft cheeses and ready-to-eat meat products. **L2**

Research Activity

Have students access the Websites for The Food Guide Pyramid: www.pueblo.gsa.gov/cic_text/food/food-pyramid/main.htm and the Dietary Guidelines: www.usda.gov/cnpp/DietGd for additional information. Which USDA recommendations would be especially important during pregnancy? **L2**

VISUAL LEARNING | **Using the Graphic**
Ask students to work in groups to plan and write out one day's menu. Then have the class evaluate all of them. Do they meet the Food Guide Pyramid recommendations for pregnant women?

LEARNING STYLES

Spatial
Provide students with a list of the vitamins and minerals in fruits and vegetables. Which fruits and vegetables would be especially good for pregnant women? Why? Have students create a graphic organizer with several columns to include the name of the food, a picture, the nutrients it contains, a description of how it benefits the baby and the mother. Which would they recommend most highly?

COMPREHENSION CHECK

1. Why do pregnant teens have special nutritional needs? (*Their own bodies are still growing and developing.*)
2. What nutrients do lactose intolerant and vegetarian women have to take special care to get? (*Calcium; protein.*)

ACTIVITIES

Discussion Activity

Ask students to list the names of their favorite foods Write their responses on the board. Help them identify the food groups to which each belongs. Would the food be a healthy choice for a pregnant woman? Why or why not? **L1**

Critical Thinking Activity

Evaluating. Have students explain why feeding a baby a nutritious diet after birth cannot make up for poor nutrition during pregnancy.

L1

VISUAL LEARNING

Using the Chart Have students work in groups to determine the percentage of total weight gain that each category represents. Then have them make a pie chart reflecting their findings..

The Food Guide Pyramid

Everyone can eat a well-balanced diet by using the Food Guide Pyramid to choose foods. The chart on page 187 shows the pyramid for pregnant and nursing women, who also need extra nutrients.

There are other important dietary recommendations for pregnant women. They should drink six to eight glasses of water daily. They should also avoid rich and fried foods, which are usually hard to digest and have few nutrients. Of course, they should avoid eating too much sugar.

Teens' Diets

Teens have special nutritional needs because their bodies are growing and developing. For this reason, it is especially important for pregnant teens to be careful about good nutrition.

Filling up on low-nutrition snacks is never a good idea, but it is even more unwise during a pregnancy. Expectant mothers need foods rich in essential nutrients. It is especially important for pregnant teens to have enough calcium and iron. See page 186 for suggestions of good sources of these minerals.

Special Diets

Some women have a problem digesting lactose, a sugar found in milk. These women feel bloated or have stomach pain when they drink milk. How can they get the calcium they need? They can choose foods such as yogurt, cottage cheese, broccoli, kale, tuna, salmon, sardines, and tofu.

Protein is an especially important nutrient during pregnancy. Meat and poultry are high in protein, but some people are vegetarians and don't eat these foods. They can still get the protein they need from fish, eggs, and dried beans and peas eaten in combination with enriched breads, grains, and seeds.

Weight Gain During Pregnancy	Pounds	Kilograms
Weight of average baby at birth	7-8	3.2-3.6
Placenta	1-2	0.45-0.9
Amniotic fluid	1½-2	0.7-0.9
Increased size of uterus and supporting muscles	2	0.9
Increase in breast tissue	1	0.45
Increase in blood volume	1½-3	0.7-1.4
Increase in fat stores	5	2.3
Increase in body fluids	5-7	2.3-3.2
Total	**24-30**	11.0-13.65

188 UNIT 2: Pregnancy and Childbirth

ISSUES IN TEEN PARENTING A Harvard University study found that low birthweight babies (under 5½ lb.) have a 40 percent higher chance of developing high blood pressure as adults than normal babies. High birthweight babies (over 10 lb.) are 62 percent more likely to develop obesity. Discuss with students why teen mothers are particularly at risk of having low birthweight babies. Have students look at the weight gain chart on page 188. Discuss the sources of maternal weight gain and the likely weight changes after birth. Have students interview older friends and relatives who have had children and report their experiences.

Weight Gain During Pregnancy

A woman usually gains about 24 to 30 pounds (11.0 to 13.65 kg) during pregnancy. The chart on page 188 shows how that weight is usually distributed.

In the first three months of a pregnancy, the woman may not gain any weight—she may even lose weight. That is nothing to worry about. Weight gain in the fourth through sixth months of pregnancy is most important for the fetus.

Doctors recommend that women gain at least 20 pounds (9.1 kg) unless they begin the pregnancy very overweight. A weight gain lower than that increases the risk of fetal death and of having a premature baby. Doctors also say that a pregnant woman should gain no more than 35 pounds (15.9 kg). However, it is not a good idea for an expectant mother to start a weight-loss diet. Pregnancy is not the time to lose weight. Moderate exercise and a diet that excludes sugary, fatty foods can help a woman have a healthy weight gain.

Some women develop diabetes while pregnant. This condition affects the body's ability to burn energy. If not controlled, it can lead to a very large size for the baby. Doctors usually give these women a special diet that controls weight gain but still supplies vital nutrients. This diet may limit the foods the women can eat from the bread, cereal, rice, and pasta group.

Personal Care and Activities

In addition to practicing good nutrition, an expectant mother should take good care of herself in other ways. She should avoid alcohol, tobacco, and all drugs or medications. She should take some other steps as well:

INFOLINK

Drugs and Tobacco

To review problems with *drugs and tobacco*. See Chapter 5, pages 158, 168-172.

- **Rest.** Women generally need more rest when they are pregnant than they did before. Taking frequent breaks during the day may revive a woman's energy.
- **Exercise.** Moderate exercise can help keep an expectant mother in good physical condition—and help make the pregnancy more comfortable. Doctors recommend walking, swimming, or biking as good exercises during pregnancy. They say that pregnancy is not a time to start any strenuous activities for the first time.
- **Hygiene.** Because the skin helps maintain correct body temperature and eliminate waste, it should be kept clean. Bathing just before bedtime also encourages relaxation and sleep.
- **Other activities.** Pregnant women can usually follow the same work routines they had before pregnancy, unless the doctor advises differently.

A woman doesn't need to change her lifestyle radically during pregnancy. Moderation may be needed in some areas, but she can continue her life as before.

Invite a dietitian to speak about the dietary needs of pregnant teens and vegetarians. Encourage students to ask questions about the different physical needs of teens and adult women. They might ask about other groups who have special dietary needs (diabetic, overweight, and underweight women). **L1**

Critical Thinking Activity

Synthesizing. Have students research the causes, effects, and prevalence of lactose intolerance. Among what segments of the population is it most common? (*90 percent of African Americans, 70 percent of Asian Americans, 50 percent of Latinos, 15 percent of whites suffer from lactose intolerance.*) What can pregnant women do to get the needed calcium if they are lactose intolerant? **L3**

Teamwork Activity

Ask small groups to discuss why women should not worry if they do not gain weight in the first three months of a pregnancy. Why is weight gain after the third month more important? What should a woman do if she is worried about her weight? **L1**

LEARNING STYLES

Mathematical

Have students create a healthy pregnancy board game. Players can answer questions written on cards and gain or lose points (or advance or go back squares) when they suggest healthy or risky behavior. Tell students to go through Section 6-1 to make up questions. Cards can be categorized and used when a player lands on the appropriate square or mixed randomly so a player has to answer one before advancing. Suggest to students that they work out their game format first and then divide the tasks.

ACTIVITIES

Critical Thinking Activity

Analyzing. Have students discuss the possible effects of pregnancy on a woman's working life. What kinds of work might she need to give up during pregnancy? Why? What special challenges might a working woman face in maintaining a nutritious diet or obtaining adequate rest? How might nausea, fatigue, and the need to wear maternity clothing affect her at work? **L1**

VISUAL LEARNING | Using the Photographs
Left—Possible answers: Biking and walking. *Right: Answers will vary.*

Emotional Changes. Women often feel ambivalent and contradictory feelings about having a baby. Some women are overwhelmed by the importance and demands of the years ahead. Some are suddenly aware of their own inadequate training and skills. A sense of grieving can be experienced as a woman shifts into a new phase of her life. It is natural to feel a full range of emotions. It is important for the mother to realize that her emotions are in reaction to the circumstances and do not reflect her ability to love and care for her baby.

Swimming is good exercise for a pregnant woman as the water relieves the feeling of added weight. *What other exercises are good?*

Maternity Clothes

By about the fourth or fifth month of pregnancy, a woman usually begins to need special clothing. Maternity clothes should be loose enough to allow for freedom of movement and circulation. Cotton knits stretch to allow room for the growing baby. Skirts and pants may include a stretch panel for comfort. Before buying any garment, a pregnant woman should consider how it will fit in the last month of pregnancy.

Comfortable, low-heeled shoes with good support are recommended. A pregnant woman should avoid wearing high heels. They throw the body out of balance and increase the risk of falling.

Emotional Health During Pregnancy

During pregnancy, expectant parents need to make emotional adjustments. It is normal for them to have concerns about the baby. Talking about these concerns with each other and with family members can be reassuring.

Pregnancy causes hormonal changes, which can produce mood swings. A pregnant woman may shift quickly from happiness to sorrow—and then back again, for no apparent reason. Even the most calm woman will feel upset and worried at times during her pregnancy. Effective techniques

---

ISSUES IN TEEN PARENTING | Pregnancy produces emotional as well as physical effects. Sometimes a woman may feel sad and other times happy. Although most of these mood swings are normal, it is usually a good idea to talk with someone about them. Teen parents often face special circumstances that can affect them emotionally. Ask students to think about the emotions of a teen parent. Have them make a list of emotions that a teen parent might feel and then note the likely reasons for these emotions. Have students identify healthy outlets for these emotions and suggest formal and informal sources of support.

Pregnancy is an emotionally charged time. *What can couples do to prevent strong emotions from causing problems?*

for reducing stress can help the woman bounce back when she's feeling down. Exercise, as long as it is moderate, not only helps a pregnant woman feel better physically but also builds emotional health. Deep breathing can reduce stress, which promotes depression. Massage can be calming as well.

SECTION 6-1 REVIEW

✔ Check Your Understanding

1. What is usually the first sign of pregnancy?
2. Why should a pregnant woman see a doctor from the start?
3. What steps are part of the initial examination of a pregnant woman?
4. How often does a woman typically see a doctor during her pregnancy?
5. Traci is pregnant. She suffers from frequent headaches. What should she do?
6. What benefits does a pregnant woman receive from vitamins A, B, C, and D?
7. What benefits does a pregnant woman gain from iron, calcium, and phosphorus?
8. What are the minimum and maximum weight gains doctors recommend?
9. What can a pregnant woman do to reduce stress?

Putting Knowledge Into Practice

1. **Applying.** Plan a day's meals for a pregnant woman using the Food Guide Pyramid.
2. **Making Inferences.** Lucinda worries about gaining too much weight during her pregnancy. She decides to begin jogging every day. Is this a good idea? Why or why not?
3. **Observing and Participating.** Look at what you and your friends eat at lunch for the next two days, and write it down. Suppose these were the lunches of a pregnant woman. Do they reflect the recommendations found in the Food Guide Pyramid or not? If not, how would you improve the nutritional value of these meals?

CHAPTER 6: Preparing for Birth **191**

ASSESS

CHECKING COMPREHENSION

Have students answer the Check Your Understanding questions. Answers appear at the bottom of this page.

EVALUATION

Give students the Section 6-1 Quiz in the *Teacher Resource Guide.*

RETEACHING

1. Assign Reteaching Activities, page 22.
2. Form the class into teams and have them play a Jeopardy-type quiz game using the parts of the section as categories.

ENRICHMENT

Have students research relaxation exercises for pregnant women and make an illustrated booklet explaining how to do the exercises and what benefits they supply.

EXTENSION

Tell students to interview older family members about attitudes towards pregnancy in the past and report to the class. How do attitudes compare today?

CLOSE

Have students write five diary entries for a pregnant woman.

FOCUS

MOTIVATOR

Have volunteers act out this scenario: A woman learns she is pregnant and hurries home to tell her husband. They begin to discuss the decisions and arrangements they must make to prepare for the baby.

VOCABULARY ACTIVITY

Ask students to match terms with synonyms.
- estimate, forecast (*budget*)
- regular, predetermined (*fixed*)
- changeable, adjustable (*flexible*)
- costs, outlays (*expenses*)
- preparation, nourishment (*formula*)
- time off (*maternity leave*)

192

Getting Ready for a Baby

The nine months of pregnancy provide expectant parents with an opportunity to learn and think about the changes to come. They can use this time to make plans and decisions as they prepare for the arrival of a new family member.

KEY TERMS

budget
fixed expenses
flexible expenses
formula
maternity leave
pediatrician

OBJECTIVES:
- Analyze how expectant parents can plan for a baby's care.
- Evaluate the preparations expectant parents should make.
- Explain how and why to make a budget.

Roles and Responsibilities

The most important question is how the parents will meet the responsibilities of child care. They need to consider many factors, such as each partner's goals, skills, schedule, and personal characteristics. Of course, they also need to take the

192 UNIT 2: Pregnancy and Childbirth

Observing & Participating

Invite to class a consumer specialist to discuss various strategies for saving money when shopping for baby equipment and supplies. Ask the speaker to bring comparative prices of different items when purchased in different outlets or by different methods to show the effectiveness of the techniques. Have students prepare questions in advance. After the visit, ask students to write a summary of the tips offered and evaluate those that they think are most useful.

Some new parents ask the newborn's grandparents to care for the child so they can return to work. *What other options are available?*

financial situation of the family into account. When both parents work outside the home, these decisions are especially important.

Many new mothers who work outside the home take a **maternity leave**. This time off from work allows a woman to give birth, recover, and begin to care for her new baby. An employer may offer employees from a few weeks to several months of leave. Some employers give time off to new fathers as well.

Federal law, the Family Medical Leave Act, requires employers with more than 50 workers to give twelve weeks of leave to workers for family reasons. This leave can be used by either parent when a baby is born. The leave is without pay, but the worker is guaranteed to have his or her job back when returning to work.

If finances allow it, a couple may decide that one parent will stay home to care for the child. This primary caregiver may be a mother or a father.

With the growing number of people who work in their homes, some couples plan to have one partner work in the home and also provide child care. This is possible, but very difficult. The needs of a baby can interfere with a work schedule.

Regardless of who takes primary responsibility for daily care, both parents should know the basics. This allows them to share the work—and the special joys—of caring for their baby.

In many families, neither parent stays home to care for the baby after the first few months. These parents need to make the best possible child care choices.

INFOLINK

Child Care Options

See Section 3-3 to review *child care options.*

TEACH

ACTIVITIES

Building Study Skills

Encourage students to preview the section before reading it: check the headings and vocabulary; look at the graphics and illustrations. Then ask students one or two content questions to show them how previewing gives purpose and understanding to reading. **L1**

Discussion Activity

Explore the decisions parents make about child rearing. How do these decisions affect a child's life and development? How do they affect the parents? How would lack of agreement between them affect the parents and the baby? What might parents disagree about? How can disagreements be resolved? **L1**

Teamwork Activity

Let groups discuss the factors that couples should take into account when deciding whether one parent should quit work to care for a new baby. Ask groups to list factors and discuss the lists as a class. **L1**

VISUAL LEARNING | **Using the Photograph**
Possible responses: One parent stays home, parents take turns, use child care.

LEARNING STYLES

Intrapersonal

Have students write an anecdote or short story about expectant parents preparing for parenthood. Tell students to show how the parents go about making their decisions. Do the parents-to-be read magazine articles or books about breastfeeding? Do they talk to friends and relatives who have children? Do they examine their income and prepare a budget? How do they look for a pediatrician? Tell students to give the characters names, to describe their thoughts and feelings, and to include dialogue when suitable.

COMPREHENSION CHECK

1. What would be the advantages of couples discussing aspects of parenting before the baby arrives? (*Can be objective, make decisions, work out differences.*)
2. How does the age of an older sibling impact the child's response to a new baby? (*Younger children understand less and emotional and behavioral responses may be stronger.*)

Teamwork Activity

Divide students into groups of four and ask them to list four ways in which parents can include an older child in preparing for a new baby. Two students should be recorders, writing down the suggestions and the reasons. One student should be the checker, responsible for the completeness of answers and grammatical correctness. The fourth student should be the speaker, presenting the group's suggestions to the class.

VISUAL LEARNING Using the Photograph *Possible responses:* Discuss how lives will change, share time with the child.

Preparing for Parenthood

Many expectant parents—especially if it is their first child—worry that they may not be able to care for their child well. Even the most confident mothers and fathers have these concerns.

Discussing ideas about parenting before the baby is born helps. For example, they might talk about how to give guidance, how to share in parenting, what goals they have for the children, and other issues. Of course, parents can't plan what they will do in every possible situation. Some ideas may also change as they become experienced in parenting. By agreeing ahead of time on general ideas about raising children, however, parents can reduce conflict later on.

Preparing for parenthood also involves anticipating changes in the other roles parents fill. Parents may also be spouses, family members, workers, students, volunteers, and citizens. As they begin to care for children, parents have less time and energy for these other roles and may need to make adjustments.

Parents can help themselves meet these roles by using good management skills—especially time management. Developing a schedule of activities—and then sticking to it—is a great help. So is using time wisely by, for instance, combining errands.

Other Children in the Family

Other children in the family will have to adjust to a new baby as well. How these children react to a new sibling depends in part on how well prepared they were before the newborn arrived. Of course, the age and emotional makeup of the children is a factor as well.

What can parents do to prepare other children for the coming arrival?

Parenting in *Action*

Very few first-time parents have completely realistic expectations about what parenting will be like. Have students interview parents to find out what was different than they expected. Tally and categorize the classes findings.

Practicing Parenting

Telling Children About a Baby

*P*arents need to help the children they already have adjust to the news that a baby is on the way.

♥ **Children under school age.** If the child is younger than school age, avoid saying anything too early in the pregnancy. Nine months is a long time for a small child to wait!

♥ **Children four and older.** If the child is at least four, be sure to tell him or her before you tell people outside the family.

♥ **Include in plans.** Including the child in making plans for the baby allows him or her to feel involved.

♥ **Changing living space.** If you are going to put the baby in the child's room and move the child to a new room, do it before the baby arrives. Allow time for the child to feel comfortable in the new room.

♥ **Changes in the child's life.** If you will be making changes in the child's life—such as toilet training—finish *before* the baby comes.

♥ **Do not create unrealistic expectations.** Do not tell the child that he or she "will have a new baby to play with." The baby won't be able to join the child in play for many, many months.

♥ **Sibling classes.** If the hospital offers a class for siblings, let the child take part.

♥ **Patience for negative behaviors.** Be patient if the child behaves like a younger child. Such behavior is often a cry for attention when the child feels pushed aside. Give some extra love. Behavior will soon return to normal.

♥ **Give reassurance and love.** Reassure the child that you love him or her. Whenever you have a chance, give the child a hug.

APPLY YOUR KNOWLEDGE

1. The parents of Shawn, aged four, are expecting a second child. If you were his mother or father, how would you tell Shawn the news?
2. Why is it important to tell a child before telling friends?

Parents should be prepared for a wide range of attitudes toward a new baby. It's normal for the child to feel jealousy and confusion—and excitement and love. Open communication and acceptance of a child's feelings will help foster a positive relationship between siblings. It may simply take time to adjust to all the changes.

CHAPTER 6: Preparing for Birth **195**

Management/Leadership Skills

The Hopi Indians have a naming ritual. Twenty days after birth, the family assembles before dawn. The grandmother washes the baby, then rubs the head four times with a perfectly formed ear of corn. She does the same to the baby's paternal aunts, who each suggest a name. As dawn approaches, the grandmother chooses a name, then takes the infant outside into the rising sun. A feast follows. When the child reaches the age of initiation, a second name is added to symbolize a new birth. Why are naming traditions of value to the baby? to the family?

COMPREHENSION CHECK

1. Why is breast milk recommended? (*Has many benefits—e.g., immunity—that formula does not have.*)
2. What is formula? (*Mixture of milk or milk substitute with water and nutrients used instead of breast milk.*)

ACTIVITIES

Teamwork Activity

Have small groups look up the differences between milk- and soy-based formula. Why is soy formula recommended for some babies?

Math Activity

Have students compute the cost of 8-ounce (240 mL) bottles of different types of formula. Include homemade, powdered, concentrated, and ready-to-use. What factors besides cost should they consider? Which would they recommend using? **L2**

VISUAL LEARNING

Using the Chart Have students look over the chart. **Ask:** What are the health advantages of breast-feeding for the baby? for the mother? What are the practical advantages? What are the advantages of bottle-feeding? Why would some women choose it over breast-feeding?

▶ Comparing Breast-Feeding and Bottle-Feeding

Breast-Feeding

Advantages
- Best source of nutrition for baby.
- Gives the baby some immunity against diseases.
- Creates a bond through physical closeness with the mother.
- May boost brain development.
- Reduces baby's risk of allergies.
- Causes fewer digestive upsets.
- Speeds the return of the mother's uterus to normal size.
- Reduces the mother's risk of later having breast or ovarian cancer.
- Reduces the risk that the mother will feel depressed.
- Is conveniently available at all times.
- Is free, though a nursing mother needs additional food.

Disadvantages
- Prevents father from participating in feeding.
- Baby has to be fed more often.
- In rare cases, may be medical reasons that suggest breast-feeding is not desirable.
- May be painful for some mothers.
- May be difficult because of work schedule.

Bottle-Feeding

Advantages
- Allows father to participate in feeding.
- Allows mother to have a more flexible schedule.
- Eliminates concern about mother's diet or medications she takes.
- Babies need feeding less often.

Disadvantages
- Can be expensive.
- Does not give the baby any natural immunities to disease.
- Involves a greater chance of baby developing allergies.
- Creates risk that baby may not be given close physical contact during feeding.

196   UNIT 2: Pregnancy and Childbirth

Parenting in Action

Write a skit in which a pediatrician examines a sick child and gives several directions to a parent for treating the child. You might include directions for administering two medications; for lowering fever; for checking the baby at night. Have volunteers perform the skit. Then have the rest of the class write down the doctor's instructions on index cards. Ask volunteers to read their cards aloud and write them on the chalkboard. Then write on the board the actual instructions. Compare the results. Ask students how parents can prevent errors in following doctors' directions.

Choosing a Pediatrician

Before the baby is born, the parents should choose a **pediatrician**—a doctor who specializes in treating children. This doctor will be the main health care provider for the child for many years. Parents should find one who meets their needs.

The parents can ask their obstetrician to suggest names of pediatricians. They can also ask friends they know who have children. Once they have a few names, they can schedule interviews with the doctors. Pediatricians are usually willing to talk to parents before the parents make a choice.

Some considerations are practical. Where is the doctor's office, and what are the office hours? What are the fees for checkups, tests, and vaccinations? Here are some other questions parents may ask:

- When is the doctor available by phone?
- How should an emergency be handled?
- Who covers for the pediatrician if he or she is not available?
- What hospital does the doctor use?
- How often will the doctor see the child, both as a baby and later?
- What are the doctor's views on breast-feeding and bottle-feeding?
- What is the doctor's philosophy on guidance?

Some parents give their children health care through a clinic or a health maintenance organization. In these cases, they may have fewer choices about which doctor they can use.

The choice of a pediatrician should be evaluated once it is put in action. If the parents don't feel comfortable about the kind of care their child is receiving, it may be best to find a new doctor.

Decisions About Feeding

Another issue the parents should consider is whether the new baby will be breast-fed or bottle-fed. Breast milk has many benefits for the baby. For this reason, health care professionals recommend breast-feeding whenever possible, for as long as possible. The chart on page 196 shows the advantages and disadvantages of breast-feeding.

Bottle-feeding with formula is a convenient alternative to breast-feeding. **Formula**, a mixture of milk or milk substitute, water, and nutrients, provides good nutrition for babies. You can buy it as a powder or a concentrate that must be mixed with water or in ready-to-use forms. The chart on page 196 shows the advantages and disadvantages of formula.

The decision to breast-feed or bottle-feed is a personal one. Many mothers successfully breast-feed for certain feedings and use bottles at others. Whatever method parents choose, they should remember that the baby responds to the feeling and care that accompany each feeding.

The Developing Brain

Breast Milk

Breast milk, unlike formula, has certain fatty acids. One study shows that when these fatty acids were added to formula, ten-month-old infants performed better on a problem-solving test than did babies the same age who fed on regular formula. The research suggests that these fatty acids make breast milk better for brain development.

ACTIVITIES

Discussion Activity

Explore the purpose of the different types of equipment. What needs of the baby do they help to meet? (*Nourishment, hygiene, warmth and protection.*) What factors should parents consider in buying equipment? (*Safety, cost, durability.*) **L1**

Critical Thinking Activity

Making Judgments. Tell students to imagine that they are planning a baby shower. Their aim is to provide the expectant mother with the basics for the first six months of her new baby's life. Have students plan a gift list for the shower. **L1**

VISUAL LEARNING **Using the Chart** Review the chart of Basic Baby Supplies with the class. Ask volunteers to explain what the different items are used for. Discuss the different variations of an item available. Bring in photographs from parenting magazines or advertisements to illustrate.

▶ Basic Baby Supplies

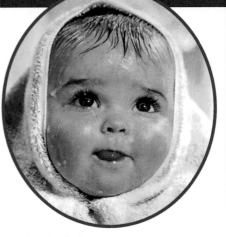

Diapering Needs
- A changing table or some surface to use for changing the baby
- If using disposable diapers: About 70 (a week's supply)
- If using cloth diapers: 3-4 dozen diapers; diaper pins; waterproof pants; a covered diaper pail; 8-10 disposable diapers for occasional use
- 6-10 washcloths
- Diaper rash ointment

Clothing
- 6-8 undershirts; 4-6 one-piece footed sleepers; 4-6 gowns
- 6 cotton receiving blankets; 1 warm outer wrapping blanket
- 1 dress-up outfit (optional)
- 1 sweater
- 1-2 sun hats or bonnets; warmer hat if needed for cooler weather
- Coat and mittens (optional)

Feeding Equipment
- If breast-feeding and mother works: Breast pump and pads; plastic bottles for storing breast milk
- If bottle-feeding: 6-8 large bottles (8-ounce or 237-mL); nipples and bottle caps (the same number as bottles, plus a few extra); bottle and nipple brush
- Bibs
- High chair

Bedding/Bedroom
- Crib and waterproof mattress (if the baby will sleep alone); bumper pad (fits around inside of crib just above mattress; keeps baby's arms and legs in, drafts out)
- Waterproof mattress cover; 2-4 absorbent pads
- 4 fitted crib sheets
- 2-3 lightweight blankets or spreads; heavier crib blanket
- Storage space, such as a chest of drawers
- Wastebasket

Bathing and Other Supplies
- Baby bathtub or other container
- Rubbing alcohol (for umbilical cord)
- Mild, pure soap; baby shampoo
- Several soft washcloths; 2 soft cotton bath towels
- Cotton balls
- Baby oil and baby lotion
- Blunt-tipped nail scissors; baby comb and brush set
- Thermometer

Travel Equipment
- Car seat, which meets the latest safety standards
- Tote bag for carrying supplies
- Stroller, carriage, or infant carrier (optional)

198 UNIT 2: Pregnancy and Childbirth

LEARNING STYLES

Mathematical

Explain that some items of baby furniture serve two purposes, such as a crib that converts to a changing table. Have students look in periodicals and the Internet to find the uses and cost of multipurpose furniture and equipment. Ask them to compare these pieces with single purpose items in terms of quality, practicality, and cost. Do multipurpose items cost less than the combined cost of the items they replace? Have students create a graphic organizer showing their findings and report them to the class.

Clothing, Equipment, and Space

Basic supplies for a baby include clothing, bedding, bathing supplies, and travel equipment. Parents who choose bottle-feeding also need equipment for that.

The chart on page 198 shows basic needs. This list merely suggests possibilities. Expectant parents may get specific suggestions from a doctor or from family and friends. Advice is also given at the hospital and at classes for new parents.

Wise parents begin with only the basic items they and the baby will need at birth. They may receive some of these items—as well as those needed later—as gifts or loans. The most appreciated baby gifts are often practical ones. A box of diapers or a sleeper that can be used often may be more welcome than a fancy outfit. People who plan to buy baby gifts should ask the parents what they need.

Baby's Room

Newborns may sleep as many as 18 to 22 hours a day. During the first six months, most babies sleep for 15 to 18 hours every day. Some parents believe that babies sleep best in the parents' room. This arrangement is convenient when it is time for a middle-of-the-night feeding. Others think babies sleep best if they have a separate place, which can be kept quiet.

The basic needs for a baby are a crib and a dresser. A changing table with storage can be helpful as well. *Why is it helpful to have a separate room for a baby?*

Of course, many families cannot provide a new baby with his or her own room. Love and pleasant conditions are more important than a spacious home. If the baby doesn't have a separate room, a quiet corner of a room can be made into the baby's special place. A room divider can be used to provide the baby—and other family members—with privacy.

The choice of a crib is of greatest importance. See pages 210–211 for specific characteristics to be checked. Keep pillows, fluffy blankets or bumper pads, and stuffed toys out of the crib when a young infant is sleeping.

Some parents like to put a monitor in the baby's room. This listening device picks

Discussion Activity

Why would babies need specialized versions of items a family would already have, such as blunt-tipped nail scissors, a rectal thermometer, or a special comb and brush set? **L1**

Critical Thinking Activity

Making Generalizations. Which items on the chart can be used long-term and which can only be used short-term? Why? Ask small groups to consider whether a second or third child is as expensive as a first one. **L2**

Teamwork Activity

Have pairs of students investigate what makes a car seat safe. Ask them to price and evaluate at least three different models. As parents, would they purchase any of the three? Why? **L3**

Discussion Activity

How do feeding arrangements help determine an infant's sleeping arrangements? Why do you think many parents like to keep the newborn near them at night? **L1**

VISUAL LEARNING | Using the Photograph
Possible response: Because they sleep so much of the day.

INFOLINK

SIDS

Positioning of the baby can help reduce SIDS death. See page 238 for more about *SIDS*.

LEARNING STYLES

Auditory

Ask students to identify the characteristics of jingles. (Easily recognizable rhythm and repeatable rhyme. The tune and lyrics should be simple and easy to mimic, so that they keep going through the listener's head.) Then have them to write a jingle advertising for supplies or equipment parents need to get for their newborn infant.

COMPREHENSION CHECK

1. What's the first step in making a budget? (*Identify income.*)
2. How do some hospitals help families with low incomes who lack insurance? (*By offering free or low-cost clinics.*)

ACTIVITIES

Teamwork Activity

Have small groups design and draw a dresser-top changing area. How would they keep the supplies tidy and dispose of trash? What would they use to make the surface comfortable? Tell groups that all students must contribute. One could draw, one write answers to questions, and one present the design to the class. **L1**

Critical Thinking Activity

Analyzing. Using an overhead projector or the chalkboard, show students how to prepare a household budget, taking into account both monthly expenses and cash flow. Discuss both fixed and flexible expenses. **L1**

VISUAL LEARNING	Using the Photograph

Possible response: In the crib.

---

up sounds from the room and sends them to a speaker. Parents put the speaker in the room where they are. This system gives the parents a chance to know if anything goes wrong while the baby sleeps.

The Diaper-Changing Area

Parents need to plan a place where the baby can be changed and dressed. Special changing tables are available, but any surface—except one used for eating—that is a convenient height and is padded can serve equally well. The top of a chest of drawers can be used as a changing table, as can a crib.

Whatever area is used, caregivers must never leave the baby unattended on it. They should pay constant attention to protect the baby from a fall and possible injury.

Making a Budget

Having a child is expensive. Prenatal care—an important expense—is costly. Equipment adds to the bills. On top of that, a growing baby seems to need new clothes every few months. Planning can help parents meet these expenses.

Do you budget your money? A **budget** is simply a spending plan used to help people set financial goals and work toward those goals. Budgets are helpful for everyone, but especially expectant parents.

Where can a baby's diaper be changed if there's no changing table?

The first step in making a budget is to identify income. How much money do the parents earn from work and other sources? If one parent will stop working to care for the child, the parents must remember that income will be reduced.

Next, the expectant parents should look at where their money currently goes. **Fixed expenses** are the costs of items that cannot be changed, such as payments for housing, taxes, insurance, and loans. **Flexible expenses** are costs for items over which people have some control—and which can be cut

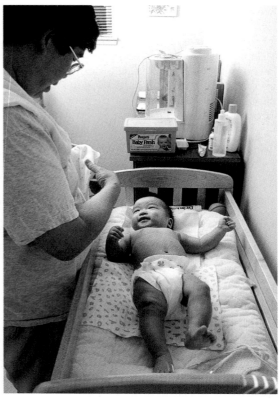

Management/Leadership Skills

Although used baby furniture can save money, it needs to be checked for safety. An old high chair may have legs that aren't stable. The paint on some older furniture and toys may contain lead. Show students pictures of various pieces of baby furniture and equipment and ask them to suggest other possible hazards. Suggest to students that baby equipment that is assembled can be tested by placing a 10-pound (4-5 kg) sack of potatoes or pet food where the baby will lie. Would this kind of testing be adequate?

Having a baby and raising a child are expensive activities. *How can planning help a couple meet the added expense?*

Discussion Activity

Ask students to identify health care expenditures having children entails, such as well-baby care, immunizations, and vitamins. Why would skimping on these expenses mean potential health problems later on? **L1**

Teamwork Activity

Determine a reasonable income for a young couple starting out in your area. Give students both the yearly figure and the weekly or biweekly pay. Have small groups create a budget for such a couple. Remind students to include fixed and flexible expenses. Provide tax tables so students can compute how much will be deducted and classified ads to estimate the cost of housing, car payments and maintenance, clothing, and food. You might wish to provide students with ledger paper, a budget worksheet or have them create a more specific graphic organizer. **L2**

back if necessary. This category includes food, household maintenance, clothing, recreation, and similar expenses.

Estimating Health Care Expenses

Medical care is a major expense. This includes the cost of health care for the mother before birth and the baby after birth. It also includes the cost of hospitalization for the birth. Hospital charges vary. They usually depend on the type of delivery, the medical needs of the baby and mother, and the length of their stay.

Health insurance can help meet these expenses. Many employers make health insurance available to their workers. These plans often cover spouses and children. A worker should find out if he or she has to pay for part of the coverage, though.

Even if there is no insurance through work, a couple can purchase health insurance on their own. Health insurance can be costly, so it pays to shop carefully. Consumers should look not only at the cost but also at what is covered.

Expectant couples should review their health insurance to see what it includes. It is also a good idea to find out whether the insurance company pays hospital bills directly or repays the parents after they have paid the hospital.

Some large hospitals have free or low-rate clinics to help people who have no insurance and can't pay the full fees. Social workers may be able to help expectant parents who have financial problems.

Estimating Other Expenses

Along with health care, expectant parents must consider other costs:
- Maternity clothes.
- The clothing, equipment, and supplies listed on page 198, as well as any other items the parents want to provide.

CHAPTER 6: Preparing for Birth **201**

ISSUES IN
TEEN PARENTING
Teen fathers are also often overwhelmed by the changes to their own plans that a baby represents. Their new responsibilities may force them to alter their plans for the future or postpone them indefinitely. Personal disappointment is added to the lack of readiness for fatherhood and financial concerns. These worries and tension can create conflict for a couple that previously got along well. Explain that one way expectant fathers can help resolve the emotional conflicts is by getting involved in the pregnancy—by taking on the joys as well as the worries. Ask students to draw up a list of ways teen fathers can get involved.

ACTIVITIES

Critical Thinking Activity

Analyzing Causes. Pregnant teens who cannot support their families may turn to the state for help. As a result, at ages 19 and 20 unmarried women with children have higher incomes than those who have no children (and may thus attend school full time). By 21, however, childless women have higher incomes—and the difference in income increases over time. Discuss the probable causes of this switch in income. **L2**

Critical Thinking Activity

Supporting Arguments. Write this statement on the chalkboard: "Babies cost too much!" Have students record their reactions to the idea in a brief essay. **L1**

Math Activity

Have students check the cost of diapers and compute the cost over a three-year period. Assume that the baby uses 350 disposable diapers in the first two months, 215 a month starting in the third month, 180 a month at one year, and 160 a month at 2½ years until 3 years. What is the total cost of diapers for one child? **L2**

In most states, laws require young children to ride in a safety seat when in a car. By shopping carefully, parents can find a good quality seat that meets safety standards.

- Formula, if the baby will be bottle-fed. Some estimates put this expense at $1,200 to $1,500 per year.
- Furnishings for the baby's room.
- Child care, if needed.

Parents must also consider the costs of raising the child in the years ahead. Food, clothing, and education will all be major expenses. Parents should think about how they will manage these expenses.

Making a Plan

Once they have a clear idea of their new expenses, the parents can plan how to meet them. The money needed for the baby must be taken from another part of the budget, often by cutting back on flexible expenses.

Parents who have some money saved will find it easier to meet the early expenses of having a baby. Although it is often difficult to save money, having a budget can make this process easier. Saving even a small amount each month can help pay for the baby's future needs.

Reducing Expenses

Parents have several ways of reducing these expenses. Many parents cut costs by shopping carefully. Good quality used clothes and furniture can often be found at

LEARNING STYLES

Kinesthetic

Ask students to attend garage, yard, or rummage sales, and locate second-hand baby furniture and equipment. Have them note the quality, condition, and price of different items. Then tell them to look for the same items at retail stores, preferably discount stores. Have them create a poster comparing the new and used items and report to the class. What conclusions did they reach? What items would they choose to buy secondhand? How much would one save? What items would they prefer to purchase new? Why?

reasonable prices. Expectant parents have several months to comparison shop for what they need.

Many people reduce the cost of having a baby by borrowing things. Relatives and friends often share clothing or equipment among themselves. Expectant parents can find bargains at yard sales, rummage sales, and secondhand stores. If you use something that is borrowed or bought second-hand, wash it thoroughly. Do so even though it may appear clean.

Special caution should be taken with equipment. Secondhand or borrowed cribs, playpens, car seats, and other items should meet current safety standards. You can find those standards by asking the pediatrician or the local health department.

SECTION 6-2 REVIEW

✔ Check Your Understanding

1. What is maternity leave?
2. How does time management help parents?
3. What steps are involved in finding a pediatrician?
4. Why are practical gifts especially good for new parents?
5. Do you think it is important for a baby to have a separate room? Why or why not?
6. What is the difference between a fixed expense and a flexible expense?
7. What factors influence the cost of hospitalization for childbirth?
8. What expenses can health insurance help with?
9. How can expectant parents save money and still get the clothing and equipment they need for a new baby?

Putting Knowledge Into Practice

1. **Making Inferences.** What factors do you think influence a mother's choice to breast-feed or bottle-feed her baby?
2. **Synthesizing.** Why might it be harder to prepare an only child for a new baby, rather than one who already has a brother or a sister?
3. **Observing and Participating.** Work in teams. Bring in ads for clothing, equipment, furniture, or supplies needed for a baby. How different are the prices? Make a list of five items and write down the prices you found. Compare those prices to the prices for the same item from different stores, as supplied by classmates. How much money can be saved by comparison shopping for these items?

ASSESS

CHECKING COMPREHENSION

Have students answer the Check Your Understanding questions. Answers appear at the bottom of this page.

EVALUATION

Give students the Section 6-2 Quiz in the *Teacher Resource Guide*.

RETEACHING

1. Assign Reteaching Activities, page 23.
2. Have students create a newspaper article with information from Section 6-2.

ENRICHMENT

Have students read at least two articles on infant feeding. Then have them create a Venn diagram showing the points in the articles and draw conclusions.

EXTENSION

Have students survey the infant department of a clothing store. What garments are sold? How many are for only one sex? Write a list of criteria expectant parents could use in selecting clothing.

CLOSE

Ask: What do you think are the most important steps in preparing for a baby? Why?

ANSWERS TO SECTION 6-2 REVIEW

1. The time a woman takes off from work to give birth, recover, and care for baby.
2. Helps parents meet demands of different roles.
3. Get a list of recommended doctors; interview them.
4. If the child is a first child, parents may need basic items.
5. Answers should be supported by reasons.
6. Fixed—must be met; flexible—vary.
7. Type of delivery; medical needs of baby; length of stay.
8. Prenatal care; hospitalization; newborn care.
9. Comparison shopping; using secondhand goods.

CAREER OPPORTUNITIES

Introducing the Feature

Ask students what health care workers help a woman who is pregnant and giving birth. Ask if they know what a midwife is. Explain that for centuries, before the delivery of babies came to be seen as a medical procedure, midwives delivered babies at home. Today all midwives must be trained and licensed, and many midwives first get their nursing degree before specializing in pregnancy and childbirth.

Answers to
CONNECTING SCHOOL TO CAREER

1. **Possible response:** May feel more comfortable or less "medical" than with a doctor.

2. Instructional videos; computer programs; posters; booklets; models.

Applying What You've Learned

Ask: What kind of person would be successful and happy as a nurse-midwife? Discuss interests, aptitudes, and personal characteristics. How might the job affect the nurse-midwife's family life?

CAREER OPPORTUNITIES

Nurse-Midwife

A CONVERSATION WITH ALICE QUINLAN

How did you become interested in becoming a nurse-midwife? What could be more wonderful than being part of the most miraculous event in life? I wanted to help pregnant women enjoy that experience in the most comfortable way possible.

What are the tasks and responsibilities of a nurse-midwife? We do prenatal checkups, counseling, and teaching. Of course, we help deliver babies. As long as the pregnancy is normal, we can handle everything.

What is the work environment like? Checkups take place in the office. I teach childbirth classes at the hospital and a local school. When it's time for a delivery, I work in the birthing rooms.

What are the working hours like? Checkups are usually during the day, but the classes are at night. Deliveries happen at any time—but it seems that babies always come at night!

What aptitudes are needed to be a nurse-midwife? Most important is to be calm and reassuring. Pregnancy and birth are natural processes, but people often become worried or concerned. We just try to help them get over that. You need to be a good communicator to be able to do that.

Career Facts

NURSE-MIDWIFE

Education and Training. Nurse-midwives need a bachelor's degree in nursing and then up to two more years of training to be a midwife.

Career Outlook. The outlook for nurse-midwives is good.

CONNECTING SCHOOL TO CAREER

1. **Thinking Skills.** Why might expectant parents want to use a nurse-midwife rather than a doctor?
2. **Technology.** What kinds of visual aids could a nurse-midwife use in teaching childbirth classes?

204 UNIT 2: Pregnancy and Childbirth

Building Career Skills

Interpersonal Skills. Have students identify the specific interpersonal skills a nurse-midwife might need in each situation.
• Team teach a childbirth class.
• Discuss a pregnant woman's worries with her.

• Give a pregnant woman a checkup with the future father present.
• Give a presentation to colleagues at a conference.
• Negotiate for classroom space and time with a hospital administrator.

SECTION 6-3

Childbirth Choices

When Ashley and Phil looked at the birthing room at the local hospital, they were thrilled. The room was large with comfortable furniture, lamps, and even a stereo. At the same time, they knew that the nursing staff was nearby, ready to help in an emergency. This, they agreed, was where they would have their baby.

KEY TERMS

alternative birth center
delivery
labor
lay midwife
nurse-midwife
postpartum
prepared childbirth

OBJECTIVES:

- Discuss the childbirth choices available to most parents.
- Describe how parents can prepare for childbirth.

What Is Prepared Childbirth?

Prepared childbirth is a method of giving birth in which pain is reduced through the elimination of fear and the use of special conditioning exercises. Though a woman knows instinctively how to give birth, most women find childbirth education classes helpful in preparing them for this event. There are

CHAPTER 6: Preparing for Birth **205**

Observing & Participating

The Bradley and Lamaze methods are the most popular preparation methods for childbirth. You can contact the American Academy of Husband-Coached Childbirth and Lamaze, International for information. They also refer callers to local childbirth instructors. Ask students to read the information or interview an instructor to compare and contrast the two methods. After discussing the two methods as a class, ask students which method they favor and why.

SECTION 6-3

Childbirth Choices

(pages 205-209)

SECTION 6-3 RESOURCES

Teacher Resource Guide
- Lesson Plan Organizer, p. 50
- Section 6-3 Quiz, p. 126

Student Motivation Kit
- Observations and Case Studies (case study), p. 103
- Reteaching Activity, p. 24
- Enrichment, p. 21
- Teen Parenting Skills, pp. 49-50

Student Workbook
- Study Guide, pp. 53-57
- It's Up to You, pp. 61-62

Effective Instruction CD-ROM

FOCUS

MOTIVATOR

Ask students if they have ever undertaken a new and difficult task. Ask volunteers to describe the experience. How did they feel facing that task alone? How would they have felt if they had had someone to help and support them? Compare the situation to that of a woman entering labor.

VOCABULARY ACTIVITY

Have students look up the words *midwife, postpartum,* and *prepared* in the dictionary. What prefixes and roots are they composed of? What do these prefixes and roots mean? What other words do students know that use them?

COMPREHENSION CHECK

1. Why do most women find childbirth classes helpful? (*Prepares them for what they will experience.*)
2. What usually takes place in childbirth education classes? (*Learning skills to cope with labor.*)
3. What is the difference between an obstetrician and a family doctor? (*Obstetrician specializes in prenatal care, childbirth.*)

ACTIVITIES

Critical Thinking Activity

Analyzing. What qualities do you think a woman looks for in a childbirth partner? Why? Why might a pregnant woman choose someone other than the baby's father? **L1**

Research Activity

Have students research what a coach does during labor. How does the coach help a laboring woman physically? emotionally? What kind of information does the coach provide? Have students organize and present their findings. **L3**

---

many different types of classes, including Bradley and Lamaze methods. In recent years, however, there has been a blending of these styles, so that most classes offer similar information.

In prepared childbirth, class members learn what happens during **labor**—the process by which the baby gradually moves out of the uterus and into the vagina to be born—and **delivery**—the birth itself. Class members see films of childbirth and receive reading material. Typically, they also tour the maternity area of the hospital. Much of the time is spent learning skills to cope with the discomforts of labor, such as relaxation techniques and patterned breathing.

Joining the pregnant woman in these classes is the father or someone else she chooses to serve as a partner or coach. The mother depends on the coach for emotional support and help when preparing for and going through labor and delivery.

Who Will Deliver the Baby?

Women can choose from among many different professionals to deliver the baby:

- **Obstetricians.** These doctors specialize in prenatal and postnatal care of the mother and baby. They are qualified to handle any emergencies or special situations that may arise.
- **Family doctors.** Some general-practice doctors also deliver babies and provide prenatal and postnatal care. If complications arise during pregnancy or delivery, a family doctor may need to call in an obstetrician.

- **Licensed midwives.** The are two types of licensed midwives, each with different education. A certified **nurse-midwife** is a registered nurse with advanced training in normal pregnancy and birth. Nurse-midwives must pass a special licensing exam before they can practice. A **lay midwife** has special training in the care of pregnant women and normal deliveries but does not have a nursing degree. Lay midwives must also pass a special exam.

Since most babies are delivered by doctors, that word will be used in this text. Remember, though, that parents have other options to choose from.

How do parents choose a doctor? They can get recommendations from their family doctor, the county medical society, or a local hospital. They can also ask friends to recommend the person they used. Some health insurance plans limit who the parents can use. Parents should find out if there are such limits before beginning their search.

What is the coach's role in prepared childbirth?

VISUAL LEARNING | Using the Photograph

Possible response: To help prepare for birth and at delivery with support, relaxation, and breathing.

LEARNING STYLES

Kinesthetic

Ask students to read childbirth preparation publications or interview childbirth educators to learn about and practice breathing and physical exercises taught to pregnant women and their coaches. What is the purpose of each kind of exercise? What are the different types of breathing taught? When are they used-during pregnancy or labor? What purpose does each one serve? Have volunteers demonstrate the exercises to the rest of the class and explain their uses.

Once the parents have a list of possible people, they should visit and talk with each one they are considering. They will want to be sure the person they choose is well qualified, makes them feel comfortable, and can answer their questions clearly.

The parents should find out how emergency calls will be handled at night and on weekends. Another consideration is which hospital or medical center the doctor is affiliated with. The parents should find out what programs and facilities that hospital has. They will also want to know whether the doctor has the same ideas about delivery procedures they do.

Although the woman should get medical care as soon as she is pregnant, she may not be ready to decide about the delivery at that time. There is no reason she cannot switch to a different doctor during pregnancy. The sooner a final decision is made, however, the better prepared both the parents and the doctor will be.

Where Will the Baby Be Born?

Until this century, almost all babies were born at home. Today, most births occur in hospitals. There, sanitary conditions, trained personnel, and special equipment make birth as safe as possible.

Many hospitals offer classes that prepare expectant parents for labor and delivery. *Why would this help them?*

Hospitals now offer a variety of services to meet the needs and preferences of expectant mothers and their families. These services, often referred to as family-centered maternity care, include the following:

- Classes help the parents prepare for delivery and for caring for an infant.
- Special programs help young children get ready for having a baby brother or sister.
- Programs encourage fathers and other family members to help the mother through labor and delivery.
- Birthing rooms provide a comfortable atmosphere for labor and birth. Medical equipment is kept out of sight but is ready for use at a moment's notice.

CHAPTER 6: Preparing for Birth **207**

COMPREHENSION CHECK

1. What is the LDRP concept? (*Arrangement in which labor, delivery, recovery, and postpartum time all take place in same room.*)
2. What is the postpartum period? (*Period after birth of baby.*)

ACTIVITIES

Discussion Activity

What options do expectant parents have in choosing a birth setting? Why is the choice of setting important? What role does insurance coverage have in the decision? **L1**

Critical Thinking Activity

Making Inferences. Why do alternative birth centers accept only low-risk mothers? What conditions might disqualify a woman from using such a facility? (*Age; existing medical conditions, like diabetes; genetic problems, like Down Syndrome, Tay-Sachs, or hemophilia; drug use.*) **L2**

Critical Thinking Activity

Comparing and Contrasting. How is giving birth in an alternative birth center similar and different from doing so at home? **L2**

- Options allow women to choose the position they prefer for labor and delivery. Instead of lying flat, a woman may walk, rock in a chair, lie on her side, sit propped up, or even shower or soak in a tub. Many women find that these positions are more comfortable and make labor easier.
- Special steps may be taken to make the birth pleasant. For example, lights in the delivery room may be dimmed so the baby can open eyes without discomfort. Music can create a pleasant atmosphere.
- Plans allow the mother and her baby to stay together for all or most of the hospital stay, instead of staying in separate rooms.

Some hospitals offer what is called the LDRP concept. In this special unit, the woman labors, delivers, recovers, and spends her **postpartum** stay all in the same room. (Postpartum is the time after the baby is born.) The baby stays with the mother; often the father can stay, too.

Expectant parents should take time to explore the various services offered by local hospitals. Many hospitals offer tours of their maternity area. After gathering information, the couple should discuss which services suit their needs.

Some couples choose not to use a hospital but go to an **alternative birth center**. This facility, separate from any hospital, has homelike rooms for giving birth. These centers emphasize prepared childbirth and usually offer the kinds of services that are part of family-centered maternity care. Usually licensed midwives handle births at these centers. Most alternative birth centers accept only mothers who have a low risk for complicated deliveries. A hospital is usually nearby, though, and mother and baby can be moved there if needed.

After learning about the alternatives, a couple has to make its own decision about what childbirth method they prefer. **What factors might they consider?**

Family-centered maternity care, whether at a hospital or an alternative birth center, usually costs less than traditional hospital maternity care. The time spent at the facility is usually shorter. If there are no complications, parents usually leave the hospital or birth center within 24 hours of delivery, compared with a two- to three-day stay for traditional births.

Whatever choice is made, safety for both the mother and the baby is the main concern. Couples should discuss the benefits and drawbacks of each type of delivery option with their doctor and then make their decision.

Delivery at home has gained popularity during recent years. The family that chooses this approach must carefully weigh the benefits and risks. This option is generally possible only for women with uncomplicated pregnancies. Statistics show that at-home births double the risk of newborn deaths. If any problems occur, emergency medical personnel should be contacted immediately.

SECTION 6-3 REVIEW

✔ Check Your Understanding

1. What is prepared childbirth?
2. Define *labor* and *delivery*?
3. What are the differences between an obstetrician and a nurse-midwife?
4. Why is it good to choose a doctor as early as possible in a pregnancy?
5. What are some of the services offered as part of family-centered maternity care?
6. What kind of health-care professional usually attends births at an alternative birth center?
7. How do family-centered maternity care and traditional childbirth compare in cost?

Putting Knowledge Into Practice

1. **Drawing Conclusions.** How can childbirth education classes reduce the fear of childbirth?
2. **Analyzing.** What are the advantages of family-centered maternity care? Of traditional childbirth?
3. **Observing and Participating.** Practice taking long, deep breaths. Does breathing in this way change the way you feel? How? Do you think this effect would help a woman in labor?

CHAPTER 6: Preparing for Birth **209**

ASSESS

CHECKING COMPREHENSION

Have students answer the Check Your Understanding questions. Answers appear at the bottom of this page.

EVALUATION

Give students the Section 6-3 Quiz in the *Teacher Resource Guide*.

RETEACHING

1. Assign Reteaching Activities, page 24.
2. Have students fill in two charts: (1) *Delivering the Baby* with columns "Health Professional"; "Services Provided"; and "Reasons for Choice." (2) *Delivery Options*, with columns "Place," "Advantages," and "Disadvantages."

ENRICHMENT

Have students investigate the Leboyer method of prepared childbirth. How does it compare to more common practices?

EXTENSION

Tell students to research alternative birth centers. What led to their creation? Who uses them?

CLOSE

Ask: Which childbirth option do you think you would choose. Why?

ANSWERS TO SECTION 6-3 REVIEW

1. Reducing pain by eliminating fear and using special exercises.
2. *Labor*: baby preparing for birth. *Delivery*: birth.
3. *Obstetrician*: Doctor who performs prenatal care and delivery. *Nurse-midwife*: Nurse who performs prenatal care and uncomplicated deliveries.
4. Parents and doctor can become familiar. Mother can get needed care.
5. Childbirth and parenting classes; sibling programs; family participation; maternal choice of position; special procedures as needed; birth rooms; keeping mother and baby together; LDRP.
6. Licensed midwives.
7. Family-centered care costs less.

Ask: Why do many parents consider the car safety seat and the crib the two most important pieces of baby equipment?

Critical Thinking Activity

Making Judgments. Point out that automobile accidents are the leading cause of death for children 14 and under. Over half the children who died in car accidents were not using restraints. Discuss why some people allow children to ride without being strapped in. What should parents do if their baby or young child was being picked up by someone who did not have appropriate safety restraints? **L2**

Writing Activity

Have students brainstorm other characteristics, besides safety, that make car seats desirable. **L2**

Teamwork Activity

Have students develop a list of ideas for entertaining an infant or young child who is in a car seat during a long trip. **L1**

Parenting With Care

Checking Baby Equipment for Safety

Parents need a car safety seat as soon as the baby is born if they will drive the baby home from the hospital.

Some parents don't obtain a crib until several weeks or even months after the baby is born. Whether this equipment is borrowed or bought, purchased second-hand or new, it should be checked for safety.

Car Seats

Regular adult seat belts simply don't keep children securely and safely in a car's seat. Laws require that young children sit in a special seat that ensures their safety in a moving vehicle. There are two kinds of car seats:

- **Rear-facing safety seats.** These seats, also called infant seats, are meant for young babies up to 20 pounds (9.1 kg) or 26 inches (66 cm) long. The seat is placed in the center of the car's back seat, with the baby facing backwards.
- **Forward-facing safety seats.** These seats are meant for children from 20 pounds (9.1 kg) to 40 pounds (18.2 kg). Some of these seats can be turned around and used as rear-facing seats for infants.

Both types of seats use straps to keep the child securely in the seat. Both also have to be correctly connected to the car. Car seats must meet safety standards set by the federal government. New cars and safety seats have a matching system of buckles. This system allows the child car seat to buckle into straps on both sides and on the top. Children of all ages are safest in the back seat.

Crib

When choosing a crib, parents should consider both safety and comfort:

- **Slat width.** The government requires that the slats on the crib cannot be wider than 2⅜ inches (6.0 cm) apart.
- **Post height.** The four posts in the corners cannot be higher than ¹⁄₁₆ inch (0.16 cm) above the sides.

210 UNIT 2: Pregnancy and Childbirth

RESOURCES ON BABY EQUIPMENT AND SUPPLIES

Shopping for baby furniture, clothes, and toys for the first time can be an exciting adventure. It can be difficult to wade through the advertising claims and stay abreast of the facts about products. Every year thousands of infants and young children are injured while using unsafe products. To learn about product safety, contact the Consumer Product Safety Commission, the agency that develops and enforces federal safety standards at: U.S. Consumer Product Safety Commission, Washington, DC 20207 or www.cpsc.gov

- **Safe decorations.** Don't use a crib with decorations cut out of the panels on either end, or a crib painted with paint that contains lead.
- **Safe edges.** The top edge of the sides should be covered with plastic because the baby might chew on them. There should be no sharp edges or rough bolts.
- **Adjustable sides.** Cribs with adjustable sides, make it easier to reach down and pick up the baby. These should be checked to make sure that they cannot slide down too easily by accident.
- **Mattress.** The mattress should fit snugly into the crib, with no space around it. The mattress and springs should be firm, not soft, to prevent suffocation.
- **Bedding.** Only use fitted sheets that fit securely around the mattress. Sheets that have shrunk could pop off and become a safety hazard.

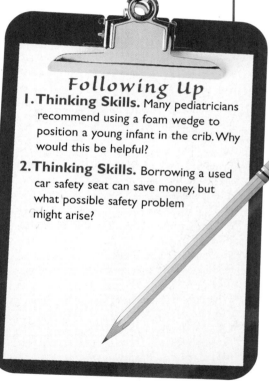

Following Up

1. **Thinking Skills.** Many pediatricians recommend using a foam wedge to position a young infant in the crib. Why would this be helpful?

2. **Thinking Skills.** Borrowing a used car safety seat can save money, but what possible safety problem might arise?

Critical Thinking Activity

Applying Standards. How can a parent who is shopping for used furniture and equipment be sure that it meets current government safety requirements? **L2**

Teamwork Activity

Have small groups design a bedroom that will be shared by an infant and a four-year-old. What needs have to be met for each of the children? What hazards have to be avoided for each? **L1**

CLOSE

1. Have students create a poster that uses callouts to highlight the safety features of a car safety seat or a crib.
2. **Extension.** Ask students to investigate the use and popularity of backyard play equipment. What do parents think of them? What do pediatricians think? Have students conduct interviews and research parent publications and on-line sources.

Answers to Following Up
1. *Possible response:* To prevent possibility of suffocation or SIDS.
2. *Possible response:* It may not meet latest safety standards.

CHECKING COMPREHENSION

Use the Summary and the Reviewing the Facts questions to help students go over the most important ideas in Chapter 6. Encourage students to ask questions and add details.

CHAPTER 6 REVIEW

Answers to Reviewing the Facts

1. She should see a doctor: first, to be sure; second, to begin prenatal care.
2. To provide a convenient and relatively simple method for planning a nutritious diet.
3. Typically 24 to 30 pounds.
4. *Possible response:* Plan for child care; tell siblings; choose a pediatrician; obtain needed supplies and equipment; make a budget.
5. *Breast-feeding:* Best nutrition; inexpensive; creates a bond between mother and child; convenient. *Bottle-feeding:* Allows others to feed; convenient. *Answers should be supported.*
6. Estimate income; estimate expenses; make a plan, possibly reducing expenses.
7. Relaxation; breathing.
8. Obstetrician; family doctor; licensed midwife (*nurse-midwife, lay midwife*).
9. Not available to women at risk for complicated births because these settings are not equipped for major emergencies.

CHAPTER 6
REVIEW &

Summary

✔ A woman should see a doctor once she thinks she is pregnant and have regular checkups during the pregnancy. (Section 6-1)
✔ Good nutrition helps both the developing baby and the mother. (Section 6-1)
✔ Expectant parents should prepare for the birth of a child. (Section 6-2)
✔ Prepared childbirth helps expectant parents get ready for labor and delivery. (Section 6-3)
✔ Expectant parents must choose who will help deliver the baby and in what setting. (Section 6-3)

Reviewing the Facts

1. What should a woman do if she notices one of the early signs of pregnancy? Why? (Section 6-1)
2. What is the purpose of the Food Guide Pyramid? (Section 6-1)
3. How much weight does a woman usually gain when pregnant? (Section 6-1)
4. In what ways should expectant parents prepare for the birth of a child? (Section 6-2)
5. Do you think you would choose breast-feeding or bottle-feeding? Why? (Section 6-2)
6. What are the steps in making a budget? (Section 6-2)
7. What methods of reducing pain are taught in childbirth education classes? (Section 6-3)

8. What three kinds of health professionals can assist at birth? (Section 6-3)
9. Are alternative birthing centers and home births available to all pregnant women? Why or why not? (Section 6-3)

Thinking Critically

1. **Analyzing.** How do you think a woman's emotional responses to pregnancy might affect how she feels physically—and the other way around?
2. **Making Inferences.** Suppose that a woman was at risk for complications in childbirth. Who would be the best health care professional to use? What setting would be best?

Taking Action

1. **Eating Well.** On a sheet of paper or an index card, write two snacks for a pregnant woman to eat, including all ingredients. Hand your paper or card to a classmate. Ask them to comment on the snacks in terms of nutrition and taste. Explain why you would or wouldn't recommend that a pregnant woman eat the snacks. (*Management*)

CONNECTIONS

2. Helping Out. A friend who moved to another town has written to say that she thinks she is pregnant but doesn't know for sure. Write a letter advising her what to do. *(Leadership)*

 Cross-Curricular Connections

1. Math. A new crib may cost from $150 to $500 and a mattress from $25 to $75. Sheets and blankets might add another $50 to $70. What is the range of the total cost of bedding? How much could be saved if expectant parents could buy these goods secondhand for half the cost?

2. Language Arts. Imagine the feelings of a three- to six-year-old whose mother has left home for the hospital and returns two or three days later with a new baby. Write a narrative of this from the child's perspective.

 Workplace Connections

1. Resources. A company offers health insurance to all its workers. This insurance adds 7 percent to payroll costs of $2 million. How much money does that represent? If the insurance cost rose to 8 percent, how much more would the employer pay for this insurance?

2. Interpersonal Skills. Suppose you are the instructor of a childbirth education class. What would you say to expectant parents on the first day of the class to ease their anxieties? Write a short talk that you would give.

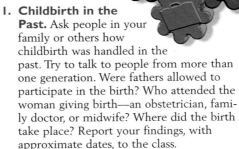 **Family and Community Connections**

1. Childbirth in the Past. Ask people in your family or others how childbirth was handled in the past. Try to talk to people from more than one generation. Were fathers allowed to participate in the birth? Who attended the woman giving birth—an obstetrician, family doctor, or midwife? Where did the birth take place? Report your findings, with approximate dates, to the class.

 Technology Connections

1. Blood Types. Research information on the Rh factor. What technology is used to test for the Rh factor? How are problems treated? Write a report with your findings.

2. Internet. Search the Internet to find the current safety requirements and recommendations for car seats or cribs. Report your findings to the class.

EVALUATION

1. Use the reproducible Chapter 6 Test in the *Teacher Resource Guide,* or create your own test using the **Exam**View® Test Generator.

2. For an alternative assessment, assign the Chapter 6 activity in the *Authentic Assessment* section of the *Teacher Resource Guide.*

ENRICHMENT

Assign students either of the two enrichment activities in the *Enrichment Activities* booklet in the *Student Motivation Kit.*

EXTENSION

Arrange a class visit by a professional such as an obstetrician, a family doctor, a nurse-midwife, a lay midwife, or a labor and delivery nurse. Ask the visitors to share their own experiences helping families with childbirth and to express their opinions about the importance of preparation during pregnancy.

CLOSE

Ask the class to create a web diagram showing the different ways that expectant parents must prepare for a baby.

Answers to Connections

Math
$225-$645; $112.50-322.50

Workplace
$140,000; $160,000

CHAPTER 7 RESOURCES

Teacher Resource Guide
• Chapter 7 Test, p. 134
• Authentic Assessment, p. 269
Student Motivation Kit
• Observ. & Case Studies
  (observation), pp. 39-40
• Teen Parenting Skills, pp. 59-60
Transparency Package
• CT-21 to CT-23
Effective Instruction CD-ROM

CHAPTER 7　OVERVIEW

In **Section 7-1**, students learn about the three stages of labor; vaginal and cesarean deliveries; and the characteristics of newborns.

Section 7-2 explains the evaluation and care of newborns; bonding between parents and infants; and care given mother and child during the hospital stay.

Section 7-3 discusses the reflexes, needs, and temperament of babies and the responsibilities and needs of parents.

CHAPTER 7　OBJECTIVES

After completing Chapter 7, students will be able to:

• Explain the three stages of labor.
• Summarize the hospital procedures and care mother and baby need after birth.
• Describe how to meet the needs of a newborn.

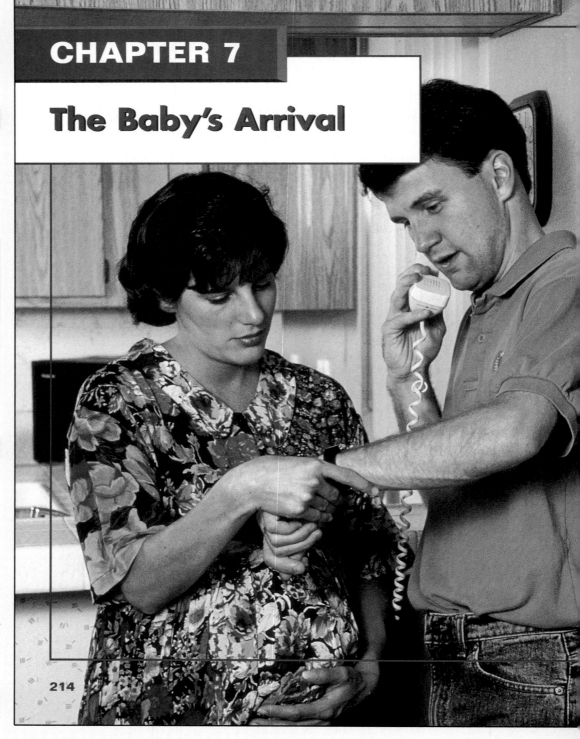

CHAPTER 7

The Baby's Arrival

214

RESOURCES TO EXPLORE

Parent Support. After the initial euphoria of birth passes, new parents experience many doubts and worries about the baby's health and their own ability to parent. All new parents benefit from ongoing support, help, and advice, but family and friends are not always available. Through classes and support groups, local organizations provide the encouragement and mentoring new parents need. Internet searches can help identify both local and online support groups, including ones for parents of children with special needs.

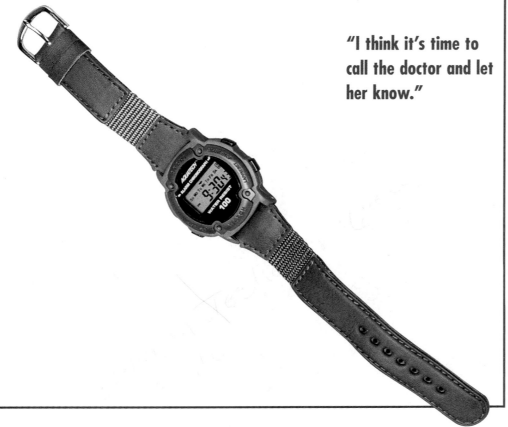

As Christine walked around the living room, she suddenly stopped. "Wow. That's a strong one," she said.

As Ed checked his stopwatch, he reminded his wife. "OK, remember your breathing. Long, deep breaths." Then he demonstrated. Christine followed his cue and did her breathing. When the contraction passed, she told him that.

"Well," said Ed, "they're 10 minutes apart and lasting about a minute."

Christine said, "This has been going on for an hour now, hasn't it?" When Ed nodded, she said "I think it's time to call the doctor and let her know. I think this is it for real!"

"I think it's time to call the doctor and let her know."

- Display items that relate to newborn babies, such as a baby bottle, a pacifier, a diaper, a grocery shopping bill, and a magazine for parents. Show one item at a time and discuss how it is used by the baby or the parent.
- Have students look at the photographs on these pages. **Ask:** What can expectant parents do to prepare for labor and delivery? How can that preparation help? If the class has any mothers, ask them how prepared they were for the experience of giving birth. What might they have done differently to prepare, if they had a chance to do it over again?

USING THE SCENARIO **Ask:** How do expectant parents feel at the start of labor? How are they likely to react? What can the mother, coach, and other family members do to stay calm and pass the time?

KEY TO ABILITY LEVELS Each section gives skill-building activities. Each activity has been labeled for use with students of various learning styles and abilities.

L1 Level 1 activities are basic activities and should be within the range of all students.

L2 Level 2 activities are average activities and should be within the range of average and above average students.

L3 Level 3 activities are challenging activities designed for the ability range of above average students.

SECTION 7-1 RESOURCES

Teacher Resource Guide
- Lesson Plan Organizer, p. 51
- Section 7-1 Quiz, p. 131

Student Motivation Kit
- Observations & Case Studies (case study), p. 104
- Reteaching Activity, p. 25
- Enrichment, p. 22

Student Workbook
- Study Guide, pp. 63-66
- Events of Labor and Birth, p. 67

Transparency Package
- CT-21 to CT-22

Effective Instruction CD-ROM

FOCUS

MOTIVATOR

Write the word *childbirth* on the chalkboard, and ask each student to write the first five words that come to mind. Compare response lists. What positive responses were given? What negative responses? What similarities and differences were there among the responses?

VOCABULARY ACTIVITY

Before students read the section, preteach the pronunciation and meaning of the Key Terms. Discuss the verb *contract* and ask students what contracts during a contraction. Analyze how all muscles work by contracting and expanding or extending.

Labor and Birth

In their ninth month, many women feel as though their pregnancy will never end. Then in just a day or so, that all changes. Giving birth is a powerful physical and emotional experience. When it is over and they are holding their babies, most women think that it is a wonderful one too.

KEY TERMS

cervix
cesarean birth
contractions
dilates
fontanels
forceps

OBJECTIVES:

- Recognize signs that labor may have begun.
- Outline the three stages of labor.
- Describe a baby's appearance at birth.

The Beginning of Labor

During the last weeks of pregnancy, women become anxious for the baby to be born. Time seems to pass slowly as they wait for labor to begin. In this time, they feel what is called "lightening." This occurs when the baby settles deep into the mother's pelvis, preparing for his or her journey into the world. When the baby moves down, the pressure on the woman's upper abdomen is

216 UNIT 2: Pregnancy and Childbirth

Observing & Participating

Years ago, women used an upright position to deliver babies. Some stood, others squatted, and some used a birth stool. For a while, it was popular to have women lie on their backs in bed during delivery. Then women began giving birth with their knees drawn up. Delivery tables with stirrups use this position. Have a small group of students research the advantages and disadvantages of different birth positions.

reduced. With a first pregnancy, lightening may occur some days or weeks before labor. A woman who has already had a baby may experience this change just before labor begins.

Early Signs of Labor

There are some definite signals that the baby is coming. One is commonly called "show" or "bloody show"; it may also be referred to as losing the mucus plug. Throughout the pregnancy, a plug of mucus seals the **cervix** (SIR-viks), the lower part of the uterus. This mucus helps prevent bacteria from moving up the vagina into the uterus where it might cause an infection. Before birth, this mucus begins to liquefy. The woman may notice a few drops of blood or a slightly pinkish vaginal staining. This bloody show may come as early as a few days before labor begins.

In some women, the onset of labor is signaled by a trickle—or even a gush—of warm fluid from the vagina. This indicates that the membrane holding the amniotic fluid surrounding the baby has broken. In most women, this membrane does not rupture until she is at the hospital or birthing center, in active labor.

When the membrane breaks, the woman should note the time, the amount of fluid, and the color and odor of the fluid. She should call her doctor or midwife and report this information. Once the membrane has broken, the doctor may want to deliver the baby within 24 to 48 hours to protect the baby from infection.

The clear sign that labor has begun is **contractions**, the tightening and releasing of the muscle of the uterus. When the uterus contracts, it gets shorter and harder—like any other muscle. Bend an arm toward your shoulder while making a tight fist. Feel the muscle in your upper arm become thick and hard. Now, slowly relax and lower your forearm. Feel the muscle stretch and soften. The uterine muscle works the same way. With each contraction of labor, it shortens and gets harder, holds the hardness for a short time, and then relaxes and rests for a few minutes.

After the amniotic sac has broken, the doctor may want to make sure the baby is born within 24 or 48 hours. *Why?*

COMPREHENSION CHECK

1. What is lightening? (*The settling of the fetus into the pelvis, relieving the pressure on the woman's upper abdomen.*)
2. Name three early signs of labor. (*Bloody show, breaking of membrane, contractions.*)

ACTIVITIES

Building Study Skills

Tell students to use the questions in the captions and in the Check Your Understanding as study questions. Suggest that they read them over before beginning the section and then read with the questions in mind. They can look for the answers as they read and write them down. **L1**

Critical Thinking Activity

Drawing Conclusions. Have students share their ideas about communication between the pregnant woman and her health care provider. Why is it important for the woman to contact her health care provider when she recognizes a pattern in her contractions? **L1**

VISUAL LEARNING	Using the Photograph

Answer: To prevent an infection from developing, which could harm the baby.

LEARNING STYLES	Interpersonal

Have pairs of students participate in "duologues," impromptu dialogues in which they take the roles of two of the people involved in the birth of a child. For example, students could play mother and coach; coach and doctor; mother and midwife; pediatric nurse and father. Encourage students to explore the questions, feelings, and points of view of the different people. Then discuss what the "duologues" revealed. What concerns do the expectant parents bring to the situation? What issues are health workers most interested in?

COMPREHENSION CHECK

1. What happens during each stage of labor? (*First: cervix opens. Second: birth. Third: delivery of placenta.*)
2. Which stage is the longest? (*First.*)

ACTIVITIES

Critical Thinking Activity

Analyzing. Why do medical personnel need to know the length and frequency of the contractions when giving advice about going to the hospital? **L1**

Graphing Skills

Ask students to create double bar graphs to compare and contrast the length of each stage of labor in a first and subsequent birth. **L1**

VISUAL LEARNING | **Using the Photograph**
Tell students that false labor is sometimes called "Braxton-Hicks contractions." Childbirth experts say the best test to distinguish false from true labor is for the woman to walk around. If contractions end, it is false labor. If they continue, it is true labor.

Are the contractions painful? Many women who have given birth say they are painful but bearable. Because there is time between each contraction, the woman can rest and recover. After the baby is born and contractions end, there is no lingering pain.

False Labor

Some women feel what is called "false labor" hours or even days before they begin real labor. They begin to feel strong contractions and believe that labor may have begun. Doctors look for three signs to see if contractions are false labor:

- They are not regular or rhythmic.
- They do not become increasingly stronger.
- They end if the woman walks around.

When contractions follow a regular pattern and grow in intensity, a woman is having real labor. The woman or her coach should time the contractions.

It can be difficult to know just when it's time to go to the hospital or birthing center. The nurses at the doctor's office, hospital's maternity ward, or the birthing center can provide helpful guidance. The nurse will want to know how long the contractions are lasting, how frequently they are occurring, how the mother is feeling, and, perhaps, additional information.

Stages of Labor

Labor moves through three stages:

- In the first stage, contractions open the cervix.
- In the second stage, the baby is born.
- In the third stage, the placenta is expelled.

When contractions become strong, regular, and close together, it's time to leave for the hospital.

The diagram on pages 220-221 shows what takes place during these three stages.

How long does labor last? The duration varies greatly, depending on the mother and the baby. Women often find that labor is longer the first time they give birth than with later babies. For a first birth, the first stage may last from 6 to 18 hours. It may be 2 to 5 hours for a later child. The second stage is typically 1 to 2 hours for a first child but might last 15 to 30 minutes for a later child. The third stage, the shortest, can be anywhere from 10 to 30 minutes.

The First Stage

In the first stage of labor, contractions prepare the mother's body to give birth. Each time the uterus contracts, the muscles of the uterus pull up on the cervix, slowly thinning and opening it, as shown in the illustrations.

During the first stage, contractions get stronger, longer (lasting about 60 seconds), and closer together (5 to 6 minutes apart). The woman begins to turn inward, searching for the strength to deal with the sensations of labor. She becomes more serious and focused on the labor and needs increasing support from her coach.

Some women become withdrawn during labor as they concentrate on their breathing. Some express anger. **Ask:** How might these responses make the woman's coach feel if they're not expected? **L1**

HEALTH TIP

Coping with Labor

*T*hroughout the first stage, the mother should try to relax as much as possible, both between and during contractions. Fear and tension cause the muscles of the body to tighten, and tight muscles can slow labor down and make it more uncomfortable.

Prepared childbirth courses teach special breathing exercises mothers can use. These exercises encourage relaxation, distract the mother from the discomfort, and help the labor progress. Fathers who attended these classes can help their wives use the techniques.

Some women change positions to become more comfortable. Most mothers may safely assume any position they find helpful. Some feel that standing or walking helps labor progress.

Some women who find the first stage very long and difficult choose to use a medication supplied by the doctor. There are several medications to choose from. Their effects vary from changing the woman's perception of pain to completing numbing the area so that no sensations are felt. All these medications have risks as well as benefits, since they have some effect on the baby. Women should talk to their doctor during prenatal checkups about the pros and cons of different medications before choosing one.

FOLLOWING UP

1. How can childbirth classes help during labor?
2. How can fathers-to-be help during labor?
3. What disadvantages do pain medications have?

HEALTH TIP

One of the coach's most important tasks is to help the mother relax. Analyze how tension increases pain and how fear can add to tension. *Ask:* What could produce fear and tension in the laboring woman? What might she be afraid of?

Answers to
FOLLOWING UP

1. *Possible response:* Give women techniques to better cope with contractions.
2. *Possible response:* Help women to remember to use techniques; encourage them.
3. *Possible response:* Have effects on mother and child.

DID *You* **Know?**

Labor. Regular exercise during pregnancy tones and strengthens the muscles used during labor and lessens some of the discomforts. Less discomfort means less reliance on pain medication.

Management/Leadership Skills

Opinions differ about the use of anesthetics during labor and delivery. Some feel the process is easier if pain medication is used. Others feel birth is a natural process that should be handled in non-medical ways. Provide students with a list of medications used during labor and ask pairs to research one. Tell them to find out how the medicine works; its effect on the mother; its effect on the baby; under what conditions it is used; and when it is discouraged. Have the pairs report their findings and their opinion about the safety of that anesthetic.

COMPREHENSION CHECK

1. What is "effacement" of the cervix? (*Thinning to allow the baby to pass.*)
2. What is "crowning"? (*The appearance of the top of the baby's head at the opening of the birth canal.*)
3. Why doesn't the baby need the placenta after birth? (*Baby is able to breathe and eat after birth.*)

ACTIVITIES

Teamwork Activity

Have small groups review the stages of labor in a round-table format. After reading the material, give each group a large piece of paper. Have students pass the paper around the group, with each student writing down one fact. Continue passing the paper until no one remembers any more information. Then have the group review what is written, consulting their textbook to verify. They can add any additional information they forgot to include. **L1**

Critical Thinking Activity

Making Inferences. Ask students to explain why a baby in a breech position may have difficulty moving through the cervix and birth canal. Why does a birth attendant have to monitor the baby and the mother, repeatedly evaluating whether or not a vaginal delivery is safe? **L1**

The Stages of Labor

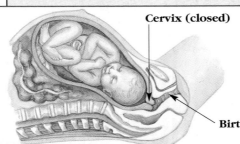

Before Labor Begins

Before labor begins, the cervix is its normal size and shape.

Cervix (closed)

Birth canal

First Stage of Labor

Contractions make the cervix **dilate**, or widen. The cervix also becomes thinner, changing from its usual thickness of about ¾ inch (19 mm) to become as thin as a sheet of paper. This thinning is called "effacement."

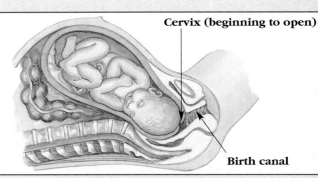

Cervix (beginning to open)

Birth canal

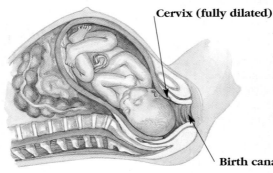

Cervix (fully dilated)

Transition

Transition completes the work of the first stage. The cervix becomes fully dilated to a size of 4 inches (10 cm) and the baby's head slips out of the uterus into the birth canal.

Birth canal

220 UNIT 2: Pregnancy and Childbirth

LEARNING STYLES

Mathematical

Ask students to create a flow chart showing the events that take place during labor and birth. Remind them that flow charts illustrate events in sequence. They should include facts about the mother and the baby. They need to find ways to distinguish events that affect the mother and those that affect the baby. Discuss whether to use illustrations (simple line drawings or pictures) on the flow chart. Remind them of the need to show variable lengths of time on their chart.

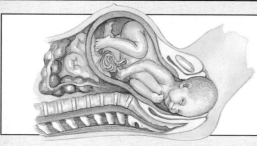

Second Stage of Labor: Crowning

First the top of the head appears at the opening of the birth canal.

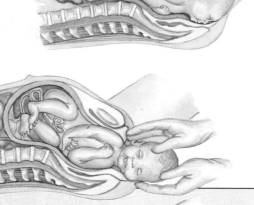

Second Stage of Labor: Head Emerges

The baby's head emerges first. The head has changed its shape to ease passage through the birth canal. It will later return to normal. After the head, the shoulders follow. The rest of the baby slips out easily.

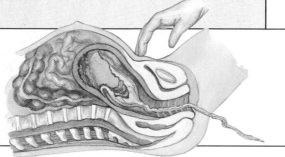

Third Stage of Labor

The woman gives birth to the placenta, no longer needed by the baby.

CHAPTER 7: The Baby's Arrival **221**

Explore how the following factors might affect labor:

- A coach is present throughout labor.
- Labor and birth take place at home.
- A nurse-midwife is the birth attendant.
- The laboring woman lives close to her parents.
- The parents have other children.

L2

Social Studies Activity

Have students research childbirth practices in other cultures. Where do women give birth? What kind of support and care do they get? From whom? What role do husbands play, if any? Have students create a chart comparing these different with those used in the United States. **L3**

VISUAL LEARNING	Using the Drawings

Discuss how the baby's shape and position conform to the shape and size of the uterus during labor. Why is this adaptation necessary?

ISSUES IN TEEN PARENTING

Many expectant fathers are eager to share the experience of childbirth. Others feel apprehensive, and teen fathers, especially, may feel hesitant. Prepared childbirth classes help a father gain confidence about participating or simply being present. Fathers who have taken part describe birth as a deeply moving and emotionally charged event. Fathers who coach know that they helped their partners through and played an active role in bringing their child into the world. Those who don't coach but do attend the birth still enjoy a special closeness to the baby and a feeling that they were part of the event.

COMPREHENSION CHECK

1. What is a "breech presentation"? (*Positioning of the baby with either the feet or the buttocks first.*)
2. What is "transition"? (*Stage of labor when the cervix becomes fully dilated.*)
3. What is relaxin, and how does it help the mother give birth? (*A hormone that makes ligaments connecting bones of the pelvis very stretchy. Makes it easier to open.*)
4. What is "cesarean birth"? (*Birth by a surgical procedure.*)

ACTIVITIES

Discussion Activity

Ask students to share their ideas about episiotomy. Why might a woman want or not want one? **L2**

Promoting Health Activity

Some people object to the use of forceps because of potential harm to the baby and mother. What dangers might be involved in using forceps? Tell them that rather than forceps some care providers use a vacuum extractor placed on the baby's head. Why might this technique be safer than forceps? **L1**

VISUAL LEARNING	Using the Photograph

Possible responses: Joy, relief, emotional exhaustion, exhilaration, togetherness.

As the cervix opens, the baby moves down into the lower pelvis, getting ready for birth. Most of the time, the baby is head down, but some babies enter the pelvis with their feet or buttocks first. These positions are called "breech presentations." Babies in these positions may have a difficult time moving through the mother's pelvis for birth. The doctor will decide whether a vaginal delivery is possible.

The first stage ends with a period called "transition," when the cervix becomes fully dilated. The contractions become very strong, last longer (up to 90 seconds), and come more frequently (2 to 3 minutes apart) than earlier. This is usually the most difficult part of labor to cope with. A woman needs her coach's support, by touching and offering loving words, at this time.

The Second Stage

The contractions of the second stage work to move the baby down through the pelvis and out of the vagina, or birth canal. This is an exciting time, as the woman's coach and the doctor encourage her by saying, "Push! Push!" It ends with the event for which the parents have been waiting—the birth of the baby.

How could a baby ever fit through what seems to be such a narrow space? The bones of the pelvis are joined together by ligaments, which are like rubber hands. At the time of delivery, these ligaments are very stretchy, as a result of the influence of a hormone called "relaxin." As a result, the bones of the pelvis stretch open as the baby passes through. The same hormone also makes the vagina very stretchy, so that the baby can safely pass through to be born.

The body of the unborn baby is well suited to this journey as well. The skull is soft and flexible so that the baby's head can become longer and narrower than normal. The skull consists of five separate bones. These bones can overlap each other to allow that baby's head to fit through the pelvis and vagina.

If the doctor decides that the fit between mother and baby is not adequate, he or she may widen the opening with a surgical cut called an "episiotomy." Although the procedure was done routinely in the past, many doctors and midwives now work with women to avoid it.

Women can give birth in a variety of positions. Many women use a position that is part sitting and part lying down, with

A baby's birth brings a great surge of emotion! *What specific feelings might be most common?*

ISSUES IN CHILDREN'S HEALTH	

After delivery, the umbilical cord is clamped in two places and cut between the clamps. The remaining stub later dries and falls off, leaving the belly button or navel. The timing of this procedure sometimes differs. The placenta contains 25 to 30 percent of a newborn's iron-rich blood, which flows to the infant through the umbilical cord after delivery. Since this iron can prevent anemia later on, some medical professionals do not clamp the cord until it stops pulsing. Others feel that too much blood can cause problems, so clamping is done immediately or very shortly after delivery.

their legs apart and their knees bent. Some women squat, sit in a birthing chair, lie on their side, or even kneel on their hands and knees. If a women is moved to a traditional delivery table, her legs may be supported by foot rests.

The doctor provides gentle support as the head is delivered. The head is followed by one shoulder, and then the other. Then the rest of the baby slips out into the world.

Sometimes a doctor uses specialized devices to help the baby emerge. **Forceps,** special surgical steel tongs, can be used to guide movement. With vacuum extraction, suction is applied to the baby's head during contractions. This helps the baby move through the birth canal.

The Third Stage

After the baby is born, the mother often experiences a period of rest. Then she may once again feel some contractions and an urge to push. These contractions usually cause very little discomfort. They help the placenta separate from the wall of the uterus. When the mother pushes and delivers the placenta, the birth process is complete.

Although this stage of labor is usually brief, it is important. If any parts of the placenta remain, bleeding, infection, and serious illness may result.

Cesarean Birth

Not all births progress through these three stages of labor. If complications arise during the pregnancy or during labor, it may be necessary to perform a **cesarean** (si-ZARE-ee-uhn) **birth.** A cesarean is the

Some newborns have hair, but others don't. *Why are the heads of newborns somewhat lopsided?*

delivery of a baby by making a surgical incision in the mother's abdomen. With some types of medication, the mother can remain awake during cesarean surgery to see her baby's delivery. The father or coach may also be present if the doctor allows.

During the pregnancy, couples may take a special class preparing them for a cesarean if such a birth seems likely. After the surgery, the mother and baby usually stay in the hospital for about three days. Women who have had cesareans may need up to six weeks to recover from birth since they are also getting over major surgery.

CHAPTER 7: The Baby's Arrival **223**

Critical Thinking Activity

Applying Concepts. Ask: How might a baby born through cesarean delivery look different from one born normally? **L1**

Teamwork Activity

Have small groups consider various reasons for cesarean deliveries. Under what circumstances is a cesarean likely to be planned? What circumstances might lead a doctor to perform a cesarean close to the time of delivery? **L2**

VISUAL LEARNING Using the Photograph
Answer: Because their shape has been changed by the pressure of the birth process.

DID You Know?

Monitoring Birth. **Fetal monitoring devices can be used during labor to continuously record the infant's heart rate and the contractions of the uterus. With this information, the medical staff can determine the degree of stress experienced by the fetus. Because it interferes with natural childbirth, some people feel that routine use is unnecessary. In high-risk births, however, fetal monitoring can be very effective in detecting problems.**

Parenting in Action

Have small groups generate lists of emotions parents might feel during the birth of their child. Then have them consider and discuss the emotions they have listed. Which emotions would be most likely to occur during each stage of labor? Why? Tell students to write down the emotions on the left side of a sheet of paper and the stages of labor and corresponding reasons on the right, next to the emotion. The answers should be the consensus of the group. Then ask groups to share their answer. What can the woman and her coach do to handle the negative emotions?

COMPREHENSION CHECK

1. What is the purpose of fontanels? (*Allow the bones of the skull to move together so the head can move through the birth canal.*)
2. How long does it take for a baby's permanent eye color to become established? (*Several months.*)

ACTIVITIES

Discussion Activity

Before reading this page, ask students what they imagine a newborn looks like. After reading the page, show them pictures of newborns and discuss how closely the description conforms to what they see. **L1**

Critical Thinking Activity

Organizing Information. Have students chart the changes that babies undergo as a result of birth. They can use a "Before and After" format. **L1**

Teamwork Activity

Have small groups examine several photographs of newborn babies and the same babies at one month. Have them try to match the photos and comment on how the babies' physical characteristics changed or remained the same after a month. Students may enjoy bringing in pictures of themselves as newborns and at a year and trying to match those as well. **L2**

The Newborn at Birth

The mother experiences amazing physical changes during labor and birth. So, too, does the baby. As a result, the baby is—for the first time—not completely dependent on the mother for life.

During its development in the uterus, the baby's lungs are collapsed. During delivery, they expand and fill with whatever amniotic fluid may have been in the baby's trachea. The pressure of being squeezed down the birth canal forces much of the fluid out. After emerging from the birth canal, the baby takes his or her first breath.

Usually, the newborn baby breathes naturally. If the baby needs help, the doctor or nurse-midwife may gently rub the baby's back to get the process started. Most of the fluid that remains in the airways or mouth is gently suctioned out.

Once the lungs have begun to take in oxygen, the baby's circulatory system changes. A valve in the heart closes and, over the next few days, becomes permanently sealed. Blood now circulates to and from the lungs, rather than bypassing the lungs as before.

The umbilical cord, through which the baby received oxygen and nourishment, is no longer needed. Within a few minutes of birth, the cord stops pulsing and begins to shrink. Health care workers clamp, tie, and cut off the cord, leaving a small stump.

How Does the Newborn Look?

What will our baby look like? When parents imagine their answers to this question, they usually picture a sturdy, smiling baby of about six months. Newborns look nothing like that.

The newborn's head is wobbly and large—about one-fourth the baby's length. The head may appear strangely lopsided or pointed because of the passage of the baby's head through the birth canal. With time, the head returns to normal.

You will recall that the bones of the skull are not yet fused together. The baby's head has two **fontanels** (FON-tuh-NELLS) open spaces where the bones have not yet joined. One of these "soft spots" is just above the baby's forehead, and the other is toward the back of the skull. These spaces allow the bones of the skull to move together during birth so that the head can fit through the birth canal. The bones come together to cover these spaces when the baby is between six and eighteen months old. In the meantime, the soft spots are protected by skin that is as tough as heavy canvas.

The face of a newborn may be swollen or puffy as a result of the birth process. The newborn typically has fat cheeks; a short, flat nose; and a receding chin. These fea-

LEARNING STYLES

Naturalistic

Have students consider labor, birth, and the newborn from the perspective of the coach. Tell them to brainstorm a list of impressions the coach would have, considering all of the senses, not simply sight. Instruct students to draw a five-pointed star and label the points *Hear, See, Touch, Smell, Taste.* Tell students to write the appropriate impressions in each part of the star. Under the star, have them write *Dominant Impression:* and a phrase or sentence stating the main idea the sensory words support.

tures make the baby's face well adapted for sucking, because the nose and chin are out of the way.

At birth, a baby's eyes are nearly adult-sized. They are usually dark grayish blue at birth. The baby's permanent eye color becomes apparent within several months.

It takes time for the baby's circulatory system to adjust to life outside the uterus. As a result, fingers and toes may be slightly cooler than the rest of their body for up to 24 hours. Wrapping the baby well and covering the head with a cap helps keep him or her warm and comfortable.

Some babies, particularly those born early, have fine, downy hair called "lanugo" over their forehead, back, and shoulders. This hair disappears as the baby grows.

While in the uterus, the baby is surrounded by warm amniotic fluid. To protect their skin from constant exposure to the fluid, babies are covered with a rich, creamy substance called "vernix." After the birth, most newborns have some vernix in the folds of their skin, particularly around their ears and neck and under their arms. It can be gently removed with warm water and a washcloth.

Many babies have tiny white bumps scattered over their nose and cheeks. These bumps are called "milia," or baby acne. They are simply plugged oil ducts, caused by stimulation from the mother's hormones, which remain in the baby's system for a short time after the delivery. The milia will disappear in a week or two.

SECTION 7-1 REVIEW

✔ Check Your Understanding

1. What are contractions? How do they feel to the woman?
2. Contrast real and false labor.
3. What is the cervix? How does it change during labor?
4. How do the bone structures of both mother and baby make birth easier?
5. Why is the third stage of labor important?
6. How does cesarean birth differ from normal birth?
7. What changes take place in the baby at birth?
8. Describe the appearance of a newborn.

Putting Knowledge Into Practice

1. **Making Inferences.** Write two paragraphs about the experience of birth from the baby's perspective.
2. **Sequencing.** Describe the stages of labor in a normal delivery.
3. **Observing and Participating.** Interview a father who was present at the birth of his baby. Ask what he did to help his wife and what the experience meant to him. Find out if he had other children whose births he did not see. How were the two experiences different? Report your findings to the class and discuss the comments of different fathers.

CHAPTER 7: The Baby's Arrival   **225**

ANSWERS TO SECTION 7-1 REVIEW

1. Tightening and relaxing of the uterus' muscles. Painful but bearable.
2. *False*—not regular or increasing in intensity; disappear when woman walks. *Real*—grow stronger and follow pattern.
3. Cervix is the base of the uterus. In first stage, it dilates and effaces.
4. Woman's pelvis becomes flexible and widens. Bones in baby's head overlap.
5. Bleeding, infection, and illness may occur if placenta remains.
6. It is a surgical procedure; requires longer hospital stay.
7. Lungs can breathe; valve closes in heart; umbilical cord no longer needed.
8. *See text on pages 224-225.*

The Postnatal Period

(pages 226-233)

SECTION 7-2

SECTION 7-2 RESOURCES

Teacher Resource Guide
- Lesson Plan Organizer, p. 52
- Section 7-2 Quiz, p. 132

Student Motivation Kit
- Reteaching Activity, p. 26
- Enrichment, p. 23
- Teen Parenting Skills, pp. 42-43, 61-62

Student Workbook
- Study Guide, pp. 63-66
- All You Need to Know About Neonatal Care, p. 68

Transparency Package
- CT-23 Babies at Birth

Effective Instruction CD-ROM

FOCUS

MOTIVATOR

Have students imagine what it must feel like for newborns to find themselves outside the dark, warm, confined space of the mother's uterus. Have each list five phrases expressing the newborn's reactions to the "outside world." Discuss the different ideas as a class.

VOCABULARY ACTIVITY

Explain to students that the Apgar scale was named after the American physician who invented it, Virginia Apgar (1909-1974). Then review what prefixes are and ask students to find the words on the list that have prefixes (*incubator, postnatal, premature*). Point out that *post* and *pre* are also antonyms.

The Postnatal Period

The moment of birth is the end of nine months of preparation—and a beginning. Soon the newborn and parents will go home to begin their new life together. First, however, the staff at the hospital or birthing center makes sure the new family gets off to a good start.

KEY TERMS

Apgar scale
bonding
colostrum
incubator
postnatal
premature
rooming-in

OBJECTIVES:

- Explain the purpose of common hospital procedures following a birth.
- Explain the special needs of a premature baby.
- Describe a mother's needs after having given birth.

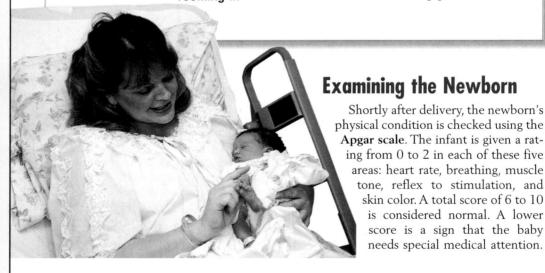

Examining the Newborn

Shortly after delivery, the newborn's physical condition is checked using the **Apgar scale**. The infant is given a rating from 0 to 2 in each of these five areas: heart rate, breathing, muscle tone, reflex to stimulation, and skin color. A total score of 6 to 10 is considered normal. A lower score is a sign that the baby needs special medical attention.

Observing & Participating

Invite a pediatric nurse to speak to the class about the procedures followed with newborns immediately after birth and during their stay in the hospital. Ask the nurse to explain the different tests, what they show, and how health care providers use them to determine how best to help the baby. What special care do newborns need that older babies might not? Have the class generate questions they would like answered. Ask the speaker to bring audiovisual materials if possible.

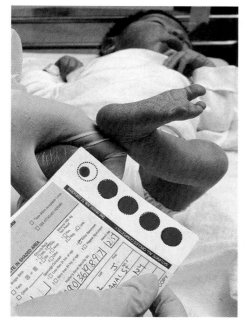

Usually, this evaluation is done one minute after birth and five minutes after birth. The baby is also given a brief examination to check for any conditions that might require special care. The baby is weighed, measured, and cleaned up.

Shortly after birth, steps are taken to identify the baby. A copy of the baby's footprint is made for public record. Two plastic bands giving the baby's family name are clamped to the baby's wrists or ankles and the mother's wrist. This prevents any confusion later.

What elements are checked in the Apgar exam?

The Apgar Scale

	SCORE		
	0	**1**	**2**
HEART RATE	Absent	Under 100	Over 100
BREATHING	Absent	Slow, irregular	Good, crying
MUSCLE TONE	Limp	Some movement of extremities	Active motion
RESPONSIVENESS (Baby's reaction when nose is irritated)	No response	Grimace	Cough or sneeze
COLOR	*Light-skinned child:* Blue or pale *Dark-skinned child:* Grayish or pale	*Light-skinned child:* Body pink, limbs blue *Dark-skinned child:* Strong body color, grayish limbs	*Light-skinned child:* Completely pink *Dark-skinned child:* Strong color with pink lips, palms, and soles

COMPREHENSION CHECK

1. What is a typical hospital stay after giving birth? (*Varies from 12 hours to three days.*)
2. Why might jaundice delay a newborn's release from the hospital? (*Untreated, it could damage the baby's nervous system.*)

ACTIVITIES

Writing Activity

Have students write their views on bonding. To help them, pose these questions: What conditions might postpone or prevent bonding? What might happen to a child who fails to bond with a parent or caregiver? What could be done to help children who were unable to bond as infants? **L1**

The Developing Brain

Crying and Comforting

Although some parents fear that responding quickly to their baby's cries may spoil him or her, researchers have found the opposite to be true. Children who are comforted quickly become calm more quickly. The baby's brain stops the body's stress response. More important, connections in the brain begin to form. Over time, babies can use these connections to calm themselves.

Later Tests

Newborns also have several other tests and medical procedures in their first few days of life. Within 60 minutes of delivery, an antiseptic is put into the baby's eyes to protect them from infection.

When they are born, babies are low in vitamin K. This vitamin is needed to help the blood clot, which puts a stop to any bleeding. Babies are given a shot with this vitamin shortly after birth.

Many hospitals administer a special hearing test. It measures whether the baby's ear echoes a light sound and can be done while the baby sleeps. Undiagnosed hearing problems cause intellectual and language delays.

Health care workers also take a blood sample from the baby. This blood is studied to see if the baby has PKU, sickle cell anemia, or some other conditions.

Bonding and Attachment

In most cases, there are no problems with the newborn, and the long-awaited moment occurs: the baby is given to the mother and father to hold. Most parents feel a deep—and memorable—thrill.

In recent years, researchers have studied the emotional needs of a newborn. They have emphasized the importance of **bonding,** or forming strong emotional ties between parent and child. Most facilities have changed their policies as a result of this research. Most now delay cutting the umbilical cord, cleaning the infant, and giving eyedrops to let parents and child begin bonding right away.

The baby may be placed in the mother's arms or abdomen to feel the mother's skin

and hear her familiar heartbeat and voice. The newborn instinctively focuses on the mother's face. Many mothers begin touching and talking to the baby.

If the baby will be breast-fed, the mother may begin nursing. While instinct helps a baby seek the nipple and suck, successful breast-feeding takes patience. A nurse or lactation specialist can provide advice. The mother's breasts supply the first breast milk, called **colostrum.** This is easy to digest and provides valuable antibodies that help protect the baby against diseases.

Some newborns have special needs that require immediate care by the hospital staff. New parents may miss the chance to bond with these children right away. Usually, though, the staff brings parents and baby together as soon as possible. Then they can begin their lifetime of love and caring.

The Hospital Stay

Birth is a momentous undertaking for both mother and baby. The newborn must adjust to a whole new world. The mother, too, needs time to adjust. In a matter of hours, her body has gone from pregnancy to labor and birth and back to being nonpregnant. Although she probably feels excited, she needs to rest and recuperate.

There are differences in the length of time mothers and babies generally stay in the hospital. In some facilities, a mother and baby who are both healthy may go home as soon as 12 hours after birth. In other hospitals, the average stay following birth is two or three days.

In the past, women and children stayed in the hospital up to four days for a normal delivery. Some critics say that insurance companies are forcing hospitals to release

---

ISSUES IN TEEN PARENTING

Discuss what teen parents can do to cope with the stresses of parenthood. **Ask:** How can support groups (whether parenting classes, parent-infant classes, or play groups) help parents avoid isolation and feel better about themselves? How do groups provide them with opportunities to discuss worries, feelings, and doubts that they may find somewhat embarrassing? Many hospitals and birthing centers sponsor parenting classes. Chat groups can be found on the Internet. Check the Website Postpartum Education for Parents (www.sbpep.org), or conduct a search for *postpartum education* sites.

Practicing Parenting

Strengthening Bonds

*B*onding with a newborn is important—but this is not the only time parents can, or should, bond with their child. Bonding remains important throughout a child's life. Here are some ideas for building strong bonds between parent and child:

♥ **Infants.** Keep the baby close to you and comforted. Take time to touch the baby; infants respond to touch. Pay attention to the baby's reactions to you and continue the actions that produce the reactions you want. If the baby is soothed by rocking, use rocking when he or she is upset. Finally, remember to play with the baby. Babies crave stimulation, especially from their parents.

♥ **Toddlers and preschoolers.** Although these children are older and more independent than infants, they still need a parent's attention. Continue using touch by giving the child an occasional hug just to say "I love you." Keep playing with the child—and take interest in the games that he or she invents.

♥ **School-age children.** Talk to the child, and encourage the child to talk to you. Keep communication open. Respect the child's feelings and desires, and value his or her opinion.

APPLY YOUR KNOWLEDGE

1. For which ages are the suggestions for bonding more physical? Why?
2. Several suggestions relate to responding to the child's needs. How would this help strengthen bonds?
3. Identify ways parents can communicate nonverbally with their children during each age span.

women and babies too soon. Some states have passed laws requiring insurers to pay for at least two days after a normal delivery if the woman and her doctor request it.

One condition that may delay release for a few days is newborn jaundice. Some babies have a yellow color on their skin and the whites of the eyes. This is caused by the blood having too much of a certain naturally occurring chemical. The newborn's liver isn't ready, just after birth, to remove that chemical from the body. If left untreated, the condition can damage the nervous system. Treatment is only a matter of putting the child under a flourescent light for a few hours each day until the liver can do its job. The treatment may also take place at home.

Critical Thinking Activity

Applying Concepts. Have students fill in a graphic organizer comparing and contrasting a newborn's bonding with siblings and with parents. Then discuss students' ideas as a class. How are the two types of bonding related? Why are both important? **L1**

Teamwork Activity

Have small groups explore the advantages of long and short hospital stays. Why would the same length of stay not be appropriate for everybody? **L2**

Practicing Parenting

Ask students what the verb to bond means. (*To bind, glue, or unite.*) **Ask:** Is it appropriate to use it with reference to parents and children?

Answers to Apply Your Knowledge

1. For infants and toddlers or preschoolers, who respond physically more than verbally.
2. *Possible response:* Makes the child feel valued and that his or her needs matter to the parent.
3. Answers will vary but should be appropriate for each age group.

LEARNING STYLES

Interpersonal

Have students work in small groups to create and perform a puppet show of the postnatal period. They can make simple sock puppets and present the information in Section 7-2 as the story of a family with a newborn infant. Have each group focus on specific aspects of the postnatal period, such as having one group address showing the new baby to siblings and another covering leaving the hospital.

COMPREHENSION CHECK

1. What documents should parents obtain for children? (*Birth certificate and Social Security card.*)
2. What is an incubator? (*A special enclosed crib that controls oxygen, temperature, and humidity.*)

ACTIVITIES

Critical Thinking Activity

Making Inferences. How does rooming-in promote bonding between parents, infant, and other relatives? **L1**

Critical Thinking Activity

Interpreting. Show the class several pictures of premature babies. Ask them how they react when they see them and why. What impression do students have of the infants? of their future? What emotional difficulties might the families of premature infants face? Why? **L1**

Teamwork Activity

Provide small groups with articles about prematurity. Have them investigate how the costs of care for premature babies differ from that for full-term babies and what risks premature babies face? How do these factors affect parents and other family members, including the ability to bond? **L2**

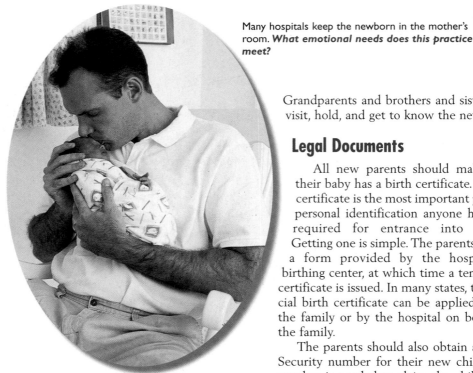

Many hospitals keep the newborn in the mother's room. *What emotional needs does this practice meet?*

Rooming-In

Many hospitals have a **rooming-in** program. With this arrangement, the baby stays in the mother's room day and night rather than in a hospital nursery. Hospitals with rooming-in generally allow the father to visit whenever he wishes.

Rooming-in programs have important advantages for all family members. Couples benefit by having a chance to get to know their baby and practice giving care before going home. The baby can be fed whenever hungry, rather than on a set schedule.

Grandparents and brothers and sisters can visit, hold, and get to know the new baby.

Legal Documents

All new parents should make sure their baby has a birth certificate. A birth certificate is the most important piece of personal identification anyone has. It is required for entrance into school. Getting one is simple. The parents fill out a form provided by the hospital or birthing center, at which time a temporary certificate is issued. In many states, the official birth certificate can be applied for by the family or by the hospital on behalf of the family.

The parents should also obtain a Social Security number for their new child. This number is needed to claim the child as an exemption on income taxes and to take part in many government programs.

Caring for Premature Babies

Between 5 and 6 percent of all babies are **premature** babies. Premature babies are those born before 37 weeks of development and weighing less than 5 pounds, 8 ounces (2.5 kg).

These babies require special care. They are not really ready to live outside their mother's body. Their systems for controlling body temperature, breathing, and feeding are not yet mature. To help them, a premature baby is usually placed in an **incubator** (IN-cue-BAY-tuhr). In this special enclosed

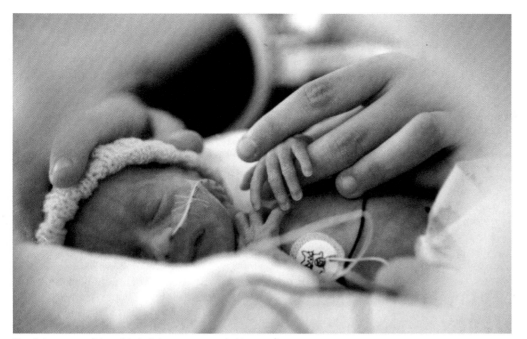

Touch is a powerful tool in helping premature babies survive.

VISUAL LEARNING Using the Photographs
Left: The need for bonding.
Right: Incubators keep them warm and supplied with oxygen.

The Developing Brain

Benefits of Breast-feeding

Breast-feeding offers special benefits to premature infants because preterm milk differs in several ways from full-term milk. It has about twice as much protein needed for growth and is easier to digest. Finally, for about the first week, it also contains almost double the usual amount of a special nutrient that boosts development of the brain and nervous system.

crib, the oxygen supply, temperature, and humidity can be closely controlled. The baby's heart and lungs can be monitored, and special steps may be taken to combat infection, breathing difficulties, and other problems. Advances in medical technology allow many premature infants—even those weighing as little as 1 pound (454 g)—to survive and become healthy.

When they become healthy enough to leave the incubator, premature babies are moved to an open bassinet. Before being allowed to leave the hospital, the baby must be able to control body temperature and gain weight at the same time.

Having a premature baby can be hard on a mother and father. They understand that the incubator is needed to save their

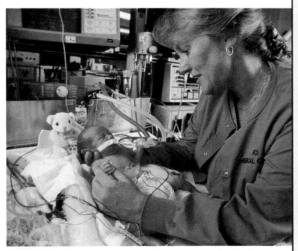

Premature babies suffer many physical difficulties. *How can they be helped by being placed in incubators?*

CHAPTER 7: The Baby's Arrival **231**

DID You Know?

Premature Infants. Twins and triplets are generally born early and need to be kept in incubators like other premature babies. Studies have found that keeping twins together in the same incubator and later in the same crib helps them thrive. The infants gain weight more quickly, they sleep more deeply, and their heart rates become more stable than when they are kept apart. The babies appear to benefit from the prolongation of the physical closeness they enjoyed in the womb.

ACTIVITIES

Teamwork Activity

Ask small groups to brainstorm suggestions for relatives and friends who want to help the parents of a newborn. Then have the groups create a chart on which to rate the different suggestions according to usefulness, convenience, and appropriateness. **L1**

VISUAL LEARNING | **Using the Photographs**

Left: **Ask:** What would you do to help a premature child lead a normal life? *Right:* To return to normal figure, correct posture.

DID *You* **Know?**

Breastfeeding. It was once thought that because nursing mothers lost calcium through the production of breast milk that they needed additional calcium in their diets. A study done at the Cincinnati Children's Hospital Medical Center has shown that although a nursing mother loses about 4% to 5% of the bone mass in her spine, she regains it quickly after the baby weans—whether she takes calcium supplements or not. Doctors now recommend that breastfeeding women continue to take prenatal vitamins and meet normal calcium recommendations for their age.

---

baby's life, but it also creates a barrier between them and their child. Steps can be taken to bring parent and child together, though. Some hospitals let parents reach into the incubator and touch the babies. Sometimes the baby is taken from the incubator for a while so the parents can hold him or her. This has been shown to improve the child's breathing and sleeping. Mothers can also breast-feed a premature baby by using a breast pump.

Good nutrition, healthy habits, good prenatal care, and an understanding of the warning signs of premature labor can all help prevent premature births. If premature labor is spotted soon enough, medication can be given to stop the contractions.

Postnatal Care of the Mother

In the period after birth—the **postnatal** period—it is natural for most of the attention to be focused on the baby. However, the new mother has special physical and emotional needs as well. A doctor or nurse will explain and discuss these needs before the mother and baby go home.

Physical Needs

The mother needs to recover from pregnancy and birth and to regain her fitness. She must take care of herself so that she can care for her child. The keys to meeting her needs include:

- **Rest.** During the first few days and weeks after the birth, the mother is likely to feel tired. She should try to sleep whenever the baby does. Relatives or friends can help the mother rest by doing household chores or caring for the baby for a few hours.

232 UNIT 2: Pregnancy and Childbirth

- **Exercise.** As soon as the mother feels able and her doctor approves, she can begin mild exercise. From just a few simple stretches, she can gradually add other exercises. Exercise helps the woman return to her normal figure and correct posture.

- **Nutrition.** Eating right is as important now as during pregnancy. As before birth, a mother who breast-feeds is supplying nutrients for

---

INFOLINK

Food Guide Pyramid.

See page 187 for the *Food Guide Pyramid for Pregnant and Nursing Women.*

---

the baby as well as herself. She should be sure to follow the recommendations of the Food Guide Pyramid for nursing women. She should also drink plenty of water and other liquids. Even if the mother is not breast-feeding, good nutrition is important to good health.

Babies who were born prematurely can often live normal lives.

Management/Leadership Skills

About 50% to 75% of women experience the "baby blues" and another 10% or more experience severe postpartum depression. Symptoms of postpartum depression include fatigue; loss of appetite; inability to sleep or concentrate; confusion; feelings of hopelessness, guilt, or inadequacy; lack of interest in the baby; anxiety; and uncontrollable anger or weeping. Have small groups of students find local and national sources of information and help. One source: Depression After Delivery, Inc. (P.O. Box 1282, Morrisville, PA 19067.

Doctors recommend that after giving birth, women begin a program of mild exercise. **Why?**

It helps the woman feel good and regain energy.

- **Medical checkup.** About four to six weeks after the birth, the new mother should have a postnatal checkup. At this time, the doctor makes sure that the woman's uterus is returning to normal and that there are no unusual problems. This is also an opportunity for the mother to discuss any questions or concerns she has.

Emotional Needs

Having a baby is a joyous but stressful event. Many new mothers go through a few days of mild depression after the birth. No one knows for certain why these "baby blues" occur. New fathers may have these feelings, too.

It helps if parents talk about their feelings. Taking good care of themselves, seeking support, getting needed sleep and avoiding isolation helps parents minimize the blues. More serious or longer-lasting depression requires the care of a doctor.

SECTION 7-2 REVIEW

✔ Check Your Understanding

1. What is the Apgar scale? When is it used?
2. Why do hospitals now delay performing some tests on the newborn?
3. What is colostrum?
4. What are the advantages of rooming-in?
5. Would a baby born in week 34 who weighs 3 pounds be premature? What about one born in week 40 that weighed 5 pounds?
6. Why do premature babies need special care?
7. What issues are involved in a mother's postnatal care?

Putting Knowledge Into Practice

1. **Predicting Consequences.** Do you think parents who have cesarean births or who adopt might have trouble bonding with their babies? If so, how much of a problem do you think that would be?
2. **Synthesizing.** What could a woman do if she was having problems with breast-feeding while in the hospital?
3. **Observing and Participating.** Talk to a mother about her feelings after birth. Did she feel any "baby blues"? When or how did they go away?

CHAPTER 7: The Baby's Arrival **233**

ASSESS

CHECKING COMPREHENSION

Have students answer the Check Your Understanding questions. Answers appear at the bottom of this page.

EVALUATION

Give students the Section 7-1 Quiz in the *Teacher Resource Guide*.

RETEACHING

1. Assign Reteaching Activities, page 26.
2. Have pairs write ten study questions on the section. Have them exchange questions with another pair and answer those they receive.

ENRICHMENT

Have students interview a grandmother or other older person about childbirth in the past and then present their findings. Have the class discuss similarities and differences in what they heard.

EXTENSION

Invite two or more recent mothers to the class. Have them discuss what their babies looked like at birth and how they responded.

CLOSE

Have students complete the sentence: "If I were the parent of a newborn, I would want . . . "

ANSWERS TO SECTION 7-2 REVIEW

1. Test heart rate, breathing, muscle tone, responsiveness, and skin color to determine newborn's general health. Done 1 and 5 minutes after birth.
2. To allow parents and infant to bond.
3. First milk that flows from mother's breasts and is easy to digest and contains antibodies.
4. The couple can get to know the baby; the baby can be fed when hungry; other family members can meet the baby.
5. 34 week: yes. 40 week: no, the baby is full-term, even if its weight is low.
6. They are not fully developed and cannot survive independently.
7. Rest, exercise, nutrition, medical checkup.

CAREER OPPORTUNITIES

Introducing the Feature

Ask students what subjects they think a nurse has to study before beginning to work. Explore the connection between the different subjects and a nurse's duties.

Answers to
CONNECTING SCHOOL TO CAREER

1. **Possible response:** They may face life-and-death situations.

2. They use machines to monitor babies.

Applying What You've Learned

Invite a guidance counselor to speak to the class about careers in nursing. He or she can discuss the different types of nursing degrees and certificates and the preparation each requires. What responsibilities does a registered nurse have that a licensed practical nurse doesn't? What are the high school requirements of the different training programs?

Encourage the class to prepare a list of topics they would like the counselor to address and to generate questions to ask during the visit.

CAREER OPPORTUNITIES

Intensive Care Pediatric Nurse

A CONVERSATION WITH JOHN RICHARDSON

How did you become interested in becoming an intensive care pediatric nurse? When I was in nurses training, I did a rotation in intensive care pediatrics. There was a baby born with many different problems—heart, lungs, kidneys. The staff worked and worked on her and saved her life. Her parents were there constantly. When I saw how grateful they were that she lived, I decided this would be a great career.

What are the tasks and responsibilities of an intensive care pediatric nurse? We have to watch the young children in our care all the time. We rely on machines to monitor their vital signs—pulse and blood pressure and breathing. But we also spend a lot of time with each one of them. They need holding and caring, just like any other babies.

What is the work environment like? It's very intense. A baby can have a crisis at any time, and you have to be ready to act immediately. It can be very difficult to wind down at the end of the day.

What are the working hours like? We work in shifts of eight hours, either day, evening, or night.

What aptitudes are needed to be an intensive care pediatric nurse? Intensive care nurses have to think clearly under pressure. We need a good memory to bring back everything ever studied or experienced to face each situation. Of course, a good background in science helps too. It's important to care—about babies and their parents.

INTENSIVE CARE PEDIATRIC NURSE

Education and Training. To become a registered nurse, a person needs to complete a two-, four-, or five-year nursing program and pass a licensing exam.

Career Outlook. Jobs for registered nurses are expected to grow much faster than average.

┌─ CONNECTING SCHOOL TO CAREER ─┐

1. **Personal Qualities.** Why do intensive care nurses need to think well under pressure?
2. **Technology.** How can technology help intensive care nurses do their work?

234 UNIT 2: Pregnancy and Childbirth

Building Career Skills

Technology. Have small groups of students work together to design a picture of an imaginary, but probable, scene in a pediatric nursery. Tell them to use images from magazines, clipart, and advertisements to make a collage illustrating their scene. They can use copiers, scanners, and printers to enlarge or reduce these images so that different parts of the scene are in proportion. Encourage them to think creatively and use portions of illustrations of other objects to piece together the picture they need.

SECTION 7-3

A New Family Member

For the first few months of life, every baby is considered "new." The baby's family, too, is newly expanded, with new relationships to establish. Welcoming home and getting to know this tiny person are exciting aspects of adjusting to life with a new baby.

KEY TERMS

grasp reflex
reflexes
rooting reflex
startle reflex
temperament

OBJECTIVES:

- Recognize a baby's reflexes.
- Describe babies' basic needs.
- Discuss how babies' needs can best be met.

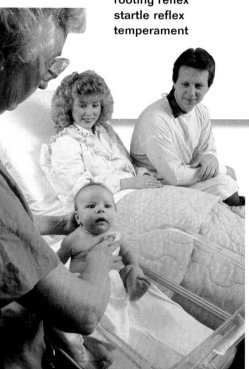

The Amazing Newborn

Newborn babies are amazing, born with remarkable capabilities. Newborns use their senses to learn about their new world.

At birth, babies are very sensitive to strong light. Some may even cry when they encounter bright lights. Newborns are sensitive to sounds—especially the sound of the human voice. Newborns

CHAPTER 7: The Baby's Arrival **235**

Observing & Participating

Have students observe the sleeping habits of an infant in their family or interview someone who has a baby.

- How do the babies go to sleep? Do they have a routine?
- What is their sleeping environment like?

Do they sleep alone or in a room with others? In a crib or in somewhere else?

- Do the babies have sleeping patterns? If so, when were they established?
- Do they have trouble staying asleep? Does noise or activity wake them?

SECTION 7-3

A New Family Member

(pages 235-241)

SECTION 7-3 RESOURCES

Teacher Resource Guide
- Lesson Plan Organizer, p. 53
- Section 7-3 Quiz, p. 133

Student Motivation Kit
- Observations & Case Studies (case study), p. 105
- Reteaching Activity, p. 27
- Teen Parenting Skills, pp. 70-72

Student Workbook
- Study Guide, pp. 63-66
- Are Baby's Needs Being Met? pp. 69-70

Effective Instruction CD-ROM

FOCUS

MOTIVATOR

Pearl S. Buck once noted, "Who can gaze at a newborn baby, and not wonder again at the miracle?" **Ask:** What did Buck mean? In what ways are newborns miraculous?

VOCABULARY ACTIVITY

Have one or two students to look up the origin of the words *reflex* (*re*: back, *flectere*: to bend) and *temperament* (*temperamentum*: proper mixing). Discuss what the origins of these words show us about their meaning. How do they help us understand the idea behind the word more completely?

COMPREHENSION CHECK

1. Why are most reflexes temporary? (*No longer needed when child gains voluntary control.*)
2. What is the average number of hours a newborn sleeps in a day? (*15.*)

ACTIVITIES

Critical Thinking Activity

Diagramming. Ask students to create a web of newborn traits as they read the section. They should include the physical, mental, and emotional characteristics of infants with a specific example. **L1**

Discussion Activity

How do new parents learn to care for newborns? What or who are the most accessible or reliable sources of information? Have them evaluate the usefulness of books, magazines, television programs, and people. **L1**

Teamwork Activity

Have small groups review a popular book about children's health, such as Dr. Spock's book or others. Have each group look at a different book. They can look at the advice given on three or four issues (such as feeding, teething, ear infections). Is the book well organized? Is the advice easy to understand? Does it seem up-to-date? Have each group report to the class and compare advice. The class might design a form that could be used to evaluate such books. **L1**

like some smells—milk, vanilla, banana, and sugar—and turn away from strong smells like vinegar. After just one week of nursing, babies turn toward nursing pads used by their own mothers, but not those used by other nursing mothers.

The newborn breathes independently. The newborn can also cry to signal a variety of needs, such as the need for food, attention, or a dry diaper.

Reflexes

Babies must be able to handle some of their needs involuntarily until they learn to do things voluntarily. **Reflexes**—instinctive, automatic responses, such as sneezing and yawning—make this possible. These coordinated patterns of behavior help the baby's body function. For example, a sneeze helps clear the baby's nose of lint. Swallowing helps the baby eat without choking.

Sneezing and swallowing continue throughout life. Other reflexes last only until the baby develops voluntary control of his or her body. Three are notable:

- **Rooting reflex.** The **rooting reflex** is a newborn's automatic response, when touched on the lips or cheek, of turning toward the touch and beginning to suck. This reflex helps the baby find food. When babies use their eyes to search for the bottle or mother's breast, around four months of age, the rooting reflex stops.
- **Grasp reflex.** The **grasp reflex** is the automatic response of a newborn's hand to close over anything that comes in contact with the palm. The grip is often so strong that it can be used to lift the newborn up. This is not a good idea, however, because the baby lets go without warning. When the baby begins to reach for objects, at about three months of age, this reflex weakens; it disappears by the time babies are one year old.

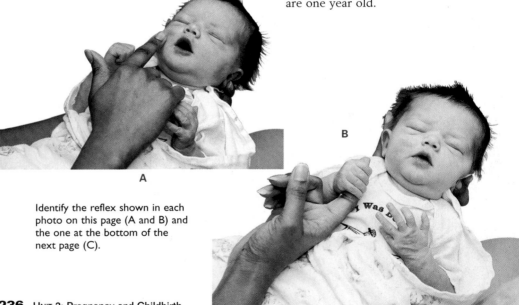

Identify the reflex shown in each photo on this page (A and B) and the one at the bottom of the next page (C).

236 Unit 2: Pregnancy and Childbirth

LEARNING STYLES

Spatial

Before assigning Section 7-3, provide students with the skeleton of a four-column chart about newborns with headings: "Behavior," "Preferences," "Needs," and "Temperament." Ask students to fill in as much as they already know about infants, After reading the section, give students a fresh chart and ask them to fill it in again. Have them compare their work before and after. Have some of their ideas about newborns changed? Have other beliefs or ideas been confirmed? What impression of infants has Section 7-3 given them?

- **Startle reflex.** The **startle reflex** is a newborn's automatic response to a loud noise or to a touch on the stomach. The legs are thrown up, fingers spread, and arms are first extended and then brought back rapidly while the fingers close in a grasping action. The startle reflex disappears when the baby is about five months old.

Learning to Care for the Newborn

At first, it may take some time for new parents to feel comfortable caring for a baby. Soon, they gain confidence and become accustomed to the baby's way of communicating. They learn how to recognize the baby's needs and adapt their responses to their baby's individual style.

C

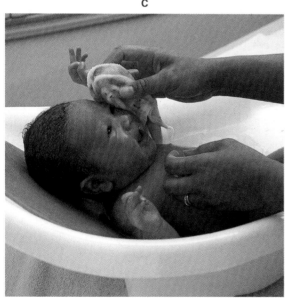

What Do Babies Need?

Later chapters in this book present detailed information about caring for a baby. Here, however, are babies' basic needs:

- **Babies need food.** A newborn shows hunger with his or her whole body. The baby squirms about, mouth searching for the mother's breast or a bottle nipple. Hungry newborns want food immediately, and it is important to meet their need quickly. Doing so helps them learn that they can trust the world.
- **Babies need sleep.** Newborns sleep and wake throughout the day and night. A newborn sleeps an average of 15 hours a day, typically in six to eight separate sleep periods. Many sleep one long five-hour stretch during the night. However, the level of alertness or drowsiness varies from baby to baby. Every baby is different; what is normal is normal for that individual baby.
- **Babies need exercise.** In the brief times they are awake, newborns wave their arms and legs. This activity helps their muscles and nervous system develop. Before a feeding, babies usually become very active, moving all parts of their body. They may kick while their diaper is changed and splash and wiggle during a bath.
- **Babies need to be kept safe, clean, and warm.** Parents diaper and bathe babies to keep them clean. They also make sure that an adult keeps an eye on the baby at all times. Anything the baby might come in contact with—a toy, a crib, a garment—should be checked for safety, and any potentially harmful objects should be kept away.

CHAPTER 7: The Baby's Arrival **237**

Critical Thinking Activity

Identifying a Course of Action. Have students create a two-column chart. In the left, list infants' needs. In the right, put actions caregivers can take to meet those needs. **L1**

Discussion Activity

Ask: How important is parents' confidence in their abilities to care for a baby? How can parents gain confidence? How does confidence affect the baby? **L1**

VISUAL LEARNING Using the Photographs
Left: (A) Rooting. (B) Grasp. *Right:* Startle.

The Developing Brain

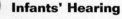 **Infants' Hearing**

Infants are very sensitive to sound. Newborns can tell the difference between two sounds that are only one tone apart. They can detect differences in the volume, length, and rhythm of sounds. Infants are frightened and stop moving when they hear sharp, high-pitched sounds. Low-pitched, rhythmic sounds soothe them. In one study, the sound of a normal heartbeat was played continuously for a group of newborns. The infants cried less, breathed more deeply, and gained more weight than those not exposed to the sound. Babies are more responsive to women's voices than to men's.

DID *You* **Know?**

Sleep. Infants have two distinct sleep patterns, regular and irregular. In regular sleep, babies breathe in a smooth, even rhythm; their eyelids are closed; eyes don't move; muscles are relaxed; and they may show the startle response. In irregular sleep, breathing is alternately slow and rapid; babies may stir, frown, flutter their eyelids, sigh, grimace, or smile. Their eyes engage in rapid eye movement (REM). Babies spend more time in irregular sleep, which scientists think may be because their brains need time to process outside stimulation.

Ask the Eperts

Dr. Van Stone
Pediatrician
Tupelo, Mississippi

SUDDEN *Infant Death Syndrome*

Q What is crib death, and what can be done to prevent it?

A Crib death is known medically as Sudden Infant Death Syndrome, or SIDS. The victims are usually infants between the ages of two weeks and six months. Children who die of SIDS seemed healthy. They die in their sleep, with no warning and no evidence of pain. SIDS strikes one or two children out of every thousand.

The cause of SIDS is unknown. Research has dismissed infection, allergy to milk, and suffocation, among other causes. The most likely explanation is long pauses in breathing.

Although the causes of SIDS are unknown, research has identified some groups who are at risk. Victims are likely to be male babies who had low birthweight. Premature babies are at risk for SIDS, as are babies living in a house where a person smokes. Babies who sleep on their stomachs are a risk group as well. Finally, SIDS most often strikes in winter.

Research has also found steps that can be taken to lower the risk:

- *Most important, put babies to sleep on their backs or sides. The American Academy of Pediatrics now recommends this position for all babies but a few.*

- *Practice good prenatal care to avoid having a premature or low-birthweight baby.*
- *Avoid smoking during pregnancy and after the baby is born. A smoke free home helps a newborn in many ways, but can also help prevent SIDS.*

Parents who suffer the loss of a baby to SIDS often feel stricken by guilt as well as grief. They can benefit from counseling.

Thinking It Through

1. Is SIDS equally likely to strike any child?
2. Why might parents who lost a child to SIDS feel guilty?

238 UNIT 2: Pregnancy and Childbirth

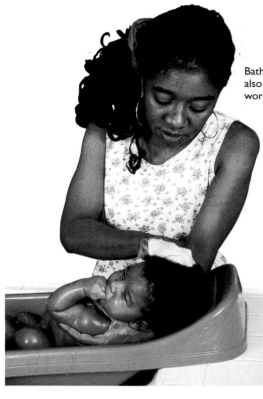

Bathing is more than a time to clean the baby. It also offers the baby a chance to learn about the world. *What needs does a baby have?*

contact with warm, affectionate adults. Love is as important as food and sleep to babies. A baby who senses that he or she is loved feels at ease and secure. Each parent should express love for his or her newborn naturally, in the ways that are comfortable.

What Do Parents Need?

Parents of newborns are often so concerned about caring for their babies that they neglect their own needs. These are some of the things that parents of newborns need:

- Knowledge of how to care for an infant.
- Resources that can provide answers to their questions.
- Information about how their babies act and change and about typical emotions they might experience.
- Time to fill their many roles.
- Emotional support from family and friends.
- Financial planning.
- Reassurance and confidence that both parents are capable and needed.
- Agreement about parenting and household responsibilities.
- Personal health, rest, and nutrition.
- Privacy and time alone.

- **Babies need medical care.** In the first year, an infant will have periodic checkups to make sure he or she is healthy and developing normally, and to receive immunizations.
- **Babies need things to look at, touch, listen to, and play with.** Stimulating surroundings help babies learn. However, babies don't need expensive toys. In fact, an infant's favorite thing to look at is a human face.
- **Babies need love.** Just like everyone else, babies want to be near the people who love them. Newborns need close

1. How can learning about newborns before birth help minimize stress after birth? (*Possible responses: less to learn, know what to expect.*)

ACTIVITIES

Discussion Activity

Encourage students to identify the new relationships that are created with the birth of a new baby. How do these new relationships affect the individual's self-image? How do they affect the family as a whole? How do they affect existing relationships between spouses, parents and children, and other combinations of family members? **L1**

Teamwork Activity

Divide the class into five groups, and assign each group two of the needs of parents. Have them devise strategies to help new parents meet those needs. Compile a complete class list on the chalkboard. **L1**

VISUAL LEARNING | **Using the Photograph**
Answer: Needs for food; sleep; exercise; to be kept safe, clean, and warm; medical care; stimulation; love.

ISSUES IN CHILDREN'S HEALTH

When a nursing mother smokes, the nicotine from the cigarette stays in breast milk for up to eight hours. Some studies have shown that smoking increases nausea, colic, and diarrhea in babies. Heavy smoking also tends to lower milk production.

ISSUES IN TEEN PARENTING Most first-time parents do not realize how exhausted and stressed they will be after a baby is born. Teen parents, with the physical demands of their own growth, may find lack of sleep and worries about the baby particularly hard to bear. They may feel overcome by emotion—and inadequate because they can't control those emotions. Discuss how emotions—even those we consider negative, like anger or hurt—can be used as a signal to "stop and think." One good way to weigh possible courses of action is what counselors call "self-talk": giving all the conflicting voices within us the opportunity to express themselves.

ACTIVITIES

Discussion Activity

What adjustments do you think parents have to make to understand their baby? to care for their baby? **L1**

Critical Thinking Activity

Defining Terms. Ask students to write a short essay explaining what *temperament* means. Tell them to provide examples of temperament in children and adults. Remind them to include an introduction with a thesis, and to provide an explanation with supporting examples for every supporting point in the body of the paper. **L1**

Parents and baby have to adjust to each other at first. Many first-time parents are surprised to learn that they have to keep adjusting—babies change quickly as they grow, and their needs and abilities change from week to week.

Adjusting to New Routines

During the first few weeks, both parents and babies have to adjust to new patterns of life. A newborn typically needs at least several weeks before he or she can settle into any predictable pattern of eating and sleeping. Parents must adjust their schedule to the baby's needs. That means feeding the baby whenever hunger strikes, day or night.

Some parents worry that this kind of response will spoil the child, making him or her too demanding. At this early stage of life, though, babies need to feel that they are important and their needs will receive attention. Later, when they are more mature, they can begin to learn to follow a schedule.

Of course, every newborn benefits from order in life. Daily patterns emerge to manage the baby's hunger, sleepiness, and wakefulness. It takes about a month, for example, to establish a fairly predictable feeding and sleeping routine. Meanwhile, the key to the baby's happiness is the parents' flexibility.

Understanding the Baby's Language

Babies have one way to communicate with the world—crying. Although newborns never cry for fun, their reasons may often be far less serious than worried new parents imagine. Babies cry because they are too hot or too cold, because they are lying in an uncomfortable position or because the sun is in their eyes, because their diaper is wet, or because they no longer hear their mother's voice.

The average newborn cries about one hour per day, but individual babies may cry less or much more than that. The important thing to remember is that a baby's crying seems to have nothing to do with the quality of parenting he or she is receiving. Parents soon learn to recognize their baby's different cries—one for hunger, another for discomfort, and so on.

240 UNIT 2: Pregnancy and Childbirth

Early Temperament

Babies differ markedly in their inborn **temperament**, or style of reacting to the world and relating to others. For example, Pete moves from sleep to wakefulness with a startled cry. Carmen awakens gradually and quietly looks around. Jake may be so easily upset that extra gentle handling and a smooth routine are necessary. Ira can be handled more playfully without objection. No two babies react in just the same way.

Parents need to be sensitive to the baby's own style. The baby, too, learns to adapt to the style of his or her parents. Studies have shown that babies as young as two weeks of age adjust their reactions, depending on how parents handle and talk to them. When parents are very gentle and soothing, the baby tends to respond with soft cooing and gentle motions. When parents are playful, the baby tends to react with excited grunts and active motions. These natural adjustments help parents and babies feel at ease with each other.

Babies reveal their own temperament soon after birth. *How do parent and newborn adjust to each other in the early weeks of the newborn's life?*

SECTION 7-3 REVIEW

✔ Check Your Understanding

1. Define *reflex* and give an example of one.
2. Describe one reflex a newborn has.
3. What do you think is the most important thing a baby needs? Why?
4. How much do newborn babies typically sleep?
5. Why is flexibility important for new parents?
6. What is temperament? Why does it matter?

Putting Knowledge Into Practice

1. **Synthesizing.** How is the way newborns respond to hunger typical of their nature?
2. **Applying.** Where can parents get the knowledge about caring for an infant that they need?
3. **Observing and Participating.** Observe parents and small infants in a public place, such as a park or a mall. Record how parents show their love for their babies. Describe how the babies respond to the parents.

CHAPTER 7: The Baby's Arrival **241**

ANSWERS TO SECTION 7-3 REVIEW

1. An instinctive, automatic response: sneezing.
2. *Possible response:* Rooting reflex; when touched on lip or cheek, baby turns mouth toward touch and begins to suck.
3. *Possible response:* Food to grow and develop.
4. Average of fifteen hours a day.
5. Newborns are too young to have a predictable routine.
6. Style of reacting to world and relating to others. *Possible response:* Shapes how baby interacts with other people.

MOTIVATOR

Ask students if they have ever looked after a baby or spent time talking and playing with one. How did the baby react?

Art Activity

Have students make a poster illustrating different occasions for speaking to a baby. Tell students to portray both the infant and the parent in the midst of the activity.
L1

Critical Thinking Activity

Making Inferences. How does talking to an infant strengthen the bonds between the caregiver and the infant? What does it show the baby about the caregiver? What does it give the baby an opportunity to do? How does it accustom the baby to being with the caregiver?
L1

Teamwork Activity

Ask small groups to act out one of the occasions for speaking to a baby listed in the feature. One student can play the parent and others can be friends or relatives visiting or people at the supermarket. **L1**

Parenting With Care

Talking Promotes Development

Current research shows that talking to a child is one of the best ways of building that child's emotional and intellectual development.

Talking helps the nerves in the baby's brain become connected, which can help with later development. Babies who are talked to often know more words by age two. Talking also strengthens the bonds between caregivers and children.

What should you talk about? The answer is just about anything at almost any time. Start talking when the baby is born—and never stop. Here are some tips for infants:

* **When feeding.** Talk about which members of the family the baby looks like or why the baby was given his or her name.
* **When bathing.** Describe water and soap or talk about how much fun it will be to learn to swim.
* **When changing diapers.** Name the parts of the baby's body.
* **When dressing.** Say the names of different articles of clothing or talk about colors.

* **When driving.** Name the roads and streets or describe memories linked to particular places.
* **When walking the baby in a stroller.** Talk about the outdoors and what is seen there or about the weather and the seasons.
* **When shopping for food.** Name the fruits and vegetables and describe their shape and color. Talk about what food tastes like or particular meals.

Will the baby understand all these facts? Probably not. The baby will still benefit, though. For the baby to benefit, this talk has to come from a live person.

RESOURCES ON PARENTING

A wonderful source of information on all aspects of child development is KidsHealth (www.kidshealth.org). It is the web site of the Nemours Foundation, which sponsors pediatric hospitals and clinics. The information can be accessed either by the age of the child (new-born to teenager) or by topic (such as growth or sleep). The site includes information on health and illness, behavior, and parenting plus news stories on recent developments in children's health. All are clearly written for a general audience.

Sitting the child in front of the television or next to the radio to listen to that talk will not help. Babies learn most when they have an emotional attachment to the person talking. The baby will benefit more if the person talking makes eye contact while talking.

All this talking benefits another person, too. The parent who spends a long day with a demanding baby can grow tired. Talking can break the quiet and help that parent stay in good spirits.

Following Up

1. **Communication.** Imagine some activity that a parent and three-year-old do and list some topics the parent could talk about.

2. **Thinking Skills.** In some families, one parent works and the other stays home with the child. Sometimes, the parent who works is faced with a torrent of words from the other parent when coming home at the end of the day. Why would that be?

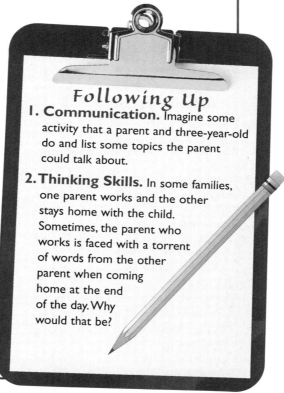

Answers to Following Up
1. *Answers will vary.*
2. *Possible response:* Because the parent who cares for the child craves adult conversation.

Distinguishing Characteristics. What nonverbal elements of speech do you think affect babies? Explore elements such as facial expression, eye contact, tone of voice, posture, and gestures. How would you predict a baby would react to a smiling face as opposed to an inexpressive face? An angry tone as opposed to a flat tone? **L2**

The Developing Brain

Reading

Another way to talk to babies is to read to them. Holding a baby and looking at picture books together provides great stimulation. Around six months of age, children begin to show excitement when read to. Studies show that it is important to read with expression, pointing out and naming things in the pictures. Ask children questions about the events, characters, and pictures once they are able to speak. Children can be asked what will happen next or to describe important people or objects. Because children learn through repetition, parents should accept with patience their children's repeated requests for the same stories. They can reinforce their children's learning by asking them to join in with them in repeating rhymes and poems.

CLOSE

How would you respond to parents who say they feel silly talking to their baby in public? Have students respond orally or in writing.

CHECKING COMPREHENSION

Use the Summary and the Reviewing the Facts questions to help students go over the most important ideas in Chapter 7. Encourage students to ask questions and add details.

CHAPTER 7 REVIEW

Answers to Reviewing the Facts

1. Bloody show: expulsion of a mucus plug from the cervix.
2. *First stage:* to dilate and efface the cervix; *second stage:* to deliver the baby; *third stage:* to deliver the placenta.
3. Both begin to function on their own.
4. Tests or procedures: Apgar scale checks physical condition; eyedrops to prevent infection; vitamin K injection to help blood clot; possible hearing test; blood test for PKU, sickle cell anemia, and other conditions.
5. Younger than 37 weeks of development; weighing less than 5 pounds, 8 ounces.
6. To regain health and energy; to be able to feed baby if she's nursing.
7. Rooting, grasp, and startle reflex. *Rooting*—when touched on cheek or lip, baby turns mouth toward touch and begins to such.
8. *Possible responses:* To reassure baby that his or her needs will be met; to build trust.
9. *Answers will vary but should be backed by examples.*

CHAPTER 7 REVIEW &

Summary

✔ In the three stages of labor, the baby emerges from the mother's body. (Section 7-1)

✔ Newborns have a unique appearance, unlike that of older babies. (Section 7-1)

✔ Health care workers examine a baby after birth to make sure he or she is healthy. (Section 7-2)

✔ Some babies and mothers have special needs that delay their leaving the hospital. (Section 7-2)

✔ Reflexes help a newborn's body function until the baby has more control. (Section 7-3)

✔ Newborn babies and parents of newborns have several needs that must be met. (Section 7-3)

Reviewing the Facts

1. What is meant by "bloody show"? (Section 7-1)
2. What purpose do contractions serve in the first stage of labor? In the second stage? In the third stage? (Section 7-1)
3. How do a baby's lungs and heart change at birth? (Section 7-1)
4. Choose one test or procedure done to a newborn soon after birth and explain why it is performed. (Section 7-2)
5. What standards are used to determine that a baby is premature? (Section 7-2)
6. Why is good nutrition important for a mother after giving birth? (Section 7-2)
7. List three reflexes a baby is born with and describe one. (Section 7-3)
8. Why is it important to feed a hungry newborn right away? (Section 7-3)

9. How might a baby's temperament affect the way parents respond to him or her? How can a parent's temperament affect a baby? Give examples. (Section 7-3)

Thinking Critically

1. **Making Inferences.** How do you think new parents would feel when they saw their first newborn if they didn't know what newborns looked like?

2. **Analyzing.** Research how labor and delivery were handled 100 years ago. Where did childbirth generally take place? Were there any problems associated with these practices? What was done to address these problems? Report your findings.

Taking Action

1. **Being Prepared.** Make a list of things an expectant couple might want to take when they leave home to have their baby. *(Management)*

2. **Lending a Hand.** How can friends or other members of the family help someone who has just had a baby? Make a chart with the headings "Food," "Cleaning," "Errands," "Child Care." *(Communication)*

CONNECTIONS

Cross-Curricular Connections

1. **Health.** Make a time line of a woman's labor. Use the time spans described in the text for each stage.
2. **Math.** Ten women, each having her first child, were in the first stage of labor for the following number of hours: 13, 16, 15, 20, 18, 12, 17, 14, 18, 10. What was the average length of the first stage? What was the range of times?

Workplace Connections

1. **Information Systems.** Create a system that could be used in hospitals or birth facilities to match newborn babies and their mothers. Make a poster or brochure describing it.
2. **Interpersonal Skills.** Suppose you worked in a hospital maternity area. How would you tell a couple that their newborn had to be taken away for emergency medical care?

Family and Community Connections

1. **Adapting to a New Baby.** Think of two or three guidelines for how a four-year-old sibling should behave with a new baby. Then write a song or story that communicates these guidelines.
2. **Finding Resources.** Find out what facilities there are in your community or nearby for giving premature babies the special care they need.

Technology Connections

1. **Medical Technology.** Bring in a news story about a premature or multiple birth. What health problems were involved? What medical procedures were used to confront these problems? Report to the class.

2. **Medications.** Find out what medications may be given during childbirth and what effect they have—on both the mother and the baby. Make a chart to present your findings.

EVALUATION

1. Use the reproducible Chapter 7 Test in the *Teacher Resource Guide*, or create your own test using the **Exam**View® Test Generator.
2. For an alternative assessment, assign the Chapter 7 activity in the *Authentic Assessment* section of the *Teacher Resource Guide*.

ENRICHMENT

Assign students either of the two enrichment activities in the *Enrichment Activities* booklet in the *Student Motivation Kit*.

EXTENSION

Invite a panel of parents and expectant parents to speak to the class. Ask the panel to discuss what their expectations were and what the reality of their experience has been. Have students prepare questions for the panel members ahead of time.

CLOSE

Ask students to complete the following sentences in writing:
- "I think the best part about becoming a parent is . . ."
- "I think the most difficult part of becoming a parent is . . ."

Answers to Connections

Math
Average: 15.5 hours.
Range: 10-20 hours.

After completing Unit 3, students will be able to:

- Describe physical growth and development during the first year of life.
- Discuss emotional and social development during the first year of life.
- Describe the intellectual development of babies.

UNIT 3 OVERVIEW

In **Chapter 8**, students examine physical growth and development during the first year of life, including the physical care a baby requires.

In **Chapter 9**, students learn to recognize signs of emotional and social development during the first year of life.

Chapter 10 introduces students to Piaget's stages of learning and discusses what caregivers can do to stimulate intellectual development.

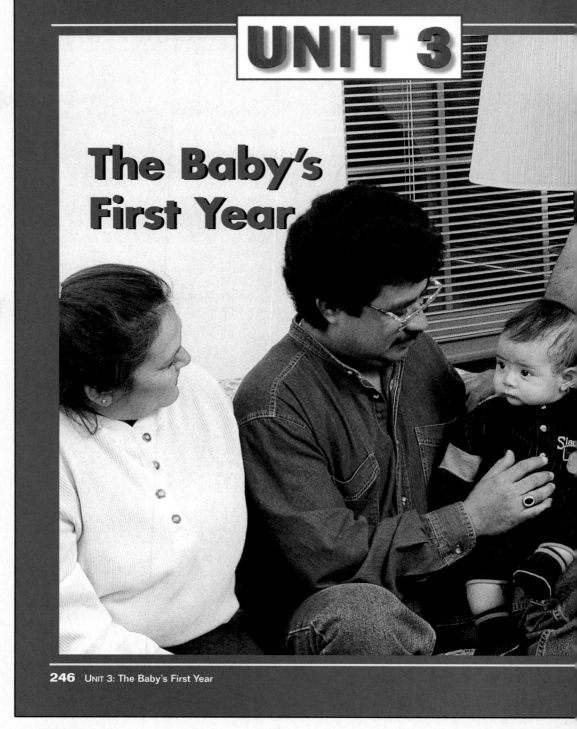

UNIT 3

The Baby's First Year

246 UNIT 3: The Baby's First Year

USING THE POEM

New parents soon discover how physically and emotionally drained they can be when caring for an infant. Yet most parents will have an equal sense of wonder at the preciousness of a baby, especially when he or she is asleep.

Ask a student to read the poem aloud, then ask the class to volunteer their thoughts and feelings about watching a baby fall asleep after a hectic day. Discuss how accurately the poet captured the images of life with an infant.

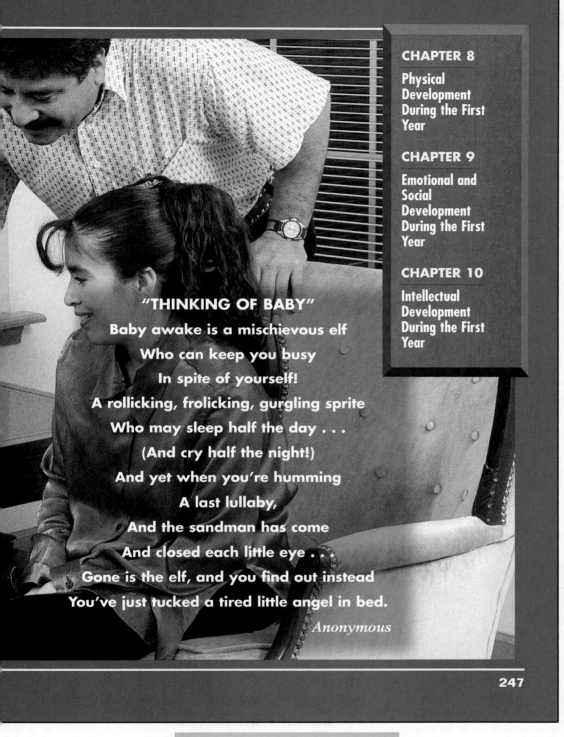

"THINKING OF BABY"

Baby awake is a mischievous elf
Who can keep you busy
In spite of yourself!
A rollicking, frolicking, gurgling sprite
Who may sleep half the day . . .
(And cry half the night!)
And yet when you're humming
A last lullaby,
And the sandman has come
And closed each little eye . . .
Gone is the elf, and you find out instead
You've just tucked a tired little angel in bed.

Anonymous

247

- Show a short video of a baby on his or her first birthday (or display several large photos of one-year-olds). Encourage students to identify some of the baby's many skills and abilities.
- Have students look at the photo and write down the first five words that come to their minds. Ask for volunteers to share their responses with the class. Then have the class discuss the ideas and feelings that infants promote.

COMPLETING UNIT 3

EXTENSION

Invite a parent to bring a one-year-old baby to visit the class. Ask the parent to bring photographs that show how the baby has developed since birth. Encourage students to ask about the baby's and parent's experiences in that year.

EVALUATION

Use the Unit 3 Test on the Exam*View®* Test Generator or use the program to create your own test.

FCCLA Connection | **A Safe Environment**

Have groups of students develop a comprehensive list of potential safety hazards during a child's first year. Each group should create a visual to present their information, such as a timeline linked to developmental changes by month. Have groups research both commercial and do-it-yourself remedies for common hazards and present those results orally as they explain their visual.

COMMUNITY AS CLASSROOM

Guest Speakers. The class could benefit by hearing from several professionals during the study of this unit. *For Chapter 8*: a pediatrician or a neurologist. For *Chapter 9*: a director of a child-care facility. *For Chapter 10*: an educational psychologist.

Field Trips. The class could take field trips to a pediatrician's office, to a infant-care center, and to an early-education department of a university to enhance their study of this unit.

CHAPTER 8 RESOURCES

Teacher Resource Guide
• Chapter 8 Test, p. 142
• Authentic Assessment, p. 271
Student Motivation Kit
• Observations, pp. 41-42
Transparency Package
• CT-24 to CT-25, CT-37
Effective Instruction CD-ROM

CHAPTER 8   OVERVIEW

In **Section 8-1**, students examine patterns of physical development in infancy. **Section 8-2** describes how the brain works and identifies activities that help develop a baby's brain. **Section 8-3** explains how to hold and feed babies. **Section 8-4** covers other aspects of providing physical care for infants.

CHAPTER 8   OBJECTIVES

After completing Chapter 8, students will be able to:

• Identify the most important milestones of growth and development during a baby's first year.
• Describe the structure of the brain and how it works.
• Describe methods for handling and feeding an infant.
• Discuss other skills involved in meeting an infant's physical needs.

CHAPTER 8

Physical Development During the First Year

248   Unit 3: The Baby's First Year

RESOURCES TO EXPLORE

Feeding Babies. Many new mothers are uncertain about whether to bottle-feed or breast-feed their babies. An excellent resource about breast-feeding concerns is the La Leche League. By contacting their main branch, you can obtain free information and referral to a local chapter leader, who may be willing to speak to your class. Contact La Leche League, 9616 Minneapolis Ave., Franklin Park, IL 60131 or www. lalecheleague.org

Brett loved the time he spent with Jason. This Saturday, they were enjoying the early afternoon sunshine. Jason cooed and giggled as they played. After a while, though, as naptime neared, Jason became a bit fussy.

"I think it's time for your bath, then a trip to your crib," Brett whispered to Jason. He swung him up to his shoulder and headed for the house, pausing to point out a cat in the yard.

Bath time, as usual, was a time for fun and splashing. Jason loved playing in the water. Once he was clean, Brett lifted Jason from the tub and wrapped him in a fluffy, blue towel. Jason wiggled as Brett put on a clean diaper and clothes. "You always make things interesting," Brett remarked. "Now it's time for kisses and a good, long nap!"

"I think it's time for your bath, then a trip to your crib."

CHAPTER 8: Physical Development During the First Year **249**

- Using about 2 yards (1.8 m) of butcher paper and pencils, markers, and measuring sticks, have students work in small groups to sketch life-size outlines of a "typical" baby at birth and at age one year. Then encourage students to compare and discuss their sketches. Save the sketches until students have finished the chapter. At that time, have them evaluate their early impressions of infants' sizes.

- Have students discuss what fathers can do to care for infants. Why is it important for the baby for the father to take a role? Why is it important for the mother? For the father?

USING THE SCENARIO Have students read the story on this page of the student text. Ask students to identify Jason's needs that Brett is meeting. Ask them to speculate on Jason's age.

KEY TO ABILITY LEVELS Each section gives skill-building activities. Each activity has been labeled for use with students of various learning styles and abilities.

L1 Level 1 activities are basic activities and should be within the range of all students.

L2 Level 2 activities are average activities and should be within the range of average and above average students.

L3 Level 3 activities are challenging activities designed for the ability range of above average students.

Growth and Development of Infants

(pages 250-259)

SECTION 8-1 RESOURCES
Teacher Resource Guide
• Lesson Plan Organizer, p. 54
• Section 8-1 Quiz, p. 138
Student Motivation Kit
• Observ. & Case Studies
  (case study), p. 106
• Reteaching Activity, p. 28
• Teen Parenting Skills,
  pp. 64-65
Student Workbook
• Study Guide, pp. 71-75
• Motor Matchups, p. 76
Effective Instruction CD-ROM

FOCUS

MOTIVATOR

Ask whether any students who have seen newborn animals. Ask them to describe to the class how the newborns look. Have them compare the skills of the newborn animals to those of older—but still immature—animals and of adult ones. Challenge them to make comparisons to a baby's first year of life.

VOCABULARY ACTIVITY

Ask students to define the terms. Then tell them that specific definitions, as they relate to child development, are provided in the text.

Growth and Development of Infants

Growth and development during the first year are the most rapid of any time in life. In twelve months, the baby who begins as a helpless newborn triples his or her birth weight, learns to stand alone, and may even begin to walk.

KEY TERMS
depth perception
hand-eye coordination
motor skills
primary teeth
proportion

OBJECTIVES:
• Analyze children's physical development to find three patterns.
• Describe physical growth during the first year.
• Describe the development of senses and motor skills during the first year.

Patterns of Physical Development

As you know, all development follows a sequence, proceeding step-by-step. Physical development, which is no exception, follows three basic patterns:

Observing & Participating

Call on volunteers to share their own experiences with the rapid growth of babies. Ask teen parents or teens with young siblings to describe the rapid changes they have observed. Let other students talk about the changes they have seen when visiting a baby at intervals of several weeks or months, for example. Have them note what differences a month makes in the size and the skills of a baby. Have them contrast what differences the same period makes in the growth and development of a teenager.

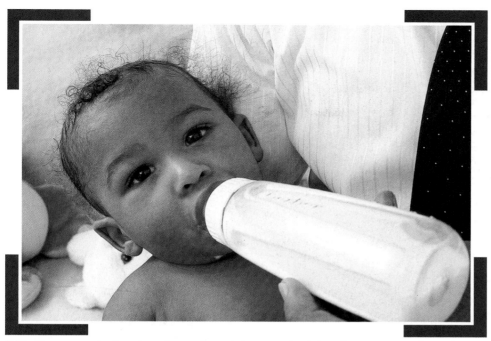

Babies first master simple tasks such as eating and sleeping and only later learn more complex tasks. *What other patterns do babies follow in their development?*

- **Head to foot.** Long before birth, the baby's head takes the lead in development. The same pattern continues after birth. First, babies lift their heads to see an object. Later, as they gain muscle control of their arms and hands, they pick that object up. Still later, they are able to walk to it.
- **Near to far.** Development starts at the trunk and moves outward. First, babies simply wave their arms when they see an object they want. Later, they grab at an object with the palm of the hand. Finally, babies learn to pick up objects with their thumb and fingers.

- **Simple to complex.** At first, babies' main activities are sleeping and eating. Gradually, they learn more complicated tasks. They eat with their fingers and later use a spoon and fork.

Growth During the First Year

Charts show the average weight, height, and abilities of children at certain ages. These charts give a general idea of growth and development, but remember that children change at individual rates.

ISSUES IN CHILDREN'S HEALTH **Weight Gain.** Monitoring a baby's weight can give many hints about the infant's health and development. Infants may fail to gain weight if they are sick, fed formula that is mixed incorrectly, or kept to a feeding schedule that is too rigid. Weight loss can also occur because babies are given inadequate love and attention. Too much weight can also be a problem. Overweight babies are sometimes fed too often, given formula that is mixed incorrectly, or given highly sugared beverages.

COMPREHENSION CHECK

1. What purpose do fontanels serve? (*They allow the head to grow.*)
2. Distinguish between growth and development. (*Growth: size increase; development: increase in skills.*)
3. Why is hand-eye coordination important? (*Necessary for skills such as eating, catching balls, tying shoes.*)

ACTIVITIES

Critical Thinking Activity

Applying. Have students imagine that they are pediatricians giving checkups to six-month-olds. What would they say to parents of the following children:

- Tonya was 6 pounds, 7 ounces (2.9 kg) at birth. Now she is drastically below the average six-month-old weight.
- Peter was 6 pounds, 7 ounces (2.9 kg) at birth. Now he weighs much more than the average six-month-old. **L1**

Discussion Activity

Ask: Why do parents compare the growth of infants with that shown on the charts? What problems might arise when parents either disregard the information on growth charts or pay too much attention to it? **L1**

From birth to age one year, babies grow by about 50 percent. *What role does heredity play in height?*

Weight

In babies, weight gain is one of the best signs of good health. Most babies lose a little weight after birth and then begin to gain weight rapidly. In the first six months, a healthy baby gains 1 to 2 pounds (0.45 to 0.9 kg) per month. In the last half of the first year, the average weight gain is 1 pound (0.45 kg) a month. A baby's weight usually doubles in the first few months and triples by the end of the first year.

The average weight of a one-year-old is 20 to 22 pounds (9 to 10 kg). An individual baby's weight may differ depending on heredity, feeding habits, and level of physical activity.

Height

Growth in height is steady in the first year. The average newborn is 20 inches (51 cm) long. By one year, the average infant is about 30 inches (76 cm) long.

Heredity more strongly influences height than weight. A baby with tall parents is more likely to be tall than the child of short parents. Of course, tall parents can have short children. Since humans carry a mixture of genes, the results of any child's mixture can't be predicted.

252 UNIT 3: The Baby's First Year

Management/Leadership Skills

Ask the following questions about caring for a baby's vision:

- How can parents recognize that their baby may have a vision problem?
- What should parents do if they think their baby's vision is not developing appropriately?
- How might parents' own expectations make it difficult for them to recognize a problem with their baby's sight?

Proportion

In child development, **proportion** refers to the size relationship between different parts of the body. Compared to the rest of the body, a baby's head and abdomen are larger than an adult's. The legs and arms are short and small.

The head grows rapidly during the first year to provide room for the swiftly developing brain. Over half the total growth of the head occurs at this time. The skull of a newborn has spaces called "fontanels," which are gaps where bones have not yet joined. These fontanels allow the head to grow. They close around the age of eighteen months.

INFOLINK

Fontanels

To read more about *fontanels*, see Chapter 7, page 224.

Development During the First Year

The terms *growth* and *development* are often used to mean the same thing, but there is a difference. Growth refers to changes in size. Development refers to an increase in physical, emotional, social, or intellectual skills. Growth and development are both rapid during the first year.

If you observed a group of teens, you could probably tell older teens from the younger ones, but it would be difficult to identify the exact age of each individual. A fifteen-year-old and a sixteen-year-old look and act much alike. In contrast, it's easy to tell a newborn from a one-year-old. A baby not only grows bigger, but also develops many skills in the first year of life.

Sight

Eyesight improves rapidly. An infant's vision is blurry at first. Within a week or so, the newborn is increasingly aware of his or her surroundings and can focus on objects that are 7 to 10 inches (17.5 to 25 cm) away. By a month, infants can focus on objects as far away as 3 feet (0.9 m). By about three and one-half months, a baby's vision is almost as good as a young adult's.

Young babies prefer patterns that show high contrast, such as alternating stripes, bull's eyes—or faces. They prefer the color red. When shown the same object in different colors, they spend a longer time looking at the red one.

In the second month, infants begin to show **depth perception**. They become able to recognize that an object is three-dimensional, not flat. By the third month, babies prefer to look at real objects rather than flat pictures of objects.

With improved vision, babies develop **hand-eye coordination**. They gain increasing ability to move their hands and fingers precisely in relation to what is seen. Around the age of three or four months, babies begin to reach for objects they see; this is an important milestone. Hand-eye coordination develops throughout childhood. It is necessary for many skills, such as eating, catching a ball, coloring, and tying shoes.

Hearing

The sense of hearing develops even before birth. In fact, babies still in the uterus often respond to sounds with altered heart rates or with changes in activity levels.

Critical Thinking Activity

Synthesizing. Have students make a list of toys and activities that help develop hand-eye coordination. **L1**

Teamwork Activity

Organize students into groups. Give each group several infant toys, such as mobiles, wall hangings, and stuffed animals. Have groups evaluate the effectiveness of each toy in developing vision. **L2**

ISSUES IN CHILDREN'S HEALTH

Strabismus. At birth, babies' eyes do not move together. By about two or three months, they should do so. Some infants, though, have a problem called strabismus (or "eyeturn"), in which the muscles that control eye movement are weaker on one side than the other. As a result, the eyes do not move together, and the child cannot focus properly. Treatment may include eyeglasses, eyedrops, or surgery. Surgery is usually done when the child is between six and eighteen months old. Sometimes more than one surgery is needed to fix the problem.

Parenting in *Action*

Evaluate an eight- to twelve-month-old baby by looking for any of the following irregularities may indicate sight problems:
- Eyes that wander in or out.
- Inability to see or recognize distant objects or people.
- Fluid discharge in eyes.
- Eyes that don't move together.
- Sensitivity to light.
- Pupils of different sizes.
- Droopy eyelids.

COMPREHENSION CHECK

1. When does the sense of hearing develop? (*Before birth.*)
2. Why doesn't the sense of smell develop much before birth? (*Because a baby is surrounded by amniotic fluid until birth.*)

ACTIVITIES

Critical Thinking Activity

Recognizing Point of View. Have students write a journal entry from a year-old baby's point of view. The entry might indicate what physical change the "baby" considers most important and how the changes in the first year affect her or his life.

L2

| **VISUAL LEARNING** | **Using the Drawings** |

Answer: Babies begin to focus on faces when very young. That is why unbreakable mirrors are good toys-they enjoy looking at themselves.

| **VISUAL LEARNING** | **Using the Photograph** |

Possible response: The danger that they'll put in their mouth something sharp, poisonous, or small enough to be swallowed.

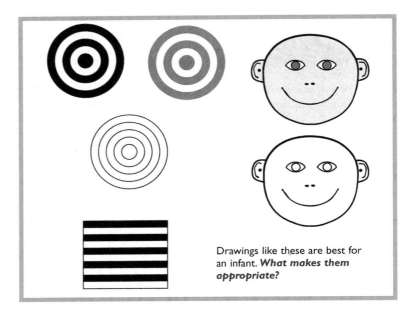

Drawings like these are best for an infant. *What makes them appropriate?*

At birth, a baby can already tell the general direction a sound comes from.

Newborns respond to the tone of a voice rather than to the words. A soothing, loving voice calms them. A loud or angry voice alarms them. Remember this when you care for a child—especially a newborn.

Babies use their mouths to explore their world. *What safety dangers does this present?*

Smell and Taste

Since a baby is surrounded by amniotic fluid until birth, the sense of smell doesn't have much chance to develop. A study has shown, however, that even newborns respond differently to different odors. Within ten days they can distinguish by smell their mother from another person.

254 Unit 3: The Baby's First Year

DID You Know?

Hearing. **Within hours after birth, babies respond to the sounds around them. Quiet, musical sounds can calm them; loud, high-pitched sounds excite or frighten them. Within weeks, babies recognize the voices** of people in their world, such as parents, grandparents, siblings, or other caregivers. By three months of age, babies cry out and listen for someone to walk toward their room. Babies also respond with smiles and movement when a parent or other caregiver talks to them, repeats their sounds, and stays near them.

Signs of Hearing Problems

*H*earing is essential for language develop-ment. Gradually attaching meanings to words that are heard is the baby's first step in learning to speak. Because hearing is so important, many physicians suggest that babies have a hearing test by about six months of age. This is especially important with premature babies, or if the baby has had fre-quent ear infections. These babies are most likely to have hearing problems.

Parents can watch for these signs of hearing prob-lems:

- A newborn isn't startled by a sharp clap of the hands.

- A three-month-old never turns toward the source of sounds.

- A baby is not awakened by loud noises, does not respond to familiar voices, and doesn't pay atten-tion to ordinary sounds.

A parent who notices any of these signs should dis-cuss them with the pediatrician. If a hearing problem is found, a referral will be made to a hearing specialist.

FOLLOWING UP
1. What groups of babies are especially likely to have hearing problems?
2. Why is it important to detect hearing problems as early as possible?

The sense of taste develops rapidly. In research studies, two-week-old babies have shown, through their sucking behavior, that they can taste the differences between water, sour liquids, sugar solutions, salt solu-tions, and milk. Even at this early age, babies show a preference for a sweet taste.

Throughout their first year, babies learn about their world by using their mouths. They put anything and everything into their mouths. Parents need to take care that the objects they do put in their mouths are clean; not too small, which could cause choking; and without edges that could cut.

Voice

The newborn's cry, initially quite shrill, becomes softer as the baby's lungs mature. This change also results from the physical growth of the throat muscles, tongue, lips, teeth, and vocal cords. The tongue and inte-rior of the mouth change in shape and pro-portion during the first months of life. This growth makes speech development possi-ble. Babies prepare for speech by making word-related sounds. They begin babbling vowel sounds, such as "ooh" and "ah" as early as three months of age.

CHAPTER 8: Physical Development During the First Year **255**

ISSUES IN CHILDREN'S HEALTH **Ear Infections.** It is common for babies to have ear infec-tions—in fact, two-thirds of all children have at least one ear infection before their second birthday. The problem typically occurs when fluid gathers in the middle ear during a cold or throat infection. The fluid becomes infect-ed with bacteria, which causes pain in the ear. Babies may signal that the ear is infected by tugging on it. Older children may say that their ear hurts. Ear infections need to be treated by doctors, who prescribe antibiotics.

COMPREHENSION CHECK

1. How do changes in the mouth and throat affect speech and feeding? (*Make speech possible; make swallowing solid foods possible.*)
2. When do the first "baby teeth" generally appear? (*About six or seven months.*)

ACTIVITIES

Critical Thinking Activity

Decision Making. Describe the following situation to the class: "Travis and Jenna have a seven-month-old daughter, Kirsten. For two days, Kirsten has been irritable and has seemed to feel unwell. She has also been drooling a lot and chewing on the front bar of her stroller."
Ask: What do you think the problem is? What would you do if you were one of Kirsten's parents? **L1**

ISSUES IN CHILDREN'S HEALTH

Baby's Teeth. Babies who are often put to bed with a bottle of juice or formula can develop early tooth decay. These babies often end up with sugary liquid in their mouths. The sugar is changed to acid by bacteria in the mouth. The acid attacks the teeth, causing tooth decay. The child could lose the baby teeth early, causing the remaining teeth to shift position to fill in the gaps. This could result in inadequate room for permanent teeth to come in.

Babies understand many words before they are able to speak. Many are physically ready for speech by the end of the first year. However, children learn to speak at different rates, and many don't say any words until after their first birthday.

The physical changes in the mouth and throat also affect feeding. At first the infant is able only to suck liquids. After these changes, the baby can swallow solid foods.

Teeth

The development of a baby's teeth actually begins about the sixth week of pregnancy. However, the first set of teeth a baby gets, called the **primary teeth** or "baby teeth," usually doesn't begin appearing until six or seven months of age. The complete set is generally finished by about twenty months. This timing varies widely.

Teething—the appearance of these teeth—is a normal process, but may be painful. As the teeth force their way up through the baby's gums, they tear the tender gum tissues. This often causes pain and swelling. During teething, a normally happy infant may become cranky or restless. Some babies refuse food and drool a lot. Teething can also cause other symptoms, including an increased desire for liquid, coughing, and fever.

Discomfort may last from two to ten days for each tooth. If teething pain persists or other serious symptoms develop, consult a doctor. For minor teething pain, these methods may be helpful:

- Offer teething biscuits or rubber teething rings so the baby can bite down hard on something to relieve the pressure on the gums.

- Since cold is a painkiller, rub an ice cube on the baby's gums to ease the pain temporarily.

You can rub a commercial teething medication onto the swollen gums. These have limited value, though, because they soon wash out with the baby's saliva.

Motor Skills

Much of the baby's development during the first year is in the area of **motor skills**. These are abilities that depend on the use and control of muscles. Mastering motor skills requires intellectual, social, and emotional development, as well as physical. This is because development in each area affects all other areas. The chart on pages 258-259 shows motor skill accomplishments during the first year.

One of the first motor skills infants acquire is control of the head. At birth, the head is large and heavy; and the neck muscles are weak. By age one month, babies placed on their stomach can lift their head slightly. By two or three months, they can lift their chest. At this age they can keep their head steady when propped in a sitting position.

LEARNING STYLES

Mathematical

Have students visit a supermarket, discount store, or pharmacy, and make a list of the medications available for easing teething pain. Ask students to include in their lists the price and size of each product, as well as notes about the directions for using it. On the basis of price and ease of use, have students decide which products, if any, they would try and explain the reasons for their decision. Compile a class list of products that students chose.

By nine months or so, the baby is crawling and beginning to explore his or her world. This is an exciting time for the baby, who has more independence than ever before. Mobility adds many new opportunities for learning.

INFOLINK

Safety

For more on *safety*, see Section 18-1.

This period also puts new demands on the parents, who have to ensure that their baby is safe while exploring. They must remove any objects that could endanger the baby, such as those made of glass. They also need to cover all exposed electrical outlets. The average home is full of things that could cause injury. Once babies start crawling, they can scoot into trouble very quickly. Parents must keep their eyes on their babies at all times.

SECTION 8-1 REVIEW

✔ Check Your Understanding

1. List the three basic patterns of physical development and give an example of one.
2. How much weight does an average healthy baby gain each month during the first year of life?
3. How do a baby's proportions compare with an adult's?
4. Describe the development of depth perception.
5. How do changes in a baby's throat muscles, tongue, lips, teeth, and vocal cords affect the ability to make sounds?
6. When do teeth generally appear?
7. List at least three motor skills that the average baby develops at seven to eight months.

Putting Knowledge Into Practice

1. **Applying.** What sensory activities could caregivers use to help stimulate hand-eye coordination in infants?
2. **Synthesizing.** Explain how speaking requires a combination of physical, emotional, social, and intellectual growth and development? Which pattern of development does it reveal?
3. **Observing and Participating.** Study the environment at an infant care center. Make a chart with headings for each of the five senses—sight, hearing, smell, taste, touch. Under each heading, list the features of the child care center that promote development of that sense in infants.

CHAPTER 8: Physical Development During the First Year **257**

Critical Thinking Activity

Applying. Have students count off the numbers for one to six. Form the students into groups organized by number. Assign all number ones the first age group in the illustration—ages one to two months. Assign three and four months to the number twos, and so on. Have each group identify and list activities that would promote the skills development of infants of that age. Compile students' suggestions into a booklet titled "Activities for Developing Motor Skills." **L1**

Teamwork Activity

Organize the class into small groups. Have them review the material regarding the development of motor skills in babies. Then have each group brainstorm safety issues that these new skills create. Ask each group to develop a pamphlet that illustrates ways to keep seven- to twelve-month-old babies safe. **L1**

ISSUES IN
TEEN PARENTING

Teen parents sometimes are not aware of the importance of giving babies activities designed to develop their motor skills. If you have teen parents in your class, you may wish to have them bring their babies to class. Encourage the parents to let their babies "show off" their motor skills. Then suggest that each teen parent demonstrate a simple game or routine he or she uses with the baby. Seeing what others do may provide new ideas to try.

Average MoTor Skills DevelopmenT from BirTh To Twelve MonThs

One to Two Months

- One month: Lifts chin when placed on stomach.
- Two months: Lifts chest well above surface when placed on stomach.

Three to Four Months

- Holds up head steadily.
- Reaches for objects, but unsteadily.
- Rolls from side to back and from back to side.

Five to Six Months

- Sits alone briefly.
- Uses hands to reach, grasp, crumble, bang, and splash.
- Turns completely over when laid on back or stomach.

258

Seven to Eight Months

- Sits up steadily.
- Reaches for spoon.
- Eats with fingers.
- Picks up large objects.
- Pulls self up while holding on to furniture.
- Propels self by arms, knees, or squirming motion.

Nine to Ten Months

- Is more skillful with spoon.
- Reaches for and manipulates objects, including medium-sized ones, with good control.
- Stands holding on to furniture or other supports.
- Crawls on hands and knees.
- Walks when led.

Eleven to Twelve Months

- Shows preference for one hand over the other.
- Holds and drinks from a cup.
- Fits blocks, boxes, or nesting toys inside each other.
- Picks up small objects using thumb and forefinger.
- Stands alone.
- May walk alone.

Writing Activity

Have students write in their journals about the growth and development of a baby during the first year. What do they consider the most important physical change to take place in that year? How does that change affect a baby's life? Caregivers' lives?

Charting Activity

Have students create a chart or timeline that shows the milestones of growth and development that parents might watch for in the first year of life.

VISUAL LEARNING | **Using the Photographs**

Refer students to the illustrations on these pages. Guide students in discussing the motor skills identified as average for babies of each age range. Encourage volunteers to share their own experiences in observing babies' motor skills. Remind students that individual babies may accomplish specific motor skills earlier or later than the period noted here.

Management/Leadership Skills

Describe the following situation to the class: "When a rattle is shaken in front of one-year-old Jamie, he responds to the noise but does not reach for the rattle. He does watch the rattle if someone moves it from side to side in front of him. If handed the rattle, he will bring it to his mouth and suck on it. Jamie crawls. When his parents stand him up, his legs fold beneath him and he plops down on the floor."

Have students evaluate Jamie's motor skill development. How might Jamie's parents use the problem-solving process (p. 127)?

The Developing Brain

(pages 260-266)

FOCUS

MOTIVATOR

Have students complete the following: "Three ways that the human body receives information are . . ." List students' responses on the board and discuss them. Point out that in this section students will learn about the brain's role in receiving information.

VOCABULARY ACTIVITY

Point out to students that many of the words in "Key Terms" have their roots in Greek and Latin. Have students find the etymologies of these terms. Then have them explain how the etymology provides a clue to meaning.

The Developing Brain

In their first year, babies grow and develop new skills. Hidden inside their heads—and powering the advances in development—are more amazing changes. How the brain takes shape in a baby's first year of life has profound effects on the baby's life.

KEY TERMS

axon
cortex
dendrite
myelin
neurons
synapse

OBJECTIVES:

• Explain what functions each part of the brain controls.
• Describe how brain cells work together.
• Explain how the brain becomes organized.
• Identify activities that support the development of brain pathways.

Structure of the Brain

Newborns learn about the world primarily through their senses—sight, hearing, smell, taste, and touch. The mobile moves when it is touched. Mother's heartbeat sounds familiar. Bananas give off a pleasant odor. A fist or a finger tastes different from milk. The blanket feels soft and fuzzy.

Observing & Participating

Have students read the subsection titles in this section and look at the illustrations. Then have them write facts about the brain that they know. Also, have them write questions about the brain and brain development that they would like to have answered. After students have completed the section, have them write responses to the questions that the section answered.

For babies, as for all of us, the information they learn through the senses is sent through the nerves to the brain. The brain is the key to intellectual development. It receives and interprets the messages from the body. The brain also develops the ability to send messages to the body, telling the muscles what to do.

In general, the responses of a newborn are physical reflexes; they don't originate in these kinds of messages from the brain. By the time the child is a year old, though, he or she has the ability to play with stacking toys, stand up, and perhaps even walk. All these skills result from the brain's growing ability to tell the body what to do.

The brain is divided into different sections, each controlling specific functions of the body. The major sections are shown in the diagram on below, along with the functions they control.

One of the most important parts of the brain is the **cortex** (CORE-teks), part of the cerebrum. Growth in this outer layer of the brain permits more complex learning. After one year of life, a baby's cortex is far better developed than it was at birth. The quality of caregiving affects brain growth.

Parts of the Brain

Cerebrum: Receives information from the senses and directs motor activities. Controls such functions as speech, memory, and problem solving. Most of these activities occur in the outer layer, called the "cortex," or "cerebral cortex."

Thalamus: Connects the spinal cord and cerebrum. Controls expression of emotions.

Pituitary Gland: Secretes hormones that regulate growth, metabolism, and sexual development.

Brain Stem: Controls involuntary activities such as breathing, heart rate, and blood pressure.

Cerebellum: Controls muscular coordination and balance.

Spinal Cord: Transmits information from the body to the brain and from the brain to the body.

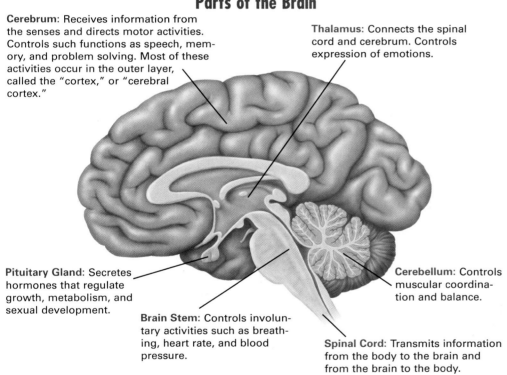

Each area of the brain has specific functions to perform.

CHAPTER 8: Physical Development During the First Year **261**

COMPREHENSION CHECK

1. How do babies learn about the world? (*Through their senses.*)
2. What does the cortex do? (*Permits more complex learning.*)

VISUAL LEARNING | **Using the Drawing** Refer students to the illustration on this page. Then provide students with a model of the brain. Have them find the sections of the brain and name the function of each.

The Developing Brain

Pregnancy

The early days of a pregnancy are important to the development of the cortex. During this time, the cells that make up the cortex have to get to the right place. As a result, it is an especially dangerous time for an expectant mother to come into contact with radiation or to take drugs. Good nutrition is essential. If the cells that make up the cortex are not developed properly in the cortex wall, the baby's brain development may be harmed.

LEARNING STYLES

Naturalistic

Have students create a model of the brain with modeling clay or play dough (a homemade version can be created with 2 cups flour, 1 cup salt, 1 cup water, and 2 tablespoons salad oil). After fashioning the material into a brain shape, have them paint different areas to identify the distinct sections of the brain. Then have them create a color coded guide that provides the name of the section and the functions it controls.

COMPREHENSION CHECK

1. Why is it important that neurons develop many links? (*The more links, the more paths the brain has, enabling it to do more tasks and control more actions.*)
2. How many neurons is a baby born with? (*All the neurons she or he will have in a lifetime.*)
3. What strengthens the connection between an axon and a dendrite? (*Repeated connections between the two.*)

Critical Thinking Activity

Synthesizing. Point out to students that the responses of newborns are generally physical reflexes. Ask students to describe the kinds of reflexes that they have observed in a newborn baby. **L1**

VISUAL LEARNING **Using the Drawing** Refer students to the "How Neurons Work" illustration on this page. Then have students create a flow chart showing the functions of the following: dendrites, axons, neurotransmitters, and synapses.

How the Brain Works

The brain is made up of billions of the nerve cells called neurons. An infant is born with all the neurons he or she will have—none are added during life.

Although *neurons* aren't added, dramatic changes do take place in the brain after birth. Neurons sprout arms called *dendrites* and *axons*. This process actually begins when the baby is developing in the mother's uterus. After birth, it happens more quickly. These arms can number in the hundreds or thousands for any neuron—or they can be only a few.

As the diagram below shows, these arms reach out toward the arms of other neurons. Although the arms from different neurons don't touch, they come very near. At the tiny gaps between them—the **synapses** (sin-AP-suhs)—messages are sent from one neuron to another.

The chemicals released by an axon are called *neurotransmitters*. These chemicals look for a dendrite to attach to—but they can only attach to those with the right kind

How Neurons Work

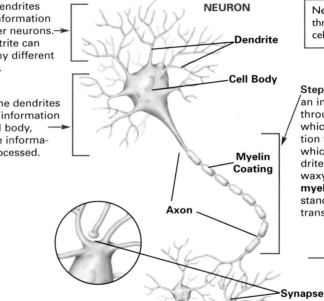

Step 1: Dendrites receive information from other neurons. Each dentrite can have many different branches.

Step 2: The dendrites pass that information to the cell body, where the information is processed.

NEURON

Neurons are divided into three parts: dendrites, the cell body, and axons.

Dendrite

Cell Body

Step 3: The cell body sends an instruction to the body through **axons** (ACKS-ons) which transmit the instruction to dendrites. Axons, which are longer than dendrites, are coated with a waxy substance called **myelin** (MY-uh-lin). This substance makes for easier transmission of information.

Myelin Coating

Axon

Synapse

OTHER NEURONS

Step 4: Chemicals called *neurotransmitters* are released by the axon and cross the gap to the dendrite of another nerve cell. That gap is called the *synapse*.

LEARNING STYLES

Kinesthetic

Organize students into small groups. Have each group choose a part of the brain and create a short skit to present to the class. The skit should show the purpose of the selected part and how the part interacts with other parts of the body. Encourage students to use props and drawings to make their skits more understandable. Call on each group to present its skit to the class.

of receptors. The more times the same axon and dendrite connect, the stronger the connection grows. As a result, they can send and receive messages more quickly.

The Developing Brain

A stimulating environment promotes the development of connections for movement, thought, and emotion.

Building the Brain

The more arms that neurons grow and the more links that develop between different neurons, the more paths the brain has.

More paths give the brain more power—it can do more tasks, control more actions. Think of a road system around a city. The more roads there are, the more places a driver can go.

These increased connections also give the brain more flexibility. Again, this is like a road system. The more roads there are, the more choices a driver has. If one road is shut down, there are alternate routes.

How the Brain Becomes Organized

Each child's brain becomes organized in a unique way. The organization is unique because it grows out of the child's experiences, which are unique to that child.

Networks in the Brain

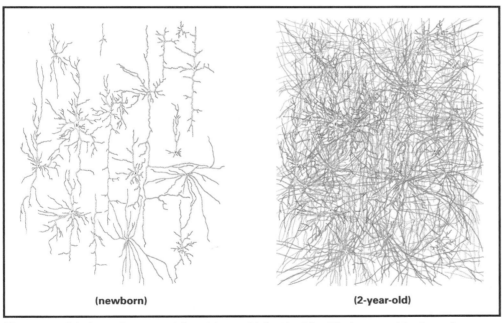

(newborn)   (2-year-old)

The image at left shows the neurons of a newborn, with few dendrites. The image at right shows the greater number of dendrites found in a two-year-old.

Parenting in *Action*

Parents of newborns and small children have a major role in their child's brain development. Parents should consider the following elements of their child's health to promote that development:
• Provide the best nutrition through breast-feeding or proper formula feeding. Providing a balanced diet throughout childhood.
• Support language development through face-to-face communication and reading.
• Raise a child in a positive, loving environment.
• Identify early developmental problems.

COMPREHENSION CHECK

1. What kind of experiences do young children need to learn? (*Physical experiences.*)
2. What kinds of activities are best to involve children in? (*Ones that they are emotionally involved in.*)

Critical Thinking Activity

Applying. Describe the following situation to the class: "Mabel and Ian wanted their daughter Brianna to learn to read early so they began using flash cards with her when she was two years old. They found that Brianna's skills developed about the same time as a neighbor child, whose parents did not use flash-cards." Have students explain why Brianna's reading skills developed as they did. **L1**

MULTIPLE INTELLIGENCES

In presenting his theory of multiple intelligences in *Frames of Mind*, Howard Gardner examines the findings of neurobiologists. After a brief survey of this work, Gardner concludes that there is "increasingly persuasive evidence" that different parts of the brain act as "functional units" that control specific kinds of mental tasks. This evidence, Gardner says, "suggest[s] a biological basis for specialized intelligences."

As connections between dendrites and axons grow stronger, a group of neurons becomes linked together. They become systems of nerve cells that control a particular action or thinking task.

For instance, one group of neurons can work together to control drinking from a cup. Each time a ten-month-old drinks from a cup, this system works together again and again. At first, the connection takes time to move the muscles. Eventually, after many repetitions, the neurons work together so well that it becomes easy for the child to drink from a cup.

These connections and systems affect all areas of behavior—not just actions. Systems of neurons work together to influence how people see and hear as well as think and remember.

The connections between neurons are not permanent. They can be broken. People

The addition of the myelin coat to nerve cells makes it easier for children to learn skills. **What areas of the brain first receive this coating?**

264 Unit 3: The Baby's First Year

lose synapses all through their lives. At the same time that some connections are being lost, new ones are added. They become part of the brain as new skills are learned or new experiences are stored as memories.

These developments have an impact on the appearance of the brain. Scientists have looked at the brains of professional violinists. These people tended to have extra large areas of the brain controlling the left hand—the one they use for their intricate fingering.

Speeding the Brain's Work

The drawing on page 262 indicates that axons have a waxy coating. This coating also plays a role in learning. Myelin makes it easier for axons to transmit signals—it speeds their work. All axons are not coated with myelin when a baby is born, however. At first, only those that control basic instincts such as nursing are.

Other axons become coated with myelin as the child grows. This process continues until about age twenty. The myelin coating is added in different areas of the brain at different times. Axons in the area of the brain that control such skills as motor abilities, vision, and hearing receive the coating the earliest. As a result, those are the areas in which babies first show development.

Observing & Participating

Have students observe parents or other caregivers with a newborn or older baby. Ask them to focus on the ways that the parents promote their baby's brain development. Examples are conversation, singing, and playing games such as peekaboo. Have them record these instances and then write a report of their observations.

Experts say that a child can benefit by having a rich environment. They aren't referring to a family with a great deal of money. **What do they mean by this comment?**

The rate at which axons receive this waxy coating may explain why children have difficulty learning certain tasks. If the nerves handling a certain activity are not yet covered with myelin, it would be difficult for a child to learn the activity. The lack of myelin does not make it *impossible* to learn the task. The presence of myelin, however, makes learning much easier.

Rules to Build a Brain By

Parents and caregivers can use these research findings to shape the environment of children and help develop their brains:

- **Keep it simple and natural.** Cuddling and hugging a baby, talking to the baby while changing a diaper or giving a bath, and playing peekaboo are all excellent ways of encouraging the baby's brain to build paths connecting neurons. Experts urge parents to give children a rich environment—one with lots of loving interaction and talking.
- **Match experiences to the child's mental capacities.** Some parents use flash cards to try to teach their babies to read. Many people say this works, but other experts say that in the long run it doesn't help the child. Young babies need physical experiences—that is how they learn. Remember that the axons for basic physical skills are the first to have myelin. Children learn to read more easily when they are older.
- **Remember that practice makes perfect.** The more times an experience is

repeated, the stronger the connections between neurons in the child's brain. When a young child asks to hear the same story every night, read it gladly.
- **Make sure the child is actively involved.** Give a child experiences in which he or she takes part. Children of all ages learn best by doing.
- **Provide variety, but avoid overloading the child.** Parents may think that by exposing their child to a many different of experiences, they can help the child become a great athlete, student, musician, *and* dancer. A more likely result is that a child would become unhappy. Give children a range of experiences engaging the senses, but avoid making them feel overwhelmed.

CHAPTER 8: Physical Development During the First Year **265**

ACTIVITIES

Critical Thinking Activity

Applying. Describe the following situation to the class: "Jamal often talks to his six-month-old daughter. He makes eye contact and uses various expressions to communicate to her." **Ask:** How is Jamal helping his daughter's brain development? **L1**

Debate Activity

Point out to students that six out of ten children under school age are enrolled in child care settings. According to the American Academy of Pediatrics, current state standards for child care settings do not provide high quality care that will promote brain development. Form students into two groups to debate this question: Should the government have more or fewer regulations of child care settings? **L2**

VISUAL LEARNING | **Using the Photographs**
Left: Those that control motor skills, vision, hearing. *Right:* They mean an environment rich in stimulation, full of language, opportunities for them to use their senses, and close physical contact.

Management/Leadership Skills

Ask students to choose two of the "rules to build a brain by" or randomly assign two "rules" to each student. Have students describe activities that they could use with a baby who is under their care that would promote the "rules" they have chosen. Call on volunteers to present their activities to the rest of the class. Ask class members to evaluate the effectiveness of each activity.

CHECKING COMPREHENSION

Have students answer the Check Your Understanding questions. Answers appear at the bottom of this page.

EVALUATION

Give students the Section 8-2 Quiz in the *Teacher Resource Guide*.

RETEACHING

1. Assign Reteaching Activities, page 29.
2. Have students create a graphic organizer that presents the basic information about the brain: its parts, how it is organized, how it develops, and what the implications of that development are.

ENRICHMENT

Have students find out what early scientists, such as the Galen and Vesalius, believed about the brain and prepare a brief report.

EXTENSION

Ask a neurologist to visit the class. Ask him or her to talk to students about the latest equipment and techniques used to measure brain activity.

CLOSE

Have students write a paragraph from the point of view of a one-year-old's brain. How has it changed in a year?

• **Avoid pushing the child.** Children learn better if they are emotionally involved in what they're doing. Look for clues as to whether the child is interested in the activity. If not, don't pursue it any more.

Is the Brain Organized Once Only?

During the first year of life, the brain becomes organized in the unique way that reflects the child's individuality. Is this the only time the brain can be organized? If basic groundwork is not set now, is a child locked out of certain possibilities in life?

The answer is "no." There are a number of situations which prove this isn't the case. Some children who suffered damage to the brain area that controls language have still learned to speak. Older people who suffer strokes—where neurons in an area of the brain die—can relearn skills by learning to use other areas of the brain.

The brain can be reorganized. In practical terms, that means a child doesn't have to be exposed to every possible activity in the first year—or even few years—of life. What is important is to give young children a stimulating environment. By doing so, parents and other caregivers help children's brains develop many pathways and connections.

SECTION 8-2 REVIEW

✔ Check Your Understanding

1. What activities does the cerebellum control?
2. What is the role of dendrites and axons in the brain?
3. How does the presence of myelin help axons work?
4. How do repeated experiences help organize the brain?
5. What happens to synapses throughout life?
6. What impact on learning results from the rate of the spread of myelin?
7. What is meant by giving infants a stimulating environment?

Putting Knowledge Into Practice

1. **Drawing Conclusions.** Name some activities that promote the growth of connections in the brain.
2. **Analyzing.** Would you agree with the statement "The brain can be reorganized, but it's easiest to organize it right the first time?" Why or why not?
3. **Observing and Participating.** Try writing your name with your opposite hand. Then use your normal hand. With which is it easier? Why?

ANSWERS TO SECTION 8-2 REVIEW

1. Motor activity; speech; memory; problem solving.
2. *Dendrites:* Receive information from other neurons. *Axons:* Pass instructions from cell body on to other neurons.
3. Helps axons send messages more quickly.
4. Dendrites and axons work more quickly.
5. Some connections are lost; some new ones form.
6. Myelin takes up to 20 years to coat all axons, so all tasks cannot be learned with equal ease at all ages.
7. *Possible response:* Provide lots of loving interaction and lots of talking.

Nuclear Medicine Technologist

A CONVERSATION WITH AARON FORD

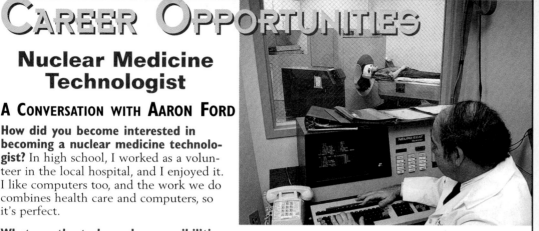

How did you become interested in becoming a nuclear medicine technologist? In high school, I worked as a volunteer in the local hospital, and I enjoyed it. I like computers too, and the work we do combines health care and computers, so it's perfect.

What are the tasks and responsibilities of a nuclear medicine technologist? We perform tests on patients by giving them safe doses of radioactive drugs. Then we position them carefully in a machine that can detect how those drugs are moving throughout the body. The results are displayed on a computer screen and can be used by doctors to understand a patient's condition.

What is the work environment like? We work in a hospital in an area that's like a lab. It's clean and quiet.

What are the working hours like? Usually we work forty-hours a week, but if there's an emergency we may have to work at night or on weekends.

What aptitudes are needed to be a nuclear medicine technologist? You need to be extremely careful and pay attention to detail. You have to follow strict procedures to protect the patient and yourself from radiation. You also have to carefully maintain medical records. It helps to be strong, too. For the test, patients need to be put on a table and sometimes they're too old or weak to do it themselves. It helps to be sympathetic—to put people at ease.

Career Facts

NUCLEAR MEDICINE TECHNOLOGIST

Education and Training. Nuclear medicine technologists need four years of training, which can include a two-year associate degree and two years in a special training program.

Career Outlook. The demand for these workers should grow much faster than average.

CONNECTING SCHOOL TO CAREER

1. **Technology.** Why is safety such an important concern for these workers?
2. **Basic Skills.** Which basic skills do you think would be more important to a nuclear medicine technologist—math or writing? Why?

CHAPTER 8: Physical Development During the First Year **267**

CAREER OPPORTUNITIES

Introducing the Feature

Ask if they have heard of MRIs, CT scans, or PET scans. All are different ways of creating images of structures and processes within the body. Have them research why each might be used on a child's head. These procedures are performed by a worker called a nuclear medicine technologist because they use radioactive substances.

Answers to
CONNECTING SCHOOL TO CAREER

1. **Possible response:** Because radioactive drugs are involved.
2. **Possible response:** Math because that will be needed more to work with the electrical equipment.

Applying What You've Learned

Ask students to evaluate the career. Have them indicate which aspects of the job they consider interesting and which not interesting. Is the career one that they might consider? Why or why not?

Building Career Skills

Interpersonal Skills. Nuclear medicine technologists often need to put people at ease before they have the procedure. Have students work in pairs and prepare a skit. One student will take the role of a technologist who is about to perform a scan on a child or adult who is very upset and won't stay still. The other student is the patient. Students should indicate the kinds of things they might say and do to ease the person's concerns and tension. Have students present the skits to the class.

SECTION 8-3 RESOURCES

Teacher Resource Guide
• Lesson Plan Organizer, p. 56
• Section 8-3 Quiz, p. 140

Student Motivation Kit
• Observ. & Case Studies (case study), pp. 107-108
• Reteaching Activity, p. 30
• Enrichment, p. 26
• Nurt. Brain Dev., p. 47
• Teen Parenting Skills, pp. 73, 75-80, 89-90

Student Workbook
• Study Guide, pp. 71-75
• Healthy Caring for Babies, pp. 79-80

Effective Instruction CD-ROM

FOCUS

MOTIVATOR

Ask students to imagine themselves as new parents who suddenly realize that they have a newborn baby for whom they have to take care of everything. Let students brainstorm a list of concerns that come to mind.

VOCABULARY ACTIVITY

The effects of inadequate nutrition is sometimes called *malnutrition*. Have students analyze the structure of *malnutrition* to better understand its meaning. The prefix *mal* means "bad" or "wrong." The root *nutrition* comes from the Latin *nutrire*, which means "to nourish." Ask them what factors contribute to undernourishment.

SECTION 8-3

Handling and Feeding Infants

An infant requires a huge amount of physical care. Learn how to lift, hold, and carry a baby gently. A baby's nutritional needs also need to be met to fuel all the physical and brain growth and development taking place.

KEY TERMS

shaken baby syndrome
weaning

OBJECTIVES:

• Explain how to hold and feed a baby.
• Identify an infant's nutritional needs.

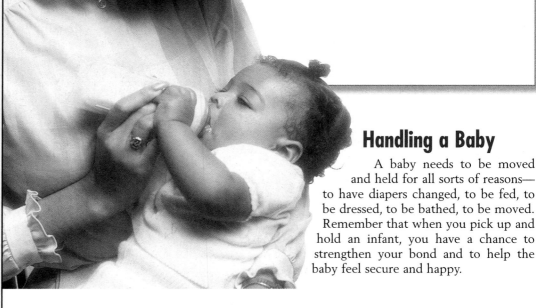

Handling a Baby

A baby needs to be moved and held for all sorts of reasons—to have diapers changed, to be fed, to be dressed, to be bathed, to be moved. Remember that when you pick up and hold an infant, you have a chance to strengthen your bond and to help the baby feel secure and happy.

268 UNIT 3: The Baby's First Year

Observing & Participating

Ask students to observe parents and their babies in public settings such as a park or a shopping mall. Have them note the ways that the parents or caregivers picked up and put down their children. Also, have them observe how they fed their babies. Discuss students' observations in class. When students have completed Section 8-3, have them compare their observations with the directives for handling and for feeding babies described in the section.

Newborns, of all babies, require the greatest care in handling because their neck muscles can't support their head. For that reason, you must keep your hand or arm under the baby's neck and head at all times. The photographs below show how to lift, hold, and put down a newborn safely.

Handling a Newborn Safely

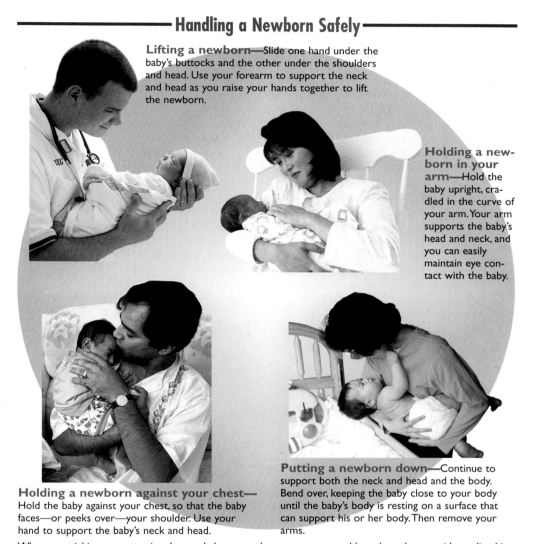

Lifting a newborn—Slide one hand under the baby's buttocks and the other under the shoulders and head. Use your forearm to support the neck and head as you raise your hands together to lift the newborn.

Holding a newborn in your arm—Hold the baby upright, cradled in the curve of your arm. Your arm supports the baby's head and neck, and you can easily maintain eye contact with the baby.

Holding a newborn against your chest—Hold the baby against your chest, so that the baby faces—or peeks over—your shoulder. Use your hand to support the baby's neck and head.

Putting a newborn down—Continue to support both the neck and head and the body. Bend over, keeping the baby close to your body until the baby's body is resting on a surface that can support his or her body. Then remove your arms.

Whenever picking up or putting down a baby, remember to move smoothly and gently to avoid startling him or her.

CHAPTER 8: Physical Development During the First Year **269**

Parenting in *Action*

Each caregiver who participates in raising a newborn may develop a personal style of holding the infant; all, however, should begin by assuming that being held comforts the baby. Some infants have distinct preferences about being held in certain ways, and some infants—though very few—do not like to be held too long or too frequently. These babies will soon make their distinct needs known. In general, however, caregivers should show their love and caring by holding and cuddling the baby frequently.

COMPREHENSION CHECK

1. What is shaken baby syndrome? (*Damage to the baby's brain caused when someone severely shakes a baby.*)
2. Why are frequent feedings necessary for newborns? (*Newborn's stomach can hold only a small amount of food.*)
3. At what point in a baby's life does a regular pattern of feeding emerge? (*About two or three months of age.*)

ACTIVITIES

Teamwork Activity

Describe the following situation to the class: "You're visiting a friend and her three-month-old son. Your friend cannot get the baby to stop crying. Finally, in anger, she picks the baby up, shakes him, and screams, 'Stop it!' and begins to cry herself."
Organize the class into small groups. Have each group suggest appropriate methods for releasing anger. Then have each group present its ideas to the class. **L1**

Discussion Activity

Ask: Have you ever seen a woman breast-feeding her baby in public? How did she handle the baby to maintain her privacy? **L1**

INFOLINK

Child Abuse

For more information on *child abuse and neglect*, see Section 19-2, pages 589-592.

By about four months, the baby can hold up his or her own head. Even then, handle the baby gently and hold the baby close to ensure a sense of security.

Gentle Handling

When you are handling a baby or young child, never—ever—shake or jiggle him or her. These actions are dangerous. Every year thousands of babies suffer serious problems due to **shaken baby syndrome**. This condition is caused when someone severely shakes the baby, usually in an effort to make the baby stop crying. It can lead to damage to the baby's brain, learning problems, mental retardation, blindness or deafness, and even death.

When babies cry a great deal, it can be very stressful to parents—especially new parents. Frustrated, they may resort to shaking. There are better—and safer—ways of handling the situation:

- Put the baby down in a safe place and go into another room to calm down before returning to the baby.
- Ask a friend or relative who is available to care for the baby.
- Take some deep breaths or look out the window to calm down.
- Call someone and talk about your problem until you are calm.

Gently rocking or playfully bouncing the baby on the knee are not dangerous. Strong shaking is.

Feeding a Baby

Mealtime provides a baby with much more than physical nourishment. The baby can also enjoy contact with other people and learn about the world. The cuddling, body contact, and nurturing that go with feeding are as important as the food.

Feeding Schedules

A newborn's schedule of eating and sleeping is unpredictable at first. Newborns need to eat as much as they want and as often as they want. In the first few weeks of life, that may be up to six to eight times—or more—in 24 hours. Frequent feedings are necessary because a newborn's stomach can hold only a small amount. Babies who are breast-fed tend to eat more often than those fed by bottle.

By the second or third month, a regular pattern generally emerges. The baby may wake for a feeding every three or four hours. Eventually, the baby will no longer need a late night feeding. By about 12 pounds (5.4 kg), a baby can usually sleep through the night. At that size, the stomach can hold more food.

As the baby grows, feeding schedules continue to change. Most one-year-olds eat three meals a day, plus snacks.

Feeding Methods

In the first year, the baby's chief food is breast milk or formula. Pediatricians recommend against cow's milk before babies are a year old. This milk is hard for babies to digest and has minerals their kidneys cannot process. Formulas based on cow's milk are acceptable—the milk has been changed to remove these problems.

A mother who breast-feeds can receive advice while still in the hospital or birthing center. Information and help are also available from La Leche League, a group that promotes breast-feeding, or the baby's pediatrician.

Management/Leadership Skills

Describe the following situation to the class: "You are the parent of a six-week old infant. An older adult relative persists in jiggling the baby in a way you consider dangerous. When you voice your concern to the relative, he says, 'Don't worry—we're just playing.'"

Ask students what they might say or do. Have class members evaluate the effectiveness of each suggestion. Which show leadership?

Whenever you feed an infant from a bottle, hold the baby close in a semi-upright position. Remember that the young baby's head and neck need to be supported, and the head should be held well above the level of the baby's stomach. Hold the bottle at an angle, so that the baby can suck comfortably. This also keeps the nipple full of milk, which prevents the baby from swallowing too much air.

Many parents prefer to give their baby a warm bottle, although this isn't really necessary. To warm formula, fill the bottle and place it in a pan of water on the stove. Then heat the water in the pan until it makes the formula lukewarm. You can also use a special bottle warmer or hold the bottle under hot running water. Check the temperature from time to time by shaking a few drops of formula onto your wrist. It should feel lukewarm, not hot.

If formula is warmed, check the temperature before feeding. **How should the formula feel?**

Never heat the formula in a microwave oven. Microwave heating can create dangerous "hot spots" in the formula that burn the baby.

If there is any formula left in the bottle, throw it away. Disease-causing bacteria can grow quickly in leftover formula and could lead to illness.

These bacteria may also stay in the bottle even after it has been emptied and cleaned. Feeding bottles should be sterilized. A pediatrician may recommend placing them in boiling water after washing, using the hot water cycle in a dishwasher, or some other method. Nipples, bottle rings, and bottle caps should be sterilized in the same way.

No matter how busy you feel, never leave a bottle propped up so that a baby can drink from it alone. The baby misses out on the important physical contact and attention. Also, the formula typically gushes from a propped bottle, which can cause digestive problems and ear infections. Finally, propping bottles can lead to tooth decay because the sugar in the formula or juice pools up around the teeth.

Whether breast-feeding or bottle-feeding, continue the feeding until the infant seems satisfied. Healthy babies usually eat the amount they need.

Burping the Baby

Whichever method of feeding is used, burp the baby at least twice— once during the feeding and once when the feeding is over. Women who breast-feed burp the baby when they

Math Activity

Infants under six months need about 55 calories per pound each day. Most formulas have about 20 calories per ounce. Have students figure out approximately how many ounces of formula a twelve-pound baby needs each day. (*2.75 ounces of formula would supply the calories for 1 pound of an infant's weight. So a 12-pound baby would need 33 ounces of formula.*) **L1**

VISUAL LEARNING	Using the Photograph

Answer: Lukewarm, not hot.

DID You Know?

Breast-Feeding. The American Academy of Pediatrics recommends that women breast-feed their babies as breast milk is the best food for infants. It is recommended that a nursing mother gives an infant about ten minutes on each breast, with a pause for burping in between. This will keep the milk supply even. Because a baby sucks most efficiently at the beginning of each feeding, the mother should alternate the breast used first from one feeding to the next.

LEARNING STYLES

Interpersonal

Discuss with students how older siblings might react when they see their parents drop everything to cuddle and feed a newborn. Have students provide suggestions for addressing this problem by focusing on the following questions:
• Should parents moderate their responses to the newborn's needs? If so, how and why? If not, why not?
• How should parents respond to the older sibling? Why?
• Who else might be available to help an older sibling? How might they help?

CHECKING COMPREHENSION

1. When should solid foods be added to a baby's diet? (*About six months.*)
2. How should the temperature of warmed baby food be checked? (*Place a drop on the wrist.*)

ACTIVITIES

Teamwork Activity

Have students work in small groups to prepare a cartoon strip titled "Things to Do When Bottle-Feeding Your Baby." The content of the cartoon strip should focus on how to prepare the formula, what to do with leftover formula, how to hold the baby during feeding, and how and why to burp the baby during the feeding. Encourage students to be creative when creating the cartoons. Display completed cartoon strips on a bulletin-board display for students to share. **L1**

VISUAL LEARNING | **Using the Photograph**
Answer: To help the baby expel any air that may have been swallowed along with the liquid. If kept in the stomach, this air could bother the baby.

How to Burp a Baby

There are two positions for burping a baby. Either lay the baby across your knees or hold the baby across your chest with the head above your shoulders. Then pat the baby gently on the back to induce the burp. Protect your clothes with a cloth on your lap or over your shoulder under the baby's head. This will catch any liquid that comes out. **Why is burping needed?**

---

switch the baby from one breast to the other.

Babies often swallow air along with the liquid. Burping helps them expel this air and avoid any discomfort. Don't be surprised, though, if the baby doesn't actually burp each time.

Introducing New Foods

Around the age of six months, other foods begin to be added to the baby's diet. The pediatrician will recommend when to introduce "solids."

With most babies, there is no rush to introduce new foods. Choose a time when the baby is well, content, and happy. Don't begin solids, for example, if the infant has been sick or the family is moving. Don't worry about postponing new foods for a while; breast milk or formula can provide all the nutrition the baby needs.

Because each new food is unfamiliar, the baby may spit back the first spoonfuls. You can reintroduce the food later, or try combining it with a favorite food to make it more acceptable. Show patience as the baby adjusts to this new experience.

Following these feeding tips will help make the experience safe and enjoyable for both the baby and you:

- For the first feedings, hold the baby comfortably in a fairly upright position.
- If the baby is used to warm formula, heat solid foods to lukewarm, too. As with formula, don't use a microwave to heat a baby's food. Check the temperature of warmed foods by placing a drop on your wrist.

272 UNIT 3: The Baby's First Year

ISSUES IN CHILDREN'S HEALTH **Feeding.** Some parents are eager to start babies on "real food," and many mistakenly think that feeding cereal to babies before putting them to bed at night will help them sleep better. A study to test this theory was conducted using 106 babies in two groups. The average age of the babies was about five weeks in one group and four months in the other. Researchers found that cereal before bed did not alter the amount of time that the babies in either group spent crying, fussing, or sleeping.

Ask the E?perts

Dr. Van Stone
Pediatrician
Tupelo, Mississippi

Giving *a Baby Solid Foods*

 How should I introduce solid foods?

Although offering babies solid food at a very early age is a common practice, the American Association of Pediatrics recommends waiting to introduce solids until approximately 4-6 months of age. Foods with a soft, pureed consistency should generally be introduced first.

A baby's first solid food is usually cereal—first rice, then oatmeal, barley, and wheat. Wheat is saved for last because it can cause allergic reactions in some young babies. These cereals can be bought dry and mixed with formula, breast milk, or water, or they can be served from jars.

After cereals, introduce vegetables, fruits, and meats. You can also give the baby fruit juices. Some foods pose particular problems and need to be handled carefully. Corn, eggs, and citrus juices usually aren't introduced before one year.

Avoid giving a cow's milk or milk products—including cheese—until the baby is a year old.

It is important to introduce foods slowly, bringing in a new food only about every four days. That way, if a certain food causes a skin rash or digestive trouble, you will be able to identify which food is causing the problem. You can continue to give the baby foods that he or she has already been introduced to. This gives the infant variety in his or her diet.

Most foods should be cooked, not raw. Bananas are an exception—they can simply be mashed.

You don't need to buy baby food. You can create your own by cooking vegetables, fruits, and meat. If you do, avoid putting seasonings—including salt—on the food. Once the food is cooked, put it through a blender or food processor and make it soft and easy for the baby to digest.

Thinking It Through

1. What kinds of foods are likely to be easiest to digest? Why do you say so?
2. What would be the advantages and disadvantages of purchased baby food versus home prepared?

CHECKING COMPREHENSION

1. What are some signs that a baby is ready to be weaned? (*Looking around while sucking, pushing the nipple away, preferring to eat from a spoon.*)
2. About what age is a baby ready to self-feed? (*Around eight or ten months.*)

ACTIVITIES

Critical Thinking Activity

Analyzing. Describe the following situation to the class: "Erica, an 11-month-old baby, often insists on feeding herself. Sometimes her parents won't let her." **Ask:** Why is it important to encourage self-feeding? **L2**

Teamwork Activity

Have students work with partners to plan, write, and illustrate a simple guide for new parents, explaining how to introduce new foods to their baby. **L2**

Research Activity

Have students research the importance of good nutrition and adequate folic acid to the development of the brain. Ask them to check folic acid levels in foods for infants. **L2**

VISUAL LEARNING	Using the Photographs

Left—Answer: Prevents spills.
Right—Answer: Hand-eye coordination.

- Be prepared for messy feedings, especially at first. Put a large bib on the baby, and be sure your own clothes are either easily washable or protected.
- When the baby starts eating cereal, make it very runny by diluting it with either breast milk or formula. Runny cereal seems more familiar to a baby—like the milk or formula he or she is used to. The cereal should be offered on a spoon, however, not in a bottle, because solid matter in the bottle may cause the baby to choke.
- If you are using baby food from a jar, take out a small portion and place it in a bowl. Then close the jar and refrigerate it immediately. Don't feed the baby directly from the jar. Bacteria from the spoon will grow rapidly in the food and cause leftovers to spoil.

Weaning

Sometimes around the first birthday, many babies are ready for **weaning**, changing from drinking from the bottle or breast to drinking from a cup. Weaning is an important sign of the baby's increasing independence.

There is no precise age at which the baby should be weaned. Nine months is common, but the age varies greatly. The baby usually shows some signs of readiness, such as playing or looking around while sucking, pushing the nipple away, or preferring to eat from a spoon. Rather than forcing weaning, wait until the baby is ready and accepts naturally. Forced weaning may result in other feeding and behavior problems for the child.

Self-Feeding

When babies can sit up steadily, usually at about eight or ten months, they start to eat with their fingers and reach for a spoon. These are signs that the infant is ready to begin self-feeding. To encourage self-feeding, provide "finger foods."

The baby's first efforts at self-feeding with a spoon will probably be fun for the baby but may not produce much actual eating. You can help by using a separate spoon and placing bits of food in the baby's mouth now and then.

It takes patience—and a sense of humor—to encourage self-feeding. You and the baby will both benefit if you allow plen-

A baby who is beginning to eat solids can also begin learning to drink from a cup. *Why is it a good idea to use a plastic cup with a lid?*

Observing & Participating

Ask students to feed—or help feed—a baby who has started eating solids. Suggest that students take notes for answers to the following questions:
- How does the baby respond to different foods?
- How does the baby show an interest in self-feeding?
- What methods does the caregiver use to meet the baby's nutritional needs?

Have students present their findings to the class.

ty of time for each meal. Then encourage the baby's efforts and enjoy his or her delight in new accomplishments.

Nutritional Concerns

Part of the responsibility of parents and caregivers is making sure that babies' nutritional needs are being met. This is usually not difficult if the child receives formula or breast milk until starting to eat a good variety of cereals, vegetables, fruits, and meats. However, problems can result if the baby is given too much food, too little food, or the wrong kinds of food.

Around the age of eight to ten months, infants show an interest in self-feeding. *Name one type of development needed for self-feeding to take place.*

ACTIVITIES

Social Studies Activity

Have students research the problem of inadequate nutrition around the world. Have them find out what is being done to address the problem. Why would inadequate nutrition be particularly harmful for infants? Ask them to prepare a written or an oral report of their findings.. **L2**

VISUAL LEARNING | Using the Photograph
Possible response: Great influence—eating habits are established in this period.

DID *You* **Know?**

Inadequate Nutrition. **Signs of poor nutrition vary depending upon the particular nutrient deficiency. Possible signs include growth that falls well below average for an age; listlessness; nervous or irritable behavior; scaling around the nose and ears; wounds that are slow to heal; hair that is dull, lifeless, thin, and easy to pull out; swollen and congested eyelids; poor posture; poor coordination; and diarrhea. The swollen stomach often associated with inadequate nutrition is the result of insufficient protein.**

These teens enjoy active lives and eat nutritious foods. *What influence does infancy have on eating habits?*

Overfeeding

As they gain weight in the first months after birth, babies may look fat. In fact, the percentage of body fat does rise in a baby's first six months. This body fat generally is not anything to worry about—most babies slim down by age three.

INFOLINK
Food Guide Pyramid
For more on the *Food Guide Pyramid*, see Chapter 6, page 187.

Bottle-fed babies may be more likely to be overfed than those who breast-feed. Parents may urge the baby to finish all the formula left in the bottle, even if the child is full. Any parent concerned about a baby's weight should talk to a pediatrician.

Healthy eating habits are established early in life. Parents can help their babies develop those healthy habits by eating in a healthy way themselves. Using the Food Guide Pyramid is a good start. Young children need the same types of nutritious foods, but the serving sizes should be smaller. Help children learn to enjoy fresh fruits and vegetables instead of salty and fatty foods.

Inadequate Nutrition

Infants have very specific nutritional needs in order to be healthy:
- Enough calories to provide for rapid growth.
- Food that contains needed nutrients, such as protein, iron, B vitamins, vitamin C, and vitamin D.

- Food that is easy to digest.
- Adequate amounts of liquid.

Babies whose diets don't meet these needs may suffer from poor nutrition, or "under nutrition"—a lack of enough food or a lack of the proper type of food. Some parents don't have enough money to provide their babies with an adequate diet. Others don't know about babies' special food needs or they feed their children high-calorie foods that are low in nutrients. Fatty foods or foods high in sugar, for instance, should be avoided. Fat-free or diet foods are also inappropriate.

Management/Leadership Skills

Have students find out where parents in their community could go to learn about the nutritional needs babies have and what foods babies need to meet these needs. Students might contact their local government to find out what programs are available. Have students compile a list of the available programs, together with addresses, phone numbers, and web sites.

Inadequate nutrition in infancy can cause lasting physical problems. Poor nutrition at any stage of childhood is also linked to poor brain development and learning problems.

Many government and community programs try to eliminate infant and childhood malnutrition. Some of these programs provide food; others teach parents about the nutritional needs of children. The federal government's Women, Infants, and Children Program (WIC) helps meet the special food needs of new mothers and young children. Other programs in your area may be funded by state and local governments or commuting groups.

SECTION 8-3 REVIEW

✔ Check Your Understanding

1. Which part of a newborn's body do you always need to support when lifting or holding the baby? Why?
2. What damage may be caused by severely shaking a baby?
3. Why should babies not be given cow's milk in their first year?
4. Describe the position in which a baby should be held for bottle-feeding.
5. Why burp a baby?
6. What nutritional needs does a baby have?
7. If a parent is concerned that a baby is overfeeding, should the parent cut back on the baby's food? Why or why not? If not, what should the parent do?

Putting Knowledge Into Practice

1. **Sequencing.** Put the following foods in the right order for introducing solids to a baby: cereals, meat, eggs, fruit, vegetables.
2. **Analyzing.** Why not start a baby self-feeding at about six months?
3. **Observing and Participating.** Ask a parent of a small baby how often the baby feeds. Find out if the parent breast-feeds or bottle-feeds the baby. Compare your findings to those of other students in the class. What patterns, based on age and type of feeding, can you find?

CHECKING COMPREHENSION

Have students answer the Check Your Understanding questions. Answers appear at the bottom of this page.

EVALUATION

Give students the Section 8-3 Quiz in the *Teacher Resource Guide.*

RETEACHING

1. Assign Reteaching Activities, page 30.
2. Give each student an opportunity to use a doll to demonstrate picking up, putting down, comforting, or feeding a newborn.

ENRICHMENT

Ask students to research commercial baby food. They might look into nutrition, safety, or cost issues. Have students present their findings in an oral or written report.

EXTENSION

Have students find out which programs in their community help meet the special food needs of new mothers and young children.

CLOSE

Have students write a list of ten rules for feeding infants.

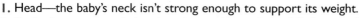

ANSWERS TO SECTION 8-3 REVIEW

1. Head—the baby's neck isn't strong enough to support its weight.
2. Brain damage, retardation, learning problems, being blind or deaf, death.
3. Hard for babies to digest; has minerals the baby's kidneys cannot process.
4. Supporting head and neck and holding bottle at an angle.
5. To help baby expel any air swallowed while feeding and avoid discomfort.
6. Enough calories for rapid growth; needed nutrients; food that is easy to digest; adequate amounts of liquid.
7. No, because babies tend to be fat. The parent should talk to the pediatrician.

SECTION 8-4

Other Infant Care Skills
(pages 278-289)

FOCUS

MOTIVATOR

Display photographs of babies' outfits clipped from catalogs or from magazines. Have students comment on whether they think each item would be appropriate for an infant and why or why not.

VOCABULARY ACTIVITY

Tell students that "cradle cap" is a condition that affects children. **Ask:** what part of the body they think it affects. (*Students should infer the head from the name.*) At what ages do they think it is prevalent? (*Infancy, since "cradle" is in the name.*)

Other Infant Care Skills

Caring for a baby can—and should—be fun. A caregiver who is competent and confident in carrying out basic care routines can enjoy the baby and contribute to the baby's appreciation and enjoyment of the world. These routines include bathing, dressing, and diapering. Proper sleep habits are also important for the baby's health.

KEY TERMS
cradle cap
diaper rash
sleeper

OBJECTIVES:
• Describe or demonstrate how to bathe, dress, and diaper a baby.
• Tell how to encourage good sleep habits.

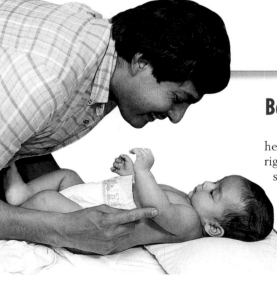

Bathing a Baby

A bath helps keep a baby clean and healthy. Any time is fine for a bath except right after feeding. Then the baby needs to sleep and digest the meal.

A newborn is given sponge baths for about two weeks, until the navel heals. After that, a tub bath may be given. Both types of baths require the parent's careful attention to ensure the baby's safety.

278 UNIT 3: The Baby's First Year

Observing & Participating

Experienced caregivers are comfortable judging safe temperatures for a baby's bath water. Students may benefit from some practice. Have students to test the temperature of running water and standing water, using their wrists, fingertips, whole hands, and elbows. Which part is most sensitive to the temperature of the water. Have students use thermometers to check their temperature estimates. Ask them to describe water that measures lukewarm, about 98° F (37° C).

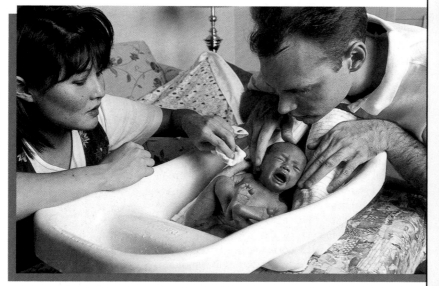

Until the navel heals, parents should give newborns a sponge bath. *About when does the navel usually heal?*

Sponge Baths

Many of the same basic supplies are needed for both sponge baths and tub baths. These include:

- Two soft bath towels
- A soft washcloth
- A diaper
- Mild soap
- Baby shampoo

Before bathing a baby, assemble these articles and the baby's clean diaper and clothes in a warm place with no drafts. The temperature of the room should be 70° to 80°F (20° to 26°C). Choose a room with a good work surface—usually the bathroom, kitchen, or baby's room. Place a soft bath towel over the work area for the baby's comfort and safety.

For sponge baths, it's convenient to put the bathwater in a basin on the work surface. Test the water temperature with your elbow, where the skin is more sensitive than on your hands. The water should feel lukewarm, about 98°F (37°C).

Remove the baby's clothes and place the infant on the towel. Lay another towel on top of the baby's body. Begin by washing the baby's face with clear water and a soft washcloth, while supporting the baby with your other hand. Then pat the baby's face dry. A young baby's skin is very tender, so never rub it with a towel.

Wash the rest of the body with baby soap and water, one area at a time. Rinse thoroughly. Pay particular attention to the skin creases. They should be gently separated, washed and rinsed, and thoroughly dried.

It isn't necessary to clean the inside of the baby's mouth, ears, eyes, or nose. Nature takes care of this. Never use cotton swab sticks. Babies move very suddenly and can easily be injured by them. Just wipe the

ACTIVITIES

Critical Thinking Activity

Analyzing. Encourage students to discuss the routine of bathing infants. Ask them what they think babies get out of bathing, in addition to being cleaned. Also, discuss what parents and caregivers can do to make the bathing experience enjoyable for them.

VISUAL LEARNING Using the Photograph
Answer: About two weeks after birth.

DID You Know?

Bathtime. Bonding between parents and children begins when parents hold and touch the baby. Stroking the baby's arm, holding the hand, circling the fingertips on the cheek all send messages of love. After bathtime, a caregiver can massage baby lotion onto the baby's back, moving the fingertips gently back and forth, or round and round. After the lotion has been absorbed, turn the baby over and apply a little more lotion to the baby's chest and tummy in the same way.

ISSUES IN TEEN PARENTING If you have teen parents in your class, or can find a volunteer teen parent, ask them to lead a demonstration on the proper technique for bathing a child. If possible, have a teen bring an infant to class and, under your supervision, bathe the baby. Ask the parent to display and describe personal preferences in bath products, equipment, clothing, and bathing methods. Be sure to include a discussion of safety procedures necessary to protect baby.

CHECKING COMPREHENSION

1. What conditions should a room in which you are bathing a baby meet? (*The room should be 70° to 80°F, or 20° to 26°C; should not have a draft; and should have a good work surface.*)
2. Why should you never use cotton swab sticks to clean a baby's mouth, ears, eyes, or nose? (*Babies move very suddenly and can easily be injured by them.*)
3. What piece of baby clothing is popular with parents of newborns? Why? (*Sleepers; probably because it is a one piece garment.*)
4. Why are socks and booties not recommended for newborns? (*Babies often get them wet or kick them off.*)

ACTIVITIES

Teamwork Activity

Organize students in small groups. Have each group write a list of "dos" and "don'ts" for bathing a baby. Have each group present their list on an illustrated poster. Display the completed posters and have the rest of the class discuss and evaluate the lists. **L1**

---

outer ears, and use a clean washcloth to remove any visible mucus from the nose.

Wash the baby's scalp with tear-free baby soap or baby shampoo once or twice a week. On other days, just wipe the scalp with clear water and pat it dry.

Sometimes babies develop **cradle cap**, a skin condition in which the scalp develops patches of yellowish, crusty scales. To treat it, apply baby oil or lanolin to the scalp at night. In the morning, gently loosen the scales with a washcloth or a soft hairbrush and shampoo the hair.

You may want to apply baby powder or lotion to the baby after a bath, but neither is really necessary. If you use powder, choose one with cornstarch, not talc. First shake the powder into your own hand, and then rub it onto the baby's skin. Sprinkling the powder on the baby, puts powder in the air the baby breathes. This may cause breathing problems or even suffocation.

Tub Baths

Once the navel has healed, the baby can be bathed in a tub. At first the "tub" can be a large dishpan or special baby bathtub. By six or seven months, use the regular tub.

Before starting the bath, gather the equipment and the baby's clean clothes. Place a rubber mat or towel in the bottom of the tub to make the baby comfortable and to prevent falls. Add lukewarm water to a depth

Appropriate clothes vary by the weather and occasion, but diapers are basic.

of about 2 to 3 inches (5 to 8 cm). The steps in bathing a baby are shown in the illustrations on page 282.

Most older babies enjoy baths, especially when they can sit by themselves in the tub. They love to splash and play in the water and with floating toys. Don't forget, though, that safety is the main concern when bathing a baby of any age.

Dressing a Baby

When choosing a baby's indoor clothes, consider the temperature in the home rather than the season of the year. Follow your own clothing needs—an infant doesn't need to be warmer than you.

The Newborn

A newborn's clothing needs are minimal. Many parents put their babies in a **sleeper**, a one-piece stretchy garment with feet, even when awake. Others dress the

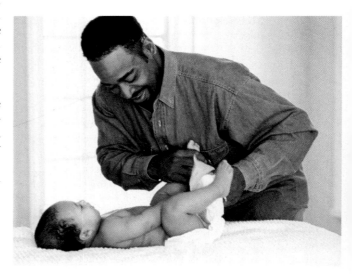

LEARNING STYLES

Auditory

Stress that bathtime should be pleasurable for both baby and the parent or caregiver. Babies enjoy being sung to. Ask students to create a song that they could sing to a baby while bathing him or her. Students might use the music of a popular song they like and write their own lyrics, appropriate for a baby's song. Students might tape their songs and share them with the class.

Safety in the Tub

*T*he bathtub can be dangerous for babies, so follow these safety precautions:

- Never leave the baby alone during the bath, not even for "just a second." A baby can drown very quickly, even in very shallow water.

- Keep the baby seated in the tub. Standing or climbing can lead to falls.

- Don't count on a bathtub seat to support an infant.

- Before you put the baby in the tub, always check the water temperature. Use your wrist or elbow, not your hand, to test the water.

- Check the temperature of the hot water heater. Water should be no hotter than 120° to 130°F (49° to 54°C). If it is warmer than that, turn the hot water heater down.

- Keep babies away from faucets, which are hard and sharp and may be hot.

- Don't let the baby drink the bathwater or suck on the washcloth. If necessary, offer a drink of fresh water or a teething ring.

FOLLOWING UP

1. Which of these safety rules do you think is most important? Why?
2. Why use the wrist or elbow to check water temperature?

baby in a cotton undershirt and a gown. In warm or hot weather (if there is no air conditioning), the baby may wear only a diaper and a short-sleeved shirt. When taking the baby outdoors in cool weather, add warm outer garments or blankets.

Socks and booties are usually not necessary for everyday wear. They may bind or get wet or kicked off. The newborn's feet usually stay covered by a sleeper or blanket. If the feet feel cool, cover them with sleeper feet or with stretchy socks.

Older Babies

When babies begin to creep and crawl, they need different kinds of clothing—more durable, allowing for movement. Overalls, especially those with legs that snap open for easy diaper changes, are good for crawling babies. Very active crawlers may need pants with padded knees. Soft, cotton knit shirts are comfortable. A sleeper keeps the baby covered even if a blanket is kicked off.

CHAPTER 8: Physical Development During the First Year **281**

ACTIVITIES

Teamwork Activity

Organize the class into small groups. Have each group review the procedures for giving an infant a sponge bath. Then have group members use life-size dolls to practice the procedure. Encourage them to point out any unexpected problems that arise in this procedure and offer solutions. **L1**

- The bathtub is not the only place where a baby's safety needs to be guarded. A bucket of water, a pool, a toilet, or a wading pool may all look inviting. Caregivers need to be careful to keep crawling and walking babies away from standing water, and always keep baby in sight when exploring the house or yard.

Answers to
FOLLOWING UP

1. Answers will vary but should be supported by sound reasoning.

2. The hand is less sensitive to temperature.

Management/Leadership Skills

Have pairs of students work together, experimenting to find the best location for bathing a baby. Using a doll, they may try a basin, a plastic dishpan or washtub, a special baby bathtub, and a regular bathtub. They might also try placing a washtub on the floor, on a table, or on a cabinet. Have students list the pros and cons of each method. Then encourage a general discussion: Which location do you recommend for bathing a baby? Why?

CHECKING COMPREHENSION

1. Why do many physicians recommend that babies who are
learning to walk do so barefoot?
(*This leaves the toes free to grip
and floor and gives the ankles flexibility.*)

Using the Graphic
Refer students to
the graphic on this
page. Then call on volunteers to
use a life-size doll to demonstrate each of the steps shown
on the illustration.

DID You Know?

Baby Shoes. **When buying
shoes for a baby, the length
and width of both feet should
be measured to ensure that the
new shoes will fit correctly.
Each foot should be considered individually, since no one
has right and left feet that
match exactly in size or shape.
Beyond choosing the best size,
parents should make sure that
the baby's shoes are breath-
able, have a flexible sole, offer
arch support, have ample
cushioning, and have a rigid
support around the heel.**

Bathing a Baby

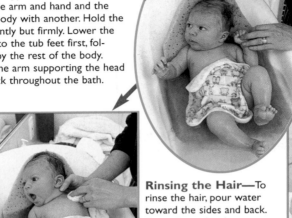

**Placing the Baby in the
Tub**—Support the head and neck
with one arm and hand and the
lower body with another. Hold the
baby gently but firmly. Lower the
baby into the tub feet first, followed by the rest of the body.
Keep one arm supporting the head
and neck throughout the bath.

Washing the Face—Begin
by washing the baby's face and
head with clear water and patting it dry. If the baby has hair,
wash it with a baby shampoo
about twice a week.

Rinsing the Hair—To
rinse the hair, pour water
toward the sides and back.
Try to keep the shampoo
out of the baby's eyes. If it
does get in the eyes, rinse
with a clean wet washcloth.

Washing the Body—Use the
free hand to wash and rinse the baby.
Then lift the baby from the water
with the same secure grip.

Drying the Baby—Place the
infant on a clean towel and wrap the
baby in it immediately to prevent chilling. Towels with hoods can prevent air
from chilling the head. Then pat the
baby dry.

282 UNIT 3: The Baby's First Year

Visual
Ask students to think of clothing for
babies that they consider attractive and
appropriate. Have them sketch their
ideas or find examples of them in magazine ads and catalogs. Students might
create mobiles or posters to display
their clothing ideas. Display students'
work. Call on volunteers to explain the
reasons for their selections.

Shoes aren't really necessary until the baby walks outdoors. Many physicians feel that the best way to learn to walk is barefoot, which leaves the toes free to grip the floor and gives the ankles flexibility. If the baby is learning to stand and walk indoors on cold floors, nonskid socks can keep the feet warm and the baby safe. Once the baby is ready for shoes, either sneakers or leather shoes are appropriate.

Dressing Tips

Dressing and undressing provide ideal opportunities for extra strokes, pats, hugs, and kisses. This is also a good time for songs, simple rhymes, or naming parts of the body or articles of clothing.

The illustrations on page 284 show how to dress a baby. As babies get older, they can help with dressing; for example, they can stretch their own arms through short sleeves. However, you may often find that even a capable baby is uncooperative. Sometimes distracting the baby with a toy or song can help make dressing easier.

Choosing Clothes

Today, most clothes for infants are simple and comfortable. Many are made of knit fabrics that contain non-irritating fibers and provide both ease of movement for the baby and ease of care for the parents.

Which characteristics are most important in choosing clothes for babies?

Baby clothes should also be flame retardant. Look for this information on clothing labels.

The size of infant wear is indicated by both weight and age of baby. Weight is the more reliable guide. It is usually best to buy nothing smaller than a six-month size for a newborn. The clothes may look large, but babies grow quickly, and the smallest sizes soon become too small. Simply fold up the hems of larger garments for a few weeks until the baby grows into them.

When choosing baby clothes, both comfort and ease in dressing are important. Since clothing is expensive, it's wise to look for clothes with generous hems and extra buttons on shoulder straps and waistbands to allow for rapid growth.

CHAPTER 8: Physical Development During the First Year **283**

ACTIVITIES

Math Activity

Ask students to make a list of basic clothing needs for a newborn. Then have them use catalogs, newspaper ads, or information from store visits to determine the cost of each item and the total cost of all the clothing items they have listed. Finally, have students compare their lists and the costs. Should they have fewer or more clothes on their lists? Do some stores have better prices than what they found? Have students discuss the findings. **L1**

ISSUES IN
CHILDREN'S HEALTH

Safety. Loose strings and ties on a baby's garment can be worse than uncomfortable; they can be dangerous. The ties may get wrapped around the baby's toes or fingers, causing discomfort and even cutting off circulation. Long strings are especially dangerous when they are out of sight, inside an infant's garment. These hidden ties may get wrapped around a baby's neck and could cause strangulation. If there is any possibility of strangulation, the ties should be completely removed from the garment.

Management/Leadership Skills

Have students list good sources for buying or borrowing these clothes. Students might find out about places in their community that sell used baby clothing. (Interested students might compare the costs of buying several clothing items for babies in the used clothing store with the same kinds of items bought new.) Then have students work in small groups to develop a checklist that can be employed to evaluate used clothing for babies.

CHECKING COMPREHENSION

1. With a pullover garment, should the head or the arms be put in first? Why? (*Head so that the opening can be as loose as possible when putting it on.*)
2. Why do you need to avoid quick, jerky movements when dressing a baby? (*To avoid startling or alarming the baby.*)
3. Why would a zipper that goes from the neck to the toes, and not just to the hips, be best for a one-piece garment? (*To allow largest possible opening.*)

ACTIVITIES

Critical Thinking Activity

Making Inferences. Discuss how a baby might be affected if a parent or other caregiver has a difficult time dressing him or her. **Ask:** How might the baby react? How might the caregiver be affected by the reaction? Then ask students for suggestions to avoid this type of problem. **L1**

Social Studies Activity

Encourage students to share what they know about infant dress at other times and in other cultures. Let interested volunteers do further research into specific times or cultures, and have them report their findings to the class. Could any of these practices be used now? **L3**

Dressing a Baby

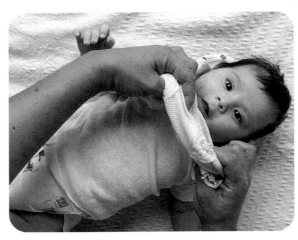

Pullover Garments. These garments have a stretchable neck opening. If the neck is small, follow these steps. If the neck opening is larger, put the opening around the baby's face first and then pull it over the back of the head.

Step 1: Gather the garment into a loop and slip it over the back of the baby's head.

Step 2: Stretch the garment forward as you bring it down past the forehead and nose. This keeps the face and nose free so that the baby doesn't feel smothered.

Step 3: Put the baby's fist into the armhole and pull the arm through with your other hand. Repeat with the other arm. Then straighten out the bottom of the garment.

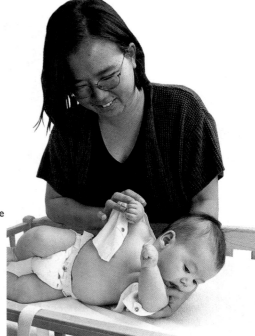

As you dress or undress a baby, work as smoothly and quickly as possible without being rough. Quick, jerking movements often frighten babies. Follow these same tips for taking each kind of garment off a baby, but reverse the order of the steps.

Open Front Shirt. For these garments, lay the baby face down to make him or her feel secure.

Step 1: Open the shirt and lay it on the baby's back.

Step 2: Gently turn the baby face up so that the shirt is underneath.

Step 3: Gently put the baby's arms through the sleeves

284 UNIT 3: The Baby's First Year

LEARNING STYLES

Visual

Have students describe or bring to class reproductions of paintings that portray infants. Focus students' attention on the clothing of the babies, and have them answer the following questions: How do you think this kind of outfit would affect an infant's comfort and activities? What might be involved in dressing a baby in this kind of outfit? What kind of care do you think this kind of infant clothing must have required?

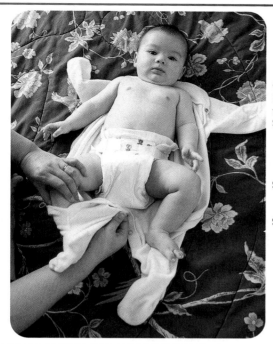

One-Piece Garment with Feet.
Putting on this type of garment is easier when the zipper or the snaps go from neck to toes.
Step 1: Start with the bottom part of the garment. Put the baby's leg on the side without the zipper or snaps into the garment leg, followed by the other leg.
Step 2: Roll the baby onto one side and pull the garment up under the baby's shoulders.
Step 3: Roll the baby back onto the garment. Then gently pull the sleeves over the baby's arms. Finish by zipping or snapping the garment closed.

Diapering a Baby

Diapers are the most essential part of a baby's wardrobe. Parents have a number of diapering options. Cloth diapers, the traditional favorite, may be the least expensive if home laundry facilities are available. Disposable diapers offer throwaway convenience, but are much more expensive than cloth diapers and add to environmental problems. Commercial diaper services, if available, are convenient and may not cost much more than using disposables. These services deliver clean cloth diapers and pick up used ones.

A very young baby probably needs a diaper change twelve to fifteen times each day. A newborn wets several times an hour, but in small amounts that don't require changing each time. An older baby probably needs fewer diaper changes a day—and is more likely to let you know when a clean diaper is needed.

Turn diaper-changing time into a period of interaction. Sing or hum while you work, or talk about what you are doing. A young baby will enjoy hearing your voice—and may even babble in response.

Keep your diapering supplies near a sturdy, padded surface such as the crib or a changing table. Cloth diapers must be folded to the correct size—the illustration on page 286 shows a good method. Disposable diapers come in several sizes, with thicker

CHAPTER 8: Physical Development During the First Year **285**

CHECKING COMPREHENSION

1. Where should the extra thickness on cloth diaper be placed for girls? For boys? (*Girls—in back; boys—in front.*)
2. Why should cloth diapers not be washed in cold or warm water? (*Either temperature leaves too many bacteria in the fabric.*)

ACTIVITIES

Critical Thinking Activity

Drawing Conclusions. **Ask:** Why diapers should not be washed with the family's other clothing. What problems may arise if the two kinds of laundry were mixed? **L1**

Using the Drawing Have students describe the process shown in the illustration on this page, and then give them an opportunity to practice folding diapers. If possible, make pre-folded cloth diapers and new-born-size disposable diapers available for comparison. Ask students to identify the advantages of each type of diaper.

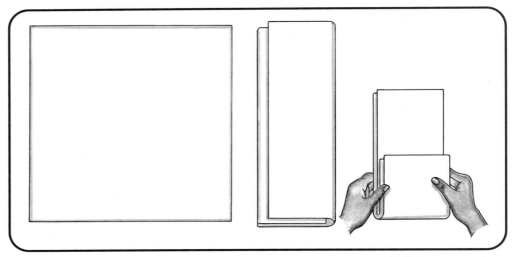

Fold a square diaper in thirds lengthwise so that it is a little wider than the baby's hips. Then turn up one end of the diaper part way.

diapers available for nighttime wear. In addition to the diaper, you will need a wet washcloth, soft tissues or toilet paper, cotton, and baby oil. Disposable baby washcloths are also available.

How to Diaper

It is never safe to leave a baby alone on a raised surface. Always keep at least one hand firmly on the baby. If you need to leave the work surface, for however short a time, take the baby with you. Babies can wriggle, squirm, or roll themselves right off the surface onto the floor, causing serious injury—and even death.

Follow these steps to change a diaper:

1. **Remove the diaper, and clean the baby.** If the diaper was merely wet, clean the baby with cotton and baby oil. If the baby had a bowel movement, use soft tissue or toilet paper to remove the soil from the baby. Then wash with a washcloth and apply baby oil.

2. **Put on a fresh diaper.** Hold the baby's ankles, and lift the body enough to slide the diaper under. If you are using cloth diapers, place the extra thickness in the back for girls, in the front for boys. With disposable diapers, be sure the adhesive tabs are under the baby. Bring the diaper up between the baby's legs. Use the adhesive tabs to fasten a disposable diaper. Use large safety pins or diaper pins to fasten a cloth diaper. If you use pins, be sure to keep your finger between the pin and the baby's skin. You can also use diaper tape, which comes off a dispenser, or diaper wraps, which are put around a diaper and closed with hooks and loops. Waterproof pants may be put on over the cloth diaper.

286 UNIT 3: The Baby's First Year

Observing & Participating

Have students describe what they have observed that helps to make a baby content while he or she is having a diaper changed. Then ask students to explain what they would do if, during the diaper changing, the baby suddenly began to squirm and fuss.

Call on volunteers to demonstrate their method to the class. Then have the class evaluate the suggested methods, explaining why they think the methods will or will not work.

3. **Dispose of used supplies.** Cleanliness is important. Dispose of used tissues, cotton, and other supplies. Roll a disposable diaper up and place it in a covered trash container. (Never flush one down a toilet. It will clog the plumbing.) Place a wet cloth diaper in a covered container filled with a mixture of water and borax or vinegar. If the diaper is soiled, rinse it before placing it in the container. A good method for rinsing is to hold the diaper firmly in a clean, flushing toilet. Be sure to wash your own hands with soap and hot water after changing a diaper.

Washing Cloth Diapers

Washing cloth diapers requires special care. Washing machines don't always wash out all the bacteria, and bacteria can cause skin problems. Wash diapers separately in the hottest water with a mild soap. Regular detergent leaves the fabric rough. Laundry sanitizers added to the wash help destroy bacteria. Be sure, too, that the diapers are thoroughly rinsed to avoid skin irritation.

Diapers may be dried in a dryer. However, drying them outdoors on a line in the sun destroys even more bacteria.

Diaper Rash

Controlling bacteria in diapers helps prevent **diaper rash**, patches of rough, irritated skin in the diaper area. Sometimes diaper rash includes painful raw spots. Sensitivity to disposable diapers can cause similar symptoms.

Treat a mild case of diaper rash by changing diapers more frequently and cleaning the baby thoroughly after a bowel movement. Spread the area with a product that contains zinc oxide and cod liver oil, which protects against diaper rash and helps it heal more quickly. Also, expose the diaper area to the air as much as possible, and avoid putting waterproof pants on the baby. If the rash continues or gets worse, ask a pediatrician for help.

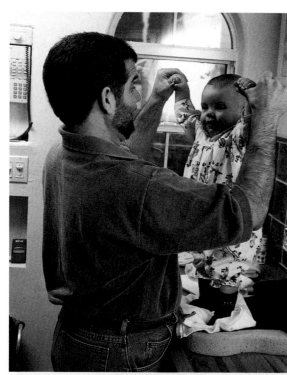

Having a set place and routine for diapering makes the process easier. Use the opportunity as a time to talk, sing, or play.

CHECKING COMPREHENSION

1. How does the amount of sleep a newborn needs change by the time the baby is one-year-old? (*A newborn may sleep from 12 to 20 hours a day. By one year, a baby often has as few as two or three sleep periods.*)

ACTIVITIES

Teamwork Activity

Organize students into small groups. Have group members recall lullabies that were sung to them or that they have heard caregivers sing to babies. Ask each group to perform the lullabies for the rest of the class. Encourage students to share lullabies from a variety of countries or cultures. **L1**

Math Activity

Provide students with the following information: A one-week-old baby sleeps about 16½ hours every day; a six-month-old baby about 14¼ hours; and a one-year-old about 13¾ hours. Ask students to make a graph illustrating this sleeping time. Have them indicate by how many hours sleeping time decreases for a baby in the first year. **L1**

| **VISUAL LEARNING** | Using the Photograph |

Emphasize to students the need to give babies a calm environment when they're being put to bed. Parents who are upset or worried need to find ways to calm down first or set those feelings aside so that the baby feels secure and comfortable.

A few minutes of rocking before bedtime can help a baby settle down more easily.

Sleep

All babies need sleep in order to grow and develop. The amount of time an infant spends sleeping decreases considerably during the first year. A newborn may sleep from 12 to 20 hours a day. By one year, however, a baby often has as few as two or three sleep periods, including naps.

The amount of sleep needed also depends on the individual baby. An active baby needs more sleep than an inactive one, just as they need more food. Babies also need more sleep on some days than others.

Preparation for Sleep

Putting the baby to bed for the night should be a relaxed and pleasant experience—for both you and the baby. Begin by washing the baby's face and hands and by changing the baby's diaper and clothes. Specific sleeping garments remind the baby that it is time to go to sleep.

Spend a few minutes rocking the baby or singing a soothing lullaby. This will be comforting and reassuring. As you put the baby to bed, keep your manner calm and unhurried, even if you don't feel that way. If not, the baby will pick up your feelings and probably not settle into sleep.

Finally, put the baby down in a safe bed. Avoid pillows, fluffy blankets or bumper pads, and stuffed toys. All increase the risk of suffocation. Dress the baby in a sleeper if extra warmth is needed. An infant too young to roll over independently should be placed on his or her back to help prevent Sudden Infant Death Syndrome.

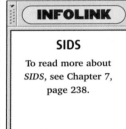

INFOLINK

SIDS

To read more about *SIDS*, see Chapter 7, page 238.

Try to follow the same routine every night. The baby learns the routine and is likely to find comfort in the ritual.

Sleep should never be brought about by the use of drugs or sleep medicines of any kind. Talk to the pediatrician if sleep problems continue.

Parenting in *Action*

Describe the following situation to the class: "When Benito and Sara brought baby Alicia home from the hospital, she was having some allergy problems. Worried, Benito and Sara hurried to comfort her at every cry during the night. A change in formula solved the allergy problem. Alicia, however, continued to cry frequently at night until a parent came to pick her up and rock her to sleep."

Have students discuss why Alicia cried after her allergy problems had been corrected. Then ask students to suggest what the parents might do.

Crying to Sleep

Many parents wonder what to do about a baby who cries when put down to sleep. Should they comfort the child? If they do, will crying and comforting become a habit that prolongs bedtime every night? If they don't, will the baby be harmed?

Some experts argue that babies should be left alone to "cry it out" so they can learn to settle themselves. Others say that this hurts the child emotionally. They urge a parent to pick up and the baby and offer any kind of comfort that will settle the baby down, even if it means letting the baby sleep with the parent.

A middle ground can be useful. If an infant cries when put to sleep, stay out of the room for two or three minutes to see if the baby settles down. If not, go in and comfort the child with voice and touch, then leave. If the crying starts again, stay away a bit longer than before. This process gives the baby some reassurance without creating an unwanted habit.

Bedtime Problems

Babies—especially active babies—often become restless while they sleep. During the night, they may waken partially and suck their fingers, cry out, or rock the crib. If you respond, your presence may become a necessary part of the baby's pattern for getting back to sleep. Infants need to learn to return to sleep on their own. Of course, provide care for a baby who needs feeding or a diaper change. A baby whose restlessness develops into crying also needs your attention.

SECTION 8-4 REVIEW

✔ Check Your Understanding

1. What should you do if you have to leave the room while you are giving a baby a sponge bath? Why?
2. At what point can a baby have a tub bath?
3. Explain what cradle cap is. What would you do to treat cradle cap?
4. How warmly should you dress an infant?
5. What are the advantages and disadvantages of cloth diapers and disposable diapers?
6. List the three main steps in changing a baby's diaper.
7. What is the benefit of a bedtime routine?

Putting Knowledge Into Practice

1. **Applying.** Using actual garments or magazine pictures, select four items of infant's clothing, ranging in size from newborn to twelve months. Evaluate each item for comfort, practicality, ease in dressing the baby, and required care. Which garment ranks highest on your list?
2. **Applying.** Tran has diaper rash. What should his caregiver do?
3. **Observing and Participating.** Using a doll, practice putting a disposable and a cloth diaper on a baby. How would this be different with a real baby?

CHAPTER 8: Physical Development During the First Year **289**

CHECKING COMPREHENSION

Have students answer the Check Your Understanding questions. Answers appear at the bottom of this page.

EVALUATION

Give students the Section 8-4 Quiz in the *Teacher Resource Guide*.

RETEACHING

1. Assign Reteaching Activities, page 31.
2. Have students work with partners to plan and prepare an illustrated poster on how to bathe a baby, dress a baby, or change a diaper.

ENRICHMENT

Ask students to research fiber characteristics and prepare a list of fibers appropriate for use in infant clothing.

EXTENSION

Ask a pediatric nurse practitioner or pediatrician to visit the class. Have the visitor discuss questions he or she is most often asked by new parents and share the responses he or she gives.

CLOSE

Put a collection of baby clothes in a bag. Have students take turns pulling out a garment and give a brief evaluation of it.

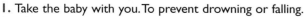

ANSWERS TO SECTION 8-4 REVIEW

1. Take the baby with you. To prevent drowning or falling.
2. After the navel has healed.
3. Yellowish, crusty scales on the scalp. Put baby oil or lanolin on the baby's scalp at night, then loosen the scales with a washcloth or hairbrush and shampoo them off in the morning.
4. *Possible responses:* About the same as you; dress for the indoor temperature.
5. *See page 285.*
6. Remove diaper and clean baby; put on fresh diaper; dispose of used supplies.
7. Baby finds comfort in consistency; baby should go to sleep more easily.

Ask students to think about games they have seen played with babies. Next, demonstrate one of the games described in this feature. Ask them if they ever played this game with an infant or saw it being played. Ask them to describe the baby's reaction.

TEACH

Teamwork Activity

Have students work in pairs to demonstrate a baby game they have learned from this lesson or one they learned about from outside reading or observation. Ask them to show how they would adapt the game when playing with two or more infants. Have the students explain how the game is beneficial to the baby and at what age it is appropriate. **L1**

Critical Thinking Activity

Categorizing. Have students group the games according to the age at which they think each is appropriate. **L2**

Parenting With Care

Spending Quality Time with Baby

As a baby grows older, you will find more opportunities to play games.

For many games, you need no toys at all—just you, the baby, and some creative imagination. Here are a few ideas:

Looking Games

- **Funny face.** Shake your head; stick out your tongue; make funny faces.
- **Shadow figures.** Shine a flashlight on the wall of a partially darkened room. Make shadow designs by placing your fingers in front of the beam.
- **Mirrors.** Sit with the baby in front of a mirror. Point to the infant's eyes, nose, mouth, and other features, and name each feature. Do the same with your own features. Eventually, the baby will point to the features you name.
- **Ping-pong.** In a variation on "Mirrors," let the baby be the leader. Watch the baby closely, and mimic everything he or she does.

Listening Games

- **Musical games.** Play or sing music and nursery rhymes. Encourage the older babies to respond by swaying or humming.

- **What's that?** Point out everyday sounds like running water, the washing machine, and the telephone. Name the sound, and then help the baby see what is making it.
- **Mimic.** Make fun sounds—the noises of cars, animals, motorcycles, and so on. Encourage the baby to imitate you.

Baby Exercises

- **Bicycle.** Lay the baby on his or her back and gently hold both ankles. Revolve the baby's legs as if riding a bicycle.
- **Tug-of-war.** Grasp one side of a large rubber ring, and let the baby grasp the other side. Gently play tug-of-war. Remember—the baby gets to win. If the baby is sitting up, don't let go entirely of the rubber ring, or the baby will tumble backward.

290   UNIT 3: The Baby's First Year

RESOURCES ON BABIES

Parents and caregivers can get advice on a range of topics from noted pediatrician T. Berry Brazelton. Brazelton published several books, including the recent popular *TouchPoints*. His views are also available from a source called "House Calls," part of the Web site established by the Pampers Parenting Institute. Interested students can visit at www.totalbabycare.com.

- **Airplane.** Playing airplane can help strengthen the back and neck muscles of a baby who can already hold his or her head steady. Hold the baby just above the waist, and then slowly lift the baby above your face. Avoid a sudden lift, which could cause the baby's head to wobble. The baby's back will arch and arms and legs will stretch out. You may want to make airplane noises, too.

Old Favorites

- **Peekaboo.** Establish eye contact with the baby. Quickly turn your head away, and then turn back again, saying "peekaboo." For older babies, cover your eyes and then uncover them.
- **Hide-and-seek.** Make a toy disappear behind your back. Let the baby crawl to find it. Help the baby find toys that you have hidden. Try hiding from the baby yourself, and then reappear quickly.

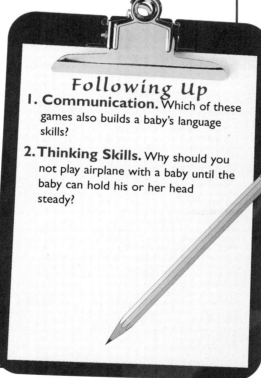

Following Up

1. **Communication.** Which of these games also builds a baby's language skills?

2. **Thinking Skills.** Why should you not play airplane with a baby until the baby can hold his or her head steady?

CHAPTER 8: Physical Development During the First Year **291**

Answers to Following Up

1. Mirrors; What's that? Peekaboo.
2. *Possible response:* It would not be safe for a baby who couldn't support his or her head.

Critical Thinking Activity

Applying. Ask students to think of one game or toy that could be used to meet three areas of a child's development (*physical, emotional, social, or intellectual*). Call on students to share their ideas and compile a class list on the board. **L1**

Discussion Activity

Have students give more examples of sounds that could be used in "What's that?"
Have them suggest actions the babies could demonstrate in "Mirrors." **L1**

CLOSE

1. Have students create a list of three to five toys that they consider essential to meeting a baby's needs and to providing a stimulating environment for him or her.
2. **Extension.** Ask students to bring used, but usable, toys to donate to a community organization that provides services for children and families. Students might tag each toy and indicate the age for which the toy is appropriate and the kind of skill the toy reinforces.

CHECKING COMPREHENSION

Use the Summary and the Reviewing the Facts questions to help students go over the most important ideas in Chapter 8. Encourage students to ask questions and add details.

CHAPTER 8 REVIEW

Answers to Reviewing the Facts

1. *Growth:* Increase in size. *Development:* Increase in abilities. *Examples will vary.*
2. *Possible response: Sight*—Change from preference for strongly patterned shapes to depth perception and preference for three-dimensional objects.
3. *Cerebrum:* Receives information from the senses and directs motor activities; controls speech, memory, and perception. *Thalamus:* controls expression of emotions.
4. Repetition makes dendrites and axons work more efficiently; it also helps to build systems of neurons.
5. *Any two:* Keep it simple and natural; match experiences to the child's mental capacities; give opportunities for practice; get the child actively involved; provide a variety of experiences while avoiding overload; avoid pushing the child.
6. Always support the baby's head.
7. Meet the baby's nutritional needs.
8. Support the baby's head during entire process; put the baby in tub feet first; wash the face with a washcloth; wash the hair with shampoo, rinsing away from the eye; wash the body; rinse; take the baby immediately out of tub and cover in a towel; pat dry.

CHAPTER 8 **REVIEW &**

Summary

✔ Children grow and develop most rapidly in the first year. (Section 8-1)

✔ Development proceeds from head to foot, near to far, and simple to complex. (Section 8-1)

✔ Parents can provide a rich environment to help a baby's brain develop. (Section 8-2)

✔ During the first year, babies begin to eat solids. (Section 8-3)

✔ An infant's clothing should be comfortable and easy to put on and take off. (Section 8-4)

✔ Babies sleep best if bedtime is handled with a soothing, familiar routine. (Section 8-4)

Reviewing the Facts

1. What is the difference between growth and development? Give an example of each from the first year of life. (Section 8-1)
2. Describe how one of the five senses changes in a baby's first year. (Section 8-1)
3. What functions do the cerebrum and thalamus control? (Section 8-2)
4. What role does repetition play in brain development? (Section 8-2)
5. Give two guidelines caregivers can follow to help an infant's brain develop. (Section 8-2)
6. What do parents always have to do when handling a newborn? (Section 8-3)
7. How can inadequate nutrition be prevented? (Section 8-3)

8. Describe how to give a baby a tub bath. (Section 8-4)
9. Why is it important to stay calm when preparing a baby to sleep? (Section 8-4)

Thinking Critically

1. **Charting.** Make a chart with three headings: "Head to Foot"; "Near to Far"; "Simple to Complex." Under each heading, list at least three examples of each pattern of development.
2. **Diagramming.** Create a flow chart showing how nerves send information to the brain and receive instructions from it.
3. **Sequencing.** Write out the proper steps for diapering a baby.

Taking Action

1. **Holding a Baby.** Hold a 10-pound (4.5-kg) sack of flour or rice in the crook of one arm while you perform various routine activities—preparing a bottle, opening the mail, putting clothes away, and so on. How much more difficult would these tasks be with a baby? *(Thinking Skills)*
2. **Dressing a Baby.** Using a doll, show the proper technique for dressing a baby. *(Management)*

---

9. To build a feeling of comfort and ease in the baby so he or she will fall asleep easily.

CONNECTIONS

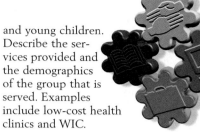

Cross-Curricular Connections

1. **Health.** Make a chart showing how you would introduce seven foods to an infant, starting with cereals and followed by vegetables. Follow the rule of allowing four days to pass between each new food.

2. **Social Studies.** Find out how many cases of Sudden Infant Death Syndrome occurred each year from 1990 to the most recent year for which statistics are available. In 1992, pediatricians began saying that babies should sleep on their backs. What happened to the rate of SIDS since then?

Workplace Connections

1. **Resources.** Look through parenting magazines or books to find out how women who work outside the home handle feeding. Do they breast-feed or bottle-feed? If they breast-feed, what do they do when they are at work and the baby is hungry? Report your findings to the class.

2. **Personal Qualities.** What personal qualities does the parent of an infant need?

Family and Community Connections

1. **Agencies and Services.** Investigate agencies in your region that provide services to benefit the health and welfare of infants

and young children. Describe the services provided and the demographics of the group that is served. Examples include low-cost health clinics and WIC.

2. **Evaluating Options.** Ask your parents and others their opinions about different kinds of infant garments: slipover gowns or shirts; one-piece shirts; and one-piece garments with feet. Which did they find most convenient? Why? Share your findings with the class.

Technology Connections

1. **Technology.** In what ways have technological advances made it easier to keep infants safe? Has technology created any new dangers?

2. **Internet.** Research on the Internet for advice about caring for a baby. What sites offer such advice? What kind of information do they have? How can you judge the reliability of the information?

EVALUATION

1. Use the reproducible Chapter 8 Test in the *Teacher Resource Guide,* or construct your own test using the Exam*View*® Test Generator.

2. For an alternative assessment, assign the Chapter 8 activity in the *Authentic Assessment* section of the *Teacher Resource Guide.*

ENRICHMENT

Assign students either of the two enrichment activities in the *Enrichment Activities* booklet in the *Student Motivation Kit.*

EXTENSION

Invite several new parents to visit the class. Have the parents discuss the aspects of infant care they have found most surprising, most difficult, and most rewarding.

CLOSE

On a poster, have each students write a "tip" that might help parents understand the growth and development of infants or meet the physical care needs of infants.

CHAPTER 9

Emotional and Social Development During the First Year

CHAPTER 9 RESOURCES

Teacher Resource Guide
• Chapter 9 Test, p. 148
• Authentic Assessment, p. 273
Student Motivation Kit
• Observations, pp. 43-44
Transparency Package
• CT-26 to CT-28, CT-37 (Also on CD-ROM)
Effective Instruction CD-ROM

CHAPTER 9   OVERVIEW

In **Section 9-1**, students learn the framework for understanding emotional and social development and how personality can be understood in terms of temperament.

In **Section 9-2**, students explore how infants develop emotionally and socially, including when and how they express different emotions and how they interact with others.

CHAPTER 9   OBJECTIVES

After completing Chapter 9, students will be able to:

• Distinguish between emotional and social development.
• Describe the importance of attachment and loving care.
• Identify different temperaments.
• Describe how children learn behavior.
• Explain how infants develop emotionally and socially.

CHAPTER 9

Emotional and Social Development During the First Year

RESOURCES TO EXPLORE

Getting a Good Start in Life. Zero to Three is a nonprofit organization dedicated to advancing the healthy development of babies and young children. The group provides training, technical assistance, research, and publication of information aimed at helping child care professionals, policymakers, and parents. Interested students might obtain information by writing to 200 M. Street, NW, Suite 200, Washington, D.C. 20036 or checking their Website: www.zerotothree.org

Kim looked forward to this time every evening. After the long day at work and the many things that needed to be done at night, this was her chance for some quiet time with Nick. The routine was simple. First Nick ate, and then she gave him a bath. After he was all cleaned up, Kim put a clean diaper and sleeper on him. Then they sat down for a book.

Of course, Nick was still too young to read, but Kim knew that he understood something. Each night, she showed him three books that he could choose from. Each night, he picked the same one.

Kim sat down in the chair and put Nick on her lap. She opened the book and said, "Look, Nick. Here's a cute little bear just like your friend Andy." The baby cooed in delight. "Let's read about the little bear. What's he going to do?"

"She opened the book and said, 'Let's read about the little bear.'"

Tiny mice yawn when the moon starts to rise.

Mother Mouse rocks her babes till they close their bright eyes.

Help Little Bear cover his mouth as he yawns.

CHAPTER 9: Emotional and Social Development During the First Year **295**

- Ask volunteers who have spent time with infants to describe what they have seen of the children's emotional and social development. At what age do they seem to notice others? How do they show that recognition? How do they show their disapproval of others?
- Have students study the photograph on the chapter opening page. **Ask:** How does the baby's expression show that he is more aware of his surroundings than he was at birth? How do the mother's actions contribute to the baby's emotional growth?

USING THE SCENARIO Have students read the story on this page of the student text. **Ask:** Why do infants find routines appealing? What benefits do they gain from following a routine?

KEY TO ABILITY LEVELS Each section gives skill-building activities. Each activity has been labeled for use with students of various learning styles and abilities.

L1 Level 1 activities are basic activities and should be within the range of all students.

L2 Level 2 activities are average activities and should be within the range of average and above average students.

L3 Level 3 activities are challenging activities designed for the ability range of above average students.

SECTION 9-1

Understanding Emotional and Social Development

(pages 296-303)

SECTION 9-1 RESOURCES

Teacher Resource Guide
- Lesson Plan Organizer, p. 58
- Section 9-1 Quiz, p. 146

Student Motivation Kit
- Observ. & Case Studies (case study), p. 109
- Reteaching Activity, p. 32
- Enrichment, p. 27
- Nurt. Brain Dev., p. 48
- Teen Parenting Skills, pp. 85-86

Student Workbook
- Study Guide, pp. 82-85
- Testing Temperament, pp. 86-87

Effective Instruction CD-ROM

FOCUS

MOTIVATOR

Have students suggest actions caregivers can take to promote infants' emotional and social development. Have students write the responses in their notebooks and save the page. After they have studied the chapter, they can review the list and see if there are any ideas they could add to it.

VOCABULARY ACTIVITY

Ask students to define the terms. Then tell them that specific definitions, as they relate to child development, are provided in the text.

Understanding Emotional and Social Development

Two babies show clear differences in their physical growth—one weighs more or is taller than the other. The same is true of social and emotional development. Watch how two babies respond to the same situation. Where one squeals in delight while crawling on the grass in the park, another may sit still. Each is becoming a unique person.

KEY TERMS

attachment
emotional development
failure to thrive
social development

OBJECTIVES:

- Define emotional and social development.
- Explain the importance of attachment to emotional and social development.
- Explain how a baby's care affects emotional and social development.
- Analyze people according to different temperament traits.

Comparing Emotional and Social Development

Emotional development is the process of learning to recognize and express one's feelings and to establish one's identity as a unique person. A child with healthy emotional development becomes an adult who has self-confidence, can handle stress, and shows empathy toward others.

296 UNIT 3: The Baby's First Year

Observing & Participating

Encourage students to observe infants and look for indications of each child's temperament, or basic way of interacting with other people. If possible, invite several parents to bring to class babies nine to twelve months old. Have students observe the babies as they react to each other, to the new surroundings, and to the unfamiliar adults. Have them notice how parents help their babies feel comfortable. After the visit, have students discuss what they saw.

Social development is the process of learning to interact with others and to express oneself to others. Healthy social development results in an adult who shows tolerance for others. A socially healthy adult can communicate well with others and listens to different points of view before acting.

Emotional and social development are connected to each other. A child's feelings about himself or herself and behavior toward others depend on one another.

Emotional and social development begin at birth and continue throughout life. Many influences shape how a child develops in these areas. The bond formed between parent and child is one. The atmosphere of the home is another. A final influence is the temperament of the child.

Attachment

Each day, Jo makes a point of going into her baby Franklin's room and giving him a hug to start the day. She does the same thing at day's end. As Jo knows, babies have a basic need for physical contact—holding, cuddling, rocking, or even just being near another person. This contact builds a bond between a parent or caregiver and a child, a bond called **attachment**. Some famous research studies have shown how important that bond is.

The first studies in this area were done with monkeys, not humans. An American experimental psychologist, Harry Harlow, made monkey-shaped forms out of chicken wire and out of soft cloth. He then used these substitute "mothers" to raise baby monkeys. He found that the baby monkeys clung to the "mothers" made of soft cloth—even if the chicken-wire "mothers" held their feeding bottles. Clearly, the monkeys needed to feel physical closeness as well as receive a feeding.

Harlow found that attachment requires more than physical contact. Once the baby monkeys were grown, they didn't know how to relate to other monkeys. They did not develop normal social relationships.

Social relationships are important for many animals as well as for humans. A famous example is Koko the gorilla's attachment to a kitten. *What animals do you know of that live in social groups?*

TEACH

COMPREHENSION CHECK

1. What three factors influence emotional and social development? (*Bond between parent and child; home atmosphere; temperament of the child.*)
2. What animals were used in the first experiments about attachment? (*Monkeys.*)

ACTIVITIES

Discussion Activity

Ask: Do you think healthy emotional development is possible without healthy social development? What about the reverse? Why or why not? **L1**

Critical Thinking Activity

Comparing. Have students explore the differences between emotional and social development by asking what are the signs of healthy development in each of these areas in teens and adults. **L1**

VISUAL LEARNING — Using the Photograph
Answers will vary but might include monkeys, chimps, bees, ants, lions, dogs, whales, dolphins, fish.

LEARNING STYLES

Visual

To help students see the differences between emotional and social development, have them create a graphic organizer. Have them draw two large boxes, labeling one "Emotional Development" and the other "Social Development." Students should then draw smaller boxes connected to one of the larger boxes. In those smaller boxes, students can list ideas related to the particular kinds of development. For instance, social development might include: healthy family relationships, close friends, teamwork, volunteering, etc.

COMPREHENSION CHECK

1. How, according to the monkey experiments, is attachment related to social development? (*Monkeys that hadn't had real mothers didn't develop normal social relations.*)

ACTIVITIES

Critical Thinking Activity

Analyzing. Do you think that the problems found in Harlow's monkeys might also be observed in children raised not in homes but in institutions? Why or why not? **L2**

Discussion Activity

Ask: Are studies done with monkeys relevant to humans? Why or why not? **L2**

Harlow believed this was caused by the lack of interaction between the babies and real mothers.

Monkeys, of course, aren't humans, but other research suggests that human babies have a similar need for contact. In the 1990s, child care experts were alarmed at the children they found in government homes for orphaned and abandoned babies in Romania. The conditions in the country were desperate, and the children had little personal care from adults. As a result, the physical and emotional development of these children was slower than normal.

Physical contact not only builds attachment, but also spurs development.

DID *You* **Know?**

Attachment. A special form of attachment, called imprinting, has been observed in swans, ducks, chickens, and geese. They walk within a short time of hatching. By instinct, they follow the first moving object they see—usually, the parent bird. Researchers have found that in geese the instinct to follow is imprinted during a specific short period after hatching. During that time, the goslings will imprint with anyone or anything they see. If mother geese are not present, goslings have been known to imprint on other animals, or humans.

More recent research has shown the benefits of giving children a gentle massage. This can sooth a baby and promote bonding. Babies need lots of love. Even young babies can experience loneliness. A baby who is left alone most of the time except for physical care, may fail to respond to people and objects. Researchers at Baylor University studied abused and neglected children. Those who failed to receive love, touch, and opportunities for learning had brains 20 to 30 percent smaller than average.

This problem is most likely to develop when physical needs are met but babies receive no emotional or social care. This may happen in institutions, but it can happen in families as well. When infants get little attention and encouragement from caregivers, their cries weaken, their smiles fade, and they become withdrawn.

Lack of love and attention may result in **failure to thrive** (also called marasmus), a condition in which the baby does not grow and develop properly. If these babies are not helped, they become unattached. Even as adults, they will be unable to develop caring, meaningful relationships with others.

Fortunately, these children can be helped. The children in the Romanian institutions improved when they went to live in loving and supportive homes. Caregivers can be given instruction and support so that they can help the baby recover and grow.

Young babies who cry to communicate their needs, gaze into the eyes of caregivers, track the movements of caregivers with their eyes, snuggle, cuddle, and become quiet when comforted show signs of growing attachment. As babies mature, they make sounds to their caregivers, embrace them, and eventually crawl or walk to them.

Building Trust Through Care

The world is a strange new place for newborns. Depending on a baby's early experiences, it may be a comfortable, secure place or a confusing, difficult one. The attitude newborns develop about their world depends on how their needs are met.

By studying a baby's responses, parents can tell if he or she is developing a healthy attachment to others. *What signs should they look for?*

CHAPTER 9: Emotional and Social Development During the First Year **299**

COMPREHENSION CHECK

1. How can a negative emotional climate affect a baby? (*Can hinder healthy development; can make baby fussy.*)
2. Why is having a pleasant emotional climate especially difficult for single parents? (*They face so many stresses.*)
3. Explain what temperament is. (*Person's style of reacting to world and to others.*)

ACTIVITIES

Writing Activity

Have students write a paragraph describing the ideal emotional climate for an infant. **Ask:** What factors might keep homes from having that ideal climate? What effects will those factors have on an infant? What can the family do to help an infant in that situation? **L1**

Discussion Activity

Ask: How does the emotional climate of the home affect older children? Is this only an issue for babies, or is it relevant for children of all ages? **L1**

VISUAL LEARNING	Using the Photograph

Answers will vary but might address such issues as benefiting from having many people to interact with.

If the newborn is kept warm and dry, fed when hungry, soothed when fussy, and talked to when awake, the infant comes to feel that the world is a comfortable place. That baby develops a sense of security.

On the other hand, if the newborn is made to conform to a rigid schedule of feeding, and crying brings no comforting adult response, the baby learns that the world is not a very friendly place.

The same result occurs when caregivers are inconsistent in their care or responses to the infant. If schedules change often, or if parents are sometimes gentle and loving and other times sharp and impatient, the baby has difficulty building trust.

Emotional Climate of the Home

Like everybody else, you probably have days when you are grumpy. Have you ever noticed how contagious such feelings are? If you snap at someone, chances are that person will snap back at you—or at someone else. Babies react the same way. Long before they know the meanings of words, babies catch the tone of adults' feelings. Worried or angry caregivers are likely to be tense in handling their baby. The baby senses these feelings and, in turn, becomes irritable and fussy.

Every family has ups and downs, and a baby adapts to them. It is essential, however, for a baby to feel that affection and caring are the basis of the family's interactions. Bitterness and mistrust can hinder a baby's healthy development.

Jess and Twana were excited when Andrea was born, but soon their feelings began to change. Jess felt left out because Twana seemed closer to the baby. Twana

loved her baby, but some days felt trapped with a child who only wet herself and cried. One night, these feelings erupted. When Andrea cried, Twana thrust her into Jess's arms, shouting, "Here, you take care of her for a change!" She stalked off into the bedroom and slammed the door.

What Jess and Twana felt isn't unusual. One outburst won't ruin the emotional climate in which Andrea lives. If their negative feelings continue to fester, though, the trouble may become more serious. They need to talk about their frustrations—when they are both calm. They need to find ways they can help each other so they can help their baby.

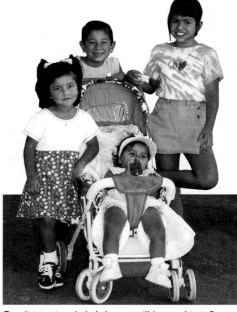

Conditions in a baby's home will have a big influence on how the baby develops. *How do you think a baby will be affected by having many brothers and sisters?*

ISSUES IN TEEN PARENTING	

For teen parents, establishing a good emotional climate for a baby can be challenging. Explore why by asking the following questions:

• Why is it difficult for teen parents to meet the physical needs of infants, which builds trust?

• What makes stress a problem for teen parents? How might that contribute to their difficulty in building trust?

• What special difficulties are faced by a teen who becomes a parent by accident and not by choice?

Parents need to find time for each other to keep their relationship healthy. **How does this benefit the baby?**

The challenge can be greater for single parents. With no other adult to share the work—or their worries—with, they may feel alone. It's important to find ways of releasing negative feelings away from the child. That way, they can have the patience and calmness to create a caring environment for their baby.

The Baby's Own Temperament

Every baby copes with life in a very personal way. This is because each baby brings his or her own individuality to a situation. For example, all babies react if the surface on which they are lying is suddenly shaken. However, one baby may respond by screaming, whereas another simply squirms a bit and quickly settles down again.

These different responses are based on the baby's temperament—his or her style of reacting to the world and relating to others. Different temperaments are revealed in how children react to a situation. Shanta, for instance, was trying to reach the mobile above her crib. She kept trying many, many times. Finally, when her father picked her up, she grabbed it. Luke, on the other hand, tried only once to reach a toy that was just out of reach. When he couldn't put his hand on it, he returned to the toy he had.

Researchers have found nine different ways of looking at temperament. Each of them has a high and low side, meaning that a child has the trait to a greater or lesser amount. Each baby—each person—needs to be looked at in terms of all of the traits together:

- **Intensity.** How strong or weak are a child's emotional responses to events or to others? A highly intense child is marked by deep and powerful responses. An intense baby may cry heartily. A less intense baby will cry weakly. Intense children are often very loud.
- **Persistence.** A persistent child is one who is determined to complete an action. Such a child may become very upset if unable to finish what was begun. A less persistent child can be easily persuaded to begin a new activity. A less persistent child accepts "no" for an answer. A highly persistent child

Discussion Activity

Ask: What can older siblings do to help create a good emotional climate for infants? What can they do directly for the infant? How can they help the infant by helping the parent? **L1**

Discussion Activity

Ask: Do you think people have the same temperament as adults that they had as children? Why or why not? What can change temperament, if anything? Can it be changed in a major way, or can people only have small shifts in what they're like? **L2**

VISUAL LEARNING	Using the Photograph

Possible response: If parents have a healthy relationship, it's likely to create a pleasant emotional climate.

DID You Know?

Birth Order. Another influence on a child's emotional and social life is birth order. First-born children tend to have more time with their parents than later children, simply because for some period of time they are the only child demanding parental attention. Parents tend to read more to first-borns than to later children. They play with them more, too.

Parenting in *Action*

Have students suggest how to respond to these situations:
- Kim is a highly sensitive baby who has difficulty falling asleep at night. Kim's crib is in her parents' bedroom.
- Juan is accustomed to a very regular schedule.

His parents both work and a neighbor cares for Juan during the day. They like everything about the neighbor except that she's disorganized. She doesn't feed Juan or give him naps at consistent times.

COMPREHENSION CHECK

1. An infant with what kind of temperament is likely to fuss at having a soiled diaper? (*High in sensitivity.*)
2. An infant with what kind of temperament is likely to accept a strict routine during the day? (*High in regularity.*)

ACTIVITIES

Discussion Activity

Another factor—in addition to temperament—that affects how others interact with children is gender. **Ask:** How does society treat infant boys and girls differently? What impact does that have on the child? **L1**

Critical Thinking Activity

Making Inferences. While a person can be high on more than one temperament characteristic, some are more likely to work as opposites. A child who is high in regularity, for instance, is likely to be low in adaptability. Have students discuss how these qualities relate to each other. Which are complementary? Which are opposites? **L2**

VISUAL LEARNING — Using the Photographs

Have students explain why the photographs show the temperaments stated in the caption. (For instance, persistence is needed to play with stacking toys, which involve trial-and-error learning.)

Babies have different temperaments. They can show energy (left), persistence (below), and intensity (right).

won't. These children want to attain a goal and are unwilling to give up on it.

- **Sensitivity.** A child who is high in sensitivity has strong reactions to his or her feelings. Such a child may be a fussy eater or may complain about clothes being uncomfortable. A less sensitive child is more likely to accept what comes. Children who are high in sensitivity may be bothered by the sights, sounds, or smells around them.
- **Perceptiveness.** The perceptive child is very aware of the surroundings. These children can be easily distracted as they become involved in new experiences. They have a hard time following directions that include several different things to do—they often lose track in some new activity after finishing the first task. Children lower in perceptiveness can handle many directions at once. They are less likely to notice things in the world around them.
- **Adaptability.** Some children find it easier than others to adjust to changes. A child who is low in adaptability wants to continue doing whatever activity is going on at the time. He or she resists change. A highly adaptable child will not be bothered by surprises. A child who is low in adaptability will dislike surprises—even pleasant ones.

302 UNIT 3: The Baby's First Year

LEARNING STYLES — Spatial, Visual

Some students might understand the idea of temperament by thinking in terms of the graphic equalizer of a sound system. These devices allow the listener to vary different aspects of the music—the bass, the treble, and so on. In the same way, a person can be thought of as having nine different temperament gauges, each of which can measure where that person stands in terms of a particular quality.

- **Regularity.** Children who are highly regular follow strong patterns. They get tired and go to sleep at the same time. They go to the bathroom at the same time. They are hungry at the same time. Children who are low in regularity are just the opposite: each day is different for them and their parents.
- **Energy.** High energy children are physically active. Even when they are sitting, they often squirm and move around in the seat. Once they are able to walk, they seem always to run. Low energy children move much less. They can play in one spot for long periods of time.
- **First reaction.** Children differ in how they face new situations. Some dive right in and take part. These children are probably open to new activities and

willing to try new foods. Others hold back and watch what others do before joining. They are less comfortable in new situations and may resist new foods.
- **Mood.** Is a child usually cheerful or cranky? Is he or she more often positive or inclined to point out the problems?

Parents and other caregivers have personal temperaments, too. Problems can arise if the adult's temperament conflicts with the child's. Understanding such a differences can help prevent clashes. For instance, a parent who is low in energy has to be prepared to accept the activity level of a high-energy child. If the high energy becomes bothersome, a trip to the park or other opportunity for vigorous play might help.

SECTION 9-1 REVIEW

✔ Check Your Understanding

1. What is emotional development?
2. What is social development?
3. What happens to children if they don't develop attachment?
4. How can a child who suffers from failure to thrive be helped?
5. How should parents and caregivers respond to a baby's needs to help the baby build a sense of trust?
6. Does it matter to a baby how the adults in the family treat each other? Why or why not?
7. How can temperament be used to understand children?

Putting Knowledge Into Practice

1. **Analyzing.** What can parents do to provide consistency in the care and attention their babies receive? What issues should they discuss with each other? What issues should they discuss with others who care for their baby?
2. **Synthesizing.** Explain how one of the following factors might affect the emotional climate in a home: the emotional maturity of parents; education; unemployment; substance use and abuse.
3. **Observing and Participating.** Look at the nine temperament traits described in the chapter. Rate yourself in each area on a scale of 1 (low in that characteristic) to 5 (high in that trait). Summarize your temperament.

ANSWERS TO SECTION 9-1 REVIEW

1. See the definition on page 296.
2. See the definition on page 297.
3. Possible response: They withdraw.
4. Possible response: By being put in loving, caring homes.
5. By being consistently loving and showing

care.
6. Yes, because poor relations between parents can hinder a baby's emotional development.
7. To identify how children respond to situations in terms of various traits.

ASSESS

CHECKING COMPREHENSION

Have students answer the Check Your Understanding questions. Answers appear at the bottom of this page.

EVALUATION

Give students the Section 9-1 Quiz in the *Teacher Resource Guide.*

RETEACHING

1. Assign Reteaching Activities, page 32.
2. Have students create a public service ad about building trust in infants.

ENRICHMENT

Have students investigate Harlow's or Ainsworth's work on attachment and report on their findings. As an alternative, students might look at the comments of critics.

EXTENSION

Invite a parent of twins to class to discuss how the children differ in temperament. (You could invite a pair of twins instead.) Have students prepare questions.

CLOSE

Give each student an opportunity to complete the statement "Temperament is . . ." Discuss the responses.

CAREER OPPORTUNITIES

Introducing the Feature

Ask students if they have ever heard of nannies before. Some may know the book and movie *Mary Poppins*. Some may have heard of celebrities using nannies for their children. Before they read the feature, **ask:** What do you think a nanny does?

Answers to
CONNECTING SCHOOL TO CAREER

1. **Possible response:** Any changes in the child's development, behavior, or health.
2. **Possible response:** Because the nanny lives with the family.

Applying What You've Learned

Tell students to pretend that they are a parent with one or more children who wants to hire a nanny. Have them write a job description outlining what the nanny would do. As an alternative, they could write a list of the qualities that they would want the nanny to possess.

CAREER OPPORTUNITIES

Nanny

A CONVERSATION WITH NICHOLE JENKINS

How did you become interested in becoming a nanny? I started babysitting in junior high school. Right then, I decided I wanted a career where I could be with children all the time. They're just such joys. I chose being a nanny instead of working in a child care center because I wanted closer involvement with children.

What are the tasks and responsibilities of a nanny? Everything that a parent would do—we feed, bathe, change, dress, and play with children. We take them to the doctor and dentist and to the park and the zoo. You name it, we do it.

What is the work environment like? That really depends on the home. The people I work for now have an apartment with an extra room for me.

What are the working hours like? Weekdays, I work from six in the morning until six at night, when both parents come home. I watch the baby some evenings when the parents are out and usually a half day or so on the weekend.

What aptitudes are needed to be a nanny? Well, you have to love children, obviously. You need patience and the ability to comfort a child. You need to watch the child at all times to make sure of safety, and you need to be creative to provide a stimulating environment. It helps to have a sense of humor. And you have to be a good communicator to let the parents know how you see the child developing.

Career Facts

NANNY

Education and Training. Nannies have a high school diploma and some additional training in child care. Some receive that training at nanny schools.

Career Outlook. The demand for nannies is expected to grow faster than average in the coming years.

CONNECTING SCHOOL TO CAREER

1. **Information Systems.** What kinds of information do you think nannies would communicate to parents?
2. **Resources.** Why do nannies receive room and board as part of their pay?

Building Career Skills

Resources. Have students assume that they are the nanny for twin infants. Have them make a chart with the following headings: "Feeding," "Cleaning," "Dressing," "Ensuring Health and Safety," "Nurturing," and "Playing." Under those headings, have them list the items they think they would need to properly care for the infants.

SECTION 9-2

Emotional and Social Development of Infants

Jo remembers how sweet the feeling was when she first felt Franklin in her arms. He had just been born. After feeling immense relief that her labor was over, she was swept up in a powerful wave of love. She promised herself—and Franklin—that she would never forget that feeling.

KEY TERMS

colic
pacifier
stranger anxiety

OBJECTIVES:

- Describe how behavior is learned.
- Describe how emotions change during infancy.
- Recognize signs of social development in babies.

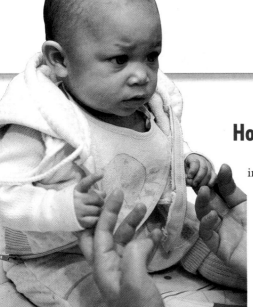

How Behavior Is Learned

As studies of attachment show, an infant learns how to behave toward others through his or her relationship with others. The type of behavior a baby learns depends on the messages he or she receives from caregivers.

305

Observing & Participating

Write several specific emotions—anger, love, fear, joy—on cards. Put each emotion on a separate card. Ask for volunteers to act out the emotion identified on a card. Students should use facial expression, body language, and sounds—but not words—to express the emotions. Have the class try to identify the emotion being shown. After all the demonstrations are done, discuss whether students think infants experience those same emotions. If so, how do they think infants show them?

FOCUS

MOTIVATOR

Ask students who have experience with babies to describe how infants change over time in terms of their relations with others. When do they seem to notice other people? How do they show this? Do they seem to favor some people over others?

VOCABULARY ACTIVITY

Ask students what it means to be anxious. From that definition, have them try to identify the meaning of "stranger anxiety."

COMPREHENSION CHECK

1. How are babies affected by routines? *(Learn through them; are comforted by the familiarity of them.)*
2. Give examples of positive and negative attention.

ACTIVITIES

Critical Thinking Activity

Understanding Point of View. Have students consider how an infant would perceive the world. Remind them that during pregnancy, developing babies have all their needs met automatically—they are warm, never hungry, never bothered by anything. Have them write a brief paragraph contrasting life in the uterus to life in the outside world. **L2**

Discussion Activity

Ask: How do you feel today—positive towards other people and upbeat, or negative and grouchy? Then have students think back to the first interactions with others they had today. How were their feelings shaped by those interactions? How can they use that experience when they are caregivers to send positive messages to infants? **L1**

VISUAL LEARNING | Using the Photograph
Answer: Babies respond more to attitudes than to words.

Babies learn about physical care through their daily routine. Running water may signal bath time; rocking signals time to sleep. They learn social behavior the same way—by seeing the same action bring about the same response repeated times. Babies learn that certain kinds of behavior are rewarded with positive responses, such as smiles, hugs, or praise. Because love is important to them, they repeat those behaviors. Babies also learn to avoid behavior that provokes negative responses like frowns or scolding.

Caregivers have to be sure to provide more positive than negative attention. When babies receive negative attention more often than positive, problems may result. The children are likely to do those things that bring on the negative response. They do so because they crave any kind of attention.

Babies are more sensitive to attitudes than to words. For example, if a mother says "no" as her ten-month-old blows food all over the high chair tray, yet laughs at the same time, the baby thinks she approves. This kind of mixed message can be very confusing.

To help a child understand what behavior is expected, parents and other caregivers must provide consistency. They must repeatedly act the same way. A baby will become confused if the same behavior provokes a positive response one time and a negative response the next. When adults change their mind often about expectations or frequently switch moods, it's difficult for their children to learn appropriate behavior.

Emotions in Infancy

Think about all the different emotions you experience. You may feel happy, angry, anxious, fearful, or excited. Babies only gradually develop such emotions.

At birth, the range of emotions is limited to pleasure or satisfaction—when the baby is quiet—and pain or discomfort—when the baby cries. Between the end of the first and second months, babies show a new emotion that most parents welcome gladly—they feel delight, which they show by smiling. In the second month, babies also show different feelings with different kinds of crying. The chart on pages 308-309 shows when other emotions develop.

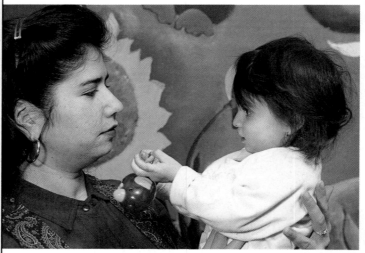

Why is it important to have tone of voice match your words when talking to a baby?

306 Unit 3: The Baby's First Year

DID You Know?

Mimicry and Better Moods. Parents and babies are quick to mimic each others' expressions. Researcher Jeannette Haviland used this fact to show how to change a baby's unhappy mood. When a baby is unhappy, the parent matches the child's facial expression for a few seconds to get the child's attention. Then the parent does something interesting or exciting such as raising the eyebrows or calling the child's name. Finally, the parent smiles—and the child usually smiles back. Ask: Why do you think the technique works?

Ask the E**x**perts

Jean Illsley Clarke
Director of J.I. Consultants in
Minneapolis, Minnesota

BABIES *and Crying*

Our one-month-old baby cries and cries some evenings, and nothing seems to help. Should we just leave her alone and let her "cry it out"?

This is a question many parents have. Most babies between the ages of three and twelve weeks have a fussy period at the end of the day.

My answer to your question really depends on what you mean by letting your baby "cry it out." For some parents, this means completely ignoring their baby. These parents believe—mistakenly—that a baby's crying is pointless and it isn't necessary to respond. This approach to crying is never appropriate.

Other parents let a baby "cry it out" during a fussy period by trying various methods of comforting the baby, one method at a time. Then they leave the baby alone for a short period—perhaps five minutes—between attempts to provide comfort. With this approach, the parents might try feeding, rocking, singing, talking, patting, carrying, adding more covers, removing covers, bundling, and loosening clothing all in turn. When they are out of the room, the baby can perhaps start learning to comfort himself or herself. This approach to crying it out can help both the baby and the baby's parents.

Crying is a baby's method of letting parents and other caregivers know about his or her needs. When the baby cries, they should be willing to listen, to respond by trying to figure out what the baby needs, and to meet the baby's needs as directly as possible. Check with a pediatrician if the problem is severe to rule out other causes.

Thinking It Through

1. What effect can letting a baby "cry it out" without any response have on the baby?
2. In the second method, why leave the baby alone after each attempt to comfort him or her?

Ask the E**x**perts

Introducing the Feature

Ask students if there is an event that they face on a regular basis that they dislike. It might be an unpleasant bus ride home or sitting next to a classmate that they don't like. Have volunteers describe how they feel as the disliked event approaches. Do they become unhappy? short tempered? Explain that an infant crying at about the same time every day is comparable. How do they think the parents would feel? How would those feelings impact on their ability to help the child?

Answers to Thinking It Through
1. *Possible response*: The baby may not develop trust.
2. *Possible response*: So the baby learns to self-comfort.

Applying What You've Learned

Have students work in groups to develop a list of strategies that parents can use on *themselves* when they have a child who fusses at the same time every day. What can the parents do to combat the frustration, anger, and lack of patience that might arise?

Parenting in *Action*

As babies grow, so does their ability to find ways to comfort themselves instead of waiting to receive comfort from others. Some experts suggest that self-comforting skills can be promoted by rocking and holding infants until just before they are asleep and then placing them in the crib so they can adjust to it and drift off to sleep on their own. A favorite toy, security blanket, or stuffed animal can help an older infant feel secure and comfortable when settling down to sleep.

ACTIVITIES

Critical Thinking Activity

Synthesizing. **Ask:** Which emotion is expressed first? *(Distress.)* When does it appear? *(Right at birth.)* Have students evaluate what impact these facts might have on parents, especially first time parents. **L2**

VISUAL LEARNING | **Using the Illustration**

Have students identify the approximate ages at which infants show each of the emotions illustrated in the chart. *Delight:* about one and a half months. *Elation:* about seven months. *Affection:* about nine months. *Distress:* at birth. *Disgust and Anger:* about four and a half months. *Fear:* about eight months.

DID You Know?

Smiling. Infants smile differently depending on what they are doing. A baby who is focusing hard on an activity will not smile broadly. The reason, researchers say, is that a broad smile, by raising the cheeks and narrowing the eyes, restricts the child's field of vision. Infants give bigger smiles to parents who enter a room because they can still see well. When trying to focus on a smaller object, though—such as another person's hands when playing pat-a-cake—the smile will be smaller.

When Emotions Develop

Babies develop their emotions gradually over time—just as their physical skills develop. They begin to show more specific responses to their world as they learn to connect their feelings to what they experience and the sensations that those experiences cause.

Delight: Babies show delight by smiling, perhaps in response to an adult who is making funny faces at them.

PLEASANT EMOTIONS

| Month 1 | Month 2 | Month 3 | Month 4 | Month 5 |

UNPLEASANT EMOTIONS

Distress: Very young babies express any discomfort or unhappiness by crying.

Disgust: Babies begin to show their dislikes very clearly.

LEARNING STYLES

Interpersonal

Form students into small groups. Have them brainstorm ideas about what circumstances might have brought about the emotions shown in the photographs on this page. Then have them identify ways those circumstances could have been changed. Would those changes have produced a different emotional response from the infant? How could a caregiver respond to that reaction?

Elation: Babies show high spirits with their whole body.

Affection: Babies first show affection for caregivers. Affection for other children comes later.

Month 7   Month 8   Month 9   Month 10   Month 11   Month 12

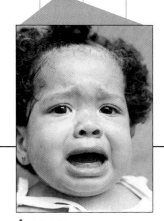

Anger: Babies first show their anger when they don't get their own way. Older babies show anger at objects as well as at people.

Fear: Babies begin to show fear of strangers at about eight months of age.

CHAPTER 9: Emotional and Social Development During the First Year **309**

Critical Thinking Activity

Analyzing. Describe the following situation to students: "A neighbor has asked you to babysit her baby daughter Angelina. The neighbor says 'You'll find it's very easy. Angelina spends all afternoon in her playpen. As long as the television is on, she's happy.'" What should you do? **L2**

Writing Activity

Have students write a scene that dramatizes an interaction between a baby and a caregiver. What emotions does the caregiver have? What emotions does the baby feel? How are the two related? Ask for volunteers to share their scenes with the class. Have the class discuss how realistic they are. **L1**

The Developing Brain

Shaken Baby Syndrome

Sometimes parents become so frustrated at a baby's loud, incessant crying that they vigorously shake the baby. Warn students that such shaking can damage the baby's developing brain. Section 8-3 of the textbook has more on the dangers of shaken baby syndrome.

LEARNING STYLES

Adapting for Various Styles

Visual. Show the class several photographs of infants. Have students try to identify what emotion the infant in each photograph shows. **Ask:** What clues suggest the infant's emotional state? What other clues would be available in a real-life situation?

Auditory. If possible, play a tape recording of infants making several different noises. Ask students to determine what emotion each sound suggests.

COMPREHENSION CHECK

1. Why are a baby's emotional needs for comforting more difficult to identify than physical needs? (*They aren't visible; the baby can't talk.*)
2. Some parents say that crying babies calm down and fall asleep in a car. Why might that be? (*It may break the cryng cycle and the motion may be soothng.*)

ACTIVITIES

Discussion Activity

Ask: What do you do when you are too cold? Too hot? Tired or sitting or lying in the same position? Bored? What can a baby who faces any of these feelings do? **L1**

Teamwork Activity

Describe the following situation to students: "Moira is a teen mother whose baby is three months old. Late one night, when Moira is doing her homework, the baby awakens crying loudly. Moira tries feeding the baby, but she pushes away, and her diaper is clean. Moira tries rocking the baby, but that doesn't stop the crying. Moira's mother calls out that it's late, and she needs her sleep." Have students work in groups to describe what Moira could do. **L2**

Crying and Comforting

The most obvious sign of an infant's emotions is crying. Newborns vary greatly in the amount and intensity of their crying. Some babies don't cry very often and are usually easy to comfort. These are what parents call "easy" or "good" babies. Other babies cry often and loudly, and it is usually hard to comfort them. These babies can be considered "difficult," because parents become frustrated when they can't calm the baby.

A young baby who is crying needs attention and care. The first step is to check for a physical problem. Is the baby hungry or in need of a diaper change? Is the infant too cold or too hot? Is there a burp left over from the last feeding? If none of these is the cause of the crying and the baby doesn't seem ill, the baby probably needs something else—your company, your cuddling, or your comforting. Remember that these are real needs, too.

As you and the baby get to know each other, you will probably discover which comforting measures work best. Here are a few to try:

- **Cuddle up with the baby in a rocking chair.** The combination of being held and rocked often soothes a crying baby. You can provide a similar combination by holding the baby close as you walk around.
- **Move the baby to a new position.** Perhaps the baby wants to lie in a different position but can't yet roll over. Maybe the baby wants to sit in an infant seat and feel involved with the rest of the family.
- **Talk softly to the baby or sing to the baby.** Even if you're not a great singer, the tone and rhythm of your voice, and the attention they indicate, may comfort the baby.
- **Offer a toy to interest and distract the baby.** The baby may be bored and want something to do. A favorite toy may end the crying.
- **Stroke the baby's back to give comfort.** Place the baby face down across your legs as you sit. Support the baby's head with one hand while gently rubbing the baby's back with the other.

Babies also develop their own techniques for comforting themselves. The most common comforting technique is sucking—on a thumb, a fist, or a **pacifier**—a nipple attached to a plastic ring.

Pacifiers, if used, must be used safely. *Never* tie the pacifier on a string around the baby's neck. To keep it from falling, use a short pacifier ribbon, which is attached both to the ring of the pacifier and to the baby's clothing. Check the pacifier often for cuts and tears on the surface. Also, clean it regularly.

Many babies also comfort themselves with a soft object such as a certain blanket or stuffed toy. They develop a special attachment to this object and use it for comfort when they are sleepy or anxious.

The Developing Brain

Most babies love to be rocked, and rocking has a variety of benefits—including for the baby's brain. Gentle rocking stimulates the cortex of the brain. This stimulation helps the baby gain weight, develops the baby's sight and hearing, and promotes regular sleep habits.

Parenting in *Action*

Describe the following situation to students: "Kelly is shopping in the supermarket with her infant son Tyler. Kelly lets Tyler suck on a pacifier whenever he wants. She finds that it calms him down, and when she's in public she doesn't want to have to handle a fussy infant. As they walk down an aisle, a stranger comes up to them and says, 'What an adorable baby you have. But why do you let him have that ugly pacifier?'" What should Kelly say or do?

Other babies comfort themselves by twisting their hair or by rocking themselves back and forth in their crib.

The baby's special self-comforting technique is an indication of his or her individuality and development. Children typically outgrow their need for such techniques and, when they are ready, give up these habits without a problem.

Colic

Catrina was at her wit's end. Little Brandon seemed to cry constantly every night, starting at about nine o'clock and going on until midnight. During the day, he was a cheerful, happy baby, but at night—when Catrina was tired and impatient—he became impossible to comfort.

When Catrina talked to the pediatrician, the doctor explained that Brandon had **colic** (COL-ick). Colic is marked by a baby's being extremely fussy every day. The periods of crying usually come any time between six o'clock in the evening and midnight. Colic is usually the worst when the baby is about six weeks old. The fussy periods then begin to grow shorter until they finally end.

If intense crying happens at all times, the problem may be something else. The baby's parents should check with the pediatrician if they are in doubt. Sometimes the baby's partially digested food comes back up.

This problem called "reflux," can cause colic-like symptoms.

Doctors don't understand why babies get colic. It may have to do with gas gathering in the stomach. One step to try to prevent colic is to eliminate food that may be causing it. Breast-feeding mothers should try avoiding milk products, cabbage, caffeine, and onions, any of which may be irritating the baby. If the baby is bottle-fed, pediatricians recommend using a soy-based, rather than a milk-based, formula.

Signs of Social Development in Infancy

Like physical and emotional development, social development follows a predictable pattern. The following list shows the common signs of social development for babies during the first year. Like all such lists, this one shows typical development for many babies. It is a general guide for what

Some parents feel frustrated until a baby begins to smile at about two months of age. **Why do you think that changes how parents feel?**

CHAPTER 9: Emotional and Social Development During the First Year **311**

COMPREHENSION CHECK

1. Would the same comforting technique used with a first baby be equally effective with a second baby? Why or why not? (*May or may not be—the babies are different.*)
2. Why are pacifiers appealing to babies? (*Satisfy their desire to suck.*)

ACTIVITIES

Critical Thinking Activity

Making an Argument. Point out to students that some people say that babies should not be given stuffed animals or special blankets as comfort objects because the children will become dependent on them. Have students debate the practice. **L1**

VISUAL LEARNING | Using the Photograph
Possible response: Because a smile shows the child responding to the parents in a positive way.

ISSUES IN CHILDREN'S HEALTH

Pacifiers. Caution students that although pacifiers come in attractive designs, parents should look for certain features to ensure safety. A pacifier should have a large handle or ring that is firmly attached. The mouthguard should be wide with a nipple that cannot be separated; this prevents choking. Mouthguards must have ventilation holes to prevent obstruction to the baby's breathing.

LEARNING STYLES | Interpersonal
Have students take the role of an expert facing questions from first-time parents worried about a baby who suffers from colic. The baby, two months old, cries loudly every night from 10:00 to 1:00 in the morning. The situation has been going on for three weeks now.

Have students work in pairs or groups to develop possible responses to the parents. Responses can include reassurance for the parents' worries and strategies the parents can use to try to relieve the child.

COMPREHENSION CHECK

1. When do children begin to respond to others? (*First few days of life.*)
2. When do babies begin to enjoy playing peekaboo? (*About six months.*)

ACTIVITIES

Critical Thinking Activity

Making Inferences. Have students write a brief essay about the effect a baby's helplessness has on others. **L1**

Teamwork Activity

Have volunteers take turns acting out the role of a parent and a stranger whose approach makes a child's cry. **L1**

Discussion Activity

Some parents join play groups where parents and children of about the same age meet on a regular basis—say, once a week—and spend an hour or two together. Babies less than a year old have little interaction with each other. **Ask:** How can these play groups benefit the babies? How can they benefit the parents? **L2**

VISUAL LEARNING | Using the Photograph
Left—Possible response: Child may crawl someplace where there is danger; may crawl out of parents' sight. *Right—Answer:* It shows that baby can remember caregivers' faces.

---

children ordinarily go through, not a checklist for helping you understand an individual baby. As you read, think about the brain development that makes each step possible.

- **The first days of life.** From birth onward, babies respond to human voices. A calm, soothing voice will quiet a baby, a harsh or loud voice will upset a baby.
- **One month.** Most babies stop crying when lifted or touched. A baby's face brightens when he or she sees a familiar person such as a parent.
- **Two months.** By two months, babies smile at people. Because their eyes can now follow moving objects, they enjoy watching people move about the room.
- **Three months.** Babies turn their head in response to a voice. Now they want companionship as well as physical care.
- **Four months.** Babies laugh out loud. They look to others for entertainment.
- **Five months.** Babies show an increased interest in family members other than parents. They may cry when they are left alone in a room. At this age, babies babble—to their toys, dolls, stuffed animals, or themselves.
- **Six months.** Babies love company and attention. They delight in playing games such as peekaboo.
- **Seven months.** Babies prefer parents over other family members or strangers.
- **Eight months.** Babies prefer to be in a room with other people. Babies who can crawl by this age may move from room to room looking for company.
- **Nine and ten months.** Now active socially, babies creep after their parents and are often

underfoot. Babies love attention. They enjoy being chased and playing games in which they throw toys again and again—with someone else picking them up each time.
- **Eleven and twelve months.** Babies are most often friendly and happy at this age. They are also sensitive to others' emotions—and know how to influence and adjust to the emotions of people around them. Babies like to be the center of attention. By this time, they are usually tolerant of strangers.

Stranger Anxiety

Another important sign of social development may seem difficult to parents and caregivers but is still a significant stage for each baby. Parents see it in the second half of the first year, often around the age of eight months. At this time, babies develop

At eight months, the baby begins to crawl and seek out company. *What dangers does this present?*

ISSUES IN TEEN PARENTING | Situations involving strangers may be more difficult for teens than for other parents because they are expected to be deferential to adults. Describe the following situation: "Alicia is standing in a supermarket line holding her baby. While they are waiting, a stranger, an older woman, comes up and stands very close and begins to tickle the baby. The baby begins to cry. Alicia tells the stranger 'The baby's very sensitive to strangers. Please stop,'"

Ask: How would the stranger respond? If Alicia were a teenager, how would the stranger respond?

stranger anxiety, a fear, usually expressed by crying, of unfamiliar people. During this period, a baby who used to sit cheerfully on anyone's lap suddenly screams and bursts into tears when an unfamiliar person approaches.

Stranger anxiety shows that the baby's memory is improving. The child can now better remember the faces of parents and caregivers. These are the people who provide comfort and security. Most other faces suddenly seem strange and make the baby feel fearful.

At this stage by remind new people to approach the baby slowly and to give the baby time to adjust. Try to keep the baby's routine as regular as possible. This is not a good time to introduce sudden changes in activities or caregivers.

How is stranger anxiety related to intellectual growth?

SECTION 9-2 REVIEW

✔ Check Your Understanding

1. How do parents' smiles and frowns help babies learn good behavior?
2. When do babies begin to smile?
3. Name two measures that might comfort a crying baby.
4. What is colic?
5. What are two signs of social development that many one-month-old babies exhibit?
6. What two signs of social development appear around the fifth month?
7. What is stranger anxiety? When does it develop?

Putting Knowledge Into Practice

1. **Analyzing.** What toys and equipment encourage caregiver-infant interaction? Which would discourage it? How could this be conveyed to parents and other caregivers?
2. **Applying.** Myong Ok's little baby is afraid of her younger brother, Sung. Suggest specific ways Myong Ok can help the baby develop a sense of comfort with her brother.
3. **Observing and Participating.** Watch one or more one-year-olds. What signs of emotions do you see? How are those emotions expressed? Share your findings with the class. Can you see any patterns?

CHAPTER 9: Emotional and Social Development During the First Year **313**

ASSESS

CHECKING COMPREHENSION

Have students answer the Check Your Understanding questions. Answers appear at the bottom of this page.

EVALUATION

Give students the Section 9-2 Quiz in the *Teacher Resource Guide.*

RETEACHING

1. Assign Reteaching Activities, page 33.
2. Have students take the role of the parent of a one-year-old. Write a letter to a friend describing the baby's emotional and social development.

ENRICHMENT

Have students prepare a brochure that contains tips parents can use to help the emotional and social development of infants.

EXTENSION

Have students create a checklist of infants' emotional and social development. Then have each student use the checklist to rate an infant. Students should record the child's age. Discuss their findings.

CLOSE

Have each student give one suggestion for encouraging emotional or social development in infants.

ANSWERS TO SECTION 9-2 REVIEW

1. They show babies which behaviors are rewarded and which are not.
2. Between the first and second months.
3. *Any two of the suggestions on page 310 or ideas generated by the student.*
4. Extreme fussiness that comes every day, usually at night.
5. Most stop crying when they are lifted or touched; their face brightens when they see a familiar person.
6. They may cry when left alone; they babble to their toys, dolls, or self.
7. Fear, expressed by crying, of unfamiliar people. Around eight months.

MOTIVATOR

Have students give examples of situations in which teens show trust in others, such as confiding a secret, sharing a possession, or arranging to meet at a certain time and place. Have them suggest how trust is developed in these situations and why it is important.

TEACH

Discussion Activity

Ask: How does consistent care help build trust? How does trust contribute to a baby's development of a healthy self-concept?

Teamwork Activity

Have students work in small groups to brainstorm ways that a family can work together to develop an infant's sense of trust.

Parenting With Care

Helping a Baby Develop A Sense of Trust

The kind of care babies receive in their first year determines how they view themselves and the world around them.

For every baby, the foundation of a strong and healthy self-concept is trust.

Responsive Care

An infant who is upset or fussy needs to be soothed. However, a content baby needs attention as well. Here are some ways to show responsiveness:

- Hold and cuddle the baby often. Carry the baby close to you as you walk, both indoors and outdoors.
- Give the baby who can crawl the freedom to explore in a safe environment, not just in a playpen.
- Answer the baby's babbles and "funny noises" with your own noises, words, and sentences.
- Let the baby sense your love in your face, voice, and touch.
- Learn to read the baby's signals. Smiling and cooing might mean, "Let's play." Turning or looking away may be the baby's way of saying, "That's enough—time to rest."

- Calm an unhappy baby with close, rhythmic movement, and soothing sounds.

Routines

Babies seem to need a predictable daily routine in order to thrive. Start with the baby's unique pattern of eating, sleeping, and waking. Then work out a routine that makes sense for you and the baby. For example, if you always hold the baby and sing to him or her after a feeding, the baby learns to look forward to it.

New Faces, New Places

Babies also need to learn to accept new situations. A caregiver can soothe fears and help the baby feel secure in unfamiliar surroundings.

Most babies go through a stage of fearing strangers. During this period, don't force a baby to sit on an

314 UNIT 3: The Baby's First Year

RESOURCES ON INFANT DEVELOPMENT

The organization "I Am Your Child" is dedicated to promote early childhood development. The group's web site has valuable information on brain research, advice from experts, and resource information. Their web address is www.iamyourchild.org. You can also write I Am Your Child Campaign, 335 North Maple Drive, Suite 135, Beverly Hills, CA 90210, or check their Website: www.iamyourchild.org

unfamiliar person's lap. Instead, allow the baby time to get used to the new person. Stay close by and show the baby that you trust this person.

You can help the baby get used to strangers by taking him or her to stores, parks, and other places where young children play. Talk to the baby in a calm, reassuring voice about what to expect and about what is happening.

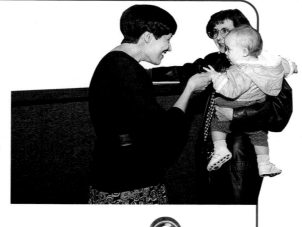

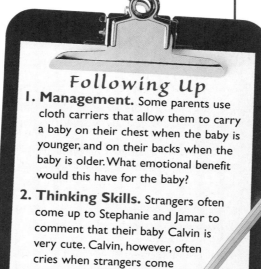

Following Up

1. Management. Some parents use cloth carriers that allow them to carry a baby on their chest when the baby is younger, and on their backs when the baby is older. What emotional benefit would this have for the baby?

2. Thinking Skills. Strangers often come up to Stephanie and Jamar to comment that their baby Calvin is very cute. Calvin, however, often cries when strangers come too close. How should Calvin's parents handle such situations when they are out shopping?

CHAPTER 9: Emotional and Social Development During The First Year **315**

Language Arts Activity

Have students write "diary" entries from an infant's viewpoint. In the entries, they should describe how the infant responds to caregivers, daily routines, and special events. Encourage students to include both positive and negative responses.
L2

CLOSE

1. Have students explain how the situations shown in the photographs in the feature demonstrate caregivers trying to develop trust in infants.

2. **Extension.** Have students observe caregivers and infants in various situations. Have them consider these questions: What did caregivers do to develop infants' trust? What did they do that would *not* develop trust? How could they change those behaviors?

CHECKING COMPREHENSION

Use the Summary and the Reviewing the Facts questions to help students go over the most important ideas in Chapter 9. Encourage students to ask questions and add details.

Answers to **Reviewing the Facts**

1. *Emotional development:* The process of learning to recognize and express one's feelings and of establishing one's identity and individuality. *Social development:* The process of learning to interact with others and to express oneself to others. They are related because an emotionally secure child is likelier to have healthier relationships with others.
2. *Possible response:* Infants need emotional closeness as well as nourishment to thrive.
3. *Possible response:* Their physical and emotional development suffers.
4. *Possible responses:* Be sure to talk through their conflicts; help each other solve problems.
5. A person's style of reacting to the world and relating to others.
6. *Possible response:* If a parent is calm when frustrated, the baby will learn not to become angry when frustrated.
7. Fear.
8. *Possible response:* With comforting measures.
9. *Possible response:* Crawling or walking late in the first year allows the baby to seek out people in the family.

CHAPTER 9

REVIEW &

Summary

✔ Emotional development deals with feelings. Social development deals with relationships with others. (Section 9-1)

✔ Attachment to caregivers is necessary for normal emotional and social development. (Section 9-1)

✔ Children and adults have different temperaments, which affect how they interact with the world. (Section 9-1)

✔ Children learn behavior through their relationships with others. (Section 9-2)

✔ Babies develop emotionally and socially through patterns. (Section 9-2)

Reviewing the Facts

1. Define emotional and social development, and explain how they are related? (Section 9-1)
2. What did Harry Harlow's experiments with monkeys show? (Section 9-1)
3. How do human babies respond when they are denied emotional support and social interaction? (Section 9-1)
4. What can parents do to create a good climate for raising a baby? (Section 9-1)
5. What is temperament? (Section 9-1)
6. Give an example of how babies learn emotional and social skills from caregivers. (Section 9-2)
7. What emotion is related to stranger anxiety and develops about the same time? (Section 9-2)

8. How should parents and caregivers respond to babies who cry? (Section 9-2)
9. How does a baby's growing mobility help his or her social development? (Section 9-2)

Thinking Critically

1. **Evaluating.** Which do you think is more important, emotional or social development? Why?
2. **Synthesizing.** Suppose that a parent was high in the trait adaptability but a child was low in that trait. Give an example of how they could come in conflict. What could the parent do to prevent problems from arising?
3. **Diagramming.** Use the information in the chapter about the stages of social development to create a chart showing how these stages appear at different ages.

Taking Action

1. **Children's Rights.** Work with a partner to write a "Baby's Bill of Rights" that lists everything you think babies have the right to receive from their parents. Make your list into a poster. *(Communication)*
2. **Helping Out.** A mother you know has become frustrated with how much her baby cries. What advice would you give her? *(Leadership)*

CONNECTIONS

Cross-Curricular Connections

1. **Health.** Find out how a child's emotional and social development is affected when a parent abuses drugs or alcohol. Report to the class.

2. **Language Arts.** Research to find suggestions to help parents who have babies who suffer from colic. Create a brochure that communicates these suggestions.

3. **Social Studies.** Choose two of the temperaments described in this chapter. Develop a list of questions that could be used on a test to determine whether a person was high or low in those temperaments.

Workplace Connections

1. **Personal Qualities.** Choose three traits of temperament. Write a paragraph explaining why you think it would be very useful for a child care worker to be high in those qualities.

2. **Basic Skills.** Create a chart showing new parents how they can expect their newborn to develop either emotionally or socially.

Family and Community Connections

1. **Father's Role.** What do you think the father's role can be in building trust? Write a list of suggestions for fathers to help build their child's emotional health.

2. **Forming Attachment.** Make a list of things parents can do to build a strong attachment to a baby.

3. **Talking to Others.** When Elijah gives his son a pacifier, his aunt criticizes the action. She says that a pacifier is bad for the child. What should Elijah say?

Technology Connections

1. **Internet.** Find an Internet site that offers advice to parents of babies. Find out what advice it gives for dealing with children who are high in any one of the nine temperament traits. Report your findings to the class.

EVALUATION

1. Use the reproducible Chapter 9 Test in the *Teacher Resources Guide,* or construct your own test using the **Exam***View*® Test Generator.

2. For an alternative assessment, assign the Chapter 9 activity in the *Authentic Assessment* section of the *Teacher Resource Guide.*

ENRICHMENT

Assign students either of the two enrichment activities in the *Enrichment Activities* booklet in the *Student Motivation Kit.*

EXTENSION

Invite a pediatrician, child care worker, or nanny to the class to discuss infants' emotions. Have students prepare questions such as: How do infants express their emotions? How do children differ in the emotions they apparently feel?

CLOSE

Have students write an essay titled "What kind of parent I will try to be to my child." Remind them to consider all the emotional support that they know a child needs based on what they've read in the chapter.

CHAPTER 10 RESOURCES

Teacher Resource Guide
• Chapter 10 Test, p. 154
• Authentic Assessment,
  p. 275
Student Motivation Kit
• Observations, pp. 45-46
Transparency Package
• CT-29 to CT-33, CT-37
Effective Instruction CD-ROM

CHAPTER 10 OVERVIEW

In **Section 10-1**, students learn a framework for understanding the intellectual development of children by reading about the periods identified by Jean Piaget.

In **Section 10-2**, students explore how to provide opportunities for infants to learn. They also learn about the acquisition of language skills.

CHAPTER 10 OBJECTIVES

After completing Chapter 10, students will be able to:

• Describe the ideas of Jean Piaget and his stages of learning.
• Explain how caregivers can provide learning opportunities for infants.
• Choose toys appropriate for infants.
• Describe the process by which infants learn language.

CHAPTER 10

Intellectual Development During the First Year

318 UNIT The Baby's First Year

RESOURCES TO EXPLORE

Developmental Delays. Some infants have disabilities and others experience developmental delays. Parents can turn to pediatricians and other specialists to address concerns about these issues. In addition, parents can turn to groups like the Family Information Network of Ohio helping parents of children with disabilities or developmental delays and professionals with information and support. The Family Information Network can be contacted at: www.familychild.org/fin.htm

Seven-month-old Daniel sat in a playpen beside a park bench. His mother was nearby, helping Daniel's four-year-old sister play on the swing and slide.

Daniel watched them from time to time, but he gave most of his attention to a red plastic cup. He turned the cup over and over, staring at it intently. Then he started chewing on its bottom, rim, and handle. Occasionally, he stopped chewing on it and banged the cup on the playpen floor.

After a while, Daniel grew tired of the cup and dropped it. He began pulling himself up to a standing position. When he succeeded, he held onto the edge of the playpen and laughed. Suddenly, he sat down again. He looked like he might cry, but instead tried to stand another time. After several tries, he managed to do so. While he stood, his mother said "Look at you, Daniel," and applauded. After two or three minutes, Daniel lost his balance and fell to a sitting position.

"When he succeeded in pulling himself up to a standing position, he laughed."

CHAPTER 10: Intellectual Development During the First Year **319**

- **Ask:** How does curiosity lead you to learn? How do you think that same impulse would work with infants? What things do infants need to learn about the world around them?
- Ask students to identify the objects in the playpen in the photograph. How would each one promote the baby's intellectual growth?

USING THE SCENARIO	Have students read the scenario in the

student text. **Ask:** What kind of temperament does Daniel seem to possess? (*High in persistence—he continued to try standing up even though he fell once.*) How will that temperament play a role in his future learning?

KEY TO ABILITY LEVELS	Each section gives skill-building activities. Each activity has been labeled for use with students of various learning styles and abilities.

L1 Level 1 activities are basic activities and should be within the range of all students.

L2 Level 2 activities are average activities and should be within the range of average and above average students.

L3 Level 3 activities are challenging activities designed for the ability range of above average students.

SECTION 10-1 RESOURCES
Teacher Resource Guide
- Lesson Plan Organizer, p. 60
- Section 10-1 Quiz, p. 152

Student Motivation Kit
- Observ. & Case Studies (case study), p. 111
- Reteaching Activity, p.34
- Enrichment, p. 30
- Nurt. Brain Dev., pp. 32-35

Student Workbook
- Study Guide, pp. 90-92
- Applying Piaget's Work, p. 93

Transparency Package
- CT-29 to CT-30

Effective Instruction CD-ROM

FOCUS

MOTIVATOR

Students may not think of infants as having "intellectual" capabilities. To make the idea more understandable, **ask:** "How do children think?" Have the class offer answers to the question.

VOCABULARY ACTIVITY

Explain that some terms on the list are related to each other and form part of a widely held theory about mental development. Ask which terms. (*The four periods.*) Explain that the others relate to concepts that children master. Have them try to identify what the concepts mean.

Understanding Intellectual Development of Infants

Consider the differences between a newborn and a one-year-old. The newborn can't move; the one-year-old can move where desired by crawling or walking. A newborn communicates only by crying; a one-year-old can use gestures and perhaps even words. A newborn can't pick up an object; a one-year-old can play with a stacking toy. In the first year of life, babies make amazing advances in their intellectual abilities.

KEY TERMS

attention span
cause and effect
concrete operations period
formal operations period
object permanence
perception
preoperational period
sensorimotor period
symbolic thinking

OBJECTIVES:
- Give examples of signs of intellectual growth in infants.
- Identify and give examples of Piaget's stages of learning.
- Explain how caregivers can make use of Piaget's ideas.

Learning in the First Year

Right from birth, babies have a number of capabilities. Newborns can hear, see, taste, smell, and feel. They use these abilities as the building blocks of learning.

Observing & Participating

Ask students to suggest toys that would be appropriate for infants from birth to one year. Write the suggestions on the chalkboard as they are made, and have students copy them into their notebooks. After the class has studied the chapter, have them consult the lists again and discuss them. What items would they take off the list? Why? What would they add? Why?

A baby's brain is fed by what he or she experiences through the senses. These experiences help the brain become organized. Babies' ability to learn from the senses, called **perception** (purr-SEP-shun), improves. As you have learned, newborns can't see objects in three dimensions, but three-month-olds can. In time, babies develop the hand-eye coordination to grasp and handle objects. They develop many skills, as shown in the chart on pages 322-323.

INFOLINK

The Developing Brain

To read more about *the developing brain*, see Section 8-2, pages 260-266.

In just the first year of life, babies also develop four abilities that show growing thinking power:

- **Remembering.** In the first few months, babies develop the ability to remember. The information from the senses can be interpreted in light of past experiences. A two- or three-month-old baby may stop crying when someone enters the room because the baby knows that he or she is now likely to be picked up and comforted.
- **Making associations.** This act—the baby's ceasing to cry—also indicates association. The baby associates a parent or other caregiver with receiving comfort.
- **Understanding cause and effect.** Babies also develop an understanding of **cause and effect**, the idea that one action results in another action or condition. When a baby closes his or her

eyes, it gets dark. When the baby opens them again, it gets light. Sucking causes milk to flow. If the baby stops sucking, the milk stops. In short, every time the infant does something, something else happens.

As babies' motor skills develop, cause-and-effect learning changes. By seven or eight months, babies can throw things deliberately. They can pull the string on a toy and make the toy move. At this age, babies have a better understanding of their own power to make certain things happen.

Of course, babies learn by repetition. That's why eight-month-old Jenny continues to drop her bowl from her perch in the high chair onto the floor.

When babies' memories improve, they will seek out a toy that they want.

COMPREHENSION CHECK

1. Give an example of how perception changes as babies age.
2. Give an example of a pleasant association a baby might have. (*Being picked up and feeling comforted.*)
3. Give an example of an unpleasant association. (*Wet diaper and discomfort.*)

ACTIVITIES

VISUAL LEARNING Using the Photograph

Ask: How do motor skills tie in with an infant's intellectual development, as shown in this photograph? (*Child can crawl in search of the toy.*)

DID You Know?

Study of Child Development. **The intellectual development of infants and small children was ignored until the 1920s. Children were considered miniature adults, who were less intelligent simply because they had not yet acquired knowledge. The work of researchers like Jean Piaget, discussed in this section, led to the discovery that children think and learn in ways that are distinctly different from adults and that mental development follows a predictable pace.**

Parenting in Action

Have students work in groups to list activities caregivers can do with children to stimulate their ability to learn and listen early in life. Give each group the following sounds and ask them to consider how an infant would respond:
- Singing a lullaby.
- Hearing soft music.
- Hearing music with a lively rhythm.
- Talking to the baby.
- People on the television talking.
- Arguing to others.

Have the groups compile their responses and compare them.

COMPREHENSION CHECK

1. Identify which skills have to do with sight, hearing, and hand control.
2. What skills listed in the chart reveal a baby's growing sense of self? (*Recognizes own name; smiles at self in mirror.*)

ACTIVITIES

Discussion Activity

What comes first, responding to language or generating language? (*Responding, which begins at 9-10 months, is before speaking, at 11-12 months.*) Why do you think that is the pattern? **L1**

Critical Thinking Activity

Making Inferences. How is the skill "Obeys simple commands or directions" related to improved memory? **L1**

VISUAL LEARNING

Using the Chart Have students identify sequences of skills—for example, preferring faces to objects (1-2 months) precedes recognizing caregivers' faces (3-4 months) and grasping objects that touch the hand (3-4 months) precedes reaching for objects (5-6 months).

▶ **Average Intellectual Development: Birth to Twelve Months**

AGES	DEVELOPMENTAL CHANGES
1-2 months	• Follows moving objects with eyes. • Gains information through senses. • Prefers faces to objects. • Cries to indicate needs. • Can distinguish between familiar and unfamiliar voices.
3-4 months	• Recognizes caregivers' faces. • Can distinguish between familiar and unfamiliar faces. • Grasps objects that touch hand. • Tries to swipe at objects. • Interested in own hands and feet. • Practices making sounds. • Responds when caregiver talks.
5-6 months	• Is alert for longer periods of time, up to two hours. • Reaches for objects and grasps them with entire hand. • Studies objects carefully. • Looks for objects that are dropped. • Plays peekaboo. • Recognizes own name. • Distinguishes between friendly and angry voices. • Makes sounds to indicate pleasure and displeasure.
7-8 months	• Imitates the actions of others. • Begins to understand cause and effect. • Remembers things that have happened. • Smiles at self in mirror. • Sorts objects by size. • Solves simple problems. • Recognizes some words. • Babbling imitates inflections of speech.

Continued

LEARNING STYLES

Naturalistic

As they study the chart, have students share their own ideas and experiences. **Ask:** Which of these developments have they observed in infants? Have them describe the situation. How did they respond to the infant's actions? How did that response affect the infant? What did they think about the child's mental abilities at the time of the interaction? What do they think now?

Average Intellectual Development: Birth to Twelve Months (Continued)	
AGES	**DEVELOPMENTAL CHANGES**
9-10 months	• Searches for hidden objects. • Handles medium-sized objects skillfully. • Takes objects out of containers and puts them back in. • Plays pat-a-cake. • Responds to some words. • May say a few words. • Obeys simple commands or directions.
11-12 months	• Manipulates objects skillfully. • Likes to look at picture books. • Fits blocks or boxes inside one another. • Knows parts of body. • Can pick up small objects with forefinger and thumb. • Recognizes many words. • Speaks some words regularly.

Teamwork Activity

Have students work in groups to identify toys and activities that help infants learn cause and effect. Have the groups compare and discuss their ideas. **L1**

Critical Thinking Activity

Applying. **Ask:** How does attention span help in learning? How is that true not only of infants, but also of older children? **L1**

The Developing Brain

Links to Piaget's Theory

The stages of intellectual development identified by Piaget are apparently paralleled by the growth of the brain. The brain grows rapidly during the first half of each stage, signaling the appearance of important new functions. During the latter half of each stage, growth levels off until the next stage is reached.

She simply wants to be sure that *every time* she drops the bowl, it will fall to the floor. Parents can become frustrated with these repeated actions—after all, for Jenny to repeat her experiment, someone needs to pick the bowl up! If they remember that their little scientists are simply learning about the world, they may find the patience to allow the game to continue.

Repetition has another benefit. Repeated actions strengthen connections between nerve cells in the brain. As a result, they can work together in a coordinated way more smoothly and quickly.

• **Paying attention.** A baby's **attention span**—the length of time a person can concentrate on a task without getting bored—grows longer. If the same object is presented over and over again, the baby's response to the object will eventually become less enthusiastic. The baby's diminishing response is a way of saying, "That's old stuff. I've seen it before." Generally, bright babies have a short attention span—they tend to lose interest sooner than babies of average or below-average intelligence. (Beyond infancy, children with above average intelligence typically have a longer attention span than others their age.)

CHAPTER 10: Intellectual Development During the First Year **323**

ISSUES IN CHILDREN'S HEALTH Have students consider the connection between intellectual and physical development. Remind them that this relationship continues in later years, and intellectual development might be affected by health changes. For instances, a child who is seriously ill may not be able to keep up with the earlier rate of development. External influences such as stress in the home can have an effect on intellectual development as well. Have students suggest other factors that might have an impact and consider strategies for minimizing any negative effect.

ACTIVITIES

Critical Thinking Activity

Analyzing. Explain to students that Piaget called children in the sensorimotor period "egocentric." They think only about themselves and see others in relation to themselves. Ask students for examples of this tendency. **L1**

Discussion Activity

Ask: What two words were combined by Piaget to create the name for this period? (*Sensory; motor.*) What do they mean? Why did Piaget combine them in labeling this period? **L2**

Piaget's Background. **Although Jean Piaget spent most of his later life researching children's mental development, his early professional life was devoted to biology. While studying mollusks, he noted how they changed structurally from one generation to another. This led him to conclude that biological development was affected by environment as well as heredity. The idea that organisms adapt to their environment carried into his study of mental development, which he also saw as a matter of adaptation.**

Piaget's Theories

Jean Piaget, a Swiss psychologist who died in 1980, had a great influence on what we know about how children learn. Piaget was trying to understand how children's intellectual skills developed. He found that intellectual development followed a pattern. Children learn to master one thinking skill before they can master another.

Children can't be forced by parents or teachers to develop understanding any faster than their abilities mature. On the other hand, children who don't get the chance to apply their developing skills may never reach their full potential. For this reason, it is important for children to have the constant opportunities for learning.

According to Piaget, learning stages appear in the same order in all children. What differs is the ages at which the stages develop, although average ages can be given. He identified four major periods.

The Sensorimotor Period

The **sensorimotor period** (SEN-suh-ree-MOE-tur), from birth to about age two, is Piaget's first stage of learning. During this period, babies learn primarily through their senses and their own actions.

Swiss psychologist Jean Piaget carried out pioneering studies of how children learn. *How can caregivers use what Piaget discovered about children's thinking?*

During the sensorimotor period, babies come to understand an important concept. Usually at about ten months, they realize that objects continue to exist even when they are out of sight. This concept is called **object permanence.** At four months, Maria drops her rubber ring toy and it rolls behind her. She simply looks for something else to play with. At eleven months, when her ball rolls out of sight, Maria actively looks for it. She has learned the concept of object permanence.

The sensorimotor period can be broken down into six shorter stages. At each stage, a baby has specific intellectual abilities. The

Parenting in *Action*

To help a baby learn object permanence, caregivers can play hiding games. First, place a special toy partly under a small blanket. When the baby consistently uncovers the toy, start putting it completely under the blanket while the child watches. Once the baby finds the toy consistently, let the baby watch as you hide the toy in more difficult places, such as in an open container or under a box. Be sure to reward each discovery with smiles and sounds of delight!

Piaget's Four Periods

PERIOD	APPROXIMATE AGES	CHARACTERISTICS
Sensorimotor	Birth to two years	Children learn through their senses and own actions.
Preoperational	Two to seven years	Children think in terms of their own activities and what they perceive at the moment.
Concrete operations	Seven to eleven years	Children can think logically but still learn best through experience.
Formal operations	Eleven years to adulthood	People are capable of abstract thinking.

chart on page 326 explains these six stages. It will better help you understand how learning occurs.

The Preoperational Period

The **preoperational period** (pree-OP-ur-AY-shun-ul), Piaget's second stage, typically lasts from age two to seven. In this period, children think about everything in terms of their own activities and of what they perceive at the moment. Children may believe that the moon follows them around. A child in this stage may think that the same amount of a liquid becomes more to drink when it is poured from a short, wide glass into a tall,

thin glass. Because the water is higher in the second glass, the child concludes that there must be more of it.

In the preoperational period, children begin to understand abstract terms like *love* and *beauty*. Concentration, though, is limited to one thing at a time. Children this age

Babies enjoy playing peeka-boo, which helps them learn object permanence. *How does this game also involve interaction?*

CHAPTER 10: Intellectual Development During the First Year **325**

COMPREHENSION CHECK

1. According to Piaget, symbolic thinking does not begin until about age eleven. What are the implications for teaching of that fact?
2. What is one criticism of Piaget's ideas? (*Children develop abilities earlier than his theory predicts.*)

ACTIVITIES

Teamwork Activity

Form students into teams for "Piaget Jeopardy." On the chalkboard, write the names of Piaget's four periods. Describe various learning skills to the class (for example, learning abstract concepts such as love; learning object permanence) and have teams identify the period to which the skill belongs. If a team is incorrect, give other teams a chance. **L1**

Discussion Activity

Ask: Why do most people never fully develop their potential for learning? Is this "a waste" or "just normal"? What could people do to further develop their potential? **L2**

| **VISUAL LEARNING** | **Using the Chart** |

Discuss with students the safety implications of the fact that hand-mouth coordination develops very early for infants. What demands does this place on caregivers?

▶ The Sensorimotor Period: Birth to Age Two

STAGE	APPROXIMATE AGES	CHARACTERISTICS
Stage 1	Birth to one month	• Practices inborn reflexes. • Does not understand self as separate person.
Stage 2	One to four months	• Combines two or more reflexes. • Develops hand-mouth coordination.
Stage 3	Four to eight months	• Acts intentionally to produce results. • Improves hand-eye coordination.
Stage 4	Eight to twelve months	• Begins to solve problems. • Finds partially hidden objects. • Imitates others.
Stage 5	Twelve to eighteen months	• Finds hidden objects. • Explores and experiments. • Understands that objects exist independently.
Stage 6	Eighteen to twenty-four months	• Solves problems by thinking through sequences. • Can think using symbols. • Begins imaginative thinking.

tend to solve problems by pretending or imitating, rather than by thinking the problems through. During this period, children may not even be aware of what is real and what is make-believe.

The Concrete Operations Period

The **concrete operations period** is Piaget's third stage of learning, lasting usually from seven to eleven years of age. In this stage, children can think logically but still learn best from direct experience. When problem solving during this stage, children still rely on actually being able to see or experience the problem.

However, logical thinking is possible. Children understand that pouring water from one container to another doesn't change the amount of water. They can also comprehend that operations can be reversed. For example, subtraction will "undo" addition and division is the reverse of multiplication. During this stage, chil-

---

Management/Leadership Skills

Babies in stages four and five of the sensorimotor period are fascinated by hinged objects. This makes opening and closing cabinet doors one of their favorite games. One mother, recognizing this, turned over a low kitchen cabinet to her child. She put a few plastic bowls and cups and similar safe items in the cabinet. Eventually, the child learned which cabinet was "hers" and which ones had to be left alone. Of course, the mother never put any dangerous objects or substances in the baby's cabinet.

dren also learn to make more complex categories, such as classifying kinds of animals or types of food.

The Formal Operations Period

The **formal operations period**, the fourth stage, lasts from about age eleven through adulthood. In this period, children become capable of abstract thinking. In other words, people in this stage are able to think about what might have been the cause of an event without really experiencing that cause. This ability allows problem solving just by thinking. People in this stage can also form ideals and understand deeper, less obvious meanings or subtle messages.

In the preoperational period, children sometimes have difficulty separating what is real and what is make-believe. *What implications does this have for children when they watch television?*

CHAPTER 10: Intellectual Development During the First Year **327**

Using Piaget's Ideas

In recent years, other thinkers have raised questions about Piaget's ideas. They point out that his experiments focused on only a certain kind of learning. They charge that the boundaries of his stages are sometimes set too rigidly. They argue that in different kinds of experiments, children have been shown to understand concepts before the stage that Piaget said they should.

Still, his work remains important. Piaget showed that young children learn in their own ways—not as adults do. Older children can learn through **symbolic thinking**, the use of words and numbers to stand for ideas. Younger children, who can't yet think in symbolic ways, rely on concrete experiences. For example, the statement "I have three blocks" means nothing to a young

CHECKING COMPREHENSION

Have students answer the Check Your Understanding Questions. Answers appear at the bottom of this page.

EVALUATION

Give students the Section 10-1 Quiz in the *Teacher Resource Guide*.

RETEACHING

1. Assign Reteaching Activities, page 34.
2. Have students prepare a concept web by writing "intellectual development" on the center and linking key concepts to it.

ENRICHMENT

Have students research to find more about criticisms of Piaget's work. What do critics say? What evidence do they use to support their position?

EXTENSION

Arrange a field trip to a child care center or an early elementary classroom. Have each student observe a different child and report on signs of that child's mental development.

Have each student complete the following sentence: "During the first year, babies learn . . ."

Why will a young child hold up three fingers while saying "three"?

child. The child has to see the blocks. A three-year-old will hold up three fingers when asked how old he or she is, even though the child may say the words, too.

The preschool child needs lessons presented with objects or activities, not just symbols. Verbal instruction from a teacher or parent has only a minor role in learning during the early years.

SECTION 10-1 REVIEW

✔ Check Your Understanding

1. What is perception? Give an example of how a baby's perception changes during the first year of life.
2. How can pull toys help a baby learn cause and effect?
3. Explain what an attention span is.
4. What are Piaget's four periods of learning and what are their approximate time spans?
5. What do babies use to learn during Piaget's first period of development?
6. Give an example of how a person can use abstract thinking, which begins in Piaget's fourth period.
7. What is the significance of Piaget's findings about symbolic thinking?

Putting Knowledge Into Practice

1. **Analyzing.** What learning ability does the game pat-a-cake build?
2. **Synthesizing.** How does the game of peekaboo contribute to the development of object permanence? How is memory linked to object permanence?
3. **Observing and Participating.** Try conducting one of Piaget's experiments with a younger child. Fill a short, wide glass with liquid and show it to the child. Then pour the liquid into a taller, thinner container and ask whether the taller glass has more liquid, less liquid, or the same amount. How do your findings compare to those of your classmates? What difference does the age of the child make?

ANSWERS TO SECTION 8-4 REVIEW

1. Learning from the senses; example—three-dimensional vision.
2. When baby pulls it, it moves and makes a noise.
3. Time a person can focus on a task and not be bored.
4. *Sensorimotor:* to age 2; *Preoperational:* 2 to 7; *Concrete operations:* 7 to 11; *Formal operations:* 11 to adulthood.
5. They learn through senses and actions.
6. *Possible response:* Teen choosing between right and wrong.
7. *Possible response:* Young children can't think symbolically, so caregivers should include physical activities.

CAREER OPPORTUNITIES

Toy Store Worker

A CONVERSATION WITH TONY NUNEZ

How did you become interested in becoming a toy store worker? Well, I've always loved to play with toys myself. In high school, I took a child development course and learned why toys are so important to children's learning. I had always enjoyed working in stores, so I thought I would combine these interests.

What are the tasks and responsibilities of a toy store worker? Much of our work is very simple—we stock the shelves, handle purchases when people know what they want, and take care of returns. What I enjoy most, though, is when customers ask about particular toys. Because I hear all the time about what children play with and like, I can give others good suggestions.

What is the work environment like? A store is a very busy place. We have areas where children can watch videos. There's music playing, so it can get noisy.

What are the working hours like? The store is open from 10:00 a.m. to 10:00 p.m. I usually work 40 hours a week except at the end of the year. Come holiday season, I work lots of overtime.

What aptitudes are needed to be a toy store worker? You have to be good with math. You really need to like children. Good communication skills and an understanding of children help you find out what people are looking for and give them advice.

TOY STORE WORKER

Education and Training. Toy store workers need a high school diploma. They usually get the training they need on the job.

Career Outlook. The demand for toy store workers should be steady in the near future.

CONNECTING SCHOOL TO CAREER

1. **Technology.** Why would a toy store worker need to be good at math if scanners and cash registers calculate the amount of a sale?
2. **Interpersonal Skills.** Suppose you were a toy store worker during the holiday shopping period. What would you say to a parent who was angry because the item he or she wanted was out of stock?

CHAPTER 10: Intellectual Development During the First Year **329**

FOCUS

MOTIVATOR

Bring in some magazine pictures of children playing. Display them at the front of the class. Have students brainstorm all the different reasons that children play.

VOCABULARY ACTIVITY

Tell students that all three terms in the section are compound words—words that are formed by joining two words or a root word and a prefix or suffix. Ask them to identify the root words in each of the terms. Have them define each term before reading the section and write that definition down. Have them to check their definitions after they have finished studying the section.

330

Helping Babies Learn

Intellectual development of an infant is closely linked to the responsiveness of others. That is, babies learn more and learn faster when parents and caregivers comfort them, smile at them, talk to them, and play with them. A baby treated this way is likely to be brighter than a similar child who does not receive loving, attentive care. Parents are babies' most important teachers.

KEY TERMS

age appropriate
childproof
recall

OBJECTIVES:

- Discuss ways parents and caregivers can help babies' intellectual growth.
- Identify toys appropriate for a baby's age.
- Explain how babies develop communication skills.

330   Unit 3: The Baby's First Year

Encouraging Learning

Even the youngest babies learn about the world from the care they receive. When Tyler feels uncomfortable in his stomach, he cries. Then his mother picks him up and nurses him. That makes the discomfort in his stomach go away. The events—discomfort, crying, cuddling, being fed—are connected. There is a pattern.

Observing & Participating

Of all the toys for babies, one ranks high above the rest. It makes noises and moves. It is creative and fascinating. It changes as the child grows. When baby plays with it, it responds. This amazing toy is a person! Notice how babies peer into faces, reach for noses, pull on ears, and laugh at silly faces. Try an imitation game with a baby. When the baby coughs, imitate the sound. Keep it up, and soon you'll hear the baby coughing just to get a response. What other such games can you think of?

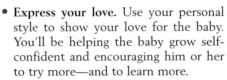
Age-appropriate toys help children develop both physically and intellectually. **How might this toy promote development?**

If the baby's cries are not answered, the baby sees no relationship between its needs and the caregiver's actions. There is no pattern.

Giving a child basic care, then, helps build that child's mental abilities. Those who care for children can influence the children's intellectual development in other ways. Encouraging learning doesn't require money or special toys. Rather, it depends on the attention, knowledge, and time of parents and other caregivers.

Here are some ways that caregivers can encourage learning:

- **Learn about child development.** Understanding how an average child develops can help you provide learning experiences that are **age appropriate**. That means they are suitable for the age and individual needs of a child.
- **Give your time and attention.** No baby needs attention every waking moment. However, you can help a baby thrive—and learn—just by talking to the baby and playing simple games.
- **Provide positive feedback.** When the baby demonstrates a new skill or tries out a new activity, show your pleasure and respond with praise. Your reaction will encourage the baby to keep trying new things.

INFOLINK

Reading to Children

For more about *reading to children*, see page 338.

- **Express your love.** Use your personal style to show your love for the baby. You'll be helping the baby grow self-confident and encouraging him or her to try more—and to learn more.
- **Talk, talk, talk.** Talking has many benefits. When parents talk to infants, they help them learn about their environment. Current research shows that the more caregivers talk to a baby, the faster the child's brain develops. Talking builds feelings of security, too.

The "Parenting with Care" feature on pages 340-341 presents more ideas for creating a stimulating environment and helping babies learn.

CHAPTER 10: Intellectual Development During the First Year **331**

Parenting in Action

Busy parents often worry about not spending enough time with their children. Here are some tips:

- Schedule some uninterrupted time each day to spend with the child. During this period, turn off the TV and ignore other distractions.

Focus on the child.

- Let a household task go undone. If you cannot ignore the chore, try to involve the child. If you must fold laundry, for instance, name the colors, count out the items of clothing, and let the child feel the different fabrics.

TEACH

COMPREHENSION CHECK

1. Why are patterns important to infants? (*Repetition helps them learn.*)
2. How can caregivers provide feedback to infants? (*With smiles, sounds, words, hugs, kisses.*)

ACTIVITIES

Discussion Activity

Have students look at the suggestions for encouraging learning. **Ask:** Which do you think parents most often neglect? Why? Which would be easiest for you to follow? Why? **L1**

VISUAL LEARNING | Using the Photograph
Possible response: Allows baby to work on hand-eye coordination.

ISSUES IN
CHILDREN'S HEALTH

In an effort to provide a baby with activities that promote development, some parents get carried away. They are so eager to have their babies accomplish new skills that they become almost competitive with other parents and babies. Babies should not be pressured to learn new things. They need to learn at their own pace.

COMPREHENSION CHECK

1. Why is safety such an important issue for infants?
2. Are stacking toys appropriate for a newborn? Why or why not? (*No; they don't have the physical abilities to use them.*)

ACTIVITIES

Discussion Activity

Write the following on the chalkboard: "A child's job is to play." **Ask:** What does this mean? How is this especially true of infants? If that is the child's job, what is the caregiver's job? **L2**

Discussion Activity

Ask: How might trying to keep a home neat stifle a baby's curiosity? Should the baby's needs always take precedence over the appearance of the home? Why or why not? **L1**

Critical Thinking Activity

Analyzing. Babies change rapidly in the first year. What responsibility does that place on caregivers in terms of providing play activities? **L2**

Safe Learning

To encourage learning, allow the baby as much freedom of movement at home as possible. In the first few months, move the baby from room to room to be with the family. A baby who spends times in different rooms and with the family learns more than a baby who is kept alone in a crib. Older babies who can crawl or walk should not be restricted to playpens for long periods of time.

It is better to **childproof** as much of the home as possible and to monitor the child's activities. Childproofing is a matter of taking steps to protect a child from possible dangers. For example, placing gates at the top and bottom of stairways prevents a child from falling. Learning occurs best when children can explore and try new things—safely.

> **INFOLINK**
>
> **Childproofing**
>
> For more about *childproofing*, see the "Parenting with Care" feature at the end of Chapter 11.

The Importance of Play

Ten-month-old Beth sits on the kitchen floor, thumping a spoon against the bottom of a saucepan. She has discovered her own "educational toy." With it, she learns that a certain action will produce a particular sound. She delights in the sound and in her own power to produce it.

For children, play is work as well as pleasure. Researchers have clearly established that playtime is essential to intellectual development. Toys are the tools for learning.

Play is also a physical necessity through which development takes place. When a baby shakes a rattle, stacks blocks, throws a ball, or chews on a teething toy, the activity is not just for amusement. These are serious, absorbing tasks through which babies strengthen their muscles, refine their motor skills, and learn about the world.

Different Toys for Different Ages

Because babies mature and change rapidly during the first year, their toys need to change, too. Here are some ideas about appropriate toys for different stages:

Add locks to low cabinets. This will provide a safe environment that gives a baby an opportunity to explore.

LEARNING STYLES

Musical

Tell students that their job is to promote a public service campaign aimed at protecting infants. They are to write a jingle that could be broadcast on the radio and would reinforce the importance of creating a safe learning environment. Students can simply sing their jingles to the class. If they wish, and if equipment is available, they could record it using either audio- or videotape.

- **Birth to three months.** A baby at this age can do little except look and listen. Bright colors and interesting sounds stimulate development of the senses. A mobile hung safely above the crib is interesting for the baby to watch. The baby's random arm and leg movements can set the objects in motion and produce sounds. Brightly colored crib liners, wallpaper, and pictures also provide interest.
- **Four to six months.** The sense of touch is important in this period. Babies need things to touch, handle, bang, shake, suck, and chew. Choose toys that are small enough to handle easily but too large to swallow. All items and pieces should be at least 1½ inches (3.8 cm) across. Teething rings, cups, rattles, and plastic toys are good choices. Stuffed toys are fun to touch, and toys that squeak give results when the baby acts. Providing objects with different textures helps the child learn by touch. Babies this age like simple picture books. Choose washable books with colorful pictures of familiar objects.
- **Seven to nine months.** Babies still need things to handle, throw, pound, bang, and shake. Anything that makes a noise fascinates babies of this age. They enjoy blocks, balls, large plastic beads that pop apart, and roly-poly toys. Safe household items are just as interesting as purchased toys. Pots and pans with lids, and plastic containers to stack make great playthings.
- **Ten to twelve months.** Babies of this age need things to crawl after. Those who are already walking like toys to push or pull. During this period, children especially enjoy toys to manipulate. Baskets, boxes, and other containers are fun. Babies like to put things into them and then dump them out again. Picture books are good for looking at alone or for brief story times during the day or before bed.

Some books not only have pictures but also different textures for a baby to touch. *Why would these be particularly good for babies four to six months old?*

Have students write warning labels that might appear on toys that aren't appropriate for children in their first year. **L1**

Critical Thinking Activity

Applying. **Ask:** How much should a baby be encouraged to play independently? How much involvement should siblings, parents, or other caregivers have? Does this change as a baby ages? **L2**

Critical Thinking Activity

Analyzing. Have students write their responses to this quotation: "For an infant, all toys are educational toys." As they respond, have them bear in mind the issue of a child's attention span and frustration level. **L2**

VISUAL LEARNING | Using the Photograph

Answer: Because the sense of touch is important in those months.

Parenting in *Action*

Along with toys, babies also benefit from activity. Here are some good exercises for an infant:
- Place babies on their backs. Hold the legs and rotate them as if the baby were riding a bicycle.
- Place babies on their stomachs. This encourages them to lift their heads.
- Once babies can move, place babies on blankets with toys slightly out of reach. This encourages them to move for the toys.

ACTIVITIES

Critical Thinking Activity

Giving Examples. Have students give examples of toys that can be used at different ages. **L1**

The Developing Brain

Brain Hemispheres

The brain is divided into two halves, or hemispheres. The left hemisphere is responsible for speaking, writing, and understanding language. It is also used in math, rhythm, analytical skills, and complex movements. The right brain is superior at spatial tasks, perception, nonverbal communication, and visualization. The left brain thinks sequentially; the right brain thinks holistically. One side or another may dominate the way a person thinks. Left-brain thinkers do well in subjects such as math, management, law, and engineering. Right-brain thinkers favor subjects such as art, music, and architecture. Still, all people need and use both sides of the brain.

Choosing Toys

When choosing playthings for a young child, look for toys that encourage participation and use. Younger children need simple toys. As a baby's abilities increase, toys can be more complex.

Toys, especially those labeled "educational," can be expensive. Sometimes they have limited usefulness. You can provide a baby with as much fun and learning by making common household items available. Try offering the baby items such as plastic measuring spoons, plastic measuring cups, a clean bucket, plastic bowls, a metal pan or mixing bowl and a large spoon, or a large cardboard box with a "window" cut in it. You'll be surprised at the variety of ways young children play with these items.

The same type of toy can serve different purposes at different ages. At five months (left), a baby explores shaped objects with his mouth to learn about texture. At eleven months (right), a child can sort the shapes.

When you buy toys, look for ones that will remain interesting and appropriate for a number of years. A set of blocks is a good example. At the age of six months, Reynaldo grasped and inspected his blocks. By his first birthday, he could stack several blocks into a tower. At the age of three, he used the blocks to make roads for his cars. Now, at age six, Reynaldo creates elaborate houses and castles, using every available block.

Developing Communication Skills

One of an infant's major tasks is to learn to communicate with others. This skill depends on development in all areas—physical, emotional, social, and intellectual. There are wide differences in the rate of development from baby to baby. However, a normal baby should show steady improvement in communication skills.

Management/Leadership Skills

Offer the following questions as a basic checklist when shopping for toys:
• Is the toy safe for my child's age?
• Does the toy have lasting play value, or will the child be quickly bored by it?
• Does the toy stimulate creative involvement from my child?
• Is it well constructed or can it be easily destroyed?
• Does it challenge my child's ability without becoming frustrating?
• Can it be used in different ways?

Safe Toys

Common household objects often make the best toys for babies—but make sure they are safe. Never allow a baby or young child to play with plastic bags. These may end up over the child's head and can cause suffocation. Small objects that could be swallowed should be off limits as well—they may cause choking. Stay away from objects that could splinter, tear, or break, especially if they can produce sharp corners that could cut the child. Finally, avoid giving a child any sharp or pointed objects. Even something as common as a pen or pencil could cause an injury.

Consumers can check on the safety of store-bought toys or equipment. From time to time, the Consumer Product Safety Commission decides to **recall** a toy—ordering that it be taken off the market or brought back to the manufacturer for needed repairs. If you have access to a computer and the Internet, you can check on product recalls by visiting the web site of the Consumer Product Safety Commission.

FOLLOWING UP

1. Would it be safe to let an infant play with a plastic container that used to hold medicine? Why or why not?
2. If you don't have access to the Internet, how could you find out if a toy was safe?

The Developing Brain

At four months, babies can respond to the different sounds of many different languages. By nine or ten months, they show more interest in the language of their parents and tend not to focus on other sounds.

Communicating Without Words

Babies communicate long before they can talk. By the end of the first year, they can effectively make most of their needs and wants known without words.

Crying is a baby's first means of communication. Babies quickly learn that crying produces a response—someone usually comes and tries to relieve their discomfort. Within a month or so, the crying takes on a pattern. A cry is followed by a pause to listen for reactions. If no response arrives, the baby resumes crying.

CHAPTER 10: Intellectual Development During the First Year **335**

Discussion Activity

Ask: Explain how each area of development is involved in learning to speak. **L1**

Safe Toys

- **Ask:** Have you ever heard of a product being recalled? What does that mean? What factors would lead the government to recall a product?

Answers to
FOLLOWING UP

1. No; there might be residue of medicine that could make the baby sick.
2. *Possible responses:* Ask at the store; call the CPSC; call local government.

Applying What You've Learned
If Internet access is available, have students visit the Consumer Product Safety Commission Web site (www.cpsc.gov). Have students draw a map of the site showing its structure and content.

LEARNING STYLES

Spatial
Have students suggest elements to include in a Venn diagram that compares verbal to nonverbal communication. The shared area might contain such concepts as goals of communication and the presence of a sender and a receiver, for instance. Write students' suggestions on the chalkboard.

After the diagram is completed, have them look at the nonverbal communication suggestions. Which are found in infants' attempts to communicate?

ACTIVITIES

Critical Thinking Activity

Making Inferences. **Ask:** Why not speak to a baby in "baby talk"? **L2**

Discussion Activity

Have students ask their parents what were the first words they spoke when they were infants. Have them share their findings with the class. Discuss patterns that are revealed by their responses. **L1**

The Developing Brain

Language Acquisition

If no one responds to an infant's babbling, the brain doesn't form the necessary connections for language acquisition.

Infants are proficient at nonverbal communication before they learn to speak. They understand an increasing number of the words they hear.

The baby soon develops different cries for different problems. A cry indicating hunger may be interrupted by sucking movements. A cry of pain may include groans and whimpers. You can learn to identify the baby's problem by the type of cry.

Babies also send messages with movements and gestures. It's clear that a wiggling baby doesn't want to get dressed. An eleven-month-old who pushes away a bowl of a usually favorite food has had enough to eat. The baby who clings with both arms to a parent's leg is showing a sure sign of fear or shyness. The use of gestures continues into adulthood, but they are used more to reinforce words than as a substitute for words.

Finally, a baby communicates by making special sounds. Some sounds, such as giggles, grunts, and shrieks, carry obvious messages.

Learning to Speak

Before learning to talk, a baby must learn to associate meanings with words. This is a gradual process. It depends on caregivers talking to the baby, even when the baby doesn't appear to respond. For example, when you take a baby for a walk, talk about what you see. Use simple words, but not baby talk. Although the infant won't understand much of what you say, you are beginning to establish an important habit. Listening to other people talk—especially

---

Parenting in Action

Few steps are awaited with greater anticipation than a baby's first recognizable word. Caregivers can promote language development in these ways:
- Use the baby's name often.
- Point to and name family members, facial features, body parts, and common objects. As the baby grows older, ask questions like "Where is your nose?"
- Talk about what you are doing as though the baby understands—soon he or she will.
- Respond to the baby's babbling.

directly to the baby—is essential for an infant's language development. This interaction also helps build the child's brain.

A newborn is physically unable to speak. Over the first year, physical changes take place that allow the baby to make the sounds necessary for speech.

Babies get ready for real speech by babbling—repeating syllables and sounds. You may have heard babies endlessly repeating consonant and vowel sounds such as "mamamamama" or "gogogogo." Babbling is a baby's preparation for saying recognizable words. You can encourage babbling—and thus language development—by responding to and imitating the baby's sounds.

You can help a baby learn language by naming objects and talking about them. *What other occasions, besides mealtime, could this be done?*

What different messages can a baby send by crying?

A child's first real words are usually understandable between the ages of eight and fifteen months. Because the infant typically has been babbling and coming close to real word sounds for some time, it isn't always easy to know exactly when a specific word is purposely spoken. First words are usually common, simple words that have special meaning for the baby, such as "mama," "dada," or "bye-bye." Most children don't have a large vocabulary or combine words into simple sentences until after their first birthday.

COMPREHENSION CHECK

1. Is a thirteen-month-old who has not yet spoken any understandable words showing signs of delayed development? Why or why not? (*No; because the range of ages for this development goes from eight to fifteen months.*)
2. Infants wave goodbye with their hands before they can say "bye-bye." How is that typical of their development? (*Waving is a simpler task than generating speech; simpler to complex is a developmental pattern.*)

ACTIVITIES

Critical Thinking Activity

Analyzing. Young children have difficult learning to use pronouns such as "you" and "me." Why might that be? **L2**

VISUAL LEARNING | Using the Photograph

Top—Possible responses: When bathing, changing the diaper, or dressing; when carrying the child to or from the car; while taking a walk, and so on.

Bottom—Possible responses: Discomfort, distress, boredom, hunger, loneliness, fear, are among the many emotions babies can express with crying.

DID You Know?

Language. Some experts believe that a child's capacity to develop language skills is inborn and genetically determined. These theorists cite research showing that individual children acquire language at different rates and with different levels of skill, regardless of their environments. Others believe that language is acquired by interacting with the environment—for instance, that children learn communication skills by modeling or imitating adults.

Ask the Eperts

Introducing the Feature

Ask: Is there any book that you remember hearing in your own childhood? What is the book? What do you remember about it? Why do you remember it? (If students have difficulty remembering, you might jog their memories by mentioning some well-known characters or titles.)

Answers to Thinking It Through
1. *Possible response:* It encourages children's language development.
2. *Possible response:* Ask a librarian for suggestions.

Applying What You've Learned

Bring in a selection of children's books. Form students into groups and distribute a sampling of books to each group. Have them examine the books and develop a consensus on what age child they would be suitable for. Have each group report to the class and compile a class list of children's books organized by age.

INFOLINK

Reading

For more on *reading,*
see Chapter 16, pages
490-491.

Ask the Eperts

Rachel Perkins
Child Development Technology
Instructor
Hinds Community College
Utica, Mississippi

READING *to Children*

Q When should I begin reading to my child?

A It's never too early to start reading to a child. In fact, I think parents should start reading to their babies even before the babies are born. This kind of reading is an extension of the natural conversing that parents do with their children, both before and after birth.

Reading is much more than a method of communicating information to a young child. Reading is a social event, and reading to a young child can help establish close emotional bonds. When you read to a young child, you have an opportunity for a special kind of personal communication and relationship.

The sense of competency and accomplishment that children gain from reading begins long before they start reading for themselves. They enjoy being part of the close relationship of adult and child.

Parents who especially enjoy reading offer their child another special gift by reading aloud. They have the opportunity to demonstrate and share a valued behavior. Of course, parents who aren't themselves avid readers shouldn't feel at a disadvantage in this situation. Whenever they take the time to read to young children and to enjoy sharing books and pictures together, they are also developing both attitudes and skills that will benefit their children. Even parents whose own reading skills are limited can participate in these activities. They can look at books with young children, talk about the pictures and enjoy reading-related games and activities together.

Whatever the age of the child, and whatever the reading skills of the adult, the most important aspect of reading to young children is enjoyment. Don't rush, and don't make reading a daily chore. Instead, enjoy sharing books, and enjoy sharing time together.

Thinking It Through

1. How does reading aloud set a good example?
2. If parents don't know what books their child would like, what can they do?

338 UNIT 3: The Baby's First Year

DID *You* **Know?**

Reading. A report by the National Research Council, "Preventing Reading Difficulties in Young Children," addressed the importance of getting an early start in reading. "The majority of reading problems faced by today's adolescents and adults," it said, "are the result of problems that might have been avoided or resolved in their early childhood years." Among the factors that contribute to reading success is "continued interest and motivation to read for a variety of purposes." Parents play a part in that motivation.

Recent research has identified certain milestones of language development and roughly at what ages they occur:

- **One to six months.** At first, the child makes sounds such as coos, gurgles, and squeals. By the end of this period, the baby begins to experiment with making different sounds by changing the shape of the mouth.
- **Seven to twelve months.** The baby starts to make more different sounds. Babies may respond to their own names at these ages and add actions to words, waving when saying or hearing "bye-bye." By the end of this period, babies connect words to their meanings.
- **Thirteen to eighteen months.** Children slowly build their language abilities in this period. At around eighteen months, vocabulary begins to grow very quickly and children use words in combinations such as "no nap" and "want juice."
- **Eighteen months to two years.** In this time, children learn as many as twelve words a day. By two years, most know a few thousand words and begin to use words to express their feelings.
- **Two to two-and-a-half years.** Children begin to construct three- and four-word sentences. They begin to use pronouns.
- **Two-and-a-half to three years.** Children speak in longer sentences that follow the rules of grammar for tense (past and present) and using plurals. They also understand that the order of words in a sentence can affect meaning.

SECTION 10-2 REVIEW

✔ Check Your Understanding

1. How does a baby learn from the care he or she receives?
2. Why should caregivers choose toys that are age appropriate?
3. What are five guidelines for parents to help children learn?
4. What is childproofing?
5. Why are bright colors and toys with sounds good for babies from birth to three months?
6. Before they learn to talk, do babies communicate? If so, how? If not, why not?
7. What age period is marked by rapid vocabulary growth and using words to express feeling?

Putting Knowledge Into Practice

1. **Applying.** Look at the list of developmental milestones on pages 322-323. Based on the skills shown, create a list of toys suitable for each age.
2. **Synthesizing.** Explain how communication skills are related to a child's physical, social, emotional, and intellectual skills.
3. **Observing and Participating.** Visit a store and identify four toys for infants. Evaluate each toy, considering appropriateness, appeal, and price. Combine your findings with those of your classmates.

CHAPTER 10: Intellectual Development During the First Year **339**

Bring to class several common everyday objects. Display them on a table at the front of the class. Hold up each and ask students how children could use it in play.

TEACH

COMPREHENSION CHECK

1. What are ways you can appeal to an infant's senses? (*Objects of different colors, textures; things that make noises.*)
2. What kind of mobile would be best for an infant—one with many small objects or one with few large objects? Why? (*Fewer, larger would be easier for an infant to focus on.*)

ACTIVITIES

Discussion Activity

Read students the following quotation from scientist Rachel Carson: "A child's world is fresh and new and beautiful, full of wonder and excitement." **Ask:** Why is it important for caregivers to remember this thought at all times? **L2**

Art Activity

Have students sketch or build a model of a baby's room decorated to provide a stimulating environment. To extend the activity, have students price out the cost of their design. **L2**

Parenting With Care

Creating a Stimulating Environment

Babies begin learning the moment they are born.

Parents and other caregivers influence both what and how a baby learns. Here are some suggestions for how they can help infants develop their senses and abilities.

Stimulating an Infant's Senses

Holding, cuddling, and gentle stroking all stimulate an infant's senses. Very young babies should have something interesting to look at, but just one or two things at a time. Simple shapes and bright or contrasting colors attract babies' interests.

A mobile hung over the crib provides both color and movement for the baby to watch. You can also hold a bright toy not close to the baby's face and then move the toy slowly, letting the baby's eyes follow it.

Infants like human faces even better than colorful pictures or toys. Let the baby look into your eyes as you hold and play with him or her or when you change a diaper.

Providing Objects the Baby Can Feel

You can also stimulate learning by surrounding the baby with interesting things to touch. Offering a variety of textures is more important than providing a great number of toys. Stuffed toys can have different textures, from a furry teddy bear to a simple beanbag. Different shapes encourage the baby to touch and explore, too. Small plastic squeeze bottles and empty plastic containers with lids are both educational and inexpensive.

Encouraging Listening Experiences

Babies learn from listening, too. The familiar voice of the primary caregiver is the first sound a baby learns to recognize. Rattles and squeak toys introduce different sounds.

RESOURCES ON CHILDREN'S LEARNING

Recent research into the development of the brain has underscored the importance of providing young children with a stimulating environment. The Families and Work Institute has an important book—*Rethinking the Brain*—full of the results of this research and what it means for parents and caregivers. Contact the institute by writing to 267 Fifth Ave., Floor 2, New York, NY 10016; or by visiting the group's Website at www.familiesanworkinst.org.

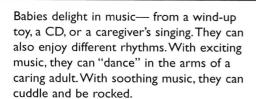

Babies delight in music— from a wind-up toy, a CD, or a caregiver's singing. They can also enjoy different rhythms. With exciting music, they can "dance" in the arms of a caring adult. With soothing music, they can cuddle and be rocked.

As babies begin to experiment with their voice, they soon learn that their sounds bring responses from an attentive caregiver.

Developing Motor Skills

A stimulating environment can help babies learn about their own abilities to move. As the baby starts to reach and grasp, reinforce these skills by encouraging the baby to reach for a special toy. As the baby's large muscle skills develop, gently pull the baby into a sitting or standing position on your lap. Once the baby is ready to take a few steps, be sure your hand is there for the baby to hold.

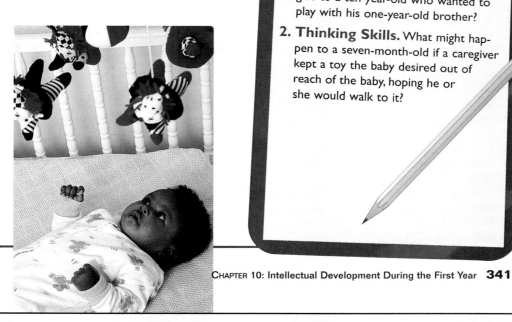

Following Up

1. **Leadership.** What advice would you give to a ten-year-old who wanted to play with his one-year-old brother?

2. **Thinking Skills.** What might happen to a seven-month-old if a caregiver kept a toy the baby desired out of reach of the baby, hoping he or she would walk to it?

CHAPTER 10: Intellectual Development During the First Year **341**

Critical Thinking Activity

Applying. Have students address the issue of an infant's attention span. How much time can a caregiver reasonably expect to spend on any given task with an infant? Have them draw up a rough schedule of activities they can do with an infant about a year old over a period of three hours. (Remind them that they should also address physical care in this period.) **L2**

CLOSE

1. Have students incorporate some of the ideas from this feature— plus their own suggestions for creating a stimulating environment—into a poster that gives advice to babysitters.
2. **Extension.** Have students try one or more of the suggestions in the feature when interacting with babies. Have them report to the class on what happened.

Answers to Following Up

1. *Answers will vary but should stress age appropriate and safe activities.*
2. *Possible response:* Baby could become frustrated and cry because he or she is probably not developmentally ready to walk.

CHECKING COMPREHENSION

Use the Summary and the Reviewing the Facts questions to help students go over the most important ideas in Chapter 10. Encourage students to ask questions and add details.

CHAPTER 10 REVIEW

Answers to Reviewing the Facts

1. Improved memory; making associations; understanding cause and effect; paying greater attention.
2. Association.
3. Stage 3, between four and eight months.
4. Understanding that an object continues to exist even when it is out of sight.
5. Preoperational period.
6. *Possible responses:* Infants are too emotionally vulnerable; they won't succeed, and it could discourage them from learning.
7. *Possible responses:* Putting plastic covers over electrical outlets; putting unsafe items out of reach.
8. Gestures; sounds.
9. *Possible response:* Responding encourages the child to continue making sounds.

Summary

✔ Babies learn through the senses, but in their first year they develop some key mental abilities. (Section 10-1)

✔ Based on his experiments, Swiss psychologist Jean Piaget said that all children go through the same four stages of learning. (Section 10-1)

✔ Children learn to think abstractly at about age eleven. (Section 10-1)

✔ Babies need a safe, stimulating environment for learning. (Section 10-2)

✔ Growing communication skills depend on a combination of mental, physical, emotional, and social development. (Section 10-2)

Reviewing the Facts

1. What are four signs of intellectual development in a child's first year? (Section 10-1)
2. Whenever Dierdra brings her daughter Brenna into the kitchen, the little girl says "Foo, Foo." What mental ability is Brenna showing? (Section 10-1)
3. In what shorter stage of Piaget's first period do children act intentionally to produce results? (Section 10-1)
4. What is object permanence? (Section 10-1)
5. In which stage, according to Piaget, are children likely to show abstract thinking? (Section 10-1)
6. Why give an infant only age-appropriate toys? Why not give the baby something that he or she will have to stretch mentally to master? (Section 10-2)

7. Give at least two ways to childproof a home. (Section 10-2)
8. What two ways of communicating other than crying do babies use? (Section 10-2)
9. How can a parent help a child develop language by responding to babbling? (Section 10-2)

Thinking Critically

1. **Making Inferences.** Why do you think caregivers should avoid using baby talk when talking to infants?
2. **Sequencing.** Put the following six activities from Piaget's sensorimotor period in the correct order: (a) can think using symbols; (b) uses reflexes; (c) imitates others; (d) develops hand-mouth coordination; (e) develops hand-eye coordination; (f) understands that objects exist independently.

b, d, e, c, f, a

Taking Action

1. **Analyzing Toys.** Think of the earliest toy of yours that you can remember. When did you start playing with it? How did you play with it? *(Thinking Skills)*
2. **Making a Mobile.** Infants enjoy mobiles. Design a mobile to hang above an infant's crib. Make the mobile or draw a picture of it in color. *(Management)*

CONNECTIONS

Cross-Curricular Connections

1. **Health.** Find out more about childproofing. Make a poster instructing parents how to childproof their homes for infants.
2. **Language Arts.** Write a scene that shows how a caregiver can provide an infant with encouragement while the baby is trying to master a new skill in intellectual development. Read your scene to the class.

Workplace Connections

1. **Information Systems.** Design a system that could be used in a child care center to record and store information on what toys children of different ages played with.
2. **Technology.** Suppose you worked in a child care center. What technology do you think would be most helpful with infants—a computer, a tape player, or a television? Explain why.

Family and Community Connections

1. **Stacking.** Infants enjoy playing with stacking toys. What objects around the house could safely be used for stacking games?
2. **First Words.** Ask an adult who has had an infant what the baby's first few words were. Compare your findings with those of your classmates. Do any words appear frequently? If so, why?

Technology Connections

1. **Print Technology.** Some books for infants show pictures of objects and include a material that shows the texture of that object. Why are these appropriate toys?

EVALUATION

1. Use the reproducible Chapter 10 Test in the *Teacher Resource Guide,* or create your own test using the **Exam***View*® Test Generator.
2. For an alternative, assign the Chapter 10 activity in the *Authentic Assessment* section of the *Teacher Resource Guide.*

ENRICHMENT

Assign students either of the two enrichment activities in the *Enrichment Activities* booklet in the *Student Motivation Kit.*

EXTENSION

Invite to class a child care expert. Have the expert give suggestions to students for promoting the intellectual development of infants. Ask students to prepare questions in advance. Discuss the visit after the expert is gone. How practical do students think the suggestions are?

CLOSE

Tell students they are to plan a pamphlet for new parents. Have them write an outline of the section dealing with intellectual development. The outline should include supporting details.

UNIT 4 **OBJECTIVES**

UNIT 4 OBJECTIVES

After completing Unit 4, students will be able to:

- Describe the physical growth and development of and care needed by children these ages.
- Discuss the emotional and social development of children these ages.
- Describe the intellectual development of children these ages and explain how to encourage their learning.

UNIT 4 OVERVIEW

Chapter 11 helps students understand the important milestones in physical growth and development up to age three, including self-care.

In **Chapter 12**, students consider patterns of emotional and social development and how to help young children express their emotions and develop positive self-concepts.

In **Chapter 13**, students examine children's methods of learning, concept development, and speech development.

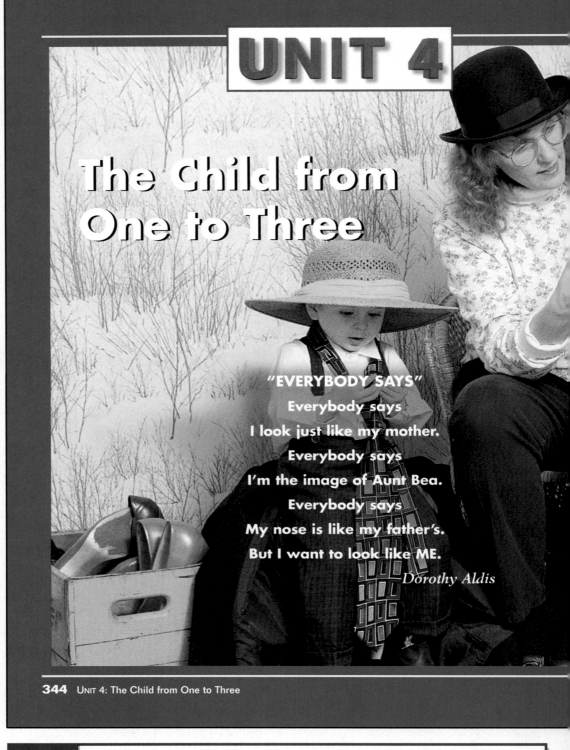

UNIT 4

The Child from One to Three

"EVERYBODY SAYS"

Everybody says
I look just like my mother.
Everybody says
I'm the image of Aunt Bea.
Everybody says
My nose is like my father's.
But I want to look like ME.

Dorothy Aldis

344 UNIT 4: The Child from One to Three

| **USING THE POEM** | As a child grows, family and friends almost cannot resist the temptation to find family resemblances. The result can be fun and well-intended, but as the poem suggests, a child is probably more interested in being a unique | individual than a younger version of someone else. **Ask:** How might such comparisons create self-fulfilling prophecies or put pressure on a child? What can caregivers do to recognize, emphasize, and reinforce a child's special uniqueness? |

CHAPTER 11

Physical Development from One to Three

CHAPTER 12

Emotional and Social Development from One to Three

CHAPTER 13

Intellectual Development from One to Three

345

- Display pictures of toys suitable for a three-year-old. **Ask:** How would a three-year-old play with these toys? Then ask students to describe how a one-year-old would react to each toy. Discuss the differences.
- Have students compare this photograph with the pictures of infants in Unit 3. Ask them to name differences. **Ask:** What demands do those differences put on caregivers?

COMPLETING UNIT 4

EXTENSION

Have students, as they go about their usual activities, study children ages one to three. Have them note physical traits, speech, and behavior. Then have them write a profile of children these ages based on their observations.

EVALUATION

Use the Unit 4 Test on the Exam*View*®, Test Generator or use it to create your own test.

FCCLA Connection

Choosing Toys

Divide students into three groups. Have each group develop a poster identifying characteristics of appropriate toys for one-, two-, or three-year-olds. Characteristics should reflect knowledge of child development. Arrange to display students' posters in a child care center, pediatrician's office, or other appropriate place.

COMMUNITY AS CLASSROOM

Guest Speakers. The class could benefit by hearing from several professionals during the study of this unit. For *Chapter 11*: pediatrician; dentist; dietician; owner of a children's clothing store. *For Chapter 12:* child psychologist; preschool teacher. For *Chapter 13:* speech therapist; preschool teacher; owner of a toy store.

Field Trips. The class could take field trips to a preschool, clothing or toy store, or pediatrician's or dentist's office to enhance their study of the unit.

CHAPTER 11 RESOURCES

Teacher Resource Guide
• Chapter 11 Test, p. 160
• Authentic Assessment, p. 277
Student Motivation Kit
• Observations, pp. 47-48
Transparency Package
• CT-34, CT-40
Effective Instruction CD-ROM

CHAPTER 11 OVERVIEW

In **Section 11-1**, students learn about changes in height, weight, proportion, posture, and motor skills that take place in these ages.

In **Section 11-2**, students learn such child care skills as feeding, dressing, toilet training, and handling bedtimes and explore strategies for teaching self-care.

CHAPTER 11 OBJECTIVES

After completing Chapter 11, students will be able to:

• Describe average changes in height, weight, posture, and proportion in these ages.
• Distinguish between small and large motor skills and give examples of each.
• Describe how to care for children these ages, including issues of nutrition, hygiene, sleep, and toilet training.

CHAPTER 11

Physical Development from One to Three

RESOURCES TO EXPLORE

Growth and Development. Information on child growth and development is continually being updated with new research. For accurate material and updates, request the National Center for Infants, Toddlers, and Families publications catalog from ZERO TO THREE, 200 M Street, NW, Suite 200, Washington, DC 20036 or online at www.zerotothree.org

Shamal watched his son Grant with pride. It seemed like just a few months ago when he or Amber had to do everything for Grant. Now, here he was putting on his own shoes and jacket. Of course, the shoes had loop and hook fasteners, and someone still had to zip up the jacket. Still, there was no doubt in Shamal's mind that Grant had made great progress—and more was sure to come. Grant's progress went beyond dressing, too. He could feed himself and wash his hands and face. Next up, Shamal thought, would be toilet training.

Before he could think any more, though, Grant spoke up. "I'm ready!" he said. "Daddy put his shoes on! Let's go outside!"

"I'm ready! Daddy put his shoes on! Let's go outside!"

- An ancient Chinese proverb says, "Give a man a fish, and he will not go hungry for a day. Teach a man to fish, and he will not go hungry for life." Read the proverb to students, then **ask:** How does this idea relate to caring for children's self-care? What factors might interfere with a caregiver's desire to teach self-care? How can caregivers prevent those factors from getting in the way of the child's learning?
- Have students look at the photograph on the student page. Ask: What can caregivers do to make self-care like dressing easier for children?

USING THE SCENARIO Have students read the scenario on the facing page of the student text. Ask students how Grant's parents have shown a sensitivity for his limited, but developing, motor skills and for his growing need for independence.

KEY TO ABILITY LEVELS Each section gives skill-building activities. Each activity has been labeled for use with students of various learning styles and abilities.

L1 Level 1 activities are basic activities and should be within the range of all students.

L2 Level 2 activities are average activities and should be within the range of average and above average students.

L3 Level 3 activities are challenging activities designed for the ability range of above average students.

SECTION 11-1 RESOURCES

Teacher Resource Guide
- Lesson Plan Organizer, p. 62
- Section 11-1 Quiz, p. 158

Student Motivation Kit
- Observations & Case Studies (case study), p. 113
- Reteaching Activity, p. 36
- Nurturing Brain Development, pp. 34-35

Student Workbook
- Study Guide, pp. 96-99
- Identifying Ages, p. 100

Effective Instruction CD-ROM

FOCUS

MOTIVATOR

Display large pictures of a one-year-old and a three-year-old. Have students make a list of at least three physical differences they see between the two pictures.

VOCABULARY ACTIVITY

Ask: What is a toddler? What age or ages does the term refer to? (*Ages one to two.*) Where does the name come from? (*Uncertain walking.*) Have them contrast the image that the word brings to mind with the control shown by the child on the wheeled vehicle in the photograph on page 353.

Physical Growth and Development from One to Three

The transition from babyhood to childhood is dramatic! The one-year-old still moves with some uncertainty, needs help dressing, and eats messily. By age three, the child is running and jumping, dressing and washing himself or herself, and using a fork and spoon.

KEY TERMS

developmentally appropriate
dexterity
large motor skills
preschoolers
small motor skills
toddlers

OBJECTIVES:

- Describe average changes in height, weight, proportion, and posture from ages one through three.
- Identify habits that build healthy teeth.
- Distinguish between large and small motor skills, and give examples of each.

Toddlers to Preschoolers

Physical growth slows considerably after the first year. However, the child's physical skills improve dramatically from the first to the fourth birthday. Most children begin to walk a few unsteady steps around age one. The term **toddlers** refers to children who make this uncertain movement. By age three, however, these children are far from "toddling." They become **preschoolers,** as

348 UNIT 4: The Child from One to Three

Observing & Participating

Bring two pictures to class: one drawn by a one-year-old and one drawn by a three-year-old. Display the pictures, giving students ample time to observe them. Then ask students to note any differences and similarities they see between the pictures. What changes in small-motor skills do the pictures show? Have students write a paragraph describing their observations and hypotheses.

children ages three to five are called. Three-year-olds not only walk steadily, they also hop, jump, and run. They make similar advances in most other physical skills.

As physical skills develop, these children need lots of space. They need time each day for active play so they can exercise their muscles and use their stored-up energy. Although their attention span is longer than that of infants, they still want to change games and activities often.

Height and Weight

Growth in both height and weight is slower in this period than among babies. Children from one to three gain only about ½ pound (0.2 kg) per month. That is less than half the average monthly weight gain during the first year of life. Growth in height also slows by about half. The chart on page 350 shows average heights and weights for children one through three.

Active Play for Growth and Development

*H*ere are some fun activities for children aged one to three:

- **Roll the Dice.** Say that each number on a die stands for an activity. Roll it once to see what the child is supposed to do—run, jump, skip, or hop. Roll a second time to see how many times he or she has to do it.

- **Batting the Balloon.** Fill a balloon and hit it into the air. Then tell the child to keep it aloft.

- **Dancing.** Pop a cassette into the tape player or just turn the radio on. Then have the child dance, dance, dance.

- **Racing Against Time.** Set a task for the child, such as running around the house or to a neighbor's and back. Time the trial run. Then have the child repeat the task to see if he or she can better the time.

- **Playing "I Spy."** You can liven up a simple walk by calling out objects the child should try to see. Each time he or she sees the desired object, the child calls out "I spy a . . ."

FOLLOWING UP

1. Which activity helps build verbal, as well as physical, skills?
2. Invent your own activity that would be fun and get a child moving. Describe it to the class.

COMPREHENSION CHECK

1. Why do children need different activities during the day? (*Attention span is short and they become bored; to develop varied skills.*)

ACTIVITIES

Art Activity

Have students draw profiles of infants and three-year-olds that show their dominant physical characteristics and label the areas that change the most during these years.
L2

Ask students why toddlers' activities must not be too difficult for their physical abilities. What problems result if games are too physically or mentally demanding?

Answers to
FOLLOWING UP

1. "I Spy."
2. *Answers will vary but should include activities with both physical activity and an element of fun.*

Parenting in *Action*

Bring two 10-pound sacks of potatoes to class. Ask for volunteers to hold both sacks at once. Point out to students that the sacks weigh a little less than the average one-year-old. Have students try to perform simple tasks, like pouring a drink or talking on the telephone while holding the sacks. **Ask:** How would carrying a child be less difficult than carrying two sacks of potatoes? (*A child would hold on.*) How are the potatoes easier than holding a child? (*They don't lean or try to struggle away.*)

COMPREHENSION CHECK

1. How does the growth of the head, chest, and abdomen change between one and three? (*After age two, the chest grows more quickly than the head and abdomen.*)
2. How does heredity play a role in tooth quality? (*Some children inherit a protective mechanism that discourages decay.*) How does environment play a role? (*Through brushing, having vitamin D and calcium, avoiding harmful foods.*)

ACTIVITIES

Critical Thinking Activity

Making Inferences. **Ask:** How do an infant's proportions and posture interfere with walking? (An infant lacks the straight spine and upright carriage necessary. The protruding abdomen throws the child off balance.) **L1**

VISUAL LEARNING Using the Photograph
Answer: Heredity and environment, including diet and exercise.

VISUAL LEARNING Using the Chart
Have students calculate the percentage increase in height (inches) and weight (in pounds) from age one to three. (*Height: 27%; weight: 44%.*)

Infants tend to be more similar in height and weight. When children are toddlers and preschoolers, however, height and weight differences begin to show. *What factors influence these differences?*

Hereditary and environmental influences on height and weight are more noticeable among children one to three than among infants. After the first birthday, children begin to show greater variation in size. Some are much larger than average; others are much smaller. Height differences are particularly significant.

These differences will probably continue throughout life. A tall two-year-old usually grows to be a tall adult. An unusually short toddler will probably be shorter than average as an adult.

Proportion and Posture

Because of changes in proportion, posture improves during the period from one to three. Until age two, a child's head, chest, and abdomen all measure about the same. All three also grow at the same rate. Between ages two and three, however, the chest becomes larger than the head and abdomen. Also during this period, the arms, legs, and trunk grow rapidly. These changes in proportion help improve the child's balance and motor skills.

By two years of age, the child stands straighter, but the posture is not completely erect. The abdomen still protrudes, and the head is somewhat forward. The toddler's knees and elbows are slightly bent. By the

Average Heights and Weights: Ages One to Three

AGE	HEIGHT		WEIGHT	
	Inches	Centimeters	Pounds	Kilograms
One year	29.8	75.7	22.5	10.2
Two years	34.0	86.4	27.7	12.6
Three years	37.7	95.8	32.4	14.7

MULTIPLE INTELLIGENCES Have students plan a class for children age three called "Taking Care of Your Teeth." The class should teach children the order in which primary teeth appear, factors that keep teeth healthy, and factors that contribute to tooth decay. For children who learn best visually, students can prepare diagrams and visual aids. For kinesthetic learners, they can prepare demonstrations. For musical learners, they might create a rhyming jingle to help children remember the principles of tooth care.

Children's bodies change a great deal from age one (left) to age three (right). The older child stands much straighter and has different body proportions. *What other differences do you notice?*

third birthday, the child's posture is more upright. The spine has strengthened, so the back is straighter. The child has lost some—but not all—baby fat.

Teeth

One-year-olds have an average of eight teeth, but there is a great deal of variation. During the second year, eight more teeth usually come in. For most children, the last four back teeth emerge early in the third year, giving them a complete set of 20 primary teeth.

The quality of a child's teeth is greatly influenced by diet. The diet of the mother during pregnancy and the diet of the child during the first two years lay the foundation for a lifetime of good—or poor—teeth. (A child's adult teeth are forming under the primary teeth.) Dairy products, which are rich in calcium and phosphorus, are especially important. The vitamin D in milk also helps the development of strong and healthy teeth and bones.

Diet can also cause tooth decay. Avoid giving children sweets, especially candy. Sugar-coated cereals often stick between the teeth and can cause decay. Avoid putting a child to bed with a bottle, unless it contains water. Other liquids can pool in the mouth and cause cavities.

CHAPTER 11: Physical Development from One to Three **351**

COMPREHENSION CHECK

1. What are small motor skills? (*Skills that involve the finer muscles of the wrist and fingers.*) Large motor skills? (*Those involving the large muscles of the back, legs, shoulders, arms.*)
2. What factors affect the rate at which children learn physical skills in these ages? (*Differences in size, health and diet, interests, temperament, opportunities for physical play, others.*)
3. What is meant by developmentally appropriate tasks or skills? (*Suitable for the child given his or her age and interests.*)

Practicing Parenting

Ask students to think about a skill they acquired recently. What did they have to do before they became comfortable with the new activity?

Answers to Apply Your Knowledge

1. *Possible responses:* Not making a fuss over failures; offering praise.
2. *Possible responses:* Remind her that she's solved similar puzzles before; Praise her for pieces connected so far.

Heredity appears to play a role in tooth quality. Dentists have identified a protective mechanism that discourages decay. Some children inherit this trait from their parents; others lack it.

Motor Skills

As you recall, physical development follows three patterns: from head to foot, from near to far, and from simple to complex. When you compare the skills of children at age one and at the end of the third year, these patterns are easy to see. Hand skills, for instance, show the pattern of simple to complex. At thirteen months, a child can bang blocks together or may stack two of them. By the fourth birthday, the same child uses blocks to make high towers, houses, and roads.

Motor skills are often divided into two types. **Large motor skills** involve use and control of the large muscles of the back, legs, shoulders, and arms. Walking, running, and throwing balls are all large motor skills. **Small motor skills** depend on the use and

Practicing Parenting

Helping Children Build Skills

*T*o develop their large and small motor skills, children need two things from caregivers— opportunities and encouragement. No one can learn to run without the chance to practice running. Learning to color requires crayons and paper. Caregivers are responsible for giving children plenty of opportunities to practice their skills.

How can you encourage children to improve their skills? First, avoid making a fuss over less-than-perfect performance. When Toby took a tumble while running, his dad made sure he wasn't hurt and then simply said, "You look fine—ready to go again?" Toby was off and running again. You can also encourage children by offering praise. Children love to know that adults recognize their efforts and accomplishments.

Practice and encouragement help children develop self-confidence. Children believe that if they keep trying, they can do it! That attitude promotes additional learning.

APPLY YOUR KNOWLEDGE

1. What are two ways of providing encouragement?
2. Suppose Valerie is having trouble with a jigsaw puzzle. How could you encourage her?

Management/Leadership Skills

Describe the following to students: "Jamie is one year old. Her mother places her on a soft mat with crayons and paper. 'Now you can make colors on the paper while I wash the dishes,' she tells Jamie. She demonstrates how to draw, then puts a crayon in the child's hand and places the paper in front of her. Jamie ends up putting the crayon in her mouth. Her mother quickly takes the crayon away."

Ask: Why did the mother's plan backfire? What could Jamie do that is more developmentally appropriate?

Child development experts distinguish between two kinds of skills based on what muscle groups are used. **What types of motor skills are these children showing?**

ACTIVITIES

Critical Thinking Activity

Analyzing Information. Have students think about a child dressing in a pair of pull-on pants and a short-sleeved shirt with buttons. Which activities require large motor skills? Small motor skills? (*Large motor:* Stepping into the pants; putting the arms through the holes; pulling the garments on. *Small motor:* Picking up the clothing; buttoning the shirt.) **L1**

Teamwork Activity

Have students work in groups to look through catalogs to find pictures of toys that promote motor skill development. Ask students to distinguish between toys that use small and large motor skills. Have students use the pictures to create a bulletin board display or poster. **L1**

VISUAL LEARNING **Using the Photographs**
Answer: Doing a puzzle: small motor skills. *Riding a tricycle:* large motor skills.

control of the finer muscles of the wrists, fingers, and ankles. Many of these skills—from using crayons and paintbrushes to turning pages of books and eating—require hand-eye coordination. This is the ability to move the hands precisely in relation to what is seen.

Children don't acquire physical skills as predictably during the period from one to three as during the first year of life. Most children learn some skills earlier than average and others later than average. These variations can be caused by differences in physical size, health and diet, interests, temperament, opportunities for physical play, and many other factors.

Experts speak of tasks or skills being **developmentally appropriate** for children. By this they mean the tasks are suitable for the child given his or her age and interests. For groups of children, caregivers need to consider the ages and interest level of all the children.

Large Motor Skills

Physical exercise and repeated practice promote the development of large motor skills. A child's improvement in any one skill is typically slow but steady. The chart on page 354 shows average large motor development of one-, two-, and three-year-olds.

Parenting in *Action*

Anyone who has been in charge of a toddler knows that those exciting early steps are not much fun when a child is injured by a fall. Ask students to explain what could happen and what they would do to prevent accidents when a toddler is walking in a room that contains the following:

- A fireplace.
- A hard floor with loose throw rugs.
- A low table with a glass top.
- A kitchen table with sharp corners.
- Open stairs to a lower level.
- A pedestal table holding a large plant.

COMPREHENSION CHECK

1. Around what age can a child catch a ball as well as throw it? (*3 to 4.*)
2. Around what age would "Big Wheels" be an appropriate toy? (*2 to 2½.*)
3. Why is walking on tiptoe more advanced than simply walking? (*Requires greater balance.*)

ACTIVITIES

Using the Illustration

Have students use the information in the chart to plan a morning's activities in a child care center. Students should suppose that the center cares for four children, of the following ages: two one-year-olds, a 2½-year-old, and a four-year-old. Remind students that the skills of all the children must be taken into account. **L2**

DID *You* **Know?**

Toddlers' Balance. Beginning in medieval times and through the eighteenth century, young children wore on their heads a "black pudding," a round, thickly wadded cap of black velvet. The purpose was to cushion their heads from the inevitable falls.

Average Large Motor Skills Development:

Ages One to Three

Ages 3 to 4
- Jumps up and down in place.
- Walks on tiptoe.
- Rides a tricycle.
- Catches a ball with arms straight.

Ages 2½ to 3
- Runs, but may not be able to stop smoothly.
- Alternates feet going up stairs, but not going down.
- Throws a ball overhand, but inaccurately.
- Kicks balls.

Ages 2 to 2½
- Walks with more coordination and confidence.
- Climbs, even in unsafe places.
- Jumps off the bottom step.
- Pushes self on wheeled toys.

Ages 1½ to 2
- Runs fairly well.
- Stands on one foot.
- Learns to walk up and down stairs, while holding on, with both feet on each step.
- Throws objects overhand.

Ages 1 to 1½
- Improves from walking a few unsteady steps to walking well.
- Slides down stairs backward, one step at a time.
- Stoops to pick up toys.

354 UNIT 4: The Child From One to Three

ISSUES IN CHILDREN'S HEALTH Ear Infections and Motor Skills. A recent study shows that children who have fluid in their middle ears lag behind others in motor skill develop-ment. Apparently, the fluid puts pressure on the part of the ear that affects balance. The resulting loss of equilibrium causes clumsiness.

As you know, most children begin to walk near their first birthday. This is an important accomplishment. It gives the child a feeling of pride—and much more mobility for exploration. At first, the toddler walks by holding on to furniture. The child's first steps are wobbly, with toes pointed outward and arms held out for balance. After a few shaky steps, the child collapses into a sitting position. Constant practice helps children improve in steadiness, balance, and body control.

Climbing skills follow a similar sequence. Even children who have learned to walk continue to climb stairs on their hands and knees for a while and slide backward when going down the stairs. Next, they begin walking up stairs with help, placing both feet on each step. Then they try walking up and down stairs on their own, holding on to a railing. They continue putting both feet on the same stair before moving down to the next stair until about age three. At that point, they can alternate feet.

Climbing isn't limited to stairs. Nothing is safe from the climbing toddler—furniture, counters, ledges, and sometimes even people are conquered like mountains! This activity, of course, makes safety an important concern for parents and other caregivers. The "Parenting with Care" feature on pages 372-373 suggests ways to make areas safe for children's explorations.

Small Motor Skills

During this stage, children's small motor skills also improve. The chart on page 356 shows average small motor development in these years.

Between their first and second birthdays, children learn to feed themselves and to drink from a cup fairly well. At first, poor

Which individual skills does this toddler need to kick the ball?

Children's growing skills can lead to difficult situations. **Ask:** How should a parent react when a child scribbles off the paper onto a table or draws pictures on the wall? How can a parent reinforce the skill while curbing inappropriate ways of practicing it? **L1**

VISUAL LEARNING | Using the Photograph
Possible answers: Balance, walking, eye-foot coordination.

DID You Know?

Practicing Motor Skills. **Children from one to three often delight themselves—and embarrass their parents—by taking off their clothes whenever the fancy strikes. This is normal and is rooted in the child's desire to show independence. Also at work is the toddler's love for doing and undoing—the same activity they pursue when they empty and refill a container or open and close a drawer. Parents can let a child undress when there is time (and the temperature allows). When time or propriety demands that clothes stay on, guide the child to see that the situation requires it—or use distraction to focus the child's attention elsewhere.**

LEARNING STYLES

Kinesthetic/Auditory

Have volunteers come to the front of the class to pantomime various everyday tasks, such as brushing their teeth, washing dishes, tying shoes, and so on. Ask the rest of the class to identify whether the task requires large motor skills, small motor skills, or both.

If possible, have students try to teach three-year-olds to perform some of the same tasks. Ask students to note where the children experienced difficulty. To what do students attribute this difficulty?

COMPREHENSION CHECK

1. Around what age would it become dangerous to leave a jar of facial cream within a child's reach? (*2½ to 3.*) Why? (*They can unscrew jar lids at that age.*)
2. Compare children's ability to build towers with blocks at different ages in this period. (*Ability improves as child develops better small motor skills.*)

ACTIVITIES

Critical Thinking Activity

Giving Examples. Ask students to identify some self-care activities that involve small motor skills. (*Possible responses: self-feeding, brushing teeth, dressing.*) Have them also name some play activities that improve these skills. Tell them to choose examples other than those in the text. (*Possible responses: Playing a toy instrument, playing with shape sorters.*) **L2**

Discussion Activity

Some children are higher or lower in energy than others. Have students give examples of activities they could use to help high-energy children—children who are always on the go—develop small motor skills. Then have them come up with ideas for activities promoting large-motor skills for children who are low in energy. **L2**

Average Small Motor Skills Development:

Ages One to Three

Ages 3 to 4
- Builds towers of about nine or ten blocks.
- Makes a bridge from three blocks.
- Cuts with scissors.
- Draws recognizable pictures.
- Uses fork and spoon with little spilling.

Ages 2 to 2½
- Turns one page of a book at a time.
- Strings large beads.
- Builds towers of about six blocks.

Ages 2½ to 3
- Builds towers of about eight blocks.
- Draws horizontal and vertical lines and circles.
- Screws lids on and off containers.

Ages 1 to 1½
- Turns several pages of a book at a time.
- Picks up small objects with thumb and forefinger.
- Scribbles.

Ages 1½ to 2
- Buttons large buttons.
- Pulls down zippers.
- Turns doorknobs.
- Stacks several blocks to form a tower.

356 UNIT 4: The Child From One to Three

Observing & Participating

Have students visit a day care center or playground to observe children at play. Have them note the types of activities children are involved in. Then ask them to single out three children and try to predict their ages based on their skills. Have students write their guesses down, along with their reasons. Have students present their observations and conclusions to the class and have the class as a whole discuss each.

hand-eye coordination causes many spills. With practice, however, their success and neatness improve. One-year-olds usually enjoy playing with blocks, large pop beads, and pyramids of different-sized rings. They also like jack-in-the-box toys, musical rolling toys, and toy pianos. Playing with these toys helps develop small motor skills.

Two-year-olds show improved **dexterity**, or skillful use of the hands and fingers. They can turn the pages of a book one at a time, peel a banana, and turn on a faucet. They enjoy using crayons—typically with a happy abandon that results in marks running haphazardly off the paper and onto the table or floor. They build towers of blocks, which usually topple once they reach five or six blocks high.

Three-year-olds show considerably more skill. They typically delight in taking things apart and putting them back together again. Children this age can draw circles as well as horizontal and vertical lines. They can also draw a cross.

SECTION 11-1 REVIEW

✔ Check Your Understanding

1. Why are children called toddlers?
2. What height and weight changes take place in these ages?
3. How do a child's posture and proportion change from age one to age three?
4. At about what age do most children have a complete set of primary teeth?
5. How do milk and milk products contribute to healthy teeth?
6. Choose a large motor skill and explain how children develop this skill from ages one to three.
7. How does improved dexterity show development of small motor skills?

Putting Knowledge Into Practice

1. **Synthesizing.** Name three toys for children ages one to three. For each, list the motor skills involved in playing with that toy.
2. **Comparing.** How do safety concerns in the home change as a child becomes one, two, and three years old? Why does this happen?
3. **Observing and Participating.** Watch a group of young children on a playground or other public place. Identify at least two children from these ages and write descriptions of their actions, explaining why you think they are one to three.

ASSESS

CHECKING COMPREHENSION

Have students answer the Check Your Understanding Questions. Answers appear at the bottom of this page.

EVALUATION

Give students the Section 11-1 Quiz in the *Teacher Resource Guide.*

RETEACHING

1. Assign Reteaching Activities, page 36.
2. Have students write down as many examples as they can of ways children change from age one to age three.

ENRICHMENT

Have students take the part of an advice columnist and write a response to a parent upset because her child's first step took place at day care while the parent was working.

EXTENSION

Have students interview a dentist or dental hygienist about caring for young children's teeth.

CLOSE

Have students write a dialogue between the mother of a child of fourteen months and her mother, worried that the child doesn't yet walk.

ANSWERS TO SECTION 11-1 REVIEW

1. Because they are unsteady when first learning to walk.
2. *See the chart on page 350.*
3. Stands upright by age three. Chest becomes larger and limbs lengthen.
4. Early in the third year.
5. Their calcium, phosphorus, and vitamin D help healthy teeth develop.
6. *Answers will vary.*
7. Dexterity involves the small muscles of the hand and fingers.

CAREER OPPORTUNITIES

Introducing the Feature

Ask: Do you recall visiting a pediatrician's office? What was the office like? How was it set up? How was it decorated? Why do you think it was made to look that way?

Answers to CONNECTING SCHOOL TO CAREER

1. **Possible response:** Name, date of birth, condition at birth, height and weight taken at each office visit, any illnesses or injuries and how they were treated, dates and types of vaccinations. Organized by patient name.

2. *Answers will vary but should reflect sensitivity to child's concerns and emphasize that the step is taken to ensure health.*

Applying What You've Learned

Have students use the information in the feature to write a short children's book that describes a day in the life of a pediatrician.

CAREER OPPORTUNITIES

Pediatrician

A CONVERSATION WITH EMILY RUTHERFORD

How did you become interested in becoming a pediatrician? When I was in medical school, I had to spend some time in pediatric care. I thought it was the most rewarding part of medicine because it gives you a chance to get people off to a healthy start in life.

What are the tasks and responsibilities of a pediatrician? We try to protect children's health by monitoring how children grow and by giving vaccinations to prevent them from catching diseases. When they are sick or injured, we help them recover. Finally, we give advice about children's diet, exercise, and behavior to parents.

What is the work environment like? I work in a practice with three other doctors. I also visit patients who are in the hospital.

What are the working hours like? Long! I see children at the hospital from 7:00 to about 9:00 each morning. Then we have office hours to either 5:00 or 8:00 P.M. We have one weekday and one weekend day free.

What aptitudes are needed to be a pediatrician? You need to know science—and psychology. It helps to be very patient and gentle. Some children are afraid of the doctor, and they need to be reassured. You need good communication skills to get information from parents—and to give it to them.

Career Facts

PEDIATRICIAN

Education and Training. Pediatricians first must complete a bachelor's degree. Then they need four years of medical school and three more years of additional training. They must also pass a state examination to receive a license to practice medicine.

Career Outlook. The demand for pediatricians should continue to grow.

CONNECTING SCHOOL TO CAREER

1. **Information Systems.** What kind of information do you think pediatricians should keep about their patients? How would you organize it systematically?

2. **Interpersonal Skills.** How would you explain to a three-year-old that he or she needed a vaccination?

358 UNIT 4: The Child from One to Three

Building Career Skills

Thinking Skills. Ask: What do you think is the most difficult part of a pediatrician's job? Why? What do you think is the most rewarding part? Why? Have students share their responses with the class, and write them on the board. Then have the class discuss the suggestions to develop an agreed-upon list of the five most difficult and most rewarding aspects. Remind students that in the discussion they have to use reasoning to support their answers.

SECTION 11-2

Caring for Children from One to Three

By their first birthday, children are already beginning to do things for themselves. If they are encouraged to practice, three-year-olds can be responsible for many self-care tasks. The typical three-year-old can dress, eat, brush teeth, and go to the bathroom independently.

KEY TERMS

hygiene
sphincter muscles
synthetic fibers
training pants

OBJECTIVES:

- Plan meals for young children.
- Explain how to help children learn and practice good hygiene.
- Choose appropriate clothes for children ages one to three.
- Describe common bedtime problems, and discuss how to minimize them.
- Discuss how to toilet train a child.

Feeding

The habits and attitudes toward food that children learn at this stage will influence their food habits throughout life. Self-feeding both depends on and helps improve their small motor skills.

CHAPTER 11: Physical Development from One to Three **359**

SECTION 11-2

Caring for Children from One to Three

(pages 359-371)

SECTION 11-2 RESOURCES

Teacher Resource Guide
- Lesson Plan Organizer, p. 63
- Section 11-2 Quiz, p. 159

Student Motivation Kit
- Observations & Case Studies (case study), p. 114
- Reteaching Activity, p. 37
- Enrichment, pp. 32-34
- Teen Parenting Skills, pp. 106-107, 110-111

Student Workbook
- Study Guide, pp. 96-99
- Planning Meals for Children, pp. 101-102

Transparency Package
- CT-34 Look for These Clothing Characteristics

Effective Instruction CD-ROM

FOCUS

MOTIVATOR

Bring to class some clothes for a toddler, including some that would be easy for a child to put on and take off and some that would be difficult. Show the items to students and discuss their merits and drawbacks.

VOCABULARY ACTIVITY

Tell students that the word "hygiene" comes from a Greek word meaning "healthful." **Ask:** What clue does this give to the word's meaning?

COMPREHENSION CHECK

1. Why do toddlers need food every three or four hours? (*Stomachs are still small.*)
2. What purpose, other than nutrition, do meals serve for a toddler? (*Practice with motor skills; time for socialization.*)
3. When should a child first be offered milk? (*After the first birthday.*)

ACTIVITIES

Teamwork Activity

Children ages one to three need about 1000 calories a day for good health. Assign each student one of the five food groups. Have them find out how many calories are present in child-size portions (p. 362) of three foods in that food group. Compile their information into a chart. Then divide the class into groups of four or five students. Have the groups use the charts to prepare a nutritious 1000-calorie diet. **L2**

VISUAL LEARNING Using the Photograph
Possible response: To prevent child from knocking it over; makes it easier for child to scoop up food.

Because they are growing less rapidly than in their first year of life, children these ages don't eat as much. However, most do need food every three or four hours because their stomachs are still small. Snacks can bridge the gap between meals, as long as they are nutritious. The amount that any child eats can vary greatly from day to day, depending on appetite and level of activity.

Meals can become a battle of wills between caregivers and young children, as many strong food likes and dislikes are developed. Children accept new foods more easily if they aren't pressured to or rewarded for eating them.

Self-feeding skills improve greatly during these years.

- **One-year-olds.** The one-year-old still eats a variety of baby foods. In addition, simple foods from the family's meals can be added. Choose foods that are low in sugar and salt. Until more teeth come in, cut foods into small pieces to aid swallowing.

  Finger foods—those easily picked up and eaten—are popular with most children this age. Most children are eighteen months or older before they can use the spoon to feed themselves with little spilling. By their

INFOLINK
Finger Foods
For more about *finger foods*, see Chapter 8, page 275.

The bowl is attached to the high chair's table by suction. *What purpose does this serve? How might the high sides help this toddler learn self-feeding?*

Parenting in *Action*

Describe the following situation: "Three-year-old Adam is sitting in his high chair happily eating a lunch of egg salad on whole wheat, green beans, peaches, and milk. His seven-year-old sister Sara sits down, refuses to drink her milk, pronounces her green beans 'yucky,' and scrapes the egg salad off her bread and eats the bread. Adam soon follows suit, refusing to eat and demanding potato chips instead." If you were the parents, what would you do?

The Food Guide Pyramid

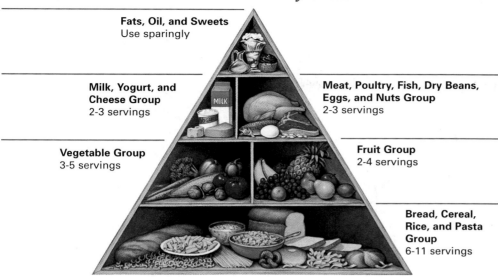

Fats, Oil, and Sweets
Use sparingly

Milk, Yogurt, and Cheese Group
2-3 servings

Meat, Poultry, Fish, Dry Beans, Eggs, and Nuts Group
2-3 servings

Vegetable Group
3-5 servings

Fruit Group
2-4 servings

Bread, Cereal, Rice, and Pasta Group
6-11 servings

second birthday, most children drink from a cup fairly well.

- **Two-year-olds.** Two-year-olds can usually feed themselves and learn to use a fork. Be patient. Remember that children often take a long time to eat. Eating not only provides nutrition, but also allows children to improve their motor skills.

    Try to schedule meals so the young child eats with the rest of the family. Conversation is an important way to help establish the social nature of meals and to reinforce family bonds.

- **Three-year-olds.** Three-year-olds have a full set of primary teeth, so chewing foods is not a problem. However, meats and other tough foods should still be served in small pieces. By this age, most children are quite handy with eating utensils.

Choosing Foods for Children

Like adults, children need a variety of nutritious foods daily. The best way to make sure a child gets this variety is to plan meals using the Food Guide Pyramid. The chart on page 362 gives some examples of a child-size serving in each food group.

Pediatricians recommend that milk or milk products not be given to a child until his or her first birthday. From one to two years, the child should drink whole milk, if not breast-fed. After the child is two, reduced-fat or lowfat milk can be given.

Be cautious in serving convenience foods to children. Many contain a great deal of salt and preservatives, colorings, and artificial flavors. Choose fresh foods when possible. Use the nutrition labels and ingredients lists on frozen, canned, and dried foods to help you make nutritious choices.

DID You Know?

Nutrition. If a child refuses to eat one food, try substituting another that contains similar nutrients. You can achieve the same dietary goals with more than one food. For example, substitute bananas, kiwi, or cherries for potatoes or squash—both groups provide potassium. Substitute cantaloupe, nectarines, or peaches for broccoli, spinach, or carrots—both groups are good sources of Vitamin A.

COMPREHENSION CHECK

1. From which food group should the greatest number of servings come? (*Bread, cereal, rice, and pasta.*)
2. From which food group should the least number of servings come? (*Meat.*) Do you think most people follow that guideline in their daily diets? (*Answers will vary.*)

ACTIVITIES

VISUAL LEARNING | **Using the Illustration**
Ask: If a child had a ½-cup of milk at lunch and then had another ½ cup with a snack, how many servings would that be? (*Two.*)

The Developing Brain

Eating Well

Recent research indicates that children do better in math and problem solving when they have eaten breakfast. When they skip this first meal of the day, attention levels and memory both decline. The best foods for breakfast are complex carbohydrates and protein. Whole-grain carbohydrates should be chosen when possible.

▶ Serving Sizes for Children Two and Three

MILK, YOGURT, AND CHEESE GROUP
2-3 servings

Milk, yogurt—½ cup
Frozen yogurt, pudding—¼ to ½ cup
Cheese, processed, American—½ to 1 oz.

VEGETABLE GROUP
3-5 servings

Carrots—¼ to ½
Corn, green beans, peas, mashed potatoes—¼ cup

BREAD, CEREAL, RICE, AND PASTA GROUP
6-11 servings

Bagel, hamburger bun—¼ to ½
Crackers—2 to 3
Whole-grain bread—¼ to ½ slice
Spaghetti, rice, macaroni—¼ to ⅓ cup
Ready-to-eat cereal—¼ to ⅓ cup

MEAT, POULTRY, FISH, DRY BEANS, EGGS, AND NUTS GROUP
2 servings

Egg—1
Chicken, hamburger, fish—1-2 oz.
Baked beans—¼ cup
Peanut butter—1-2 Tbsp.

FRUIT GROUP
2-4 servings

Apple, banana— ¼ to ½
Fruit juice—⅓ cup
Grapes, peaches, strawberries—¼ cup

A healthy diet includes at least the minimum number of servings from each food group *each day*. This chart will help you see how much of several different foods equals a servings. Older children need more food.

362 UNIT 4: The Child From One to Three

Adapted for Various Styles

Have students devise ways of demonstrating their mastery of the concepts in the Food Guide Pyramid. Spatial learners could create a model. Mathematical learners could devise a chart that calculates the total number of servings of the different groups in a set of menus. Whatever the method chosen, have students share their results with the class.

To promote interest in nutritious foods, give children appealing meals. Color, texture, shape, temperature, and ease of eating are the keys.

- **Color.** A variety of bright food colors adds interest. A meal of cream of chicken soup, applesauce, milk, and vanilla pudding looks boring. Changing the soup to split pea and serving cut-up apple slices instead of applesauce would make the meal more visually appealing.
- **Texture.** Include foods with different textures at the same meal. Crunchy crackers, chewy cheese, and juicy grapes, for example, all give different sensations.
- **Shape.** Foods with a variety of shapes add appeal. Cut sandwiches into rectangles or squares—or even triangles. Carrot coins, zucchini sticks, and orange wedges might round out the meal. Help the child identify each shape. Another day, use a cookie cutter to cut bread into special shapes or shape pancakes like animals.
- **Temperature.** Try serving both hot and cold foods at a meal. Safety is also a concern, so check the temperature of all hot foods before serving them. If a food has been cooked or warmed in the microwave, stir it thoroughly to even out the temperature. "Hot spots" can burn the mouth.
- **Ease of eating.** Certain foods are easier than others for young children to eat. Ground beef is easier to chew and swallow than a pork chop. Many children like spaghetti, but they can handle it more easily if it is cut into short pieces.

Mealtime Tips

Are you prepared for the challenge of planning and preparing nutritious, appealing meals for young children? Meals are important events in the child's day. They provide a chance to practice skills, learn independence, explore the texture of foods, and talk to others. The following guidelines can help you make mealtimes with a young child more enjoyable:

Meals need to be nutritious, appealing, and easy for young children to eat. **How does this meal satisfy those requirements?**

COMPREHENSION CHECK

1. Why is it important for caregivers to use good table manners and to practice good nutrition? (*Children imitate the behavior of others.*)
2. What are two dangers of bathing a toddler? (*Slipping and drowning.*)
3. Upon what factors does a child's readiness for showering depend? (*Child's ability to control the water temperature, stand in the shower safely, and get him- or herself clean.*)

ACTIVITIES

Discussion Activity

Discuss with students the role that snacks might play in a child's diet. What are good food choices for snacks? What snack would they suggest for an overweight child? Remind them that snacks should not become a substitute for meals and that snacks should include nutrient-rich, not nutrient-poor foods. Point out that the American Dietetic Association suggests that children not have snacks too soon before a meal. **L1**

VISUAL LEARNING	Using the Photograph

Possible response: They might eat more than they really need. They should eat only as long as they're hungry.

Some parents tell their children to eat all the food that they are served. **How can this lead to the child being overweight? What guidelines should parents follow in terms of how much children should eat?**

- Include children in meal preparation whenever possible. For example, young children can mix raisins in applesauce, wash potatoes with a scrub brush, and wash vegetables.
- Follow a regular schedule for meals and snacks. Children find it difficult to wait—especially when they're hungry.
- Keep meals pleasant. Remember that the child's table manners will improve with age. Be sure to model the behavior that you want the child to follow.
- Use a sturdy, unbreakable dish or plate with sides for serving the child's food. Food can be scooped up against the sides for easier eating.
- Choose a cup that the child can hold easily and that doesn't readily tip.
- Provide child-sized eating utensils. Young children have trouble handling full-sized forks and spoons.

- Let a toddler sit in a high chair for meals. As the child grows, use a high stool with a back or a booster seat on a regular chair.
- Remember that children imitate others. Set a good example in food choices and in table manners.

Avoid using food as a punishment or a bribe. If you say, "You can't have a cookie until you finish your vegetables," you give the impression that vegetables are bad and cookies are good.

Bathing

Parents and other caregivers need to help young children develop both good attitudes about **hygiene**—personal cleanliness—and good hygiene skills. For instance, when they begin toilet training, children

364 UNIT 4: The Child From One to Three

LEARNING STYLES	Intrapersonal

Have students analyze their own diets by keeping track of what they eat for three or four days. At the end of that time, have them tally the number of servings in each of the four food groups. What eating patterns do they notice? What corrections, if any, should they make to their diets? Have students chart the results of their study, writing their observations and recommendations for improvement below the chart.

should be taught to wash their hands each time they use the bathroom.

A daily bath also helps develop good habits. Evening baths are usually most practical and can become an enjoyable part of getting ready for bed. Children these ages typically have fun in the water.

One-year-olds begin to want to wash themselves. At first, this means merely rubbing the washcloth over the face and stomach. By age two, however, most children can wash, rinse, and dry themselves fairly well, except for the neck and back. By age three, children can bathe themselves with little supervision.

Bathtubs are still dangerous for children, though. A child can drown in as little as one inch of water. You should never leave a young child alone in the bath—not even for one minute. Another way of making the tub safe is to cover the bottom of the tub to prevent slipping. Attach rough plastic stickers or place a rubber mat on the bottom of the tub.

There is no set age at which all children can safely shower. It depends on the child's ability to control the water temperature, stand in the shower safely, and get himself or herself clean. If a child does shower, some kind of covering for the shower floor is a good idea. This will prevent the child from slipping and falling.

Caring for the Teeth

At age one, most children have several teeth. Teach them to brush their teeth right after eating. The longer food remains in the mouth, the more it can damage the teeth.

To encourage children to begin brushing, give them a small, soft toothbrush and a bit of toothpaste. Their first attempts will

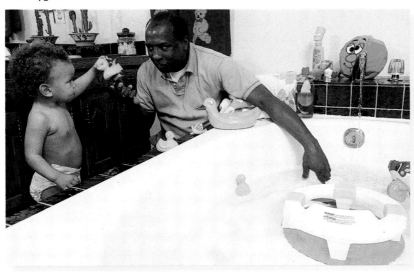

Bath time provides an opportunity for positive parent-child interaction, as well as learning about hygiene.

Art Activity

Explain to students that many children become frightened of the bath at some point. It is common, for example, for toddlers to fear that they will slip down the drain with the used bath water. Have students create short board books for toddlers that ease their fears of the bath. Text should be minimal, and pictures should be clear and colorful. Use cardboard for the pages and bind them together with ribbon. **L2**

VISUAL LEARNING **Using the Photograph**

Ask: What should parents look for to see if a young child is ready to eat in public? (*Eating quietly; not throwing food.*)

Hygiene. **During the summer months, daily bathing is important for more reasons than just washing away the dirt. It also:**
• **minimizes the skin's absorption of chemical-based insect repellents.**
• **reduces the drying effects of chlorine from swimming pools.**
• **decreases the chances that small cuts may become infected by bacteria.**

Observing & Participating

Have students refer to the information in Section 11-1 about small and large motor skills. Then have them identify the small and large motor skills necessary for a toddler to bathe himself. Why does it generally take until the age of three before a child can wash herself completely? What games might parents use to interest children in learning how to bathe themselves?

COMPREHENSION CHECK

1. When should children have their first dental checkup? (*Eighteen months.*)
2. When should parents encourage self-dressing? (*When a child shows interest.*)

ACTIVITIES

ISSUES IN CHILDREN'S HEALTH

Fluoride. Fluoride, while beneficial in adult oral hygiene, is potentially harmful to a young child. Because children tend to swallow toothpaste rather than spitting it out, they ingest the fluoride in the paste. This can result in white spots on the teeth, weakening of tooth enamel, and, in cases of overdose, vomiting. For this reason, use only a small amount of toothpaste.

One way that parents teach children good hygiene is by setting a good example. If they brush after every meal, children will learn this habit. *How else can parents help children have clean teeth?*

not be very successful, but the opportunity to try is important. Even up to age three, children still need adult help.

Many dentists recommend that parents also begin flossing the child's teeth and showing the child how to hold and use dental floss. Start with the top teeth one night and do the bottom teeth the next. Creating the habit of flossing is the most important thing. Dentists also suggest that eighteen months is a good age for children to have their first dental checkup.

Dressing

Children are eager to learn dressing skills; adults and other caregivers should encourage self-dressing whenever a child begins to show interest. Dressing involves a number of large and small motor skills that must be learned one step at a time. Patience is important! A child learns these skills only through practice. If others insist on dressing the child because they can do it faster, they will probably have to continue dressing the child when older.

A child usually starts trying to help with dressing around the age of thirteen or fourteen months, perhaps by holding out an arm

As children become older, they wish to have greater power over issues that touch their lives. Giving them choices of what outfit to wear helps them gain that feeling of power.

Management/Leadership Skills

Dentists suggest that adults and children change toothbrushes every three to four months. Wear and tear on the toothbrush makes it a less effective cleaning tool at that point. If the bristles are flattened or fall out, the toothbrush should be replaced sooner. To avoid passing bacteria from one person to another, people should never share toothbrushes. Assign a brush of a specific color to each member of the family and consistently buy brushes of that color for that person.

for the sleeve of a shirt. Next, the toddler may learn to actually push his or her own arm through a sleeve. By two years, the child can pull up pants, but putting on shirts continues to be difficult. At this age, children often end up with their garments inside out or backwards. By age three, the child can dress independently, except for some help with difficult fasteners like buttons and with shoelaces.

With self-dressing, a child learns independence, responsibility, and self-esteem. You can encourage it by providing clothes that are easy to put on and take off.

Choosing Clothing

Comfort, durability, and economy are the most important characteristics to look for in clothing for young children.

- **Comfort.** Look for clothes that allow freedom of movement. Knits that stretch as the child moves are good choices. Avoid stiff or scratchy fabrics.

Size is an important factor in comfort. Clothes that are too small restrict movement. Clothes that are a little large allow the child to move comfortably. Of course, even clothes labeled the same size may not fit the same way. If the child will cooperate, let him or her try on clothing before you buy. Otherwise, have the child try the clothes on at home. Remember to allow for some shrinkage.

- **Durability.** Children's clothes must withstand hard wear and repeated washing. Durability is influenced by the quality of the fabric and the construction of the clothing. Denim, used for jeans and overalls, is an example of a durable fabric. In checking construction, look for close, even stitching with strong thread. The stitching should be

What factors should you consider in buying clothing for children these ages? How can labels help you as you shop for clothing?

ACTIVITIES

Discussion Activity

Have volunteers attempt to put on one of the following while wearing gloves or mittens: a sweater with small buttons, a jacket with a zipper, sweatpants with a drawstring, or a garment with small hooks or snaps. Then lead the class to see how this activity helps them understand the challenge a child faces when learning self-dressing. **L1**

Critical Thinking Activity

Comparing and Contrasting. Have students do research to compare and contrast the way children are dressed today with the clothing styles available in previous times. They might check advertisements in old newspapers or catalogs, or look in books that describe everyday life in the past. Suggest that students focus their research and report on the following topics: comfort, fabrics, and child-friendliness. **L3**

VISUAL LEARNING	Using the Photograph

Answers: Factors: comfort, durability, economy. *Labels* can tell size; fiber content, which suggests comfort; and cleaning needs.

ACTIVITIES

Discussion Activity

Have students discuss the advantages of buying second-hand clothing for children. (*Cost savings; recycling clothing reduces the negative impact of human activity on the environment.*) **L2**

Teamwork Activity

Have students work in groups to develop lists of features that ensure comfort, durability, and economy. Combine the groups' lists into one checklist. Reproduce the checklist to share with parents of young children. **L2**

VISUAL LEARNING | **Using the Photograph**

Possible responses: Sympathetic to the child but tired.

MULTIPLE INTELLIGENCES | Children of differing learning styles can be taught the skills needed for self-dressing in ways that meet their needs. Provide a visual learner with books that explain the basics of buttons, zippers, and the like. Auditory learners will benefit from a verbal description of what needs to happen: "Put your arm through the sleeve."

---

reinforced at points of strain. All fasteners and trims should be firmly attached.

Cotton is a good choice, especially for T-shirts and underwear. Cotton wears well, doesn't irritate the skin, and washes well—though it may shrink. Since it absorbs moisture, cotton is also comfortable.

Synthetic fibers are made from chemicals rather than natural sources. Fabrics made from synthetic fibers—like polyester and acrylic—are durable, wrinkle resistant, and quick drying. Unlike cotton, though, most synthetic fibers don't absorb moisture well. They hold heat and perspiration against the body.

A blend of cotton and synthetic offers the benefits of both kinds of fibers. By law, all clothing must have a label that identifies the fibers used.

Clothing labels also state how to care for each garment.

- **Economy.** Since young children grow rapidly, they outgrow their clothes often. Many parents exchange outgrown clothes to cut costs. Others find good used clothes at yard sales, secondhand stores, and thrift shops.

Choose clothes that allow for growth. Look for deep hems or cuffs that can be let down after the child has grown. Check that the straps on overalls or jumpers are long enough to allow the buttons to be moved. Pants often can be bought a size larger and the pant legs rolled up.

When possible, let children help choose their own clothes. They usually love bright colors. In fact, young children choose their clothes more by color than by anything else. Other favorites include clothes printed with pictures of animals, toys, or story characters.

Sleeping

Near their second birthday, the sleeping habits of most children change. They usually require less sleep than before, and they may not go to sleep as easily or as willingly. By age two, most children no longer take a morning nap. Most three-year-olds give up the afternoon nap as well.

Children often need comfort at night. Younger toddlers may fuss before settling down. They may also suffer from nighttime fears. *How might these nighttime demands make a parent feel?*

Parenting in Action

During the toddler stage, children will learn to dress themselves faster and more easily if their clothing is chosen with this goal in mind. Front zippers or other front openings allow children to fasten their garments themselves. A garment that has a distinct front and back can help the child know how to put it on. Otherwise, the front and back of the garment should be clearly marked. Big buttons are easier than tiny ones for small hands to handle. Pants and skirts with elastic waistbands are also easy to master.

Bedtime and sleep patterns can change in another way. A two-year-old may seem to be more emotionally dependent on adults than during the previous year. Many two-year-olds call a parent back repeatedly at bedtime. They may ask for a drink of water, another story, and one more trip to the bathroom. What they really want is someone near. Children of this age often use self-comforting techniques at bedtime, such as thumb sucking, rocking the crib, or cuddling a favorite blanket or soft toy.

It isn't unusual for three-year-olds to wake in the middle of the night and even get out of bed. Emotional experiences of the day, excitement at bedtime, or nighttime fears may cause them to feel insecure at night.

Fear of the dark is common among two- and three-year-olds. There are many possible causes. For example, the child may have overheard talk or news reports about prowlers, fires, accidents, or other dangers. The child's fears are very real and usually very troubling. Unfortunately, there is rarely a quick solution. A calm discussion may help some children. Others may feel more comforted by a night-light. All children who feel afraid of the dark need patience and understanding. Ridicule or shaming the child only makes the problem worse. If you were afraid of the dark as a child, try to remember what it felt like.

Toilet Training

Most children begin toilet training sometime after eighteen months of age. There is no set age at which the process should begin. Rather, each child should start toilet training when he or she is physically mature and emotionally ready.

Readiness

To be physically mature enough for toilet training, a child must be able to control his or her **sphincter muscles** (SFINGK-tur), the muscles that control elimination. The child must also be able to recognize the body sensations that precede elimination. Only then is the child ready to start learning to control and release these muscles.

A child who is emotionally ready is happily settled into a familiar daily routine. During a family move or any similar event that requires adjustments is not a good time to start toilet training.

Giving Help

The attitudes of parents and other caregivers toward toilet training are very important. Calm encouragement is more effective than rules and punishment. It also helps build self-esteem. Remember that the child who is physically and emotionally ready for toilet training genuinely wants to succeed. If the child resists, wait for readiness. Even after a child is toilet trained, some accidents should be expected.

When children begin to use the toilet, they may prefer to use a special child seat on the toilet or a separate potty chair. Using a child seat eliminates the need for another adjustment later, when the child is ready to

COMPREHENSION CHECK

1. How do the sleeping habits of children change around age two? (*Two-year-olds require less sleep and do not go to sleep as easily or willingly as before.*)
2. Why is it often better to flush the toilet after the child has left the bathroom? (*Many children are frightened by the flushing of a toilet.*)

ACTIVITIES

Critical Thinking Activity

Formulating Ideas. Pedro is three years old. He is terrified that a lion lives in his closet, waiting to leap out and devour him as soon as he is alone at night. Suggest strategies his parents could use to help him handle his fear. **L1**

Discussion Activity

Ask students whether they have had any experiences with children having problems sleeping at night. Have them describe the situation, how they responded, and how the child reacted to that response. Have the class discuss these responses. **L1**

ISSUES IN CHILDREN'S HEALTH

Night Terrors. Around the age of three, some children begin to experience night terrors. These episodes involve screaming, sobbing, sleepwalking and thrashing around. Although the child's eyes may be open, he or she is unresponsive; in the morning, the child will probably not recall the incident. Researchers do not know what causes night terrors, but they seem more frequent in sleep-deprived children. When night terrors strike, do not wake the child. Be sure all your doors are locked to prevent the child from wandering outside. Avoid discussing the event in the morning, since doing so will only frighten the child.

Ask the E✗perts

Introducing the Feature

Point out to students that a parent changes an average of six to eight diapers in a twelve-hour period. How long do students think a diaper change takes? Why might parents be eager to begin toilet training?

Answers to Thinking It Through
1. *Possible response:* It shows awareness of bodily functions.
2. *Possible response:* Self-dressing skills make it easier for a child to undress before using the toilet.

Applying What You've Learned

Have students create a checklist for parents to use when deciding whether their child is ready for toilet training.

Ask the E✗perts

Dr. Van Stone
Pediatrician
Tupelo, Mississippi

Signs of *Readiness for Toilet Training*

Q What are the signs that a child is ready for toilet training?

A The most important thing to remember about toilet training is not to begin it until the child is ready. Beginning this training before the child is ready can make it longer and more difficult.

A child who is aware of the process of going to the bathroom is probably ready to use the toilet. If your child stops playing and grunts while having a bowel movement, he or she can probably begin toilet training. A child who is curious about the body and about elimination is probably ready as well.

The child with a less frequent need to urinate—sometimes going from one meal to the next—is ready for bladder training. So is a child who tells you that his or her diaper needs changing.

A child will do better at potty training if he or she has mastered self-dressing. Some children have accidents because they head to the bathroom without enough time to manage their clothes.

Having the language skills to talk about elimination can help with training as well. Some children make it fairly easy for parents. They simply announce that they're ready to get out of diapers!

When you do begin toilet training, be sure to keep the whole process as free of stress as possible. Avoid pushing the child, and be sure not to punish him or her for the accidents that will inevitably occur. Instead, praise the child when he or she does use the toilet correctly.

Thinking It Through

1. Why does a child's saying that a diaper needs changing suggest the child is ready for toilet training?
2. What role does self-dressing play in readiness for toilet training?

370 Unit 4: The Child from One to Three

Parenting in *Action*

Experts agree that children are ready for toilet training when they become aware of bowel movements or bladder fullness. The age a child reaches this awareness is unpredictable, but caregivers can look for telltale signs of this awareness. For example, at almost age two,

Maleese would hide behind a chair for a while or slip into another room. Theo, at the same age, would stop what he was doing, stand still, and look preoccupied. Both children are good candidates for toilet training.

move from a potty chair to the toilet. On the other hand, using a potty chair allows the young child more independence than the special seat.

Some children are frightened by the flushing of a toilet. Unless the child is particularly interested in flushing, it may be better to flush the toilet after the child has left the bathroom.

Bowel training usually comes before bladder training. Most children are ready when they show an awareness that a bowel movement is imminent. When you see this awareness in the child's facial expressions or gestures, suggest that he or she might try sitting on the toilet seat or potty chair. Be available and encouraging. However, being too forceful or demanding will make toilet training more difficult both for the child and for you.

Bladder training typically follows bowel training by several months, although some children learn both at the same time. Many young children are encouraged in toilet training when they are given **training pants**, heavy, absorbent underpants, in place of diapers. Wearing training pants makes it possible for a young child to use a potty independently. Most children also recognize that wearing underpants instead of diapers is a sign of maturity.

SECTION 11-2 REVIEW

✔ Check Your Understanding

1. What is the most important consideration in preparing meals and snacks for young children?
2. What choices in plates, cups, and utensils can make it easier for toddlers to learn self-feeding?
3. How can parents build the bathing skills of children from one to three?
4. What should caregivers do to teach children to care for their teeth?
5. Why are comfort, durability, and economy important in children's clothing?
6. How should caregivers respond to a young child's fear of the dark?
7. How are sphincter muscles involved in toilet training?

Putting Knowledge Into Practice

1. **Comparing.** How do an infant's sleep patterns compare to those of a two-year-old? How do they compare to those of a three-year-old?
2. **Applying.** When Michael was one year old, his older sister Maria dressed him every day. Now that Michael is one-and-a-half, what should she do?
3. **Observing and Participating.** Plan a lunch or dinner for a toddler that takes into account nutrition and the color, texture, shape, and ease of eating the foods.

CHAPTER 11: Physical Development from One to Three **371**

ASSESS

CHECKING COMPREHENSION

Have students answer the Check Your Understanding questions. Answers appear at the bottom of this page.

EVALUATION

Give students the Section 11-2 Quiz in the *Teacher Resource Guide*.

RETEACHING

1. Assign Reteaching Activities, page 37.
2. Have students write one question for each subheading in the section and then exchange papers and answer one another's questions.

ENRICHMENT

Have students design a product that would help make bathtime safer or more enjoyable for either the parent or the child. Ask them to create an advertisement for their new product.

EXTENSION

Have students research and report on childhood illnesses related to diet deficiencies.

CLOSE

Have each student write an ending to this sentence: "When caring for a child between ages one and three, it is important to remember…"

MOTIVATOR

Tell students that some 130,000 children in the United States are victims of poisoning every year. Explain that many more are injured in other household accidents that could have been prevented.

TEACH

COMPREHENSION CHECK

1. Why should a caregiver always turn the handles of pots and pans toward the center of the stove? (*To avoid a child grabbing the handle and burning himself or herself when pan spills.*)
2. Why should the doors of unused refrigerators be locked or removed? (*To avoid a child being trapped inside and suffocating.*)

ACTIVITIES

Critical Thinking Activity

Identifying Alternatives. Ask students to inspect their yards or the immediate surroundings of their homes. Have them make a list of objects or conditions that are potentially dangerous to an infant or small child. For each item on their lists, have students suggest a remedy or a precaution that parents or caregivers could make to ensure the safety of a child.

L1

Parenting With Care

Keeping Children Safe and Healthy

Children from one to three are capable of—and interested in—exploring their environment.

They open drawers and cabinets. They turn knobs and stick their fingers into tiny holes. As they try to learn about their world, they often put themselves in danger. It's not fair to the child to put a stop to this exploration. The best solution is to childproof the home, making it as safe as possible for the child.

Parents can follow these tips to make a safe environment for a child:

To Prevent Falls
* Keep the floor and stairs free of anything that the child might trip over.
* Wipe up spills immediately—before someone slips and falls.
* Use safety gates on stairways until the child can navigate them independently.
* Always use the seat belt when the child is in a high chair.
* Be sure that all open windows have secure screens. Windows in high-rise buildings should have safety latches the child cannot open.
* Remove loose rugs and any furniture that might tip easily.

To Prevent Burns
* Teach the child that the range is hot and must not be touched.
* Always turn the handles of pots and pans toward the center of the range.
* Check the temperature of the hot water. It shouldn't be higher than 120° to 130°F (49° to 54°C) to prevent burns. If the water is hotter than that, lower the thermostat of the hot water heater.
* Put safety caps on all unused electrical outlets.
* Keep small appliances, such as toasters and irons, unplugged and out of reach when they are not in use.

To Remove Other Hazards
* Keep all dangerous materials, such as cleaning supplies, medicines, paints,

372 UNIT 4: The Child from One to Three

RESOURCES TO EXPLORE

Safety at Home. The American Academy of Pediatrics has published a guide for parents called *Caring For Your Baby and Young Child: Birth to Age 5* (Steven P. Shelov and Robert E. Hannemann, editors). The book contains a detailed chapter on safety as well as a "Safety Check" at the end of each chapter on developmental stages. More information on safety—and on many other topics—can be found at the AAP's web site, www.aap.org.

and insecticides, out of the child's reach. Keeping these materials on a high shelf is not enough—children like to climb. They should be stored in locked cabinets or containers.

- Keep sharp knives, razor blades, scissors, and matches locked out of children's reach as well. Never let a child have such an object.
- Check toys and equipment for broken parts or sharp edges.
- Keep the toilet lid down whenever the toilet isn't in use.
- Lock unused refrigerators and freezers or remove their doors.

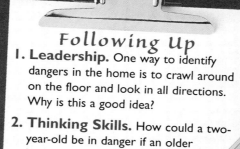

Following Up

1. **Leadership.** One way to identify dangers in the home is to crawl around on the floor and look in all directions. Why is this a good idea?

2. **Thinking Skills.** How could a two-year-old be in danger if an older brother or sister often ran up and down stairs?

CHAPTER 11: Physical Development from One to Three **373**

Teamwork Activity
Divide the class into groups. Give each group an object that can be used to prevent accidents by one- to three-year-olds, or give them a picture of such an object. Ask each group to produce a report explaining how the item could be used in toddler-proofing the home. **L2**

DID You Know?

Childhood Accidents. More children die or are injured from accidents than from the next five most frequent causes of childhood deaths combined. For children ages one to four, 37 percent of all deaths are caused by accidents. Of these, 34 percent die in cars; 19 percent in fires or of burns; 16 percent from drowning; 6 percent in falls; and 6 percent from poisoning. For children five to fourteen, 46 percent of all deaths are due to accidents.

CLOSE

1. Have students look in books, magazines, and web sites to collect safety tips for families with children. Then ask students to develop a poster about safety.
2. **Extension.** Have students contact the people in charge of community education for local hospitals to find out what information they offer about home safety.

Answers to Following Up

1. *Possible response:* Because it puts a person on a child's level, seeing what the child sees.
2. *Possible response:* The toddler could be near the stairs and, if the older child doesn't see him or her, be knocked over and seriously hurt.

CHECKING COMPREHENSION

Use the Summary and the Reviewing the Facts questions to help students go over the most important ideas in Chapter 11. Encourage students to ask questions and add details.

CHAPTER 11 REVIEW

Answers to Reviewing the Facts

1. One-year-old has head, chest, and abdomen that measure about the same; after two, the chest becomes larger. Three-year-olds stand straighter.
2. Calcium, phosphorus, and vitamin D build strong teeth; sugary foods harm teeth. Some may inherit protection against tooth decay.
3. *Large:* involve the large muscles (back, legs, shoulders, arms). *Small:* Involve smaller muscles (wrists, hands, fingers).
4. *Large motor (any two):* Walks with more coordination; climbs; jumps; pushes self on wheeled toys. *Small motor (any two):* Turns one page at a time; strings large beads; builds six block towers.
5. They affect attitudes toward food throughout life.
6. Color, texture, shape, temperature.
7. Uncomfortable; larger clothes allow for shrinkage and growth of the child.
8. May use delaying tactics at bedtime; may suffer nighttime fears.
9. Extra-absorbent underwear that make it easier for children to move out of diapers.

CHAPTER 11   REVIEW &

Summary

✔ Children one to three years old grow more slowly than infants. (Section 11-1)
✔ Large and small motor skills improve greatly during this period. (Section 11-1)
✔ Children from one to three develop eating and cleanliness habits that will last throughout their lives. (Section 11-2)

✔ Clothing for children these ages should be comfortable, durable, and economical. (Section 11-2)
✔ Bedtime problems are common in this stage. (Section 11-2)
✔ Toilet training should begin when a child is physically and emotionally ready. (Section 11-2)

Reviewing the Facts

1. How do body proportions and posture change from ages one to three? (Section 11-1)
2. Explain how heredity and diet affect the health of teeth. (Section 11-1)
3. What is the difference between large and small motor skills? (Section 11-1)
4. List two large and two small motor skills of two-year-olds. (Section 11-1)
5. Why are the attitudes of children ages one to three toward food so important? (Section 11-2)
6. What can caregivers vary to make meals appealing? (Section 11-2)
7. Why shouldn't children wear clothes that are too small for them? (Section 11-2)
8. What bedtime problems may arise with children these ages? (Section 11-2)

374 UNIT 4: The Child from One to Three

9. What are training pants? How can they help with toilet training? (Section 11-2)

Thinking Critically

1. **Making Inferences.** What should a parent do if a child doesn't master large motor skills at the average ages described in the chapter?
2. **Supporting.** The text says "Self-feeding both depends on and helps improve small motor skills." Explain how that is true.
3. **Analyzing.** Make a display for the bulletin board that includes a picture of a child's garment and captions explaining what features the garment should have to be useful to a child one to three.

Taking Action

1. **Handling Food Preferences.** Write a scene showing how a parent should respond when a two-year-old refuses to eat a particular food. *(Leadership)*
2. **Scheduling.** Make a chart of a day's activities for a three-year-old. The schedule should include time for physical activity, meals, practice in small motor skills, and good hygiene. Explain why such a schedule would—or would not—work. *(Management)*

CONNECTIONS

Cross-Curricular Connections

1. **Language Arts.** Write a brochure giving parents advice on how to choose clothes for toddlers.

2. **Math.** A cup of whole milk has 8 grams of fat, a cup of reduced-fat milk has 5 grams of fat, and a cup of lowfat milk has 3 grams of fat. If a three-year-old drinks 3 cups of milk a day, how much less fat does he or she drink by switching from whole milk to reduced-fat milk? From whole milk to lowfat milk?

3. **Science.** Older homes may contain surfaces coated with lead paint. Research the effects of lead poisoning on young children. Predict which groups of children are at highest risk.

Workplace Connections

1. **Interpersonal Skills.** Suppose you work in a toy store. What would you suggest to a customer who asked for your help in buying a toy for a niece aged three?

2. **Basic Skills.** Calculate the average weight of ten three-year-olds with the following weight in pounds: 25, 30, 32, 24, 28, 29, 23, 27, 26, 27. Then multiply the answer by 0.45 to find their average weight in kilograms.

Family and Community Connections

1. **Analyzing Meals.** Write down the food eaten by your family at dinner for two nights. Analyze the foods according to the Food Guide Pyramid. Would these meals be appropriate for a three-year-old? If not, what changes would need to be made?

2. **Community Outreach.** Explore possible sources of low-cost children's clothing in good condition. Try to name at least three places where preworn apparel would be sold. Are any run by community groups, religious organizations, or social service agencies?

Technology Connections

1. **Internet.** Search the Internet for reliable advice on toddlers' sleeping problems. You could visit the sites of the American Academy of Pediatrics or some other authoritative source. Based on your research, devise a list of ten tips for parents. Include a list of the sites you visited.

EVALUATION

1. Use the reproducible Chapter 11 Test in the *Teacher Resource Guide*, or construct your own test using the **Exam***View*® Test Generator.

2. For an alternative assessment, assign the Chapter 11 activity in the *Authentic Assessment* section of the *Teacher Resource Guide*.

ENRICHMENT

Assign students either of the two enrichment activities in the *Enrichment Activities* booklet in the *Student Motivation Kit*.

EXTENSION

Have students develop a plan for an interactive CD-ROM for parents of one- to three-year-olds. Their CD-ROM may focus on any one of the following topics: dressing, eating, hygiene, bedtime, toilet training. Students might include sketches showing the various screen and menu options.

CLOSE

Have students draw a graphic organizer that summarizes the physical development of a child from ages one to three. They may use various types of organizers, such as a tree or a time line.

CHAPTER 12 RESOURCES

Teacher Resource Guide
- Chapter 12 Test, p. 166
- Authentic Assessment, p. 279

Student Motivation Kit
- Observations, pp. 49-50

Transparency Package
- CT-35, CT-36, CT-40

Effective Instruction CD-ROM

CHAPTER 12   OVERVIEW

In **Section 12-1**, students study general patterns of emotional development in these ages and examine how children handle specific emotions.

Section 12-2 explores social development in this period, focusing on making friends, imaginary friends, sharing, and guidance techniques.

CHAPTER 12   OBJECTIVES

After completing Chapter 12, students will be able to:

- Describe general patterns of emotional and social development in these ages.
- Explain the importance of a positive self-concept and ways it can be nurtured.
- Describe how young children gradually learn to play with each other.
- Explain general guidance techniques and how to promote sharing.

376

CHAPTER 12

Emotional and Social Development from One to Three

RESOURCES TO EXPLORE

Advice to Parents. The Educational Resource Center (ERIC) is a rich depository of research information on children. Some of this information has been gathered in a web site called the National Parent Information Network. The site offers up-to-date information on childhood issues, reviews of books about children and parenting, a question-and-answer resource called Parents Ask ERIC, and much more. You can access the Website at: www.ericeece.org/askeric.html

Mark and Michael watched their children on the seesaw. Matt and Jordan were having so much fun together. The two fathers enjoyed seeing it. "Remember how they used to play?" asked Mark. "They would sit back to back in the sandbox as though the other one wasn't even there."

Michael nodded. "There has been a real change," he said. "Now Jordan really looks forward to getting together with Matt. It's great, actually. Most mornings it takes a long time for him to get dressed—he gets distracted by everything in the room. But on days that we're meeting Matt, well, it's all different. He cleans up after breakfast and has his clothes on in a hurry. Then he's ready to play!"

> **"Remember how they used to play? They would sit back in the sandbox as though the other one wasn't even there. Now Jordan really looks forward to getting together with Matt."**

- Describe the following situation: "Two-year-old Jerry and his father go to the supermarket to buy food for the week. Jerry is tired and hungry, and the trip ends with him face down in the cereal aisle, kicking and screaming because his father won't buy the sugary cereal he wanted." **Ask:** What might have caused the situation? How could it have been avoided?
- Have students examine the photograph on the opening page of the chapter. **Ask:** How can caregivers help children learn to play together?

USING THE SCENARIO Have students read the opening scenario and name the developmental change the fathers have noticed. (*Playing with others*.) Then have them identify other ways that this change might be manifested.

KEY TO ABILITY LEVELS   Each section gives skill-building activities. Each activity has been labeled for use with students of various learning styles and abilities.

L1 Level 1 activities are basic activities and should be within the range of all students.

L2 Level 2 activities are average activities and should be within the range of average and above average students.

L3 Level 3 activities are challenging activities designed for the ability range of above average students.

SECTION 12-1 RESOURCES
Teacher Resource Guide
• Lesson Plan Organizer, p. 64
• Section 12-1 Quiz, p. 164
Student Motivation Kit
• Observ. & Case Studies
  (case study), pp. 115-116
• Reteaching Activity, p. 38
• Enrichment, p. 35
Student Workbook
• Study Guide, pp. 103-106
• Solving the Puzzle of
  Emotional Development,
  p. 107
Transparency Package
• CT-35 Stepping Stones to a
  Positive Self-Concept
Effective Instruction CD-ROM

FOCUS

MOTIVATOR

Ask students whether they have ever seen a child age one to three behave in a way that they disapproved of. What did the child do? How did the parent respond? Did they think to themselves, "No child of mine will ever do that"?

VOCABULARY ACTIVITY

Explain that the meanings of the words that make up a compound word provide clues to the meaning of the compound word. Have volunteers try to define the terms that are compounds.

378

Emotional Development from One to Three

Between one and four, children undergo many emotional changes. They develop new emotions, such as jealousy, they had not felt before. They display their emotions very clearly. By the end of their third year, children begin to control their emotions and to express them in more socially acceptable ways. Emotional development depends upon brain development and personal experiences.

KEY TERMS

empathy
negativism
self-centered
self-concept
separation anxiety
sibling rivalry
temper tantrums

OBJECTIVES:

• Describe patterns of emotional development from ages one to three.

• Identify the common emotions of young children and the changing ways they express those emotions.

• Analyze how individual differences affect emotional development.

• Explain how self-concept develops.

General Emotional Patterns

Throughout childhood, emotional development tends to go in cycles. That is certainly the case with children at this stage. They go through periods of negativism and rebel-

378 Unit 4: The Child from One to Three

Observing & Participating

Ask volunteers who have photographs or home videos from the time when they were one to three years old to bring them to class. Without identifying who is shown, have the class look at the images, looking particularly for different emotions being displayed. Can students pick out any general emotional patterns? Can they identify any major differences between the emotional development of one-year-olds and that of three-year-olds?

lion, but also periods of happiness, calmness and stability. These periods tend to alternate, and they are generally related to the age of the child.

Of course, each child is an individual. Jasmine may not go through the negativism of eighteen months until she is two. Manuel may not seem to go through it at all. Generally, however, you will find the following characteristics in children at about the ages given.

Eighteen Months

Eighteen-month-old children are primarily **self-centered**, that is, they think about their own needs and wants, not those of others. This isn't surprising. During infancy, caregivers promptly meet a child's needs and desires. At eighteen months, however, they begin to teach the child that some desires won't be met immediately—and others never will be met. This is a difficult lesson, and the eighteen-month-old is only beginning to learn it.

Spoken instructions aren't always successful with children this age. The young toddler is likely to do the opposite of what is requested. At this age, the child's favorite response to everything is "No."

Negativism, or doing the opposite of what others want, is normal for a young toddler. It has a number of causes:

- **The desire for independence.** Saying "no" is a way of saying, "Let me decide for myself." The child may even say "no" to things he or she would really like to do—just for the chance to make the decision!
- **Frustration.** The bodies of toddlers aren't developed enough to obey their wishes, and they don't have the language skills to express their feelings.

The frustration that results is often expressed in a simple and emphatic "No!"

- **The child's realization of being a separate person.** This idea is both exciting and frightening. The child likes the power of being a separate person but misses the close bond with a primary caregiver.

This negativism might produce a battle of wills between child and caregiver. Some strategies can help prevent clashes. One is to eliminate as many restrictions as possible. For example, rather than asking an eighteen-month-old not to touch certain objects, put them away. As the child gets older, they can be put back in place.

Toddlers begin to show independence. Being negative is one way for them to do so. *What strategies can parents use to deal with a child's negativism?*

CHAPTER 12: Emotional and Social Development from One to Three **379**

1. What difficult lesson are eighteen-month-olds beginning to learn? (*That not all of their desires will be met.*)
2. What are three reasons for toddlers' negativism? (*Desire for independence; frustration with their skills; realization that they are a separate person.*)

ACTIVITIES

Teamwork Activity

Have students work in groups to create a plan for a new business. The idea is to create an activity center for children and parents that caters to children eighteen months to two years old (similar to Gymboree). For example, one corner of the room might contain a "Whack Me" pillow, which frustrated toddlers are allowed to hit, but that diffuses their anxiety by making a funny noise. Have students draw up a floor plan and write a description of the products and activities available in their center.
L2

LEARNING STYLES

Spatial

Have students create a time line showing the years from one to three. As they read through the section, they can add to it. Suggest that they place the time line down the center of the page. On one side, they can they write information reflecting the emotional development of children. On the other side, they can include suggestions for caregivers to foster that development. They might illustrate their time line with photographs or drawings that show a child's emotions.

COMPREHENSION CHECK

1. Name two strategies for coping with negativism. (*Eliminate restrictions where possible; offer choices when reasonable.*)
2. How is emotional development during the toddler years like a roller coaster? (*Because emotional development moves in cycles from "low" periods of negativism to "high" periods of happiness and stability.*)

ACTIVITIES

Discussion Activity

Ask: How are the emotional lives of children one to three like those of teens? **L1**

VISUAL LEARNING	**Using the Graphic** Have students use the illustration to answer the following questions. (1) At what age is a child most likely to refuse to eat the food offered at mealtime? (*Eighteen months.*) (2) At what age would a book titled *What's That Under My Bed?* be appropriate for a child? (*Three and one-half years.*)

Positive guidance can help caregivers handle a child who is negative:

- **Give choices.** Cleaning up can become a game when the caregiver asks, "Which will you pick up first—the books or the toys?" Having choices allows the child to exercise control. Limit choices to two alternatives, however. Toddlers can't think about three or four things at a time.

- **Redirect the child.** If possible, take the child's attention off the issue that is causing the negative response. You may be able to return to it later when the child is calmer.

- **Encourage talking.** Help children learn to use words to communicate how they feel. This will help both you and the child understand and deal with those feelings.

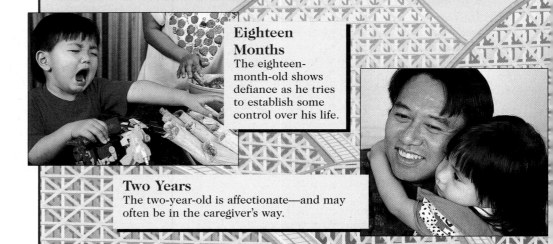

An Emotional Roller Coaster

Parents may be bewildered when a cheerful three-year-old suddenly becomes insecure and uncertain at three-and-a-half. Shifts in behavior become easier to bear when parents realize that they are normal—and that the times when children are more difficult to handle will pass.

Eighteen Months
The eighteen-month-old shows defiance as he tries to establish some control over his life.

Two Years
The two-year-old is affectionate—and may often be in the caregiver's way.

ISSUES IN TEEN PARENTING	Teens should be able to relate to a toddler's rebellion against being told what to do. Ask students to discuss recent experiences in their own lives that point out the emotional value of having

choices. Ask students whether having choices can sometimes seem overwhelming or frightening and ask them to give examples. Finally, point out to them that having too many choices, or choices that are not familiar, is also frightening for a toddler.

Around eighteen months, many children start to have **temper tantrums**. In a tantrum, the child releases anger or frustration by screaming, crying, kicking, pounding, and sometimes holding his or her breath. These tantrums may occur until age three or four. Sometimes, even seemingly minor frustrations can cause temper tantrums. Try to help the child find less explosive ways of expressing these feelings.

Two Years

Emotionally, the two-year-old is less at odds with the world than he or she was at eighteen months. Speech and motor skills have improved, relieving much frustration. The child also understands more and is able to wait longer for needs to be met.

The two-year-old expresses love and affection freely and seeks approval and

Two and One-Half Years
At two and one-half, the child feels overwhelmed, and frustration becomes anger.

Three Years
The three-year-old is generally a happy child who is eager to help.

Three and One-Half Years
At three and one-half years, a child is often bothered by fears.

CHAPTER 12: Emotional and Social Development from One to Three **381**

Discussion Activity

Ask: Why is the move for independence difficult for children and parents? Why is it important?

Critical Thinking Activity

Analyzing. **Ask:** What problems might arise if caregivers offer choices in these situations:
- The child is tired. He or she may not make a good choice and may be unhappy with any choice.
- The child is in a new situation and is unfamiliar with the choices.
- The caregiver is not prepared to accept the child's decision. **L1**

ISSUES IN
CHILDREN'S HEALTH

Anger. Research shows that a two-year-old displays more aggression than a child of any other age between birth and age twenty. Kicking, biting, pushing, and other physically aggressive behaviors at this age are normal reactions to frustration and anger and normal testing of limits. Research also shows that some children are more aggressive than others. Children who exhibit high levels of violent aggression early on are more likely to commit crimes or fall into substance abuse later in life.

Parenting in Action

Children one to three can feel frustrated when faced with changes to their routine. To ease these transitions:
- Give advance warning of an impending change. Remind the child five minutes before it's time to stop an activity.
- Prepare children for what they will do or see in the new activity.
- Use language the child can understand. Say, "We're going out after lunch," not "We're going out in a little while."
- Allow extra time so the child won't have to be rushed.

COMPREHENSION CHECK

1. Why is a two-year-old less prone to anger and frustration than an eighteen-month-old? (*Speech and motor skills have improved; the child better understands explanations and is less impatient.*)
2. What tactics help a two-and-one-half-year-old cope with emotional changes? (*Routines; love; patience; flexible limitations.*)

ACTIVITIES

Discussion Activity

Ask: How does the desire for approval and affection influence a child's behavior? Could this desire ever be too strong? Explain how.
L1

Practicing Parenting

Ask students why a parent might be tempted to give in to a child's demands when a tantrum occurs in a public place. How is this action self-defeating?

Answers to Apply Your Knowledge

1. *Possible response:* More tantrums to get her way.
2. *Possible response:* Because children are more likely to accept an explanation when they are calm.

---

praise. Though the child still has some emotional outbursts, they are fewer and less intense. Two-year-olds are easier to reason with. They usually get along better with parents and other children because they tend to be more outgoing and friendly and less self-centered.

Practicing Parenting

Handling Temper Tantrums

In handling a tantrum, there are two goals. First, prevent the child from being hurt or hurting anyone else. Second, enforce the limits you have set. Tantrums usually occur when the child has been denied something that he or she wants. If you give in to the child's demands, tantrums are more likely to be repeated.

If you see a tantrum coming, try to distract the child to head it off. Sometimes holding the child in a firm hug will work. Some children, though, react strongly against that technique.

If a tantrum occurs at home, the caregiver may be able to ignore it. The child who finds that tantrums produce no attention is likely to stop having them.

When a tantrum occurs in a public place, move the child to a quiet spot to cool down. If possible, take the child home.

The most important thing is always to remain calm. Resist giving in to your own frustration by raising your voice—it will only heighten the tension. Acknowledge the child's feelings while reemphasizing why his or her demands can't be met.

Remember that the child isn't old enough to understand rational arguments—don't bother with long explanations. A firm and direct statement of the rule or your decision with a brief reason is enough.

APPLY YOUR KNOWLEDGE

1. Renee was shopping in the supermarket with her father. When her father said he would not buy some candy she wanted, Renee began to have a tantrum. Her father then put the candy in the shopping cart. What problems might this action cause?
2. Many tantrums arise when a child is denied something he or she wants. Why would it be helpful to talk to a child about the reason for the denial after the child has calmed down?

382 UNIT 4: The Child from One to Three

Two and One-Half Years

Just as parents and caregivers begin to adjust to a smoother, less intense toddler, the child enters another difficult stage. In fact, this period may seem even more difficult for caregivers than the eighteen-month-old stage. At two and one-half, tod-

---

ISSUES IN CHILDREN'S HEALTH **Toddler Speech.** Speech difficulties—called "speech disfluencies" are normal in these years. Some children stumble over the first letter of words; others repeat the first word of a sentence several times. One cause of these problems is stress, which creates tension in the child's throat. In their struggle for emotional control, other toddlers may be unable to speak about their feelings. Children may need help if they repeat the first syllable of a word four or five times or draw out the beginnings of words.

Have you ever seen a child have a temper tantrum in a supermarket? It can be very tempting for a parent to give in so that the noise and emotional turmoil end. **What is the negative result?**

but can't always make themselves be understood. These situations produce frustration that may boil over.

At two and one-half, the drive for independence is strong. This causes children to resist pressures to conform. They are sensitive about being bossed, shown, helped, or directed. Independence and immaturity clash head-on during this stage. Children this age can be stubborn, demanding, and domineering. However, their moods change rapidly, and within a short time they can become lovable and completely charming.

dlers are not so easily distracted as they were at eighteen months.

Children this age are learning so much that they often feel overwhelmed. Their comprehension and desires exceed their physical abilities. For example, they may want their blocks placed in a certain way but succeed only partially before accidentally knocking them over. Two-and-one-half-year-olds know what they want to say

Since two-and-a-half-year-olds like things to be in the same place and like to do things themselves, they can begin to learn to pick up their toys. **What emotional tendency of children this age might make it more difficult to convince them to pick up toys?**

383

Critical Thinking Activity

Analyzing. Describe the following situations to students and ask them to identify how they, as the child's caregiver, would offer each child a choice:

- Esperanza wants to wear a new top while working in the garden.
- Huang wants to eat candy for breakfast.
- Bobby wants the toy that Masahiko is using.
- Katrina wants to take a plastic toy with her to bed. **L1**

VISUAL LEARNING	Using the Photographs

Top—Answer: The child is likely to have other tantrums, hoping to get his or her way again.

Bottom—Answer: They resist pressures to conform.

MULTIPLE INTELLIGENCES	Having imaginary friends is one way that some children express their emo-

tional lives. Other children may find other outlets that derive from their personal talents and interests. A spatial child may draw using colors like red when upset and colors like blue when calm and at peace. A verbal child is likely to express emotions in words and tone of voice. A musical child may wish to hear songs or music that reinforce a mood.

LEARNING STYLES	Auditory

Have students contact a local child care center for permission to visit and tape record the children, or provide a tape that you recorded. Then, have students listen to the recordings and discuss the speech patterns they hear. Have them try to identify the ages of the children from what they hear. Have them give reasons to support their inferences. What conclusions do they draw about children's speech?

ACTIVITIES

Critical Thinking Activity

Comparing and Contrasting. Have students analyze the differing ways a two-year-old and a three-year-old might respond to these situations:

- An adult who wants to help the child with everything.
- Starting a new child care situation.
- Visiting a parent's workplace. **L2**

Language Arts Activity

Read the following to students: "Just about the time he turned three and one-half, Colin began sucking his thumb before sleeping. Then he began sucking it during the day."
Have students write what they would do if they were Colin's parents. **L1**

Discussion Activity

The subtitle to a book about two-year-olds is "Terrible or Tender." The book in the same series about three-year-olds is subtitled "Friend or Enemy." **Ask:** Are these appropriate subtitles? Why or why not? **L2**

VISUAL LEARNING | Using the Photograph

Possible responses: It gives them a sense of how they sound to the child—whether they sound harsh or caring.

Children this age have a need for consistency. They want the same routines, carried out the same way, every day. This is their way of coping with a confusing world. Following a routine helps build confidence and a feeling of security.

At two and one-half, children are both independent and dependent. Sometimes they seek help; at other times, they want to do things themselves. Love and patience are essential—especially when the child is neither lovable nor patient. Two-and-one-half-year-olds need flexible limitations rather than hard-and-fast rules.

Three Years

Three-year-olds are generally sunny and cooperative and are learning to be considerate. As preschoolers, they are more physically capable. They don't have to deal with as many frustrating situations as two-year-olds.

Three-year-olds are more willing to take directions from others. They will modify their behavior in order to win praise and affection—which they crave. Three-year-olds generally have fewer temper tantrums than younger children.

At three, children like to talk and are much better at it. They talk to their toys, their playmates, their imaginary companions, and them-

While three-year-olds play, they may talk for the imaginary people in their games. When they take the parents' role in these games, they often imitate the way their caregivers speak to them. *How can this help caregivers?*

selves. They also respond to others' talking; they can be reasoned with and controlled with words.

Three and One-Half Years

The self-confident three-year-old is suddenly very insecure at three and one-half. Parents may feel that the child is going backward rather than forward emotionally.

Fears are common at this age. The child may be afraid of the dark, lions and tigers, monsters, strangers, or loud noises—even

Management/Leadership Skills

Have students suppose they are parents of a three-year-old and expecting a baby. Tell them to develop a list of tasks for the child to help them care for a new baby. Ask them to explain how these tasks could help the child feel like a valued part of the family. Have students turn their lists into a checklist that the child could easily understand. For example, if the task is "Putting the baby's bibs away," the list might show a picture of a bib. You might wish to have students prepare this assignment in groups.

though none of these was frightening before. Emotional tension and insecurity often show up in physical ways, too. Some children may start habits—such as thumb sucking, nail biting, or nose picking—to release tension. Others stumble or stutter.

At three and one-half, children try to ensure their own security by controlling their environment. They may issue insistent demands, such as "I want to sit on the floor to eat lunch!" or "Talk to me!"

Specific Emotions

Children express their emotions openly until the age of two or three. The three-year-old begins to learn socially acceptable ways of displaying feelings. For example, eighteen-month-old Marta shows anger by kicking and screaming. Three-year-old Jonathan uses words.

Anger

Anger, as we have seen, is often the child's way of reacting to frustration. How children in this stage show that anger changes over the years. Three-year-olds are less violent and explosive—they are less likely to use hitting or kicking. Physical attacks give way to name-calling, pouting, or scolding.

The target of anger changes in these years as well. An eighteen-month-old who has a tantrum usually doesn't direct the anger toward a particular person or thing.

Biting and Hitting

Children ages one to three sometimes express their anger by biting or hitting another person. This can be a serious situation. Children do need to be told that biting and hitting are inappropriate ways to express their anger. They should be told that physical attacks can hurt others. Of course, caregivers need to take the situation into account, too. If the child lashes out during a temper tantrum, that is not the time for a discussion of how it is wrong to hit.

At the same time, children may need physical release for their anger. One way is to provide a safe substitute. A child who is prone to biting may be given a soft cloth or a teething ring—something the child can bite into without hurting others. A child who hits could be given an air-filled punching bag or a pillow to strike.

FOLLOWING UP

1. Why isn't it a good idea to talk to a child about not hitting while the child is having a tantrum?
2. Give some examples of objects that it would be safe for a child to hit.

Depression and the Brain

Children whose parents suffer from depression are more likely to suffer from that emotional problem themselves. Researchers are currently testing new procedures that use brain-imaging techniques to identify those children at an early age. Brain scans can help researchers identify a distinctive pattern of metabolic activity in the area of the brain where strong emotions are registered. It is hoped that early detection can result in early intervention to help prevent serious depression later in life.

Biting and Hitting

- Some parents provide plastic inflatable punching bags for children who hit when angry. **Ask:** Is this a good idea because it's a safe way of physically venting anger? Is it a bad idea because it reinforces hitting?

Answers to
FOLLOWING UP

1. *Possible response:* Child is so overcome with emotions that words won't be heard.
2. *Possible responses:* Pillow, cushion, mattress, inflatable punching bag.

LEARNING STYLES	Intrapersonal

Intrapersonal

Have students explore their own ways of dealing with anger by asking these questions: When was the last time you felt really angry about something? Did you show your anger or try to hide it? If you showed your anger, how did you do so? Is suppressing anger a good way of handling this emotion? Why or why not? What are some healthy ways to express anger? How can you improve the way you handle anger? Which of those techniques could be used by young children?

COMPREHENSION CHECK

1. How might separation anxiety be apparent at night? (*Child may have difficulty going to sleep or be unwilling to let parent leave the room.*)
2. At what ages does jealousy first appear, peak, and then recede? (*First appears in second year, peaks by age three, and then begins to lessen.*)

ACTIVITIES

Discussion Activity

Some parents think it's a bad idea to allow children to sleep with a night light on. They say the child will never get used to sleeping in the dark. Others say that if the light helps the child sleep, there's nothing wrong with it. Have students debate the matter. **L1**

Critical Thinking Activity

Understanding Cause and Effect. Ask students to write about a fear that they had when they were a child. They should identify the fear and, if possible, explain how it arose and how they learned to overcome it. **L1**

VISUAL LEARNING	Using the Photograph

Possible response: By offering comfort, support.

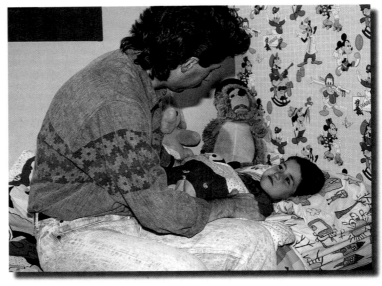

At age three and a half, children often feel fears at night. *How can parents best respond?*

From age two to three, children are more likely to aim their anger at the object or person they see as responsible for their frustration.

A number of factors can cause a child to be angry more often than normal. Anger is more frequent in anxious, insecure children. The child who hasn't learned self-control also tends to have frequent outbursts. Children whose parents are overly critical or inconsistent become frustrated easily and show anger. Make sure that the demands on children are both limited and reasonable as they are learning self-control.

Some common causes of anger are temporary—and felt from time to time by almost all children. If a child is sick, tired, uncomfortable, or hungry, frustration is more likely to turn into anger.

Caregivers must remember to respond to a child's anger in a controlled way. Reacting angrily themselves will only make the situation worse.

Fear

At each age, children have particular fears. A one-year-old may be frightened of high places, strangers, and loud noises. A three-year-old might be afraid of the dark, animals, and storms. Some fears are actually useful, since they keep the child from dangerous situations. Others must be overcome for the child to develop healthily.

Adults sometimes communicate their own fears to children. Even if the fear is never discussed, the alarmed call of a parent whenever a dog comes near may cause a child to become afraid of dogs.

One fear commonly arises some time or another between the first and fourth birthdays. Many children suffer from **separation anxiety**, a fear of being away from parents, familiar caregivers, or their normal environment. Nicole cried when her parents left her with a new babysitter. Jake cried when his father left on the first day of preschool.

Parenting in Action

Separation anxiety usually begins sometime in the first year, peaks at eighteen months, and then declines. Children are most likely to be upset when they do not understand where parents have gone or when they will come back. Toddlers should be given a brief, reassuring explanation before parents leave. Separation can be difficult for parents as well. Working parents may feel guilty about being away from their children. However, research has failed to show that all-day child care harms children.

Separation anxiety can upset parents. If they have placed the child in a child care situation, the child's fears may make them feel guilty. The parents need to remind themselves that they chose a safe, secure caregiver for the child. This is simply a stage that the child will go through—and grow out of. Parents can try to speed that process by spending special time with the child at home. They can also be specific about when they will return. "I'll be back after you've had your nap," gives the child a better sense of what to expect.

Many children who feel separation anxiety have trouble going to sleep at night. Some have nightmares. A bedtime routine and a reminder that a parent is nearby can help lessen these fears. Asking the child to describe a nightmare can help as well. It can be a relief to talk about the bad dream, instead of holding it inside. Also, by hearing what the child dreamt, the parent may understand the underlying cause of the nightmare.

The following suggestions will help you deal with the fears of toddlers:

- Offer support and understanding. Avoid shaming a child for his or her fears.
- Encourage the child to talk about the fears and listen seriously. Admitting to fears might diminish their impact.
- In some cases, it is best to accept the fear and avoid trying to force the child to confront it. Often, it will simply go away on its own.

- Read books together about a child who experiences fear. Talking about the book can help relieve the toddler's fears.
- Make unfamiliar situations more secure. Discuss new experiences and events in advance to help the child know what to expect. If possible, accompany the child. A first visit to the dentist, for example, goes more smoothly in the company of a caring adult.
- Teach the child how to control frightening situations. Fear of the dark can be lessened by knowing how to turn on the light.

Jealousy

Jealousy becomes a recognizable emotion some time in the second year. The one-year-old shows no jealous reactions, but by eighteen months, jealousy is very pronounced. It reaches its peak at age three and then lessens as outside relationships begin to replace the close ties to home and parents.

A new baby sometimes causes jealousy. Giving the older child a caring role can help minimize these feelings. *Why might a preschooler handle this situation better than a toddler?*

CHAPTER 12: Emotional and Social Development from One to Three **387**

ACTIVITIES

Critical Thinking Activity

Analyzing Primary Sources. Read students the following quotation by child care expert Dr. Marianne Neifert: "By giving your child your undivided attention, you let her know that she's more important than anything else at that moment. Put down the newspaper when she's trying to talk to you. Maintain eye contact and listen to what she's saying."
Ask: How does this advice relate to the issue of jealousy? **L1**

Teamwork Activity

Have students write the beginning of a story about a child aged two to three who has done something to hurt the feelings of another person. The story should end at the point where the other person's hurt feelings become known. Then have students exchange papers with a partner. Each student should complete the story received, explaining how a caregiver responded to the situation. Ask for volunteers to read their completed stories to the class. **L2**

One focus of jealousy may be the parents. The toddler may resent any show of affection between parents. Children may not understand that parents have enough love for everyone.

Sibling rivalry, or competition between brothers or sisters for parents' affection and attention, is another common cause of jealousy. This often arises when a new baby is born. Suddenly, a child finds that the attention he or she once received is now focused on the baby. For this reason, many experts say it is never safe to leave a baby alone with a toddler.

Some children react to a new baby by trying to get attention. They may show off, act in inappropriate ways, or revert to baby-like behaviors, such as wetting the bed or using baby talk.

If parents act shocked or threaten not to love the child anymore, they only make the problem worse. Fear of losing the parent's love caused the negative behavior in the first place. What the child needs is more affection and reassurance.

Sibling rivalry doesn't occur only when there is a newborn, however. Ask Todd, who came home from work to find himself overwhelmed by hugs from both four-year-old Becky and three-year-old Curt. Soon each child was trying to gain a position that would block the other from their father.

There are steps a parent can take to cut down on sibling rivalry:

- Make sure that all children know that they are loved and appreciated.

INFOLINK

Accepting a New Baby

For more about *preparing an older child to accept a new baby*, see Chapter 6, pages 194-195.

- Try to set aside time to be with each child so that there is less need to compete for attention.
- Avoid making comments that compare one child to the other.
- Let the children take turns in choosing activities—the game the family plays together or the video that's rented.
- Make clear that you will not accept one child tattling to get the other in trouble.

Love and Affection

The relationships that children have with others in these years form the basis of their capacity for love and affection in later life. Young children must learn to love.

The Developing Brain

In studying brain scans of children who have suffered severe neglect, researchers found that the area of the brain used for attachment to others is smaller than usual.

First comes "love" of those who satisfy the baby's physical needs. Gradually, the baby's affection expands to include siblings, pets, and people outside the home.

Relationships between parents and children should be strong, but not smothering. A child who depends too much on caregivers has difficulty forming other relationships.

Empathy

For years, people believed that infants and toddlers were so self-centered that they wouldn't feel anything toward another person who was unhappy. Research has over-

DID You Know?

Affection. Infants who have one primary caregiver tend to become strongly attached to that person. What about children who regularly spend time with different caregivers? Is the attachment to parents weakened? The evidence suggests otherwise.

Studies have shown that children who receive quality substitute care have no problems forming secure attachments to parents. Studies have also shown that as long as children receive responsive, stable, sensitive care, having a number of different caregivers does not adversely affect development.

turned that view. Between their first birthday and eighteen months, children begin to understand that their actions can hurt others. This is the first step toward **empathy**, or the ability to put oneself in another's place. Children as early as a year old may pat and talk to an unhappy child. By two, a child can show empathy. When Jesse saw that Nathan was upset, he offered Nathan his favorite stuffed animal to try to cheer him up.

Caregivers can teach children to show empathy. If a child does something to hurt another's feelings—taking a toy, for instance—tell the child to apologize. Then the child should also take an active step to making the wronged child feel better.

Individual Differences

Each child, of course, is unique and will develop emotionally in a special way. Individual differences can be very striking during this stage. These differences grow in part out of the different set of experiences that each child has. Roberto, an only child, will have different opportunities than Andrea, one of five children. Larissa's and Nadia's development will be affected by the fact that they are twins. Muhammad's experience will differ because his only brother, Rasheed, is ten years older.

Another factor is the child's temperament. As you recall, temperament is how a child naturally responds to other people and to events. An intense child may react more strongly to frustration than an adaptable child. A more perceptive child may show more empathy than one who is less perceptive.

Keep these differences in temperament in mind as you teach children how to control their emotions. Cody is very perceptive—he is very aware of his environment. At the same time, he can be easily distracted. When his mother sees a temper tantrum coming, she can try to turn his attention to something new. Such a technique may not work with a child with a different temperament. Nicole

Parents make an effort to be fair to all of their children. *Is it wise for them to handle each child the same way? Why or why not?*

INFOLINK

Temperament

For more about *Temperament*, see Chapter 9, pages 301-303.

CHAPTER 12: Emotional and Social Development from One to Three **389**

Discussion Activity

Do you agree or disagree that children can show empathy as early as age two? Why? **L1**

Discussion Activity

Have students discuss how number of siblings and birth order affect a child's experiences. **L1**

Critical Thinking Activity

Analyzing. Describe the following situation to students: "Carmen Rodriguez is bringing her two-year-old to the child care center for the first time."

Have them describe how they would handle this situation if they were Carmen Rodriguez. They should prepare two versions, showing the different approaches they would take for children of two different temperaments. **L2**

VISUAL LEARNING | Using the Photograph

Possible response: Because each child has a different temperament and responds differently to the same approach, parents need to adjust how they respond to children's actions. Fairness may not mean handling children exactly the same way, but treating them comparably.

MULTIPLE INTELLIGENCES

Stimuli for arousing empathetic feelings vary depending on the child's learning style. A visual learner, for example, may be roused to sympathy by seeing a sad face; an auditory learner may find distressing sounds more disturbing. Responses may vary similarly. A kinesthetic learner, for example, may hug someone who is unhappy, while a verbal person will use words. Discuss with students how, by identifying what kind of learner a particular child is, caregivers can better respond to distress in a way that will be meaningful to that child.

COMPREHENSION CHECK

1. Does self-concept originate from within or derive from external influences? (*Originates in response to the actions, attitudes, and comments of others.*)
2. Why is it important to avoid being overly critical of a child's efforts? (*To avoid negatively affecting child's self-concept.*)

ACTIVITIES

Discussion Activity

Have students discuss the text example of a three-year-old helping to set the table. What steps can parents take to become more conscious of the effects of interactions such as this on their child? **L1**

Discussion Activity

Ask: How is a child's self-concept likely to be affected if a parent's expectations are unreasonably high or low? What can parents do to develop reasonable expectations? **L2**

VISUAL LEARNING | Using the Photograph
Answer: If it is healthy, the child will probably develop in an emotionally healthy way.

---

adapts to change slowly. Her parents have to be sure to give her plenty of warning and time before any upcoming changes. She also dislikes surprises—even pleasant ones.

Parents have a range of tools that they can use to try to lead a child to a desirable behavior. This is true whether the issue is negativism, tantrums, sibling rivalry, or changing activities. For each child, with his or her unique combination of experiences and own temperament, some of those tools are more effective than others.

Developing a Positive Self-Concept

As children grow, they become more aware of their individual differences. Those traits that make them special become part of their **self-concept**—how they see themselves. Self-concept can be positive—if you see yourself as a good person, or a capable person, or one who can control emotions. It can also be negative—you could see yourself as a bad person, or an incapable person, or one who loses emotional control.

Self-concept is different from self-esteem. Self-concept is what you think you are like as a person. Self-esteem is how highly you value yourself.

A child forms his or her self-concept in response to the actions, attitudes, and comments of others. Parents usually spend the most time with the young child, so they have the strongest influence on the child's self-concept. The years from one to three are crucial in the child's development of self-concept.

Young children believe what others say about them—and that belief influences how they behave. If children hear they are good, they try to act the part. However, if

they constantly hear that they are "bad" or "stupid," they will live up to that image. Even young toddlers are tuned in to adults' body language and tone of voice. The strong influence of adults' words and actions doesn't diminish until children are older and can judge their own actions. By that time, however, their self-concept is firmly established.

Another factor in building a positive self-concept is mastery of skills. For this reason, it is important to give infants and toddlers the chance to explore their world. Then they have the opportunity to master skills. Success gives a sense of competence, which leads to a positive self-concept.

Some parents unintentionally act in ways that hurt a child's self-concept. For example, when three-year-old Jackie set the table her mother smiled and said, "You did a very nice job, Jackie!" Then, however, the mother moved the forks to their correct positions. This showed Jackie that her efforts weren't worth much. A better approach would have been for Jackie's mother to avoid making any changes. Then at dinner she might have said,

The child's first important relationship is with parents. *How can that relationship be used to gauge emotional development?*

Management/Leadership Skills

Have students create "report cards" for parents to use in evaluating their child's emotional health. Students can use the indicators listed in the text, supplementing it with outside research if they desire. Students should set up a grading system and explain that system on the report card. Advise students to use a scale that avoids traditional letter grades. Remind them to explain each rating of a level of emotional health.

"Jackie set the table tonight. Didn't she do a nice job? She already knows where the knives and spoons go."

Evaluating Emotional Adjustment

How can parents tell whether their child is developing well emotionally? Between the first and fourth birthdays, the most important clue is the child's relationship with his or her parents. The early pattern established between parents and child will shape the child's relationships later in life as a friend, a co-worker, and a spouse.

These are signs of a healthy relationship between parents and child:

- The child seeks approval and praise from parents.
- The child turns to parents for comfort and help.
- The child tells parents about significant events so that they may share in the joy and sorrow.
- The child accepts limits and discipline without unusual resistance.

Another indicator of emotional adjustment is a child's relationship with siblings. Some quarreling with brothers and sisters is bound to occur. However, the child who is continuously and bitterly at odds with brothers and sisters, in spite of parents' efforts to ease the friction, may need counseling. If emotional problems are dealt with early, it can make a difference for a lifetime.

SECTION 12-1 REVIEW

✔ Check Your Understanding

1. Explain what it means to be self-centered.
2. What is negativism? What does negativism in a toddler indicate?
3. What changes occur in emotions between three and three and one-half years?
4. What children are more likely than others to feel anger?
5. What is separation anxiety?
6. What emotional problems do nightmares often reveal?
7. What individual factors affect a child's emotional development?
8. Distinguish between self-concept and self-esteem.

Putting Knowledge Into Practice

1. **Comparing.** Compare two- and two-and-one-half-year-olds in terms of how they handle being told what to do.
2. **Applying.** Suppose a toddler who was toilet trained begins to have accidents after a new baby enters the family. What would you do?
3. **Observing and Participating.** Write down your self-concept—what you think you are like. With each idea you write down, try to determine when in your life it arose.

ASSESS

CHECKING COMPREHENSION

Have students answer the Check Your Understanding Questions. Answers appear at the bottom of this page.

EVALUATION

Give students the Section 12-1 Quiz in the *Teacher Resource Guide*.

RETEACHING

1. Assign Reteaching Activities, page 38.
2. Have students write ten questions based on the section, exchange questions with a partner, and answer the questions they receive.

ENRICHMENT

Have students research the importance of a positive self-concept for teens. What problems are related to a negative one?

EXTENSION

Have students visit the library to find advice on how to handle temper tantrums. Have them bring their findings to the class and debate the different suggestions.

CLOSE

Have students make a chart summarizing the emotional characteristics of each age described in the text.

ANSWERS TO SECTION 12-1 REVIEW

1. To be focused on oneself.
2. Doing the opposite of what others want. *Indicates:* desire for independence, frustration, separate identity.
3. Three's are sunny and cheerful; three-and-a-half's can be fearful.
4. Those who are insecure or lack self-control or consistent guidance.
5. Fear of being away from familiar caregivers or normal environment.
6. Separation anxiety.
7. Individual experience; temperament.
8. *Concept:* What you think you're like. *Esteem:* How you value yourself.

CAREER OPPORTUNITIES

Introducing the Feature

Ask students whether they think a clown can make a difference in the life of a child. Then ask them to consider the case of a clown visiting a sick child in the hospital. Does this example change their response?

Answers to
CONNECTING SCHOOL TO CAREER

1. **Possible responses:** Softer because it is likely to be a small space and the young children may be upset by loud behavior.

2. **Possible responses:** Yes, because there are more people who want to be clowns than there is demand for them.

Applying What You've Learned

Ask: What can caregivers do "to help children see the magic and fun of life"? Have students develop a list of five activities to do or places to visit with a child from one to three. Have each student present these suggestions to the class and discuss how enjoyable they would be to children.

Ask: What would be the advantages and disadvantages of being an entrepreneur? Of working part-time?

CAREER OPPORTUNITIES
Clown

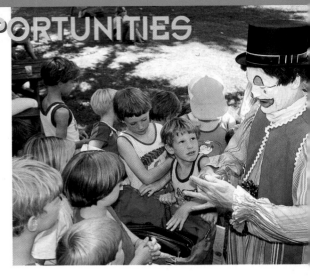

A CONVERSATION WITH DAVE JACKSON

How did you become interested in being a clown? I saw the circus when I was a child. I just loved the clowns—they were so funny. I guess the experience stayed with me.

What are the tasks and responsibilities of a clown? Well, to entertain! I try to help children see the magic and fun of life. What I do depends on where I'm working. At a birthday party, we're in a small space, and I'll do simple things like make balloon animals or paint the children's faces—if they want. At a child care center, I'll try to get the children involved in dancing games. In a larger setting, like a fair, I'll do funny routines with my dog.

What is the work environment like? As you can see, I work in many different places—in people's homes, in centers, or at county fairs. I also visit children in hospitals.

What are the working hours like? I work part-time as a clown and part-time at another job. My clown work is usually a few days a week, but it varies from week to week.

What aptitudes are needed to be a clown? You need creativity, a sense of humor, and a real interest in children. For clowning, you need good physical skills because sometimes we do pantomime. The actions need to be clear so children can understand them.

CLOWN

Education and Training. Many clowns take courses in clown or acting schools.
Career Outlook. The demand for clowns is expected to remain steady, though the number of people trying to become clowns is expected to grow.

CONNECTING SCHOOL TO CAREER

1. **Personal Qualities.** Should a clown performing at a three-year-old's birthday party use a loud or soft voice? Why?

2. **Thinking Skills.** Is clowning a very competitive career? Why or why not?

392 UNIT 4: The Child from One to Three

Building Career Skills

Basic Skills. Have students write a training manual for clowns based on what they've read in the feature. The manual might cover such topics as: aptitudes and characteristics needed; skills needed; training; activities to perform with children; locations or events at which clowns can perform; business aspects (scheduling, handling payment, and so on). You could divide the class into groups and have each group take one topic.

SECTION 12-2

Social Development from One to Three

The period between ages one and four is also an important time for social development. In these years, children develop attitudes and skills that remain with them throughout their lives. Their experiences in the family help them learn how to live with others.

KEY TERMS

cooperative play
parallel play
socialization

OBJECTIVES:

- Describe patterns of social development from ages one to three.
- Explain how children make friends.
- Give principles for guiding toddlers.

General Social Patterns

Young children gradually learn to get along with other people, first in their own families and then in groups. This process is called **socialization**. Through this process, children can be expected to learn certain social skills at different ages. Of course, as with other areas of development, individual differences may influence these patterns.

Observing & Participating

Divide the class into groups, purposefully including in each group students who do not know each other very well. Tell students to spend ten minutes "getting acquainted." At the end of the time, reconvene the class and hold a discussion about the different methods students used and observed among their peers for getting to know new people. Ask students to keep these methods in mind as they read the section.

SECTION 12-2 RESOURCES

Teacher Resource Guide
- Lesson Plan Organizer, p. 65
- Section 12-2 Quiz, p. 165

Student Motivation Kit
- Observ. & Case Studies, (case study) p. 117
- Reteaching Activity, p. 39
- Enrichment, p. 36
- Teen Parenting Skills, pp. 102-104

Student Workbook
- Study Guide, pp. 103-106
- Guiding a Child to Desirable Behavior, pp. 108-109

Transparency Package
- CT-36 Sequence of Play

Effective Instruction CD-ROM

FOCUS

MOTIVATOR

Have students think back to their very first friendship. Do they remember who the person was? How did the friendship begin? Are they still friends with that person? Invite volunteers to share their memories with the class.

VOCABULARY ACTIVITY

Ask volunteers to define the words cooperate (*to act or work with others*) and parallel (*everywhere equally distant and not meeting*). Then challenge students to come up with definitions for cooperative play and parallel play.

COMPREHENSION CHECK

1. How do family experiences achieve the socialization of a child? (*By teaching how to live with others.*)
2. What social skills does a two-year-old typically exhibit? (*Good at understanding and interacting with main caregiver; able to communicate increasingly well; beginning to understand idea of sharing.*)
3. How is child's self-centeredness apparent in the understanding of fairness? (*They are mostly concerned with what is fair to them.*)
4. At what age do parents begin to be less important in a child's social life? (*Age three.*)

ACTIVITIES

Critical Thinking Activity

Interpreting Information. Review with students the emotional state of an eighteen-month-old (*self-centered, prone to negativism*). How do these emotional characteristics surface in a child's social development at this age? **L1**

| VISUAL LEARNING | Using the Photograph *Answer:* Parallel play. |

Eighteen Months

At eighteen months, children begin developing independence from the family. For most children, the closest relationships are—and remain—those with family members. However, toddlers need to learn about the outside world. This may mean trips to the playground or other opportunities to be with children and adults who are not part of the family. Some children attend child care all day.

At about eighteen months, there is little real interaction between children, even when they are playing in the same area. Instead, children engage in **parallel play**, meaning that they play independently near, but not actually with, another child. More than one child may want—and grab for—the same toy, but the children aren't really playing with one another.

Eighteen-month-olds often seem to treat other people more as objects than as human begins. At this stage, the toddler is intent on satisfying strong desires without regard for anyone who interferes. There may be conflicts over toys that result in screaming, hitting, biting, or hair pulling.

The child this age can understand that his or her actions have consequences for others, though. This understanding is limited to actions that have direct, immediate, and physical results, however. When an eighteen-month-old hits another child, and that child cries, the first child can see that he or she caused the upset.

Parents look forward to when their children begin to play with other children, since this is a step in the child's social development. Many parents are surprised, then, when eighteen-month-olds play not *with* but *alongside* children their own age. **What is this kind of play called?**

394 UNIT 4: The Child from One to Three

Parenting in *Action*

Caregivers can foster social development by providing different play experiences:
- For one-year-olds, talk to the baby about the names of the toys or their characteristics (color, shape).
- For two-year-olds, provide a child with toys that require some decision making, such as shape sorters. Begin to teach taking turns.
- For three-year-olds, encourage activities that allow the child to play with others without your involvement.

Two Years

By age two, children already have an impressive list of social skills. A two-year-old is especially good at understanding and interacting with his or her main caregiver. The child can read that person's moods and gauge what kind of behavior he or she will accept. As speech develops, the young child is increasingly able to communicate with others.

Two-year-olds find it is fun to have someone to play with, although they usually still engage in parallel play. At two, they begin to be able to understand the ideas of sharing or taking turns. Children this age like to please other people. Occasionally, they are willing to put the wishes of someone else (usually an adult) above their own wishes.

Two and One-Half Years

The negativism that is characteristic of the child at two-and-one-half carries into the child's social relationships. During this stage, a child who refuses to do anything for one person may do things happily for another. The reasons for these different responses are impossible to understand.

At this age, children are beginning to learn about the rights of others. They can respond to the idea of fairness—though at first, they are more concerned with what is fair to them. Social play is still parallel and works best with only two children. Squabbles are frequent, but brief. Children forget them quickly and resume their play.

Three Years

Most three-year-olds are sunny and agreeable. This shows in their relationships

What type of play is shown by these children? At about what age do children begin this kind of play?

with others. People are important to children of this age. A three-year-old will share, help, or do things another person's way—just to please someone.

Three-year-olds begin **cooperative play**, actually playing with one another. They build sand castles together, push toy tractors down the same roads, and park their toy cars side by side in the same area—with little friction. They can also work together in small groups to build with blocks, act out events for doll families, and fit puzzles together.

Parents, though still very important to three-year-olds, are no longer all-powerful in children's social lives. Most children this age seek friends on their own. They may prefer some companions over others.

Three and One-Half Years

By three and one-half, children's play becomes more complex and includes more conversation. Disagreements with play-

CHAPTER 12: Emotional and Social Development from One to Three **395**

DID *You* **Know?**

Play Personalities. Toddlers often show one of two opposing types of behavior when they are with other children. Some toddlers will give up every toy they have in order to avoid conflict. Others will monopolize every toy in sight. In each case, caregivers can help children learn appropriate negotiating skills—either to share more willingly or to give up less easily.

COMPREHENSION CHECK

1. How do three-and-a-half-year-olds typically solve conflicts? (*Through conversation and negotiation.*)
2. What evidence can you find that a three-and-a-half-year-old is less self-centered than before? (*They are more likely to compare themselves with others.*)

ACTIVITIES

Critical Thinking Activity

Analyzing. Have students develop a list of toys that would encourage cooperative play in children. Have them share their suggestions and discuss them. **L1**

VISUAL LEARNING	Using the Illustration

Have students answer the following questions: To whom does an eighteen-month-old direct most of his conversation? (*Himself.*) At what age does this change? (*Two and one-half years.*) How is a child's increasing socialization shown in patterns of talking? (*As the child becomes older, he directs less of his talk to adults and more to peers.*)

Patterns of Talking

From eighteen months to four years, the patterns of children's conversations change. The thick arrow shows the person they speak with the most. The thinner arrow shows other targets of talk. If there is no arrow, the toddler directs little or no talk to that person.

Eighteen Months

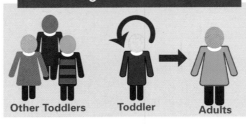

Other Toddlers   Toddler   Adults

Two Years

Two and One-Half Years

Three Years

Three and One-Half Years

Four Years

396   UNIT 4: The Child from One to Three

LEARNING STYLES	Spatial

Have students create a chart, graphic organizer, concept web, or other visual device to summarize the general social patterns exhibited by children from eighteen months to three and one-half years. Visuals should provide the main points under each subheading in the textbook. Suggest that students use their charts as study aids.

mates occur less often. Because children this age enjoy the company of others, they realize they must share toys and put up with some things they don't like in order to have it.

Children this age can use several different strategies to solve these conflicts. Jorge tried to take a block that was nearer to Ramon, who was also playing with blocks. When Ramon said, "That's my block," Jorge replied, "Oh, OK" and put it down. Julia and Latishia were playing with trucks. When Julia reached for one of Latishia's trucks, Latishia objected and then said "You can have it if you give me that one of yours."

There is an increasing ability to evaluate friendships. For example, a three-and-one-half-year-old may say, "I don't like to have Kevin come here. He doesn't play nice."

Close friends begin to exclude others, although most friendships don't last.

Children this age also take more notice of what other children are like. They become more likely to compare themselves to other children—not always to their own advantage. One day, Allison asked her mother, "Why does Libby always win when we race?" Her mother agreed that Libby was faster, but pointed out things that Allison did well. In this way, she acknowledged that Allison wasn't as skilled as the other child in one area but had other skills of her own.

Making Friends

The ability to make friends is important to normal social development. A child who is comfortable and friendly with others and who has at least one friend at a time is usually developing normally. However, if a child is unable or unwilling to make friends, try to discover the cause and take steps to help.

Even very young children need contact with other people. This is how they learn the give-and-take of socializing. Sometimes a caregiver needs to help a child learn what to say or how to act to join others in play. Those who begin to play with others early aren't as likely to be afraid of other children. They learn to cope with the occasional blows and snatching of other one- and two-year-olds.

Three-year-olds begin to develop friendships. They also begin to compare themselves to others. *What impact might that have on their self-esteem?*

CHAPTER 12: Emotional and Social Development from One to Three **397**

Discussion Activity

Ask: How does living with siblings contribute to social development? Ask for examples. **L1**

VISUAL LEARNING | Using the Photograph

Possible response: Self-esteem could suffer if they only focus on areas where friends perform better than they do.

The Developing Brain

 Gender Differences in Play

When playing, boys and girls often exhibit differing behaviors and preferences for different toys. New brain imaging techniques, such as the Functional Magnetic Resonance Imaging (FMRI) and the Positron Emission Tomography (PET) scans, have revealed that brain activity in males and females differs. Males show patterns that lead to more aggressive behavior and better understanding of spatial relationships. Female brain patterns show a tendency toward better language skills and susceptibility to depression. Researchers still aren't sure, however, whether these brain patterns are inborn or the result of environmental influences.

Observing & Participating

While watching a group of three-year-olds at play, the actions of an aggressive child will stand out. Instead of asking to borrow a toy, this child will grab it. Whereas a parent or caregiver might perceive this behavior as a problem, the aggressive child sees it merely as a solution. Have students brainstorm ways to guide such a child to share. For example, a parent might say, "I see you really wanted to play with Jesse's toy. Next time, ask to borrow it or offer a toy you have in trade for the one you want."

COMPREHENSION CHECK

1. Why might children who have only adult companions have difficulty interacting with children their own age? (*Because adults are more polite and considerate, the child doesn't learn to deal with the rougher world of child's play.*)
2. How should a caregiver handle a conflict between two toddlers? (*If no one is being hurt, allow the children to solve the problem themselves. If intervention is necessary, try to guide the children to a solution rather than imposing one.*)

ACTIVITIES

History Activity

Have students research the social life of young children during another period in history, such as the colonial era or the Victorian era. Ask students to present their findings in a written or oral report.

VISUAL LEARNING	Using the Photograph

Answers will vary but should reflect effective responses.

ISSUES IN
CHILDREN'S HEALTH

Misbehavior. The child who is misbehaving more than normal may not be feeling well. A frustrating inability to communicate or understand physical symptoms of illness, as well as the bad humor that results from not feeling well, can push many children to misbehave.

Give an example of a situation when caregivers should take action when children these ages disagree. What action would you take?

Children who have only adult companions may have difficulty interacting with others their own age. Adults are more polite and considerate than children. Each child needs to learn to enjoy the rough-and-tumble companionship of other children. If this learning is delayed until school age, the child may face a difficult adjustment. At five or six, feelings are more easily hurt.

All children sometimes have disagreements and arguments. Whether or not a caregiver should step in depends on the situation. If two children are relatively evenly matched and there is no physical or emotional harm being done, the caregiver can simply observe the situation. Children need to learn how to solve their problems.

If the situation is more hurtful to one child, the caregiver will probably need to step in and help the children solve the problem. It is best for the children if the caregiver doesn't impose a solution but instead guides the children to find one for themselves.

398 Unit 4: The Child from One to Three

Imaginary Friends

In this period, many children begin to have imaginary friends. Some have the same friend for a long period of time—from several months to a year. Others have different friends. Some have imaginary animals rather than friends.

Imaginary friends may start as early as age two. They are more common from ages three to four. In that year, children have rich imaginations and are interested in fantasy and reality.

Some parents are concerned that children invent imaginary friends because they are unable to make real friends. They worry that an imaginary friend is a sign of unhappiness or problems coping with life.

In fact, an imaginary friend can be a very helpful way for a child to experiment with different feelings. Some children use an imaginary friend as a way of working through their negative feelings. For others, the friend mirrors everything the child does or experiences. Then the child talks to the family about how the imaginary friend felt about these experiences. In this way, the child finds a way to examine his or her own thoughts and feelings.

Usually imaginary friends fade away. Crystal simply stopped talking about her

---

DID You Know?

Play Groups. One way to help a toddler learn to get along with others is through play groups—informal gatherings of caregivers and children in a home setting. Many parents find that setting a scheduled time for playing with others eases the child into a social life. One suggestion when establishing a play group: avoid groups of three children, since two will almost always pair off, leaving the third to feel left out.

friend when she started school. Paul had an imaginary friend when he was three, but he was gone by age four. There is no cause for concern unless the imaginary friend continues into adolescence.

Guidance Guidelines

The purpose of guidance is to help children learn self-discipline—the ability to control their own actions. There is no single best approach to guidance. Parents should consider the individual personality of each child, as well as their own personal beliefs. They should also consider each child's age and stage of development and understanding. Different approaches may be especially effective at various ages.

- **Eight to twelve months.** At this age, inappropriate behavior can usually be controlled by distraction. If the baby is chewing on a newspaper, for example, you might jingle a bright rattle in front of the child. As the rattle catches the baby's attention, simply move the newspaper out of the way.
- **Twelve to fifteen months.** Distraction and physically removing the child from forbidden activities or places work best. For example, Jared was fascinated by the lawn mower and tried to follow it around the yard. His older sister picked Jared up and took him into the house, saying, "Let's see if we can find the book about the teddy bear."

- **Fifteen to twenty-four months.** Children this age require distraction, removal, and spoken restrictions. Hassan started playing with toy cars on the driveway, where a repair truck was parked. His father said, "Let's take your cars into the backyard. You'll have more room there. The driveway isn't a safe place to play."
- **Two to three years.** By the age of two, children are better at responding to spoken commands and explanations. Two-year-olds can more easily understand adults' reasoning. Caregivers who explain their reasons get better results than those who only issue sharp commands. When she saw that her two-and-one-half-year-old was still not dressed, Kerri's mother said, "Kerri, you need to get dressed now because Grandma will be here soon to go shopping with us. We can't go unless we are ready."
- **Three to four years.** Three-year-olds take reasonable, loving guidance more readily than children of other ages.

Children learn how to behave as a result of parents' guidance. *Why is it a good idea for parents to discuss guidance issues together? How should parents interact with other caregivers?*

Ask the Experts

Introducing the Feature

Read to students the adage "An ounce of prevention is worth a pound of cure." **Ask:** How is this related to the issue of guiding behavior?

Answers to Thinking It Through
1. *Possible response:* "Take your shoes off at the door because they are muddy."
2. *Possible response:* It is fine to give children explanations, but they should be brief and simple

Applying What You've Learned

Divide the class into five groups. Assign each group one child development authority: Dr. Benjamin Spock; Penelope Leach, Dr. T. Berry Brazelton, Dr. James Dobson, Dr. William Sears. Assign each group the same common behavioral issue such as tantrums or biting to research their expert's views. Have a class discussion comparing the advice. Which approach do students think would be most effective? Why?

ACTIVITIES

Critical Thinking Activity

Supporting an Opinion. Ask students to consider the following statement: "Although sharing is a useful social skill, it is not essential; it is possible for an adult to function in society without ever having learned to share." Have students write whether they agree or disagree with this idea and use examples to support their position. **L2**

Ask the Experts

Jacqueline Mault
Director of Special Services for the Toppenish School District in Toppenish, Washington

GUIDING *Toddlers' Behavior*

Q How can I guide my toddler's behavior?

A One of the best ways of guiding a toddler's—or any child's—behavior is by setting a good example. Children learn by imitating.

As toddlers grow older, they become increasingly able to take verbal direction. Caregivers get the best results by speaking in certain ways:

- **Be clear and specific.** *Speak to the child using very specific language. To say "I want you to behave at dinner" does not tell a child how to act. It's more effective to say, "I want you to sit still at the table" or "Remember to use your knife and fork."*

- **Limit the instructions.** *Focus on just one behavior at a time. You can't expect a young child to sit still at the table __and__ eat with a knife and fork __and__ stop talking with a mouth full of food __and__ use the napkin. Work on one behavior. When the child learns that, it is time to move to the next one.*

- **Use positive words.** *Avoid saying "don't." Tell the child what he or she __can__ do, not what is not allowed.*

- **Keep it simple.** *Use as few words as possible while still being clear. Toddlers can't remember too many directions at once. Some caregivers give lengthy reasons, explaining why they gave a child a certain direction. Give the next direction after the child has completed the first.*

- **Be firm.** *State the direction firmly and without apologizing so the child knows you mean it.*

Thinking It Through

1. Reword the following direction to make it more effective: "Don't track mud into the house."
2. Does this advice mean a caregiver shouldn't give any explanations for a direction? Why or why not?

400 UNIT 4: The Child from One to Three

ISSUES IN TEEN PARENTING Teen parents, as well as many older parents, won't always have the emotional maturity to handle a toddler's negativism, tantrums, or stubbornness. They may believe the child is being deliberately naughty or take negativism as a personal rejection. Point out the fallacies of these beliefs. Discuss how the family interaction is apt to change during the toddler years. How can teens cope with a negative toddler? How might the development of language skills affect the child's behavior?

They like to please, and they may be quick to remind a parent that they are obedient. Marcus came inside on a rainy day and said, "I remembered to wear my boots today. See my clean shoes? I'm a good boy, right?"

Promoting Sharing

One of the first social skills that children learn is to share, and that learning begins at this stage. Caregivers can help children develop this skill in various ways:

- Lead children to activities in which they need to share—or at least take turns—such as the seesaw or going down a slide.
- Limit the materials on hand for an activity so that sharing or taking turns is required. If there is only one pair of scissors, for instance, children will have to take turns.
- When you're handing out snacks, use the children to pass them to one another. That gives children an opportunity to practice sharing.
- Make clear what behavior you're trying to encourage. Call it "sharing" or "taking turns."

Some toys are very special to a child. They may have a strong emotional attachment to a stuffed animal or be very pleased about a new birthday present. It can be very difficult for the child to share these objects. Sometimes, too, there is legitimate concern that another child may accidentally break it. If the toy is visible, however, odds are that another child will see it and become interested in it. In these cases, it might be a good idea to put that toy away when other children visit.

SECTION 12-2 REVIEW

✔ Check Your Understanding

1. What is socialization?
2. Compare parallel and cooperative play. At about what age does cooperative play begin?
3. How do two-and-one-half-year-olds often show negativism in their social relationships?
4. How do children change in the way they handle disagreements from eighteen months to three and one-half years?
5. Why is it important to give young children opportunities to play with friends?
6. Distraction is effective for children of which ages?
7. What can parents do to promote sharing?

Putting Knowledge Into Practice

1. **Synthesizing.** Jeremy has an imaginary friend. If you were his parent, what would you do?
2. **Applying.** Eric and Chris, both two years old, were playing when they suddenly began to argue. What would you do?
3. **Observing and Participating.** Visit a park or a child care center and observe one or more groups of one- to three-year-olds. Report to the class on how they played.

CHAPTER 12: Emotional and Social Development from One to Three **401**

CHECKING COMPREHENSION

Have students answer the Check Your Understanding questions. Answers appear at the bottom of this page.

EVALUATION

Give students the Section 12-2 Quiz in the *Teacher Resource Guide.*

RETEACHING

1. Assign Reteaching Activities, page 39.
2. Have students write a paragraph contrasting the social development of eighteen-month-olds and of three-and-one-half-year-olds.

ENRICHMENT

Have students assume the role of an advice columnist and respond to a parent concerned about a three-year-old who often fights with children.

EXTENSION

Invite a child care worker to speak to the class about the social behavior of children one to three. Have students prepare questions in advance.

CLOSE

Have students write an ending for this statement: "To develop social relationships, toddlers must learn to . . ."

Tie a large towel around a student volunteer's neck. Have the student eat a serving of rice or macaroni from a bowl, using a large cooking spoon held in the non-dominant hand. When he or she is finished, ask the student to describe the experience. **Ask:** How is this similar to a child's learning to eat?

TEACH

COMPREHENSION CHECK

1. How can a caregiver minimize the mess when a child is learning self-feeding? (*Use unbreakable dishes, child-sized utensils, and a cup with a spill-proof lid.*)
2. What features make self-dressing easier? (*Loose clothing; elastic waistbands; front openings; large buttons, zippers, and tape and loop fasteners.*)
3. What is the best way to persuade a child to follow good grooming habits? (*Display good grooming habits yourself.*)

Parenting With Care

Encouraging Independence

Between one and four, children long to be more independent.

Caregivers can help them achieve that. Of course, caregivers still have the main responsibility of meeting a child's basic needs. They can, however, help toddlers and preschoolers help themselves grow toward independence.

Self-Feeding
- Expect—and accept— some messiness as a child learns self-feeding. Minimize that mess with unbreakable dishes and a child-sized spoon and fork. Serve food in small servings. Use a cup with a spill-proof lid in this learning stage.
- Choose foods that are easy to handle and eat. Cut food into bite-sized pieces before serving.
- Be sure the child is comfortable. For eating at a table, use a high chair with the tray removed or a booster seat to raise the child to the right height.

Self-Dressing
- Choose clothes that are easy to put on and take off. Look for roomy shirts that slip on easily. Elastic waistbands make pants, skirts, and shorts easier to handle. Clothes with buttons or zippers in the front are more convenient than those with back openings.
- Fasteners often cause problems. Hook-and-loop fasteners, large buttons, and zippers are easiest for toddlers to manage.
- If a dressing task is too difficult for the child to do completely, let him or her do at least one part of it. Pulling up a zipper or slipping a foot into a shoe can be the first step toward learning a more complex task.

Grooming Skills
- Provide the child with his or her own towel, washcloth, brush or comb, and toothbrush. Be sure that all are within easy reach.
- A small stool can help small children cope with adult-sized bathrooms.
- Establish grooming routines, and help the child follow them every day.

RESOURCES TO EXPLORE

Guides to Raising Children One to Three. Encourage students to explore the library for books that offer advice to parents on coping with and caring for a toddler. *What to Expect the Toddler Years* by Arlene Eisenberg, Heidi E. Murkoff, and Sandee E. Hathaway, is a good, all-round reference book. *The Girlfriend's Guide to Toddlers* by Vicki Iovine, geared to mothers, is a humorous and helpful source that includes chapters on eating and fashion.

- Set a good example yourself. The child is more likely to wash hands before eating if you do it, too.

Helping Others
- Putting away toys can start as a game. Be sure there is adequate storage space within the child's reach.
- Let young children help with simple chores around the house, such as sweeping, carrying laundry, and setting the table.

Above all, remember to be patient. A child's efforts will always be slower and less efficient than your own, but learning can't take place without practice.

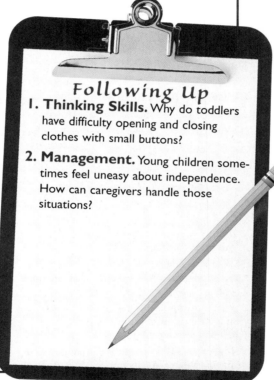

Following Up
1. **Thinking Skills.** Why do toddlers have difficulty opening and closing clothes with small buttons?

2. **Management.** Young children sometimes feel uneasy about independence. How can caregivers handle those situations?

403

ACTIVITIES

Teamwork Activity
Have students work in groups to plan an "Independence Seminar" for toddlers modeled on the seminars that adults sometimes attend to enhance their careers. Divide the class into four groups. Have each group address one of the four areas discussed in the feature. Group members should outline ways they could teach these skills to children one to three. **L3**

VISUAL LEARNING | **Using the Photographs** Have students look at each photo in the feature and describe how the children are showing independence. What have caregivers done to give the child these opportunities?

CLOSE

1. Have students explain how a caregiver can respond when a toddler says, "Me do it."
2. Extension. Have students research and report on products for grooming, dressing, and eating that are designed to teach self-help skills.

Answers to Following Up
1. Their small motor skills are not yet fully developed.
2. *Possible response:* By giving them more help with feeding, dressing, and grooming at those times.

CHECKING COMPREHENSION

Use the Summary and the Reviewing the Facts questions to help students go over the most important ideas in Chapter 12. Encourage students to ask questions and add details.

Answers to Reviewing the Facts

1. *Eighteen months:* Negativism. *Two:* More patient and affectionate. *Two and one-half:* Difficult period; child resists direction. *Three:* Sunny and cheerful. *Three and one-half:* Fearful.
2. *Young:* More likely to be physical. *Older and age three:* Are more likely to use words.
3. Separation anxiety.
4. Competition between brothers and sisters for parents' affection and attention.
5. By age two.
6. *Parallel:* Children play alongside but not with each other. *Cooperative:* Children play together; begins to appear around age three.
7. So they can learn how to get along with other children.
8. Opportunity to experiment with and examine different emotions and thoughts.
9. Promote activities that require sharing; limit materials on hand so they have to share; have children pass out snacks; label as "sharing."

Summary

✔ Young children pass through emotional ups and downs but become increasingly able to control emotions. (Section 12-1)

✔ Toddlers show negativism as they try to exert control over their lives. (Section 12-1)

✔ Individual differences affect emotional development. (Section 12-1)

✔ As they grow, young children become more interested in other children. (Section 12-2)

✔ Learning to be friends helps toddlers and preschoolers develop skills they use later. (Section 12-2)

✔ Caregivers can help toddlers learn to share. (Section 12-2)

Reviewing the Facts

1. Describe the emotional ups and downs during ages one to three. (Section 12-1)
2. Contrast how younger and older toddlers and three-year-olds express anger. (Section 12-1)
3. What concern often underlies children's fears? (Section 12-1)
4. What is sibling rivalry? (Section 12-1)
5. About when do children begin to show empathy? (Section 12-1)
6. Explain the difference between parallel and cooperative play. About what age does cooperative play begin? (Section 12-2)
7. Why is it important for children to spend time with other children and not just adults? (Section 12-2)
8. How can a child benefit from having an imaginary friend? (Section 12-2)

9. What techniques can caregivers use to teach children to share? (Section 12-2)

Thinking Critically

1. **Synthesizing.** Rosalie often tells her son Eric, "You're always messy" and "You never do anything right." How can such statements, when said frequently, affect his self-concept?
2. **Drawing Conclusions.** Are all children in a family likely to have the same temperament? Why or why not? What impact will that have on how parents interact with each of the children and the children as a group?
3. **Diagramming.** Make a time line that charts the typical social development of a child from one to three.

Taking Action

1. **Living with Differences.** Claire and Carrie are twins. Claire finds it very easy to switch from one activity to another, but Carrie needs more time. If pressured to move faster, she has a tantrum. What can their parents do? *(Leadership)*
2. **Learning to Get Along.** Draw up a set of a few simple rules about getting along with other people that you think two- and

CONNECTIONS

three-year-olds can—and should—follow. Word the rules so that the children could understand and follow them. *(Communication)*

Cross-Curricular Connections

1. **Language Arts.** Write an objective description of a scene in which two toddlers at a child care center become involved in a conflict over toys. Write from the point of view of a center worker who describes what happened and what he or she did about it.

2. **Social Studies.** Explain how a child's culture and how his or her caregivers handle their own emotions could influence the ways the child expresses emotions.

Workplace Connections

1. **Interpersonal Skills.** You and a partner should each write down six negative statements that a caregiver could make about a toddler or preschooler. Exchange papers and turn each negative statement into a more positive one. In what ways would this skill help in working with adults?

2. **Information Systems.** Create a poster that would remind child care center workers about how to guide children's behavior.

3. **Resources.** Discuss how working parents with low incomes can find quality, affordable care for young children. What obstacles may they face? Predict possible consequences of inadequate care.

Family and Community Connections

1. **Guiding an Only Child.** Children with siblings have many opportunities to learn to share in the home. How can parents of an only child encourage the child to learn sharing?

2. **Handing Tantrums.** Ask a parent to describe how he or she once handled a child's tantrum. Report your findings to the class and evaluate them to determine which are the best techniques.

Technology Connections

1. **Internet.** Search on the Internet for advice to parents in handling any of the following topics: temper tantrums, separation anxiety, sibling rivalry, nighttime fears. Keep track of your sources. Compare the advice you found with others in your class. What might be the reasons for the differences?

2. **Television.** Some people argue that violent television shows and movies teach children to settle conflicts in violent ways. Do you think that the content of young children's programs should be controlled? Why or why not?

EVALUATION

1. Use the reproducible Chapter 12 Test in the *Teacher Resource Guide*, or construct your own test using the **Exam***View*® Test Generator.

2. For an alternative assessment, assign the Chapter 12 activity in the *Authentic Assessment* section of the *Teacher Resource Guide*.

ENRICHMENT

Assign students either of the two enrichment activities in the *Enrichment Activities* booklet in the *Student Motivation Kit*.

EXTENSION

Have students research several issues of parenting magazines and compile a scrapbook of worthwhile, informative articles and tips for handling toddlers.

CLOSE

Have students write a description of a typical situation involving a child from one to three and a caregiver. The situation could be a conflict or an attempt to guide the child. Have them exchange situations with a partner and write an explanation of how they would respond.

CHAPTER 13 RESOURCES

Teacher Resource Guide
- Chapter 13 Test, p. 172
- Authentic Assessment, p. 281

Student Motivation Kit
- Observations, pp. 51-52
- Creative Activities, pp. 45-69, 75-79

Transparency Package
- CT-38 to CT-40

Effective Instruction CD-ROM

CHAPTER 13 **OVERVIEW**

In **Section 13-1**, students learn about different methods of learning, how children from one to three develop certain concepts, and the seven basic elements of intellectual activity.

In **Section 13-2**, students learn how to encourage learning. They also examine language development, especially development of speech patterns and common speech problems.

CHAPTER 13 **OBJECTIVES**

After completing Chapter 13, students will be able to:

- Describe methods of learning and how children develop an understanding of concepts.
- Explain the seven basic intellectual activities.
- Suggest ways to encourage young children to learn.
- Describe how speech develops.

CHAPTER 13

Intellectual Development from One to Three

406 UNIT 4: The Child from One to Three

RESOURCES TO EXPLORE

Kindermusik. Kindermusik is program of music and movement specially designed for children from birth to seven. The program claims to contribute to the musical, physical, social, emotional, and cognitive development of children, as well as aiding language development. Students can find out more about the program and the research on which it is based by contacting Kindermusik International, P.O. Box 26575, Greensboro, NC 27415. Their Website address is www.kindermusik.com

First, Drew, age three and one-half, molded the clay into a flat, round shape. Then he rolled up a smaller ball and attached it to the top of the first shape. He put two small cylinders of clay on the front and then picked up his creation. "Emperor," he said, "the new Star Avenger has been completed." As he spoke, he moved his clay spaceship through the air, making zooming sounds.

Drew put down his spacecraft and began to make something else. This time he made a long cylinder of clay and attached another piece of clay to it. He picked that creation up. "The rebel attack force nears the imperial base," he said. Then he picked up his first ship again and began to maneuver the two clay models through the air.

> **"He moved his clay spaceship through the air, making zooming sounds."**

- Take an imaginary walk with a toddler through your neighborhood or community. Make a list of the people you would meet, the sounds you would hear, and the sights you would see. Describe how you might use the walk to encourage the child's intellectual development.
- Ask students to look at the photograph. **Ask:** What is the expression on the child's face? What does it indicate?

USING THE SCENARIO After students have read the opening scenario, explain that imaginative play usually begins around age two. Parents can encourage such play by providing ordinary materials that children can transform into spaceships, animals, and the like. Modeling clay is one such material. Ask students to suggest other items that could be used to foster imaginative play. Write their responses on the chalkboard and discuss each one as a class.

KEY TO ABILITY LEVELS Each section gives skill-building activities. Each activity has been labeled for use with students of various learning styles and abilities.

L1 Level 1 activities are basic activities and should be within the range of all students.

L2 Level 2 activities are average activities and should be within the range of average and above average students.

L3 Level 3 activities are challenging activities designed for the ability range of above average students.

SECTION 13-1 RESOURCES

Teacher Resource Guide
- Lesson Plan Organizer, p. 66
- Section 13-1 Quiz, p. 170

Student Motivation Kit
- Observ. & Case Studies (case study), p. 118
- Reteaching Activity, p. 40
- Enrichment, pp. 37-38
- Nurturing Brain Development, pp. 34-36

Student Workbook
- Study Guide, pp. 110-112
- Planning Activities, p. 113

Transparency Package
- CT-38 How Do Children Learn?

Effective Instruction CD-ROM

FOCUS

MOTIVATOR

Write on the chalkboard: "I'll never do that again!" Ask students to offer examples of times they've used the phrase. Most incidents will illustrate trial-and-error or incidental learning. Discuss their advantages and disadvantages as methods of learning.

VOCABULARY ACTIVITY

Incidental is derived from "incident" and means occurring in connection with some other event. Thus, incidental learning results from something else. In contrast, "to direct" is to show the way; directed learning involves being taught.

Understanding Learning and the Mind

Tiffany put the toy stethoscope on. She bent over the doll to listen to its heart. Then she looked into its ears. As she put her tools away, she smiled at the doll and said, "You healthy girl!"

KEY TERMS

concepts
creativity
directed learning
imitation
incidental learning
intelligence
trial-and-error learning

OBJECTIVES:

- Identify ways children learn.
- Explain how children develop concepts.
- Explain how one- to three-year-olds develop in several areas of intellectual activity.

The Role of Intelligence

Tiffany, age two, recently had a checkup. A few days later, she checked on the health of her doll. In the process, she revealed the growing power of her own mind.

A one-year-old is still much like a baby, just learning to make sense of the world. In contrast, a child of three and one-half talks freely, solves simple problems, and constantly seeks out new things to learn.

408 UNIT 4: The Child from One to Three

Observing & Participating

Bring to class the following items: a family portrait, a variety of educational toys, and signs that read, "Way to go!" and "You can do it!" Display the items. Then ask students what these items represent. (Families, play-things, and encouragement.) Ask: How can the ideas that these things represent promote intellectual growth? How might the absence of these items affect intellectual growth?

Intelligence is the ability to interpret or understand everyday situations and to use that experience when faced with new situations or problems. Intelligence is shaped by heredity and by environment. Everyone is born with certain limits of intellectual development. However, the extent to which an individual's potential is actually developed is greatly influenced by that person's environment.

It is crucial for young children to have an environment that promotes learning. Such an environment includes interactions with family members, the availability of playthings, and encouragement. Toddlers and preschoolers form attitudes toward learning that last a lifetime. If curiosity—a natural quality—is encouraged and enhanced, the child develops a positive attitude toward learning.

Methods of Learning

Children learn on their own through everyday experiences and through play. In the course of this learning, they use four different methods.

Incidental learning is unplanned learning. Five-month-old Josh happens to push both feet against the bottom of the crib and discovers that this motion moves his body forward. After this happens accidentally a few times, Josh sees a cause-and-effect situation. He then pushes against the crib on purpose.

Trial-and-error learning takes place when a child tries several solutions before finding one that works. At twelve to eighteen months, this means experimenting: "What happens when I touch the cat? Try to pick up the cat? Pull the cat's tail?" Krista, age three, uses trial-and-error learning differently when she wants her younger brother's truck. First, Krista grabs the truck from her brother, but he screams and her mother makes her give it back. Next, she tells her brother to go outside and play, but he doesn't want to. Finally, Krista offers to let her brother use her clay if she can play with his truck. He agrees, and Krista gets what she wants.

Imitation is learning by watching and copying others. Perhaps you have been annoyed by a younger brother who copied everything you did. Did you realize that he was trying to learn from you? Both skills and attitudes are learned by imitation.

Directed learning is learning that results from being taught. Umberto's first grade teacher helps him learn to read. Kara's mother teaches her the names of parts of her body by saying them while pointing to them. That's directed learning, too—it's just less formal. Directed learning begins in the early years and continues throughout life.

What type or types of learning help a child develop food preferences?

409

ISSUES IN
TEEN PARENTING

Research shows that children who have regular contact with a caring adult have a step up when it comes to thinking skills. Teen parents can help their children by:

- Giving them time to master new skills by themselves.
- Giving advice to help them solve a problem, and especially by phrasing that advice as a question.
- Praising appropriately.
- Building on existing knowledge.

COMPREHENSION CHECK

1. What are concepts? (*General categories of objects and information.*)
2. What three principles guide learning of words? (*Labels are for wholes, not parts; labels apply to the group to which an object belongs, not to the object; any object has only one label.*)

ACTIVITIES

Discussion Activity

Have students identify the method used to learn each of the following:

- A dog wags its tail when scratched. (*Incidental.*)
- Licorice ice cream tastes terrible, but peanut butter sandwiches taste good. (*Trial-and-error.*)
- New dance moves. (*Imitation, directed learning.*)
- How to make pasta. (*Directed.*)

L1

Teamwork Activity

Assign groups one of the four types of learning. Have students brainstorm as many examples of their type of learning as possible. Then have groups share their ideas. **L1**

VISUAL LEARNING	Using the Photographs

Left: Trial-and-error. *Right:* Directed learning. *Bottom:* Imitation.

What kind of learning is each child demonstrating?

Concept Development

As they learn to think, young children begin to organize the information they receive from their senses. They start to form **concepts**, general categories of objects and information. Concepts range from categories for objects such as "fruit" to qualities such as color or shape and to abstract ideas such as time.

Children learn words and concepts by using three principles. Suppose Desmond's father points to an animal and calls it a dog. How does Desmond know that the label "dog" applies to that animal and not to its legs or its nose? Children start by thinking

410   UNIT 4: The Child from One to Three

Intrapersonal

Have students choose the type of learning they feel works best for them and explain it in an essay. They should include examples of what they have learned by the method as well as an explanation of why they feel that method is best for them.

If students do not believe they learn better by one particular method, have them select a particular area of study and write about how two learning methods apply to that field.

that labels are for whole objects, not parts. Also, children believe that labels apply to the group to which the individual objects belong, not the particular object. Dog means creatures like that one, not that particular dog. Finally, young children believe that any object can only have one label. That may be why it takes time for children to learn to use pronouns. It is hard for them to understand that "mommy" and "she" can mean the same person.

As a child matures, concepts become more accurate. Babies begin with two broad concepts—"the baby" and "not the baby." Young toddlers make very broad distinctions between people and things. For example, at first all women are "mama." A three-year-old understands the concepts of "woman," "man," "girl," and "boy."

Young children also learn to categorize objects by shape, color, and size. Balls are round, and so are biscuits and plates. Grass and trees are both green. Size distinctions come in two steps. The relationship between two items—"big" and "little"—may be recognized as early as eighteen months. Not until age three, however, can children pick out the middle-sized ball from three possibilities.

Concepts of life are not learned until later. A young child believes that anything that moves or works is alive—clouds, toys, and the washing machine!

Concepts of time improve during the second and third years. Two-year-olds may show more patience because they know what "soon" means and can wait a short time. They know the difference between "before" and "after." However, a child may not understand "today," "tomorrow," and "yesterday" until kindergarten.

The Mind at Work

Intellectual activity can be broken down into seven areas: attention, memory, perception, reasoning, imagination, creativity, and curiosity. All these areas develop throughout life. However, their development from one to three is especially remarkable.

> **INFOLINK**
>
> **Piaget**
>
> For more on Piaget's preoperational period, see Chapter 10, pages 324-328.

Attention

Every moment, the five senses are bombarded with information. Right now, for instance, you see the words on the page. At the same time, you are also aware of such things as the size, shape, and color of the book and the amount of light in the room. You can probably hear pages being turned. You may be able to smell lunch being prepared in the cafeteria. Your skin can tell you that the paper of the book is smooth and cool.

You have the ability to block out most of this sensory information and focus only on the book. You can concentrate. A baby isn't able to concentrate. The infant's attention flits from one bit of sensory information to another.

As children mature, they gradually develop the ability to ignore most of the information their senses provide and to concentrate on one item of interest. Their learning is more focused on a particular topic. One- to three-year-olds have short attention spans. However, a three-year-old can focus on one activity for much longer than a one-year-old.

For more on Piaget's preoperational period, see Chapter 10, pages 324-328.

Discussion Activity

Have students offer definitions of the words "today," "tomorrow," and "yesterday." Then have the class discuss whether a child of two or three could understand the concepts from those definitions. **L2**

Critical Thinking Activity

Comparing. Have students reread the material on Piaget's stages of intellectual development in Chapter 10 (pages 324-327). Have them use the material in the section on concept development to compare the discussion of Piaget's work. Do the examples here support Piaget's theory or not? **L2**

Critical Thinking Activity

Applying. Describe the following situation to the class: "Becky holds up a blue block and says to her younger brother, 'blue.' Her brother holds up an orange block and says, 'blue.' Becky points to her yellow sweater and says 'yellow.' Her brother points to his green sweater and says 'yellow.'" **Ask:** What concept does Becky's brother need to learn? (*Color.*) What can Becky do to teach it? (*Point to several different objects that are the same color.*) **L1**

The Developing Brain

Premature Babies

Premature babies face many problems due to incomplete development before birth. Many lack the close attachment that helps build the brain's synaptic connections. One study showed that these effects need not be permanent. The Infant Health & Development Program gave children born prematurely a rich child care environment and meetings for parents. By age three, the children showed higher IQ scores.

COMPREHENSION CHECK

1. How does memory help children know how to react to situations? (*They can base reactions on what they recall from the past.*)
2. What is the difference between the perceptions of a newborn and those of an older child? (*Newborn can't interpret perceptions.*)
3. At what age does a baby begin to show simple problem-solving abilities? (*Four to six months.*)
4. How can caregivers help children learn to make good decisions? (*By giving them the opportunity to make real decisions.*)

ACTIVITIES

Critical Thinking Activity

Making Inferences. **Ask:** Why are memories linked to strong emotions most firmly imprinted in the brain? Have students write a paragraph explaining why—especially for children in this age group. **L1**

Toddlers can describe their experiences during the day to adults who did not share them. *What intellectual development makes this possible?*

Memory

Without memory, there would be no learning. Experiences that leave no impression cannot affect later actions or thoughts.

 The Developing Brain
Memories linked to strong emotional reactions are most firmly imprinted in the brain.

As children develop, they become able to react to a situation by remembering similar experiences in the past. A one-year-old who was frightened by a dog may be afraid of all animals for a time. A three-year-old can remember the particular dog and compare it with others.

By age two, a toddler has a fairly good memory. Tyler knew his daddy who had been away for ten days. He can deliver simple messages. He also can repeat bits of favorite stories and talk about going to the park. Three-year-old Keisha remembers simple requests or directions, uses numbers as if counting, and is able to identify most colors.

Perception

A newborn learns about the world through perceptions—the information received through the senses. This sensory information reinforces established connections in the brain and sparks new ones. Gradually, the brain organizes itself for increasingly complex learning. The newborn, however, is just beginning to interpret this information.

Caregivers play a key role in toddlers' and preschoolers' development of perception. By talking about what they and the children are doing, they help the children become more perceptive. Use descriptive observations that the child can understand and expand on. For example, when passing a store window, you might say, "Look at the

412 UNIT 4: The Child from One to Three

MULTIPLE INTELLIGENCES

Form students into groups and have each group brainstorm how to create a memory game that could be played with two- or three-year-olds. When the groups present their ideas to the class, have the class determine which kind of intelligence—linguistic, spatial, musical, mathematical, kinesthetic, interpersonal, intrapersonal, or naturalistic—the game is most suited to.

blue coat. Your shirt is blue, too. Let's see what other blue things we can find as we walk."

Two- and three-year-olds seem to ask questions constantly. Answering questions of "Why?" "What is that?" and "How does it work?" helps improve a child's perception. When questions are ignored or brushed aside, though, a child loses opportunities for learning. If the response is usually an absent-minded "Uh-huh" or "Don't bother me right now—I'm busy," the child eventually stops asking questions.

Reasoning

Reasoning is basic to the ability to solve problems and make decisions. It's also important in recognizing relationships and forming concepts.

Babies show the beginning of simple problem-solving ability at about four to six months of age. One-, two-, and three-year-olds gradually learn more sophisticated reasoning skills. At fourteen months, Omar solves problems by actually trying out all possible solutions. For example, when playing with a shape sorter box, he picks up a triangle and tries to fit it into each shape of hole until one works. By his third birthday, Omar's problem solving is less physical and more mental. He can think through possible solutions and eliminate those that won't work without actually trying out each one. He can usually find the triangle hole on the first try!

Discussion Activity

Have students describe all the sensory information they have around them. What could a young child learn from each of these sensory inputs? **L1**

Critical Thinking Activity

Finding Supporting Details. Have students look through the photographs in this chapter. What sensory experiences could a child learn from the situations shown in each? **L1**

Practicing Parenting

Learning from Nature

*S*tep outdoors for a new world to explore! Children learn through their senses, and nature has many different sounds, smells, textures, and tastes.

Outdoors, children discover that sticks make wonderful pencils for scratching designs or letters in the earth or sand. They find that rocks come in a variety of shapes and sizes. Flowers have different scents. Some birds feed in the water and others on land. The bark of trees can feel rough or smooth. Help children make these discoveries by talking about nature and providing opportunities for children to ask questions.

APPLY YOUR KNOWLEDGE

1. How can children learn from nature even in cold or rainy weather?
2. Is it safe to let children experiment with the different tastes of nature? Why or why not?

Practicing Parenting

Give students five minutes to list as many nature-related activities to do with a child as possible (for example, collecting colorful leaves in the fall and ironing them between sheets of waxed paper).

Answers to Apply Your Knowledge

1. *Possible response:* You can talk about the weather and seasons; you can bring leaves or seeds into the classroom.
2. *Possible response:* No, because children may think they can taste anything in nature, but some things can make them ill.

CHAPTER 13: Intellectual Development from One to Three **413**

Parenting in *Action*

Here are three ways to communicate positive attitudes toward learning:
• Encourage the child's curiosity about the world. Take walks together and talk about things that fascinate you.
• Welcome the child's questions—and ask your own. Discuss where you might go to find the answers.
• Praise the child's efforts to learn new skills. Help children feel that learning is an important accomplishment.

ACTIVITIES

Discussion Activity

The textbook states that creativity is an asset throughout life. Do students agree or disagree with this statement? Why? Ask for examples of situations in an adult's life in which creativity might be helpful. **L1**

Discussion Activity

Why do some parents discourage such creative activities as finger painting or making things with clay? What can parents do to overcome that tendency? **L1**

Teamwork Activity

Divide the class into seven groups. Assign each group one of the seven areas of intellectual activity. Have group members take the following roles: researchers; writers; presenters. Have each group do further research to learn more about their topic. Writers should then take the information provided by the researchers to prepare an oral presentation on the topic. Presenters should then report the information to the class. **L2**

VISUAL LEARNING | **Using the Photograph**

Ask: What different things could the box be used to represent? Write students' suggestions on the board. Lead them to see that objects that are open-ended allow children great variety of play by giving opportunities to use their imaginations.

As children solve problems, they basically are answering these questions:

1. What is the problem?
2. What do I already know about it?
3. What are the possible solutions?
4. Which is the best solution?
5. Did I make the right choice?

Decision making involves choosing between alternatives. Children learn to make good decisions through practice. It's important to give one- to three-year-olds opportunities to make real decisions. At first, these decisions should be based on limited choices in which either choice couldn't cause any harm. An eighteen-month-old can choose between two toys. At two, "Would you rather wear your yellow shirt or your green striped shirt?" What kinds of decisions might be appropriate at age three?

Imagination

Imagination becomes apparent at about two years of age. (No one knows whether babies may have an imagination.) An active imagination enhances learning because it allows the child to try new things and to be different people—at least in the mind. Chairs become trains, boxes are buildings, and closets are caves. The child becomes a ferocious lion or a busy mail carrier.

Children can be and do almost anything through imagination. They can play with ordinary objects like an empty box, turning it into a house, a spaceship, a fort, or many other things.

Children use their imagination to connect what they see and hear with themselves. A child may see an airplane and wonder, "Will I fly in a plane someday?" A child may hear about death and ask, "Will I die, too?"

Respect a child's imagination and respond carefully. When three-year-old Emma makes up a story, she isn't lying—she's using her imagination. In fact, until about the age of five, children are simply not sure where reality ends and imagination begins. However, if Emma's mother says, "Don't be silly. You know that didn't really happen," Emma will be discouraged from using her imagination.

Creativity

A related mental ability is **creativity**, in which the imagination is used to produce something. The product is usually an object that others can see, such as a finger painting.

Management/Leadership Skills

Tell students that some communities offer special recreational options for young children, for example, hands-on science museums or history museums that include period costumes or objects that children can wear or manipulate. Have students work in groups to devise their own creativity- and curiosity-fostering museum. What would be its theme? How would the museum encourage creativity and curiosity in toddlers? Ask each group to write up a plan for their museum and present it to the class.

Ask the Eperts

Rachel Perkins
Child Development Technology
Instructor
Hinds Community College
Utica, Mississippi

ENCOURAGING *Creativity*

 How can I encourage creativity in my toddler?

 Encouraging creativity is very important for children. Fortunately, it is not that difficult.

- *Encourage play activities that depend on exploration and imagination. Drawing, playing with clay, building things, dressing up in grown-up clothes, and telling stories are all examples. You can make up part of a story and ask the child to finish it.*

- *Provide toys that can be used in more than one way. Small wooden blocks can become microphones, cars, sandwiches, or the walls of a castle. Empty cardboard boxes can be caves, fire trucks, or doll beds.*

- *Provide unstructured time. Children need time to themselves to have a chance to let their imagination roam. The less television they watch, the better for their imagination, too.*

- *Remember that the process of creating is more important than the product. You might respond to a child's drawing this way: "Amanda, I've never seen a cat with three eyes before! I wonder what it would be like to have three eyes."*

- *Praise the child's efforts with deeds as well as words. Display the picture of the three-eyed cat on the refrigerator and let the child hear you tell others about it.*

Of course, the main idea behind all these methods is a simple one. To encourage a child's creativity, you need to provide opportunities—and then sit back and watch. Allow the child to control and direct the creative play. Try not to set limits—as long as the child is safe. You'll be amazed at what your child can come up with!

Thinking It Through

1. Why are toys that can be used in more than one way good for developing creativity?
2. Why do you think television does or doesn't promote creative play?

Ask the Eperts

Introducing the Feature

Have students write at least three questions they would ask a child psychologist about how to foster creativity in young children.

Answers to Thinking It Through
1. *Possible response:* Because they allow the child to determine what the toy is in a variety of play situations.
2. *Possible response:* It doesn't, because it leaves little to the imagination.

Applying What You've Learned

Have students predict the ways the following household items might be used by a two- or three-year-old in creative ways: scrap paper, paper bags, tubes from rolls of paper towels, refrigerator magnets, empty spools of thread.

Parenting in *Action*

Curiosity about the way the world works prompts children to ask a seemingly endless stream of questions. This is because children see their parents as their interpreters of a sometimes confusing world. Children also tend to ask questions when they are lonely, afraid, or need reassurance. In these instances, it is important to realize that your child is not really seeking information. Try to perceive the real motive behind the questions and respond accordingly.

Have students answer the Check Your Understanding Questions. Answers appear at the bottom of this page.

EVALUATION

Give students the Section 13-1 Quiz in the *Teacher Resource Guide*.

RETEACHING

1. Assign Reteaching Activities, page 40.
2. Have pairs of students act out examples of each of the four methods of learning.

ENRICHMENT

Have students write a plan for a game or activity that requires attention, memory, perception, or reasoning.

EXTENSION

Have students make a list of imaginative activities, toys, and games appropriate for one- to three-year-olds. Include an explanation of how each item promotes imaginative play.

CLOSE

Have students create a concept web based on the phrase "intellectual development."

Sometimes, though, the creative product is not an object. Examples are daydreams and dramatic play. Creativity, an asset throughout life, is most readily developed in early childhood.

Curiosity

Children are curious about the world around them, and that curiosity fuels brain development and learning. It's curiosity that causes children to wonder why or to try new activities. However, parents sometimes sti-

> **INFOLINK**
>
> ### Childproofing
>
> For more about *child-proofing*, see Chapter 11, pages 372-373.

fle that curiosity by overprotecting the child—or by overprotecting the home. Children need a safe environment and the freedom to explore it.

Young children seem to be into everything. They poke into every corner and closet. They touch and examine everything within reach. It's impossible to anticipate what a one-, two-, or three-year-old may do next. A doll or truck may turn up in the washer because "it was dirty." Patience and a healthy dose of humor are essential!

SECTION 13-1 REVIEW

✔ Check Your Understanding

1. What is intelligence?
2. Which method of learning is based on watching and copying others? Which type is based on trying different approaches to solving a problem?
3. What concept is developed by a shape sorter toy? By stacking boxes?
4. How does memory support learning?
5. How can caregivers help children sharpen their perception?
6. Why is curiosity important?

Putting Knowledge Into Practice

1. **Comparing.** Which of the four methods of learning do you use most? Why? Which do you think you found most useful and enjoyable as a three-year-old? Why?
2. **Applying.** Choose a toy for children ages one to three (other than one mentioned in this chapter). Identify the concepts that the toy helps a young child learn.
3. **Observing and Participating.** In writing, describe a learning situation that occurred in one of your classes this week. Identify the learning method used. Develop another version of the same situation in which a different learning method could have been used.

416 UNIT 4: The Child from One to Three

ANSWERS TO SECTION 13-1 REVIEW

1. The ability to interpret or understand situations and to use that experience when faced with new situations.
2. Imitation; trial-and-error learning.
3. Shape of objects; size of objects.
4. *Possible response:* Need memory for learning to take place because only with memory can situations be compared and then analyzed.
5. By responding to their observations and answering their questions.
6. It fuels learning.

CAREER OPPORTUNITIES

Preschool Teacher

A CONVERSATION WITH RACHEL QITSAULIK

How did you become interested in becoming a preschool teacher? I always wanted to be a preschool teacher. The early years are crucial for children. I help them get off to a good start.

What are the tasks and responsibilities of a preschool teacher? Our main goal is to help children develop and learn. We provide opportunities to experience new things and explore new situations. We help them learn to get along with others. Of course, we stay in close contact with parents.

What is the work environment like? The classroom is a friendly place with lots of light and bright colors. You have to get used to being busy all the time. Still, the children bring energy, curiosity, and joy so that it's easy to stay energized.

What are the working hours like? We have morning and afternoon sessions. We also prepare materials for classes. I have summers off, but some programs run year round.

What aptitudes are needed to be a preschool teacher? It's a long list—energy, creativity, patience, self-control, initiative, flexibility, knowledge of child development. We need skills in problem solving, time management, and communication. We also need to be able to work with others.

PRESCHOOL TEACHER

Education and Training. Preschool teachers usually have a college degree in early childhood education. In some states, a degree from a two-year college is accepted. In most states, teachers have to be certified. This means getting an official document that declares they meet minimum qualifications.

Career Outlook. The demand for preschool teachers should rise.

CONNECTING SCHOOL TO CAREER

1. **Thinking Skills.** Why would states require preschool teachers to be certified?
2. **Basic Skills.** Why would preschool teachers need good communication skills?

CHAPTER 13: Intellectual Development from One to Three **417**

Building Career Skills

Personal Qualities. Have students consider the list of aptitudes needed to be a preschool teacher. Then have them give an example of a situation in which that aptitude would be needed. Have students describe the situation to the class. Have the class as a whole discuss the individual examples and reach a consensus on whether or not the aptitude does apply.

FOCUS

MOTIVATOR

Read the following scenario to students: "Three-year-old Scott's father is proud of his son's ability to recognize many letters of the alphabet. The father decides to teach Scott how to write the letters. The lessons, however, usually end with Scott crying." Why did this happen?

VOCABULARY ACTIVITY

Ask students to look up the words articulate, flammable, and pathologist in the dictionary. Then have them use each term in a sentence.

Encouraging Learning from One to Three

Caregivers have a major effect—either positive or negative—on a child's learning. Those who provide a relaxed, accepting atmosphere and a variety of experiences encourage young children to learn. But adults who are overly harsh, too busy with their own lives, or who show children that they don't really care about learning discourage it.

KEY TERMS
articulation
flammable
speech-language pathologist

OBJECTIVES:
• Suggest ways to encourage young children to learn.
• Choose safe, appropriate toys that promote mental, physical, and social skills.
• Describe how speech develops.
• Name common speech problems and approaches to solving them.

418

Readiness for Learning

Children can learn a new skill only when they are physically and intellectually ready. It's a waste of time trying to teach a six-month-old to pull a zipper closed—the baby has neither the physical nor intellectual maturity that skill requires. In the same way, most two-year-olds lack the physical and intellectual development needed to

Observing & Participating

Children participate in five types of play. Sensory play involves experiencing new sounds, tastes, odors, and textures. Motion play includes running, jumping, twirling, and skipping, giving children practice with their coordination. Language play involves words, syllables, and phrases. Dramatic play allows children to act out real-life and imaginary situations. Competitive play includes games and rituals. Have students observe a group of one- to three-year-olds and write down examples of these types.

Toddlers can enjoy many different organized activities, but they also need unstructured time in which they can simply do what they are interested in. Caregivers help children by allowing some of this free time every day.

learn to print letters. When adults push children to learn things they aren't ready for, the children can't succeed. A sense of failure may slow the child's learning, rather than increase it as the adult had intended.

Avoid delaying skills that children are ready to learn. Because he struggled with the task, Ben's mother put his shoes on for him. She later discovered that this "helping" caused problems. When Ben was well past the age when he should be able to put on his own shoes, he continued to ask for help.

Guiding Learning

These suggestions will help you guide the learning of young children:

- **Give your time and attention.** Children learn best when they are encouraged by someone who cares about them.
- **Take advantage of simple learning opportunities.** Everyday life provides many chances to help a child's understanding grow. Erin took two-year-old Colin to the supermarket. As she chose oranges, she said, "I'll buy five oranges" and then counted out five. This helped Colin learn the concept of five, counting skills, and the name of the fruit.
- **Allow time for thinking.** Problem solving and decision making are new experiences for young children. They need time to consider choices and make decisions.

- **Give only as much help as the child needs to succeed.** If a toddler is struggling to pull on socks, don't take over. Instead, just help slip the sock over the child's heel before it gets caught. The child learns how to put on socks and enjoys the sense of accomplishment. If at all possible, let children do the final step in any task they are struggling with.
- **Encourage children to draw their own conclusions.** "Let's find out" is better than an explanation. Seeing and doing helps reinforce learning.

CHAPTER 13: Intellectual Development from One to Three **419**

DID *You* **Know?**

Computers and Learning. Some parents buy computer programs for children these ages. In fact, software aimed at children from nine months to five years old is a fast-growing category of software. The programs, intended for joint use by parent and child, are called "lapware." Some experts think computer learning is too restrictive for children this young, who learn better using their senses. Some say the software is harmless as long as caregivers don't put too much emphasis on this play at the expense of reading and experiential play.

COMPREHENSION CHECK

1. Why is it important to keep explanations simple and on the child's level? (*Too much information can cause child to stop listening.*)
2. How might constant reminders to keep her clothes clean inhibit Sierra's learning? (*She may limit exploring from concern over being dirty.*)
3. How do toys help a toddler's development? (*Allow children to experience imaginary situations; encourage development of large and small motor skills; help children learn to share.*)

ACTIVITIES

Critical Thinking Activity

Analyzing. What happens to a caregiver if a young child asks "Why?" many consecutive times? How does the caregiver's response affect the child? **L1**

- **Show how to solve problems.** When a toddler's tower of blocks keeps toppling, demonstrate that stacking one block directly on top of another provides balance. Then leave building the tower to the toddler.

  You can also model problem solving. Talk out loud as you solve problems or make decisions. That way, the child can hear the way you think your way to a solution.

- **Maintain a positive attitude.** Express confidence in the child's abilities. One way is to praise the child's efforts: "You worked very hard putting your toys away."

- **Keep explanations simple and on the child's level.** Too much information can cause a young child to stop listening. When a child asks about the fish in the aquarium, explain, "The fish live in water. People live outside the water. We need air to breathe."

- **Allow children to explore and discover.** Let them roll in the grass, climb trees, and squeeze mud through their fingers and toes. Constantly saying "Don't do this" and "Don't touch that" limits the sensory and motor experiences needed for learning.

- **Help the children understand the world and how it works.** Take young children along, even on routine errands. The library, the supermarket, and the gas station can all be learning experiences. Talk about what is happening and why it's happening. Helping at home also boosts learning.

The outdoors is a great place for learning. An adult's participation can increase the fun.

Management/Leadership Skills

Tell students that their task is to create report cards for caregivers to use to measure how well they are contributing to a child's learning. Suggest that the report cards be applicable either to caregivers or parents. Have students indicate the criteria that they would use to judge caregivers' effectiveness. Remind them to focus on issues appropriate for children in the one-to-three age group. Have students share their suggestions with the class, and have the class discuss which criteria seem most appropriate.

Many traditional toys encourage a child to use his or her imagination.

As toddlers help rake leaves, for example, call attention to the different colors and the crackling sounds. Discuss the changing seasons.

- **Take frequent breaks.** A child needs stimulation—but a child also needs a chance just to have fun. Watch for clear signals that a child has had enough of an activity. Fussing, wiggling in a chair, or a distracted look all suggest that it's time to stop.

Play Activities and Toys

Toys are an important part of play. They allow children to experience imaginary situations and act out different roles. They encourage the development of large and small motor skills. They also help children learn to share and cooperate with others.

Evaluating Toys

With thousands of toys to choose from, knowing what to buy is important. Ask yourself these questions:

- **Is the toy safe?** This is the single most important consideration. Make sure there are no small parts that could be swallowed or sharp edges that could cut a child. Make sure that the toy is not **flammable,** or easily burned.

Finally, make sure that the toy has no lead-based paints, which are poisonous. The government's Consumer Products Safety Commission alerts the public about toy safety problems.

- **Is it well made and durable?** There is nothing more discouraging for a child—or an adult—than having a toy break the first time it's used. Is the toy

Have students design posters titled "Guiding Children Along the Path of Learning." Their posters should illustrate one or more ways to encourage learning. Display completed posters in the classroom. **L1**

Critical Thinking Activity

Hypothesizing. Point out to students that many toys for children two and up are child-size versions of adult items, such as tools and kitchen sets. Ask students why. What type of learning do these toys foster? Why are they appropriate for a two-year-old but not a younger child? **L2**

Management/Leadership Skills

Older siblings can also help children learn. Some students may have siblings, other relatives, or neighbors of the young ages discussed in the chapter. Those young children often follow their older relatives around, eagerly looking for atten-tion. Have students form into groups and suggest ways that teens can help younger children learn. What can they do or say during their daily routines to teach children about the world?

COMPREHENSION CHECK

1. Why are children's toys often painted in primary and secondary colors? (*They are vivid.*)
2. What skills should be encouraged by a toy for a child from one to two years old? (*Balance, large and small muscle skills, exploration.*)

ACTIVITIES

Critical Thinking Activity

Ranking. Have each student rank the list of ways of evaluating toys from most important to least important. Tabulate students' rankings. Is there a consensus on which criteria are most important? **L1**

History Activity

Have students go to the public library to review newspapers and magazines from 1940 or earlier. Ask them to find advertisements for toys. Other sources include popular history books that focus on everyday life. Then have students critique these toys in terms of today's standards. Would the toys be considered suitable for children today? Why or why not? **L3**

Different toys provide different learning opportunities. Playing with dolls or small figures encourages language development and dramatic play. Blocks and construction toys build spatial and small motor skills. ***What skills are developed by a riding toy?***

made to withstand the use it will receive?

- **Will it be easy to care for?** A stuffed bear that takes a ride through a mud puddle may be ruined unless it can be washed. Similarly, books with wipe-clean covers are the most practical choice for young children.
- **Will it encourage the use of imagination?** Many toys do everything for the child. With no need to pretend, the

child's imagination develops more slowly. Look for simple toys that can used in a variety of ways. A talking doll may say ten phrases, but a child can make a nontalking doll say anything!
- **Is it colorful?** Young children respond more readily to colorful objects. They also encourage children to learn the names of colors.
- **Will it be easy for the child to handle?** Think about the size of the child in relation to the toy. The excitement of a new tricycle is quickly lost if the child's legs are too short to reach the pedals.

Age-Appropriate Toys

Toys should also be appropriate for a child's age. Infant toys are usually not challenging enough for three-year-olds. Neither will an older child's toys hold the attention of most fourteen-month-olds for long.

Children at different ages enjoy different kinds of toys:

- **One to two years.** At this age, a child practices body control and learns through exploration. Many of the best "toys" are items found in the home, such as metal pans, wooden spoons, and plastic storage containers. Anything that allows the child to use large muscles is popular. This may include swings, riding toys with wheels, balls, small wagons, boxes, and low furniture. Children of this age also enjoy small dolls and stuffed animals, sturdy books, simple puzzles, and toy cars. Be careful to avoid small toys or toys with small parts that could be swallowed.
- **Two to three years.** Coordination and understanding improve greatly during this year. In addition, the child wants to do what adults are doing. The desire to

DID *You* **Know?**

Picking Up. Most parents think their children should pick up their toys throughout the day, or at least at the end of the day. Toddlers, however, rarely understand the need for tidiness. Researchers have found that when adults participate in picking up, children cooperate more willingly because the chore becomes a social experience. In addition, when adults help, picking up takes on more importance. Even if parents have to help children at this age, when the children are older they'll do it more willingly.

How does finger painting help children express their creativity?

imitate suggests a variety of toys: a child-sized broom, a small shovel, plastic or wooden tools, play dishes, and empty food containers. Crayons, clay, large beads to string, books, large blocks, and blunt scissors are popular. A sandbox can provide hours of enjoyment.

- **Three to four years.** Preschoolers' improved motor skills and increased imagination bring interest in toys requiring small motor skills. Dolls to dress, cars and trucks, and similar toys are popular. Children of this age love to mold clay, color, and paint—especially with finger paint. Three-year-olds spend longer periods with books and enjoy listening to records or cassettes. They enjoy puzzles and using ladders, swings, and slides. Most three-year-olds love the mobility of a tricycle.

Speech Development

In the toddler and preschool years, language abilities grow at a very rapid pace. As with other areas of development, though, children vary greatly in the timing of their speaking skills.

One of the early signs of developing language is that a child can point to or pick up an object that has been named. **What does this show?**

423

Teamwork Activity
Divide the class into small groups. Provide each group with a toy. Give them time to examine the toy. Then ask each group to prepare a report in which they rate the toy ("1" being "excellent" and "5" being "poor") for how well it satisfies each requirement given in the textbook for appropriate toys. What age or ages would it be most appropriate for? **L1**

VISUAL LEARNING | **Using the Photograph**

Top—Possible response: They can create their own pictures; express feelings with colors.
Bottom—Possible response: It shows that the child can process the words heard.

ISSUES IN
CHILDREN'S HEALTH

Hand-crafted toys are frequently purchased at craft shows or received as gifts from creative family members and friends. With handmade toys, however, safety codes are more difficult to monitor and enforce. Parents should always question the materials used to make these gifts and check for potential choking and other hazards.

LEARNING STYLES | **Mathematical**

Tell students that they are parents shopping for birthday presents for their two-year-old. They have budgeted $50 for the child's birthday. Provide them with toy catalogs or tell them to spend some time outside class visiting local toy stores. Tell them they to prepare a list of toys they would buy, staying within the limits of the budget. Have students present their lists of toys to the class and have the class discuss them. Do any suggestions seem inappropriate? How easy or difficult was it to stay within budget?

COMPREHENSION CHECK

1. At about what age does a child begin to use pronouns? (*About age two.*)
2. How do children learn most words and the rules of grammar? (*By listening to others talk.*)

ACTIVITIES

Critical Thinking Activity

Determining Cause and Effect. Have students consider the text information on speech development. With this information in mind, ask students to write a paragraph in response to the following: What would be the likely effect on a hearing child who is being raised by parents who are deaf or mute? Discuss their responses. **L1**

VISUAL LEARNING	Using the Photograph **Ask:** Why do listening and responding have this effect?

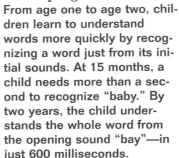

The Developing Brain

From age one to age two, children learn to understand words more quickly by recognizing a word just from its initial sounds. At 15 months, a child needs more than a second to recognize "baby." By two years, the child understands the whole word from the opening sound "bay"—in just 600 milliseconds.

Brain development research has brought new insights into how children learn to use language. They appear to have an inborn instinct to decode sounds, words, sentences, and grammar from the language they hear. The first three years of life are a window of opportunity for learning words.

Between their first and second birthdays, children work at learning new words. They like to learn the names of everything, and they enjoy listening to the sounds the words make. At twelve months a child may speak two to eight words. By age two, that jumps to about 200 words. During this period, most children use one or two words rather than a whole sentence to express a thought. For example, a child might hold out a cup and say "water" to mean "I want a drink of water."

A child's language development is strongly influenced by how caregivers and older children speak to him or her. For example, Jason's mother usually used baby talk with him. Not surprisingly, at three and one-half, Jason still has trouble speaking plainly enough for others to understand him.

Listening to a young child and giving a personal response help encourage language development.

424　UNIT 4: The Child from One to Three

Parenting in *Action*

One way parents can build their child's language skills is to interrupt stories for discussion and to ask open-ended questions. Parents can also praise and expand on the child's answers. In an experiment, the verbal expression and vocabulary skills of children were tested after one month of their parents using these techniques. Their scores were compared with those of a control group whose parents read stories without incorporating the questioning, praise, and expansion. The children in the experimental group scored six months ahead of those in the control group.

Signs of Language Development

Children's language abilities develop at different rates. Still, most three-year-olds can do the following:

- Say their name and age.
- Make all the vowel sounds and speak the consonants P, B, M, W, H, D, T, and N.
- Speak without repeating a word or syllable.
- Use sentences of at least four words.
- Usually be understood by others, even strangers.
- Answer questions of "what" and "where."
- Understand what is meant by "on," "in," and "under."
- Follow a command with two or three parts.

FOLLOWING UP

1. Why would it be significant that a child can be understood by strangers rather than by usual caregivers?
2. How does following a multiple-part command indicate improved memory as well as language skills?

Encourage language development and learning in toddlers by talking to them about their lives. Speak in a clear and engaging way. For example, you can take the time to describe—and guide children in talking about—whatever they are seeing or doing. "Look at the big bite you've taken out of that shiny red apple. Can you hear the crunch it makes when you put your teeth into it?"

At about age two, the child usually starts combining a few words to make short sentences: "Doggie bark." "Jimmy fall down." From age one to two, a child typically calls himself or herself by name. At about two years, children begin to use pronouns.

At about two and one-half, children begin to learn some of the rules of grammar.

They learn by listening to other people talk rather than by any formal teaching. For example, a child begins to add an *s* to words to make them plural. The child then—quite logically—applies this rule to all words. At two and one-half, *foot*s and *tooth*s make as much sense as *hands* and *eyes*. At three, Katie responded to "I'm going to Eureka" with "You're going to *my* reeka?"

Speech Difficulties

Many parents are concerned about "late talkers." Some make the mistake of pressuring the child who talks late or whose speech is unclear. Most often, this pressure just makes the child aware of the problem and may make it worse.

Discussion Activity

Ask whether any students in the class have learned a second language. What aspects of the new language did they find difficult? Which were easy? Does their experience shed any light on how young children learn language? **L1**

Teamwork Activity

If a child says "apple," a caregiver might say, "Yes, it's a shiny red apple." This is called elaboration. Have students work in groups to write ten statements a child might make and at least one way a caregiver could elaborate on each one. **L1**

HEALTH TIP

Bring to class an audio- or videotape on which a toddler is talking. Ask students to try to interpret what the child is saying. Then ask them to comment on whether it was easy or difficult to understand the child. Why?

Answers to FOLLOWING UP

1. *Possible response:* Familiar adults can learn to understand a child, despite problems with articulation, simply through practice.
2. It shows that a child can retain multiple instructions.

The Developing Brain

Plasticity

Scientists marvel at the brain's "plasticity"—its ability to change. This is shown by the capacity of some children to recover from severe brain trauma. In rare cases, children have strokes and lose the capacity to speak. Research shows that other areas of the brain—including the other hemisphere—take over this function. Research has shown that the brain's ability to rebound is most pronounced from birth to age ten.

COMPREHENSION CHECK

1. What is a speech-language pathologist? (*Specialist trained to detect and correct speech problems.*)
2. What types of physical problems might hinder a child's language development? (*Poor hearing, mental retardation, learning disabilities, and emotional problems.*)
3. What is the best way to handle a child's stuttering? (*Give child time to say the word; be supportive and loving.*)

ACTIVITIES

Discussion Activity

Discuss with students the ways that a child's life might be affected by a speech difficulty. How might it affect, for example, school work? participation in extracurricular activities? ability to form friendships? What factors in the child's life might make handling a speech difficulty easier or harder? **L1**

Promoting Health Activity

Ask students to research the methods used by speech-language pathologists to correct stuttering. Have them prepare a written report about their findings. **L2**

VISUAL LEARNING	Using the Photograph

Possible responses: Stutter, lisp.

What speech difficulties may require the help of a speech-language pathologist?

A child who doesn't seem to understand what is said and doesn't speak at all or who speaks very little should have a thorough examination. Free screenings may be available from a **speech-language pathologist** through the local public school. These specialists are trained to detect and correct speech problems. It is important to identify, as soon as possible, any physical problem that may be hindering the child's language development. Poor hearing, mental retardation, learning disabilities, and emotional problems may all slow a child's speech.

Problems with **articulation**, the ability to use clear, distinct speech, are common until at least age three or four. Some children skip syllables or leave off the endings of words. These problems usually correct themselves in time. A speech-language pathologist can determine whether a problem is likely to go away over time or if therapy is needed.

Avoid constantly correcting a child's pronunciation. Instead, be careful to set a good example with your own speech. If the toddler says "ba" and reaches for a bottle, hand the bottle over, saying, "Bottle. Selena wants her bottle."

Stuttering is a more serious speech difficulty for young children. However, many adults mistake normal speech hesitations for stuttering. A child may repeat whole words or phrases: "Johnny... Johnny... Johnny. He... he... he hit Zoe!" This is not true stuttering. In this case, the child's speaking and thinking abilities are still immature. He or she simply can't get the words out as rapidly or smoothly as desired.

Parenting in Action

By playing conversational games, caregivers can promote not only language development, but also learning in general. One such game is "What if?" A caregiver might ask a child "What if it rained today?" or perhaps even something as silly as "What if it rained tomato sauce?"

Once the child responds, more "What if" questions can follow. This kind of interchange can be useful for preparing children for diffult situations, such as "What if someone you didn't know offered you candy?"

A true stutter can be identified by the rhythm, pitch, and speed of speech. It is rapid, forced, and short and sharp in sound. Usually, the child repeats only the beginning sound of a word: "I c—c—c—can't g—g—g—go outside." The child often also shows tenseness in some way—with gasping, sputtering, or rapid blinking, for instance.

The cause or causes of stuttering are still not clearly understood. Some children need the help of a speech-language pathologist to overcome the problem. Most children who stutter, however, outgrow it. Experts advise against finishing words for a child. Children who stutter need time to say the word on their own.

Children with speaking difficulties need to know they are loved. Such an attitude will help the child cope with—and perhaps even overcome—the problem. Ridicule or constant corrections only make the problem worse.

SECTION 13-2 REVIEW

✔ Check Your Understanding

1. What kind of readiness is needed before a child can learn a skill?
2. Choose one of the principles of how to guide a child's learning and give an example of a caregiver putting it into practice.
3. Which kinds of development—physical, emotional, social, or intellectual—does play promote?
4. What should be the most important consideration when choosing toys for children? Why?
5. List at least four toys that are appropriate and fun for toddlers between the ages of one and two.
6. What age group most enjoys songs, playground equipment, and tricycles?
7. What is the disadvantage of speaking to a child using "baby talk"?
8. What kinds of problems might indicate that speech therapy is needed?

Putting Knowledge Into Practice

1. **Making Inferences.** Identify three local activities or events appropriate for young children. Explain what you think children would learn from each.
2. **Applying.** While at a friend's birthday party, the friend's mother asks Jake which balloon he wants. He answers, "I . . . ah . . . ah . . . want the . . . ah . . . green one." Does Jake's answer suggest that he needs speech therapy? Why or why not?
3. **Observing and Participating.** Write a description of a routine chore such as shopping for food, washing dishes, or cleaning. Then describe how you could talk about this activity to a toddler who was watching you do it. How could the child help?

ASSESS

CHECKING COMPREHENSION

Have students answer the Check Your Understanding questions. Answers appear at the bottom of this page.

EVALUATION

Give students the Section 13-2 Quiz in the *Teacher Resource Guide*.

RETEACHING

1. Assign Reteaching Activities, page 41.
2. Have students write one question and answer for each topic in the section. Then have them exchange papers with a partner and answer the questions.

ENRICHMENT

Have students research normal speech acquisition in this period and present their findings in a chart.

EXTENSION

Invite a child care worker to the class to talk about promoting learning in children these ages. Have students prepare questions in advance.

CLOSE

Have students prepare a handout of ten suggestions for parents to promote learning.

ANSWERS TO SECTION 13-2 REVIEW

1. Physical and intellectual.
2. *Possible response:* A parent helps the child put on one shoe, then lets the child put on the other shoe alone.
3. All four.
4. Safety, because you must protect the child from being hurt.
5. *Possible response:* Household items; rocking horses; puzzles; books.
6. Three to four years old.
7. It can slow the child's acquisition of language skills.
8. Articulation problems; stuttering.

Ask students to name their favorite children's books. On the board, list the titles as students call them out. Ask students how many of the books they remember from when they were young children.

COMPREHENSION CHECK

1. How do children benefit by being read to? (*Nourishes relationships, builds vocabulary, encourages language and listening skills, helps the child separate reality and fantasy, fosters reading throughout life.*)

2. How does asking questions as you read a book help a child? (*Makes them a participant; increases learning.*)

3. Why should the reader keep his or her focus on the child, rather than on insisting that the story be read through to the end? (*If the child has lost interest, such insistence will make reading seem more like a chore than an enjoyable activity.*)

Parenting With Care

Reading to Children

Sharing a book with a child can be a special experience, both for you and for the child.

Books are wonderful learning tools. In addition, reading to a child nourishes close relationships, builds vocabulary, encourages language and listening skills, and helps the child separate reality from fantasy.

Children who learn early in childhood that books are fun are more likely to remain readers throughout life. They also learn to read more easily. Chapter 16 gives more information on reading to children.

Choose Appropriate Books

Children of different ages respond to different types of books:

- One-year-olds need short, simple books with large, uncomplicated pictures. They like picture books with objects they can name and books with rhymes.
- Two-year-olds prefer simple stories they can relate to. Like one-year-olds, they never tire of hearing their favorite stories again and again.
- By age three, children enjoy longer stories with more of a plot. They like realistic stories and stories that help them use their imagination. They enjoy books about how things work and why things happen.

Become a Master Storyteller

Reading a story is like putting on a play. Create excitement and interest by varying the tone of your voice, giving each character a different voice, and using gestures and facial expressions.

If you are reading to one or two children, snuggle up close and hold the book so they can see. If you are reading to a group, arrange the children in a semicircle facing you. Read loudly enough for everyone to hear. Take time to learn the book beforehand so you can keep the pictures facing the children.

Encourage Participation

Even before they can read, children can participate in stories to increase learning and fun.

RESOURCES TO EXPLORE

Books. The American Library Association has many programs to foster love of reading. Many local public libraries hold story hours for children of different age groups. In addition, the ALA has a Website that includes a special section called "Read! Learn! Connect!" This has a list of suggested children's books and Websites (divided by age), and information for parents. Contact www.ala.org

- Very young children can turn the pages, which builds hand-eye coordination.
- Relate the action and pictures in the book to the child's own life. "You have a red ball, too, don't you?"
- Ask questions as you read. "What do you think Melissa will find when she opens the box?"
- With familiar books, let the child play the part of one character.
- With older children, point out the words for familiar objects. Practice recognizing letters and their sounds.
- Encourage children to dramatize a story by themselves or with puppets. Have them draw pictures to go with a story.
- Remember to keep your focus on the child—not on the story. Reading together should be fun. If the child has stopped enjoying the story, put the book away.

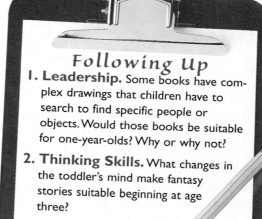

Following Up

1. **Leadership.** Some books have complex drawings that children have to search to find specific people or objects. Would those books be suitable for one-year-olds? Why or why not?

2. **Thinking Skills.** What changes in the toddler's mind make fantasy stories suitable beginning at age three?

429

Answers to Following Up
1. *Possible response:* No, because the pictures are too complex for them.
2. *Possible response:* A child's growing imagination.

ACTIVITIES

Critical Thinking Activity

Identifying Alternatives. Ask students to respond to the following question: Other than reading to a child, how might a caregiver encourage a love of books and reading? **L1**

DID *You* **Know?**

Preparing Children for Reading. **Dr. Shelley K. Lindauer of Utah State University advises:**
- **Read things other than books aloud, for example, road signs, store names, menus.**
- **Let children choose books to buy or borrow from the library.**
- **Give children easy access to writing instruments and paper.**
- **Post labels on objects in the home.**

CLOSE

1. Have students take turns reading children's books aloud in small groups. Have the other students comment on the reader's strengths and suggest improvements.
2. **Extension.** Arrange for students to observe the story hour at a library. Assign some students to observe the storyteller; ask others to observe the children's reactions.

CHECKING COMPREHENSION

Use the Summary and the Reviewing the Facts questions to help students go over the most important ideas in Chapter 13. Encourage students to ask questions and add details.

Answers to **Reviewing the Facts**

1. *Possible response:* Children whose parents do a great deal of talking have larger vocabularies.
2. Imitation.
3. *At two years:* They can understand before and after. *In kindergarten:* They can understand yesterday, today, and tomorrow.
4. A three-year-old can focus on one activity whereas an infant cannot.
5. *Possible responses:* By giving them opportunities; by modeling problem solving for them.
6. Learning may actually slow down rather than accelerating.
7. *Principles appear in the list on pages 419-421; examples should reflect the principle stated.*
8. In a clear and engaging way.
9. By modeling good speech rather than correcting them.

CHAPTER 13

REVIEW &

Summary

✔ Intelligence is determined by heredity and environment. (Section 13-1)

✔ Children use four different methods to learn. (Section 13-1)

✔ Imagination and creativity are areas of intellectual activity. (Section 13-1)

✔ Toys should be safe, appealing, and appropriate for a child's age. (Section 13-2)

✔ The way in which caregivers speak to children shapes language development. (Section 13-2)

Reviewing the Facts

1. Give an example of the effect of environment on intelligence. (Section 13-1)
2. Noemí used the hose to wash her toy trucks, just as her father washed the car. What kind of learning is this an example of? (Section 13-1)
3. When do children learn concepts of time? (Section 13-1)
4. What is the difference between an infant and a three-year-old in terms of attention? (Section 13-1)
5. How can caregivers teach children to solve problems? (Section 13-1)
6. What may happen to children who are pushed to learn something before they are ready? (Section 13-2)
7. Name a principle for guiding learning and give an example of that principle at work. (Section 13-2)

8. In what way should caregivers talk to children to help them learn speech? (Section 13-2)
9. How should parents respond to children who have problems with articulation? (Section 13-2)

Thinking Critically

1. **Drawing Conclusions.** What can parents do to persuade children to value learning? Why would their actions matter?
2. **Charting.** Make a chart that shows the kinds of skills—large motor, small motor, or language—that children can learn from three of the toys listed on pages 422 to 423 for each age group.
3. **Synthesizing.** What method of learning do children use as they build language skills? Explain how they use that method.

Taking Action

1. **Promoting Creativity.** Write the beginning of a story that would inspire children to use their creativity by finishing the story or by drawing a picture of it. *(Leadership)*
2. **Testing Memory.** Create a simple memory game that could be played by toddlers to improve their memory. *(Thinking Skills)*

CONNECTIONS

 ## Cross-Curricular Connections

1. **Art.** Draw a series of pictures that you could show to toddlers to help them learn the concepts of color, shape, or size.
2. **Science.** Find out what scientists have learned about how the brain stores memories. What sights, sounds, words, or colors are remembered? What makes them memorable? Prepare a summary of your findings.

 ## Workplace Connections

1. **Resources.** Suppose that you are about to start a child care center for children from one to three years old. Choose one kind of activity—such as art or music or reading—and make a list of the toys and play activities that you would have to promote that activity.
2. **Basic Skills.** Write a brochure that explains to parents the philosophy and goals of a fictional child care center in terms of children aged one to three.

 ## Family and Community Connections

1. **Library Resources.** Visit a local library to learn about services that are offered for young children. Share your findings with the class.
2. **Learning in the Home.** Identify an object or activity that is commonly found in the home. List ways that this object or activity could be used for learning. Find at least one example for each of the four methods of learning.

 ## Technology Connections

1. **Internet.** Search on the Internet to find information about stuttering. About how many children stutter? At what ages does stuttering commonly develop?
2. **Television.** Watch a half hour of an educational children's television show such as *Sesame Street*, *Mister Rogers' Neighborhood*, or *Reading Rainbow*. Describe the show to your class, pointing out what skills or concepts a toddler or preschooler could learn from the show.

EVALUATION

1. Use the reproducible Chapter 13 Test in the *Teacher Resource Guide*, or construct your own test using the Exam*View*® Test Generator.
2. For an alternative assessment, assign the Chapter 13 activity in the *Authentic Assessment* section of the *Teacher Resource Guide*.

ENRICHMENT

Assign students either of the two enrichment activities in the *Enrichment Activities* booklet in the *Student Motivation Kit*.

EXTENSION

Invite a children's librarian to speak to the class about book selections for young children and about reading to them. Have students prepare questions in advance.

CLOSE

Have students debate, orally or in written form, the following statement: "Intelligence is related more closely to inherited abilities than it is to the child's environment."

After completing Unit 5, students will be able to:

- Describe the physical growth and development of children from four to six and plan for the physical care they require.
- Act appropriately to meet the emotional and social needs of children from four to six, based on their development.
- Explain intellectual development of children from four to six and discuss school experiences appropriate for children with different needs.

UNIT 5 | OVERVIEW

In **Chapter 14**, students learn about the physical growth and development of four- to six-year-olds and consider how caregivers can encourage good self-care habits.

Chapter 15 helps students understand emotional and social development in these years, including issues that arise from adjusting to school.

In **Chapter 16**, students examine the learning and intellectual development in these years, examine different ideas of intelligence, and consider children with special needs.

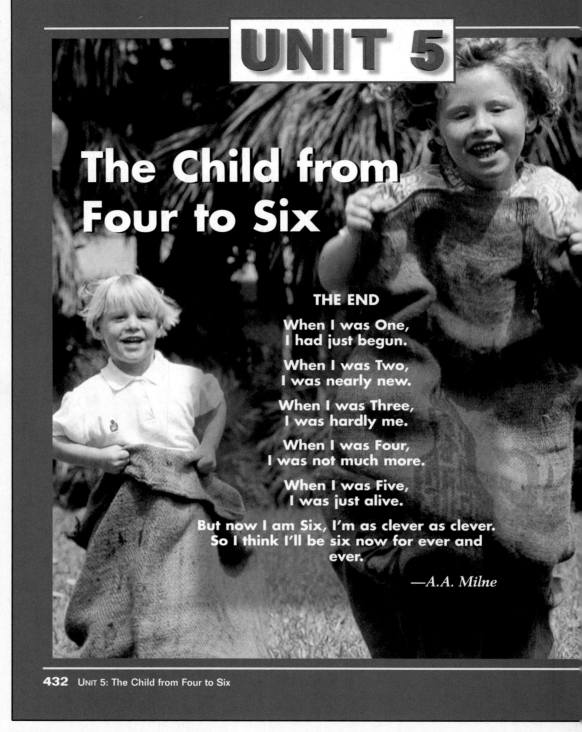

UNIT 5

The Child from Four to Six

THE END

When I was One,
I had just begun.

When I was Two,
I was nearly new.

When I was Three,
I was hardly me.

When I was Four,
I was not much more.

When I was Five,
I was just alive.

But now I am Six, I'm as clever as clever.
So I think I'll be six now for ever and
ever.

—*A.A. Milne*

432 UNIT 5: The Child from Four to Six

USING THE POEM A. A. Milne has delighted children of all ages with the whimsical stories of Christopher Robin, Winnie-the-Pooh, and their friends. In this poem, from *Now We Are Six*, the speaker reflects on his accomplishments since birth. Have a volunteer student read the poem aloud, using the animated voice and tone of an exuberant young boy. **Ask:** From whose point of view is the poem written? What attitude does the speaker show to each age? How do the speaker's words show his enthusiasm for this new plateau he has reached? Why would he be content to stay six "for ever and ever"?

CHAPTER 14

Physical
Development
from Four to Six

CHAPTER 15

Emotional and
Social
Development
from Four to Six

CHAPTER 16

Intellectual
Development
from Four to Six

433

- Have students recall their own experiences in preschool or kindergarten. **Ask:** What do you remember about that school? How did you feel when you started at that school? How did your feelings change as you spent more time there?
- **Ask:** What areas of development are included in the activity shown in the photograph in the student book?

COMPLETING UNIT 5

EXTENSION

Have students write a preschool teacher's report on a fictional student. He or she should describe the child's development in all areas during the past year at preschool and address the child's readiness to begin kindergarten the following fall. Students should be cautioned not to make the child perfect.

EVALUATION

Use the Unit 5 Test on the Exam*View®* Test Generator or use the program to create your own test.

FCCLA Connection	**Rating Visual Media**

Have groups of students develop a rating scale that could be used to evaluate one form of visual media, such as television programs, children's videos, or video games. Students should consider four- to six-year-olds' intellectual, social, emotional, and moral development. Have the students use their rating scale on five to eight programs or products. What conclusions did they draw? Would they revise their scale in any way?

COMMUNITY ᴀꜱ CLASSROOM

Guest Speakers. The class could benefit by hearing from several professionals during the study of this unit. *For Chapter 14*: pediatrician; dentist; public health nurse; dietitian; retail store clothes buyer. *For Chapter 15*: child psychologist; family counselor; recreational program director. *For Chapter 16*: kindergarten or special education teacher; school librarian.

Field Trips. The class could take field trips to a preschool, a kindergarten class, or a school cafeteria to enhance their study of the unit.

CHAPTER 14 RESOURCES

Teacher Resource Guide
• Chapter 14 Test, p. 178
• Authentic Assessment, p. 283
Student Motivation Kit
• Observations, pp. 53-54
Transparency Package
• CT-41, CT-42, CT-49
Effective Instruction CD-ROM

CHAPTER 14 **OVERVIEW**

In **Section 14-1**, students learn about changes in height, weight, proportion, and posture in these years. They also read about the appearance of permanent teeth and changes in large and small motor skills.

In **Section 14-2**, students learn about caring for children of these ages. The text addresses self-feeding and how to teach healthy eating habits. They also learn about washing and bathing, brushing teeth, dressing, choosing and caring for clothing, sleeping, and toileting.

CHAPTER 14 **OBJECTIVES**

After completing Chapter 14, students will be able to:

• Describe normal physical growth for four- to six-year-olds.
• Compare motor skill development of four-, five-, and six-year-olds.

CHAPTER 14
Physical Development from Four to Six

434 Unit 5: The Child from Four to Six

RESOURCES TO EXPLORE

Safety. Children from four to six enjoy playing on playgrounds. The National Playground Safety Institute has identified the twelve leading causes of injury on playgrounds. The top five are: hard surfaces; inadequate space for children to fall safely; protruding equipment that can hurt a child or catch clothing; open-ings in which heads can be trapped; and inadequate space between pieces of equipment. For more information on playground safety, contact: National Recreation and Park Association, 22377 Belmont Ridge Road, Ashburn, VA 20148. You can also go to the NRPA Website: www.nrpa.org

Shawna Simons teaches kindergarten at Great Oaks Elementary School. Today she is the guest speaker on motor skill development at Jefferson High.

"You only have to look at my class of four- and five-year-olds," Mrs. Simons said, "to realize that motor development varies greatly from child to child. You can't necessarily tell a child's age just by how well the child runs or colors. I have one child who's among the youngest but skips better than anyone else in class.

"Think back to the activities during your own days in kindergarten. Many are chosen to help children improve their large and small motor skills. Painting is not only a great creative activity, but it also helps hand-eye coordination. Cutting and coloring do, too. We play games that involve running, jumping, and throwing—all large motor skill activities.

"Children need well-developed motor skills to learn to read and write successfully. Forming letters takes the same kind of small muscle control and hand-eye coordination as coloring, doesn't it?

"Your teacher will be bringing you to observe my kindergarten class next week. I think you'll find the kids interesting and very individual. If you look closely, you will also see lots of learning going on—whether they are flying a kite or listening to a story. I'll be back to answer questions after you have observed my class."

"We know that children need well-developed motor skills to learn to read and write successfully."

- Identify ways to encourage good nutrition and healthy eating habits.
- Explain how to help children develop good self-care habits.
- Describe ways to prevent and handle toileting accidents among children ages four to six.

INTRODUCING CHAPTER 14

- Have students look at the photographs. Ask them to recall the difference between growth (*increasing in size*) and development (*increasing in skills*). Ask which of these changes the photographs exemplify. (*Page 434: growth, as children are measuring each other. Page 435: Development, as children's growing skills facilitate work in crafts.*)
- Have students study the photographs of children ages four to six in this unit and compare them to the photos of toddlers in Unit 4. Ask them to describe the differences in body proportion and shape.

USING THE SCENARIO Have students read the story on this page of the student text. Write the following common kindergarten activities on the board: coloring; marching to music; playing with blocks; pressing leaves; playing musical chairs; serving snacks. Ask volunteers to identify the physical skills children can learn from these activities.

KEY TO ABILITY LEVELS   Each section gives skill-building activities. Each activity has been labeled for use with students of various learning styles and abilities.

L1 Level 1 activities are basic activities and should be within the range of all students.

L2 Level 2 activities are average activities and should be within the range of average and above average students.

L3 Level 3 activities are challenging activities designed for the ability range of above average students.

SECTION 14-1

Physical Growth and Development from Four to Six

(pages 436-443)

FOCUS

MOTIVATOR

In learning self-care, children in these ages are becoming more independent. Ask students how this compares to their own experiences in adolescence.

VOCABULARY ACTIVITY

Ask students for the meanings of the words *ambiguous* (having more than one meaning) and *ambivalent* (having more than one feeling on an issue). These meanings give clues to the meaning of *ambidextrous* (being able to use more than one hand).

Physical Growth and Development from Four to Six

If you've ever been around a four-, five-, or six-year-old, you know how active children are during this period. They run rather than walk, and they wiggle when they sit, yet there is a purpose behind all this activity. Children are constantly practicing and refining their physical skills.

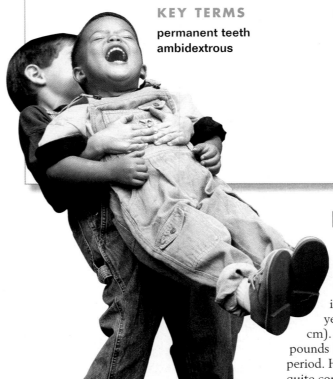

KEY TERMS

permanent teeth
ambidextrous

OBJECTIVES:

• Describe how an average child's height, weight, proportion, and posture change from ages four to six.

• Explain the changes to a child's teeth that generally begin around age six.

• Compare average motor development of four-, five, and six-year-olds.

Height and Weight

The rate of physical growth from ages four to six is only slightly slower than from ages one to three. The average yearly increase in height during these years is 2½ to 3 inches (6.4 to 7.6 cm). Most children gain about 4 to 5 pounds (1.8 to 2.3 kg) per year during this period. However, larger or smaller gains are quite common. Boys are often slightly taller and heavier than girls.

436

Observing & Participating

Bring to class a selection of drawings created by children of different ages. Try to find drawings done by children about age three and about age five or six. Show them to the students. Ask them to analyze the drawings. How does the quality of the line work compare in the work by the younger and older children? What about the use of color and the skill at coloring? What conclusions does the class draw about the small motor skills of children ages four to six?

The chart below shows average heights and weights for four- to six-year olds. Of course, height and weight charts give average measurements. Most children who are smaller or larger than the averages are still developing normally.

Children from ages four to six seem to be always active. *How does the posture of children these ages differ from that of a toddler?*

The Developing Brain

One of the fastest-growing parts of the child ages four to six is the brain. At age three, the brain is about 75 percent of its adult weight. Over the next three years, it grows to around 90 percent of its adult weight.

Proportion and Posture

Between a child's fourth and seventh birthdays, the body becomes straighter and slimmer. The protruding abdomen of babyhood flattens. The shoulders widen and are held more erect. The chest, round from birth to age three, broadens and flattens. The neck also becomes longer. The legs lengthen rapidly, growing straighter and firmer.

Average Heights and Weights for Four- to Six-Year-Olds		
YEARS	HEIGHT	WEIGHT
Four Years Old	40.7 inches *(103 cm)*	36.0 pounds *(16.3 kg)*
Five Years Old	43.5 inches *(110 cm)*	40.5 pounds *(18.4 kg)*
Six Years Old	46.0 inches *(117 cm)*	45.0 pounds *(20.4 cm)*

Differences in height and weight increase as children grow older. *What differences do you see in your own class?*

Parenting in *Action*

The constant motion of four- to six-year-olds can be physically and emotionally draining on an adult. Here are some tips for preventing the child's level of activity from being a problem:
• Give the child plenty of time for active play. This will make it easier to set aside quiet time.
• Have the child do physical chores around the home. A six-year-old who empties the wastebaskets uses up some energy.
• Identify what time of day the child feels more energetic and active. Make sure that you schedule active play at this time.

ACTIVITIES

Teamwork Activity

Divide students into four groups. Have each group measure the height of each group member and then calculate the group's average height and range in height. How do the averages and ranges compare? What does the size of the range suggest about averages? **L1**

VISUAL LEARNING Using the Photograph
Four- to six-year-olds stand much straighter than do younger children.

VISUAL LEARNING Using the Chart
Answers will vary. If the Teamwork Activity described above has been assigned, students will have quantifiable measures of the differences in their class.

DID *You* Know?

Body Proportions. **Scientists measure "sitting height," which is the distance from the top of the head to the surface on which a child is seated. Newborns' sitting height is about 70 percent of the total body length, because their legs are relatively short. By age three, it is only 57 percent. By the early teens, it is 52 percent.**

ACTIVITIES

Critical Thinking Activity

Making Inferences. Ask students how caregivers might treat a child who is much taller or shorter than average. *(May expect more advanced skills from a taller child; may treat a smaller child as younger.)* How might that affect the child? (*Could cause frustration.*) What can caregivers do to prevent this problem? (*Focus on child's ability level, not appearance.*) **L1**

ISSUES IN CHILDREN'S HEALTH

Organized Sports. During this period, many children join organized sports for the first time. Experts suggest these basic guidelines:

- Look for leagues in which children have fun without an overemphasis on winning.
- If the child doesn't enjoy competitive sports, try non-competitive activities such as martial arts and swimming.
- Set a limit of one sport a season to allow for other activities.
- Take an interest in the child's sport. Children crave parents' attention.

The child's balance and coordination improve in these years as well. Four- to six-year-olds hold their arms nearer their body when they walk or run.

Teeth

A smile showing missing teeth is typical of a six-year-old. At about that age, children begin to lose their primary teeth. Over time, the primary teeth are replaced by **permanent teeth**, the set of 32 teeth that will not be naturally replaced.

The six-year old molars, or "first molars," are the first permanent teeth to appear.

There are four of them—two upper and two lower—positioned in back of the 20 primary teeth. Because they appear first, these molars act as a lock to keep all the teeth in position. Later, when the child's front teeth are replaced by their larger permanent front teeth, the molars prevent the new front teeth from pushing other teeth farther back in the jaw.

In general, the primary teeth are lost in the same order as they came in. The two lower front teeth are the first to be replaced, followed by the two upper front teeth.

Thumb Sucking

Some four-, five-, and six-year-olds continue to suck their thumb, usually to comfort themselves or to handle tension. Adults may worry about this habit, but in most cases, it is best ignored. Trying to force a child to quit can cause more problems than the habit itself. Generally children stop on their own.

If thumb sucking seems excessive or continuous, check with a dentist. A problem exists if the position of the permanent teeth and the shape of the jaw are being altered.

Some children from ages four to six continue to suck their thumbs. *What are some reasons that children suck their thumb, and what should parents do about the habit?*

438 Unit 5: The Child from Four to Six

Management/Leadership Skills

Read the following to students: "Kerri started sucking her thumb as an infant. Now five, she still does it from time to time as a way of comforting herself. Recently, when her father saw her sucking her thumb, he yanked her thumb out of her mouth and said, 'What do you think you are, a baby?'"

Have students explain whether they think her father's words and actions would lead Kerri to stop sucking her thumb. If so, why? If not, what would they have done?

CAREER OPPORTUNITIES

Dental Hygienist

A CONVERSATION WITH RAMON REYES

How did you become interested in becoming a dental hygienist? At eleven, I needed braces. I spent lots of time in the dentist's office and got to know the people well. I love science, and helping other people always gives me a boost.

What are the tasks and responsibilities of a dental hygienist? My main job is to clean and polish people's teeth. I also take x rays. I keep records and let the dentist know about any problems. I also teach patients how to care for their teeth.

What is the work environment like? Dental hygienists work indoors in offices. Working in health care, we have to be clean and well organized, and our work space must be that way too. Safety guidelines require us to wear masks, gloves, and glasses while we work to prevent the spread of infection.

What are the working hours like? The office where I work is open six days and three evenings a week. That makes it easier for patients to schedule visits. Some hygienists work two or three days a week for two different dentists.

What aptitudes are needed to be a dental hygienist? You need good hand-eye coordination and a sensitive touch so you don't hurt or bother the patients. You need to able to work carefully and thoroughly. Hygienists must be clean and neat, giving a professional appearance. If you are pleasant and reassuring, you can help patients feel more comfortable. Finally, hygienists have to be able to communicate well with people.

DENTAL HYGIENIST

Education and Training. Hygienists can either earn a certificate in a two-year program or receive their training at a four-year college. To practice, they need to pass a state licensing test.

Career Outlook. Jobs for dental hygienists are expected to grow faster than the average in coming years.

CONNECTING SCHOOL TO CAREER

1. **Interpersonal Skills.** If you were a hygienist, how would you introduce yourself to a six-year-old having her teeth cleaned for the first time?
2. **Personal Qualities.** Self-management involves setting personal goals, having self-control, and evaluating one's own work. Why would these characteristics be essential in this career?
3. **Technology.** What are some ways dental hygienists could stay up-to-date on new technological advances in their field?

CHAPTER 14: Physical Development from Four to Six **439**

COMPREHENSION CHECK

1. How do good small motor skills help children in school? (*Make it easier to learn how to read and write.*)

ACTIVITIES

Critical Thinking Activity

Making Inferences. **Ask:** What inconveniences might a left-handed person face in a right-handed world? **L1**

| VISUAL LEARNING | **Using the Photograph** |

Possible responses: Building with blocks, making puzzles, cutting and pasting, stringing beads.

DID *You* **Know?**

Handedness. **A study looked at handedness in relation to children's visits to emergency wards for injuries. Left-handed people make up about 10 percent of the population, but left-handed children accounted for more than 16 percent of the injury patients.**

Motor Skills

During this period, most basic large and small motor skills improve significantly. How Motor Skills Develop on the next page gives examples of average physical skills by age. The timing of the development of these skills varies, of course. Ahmad can put together puzzles with 75 to 100 pieces but has not yet mastered skipping. Reilly is more comfortable with puzzles of 35 pieces and loves jumping rope.

Four-, five-, and six-year-olds are very energetic. Their favorite activities are usually physical— running, jumping, climbing, and turning somersaults. At four, children are learning to throw and catch both large and small balls. Five-year-olds show improved speed and coordination in all their activities. The movements of six-year-olds are smoothly coordinated. They enjoy balancing activities, such as walking a curb or riding a bicycle. Rhythm intrigues them—they like keeping time to music and jumping rope to chanted jingles.

Four- and five-years-olds show improved dexterity, the skilled use of the hands and fingers. Most four-years-olds learn to lace their shoes, but generally cannot tie them until about age five. Five-year-olds can pour liquids from a pitcher into a glass, showing improved hand-eye coordination. They like to cut and paste and can print some letters, but often not words. Six-year-olds show even greater ease and skill.

Children need plenty of opportunities for skill development. Giving them time and space to run, jump, and climb helps them develop their large motor skills. Providing activities such as coloring, painting, drawing, tracing, cutting, and writing helps them build small motor skills. Children with well-developed small motor skills will find learning to read and write easier.

Hand Preference

By about age five, most children consistently use either their right or left hand for most activities. The hand used most often becomes the most skillful. Only a few people are **ambidextrous**, or able to use both hands with equal skill.

With better fine-motor skills, children of these ages can paint with brushes instead of using finger paint. Hand preference is becoming established. *What other fine-motor activities are good practice for children ages four to six?*

440 UNIT 5: The Child from Four to Six

| MULTIPLE INTELLIGENCES | Have students join in pairs to develop different techniques for teaching a child how to tie shoes. They should develop instructions for at least two learning styles. Instructions might include, for example, verbal instructions for verbal learners, a diagram for visual learners, or moving the child's hands through the motion for kinesthetic learners. After they have created their instructions, have another group try to follow them. |

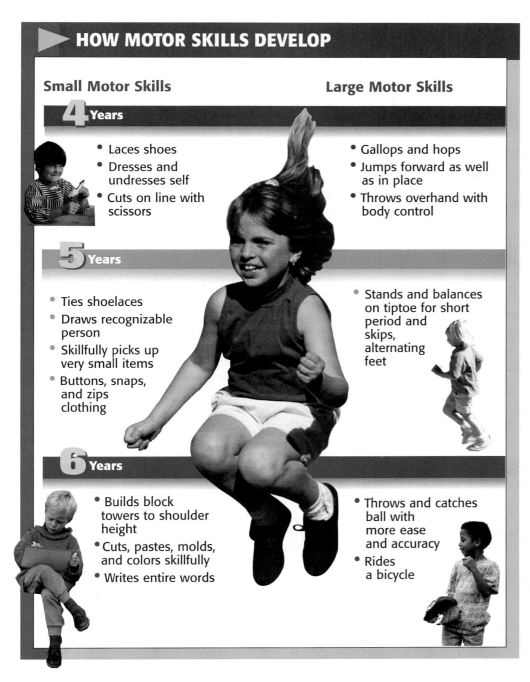

HOW MOTOR SKILLS DEVELOP

Small Motor Skills	Large Motor Skills
4 Years	
• Laces shoes • Dresses and undresses self • Cuts on line with scissors	• Gallops and hops • Jumps forward as well as in place • Throws overhand with body control
5 Years	
• Ties shoelaces • Draws recognizable person • Skillfully picks up very small items • Buttons, snaps, and zips clothing	• Stands and balances on tiptoe for short period and skips, alternating feet
6 Years	
• Builds block towers to shoulder height • Cuts, pastes, molds, and colors skillfully • Writes entire words	• Throws and catches ball with more ease and accuracy • Rides a bicycle

CHAPTER 14: Physical Development from Four to Six **441**

ACTIVITIES

Critical Thinking Activity

Understanding Point of View. Have students try to simulate the process of a child learning how to write by attempting to write using the hand they *don't* prefer. Have volunteers describe to the class what the experience was like. **L1**

Practicing Parenting

Ask students to imagine that they just won an award that is important to them. Suppose that they tell their friends the news, but no one says anything. How would they feel? How do they think a child who is not praised will feel?

Answers to Apply Your Knowledge

1. *Possible response:* "You did great jumping rope! That's a hard skill because you have to get the timing just right."

2. *Possible response:* Concern that they will think too highly of themselves.

Although handedness becomes apparent about age five, preference for one hand actually begins early in life. Researchers still don't know how hand preference develops. Some point to heredity as the probable source. Others think it depends on which hand parents usually put objects into during the first years of a child's life. Whatever the cause of hand preference, professionals agree that there is no reason to try to influence a child to prefer one hand rather than another.

Practicing Parenting

Making Compliments Count

For children ages four to six, the praise and compliments that they receive play a hidden, but important, role in development. Giving praise does more than just build self-esteem. That self-esteem encourages the child to try and master even more difficult tasks. When Janette learned how to do a forward roll, her dad commented, "Look how well you tucked your head under!" At her next tumbling class, Janette was ready to try doing somersaults. All areas of development can be enhanced through positive reinforcement. How can you use praise effectively?

♥ **Make it special.** Don't just give automatic compliments. Constant praise loses its power. Children know whether you really mean what you say.

♥ **Make it specific.** "You did a fine job putting your books away. They're so neat and organized," tells the child more than "You did a great job!"

♥ **Target problem areas.** If a child needs to work on learning to button clothes or share toys, look for opportunities to encourage improvement of those skills.

♥ **Notice positive behavior.** Children crave attention. By complimenting what the child does well, less desirable behavior will diminish.

APPLY YOUR KNOWLEDGE

1. How might you compliment a child who just learned to jump rope?

2. Why might some people feel children should not be praised very often?

Parenting in *Action*

Caregivers can encourage dexterity by providing appropriate materials and activities. Here are some ideas:
• Make figures and shapes from pipe cleaners.
• Glue ice cream sticks together to make boxes.
• Let children mix flour, sugar, salt, and other foods as they pretend to make bread.
• Glue paper strips together to make a paper chain for decoration.

Outdoor play with friends promotes development in all areas, not just physical.

SECTION 14-1 REVIEW

✔ Check Your Understanding

1. What changes in height, weight, and proportion generally take place in four- to six-year-olds?
2. Describe the posture of children ages four to six.
3. Which are the first permanent teeth to appear? What function do these teeth perform?
4. What would you say to a parent who asked you for advice on how to handle a five-year-old who sucks his thumb?
5. List at least four large motor skills you could place on a developmental checklist for four-year-olds.

Putting Knowledge Into Practice

1. **Analyzing.** Six-year-olds—especially boys—are very active and have difficulty sitting still. What effects might that have on their behavior in school?
2. **Synthesizing.** Put together a list of typical activities for a half day of kindergarten. For each appropriate activity, indicate which specific small and/or large motor skills would be practiced.
3. **Observing and Participating.** Go to a park or playground where young children are playing. Watch them play and record what they do and how they behave. Try to determine which of the children are aged four to six based on their behavior. Share your notes and your conclusions with the class.

CHAPTER 14: Physical Development from Four to Six   **443**

ANSWERS TO SECTION 14-1 REVIEW

1. *Height:* Grow 2½ to 3 inches (6.4-7.6 cm) a year. *Weight:* Gain 4-5 pounds (1.8-2.3 kg) each year. *Proportion:* Shoulders widen, neck and legs become longer.
2. Body becomes straighter and slimmer.
3. Molars. Keep all teeth in position and prevent new front teeth from pushing others back in jaw.
4. *Possible response:* Let child outgrow it.
5. *See the chart on page 441.*

CHECKING COMPREHENSION

Have students answer the Check Your Understanding questions. The answers appear at the bottom of this page.

EVALUATION

Give students the Section 14-1 Quiz in the *Teacher Resource Guide*.

RETEACHING

1. Assign Reteaching Activities, page 42.
2. Have students compare children aged four to six and children aged one to three in physical development.

ENRICHMENT

Have students describe their own experience learning how to ride a bicycle. When did they learn? How did they learn?

EXTENSION

Take students to observe a Pre-K or a kindergarten class. Tell them to pay particular attention to differences in height, weight, and balance.

CLOSE

Have students write an ending to this sentence: "Between ages four and six, children . . ."

SECTION 14-2

Providing Care for Children from Four to Six

(pages 444-451)

SECTION 14-2 RESOURCES
Teacher Resource Guide
- Lesson Plan Organizer, p. 69
- Section 14-2 Quiz, p. 177

Student Motivation Kit
- Observ. & Case Studies (case study), pp. 123-124
- Reteaching Activity, p. 43
- Enrichment, pp. 41-42
- Teen Parenting Skills, pp. 129-130

Student Workbook
- Study Guide, pp. 115-118
- Reading Nutrition Labels, pp. 120-121

Transparency Package
- CT-41, CT-42

Effective Instruction CD-ROM

FOCUS

MOTIVATOR

Remind students how much physical care children need before age four. Ask them to write in their notebooks an hypothesis about how that might change for children ages four to six. After reading the section, have them check their hypotheses.

VOCABULARY ACTIVITY

Tell students that two of the terms are formed by combining a root word and a suffix (*identity* and *identification; seal* and *sealant*). Point out that they can get clues to the meaning of the terms by knowing the meaning of the root words. Suffixes also give clues to the function of words. In this case, both are nouns.

444

SECTION 14-2

Providing Care for Children from Four to Six

Four-, five-, and six-year-olds need less actual physical care than younger children. However, they still need guidance in developing self-care skills. This increasing independence is needed as children start school. Many four-year-olds go to preschool programs, and most five-year-olds go to kindergarten for a full or half day. By age six, children are typically in school for a full day.

KEY TERMS
fluoride
group identification
sealant

OBJECTIVES:
- Explain why good nutrition is essential for children ages four to six.
- Give examples of ways to encourage good nutrition in children of these ages.
- Explain how to help children ages four to six develop good self-care habits.

Feeding

The energy children need for growth, learning, and activity depends on a steady supply of nutritious foods. Following the Food Guide Pyramid, shown on page 361, is an easy way to ensure good nutrition. Serving sizes are smaller for children. Young children often eat the minimum number of servings from each food group.

Observing & Participating

Ask students what establishments they have seen in the community that sell prepared food that appeals to children. Write the suggestions on the chalkboard. Ask how popular the different establishments are. Do they employ marketing techniques that make them popular with children? Ask them to think about the kinds of foods that are available from these places. Do they promote good nutrition or not? If not, how could the nutritional value of the food be improved?

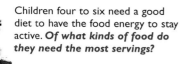

Children four to six need a good diet to have the food energy to stay active. *Of what kinds of food do they need the most servings?*

Of course, the actual amount of food an individual child needs varies. It depends on such factors as height and weight, temperament, and level of physical activity. A girl who runs and bikes a great deal needs more food energy than one who spends more time playing quietly indoors.

Research has shown that many children do better with five or six small meals and snacks a day than three large ones. Why? A child's stomach is still small. Eating more frequently provides a more constant level of energy.

Poor Nutrition

Poor nutrition—not getting the key nutrients needed through food—has many causes. Lack of money to buy healthful foods is *not* the most common one. Some caregivers don't understand the need for or principles of good nutrition. Others have poor eating habits themselves and set a poor example. Sometimes children are simply allowed to choose their own food. It is the responsibility of parents and other caregivers to provide children with healthful food choices and make sure they are well-nourished.

Poor nutrition has negative effects. Children with inadequate diets have less

resistance to colds and other illnesses. Their growth may be limited. Learning, too, may be more difficult because they are tired and easily distracted.

Weight Problems

During this age span, children may look chunky or slim and still be healthy. Check with a doctor before deciding that a child is overweight or underweight. If a problem is detected, the doctor or a dietitian can help determine what eating and activity changes are needed. What works for adults may not be appropriate for children. For an overweight child, for example, a low-calorie diet may not supply the nutrients and energy needed for growth, development, and learning.

When a child consistently consumes more calories than the body uses, the extra calories are stored as fat to meet future energy needs. A child who is underweight is not eating enough food to supply his or her energy needs. Neither of these conditions occurs suddenly, although a child may lose weight quickly when ill. Both result from long-term eating habits that do not match the child's needs. Often it's not just the quantity of food eaten, but the quality that's the problem.

Poor food choices can also be a cause of weight problems. With help, children can learn to balance the types and amount of food they eat with the specific needs of their body.

CHAPTER 14: Physical Development from Four to Six **445**

TEACH

ACTIVITIES

Promoting Health Activity

Some researchers urge family fitness as a way of helping young children develop good health habits. They suggest that the family can be instrumental in developing a fitness program that matches the interests of all family members. Have students create a poster promoting the idea of family fitness. **L1**

| **VISUAL LEARNING** | Using the Photograph |

Answer: Foods from the Bread, Cereal, Rice, and Pasta Group.

The Developing Brain

The Effects of Malnutrition

Studies show that malnutrition can have a powerful negative impact on brain development. Children who are malnourished show slow and simple responses. Lack of protein or calories is not the only factor, though. Along with diet improvements, these children benefit from social and educational help that fosters exploration and social interaction.

Parenting in *Action*

Students should take the role of parents in a family with two children. Have them develop ways of handling these situations:
- When the family goes to eat at another family's house, six-year-old Adam looks at the food on the table and announces which items he does not like.
- Four-year-old Wendy refuses to eat anything that is green.
- At the grocery store, both children beg you to buy Crispy Crunchies, a cereal they have seen advertised but which is high in sugar.

Ask the E❓perts

Introducing the Feature

Because their capacity for food is small, children cannot afford to eat low-nutrient foods such as pretzels, potato chips, candy, or cookies. These foods are high in calories and have few nutritional benefits. Many of them also have high levels of salt, fat, and sugar, all of which should be limited in any person's diet.

Answers to Thinking It Through

1. *Possible responses:* Invent silly names for foods (Carrie Carrot, Nana Banana); work with child to create rhyming jingles.

2. *Possible responses:* Cooking large quantities of nutritious foods when they have time and freezing portions to be reheated later; preparing quick but nutritious meals such as broiled meats and raw vegetables.

Applying What You've Learned

Allie tends to eat in streaks at dinner—mostly grains one day, mostly meat the next, and mostly vegetables on another day. Ask students what Allie's parents should do.

Ask the E❓perts

Pat Brodeen
Teacher and Teen Parent Coordinator
at Theodore Roosevelt High School
San Antonio, Texas

PROMOTING *Good Eating Habits*

How can I encourage my child to eat a balanced diet now, and how can I help her build healthy eating habits that will last a lifetime?

A Many parents worry about their children's eating habits. It's a natural concern, but worrying isn't part of the solution. Because children begin to eat less and become more choosy as they get older, the best approach to helping a child develop good eating habits has three steps:

1. **Understand children's nutritional needs.**
2. **Make nutritious foods available and attractive.**
3. **Set a good example, but don't make eating an issue.**

The first step is easy. Become familiar with the Food Guide Pyramid. The pyramid makes it clear that children—like the rest of us—should be eating more foods made from grain, fruits, and vegetables than from meat.

The second step can be fun for both parents and children. Involve the children in selecting, preparing and serving nutritious foods. Find ways to enjoy familiar foods and to experiment with new ones. Try making frozen pops from juice or dipping broccoli "trees" in cheese. Let children create—and then eat—their own necklaces of oat cereal rings.

For many parents, the third step is the most challenging. Offer your child nutritious,

appealing foods; then let go. Treat your child's food preferences—and your child—with respect. Forcing a child to eat can cause problems beyond food choices. Given opportunities, good examples, and respect, children will likely develop healthy, long-lasting eating habits.

Thinking It Through

1. Children these ages enjoy silly names and rhymes. Suggest specific ways you could build on these interests to encourage good nutrition.

2. In many families, parents work outside the home so preparing a nutritious dinner quickly is a challenge. What techniques could parents use to avoid frequent take-out meals which often are high in fat?

446 UNIT 5: The Child from Four to Six

Parenting in *Action*

Some experts point out that when children reject a food the first time they see it, they may still grow to like it. As Dr. Isobel Contento of Columbia University says, "Research shows that it may take up to fifteen or twenty tries before the kid will like" a new food. Dr. Leann Birch of Pennsylvania State University says parents can reintroduce the food every two or three days.

Have students suggest different foods that they now enjoy but that they did not like at first. Ask them to consider why their attitudes changed.

Teaching Children About Nutrition

One of the best gifts parents and other caregivers can give young children is good eating habits. Nutrition lessons learned at this stage can lead to a lifetime of better health.

As children begin school, they start making more decisions on their own about what they will and will not eat. By learning about nutrition, children can make wise food choices. They are more than happy to tell others what they have learned, too. Just before four-year-old Chris popped a carrot stick in his mouth, he announced, "This gives me good eyes." Both home and school play a part in teaching good food attitudes and habits.

At Home

Parents can take advantage of children's natural curiosity at this stage. Food is a rich resource for learning. For example, involving children in caring for a garden has been shown to increase the variety and quantity of vegetables they eat.

Children also can help in the kitchen in many different ways. They can tear lettuce for salads, scramble eggs, or mix batter. They enjoy cutting shapes out of bread. They can make mini pizzas by flattening biscuit dough, pouring on tomato sauce, and sprinkling on cheese or other toppings. Teaching children about nutrition in this way offers other advantages as well. Children

Children aged four to six are eager to help around the kitchen. *What tasks can parents ask them to perform?*

feel proud of the contributions they have made to a meal. The parent and child spend positive time working together. Such activities also help children improve their small motor skills.

At School

Schools, too, use food as learning tools. For a preschooler, spreading peanut butter inside a celery stick and sprinkling raisins on the top provides lots of lessons. Celery, peanut butter, and raisins are all good for you and help you grow. The textures of these ingredients are quite different. What words describe their texture? How many raisins are on the peanut butter? How does

Critical Thinking Activity

Analyzing. **Ask:** What effect do television commercials have on food choices? At what age do they think that effect begins? At what age does it lessen or disappear? **L1**

Nutrition Activity

Have students bring nutrition labels for prepared foods such as pizza, canned soup, rice or pasta mixes, and microwaveable meals. Have students form into groups according to the kinds of food the labels represent. Have each group prepare a chart showing the type of food; brand name; and nutrient, fat, sodium, and sugar content. Display all the charts. **Ask:** Which foods are high in nutrients? Which are high in fat, sodium, and sugar? Do certain brands offer better nutrition? **L2**

VISUAL LEARNING	Using the Photograph

Possible responses (other than examples in the text): Washing vegetables or fruit, putting bread in toaster, serving cereal.

LEARNING STYLES	Visual

Have students create an illustration showing what factors influence a child's food preferences. Students can prepare their illustration in one of several ways: by drawing symbols representing the different influences, by making a collage with pictures cut out of magazines, or by using a computer drawing program. You may wish to begin by having the class brainstorm what factors to include (for example, family, peers, advertising, ethnic background, region of the country).

COMPREHENSION CHECK

1. What kinds of self-care can four- to six-year-olds manage? (*Clean bodies and teeth, dress selves, care for clothing.*)
2. What are sealants and fluoride? (*Both protect teeth from cavities.*)
3. How do low rods and handy shelves help children care for clothing? (*Make storing easy.*)

ACTIVITIES

Critical Thinking Activity

Applying. Have students develop a list of basic rules of cleanliness that they think a child aged four to six can follow. Ask for volunteers to read their ideas to the class. **L1**

> ► **In the Lunch Bag**
>
>
>
> **What other tips for great packed lunches can you add?**
>
> - **Let them choose their own lunch box or bag.**
> - **Don't get in a rut**—send different foods each day.
> - **Make foods easy to eat.** Try pita bread or a tortilla wrap to keep the filling inside.
> - **Think finger foods**—chunks, strips, cubes, and shapes.
> - **It doesn't have to be a sandwich.** Lowfat yogurt with sprinkles, a hearty soup, crisp salad, or casserole favorites can travel in insulated containers.
> - **What about sweets?** Ripe fruit, raisins, fig bars, and graham crackers are all good choices.
> - **Add a surprise!** This could be a special treat, a fancy napkin, a riddle, or a note that says you care.

the celery sound when you bite it? What does the finished snack look like? Maybe ants on a log!

Children who are in school all day usually bring their lunch from home or eat one provided by the school. However, what children are given to eat and what they actually eat may be quite different. Food is often traded or thrown away. To entice children to eat all of their packed lunch, try the tips shown above.

Teaching Self-Care Skills

As four- to six-year-olds' physical abilities improve, they are increasingly able to care for themselves. They can keep themselves clean, dress themselves, and begin to care for their clothes.

Washing and Bathing

Many children this age are less interested in washing and bathing. Performing these tasks has lost its novelty. Praise for a job well done works better than nagging and scolding.

Setting up and maintaining hygiene routines helps children accept these tasks as expected behavior. Malcolm and his sister take turns using the bathroom to wash up before bed. While one is washing, the other gets his or her backpack ready for the next day.

Brushing Teeth

Regular tooth brushing is another essential routine. Make sure children know how to brush effectively and learn how to floss their teeth.

Tooth decay is a real concern at this age since permanent teeth are beginning to emerge. The dentist may recommend using **sealants**, thin plastic coatings that prevent plaque from developing. Toothpaste with **fluoride**, a chemical that strengthens the outer coating of teeth, helps also. These two steps can prevent about 90 percent of cavities from developing.

Dressing and Choosing Clothes

Four-, five-, and six-year-olds are usually able to dress themselves independently.

Parenting in *Action*

Point out to students that developing self-care habits may be more difficult for children whose parents are divorced if they spend time in two different homes. Sometimes they receive inconsistent instruction. Tell them the following story: "When Sarina lives with her father and stepmother, they don't require her to bathe every day. Her mother wants her to bathe each night, but she's having trouble enforcing that rule."

What do students think Sarina's mother should do?

Molars, in back, are the first permanent teeth to appear. *What order do the remaining teeth follow?*

of belonging—begins to be important. That may bring a desire to wear clothes that are popular with others. Take the child along on shopping trips, if possible.

Caring for Clothes

Once children begin to care about what they wear, they can learn basic clothing care. To start, they can fold and hang up clothes and put dirty items in the appropriate place. Putting clothes away is simpler if the child has storage within reach. Hooks at eye level, low rods, and handy shelves encourage children to take care of their clothes.

Developing these habits will probably take a long time and require consistent reminders. To some parents, it just seems easier to continue doing such tasks for their

Some may need help with complicated fasteners, such as shoelaces or buttons down the back of a garment.

Many children have difficulty figuring out which clothes match. Mismatched outfits can usually just be ignored. Another approach is to help children select coordinating outfits ahead of time and store them together.

Comfort, durability, and economy remain the guidelines for choosing clothes. Two other factors are important in selecting clothes. First, children this age have definite likes and dislikes. Some become attached to a favorite garment, as they do to a particular toy. Second, **group identification**—a feeling

Children will be interested in taking care of clothes that they were able to choose themselves. *What kind of clothing is best for active children?*

CHAPTER 14: Physical Development from Four to Six **449**

Teamwork Activity

Have students form into groups and write down recipes for nutritious snacks. Then have them combine their ideas into a snack book. If possible, they could use a computer program to put their suggestions in a more finished form. They could decorate the recipes with clip art or other illustrations. **L2**

Discussion Activity

Ask students to identify advantages of hand-me-down clothing. (*Economical, save shopping time.*) What are the disadvantages? (*May not fit exactly, may be out of style, may look worn.*) **L1**

Critical Thinking Activity

Sequencing. Have students develop a way of explaining to children how to brush their teeth. They can do it in writing, in a diagram, or by performing the actions. **L2**

VISUAL LEARNING	Using the Photographs

Top—Answer: Two lower front and upper front teeth follow the molars. *Bottom—Answer:* Comfortable, durable, and economical clothes. It is best if clothes do not have complicated fasteners.

Management/Leadership Skills

Many hours of imaginative play can come from a box of old clothes. Through playing dress-up, children not only test their creativity and imagination but also practice dressing skills, including manipulation of buttons, zipper, and other fasteners. Before throwing away old clothes, people might think of a child who could enjoy them. Even if there is not a child in the family, people can take steps to get old clothes into the hands of a child. Have students brainstorm ways to distribute old clothes to children for play.

Right:—Possible responses: Improves child's language skills, helps child feel close to person who is reading.

HEALTH TIP

Ask if students ever felt embarrassed about something they did. Ask if that feeling made it harder for them to control their actions. Point out that the same situation can affect children who have lapses in bladder control. If they are made to feel ashamed, they are likely to have more accidents. They need encouragement and support.

Answers to
FOLLOWING UP

1. *Possible response:* Ashamed, fearful, discouraged.

2 *Possible response:* Check with the pediatrician to see if the child needs medical attention; limit how much liquid the child drinks at night; remind child to go to the bathroom before going out.

HEALTH TIP

Handling Bedwetting

*I*t is not unusual for children who have completed toilet training to occasionally wet the bed at night. Bedwetting tends to happen more frequently soon after a child learns bladder control. Over time, it usually happens less often, and by five it typically disappears.

Still, about 10 percent of children older than five occasionally wet their bed at night. About two-thirds of these children are boys. There are several possible causes. Either the child's bladder is not large enough to hold urine during the night, or he or she is not awakened by the feeling of a full bladder. Sometimes the cause is an infection in the urinary tract.

Treat toileting accidents casually. Shaming or scolding the child doesn't help. Concerned parents should talk to the child's pediatrician.

FOLLOWING UP
1. How are children older than five likely to feel when they wet the bed at night?
2. If you were a parent of a six-year-old who occasionally wets the bed, how, specifically, would you handle the situation?

---

children. However, this is the stage of development when children need to increase their independence and sense of responsibility. Parents who pick up and put away clothes for a five-year-old shouldn't be surprised when the child expects the same service as a teen.

Sleeping

By four, many children no longer take an afternoon nap. Some continue a daily nap until they begin a full day of school. It depends on the needs of the individual child.

Children this age are generally more cooperative about going to bed. A few use delaying tactics, but many actually ask to go to bed. After saying goodnight and perhaps looking at a book or listening to soft music for a while, most go to sleep easily. Some children may need conversation, compan-

ionship, or a stuffed toy to sleep. Bedtime stories offer a time for closeness and develop an interest in books and reading.

Toileting

By their fourth birthday, most children have few toileting accidents. When accidents do occur, it is often because the child is concentrating so fully on an activity that he or she forgets to go to the bathroom. Sometimes a child is in a new place and feels uncomfortable asking where the bathroom is. Sickness—even a cold—may also lead to accidents. A persistent problem should be checked by a doctor.

These steps can minimize accidents:
• Before leaving home for an activity, make sure the child goes to the bathroom.

| ISSUES IN TEEN PARENTING | When teens become parents, they must change roles, often very quickly. As teens, they were cared for by someone else. As parents, they are now the caregivers. Ask students to make a list of | responsibilities associated with caring for a child. (Encourage them to consider more than just physical needs.) Which responsibilities do they think would be easiest for a teen parent to assume? Why? Which would be the most difficult? Why? |

A bedtime story can help settle a child after an active day. *What other benefits does reading together provide?*

• When arriving at a new place, help the child find where the bathroom is.
• Keep an extra outfit available so that if an accident does happen, the child has clean clothes to wear.

When they begin school, some children may suffer from constipation or sometimes wet their pants. These problems can be caused by the tension children feel in their new school surroundings. The length of time for adjustment depends on the individual child. Most children adjust within a few weeks. For some children, the problem may recur at the beginning of school for several years.

SECTION 14-2 REVIEW

✔ Check Your Understanding

1. What factors influence the amount of food a child needs?
2. How can parents and other caregivers help children learn good nutrition in the home?
3. What would you do if you found out that a child you care for usually trades away her school lunch for others' cookies and candy?
4. How can caregivers teach children to make cleanliness routines a habit?
5. What practices should children follow to care for their teeth?
6. Why is it helpful to take children along when shopping for their clothes?
7. What steps can be taken to make it easier for children to care for their clothes?
8. How should parents and other caregivers handle toileting accidents by four- to six-year-olds?

Putting Knowledge Into Practice

1. **Comparing and Creating.** Compare the three-year-old's interest in bathing and washing to that of a four- to six-year-old. Working with a partner, brainstorm a list of suggestions for increasing interest.
2. **Applying.** Imagine that you are the parent of a six-year-old who wets the bed about once a month. What might be your reactions? What would you actually do?
3. **Observing and Participating.** Watch a group of four- to six-year-olds eat a meal. Choose one child and analyze his or her food choices. Were they nutritious? If not, what would you do to make them more nutritious? Share your notes and conclusions with the class.

CHAPTER 14: Physical Development from Four to Six **451**

ASSESS

CHECKING COMPREHENSION

Have students answer the Check Your Understanding questions. Answers to the questions appear at the bottom of this page.

EVALUATION

Give students the Section 14-2 Quiz in the *Teacher Resource Guide.*

RETEACHING

1. Assign Reteaching Activities, page 43.
2. Have students develop a plan for a child's nightly self-care routine that includes good hygiene and a calm preparation for sleep.

ENRICHMENT

Have students evaluate different fabrics used in children's clothing in terms of comfort, care, durability, and cost. Have them make a chart compiling their findings.

EXTENSION

Invite a pediatrician, pediatric nurse, or nurse practitioner to the class to speak about what they look for in a healthy child's four-, five-, and six-year checkups.

CLOSE

Have students write a checklist of self-care skills for a six-year-old.

ANSWERS TO SECTION 14-2 REVIEW

1. Height, weight, temperament, level of activity.
2. *Possible response:* By letting them help grow and prepare food.
3. *Possible response:* Be sure to pack nutritious foods that the child likes.
4. By setting up and maintaining routines.
5. Brushing after eating.
6. So they can choose clothing they like, which they are more likely to wear.
7. Providing adequate storage within the child's reach.
8. *Possible response:* With patience and support.

MOTIVATOR

Ask students to recall their favorite television shows when they were children. Write the names of the shows on the board. Ask for a show of hands, and record how many students recall watching each show. Ask students why those shows were popular.

Discussion Activity

Have students stage a debate on the statement by the American Academy of Pediatrics reproduced on this page. Do they agree or disagree with the policy? Do they think this organization should be making statements about TV viewing? Why or why not? **L2**

Critical Thinking Activity

Analyzing. Ask students to respond to the following questions:
• How can children benefit from watching television? What can they learn?
• What are some negative effects—physical and emotional—of watching television? **L2**

Teamwork Activity

Have students work in groups to write a scene in which parents tell a young child that they do not want the child to watch a particular TV show. Then ask volunteers to perform their scene for the class. Have the class discuss whether the approach would be effective. **L2**

Parenting With Care

Monitoring Television Viewing

If you ask whether young children should watch television, you'll likely get strong opinions.

Actually parents and other caregivers should think about different questions: Which TV programs are right for young children? How much TV should they watch? With whom should they watch TV?

There are certainly many valuable TV shows. Shows like *Sesame Street*, for example, teach the alphabet and numbers, help children learn about different cultures, and help them understand their feelings. Nature shows teach and entertain at the same time.

Programs about current events can help children develop an interest in the world around them. Letting the TV serve as an "electronic babysitter," however, isn't healthy. The more children watch TV, the less time they have for other activities. Drawing and cutting and pasting, running and jumping, and playing with other children are all important to the child's physical, social, emotional and intellectual development.

Many TV programs simply aren't suitable for children.

Some programs frighten or confuse them. Others present topics that are too mature for them to understand. The amount of violence shown on TV—even in children's programs, such as cartoons—is a particular problem. Research is still being conducted on the effect of TV violence on children, but the extent of violence is clear. One study found that more than 60 percent of all TV shows surveyed had violence—and in almost three quarters of them, the person who committed the violence suffered no punishment. The American Academy of Pediatrics has taken a firm stand on the issue:

"We believe that televised violence has a clear effect upon the behavior of children and contributes to the frequency with which violence is used to resolve conflict."

452 UNIT 5: The Child from Four to Six

RESOURCES ON TELEVISION

One aspect of television that troubles many parents is advertising aimed at the very young. Parents are concerned both about the type of products advertised and how the commercials influence their children. Your students may be interested in writing for the free publications "Parent's Guide: Advertising and Your Child" or "Self-Regulatory Guidelines for Children's Advertising." These brochures are available from: Council of Better Business Bureaus, Children's Advertising Review Unit, 845 Third Avenue, New York, NY 10022.

TV watching can be helpful or harmful to a child's development. These steps can help make it a positive experience.

- Limit the amount of time children spend watching TV.
- Choose programs that are appropriate for the child's age and promote development.
- Check out shows the child wants to watch to see if they are acceptable.
- Whenever possible, watch along with the child. You can help the child separate reality and fantasy by explaining things that may be confusing. If violence is shown, explain other ways that the problem could have been solved.

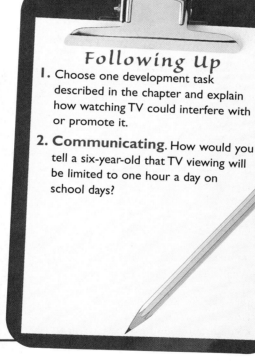

Following Up

1. Choose one development task described in the chapter and explain how watching TV could interfere with or promote it.

2. **Communicating**. How would you tell a six-year-old that TV viewing will be limited to one hour a day on school days?

CHAPTER 14: Physical Development from Four to Six **453**

DID You Know?

The V Chip. **Parents can block some programs from appearing on their TVs if the television set is equipped with a "V [for violence] chip." In 1998, the Federal Communications Commission approved program ratings from Y (acceptable for children of all ages) to MA (inappropriate for children under 17). There are also codes telling whether a show has violence, offensive language, or sexual activity. V chips must be installed on all sets from the year 2000 on. Parents can choose which programs they want to block by selecting the relevant codes.**

CLOSE

1. Have students assume that they are about to begin a job babysitting for a young child. Have them write a list of questions they would ask the parents about television viewing.

2. Extension. Have each student observe a child while watching a television program. Ask the students to note the child's age and physical and emotional reactions to the television program and the commercials. Have them prepare their observation in written form.

Answers to Following Up

1. *Possible response:* TV viewing interferes with large motor skills because time spent in front of the television is time that a child cannot practice running, jumping, and so on.

2. *Possible response:* "We have to limit your TV viewing to one hour a day during school. You spend many hours a day in school, and you need time to have fun in many different ways after school. You can choose to watch one hour-long show or two half-hour shows."

CHECKING COMPREHENSION

Use the Summary and the Reviewing the Facts questions to help students go over the most important ideas presented in Chapter 14. Encourage students to ask questions and add details.

CHAPTER 14 REVIEW

Answers to Reviewing the Facts

1. *Height:* They grow an average of 2½-3 inches (6.4-7.6 cm) each year. *Weight:* They gain an average of 4-5 pounds (1.8-2.3 kg) per year. *Posture:* They stand straighter and slimmer.
2. Four molars appear first. They are followed by two lower front teeth and then the two upper front teeth.
3. *Possible responses:* They gain comfort; to handle tension; it becomes a habit.
4. At four years, children can gallop and hop, jump forward and in place, and throw overhand. At five, they can stand and balance on tiptoe and alternate feet while skipping. At six, they can throw and catch a ball with more ease and accuracy.
5. *Any four:* Coloring, painting, drawing, tracing, cutting, writing, etc.
6. Setting a good example; providing healthy food choices; involving children in growing or preparing food so they become more interested in it.
7. Help children select outfits with clothes that match in advance of the time that children will be making decisions about what clothes to wear.

Summary

✔ Children ages four to six grow rapidly, and their body shape changes. (Section 14-1)

✔ Permanent teeth begin to appear around age six, replacing primary teeth. (Section 14-1)

✔ Children ages four to six refine their large and small motor skills. (Section 14-1)

✔ Good eating habits can influence nutrition habits as an adult. (Section 14-2)

✔ Four- to six-year-olds can wash and dress themselves and can help care for their own clothes. (Section 14-2)

✔ Children ages four to six may still have toileting accidents. (Section 14-2)

Reviewing the Facts

1. Describe how children ages four to six change in height, weight, and posture. (Section 14-1)
2. In what order do permanent teeth appear? (Section 14-1)
3. Why do some children continue to suck their thumb? (Section 14-1)
4. How do children's large motor skills improve during this age span? (Section 14-1)
5. Give at least four examples of activities which can help four- to six-year-olds improve their dexterity. (Section 14-1)
6. What are three ways parents can help young children learn good nutrition? (Section 14-2)
7. How can parents make it easier for children to choose clothing that matches? (Section 14-2)

454 UNIT 5: The Child from Four to Six

8. Name two possible causes for toileting accidents by children ages four to six. (Section 14-2)

Thinking Critically

1. **Analyzing.** By the end of kindergarten some children haven't yet mastered such small motor skills as writing letters. Do you think these children should repeat kindergarten or be allowed to advance to first grade? Explain your answer.
2. **Synthesizing.** Suppose you worked at a child care center. Describe three steps you could take to help the children prevent bladder-control accidents.

Taking Action

1. **Which Hand Is It?** Draw two pictures of a house with trees and flowers—one with your right hand and one with your left. (Mark them with an "R" and "L".) As a class, compare all the right-handed drawings and all the left-handed ones. Can you identify which were drawn with the preferred hand? How might drawing with your "wrong" hand be similar to a young child's experience drawing pictures? (*Thinking Skills*)

---

8. *Any two:* Child may be concentrating so fully on an activity that the need to go to the bathroom is ignored; child may feel uncomfortable asking where the bathroom is in a new place; illness.

CONNECTIONS

2. **Tie It Up.** How would you teach a five-year-old to tie shoelaces? Make a simple chart or give a visual demonstration of the steps you would use. Be sure your verbal explanation will be understood by the child. *(Leadership)*

Cross-Curricular Connections

1. **Math.** Using the heights and weights of the children in a preschool or kindergarten class, calculate the children's average height and weight. Next find the range of differences in weight and height. Make a visual of your findings.

2. **Language Arts.** Ask a librarian to recommend a book that would be suitable as a bedtime story for a four- to six-year-old. Read the book and tell the class why you agree or disagree with the recommendation.

Workplace Connections

1. **Interpersonal Skills.** You see Tonya, a five-year-old, bouncing a ball near a group of three-year-olds. Being older, Tonya is faster and more sure on her feet, but she still isn't very aware of others. As she bounces the ball harder and harder, you are concerned that it may hit and knock down one of the younger children. What would you do?

2. **Basic Skills.** You work in a child care center and have been asked to devise a set of cleanliness rules for the children. The rules should include what children should do before and after meals or snacks and after they have used the bathroom.

Family and Community Connections

1. **Eating Right.** Design a poster about good nutrition or healthful snacks for kindergarten students. Display the posters in a classroom or other appropriate community site.

2. **Clothing Care.** If you have a younger child living with you, look at how his or her clothes are stored. Would you recommend any changes to make it easier for the child to care for his or her clothes?

Technology Connections

1. **Computer.** Using a nutrition analysis program, find the nutritional value of the foods that you ate today for breakfast and lunch. Include serving size, number of calories, and grams of fat, protein, and carbohydrates. Based on your findings, what would you do to improve your diet to be a good example for a child? Explain whether or not you would use this software to analyze a child's diet.

1. Use the reproducible Chapter 14 Test in the *Teacher Resource Guide*, or construct your own test using the **Exam**View® Test Generator.

2. For an alternative assessment, assign the Chapter 14 activity in the *Authentic Assessment* section of the *Teacher Resource Guide*.

ENRICHMENT

Assign students either of the two enrichment activities in the *Enrichment Activities* booklet in the *Student Motivation Kit*.

EXTENSION

Have students prepare a lesson that would teach four- to six-year-olds about the Food Guide Pyramid and how to use it.

CLOSE

Have students create a timeline of physical development from ages four to six. Above that timeline, they should show what skills a child acquires and about when. Below the timeline, they should place labels describing care of children these ages. Those labels should indicate whether the activity is performed by a caregiver or is a matter of self-care.

CHAPTER 15 RESOURCES

Teacher Resource Guide
• Chapter 15 Test, p. 184
• Authentic Assessment, p. 285

Student Motivation Kit
• Observations, pp. 55-56
• Creative Activities, pp. 13-41,
106-124

Transparency Package
• CT-43, CT-44, CT-49

Effective Instruction CD-ROM

CHAPTER 15 | OVERVIEW

In **Section 15-1**, students study
patterns of emotional and social
development in ages four and six.
In **Section 15-2**, students explore
how these patterns apply to family
and other relationships.

CHAPTER 15 | OBJECTIVES

After completing Chapter 15,
students will be able to:

• Describe general patterns of
emotional and social development of children ages four to six.
• Describe the effects of competition on children these ages.
• Analyze how beginning school
affects a child's emotional and
social development.
• Describe a child's relationship to
other family members in these
ages.
• Explain how children develop a
sense of right and wrong.

456

CHAPTER 15

Emotional and Social Development from Four to Six

RESOURCES TO EXPLORE

Child Abuse. Children under the age of
six are the most likely to be victims of child
abuse. Childhelp USA sponsors a national
toll-free number to report suspected
abuse. It is 800-4-A-Child (800-422-4453).
Founded in 1959, the organization's Website
is www.childhelpusa.org

The children crowded around the aquarium's children's exhibit to touch the baby shark. Angela pushed her way through the rest to get right to the front where she could feel it. Dustin hung back from the others although he moved to a position where he had a good view. Rachel and Briana talked the whole time—although their conversation did not seem to be about the shark. Kaleel told Bobby what kind of shark it was, and what it ate. Molly named it, and Shoma tried to tell a story about sharks.

Jed Washburn, who taught this preschool class, simply watched the children be themselves. He smiled to himself and realized how much the children had changed since the class started in the fall. "They're really growing up," he thought, and then said aloud, "OK, Briana, tell me what you know about sharks."

"He realized how much the children had changed over the year."

INTRODUCING **CHAPTER 15**

- Read the following statements to the class, and ask whether they think child care professionals would agree.
  "Five-year-olds are more cooperative and receptive to rules than four-year-olds."
  "Competition is unhealthy for children."
  "Children from four to six behave in acceptable ways only to escape punishment or win approval."
- Have students examine the children in the photograph. **Ask:** How do they reflect the physical changes that occur in this period? Tell them the chapter will focus on emotional, social, and moral development.

USING THE SCENARIO Have students read the story on this page of the student text. Ask students to describe the skills the children in the story exhibited. Ask them why the teacher thought the children were growing up.

KEY TO ABILITY LEVELS Each section gives skill-building activities. Each activity has been labeled for use with students of various learning styles and abilities.

L1 Level 1 activities are basic activities and should be within the range of all students.

L2 Level 2 activities are average activities and should be within the range of average and above average students.

L3 Level 3 activities are challenging activities designed for the ability range of above average students.

Emotional Development from Four to Six

(pages 458-467)

FOCUS

MOTIVATOR

Write the following on the board for students to complete: "The biggest change between a three-year-old and a six-year-old is . . ."

Have students record their answers. After completing Section 15-1, have them compare their responses with information in the section.

VOCABULARY ACTIVITY

Point out that the key term derives from initiate, which means "to start or begin." Ask students what the term might mean based on this derivation.

Emotional Development from Four to Six

Heather walked to school with Justin on his first day. As they reached the block where the school stood, Justin turned to his mother. "OK, Mommy," he said. "You can go home now." Heather gave him a hug and a kiss, and Justin walked the rest of the way, swinging his lunch bag. Heather's eyes clouded as she thought of how her baby had grown up in just five years.

KEY TERMS

initiative

OBJECTIVES:
- Describe emotional development in children ages four, five, and six.
- Identify ways children show anger, fear, and jealousy.
- Develop ways to respond to anger, fear, and jealousy in children ages four to six.
- Analyze the effects of competition on children.

General Emotional Patterns

Four-, five-, and six-year-olds face many changes. Many, like Justin, begin regular school attendance during this period. School takes children away from their home and into a new environment that they share with unfamiliar adults and large groups of other children. In

458 UNIT 5: The Child from Four to Six

Observing & Participating

Have students observe four-year-olds at play, paying special attention to the language used. Have them focus on the following questions: Did the children use silly names or plays on words? How much boasting or telling of tall tales did students hear? Did the children tell jokes? Have your students prepare objective evaluations of the observations and share their observations with the class.

addition, children of this age begin to assume more responsibility and become aware that they have left babyhood forever. Feelings of independence and self-worth help children develop initiative—motivation to accomplish. Each child differs in response to these challenges.

Four Years

Most four-year-olds seem intent on asserting their independence. They are more self-centered, impatient, defiant, and boastful than they were at age three. They often argue and compete, and they are bossier than in the past.

Children four years old spend more time playing with others than do younger children, but relations are not always smooth. This four-year-old is telling her playmates where to play. *What quality typical of four-year-olds is she showing?*

Four-year-olds can also be unusually loving and affectionate. They need and seek parental approval. One minute, a four-year-old may stamp her foot and scream, "I hate you, Mommy!" Three minutes later, she may smilingly offer her mother a flower.

Because they feel more independent and have more skills, four-year-olds can wash and dress themselves. They are typically proud of their accomplishments, abilities, possessions, and creations. They can still fall back into younger behavior, though, when you least expect it.

Four-year-olds use language with enthusiasm. They enjoy the sounds of language. "Antsy-Wantsy-Nancy"—or some similar nonsense—can send them into hysterical laughter. They enjoy trying out bathroom-related words and seeing how others react. They also want to talk the way adults do, although they don't yet have the language skills for mature conversations.

Four-year-olds enjoy having other people laugh at their jokes, but they dislike it when people laugh at their mistakes. It is important to them that they are no longer seen as babies.

Most four-year-olds are in a rather difficult phase of normal emotional development. You can help children of this age by respecting their need to explore and test themselves. Avoid treating four-year-olds like toddlers. Try to use flexible rules when guiding their behavior.

TEACH

ACTIVITIES

Critical Thinking Activity

Synthesizing. Ask students why the characteristics of four-year-olds make it important for parents and caregivers to set limits on their behavior. **L2**

Discussion Activity

Brainstorm ways that caregivers can handle the bossiness of four-year-olds. **L1**

VISUAL LEARNING Using the Photograph
Answer: They are typically bossy.

ISSUES IN CHILDREN'S HEALTH

Praise is obviously important for preschoolers, who derive much of their self-image and self-worth from caregivers. Remember to praise children, when appropriate, for their ability to do things like fix their own peanut butter and jelly sandwich. Giving praise is essential for children this age—it affirms their sense of self, builds confidence, and creates a more independent child.

LEARNING STYLES

Kinesthetic

Give students index cards. Tell them to track the lines of text with a card as they read each subsection to stay focused on the words. When they finish reading the material under each heading, have them paraphrase on the card what they read. Use a fresh card for each section.

Remind students that to avoid plagiarism, they must change both the sentence structure and the words that are used to express ideas. Material used directly should be placed in quotation marks.

COMPREHENSION CHECK

1. What are some characteristics of five-year-olds? (*They're practical, sympathetic, and serious and have improved attention span and memory.*)
2. How do five-year-olds compare to four-year-olds regarding humor and language? (*Both ages enjoy slapstick humor. Unlike four-year-olds, five-year-olds are more able to carry on real discussion and ask meaningful questions.*)

ACTIVITIES

Teamwork Activity

Point out that the average attention span for five-year-olds is less than 15 minutes. Have students work in groups to develop a list of activities suitable for five-year-olds that could be completed within that length of time. Students might try the activities with a group of five-year-olds and report on their effectiveness. **L2**

VISUAL LEARNING Using the Photographs
Top—Answer: They are seeking more independence. *Bottom—Possible response:* Greater attention span will help children in school.

Four-year-olds can be difficult, but they are also very loving. **What needs mark their relationship with parents?**

Having learned that others won't accept tall tales and lies, five-year-olds are increasingly realistic. Like four-year-olds, they continue to enjoy slapstick humor. At the same time, they are more able to carry on real discussions and ask meaningful questions than four-year-olds.

At this age, children conform to rules more easily. They willingly mind their parents and teachers—at least most of the time. However, adult criticism is very hard for them to take.

Children at age five are more patient, generous, persistent, and conscientious than earlier. They sometimes feel anxious, often out of a desire to achieve acceptable results rather than as a result of general insecurity.

Five Years

Five-year-olds enter a quieter period of emotional development, similar to that of age three. Children of five are generally rather practical, sympathetic, and serious. Their improved attention span allows them to finish what they have started, rather than moving from one thing to another. Having a better memory allows them to go back and finish uncompleted tasks.

Because they have improved attention spans, five-year-olds can take on more complex tasks than they could before. **How will this help them in the future?**

460 UNIT 5: The Child from Four to Six

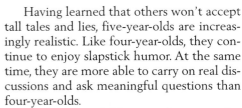

DID *You* **Know?**

Children's Humor. **Children see humor in repetition. When a preschool child discovers something funny, whether it is an action, joke, or humorous phrase, all the other children want to participate by repeating it themselves. They are likely to continue repeating it, again and again, still finding the joke funny long after adults have become exasperated with the repetition. Adults need to bear in mind that children outgrow the behavior.**

Six Years

Like children of four, six-year-olds are often stubborn and quarrelsome. They resent directions, and they think they know everything. They are the center of their own universe—and determined to stay there. Six-year-olds are often at their worst with their own parents.

At six, children have rapidly changing moods. They love and hate, accept and reject, smile and storm—sometimes for no apparent reason. Even a favorite playmate is likely to get a swift whack before being told, "You bumped into my truck." Of course, a six-year-old playmate will probably immediately hit back.

Six-year-olds are learning to appreciate humorous situations and jokes. They throw themselves into their fun with the abandon that characterizes all they do.

It is easy to understand why six is a difficult age for children. Many are in school all day for the first time. They are faced with the task of finding their status outside the home. It's also a time when children long to feel grown-up—but often feel small and dependent. Six-year-olds crave praise and approval. They are easily hurt and discouraged.

Specific Emotions

During the years from four to six, children need help in recognizing and expressing their emotions. Caregivers should accept and help children identify all the emotions they experience.

Six-year-olds have rapidly changing moods. *What new change in their lives contributes to their emotional upheaval?*

COMPREHENSION CHECK

1. What are three ways to help children overcome their fears? (*Accept the fear; let the child express the fear without ridicule; help the child feel able to face the fear.*)

ACTIVITIES

Critical Thinking Activity

Synthesizing. Read students the following situation: "When six-year-old Hannah's parents wouldn't let her watch the TV show, she yelled, 'I hate you!' and left the room." Have them put themselves in the parent's place. How would they respond? **L2**

Teamwork Activity

Have students work in groups to create a time line about children and anger. The time line should include different ages with labels indicating what factors cause anger and how children express that anger. Display the time lines in the class. **L2**

| **VISUAL LEARNING** | Using the Photograph *Answer:* Other children. |

Self-Confidence

As children find success at accomplishing new skills and facing unfamiliar situations, their confidence improves. These feelings of independence and self-worth help them develop **initiative**—motivation to accomplish more.

Anger

How children express anger changes more during childhood than any other emotion. Young children show anger freely, with no effort to restrain themselves. As children grow, they use more subtle means of expressing their anger:

- **Four years.** Four-year-olds may still show anger by physically fighting. Their anger lasts longer than before. They often threaten and attempt to "get even."
- **Five years.** Five-year-olds are more likely to try to hurt other children's feelings rather than hurting them physically.
- **Six years.** Six-year-olds are even more stinging with words. They tease, insult, nag, and make fun of others.

The frequency of anger decreases from age four to age six, but the effects of anger last longer. There are a number of reasons for these changes. A child's tolerance for frustration generally increases with

age. Also, some sources of earlier frustration are eliminated as the child's skills improve. Finally, by age six, children have better social skills, which can reduce situations that lead to anger. They usually recognize some things belong to other people, can work well in groups, and begin to learn about and accept the differing personalities of others.

Disagreements with other children are the most common cause of anger. Although quarrels are still loud and verbal, five- and six-year-old children begin to conceal and disguise their feelings. Sometimes their methods of revenge are indirect. They may pretend indifference, sneer, or make sly remarks. Often they make exaggerated threats. Occasionally, they take their anger out on a scapegoat, such as a younger sibling, a pet, a toy, or the furniture.

Parents can also be the object of the child's anger. Children who are chided for

Because parents are the ones who make rules, children may turn their anger toward their parents. *Who are children more commonly angry with?*

Parenting in *Action*

Adults who have not learned to deal with anger in a constructive way offer a poor example to children between four and six years of age who are learning to recognize and vent anger. Caregivers who use positive ways of expressing anger set a good example. A parent who says "I can't talk about it right now. I need to calm down" or "Let me count to ten and calm down first" sends an important message to an impressionable child.

The fears felt by children in this age group may lead to nightmares. *What kinds of fears are common in these ages?*

doing something wrong will "punish" a parent by breaking yet another rule. When six-year-old Hanna was told to go to her room for kicking her brother, she retorted, "Okay, I'm not going to hang my clothes up for a week—or maybe a year!"

Children vary greatly in how much anger they show and how they show it. Some of these variations depend on a child's personality, but the way parents express their own anger—and respond to the child—are also important. Caregivers need to set an example by sharing and talking—but not acting out—their own anger. It's important to teach the child self-control early in life before inappropriate expressions of anger become a habit. Encourage children to use words—not their bodies—in expressing anger.

A child who is very physical may need action to release the anger. Teaching the child to hit something soft, like a pillow, may help.

Fear

Children from four to six have a well-developed imagination, and many of their fears center on imaginary dangers. They may be afraid of ghosts, robbers, kidnappers, or vampires. Sensitive and insecure children are especially prone to fears. Many children of this age are afraid of the dark. Some may worry about the possibility of being left alone or abandoned.

Many children fear school. Some are afraid to be leaving the security of home. Others may fear a bully or a teacher. Social acceptance is very important at this age, and the threat of losing it worries children.

You can help children overcome these fears in three ways:

- **Accept the fear.** Having someone older who listens and understands can greatly help a fearful child. Don't just say that what the child fears doesn't exist. It's very real to the child.
- **Let the child express the fear without ridicule.** If they worry that they will be made fun of, children may not show their other fears openly.
- **Help the child feel able to face the fear.** Use talking and acting out to help the child learn to face the fearful situation. By practicing how to face a large dog, Kyle found the strength to overcome his fear of large dogs.

Sometimes, of course, a child's concern over a situation is justified. A bully at school or danger on the streets are reasonable con-

CHAPTER 15: Emotional and Social Development from Four to Six **463**

Critical Thinking Activity

Analyzing. Have students watch a children's television program or read a fairy tale. Ask them to analyze the work in relation to children's fears and share their conclusions with the class. **L3**

Discussion Activity

Have students discuss their own fears as children or those experienced by children they know. How did they or the other children overcome those fears? **L1**

Discussion Activity

Ask: What fears do children have that might help keep them safe? How can caregivers talk to children about those fears to encourage safe behavior without leading children to worry too much? **L2**

VISUAL LEARNING | Using the Photograph

Possible responses: Imaginary dangers, dark, being left alone, being abandoned.

ACTIVITIES

Discussion Activity

Ask: Is sibling rivalry all bad? Are there any benefits that can be gained from competition between siblings? **L1**

Critical Thinking Activity

Synthesizing. Have students write about sibling rivalry in blended families. What issues might arise that would cause jealousy or other upset feelings? How are those feelings exacerbated by the way the family was formed? What could parents do to try to diffuse the situation? **L2**

Teamwork Activity

Form students into pairs. Have each member of the pair write five statements that parents might make comparing one child to another in an unfavorable way. Have students in the pair exchange papers and write a different, non-comparative statement the parent could make. **L2**

cerns. In these cases, parents need to take action to help remove the source of those fears.

Jealousy

Sibling rivalry—jealousy of brothers and sisters—is common during this period. Some parents worsen the problem, often without meaning to, by showing favoritism to one child. Sometimes they try to improve behavior by comparing one child with another. For example, one father asked his daughter, "Why can't you be neat and clean like Jennifer? I never have to tell her to put her toys away." Such comparisons are rarely effective. Instead, they damage a child's self-esteem and undermine good family relationships.

At this age, jealousy often takes the form of tattling, criticizing, or even lying. Some children react to their own feelings of jealousy by boasting. Jealousy may also result in tensional outlets such as nail biting, bed-wetting, and tantrums. By encouraging empathy you can help lessen jealousy. Sometimes a bit of additional attention helps. Sibling rivalry tends to fade as the child matures and finds interests outside the family.

Children and Stress

Children, like teens and adults, lead stressful lives. Children may worry about everything from fires to their own popularity, the illness or death of a family member,

Habits like twirling hair, rapid blinking, or biting nails can be signs of stress. *What kinds of events or feelings can bring on this stress?*

or news about missing children. One expert says that more than one in three children suffers from stress.

As with adults, this stress can result in problems. Stress can cause stomachaches, headaches, moodiness, irritability, and trouble eating or sleeping. Other signs of stress include problems at school, pulling away from groups, clinging to adults, or stuttering. A child who often blinks rapidly, taps pencils or pens, or shuffles his or her feet may be under stress as well.

What should parents and other caregivers do? Hugs help. The "Health Tip" on the next page has other suggestions.

Is Competition Good or Bad?

People have differing views about the role competition should play in children's

ISSUES IN CHILDREN'S HEALTH Children can feel too much stress when they are given too much responsibility, are expected to deal with too many changes, or are overloaded emotionally. The following can help children cope with stress:

- Spending time with the child shows that he or she has support.
- During private conversations, encouraging the child to examine and express feelings.
- Finding ways to minimize the causes of the stress.

Handling Stress

*Y*ou can take these steps to help children reduce stress:

- **Find the cause.** Children's drawings can reveal the causes of stress. A child whose parents had just divorced drew a picture of herself split in two. Another approach is to say that a favorite puppet or stuffed animal is not feeling well and then ask the child what the problem is. The child may describe his or her own problems. Once the cause of the stress is known, work on that problem.

- **Give them chances to get rid of tension.** By giving children a physical way of releasing tension, you can relieve their stress. Have them run around the home, jump off a cushion, or color very rapidly.

- **Read a book about the issue causing the stress.** There are books that deal with issues that can cause stress in children, from moving to a new home to facing someone's death. Reading a book can help the child learn ways to handle the situation.

- **Maintain normal limits on behavior.** Some parents ease up on rules because they want to make life easier for a child feeling stress. Such an approach can actually backfire by confusing the child—and causing additional stress.

FOLLOWING UP

1. Chad, a five-year-old, has three brothers and sisters, including a newborn. He drew a picture of himself and his whole family, but he was toward the edge of the page and smaller than the other figures. What might this drawing reveal as a likely cause of the stress he is experiencing?

2. What techniques for handling stress have you found to work? Would they work with young children? Why or why not?

---

lives. Some say that children benefit from it because competition:
- Stimulates individual effort.
- Promotes higher standards.
- Creates an interest in completing tasks.
- Helps a child gain a realistic view of his or her own ability in relation to others.
- Encourages speed in accomplishment.
- Helps children excel and prepares them for the adult world.

Others feel that competition harms children because it:
- Instills the idea that success depends on the ability to outdo others.
- Leads to hostile relationships with others.
- Results in lack of effort among those who never or rarely win.
- Points out children's inadequacies.
- Lowers the status and self-esteem of those who lose.

The Developing Brain

Exercise and the Brain

Research suggests that exercise is good for the brain. Apparently, exercise increases brain levels of norepinephrine, a neurotransmitter. Scientists note that antidepressant drugs have the same effect. One researcher suggests that just as exercise tunes the muscles to make them respond more efficiently, so it tunes the brain to make it handle stress more effectively. Other research suggests that, in animals, forced exercise had little beneficial effect while voluntary exercise did.

Discussion Activity

Have students offer their first impressions when they hear the word "competition." Are these responses generally positive or negative? **L1**

Critical Thinking Activity

Analyzing. Have students suggest activities for children these ages that encourage cooperation rather than competition. **L2**

Discussion Activity

Ask: What does the phrase "good sport" mean to you? How important is it to be a good sport? **L2**

Critical Thinking Activity

Analyzing. **Ask:** Do boys and girls handle competition differently? In what way? Why is that the case? **L2**

VISUAL LEARNING | Using the Photograph
Possible responses: Coaching, helping children practice, attending games.

Many children these ages begin to play competitive sports on teams. *How can parents take part in these activities?*

Competition can be very difficult for six-year-olds. Children this age don't take criticism well, and they hate to lose. Cal, playing a board game with his father, tried a six-year-old's typical solution to losing. When his father wasn't looking, he cheated. Such behavior fades after a year or so. If a child shows that he or she has difficulty handling losing, it may be best to set aside competitive games for a while. As the child matures, they can be played again. Of course, caregivers who show what it's like to be good sports help children learn to lose graciously.

When competitive games are played, be aware of the possible impact on children's feelings. If children are being grouped into teams, use some system other than letting the children choose teammates.

Another issue with competitive games is playing time. Most children, regardless of their skill level, want to join in when games such as soccer or kickball are being played. If only a few children are given a chance to play, others feel left out. Not only do these children feel rejected, they also lose the chance of working to improve their skills. At this age, choose games that give everyone a chance to play.

Teamwork and Cooperation

Most four-, five-, and six-year-olds prefer cooperative play to competitive games. You can encourage children to play cooperatively in competitive games by working together with their teammates. Any children who are not playing at a particular

MULTIPLE INTELLIGENCES Sports can be enjoyable and beneficial for children—especially those with bodily-kinesthetic intelligence. Other children, though, have talents in other areas, and parents can help them by encouraging them to pursue those abilities. Musical children can learn an instrument. Spatial children might enjoy art classes. Naturalistic children can savor the outdoors activities promoted by scouts or groups like the 4-H Club. There are many activities that give children a chance to interact with others.

time can cheer for their teammates. When they are playing, children can share by, say, passing the ball to one another.

Whatever the game, teach children not to compare themselves to others. Instead, they can compare their skills today to their skills in the past. Is Jennie dribbling the ball better? Is Carlos running faster than last month? Most children can see improvement—and feel some satisfaction.

SECTION 15-1 REVIEW

✔ Check Your Understanding

1. What major change takes place for most children between the ages of four and six?
2. Compare four- and five-year-olds in terms of their willingness to cooperate.
3. Which group—four-, five-, or six-year-olds—is most likely to have major swings in mood?
4. How do children aged four to six show anger? How should a caregiver respond?
5. Mandy's mother said, "Silly, don't be afraid of the dark. There's nothing that can hurt you." Was that an effective way of dealing with Mandy's fear? If not, what would have been better?
6. What behaviors may be signs of stress in a child?
7. List three advantages and three disadvantages of competition among children.

Putting Knowledge Into Practice

1. **Applying.** Children in all three ages from four to six have difficulty handling criticism. Develop a list of four rules for caregivers to use when they try to correct the behavior of a child during this period.
2. **Interpreting.** Derrick was angry when he was kicked by another child. Instead of hitting, he said, "That felt just like a minnow swimming by me." What age is Derrick likely to be? Why?
3. **Observing and Participating.** Working in a small group, develop a game that children four to six could play that would encourage cooperation. Explain the rules of the game to your class.

ANSWERS TO SECTION 15-1 REVIEW

1. They start school.
2. *Fours:* Want to show independence; may not cooperate. *Fives:* More willing to conform.
3. Six-year-olds.
4. *Fours:* By fighting or making threats. *Fives:* By hurting feelings. *Sixes:* Teasing, insulting, and making fun of others.
5. Not. *Possible response:* "Let's look around and see if we see anything."
6. *See page 464 for possible answers.*
7. *See page 465 for possible answers.*

CAREER OPPORTUNITIES

Introducing the Feature

Discuss with students what their favorite childhood books were and who the authors were. Discuss how the author's style contributed to their enjoyment of the book.

Answers to
CONNECTING SCHOOL TO CAREER

1. **Possible responses:** So that readers are convinced by the characters' actions; so that readers can draw parallels from the characters' lives to their own.

2. **Possible response:** For research.

Applying What You've Learned

Ask students to decide on a concern that faces four- to six-year-old children. Have them describe a story line for a children's book that they think would be interesting and would help children in dealing with that concern.

CAREER OPPORTUNITIES

Children's Book Writer

A CONVERSATION WITH PAUL ZARSKY

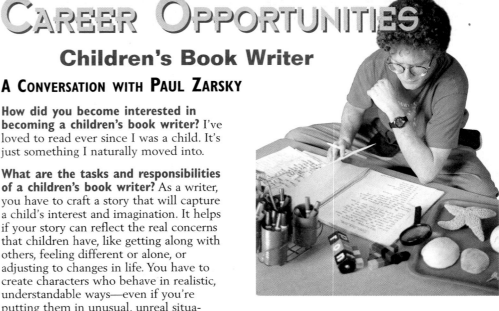

How did you become interested in becoming a children's book writer? I've loved to read ever since I was a child. It's just something I naturally moved into.

What are the tasks and responsibilities of a children's book writer? As a writer, you have to craft a story that will capture a child's interest and imagination. It helps if your story can reflect the real concerns that children have, like getting along with others, feeling different or alone, or adjusting to changes in life. You have to create characters who behave in realistic, understandable ways—even if you're putting them in unusual, unreal situations, like a magical trip to another world.

What is the work environment like? Most writers work in offices in their own homes. They are entrepreneurs. What that is like is really what you make it like.

What are the working hours like? Because you're working at home, you can create the hours that you want. Of course, when a deadline looms, you have to put in extra hours if you're behind.

What aptitudes are needed to be a children's book writer? You need a good imagination and excellent language skills. You need to know the meanings of words and their sounds so you can put them together in pleasing ways. You need to be able to do research—for instance, if you're writing about a medical problem, you need to learn about it to make your story convincing. You must have self-discipline when you work at home.

CHILDREN'S BOOK WRITER

Education and Training. Writers usually have college degrees in English. Some begin writing in their teens or college years.

Career Outlook. The demand for writers is expected to continue to grow in the future, but competition for writing jobs is high.

CONNECTING SCHOOL TO CAREER

1. **Thinking Skills.** Why is it important for characters to behave realistically even if they are in fantasy worlds?

2. **Technology.** How could children's book writers use the Internet in their work?

468 UNIT 5: The Child from Four to Six

Building Career Skills

Personal Qualities. Ask students to refer to the information in the feature and create a chart in which they list the positive and negative aspects of being a children's book writer. Students should focus on the tasks and the working environment of a writer. Have them think of other careers that would present the opposite kind of environment. Which do they think they would prefer? Why?

SECTION 15-2

Social and Moral Development from Four to Six

School brings four-, five-, and six-year-olds into contact with many new people. Children must learn how to meet strangers, make friends, work and play in groups, and accept authority from new people. As they enter school, children broaden their world.

KEY TERMS

moral development
peers

OBJECTIVES:

- Describe social development in children ages four, five, and six.
- Describe a child's relationship to family at ages four, five, and six.
- Create strategies for helping children develop a sense of right and wrong.
- Debate ways of handling outside influences on children's behavior.

General Social Patterns

During the preschool and early school years, development of social skills is a major task. As children spend more time outside the home, they refine skills in getting along with **peers**, others their age.

CHAPTER 15: Emotional and Social Development from Four to Six **469**

Observing & Participating

Provide students with an opportunity to observe the social interactions of four- and five-year-olds. Have them focus on how children in each age group cooperate and share with one another. How do they speak to one another? How often do they quarrel? How are those arguments settled? Ask students to compare those interactions to those of their own age group. How are they similar and different?

SECTION 15-2

Social and Moral Development from Four to Six

(pages 469-477)

SECTION 15-2 RESOURCES

Teacher Resource Guide
- Lesson Plan Organizer, p. 71
- Section 15-2 Quiz, p. 183

Student Motivation Kit
- Observ. & Case Studies (case study), pp. 127-128
- Reteaching Activity, p. 45
- Enrichment, pp. 45-46

Student Workbook
- Study Guide, pp. 122-125
- Guiding Children's Behavior, p. 127

Transparency Package
- CT-44 The Road to Moral Development

Effective Instruction CD-ROM

FOCUS

MOTIVATOR

Ask: How do you determine what is the right thing to do when faced with a moral question? How do you choose whether to take that action or a different course? Explain that this section will describe how young children learn to make these choices.

VOCABULARY ACTIVITY

Explain that the word peer comes from the Latin term "par," which means "equal." Peers, then, are people who are equal in age.

COMPREHENSION CHECK

1. At which age is family likely to be most important, four, five, or six? (*Four.*)
2. At which age would you say children are easiest to get along with, four, five, or six? Why?

ACTIVITIES

Discussion Activity

In 2001, the National Institute of Child Health and Human Development (NICHD) reported findings of the most comprehensive long-term study of child care ever conducted. One statistic in particular made headlines—16% of 4½-year-olds in child care (30 or more hours weekly) displayed aggressive behavior; the number rose to 17% in kindergarten. Do students believe that there is a link between child care and behavior problems? Why would working parents find the report so disturbing? **L2**

| **VISUAL LEARNING** | Using the Photograph |

Top—Possible response: They will find the adjustment easier because they are accustomed to taking directions, to taking turns, to sitting quietly, and so on.

Preschool gives children opportunities for social relationships outside the home. *Do you think children who attend preschool are more likely to make the transition to grade school more easily? Why or why not?*

Four- and five-year-olds have the social skills to participate in group activities.

470 UNIT 5: The Child from Four to Six

DID *You* **Know?**

Role Models. An important social and emotional task for children is finding role models, especially of their own sex. Children learn these roles from family members, friends, neighbors, and teachers. These people show, through words and deeds, how people should behave. Watching family members who are the same sex helps boys and girls learn how to become men and women.

Adult authority figures other than parents also gain more importance. Although the rate at which individual children learn social skills varies, there are general patterns common at each age.

Four Years

Four-year-olds form friendships with their playmates. At this age, children spend more time in cooperative play than they do playing alone. They seem to play best in groups of three or four. Children this age share toys and take turns. Since four-year-olds are still often bossy and inconsiderate, fighting can be common.

Although friends are important to four-year-olds, the family is still more important. Children this age often ask for approval by making such remarks as "I'm a good builder, right?" or "Look how high I can climb!" If things go wrong, they look to adults, including teachers, for comfort.

At age four, children enjoy helping around the house. **What kinds of tasks could they be given?**

Five Years

Most five-year-olds are more outgoing and talkative than they were at age four. They play best in groups of five or six, and their play is more complicated. Quarreling is less frequent. When they do quarrel, five-year-olds typically resort to name-calling and to wild threats.

At age five, children have more respect for others' belongings. This doesn't mean that a five-year-old will never snatch someone else's toy. Such behavior, though, is less common than in earlier years.

As children begin school, social acceptance by peers becomes more important. Children are concerned about what their friends say and do. They don't like to be different, and they fear ridicule. This is why teasing can be very hurtful for children this age.

At about this age, children often begin to gossip about other children. Typically, this talk involves which children are friends or who has what toys. Sometimes, though, the talk can be personal—and very critical. Gossip indicates what behaviors children as a group value. Undesirable actions are criticized. If such talk turns nasty, though, discuss the matter with the children, pointing out that gossip can be hurtful.

Six Years

At age six, social relations are often characterized by friction, aggression, threats, and stubbornness. Children this age want everything, and they want to do things their own way. When playing with other children, they may not want to share their own toys, and they are likely to be jealous of others' toys.

CHAPTER 15: Emotional and Social Development from Four to Six **471**

COMPREHENSION CHECK

1. Why are six-year-olds less in harmony with family members than four- and five-year-olds? (*They're more self-centered*).

ACTIVITIES

Teamwork Activity

Form students into groups and have each group brainstorm toys or games that would help children develop social skills. Have them list the toy or game and the skill it would promote. Ask each group to share its findings with the class, which should discuss the suggestions. **L1**

Discussion Activity

Ask: What impact can a peer group's criticism have on a five- or six-year-old? **L1**

VISUAL LEARNING | **Using the Photograph**
Possible response: As the photograph shows, they are learning to follow rules such as raising hands. Ask for other examples.

Children in this stage follow rules to avoid being punished. They do not yet have the ability to understand the reasons for these rules. *What development shows that they are beginning to internalize rules of behavior?*

Best friends are usually of the same sex, although six-year-olds play readily in mixed groups. Friendships are closer and longer lasting now than at age five.

At this age, children like the group play and organized teams of school games. As soon as they tire of playing, though, they will drop out of a game with no regard for the team effort.

Family Relationships

Four-year-olds have a strong sense of family and home. They want to feel important in the family. They are proud to perform household chores. However, they are also apt to quarrel and bicker with their brothers and sisters.

The family relationships of five-year-olds are similar to those of four-year-olds. They are proud of their parents and delight in helping. At five, though, children play much better with their younger brothers and sisters. They are usually protective, kind, and dependable with younger siblings.

Six-year-olds are less in harmony with their family members, in part because children this age are more self-centered. Their own opinions and needs come first. Arguing with adults is common. At six, children are often rough and impatient with younger brothers and sisters, and they may fight with older siblings.

Moral Development

Moral development—the process of gradually learning to base one's behavior on personal beliefs of right and wrong—begins early in life. Parents have a responsibility to help their children develop a moral sense that will guide their behavior.

As toddlers, children begin to learn the rules their parents and other caregivers set. At this age, though, they can't understand the reasons behind the rules or the difference between right and wrong. They just know that some actions—such as hitting another person—make their caregivers unhappy with them. They learn to avoid such behavior because they don't want to lose love and approval.

LEARNING STYLES | **Interpersonal**

As part of growing up, children learn what makes a valued group member. Children who are popular tend to be considerate, cooperative, generous, sharing, and cheerful. They have a good sense of humor. In contrast, children who are unpopular often tease, insult, tattle, and bully. They are often stingy and bossy. They cry when they lose, gloat when they win, and get their feelings hurt easily. Have students, working alone or in groups, write a skit in which children show these positive or negative behaviors.

Between the ages of five and seven, children gradually develop the beginning of a conscience, that inner sense of right and wrong that leads people to good behavior and causes them to feel guilt following bad behavior. The rules learned in early childhood form the basis of the conscience in the early school years.

Lying

As children begin to learn the difference between truth and lies, that understanding isn't always accurate. For example, they may exaggerate the details of stories they tell.

During this process, help children separate fact from fiction. At the same time, punishing children when they are simply being imaginative isn't appropriate. Children need to know that telling the truth is important because people rely on what others say as they decide how to act. Point out that someone who consistently tells the truth is trusted by others. Telling the story of "The Boy Who Cried Wolf"—who suffered because he couldn't be trusted—can help the child see this point.

Sometimes children lie because they fear the consequences of something they did wrong. Punishment for undesirable behavior shouldn't be so severe that a child would rather lie than accept responsibility for an action.

There are many ways that parents can use to guide children in their moral development. *Why is setting a good example such an important one?*

As children learn right from wrong, try to avoid direct confrontations. When Brad saw the flower pot overturned, he didn't challenge his son Lee directly. He simply said, "Look at this! I wonder how this happened?" Then Lee explained that he had accidentally knocked it over. If Lee hadn't offered the information, Brad could have asked him, "Do you know anything about it?" to try to prompt a response. When asked in a nonthreatening way, children can be more willing to tell the truth. This helps establish the pattern of truthfulness.

Guidelines for Moral Development

Here are some guidelines for teaching moral behavior:

- **Consider the child's age and abilities.** For example, at preschool, Chrystal was playing at the shallow table filled with rice and containers. She started tossing the rice into the air and watching it land on the floor. The teacher

CHAPTER 15: Emotional and Social Development from Four to Six **473**

Parenting in *Action*

The moral attitudes and beliefs of parents are generally thought to be the most powerful influences on a child's conscience. The methods parents use in guiding children's behavior may also have an influence. Studies have shown that children with the most highly developed consciences have parents who are consistent in imposing and enforcing rules, provide firm but not severe discipline, and use physical punishment sparingly.

Ask the Experts

Introducing the Feature

Ask students to read the question at the beginning of the feature. Ask how they would answer this question based on their experience with four- to six-year-old children.

Answers to Thinking It Through
1. *Answers will vary.*
2. *Possible response:* Talk to the child about what he or she did wrong.

Applying What You've Learned

Point out to students that children are not entirely able to separate fantasy from reality until age seven. Ask students to write a paragraph explaining how this fact affects younger children's concept of what constitutes a lie. Call on volunteers to read their paragraphs and discuss them with the class.

Ask the Experts

Jean Illsley Clarke
Director of J.I. Consultants in Minneapolis, Minnesota

CHILDREN *and Lies*

Q Do young children lie?

A Of course children lie. Children learn about their world by exploring it, by trying it out. So we can expect children to learn about lies by lying. However, their lies are often not deliberate attempts to deceive.

Many children, especially four- and five-year-olds, tell tall tales. Telling such tales helps children develop their imagination and creativity. It may also help them deal with their own fears and frustrations.

It's not unusual for young children to mix exaggerated stories with reality. When you need information from a child, you can show the child that you know the difference. You might explain, "I will listen to your story, and then I need to know what really happened."

Sometimes a statement that sounds like a lie really reflects the child's misunderstanding. For example, a child might feel that he or she has completed a task, but a caregiver is not satisfied that it has been done fully. When the child says, "I did what you told me," he or she is not lying.

Children sometimes tell lies simply to get a response from adults. In these cases, it's usually best to give the child more attention at other times, but to avoid special attention in response to the lying. Remember that all children want—and need—to be noticed.

Children may also lie to protect themselves or to please others. They may not want to risk an adult's anger or disappointment, so they lie about their behavior. Parents and other caregivers can help by encouraging children to accept and deal with their own mistakes or with their own deliberate misbehavior.

As we help children learn when and where and how to tell the truth, we should remember that the development of a conscience as an internal behavior guide takes many years. We should remember, as well, that children learn from our examples.

Thinking It Through

1. Can you remember a time when you were younger that you lied? Why did you lie? What happened?
2. What would you do if a five- or six-year-old lied to you about having taken a cookie?

DID You Know?

Cheating. By age five, most children can follow rules and play simple games. Still, almost all preschoolers, at one time or another, cheat at games. Preschoolers tend to believe that what's fair is what's good for them. They may very loudly insist that the person they're playing with strictly follow the rules even if they don't do so themselves. Adults may become concerned, feeling that the child is showing moral laxity. It is a stage that most children pass through.

reminded Chrystal to keep the rice in the table. Then she handed her a broom and a dustpan to sweep up the mess. Chrystal's teacher knows that children this age can't always remember the rules but will learn from the consequences of their actions.

- **Set a good example.** Children learn best by following an example. They receive a mixed message if, for example, they are told that lying is wrong, but hear their parents telling lies. You must behave around children the way you want them to behave.
- **Remember that learning self-discipline is a lifelong task.** It is unfair to expect perfection from children. Instead, help children learn from their mistakes—and recognize their steps in the right direction.
- **Talk about mistakes in private.** Children don't like to be put in a position where others can ridicule or make fun of them. Correcting their behavior in front of others may make them feel humiliated. The teacher took Jason to the side to talk to him about his loud talking.
- **Continue to show love despite misbehavior.** Children need to know that, although you don't like what they did, you continue to love them. Separate the deed from the doer.

Talking about a behavior problem can help a child improve. Remember that such changes take time.

Handling Outside Influences

The influence of peers increases as children spend more time away from home. They pick up the words and speech patterns of their friends. They come to want toys or clothes like other children have. Of course, every request can't be met. Children need to learn that each family has its own set of rules.

As they gain independence, many children watch more television. Some of the shows they see may reflect values that run counter to those of the family. Some preschoolers spend time on the computer,

Critical Thinking Activity

Evaluating. Describe the following situation: "Richard's mother found out that Richard had lied about eating candy. His mother said that he had to be punished but she wasn't sure what his punishment would be. Later, she told Richard that she had decided he would set the punishment."

Have students evaluate how Richard's mother handled the situation. **L2**

VISUAL LEARNING | **Using the Photograph**

Choose a common behavioral problem—not sharing, not taking turns, interrupting are all examples—and ask students for suggestions on how to lead a child to improve the behavior.

Management/Leadership Skills

Describe to students the following situation: "Erin is angry with her five-year-old sister, Deanna, because she broke her favorite necklace. Erin yelled at Deanna for breaking the necklace. Deanna said she didn't do it, although she really had accidentally broken it."

Ask students why they think Deanna lied to Erin and how Erin could have handled the situation in a way that would have made it easier for Deanna to tell the truth.

ACTIVITIES

Discussion Activity

Have the class debate the use of ratings for movies, television programs, and video and computer games. Are the ratings useful to parents? To children? If not, what would make them more useful? **L1**

Critical Thinking Activity

Synthesizing. Have students consider what parents can do to minimize the influence of undesirable habits or behaviors of other children on their own children. **L2**

Teamwork Activity

Organize students into small groups. Ask students in each group to talk to the parent of a young child. Have them ask what methods the parent thinks are most effective for teaching moral behavior to children. Have students share their findings with the class and discuss them. **L2**

Some critics say that another problem with video games is that they lead children to be isolated from other people. **What do you think of this criticism?**

---

where games may include images that parents object to. What can parents do about these issues?

The television industry has adopted a series of ratings meant to advise parents of the content of each show. One study argued that the rating system doesn't work. The study identified shows that had "fantasy violence"—the kind found in cartoons, in which characters act violently but don't suffer any harm. Researchers said that only one-quarter of the shows they identified as being violent in this way were given the appropriate rating. The study also found that of all the shows that networks said were educational, under one-third were highly educational.

Parents and caregivers are responsible for what children watch and how much they watch. One way to prevent television from having a negative effect is to lead young children away from television as a way of passing time. If children develop other ways of learning and playing, watching television is less likely to become a habit.

Video and computer games can be violent as well. Software boxes have labels indicating the level of violence. Parents can check with store personnel for more details if they are unsure of what the labels mean.

INFOLINK

Children and Television

For more about *children and television*, see "Parenting With Care," pages 452-453.

476 UNIT 5: The Child from Four to Six

LEARNING STYLES

Kinesthetic

Review with students the information in this section about guidelines for teaching moral behavior to children. Then organize students into groups of two or three. Have each group develop situations for a skit showing parents setting good moral examples for children. After the groups present their skits, have the class evaluate how effective each set of "parents" was in guiding their children's moral behavior.

What social and moral values would this type of activity encourage?

CHECKING COMPREHENSION

Have students answer the Check Your Understanding questions. Answers appear at the bottom of this page.

EVALUATION

Give students the Section 15-2 Quiz in the *Teacher Resource Guide*.

RETEACHING

1. Assign Reteaching Activities, page 45.
2. Have students write ten questions about the social and moral development of children these ages. Have them exchange their questions with a partner and answer the questions.

ENRICHMENT

Have students read more about peer pressure and report on its relevance to children these ages.

EXTENSION

Have students watch several children's television programs and evaluate the positive and negative influences of the shows on four- to six-year-olds.

CLOSE

Have students compare the moral development of four- to six-year-olds to that of one- to three-year-olds.

SECTION 15-2 REVIEW

✔ Check Your Understanding

1. Who are a person's peers?
2. What kind of play is typical for four-year-olds?
3. How do five-year-olds' feelings about teasing show the influence of peers?
4. Compare how four- and five-year-olds typically play with younger siblings.
5. What is moral development?
6. Give three suggestions for helping children learn right from wrong.
7. How can parents minimize the effects of television violence on children?

Putting Knowledge Into Practice

1. **Comparing.** What is the difference between a four-year-old's imaginative story and a teen's lie? How would you, as a parent, handle each situation?
2. **Applying.** Five-year-old Savanna often takes playthings away from neighbor children in the child care center. You work at the center. What would you do?
3. **Observing and Participating.** Based on how you and your friends interact, how would you define "friend"? How differently do you think a child four to six would define "friend"?

ANSWERS TO SECTION 15-2 REVIEW

1. Other people the same age.
2. Cooperative play.
3. They dislike teasing because they fear ridicule.
4. Five-year-olds are more likely to play well with younger siblings.
5. Learning to base one's behavior on personal beliefs of right and wrong.
6. *Any three:* Consider the child's age and abilities; set a good example; do not expect perfection; talk about mistakes in private; continue to show love despite misbehavior.
7. *Answers will vary.*

Teaching Manners

FOCUS

MOTIVATOR

Ask students to define "manners." What purpose do they serve? What would a society without manners be like?

TEACH

ACTIVITIES

Discussion Activity

Ask: Where should manners fit in a caregiver's priorities for guiding the behavior of children between four and six? Have students give reasons for their opinions. **L1**

Critical Thinking Activity

Analyzing. **Ask:** Do you think manners are important in social situations? Why or why not? Have students write a paragraph explaining their answer. **L2**

VISUAL LEARNING | **Using the Photograph**
Have students identify what manners are involved in the situations shown in the photographs on both pages.

As children become older, they are ready to learn how to behave politely.

As with all behavior, children learn manners from the example set around them. When parents say "Pass me the bread, please" at the dinner table, children learn that this is the way requests are made.

What kinds of manners are young children capable of learning? Although they can't be expected to act with all the polished manners of an adult, they can manage some simple steps:

- To say "please" and "thank you"—although, being children, they may not remember to do it all the time.
- To say "excuse me" when they wish to interrupt a conversation or when they cross in front of someone.
- To say "hello" and "goodbye" to people when they enter and leave the home.
- To speak clearly instead of mumbling and to look people in the eye.
- To follow basic table manners such as using a knife and fork, wiping the mouth with a napkin, and chewing with the mouth closed.

Parents can use the following technique to teach these manners to their children:

- **Focus on one area of behavior at a time.** It's easier for children to learn one skill at a time, rather than trying to master many instructions at once. Parents may choose to focus first on learning to say "please" and "thank you" before moving to table manners in general. Once the child is mastering these two areas, it is possible to move on to, say, greetings or phone manners.
- **Be prepared to accept mistakes.** Children will slip. They should not be berated or severely criticized for these lapses. Give them a chance to show that they know what to do by asking them how they should behave.

RESOURCES ON ETIQUETTE

Courses designed to teach manners to young people can be found in many communities. Most accept students as young as age six. Videos focusing on manners are also available. Interested students can learn more about etiquette by consulting one of the many books on the subject. Some have been written with children in mind. One is called *Miss Manners' Guide to Rearing Perfect Children.*

- **Notice—and comment on—what children do right.** Caregivers sometimes fall into the trap of only talking about what children do wrong. Children need to hear praise when they have acted correctly so they know that those actions matter.
- **Review the basics.** Before a social occasion, talk to the child about what situations might arise and what the child should do. By being prepared, the child will be more likely to behave as desired.

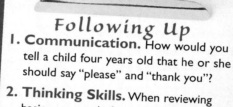

Following Up

1. **Communication.** How would you tell a child four years old that he or she should say "please" and "thank you"?

2. **Thinking Skills.** When reviewing basic manners before a special occasion, how would it help to have the child act out the desired behavior?

CHAPTER 15: Emotional and Social Development from Four to Six **479**

Answers to Following Up
1. *Possible responses:* We show respect for other people by saying "please" when asking them to do something and "thank you" when they have done it. Saying "please" and "thank you" is a way of recognizing that people are doing us a favor.
2. *Possible response:* It would help children because by acting it out physically they may remember better.

Teamwork Activity

Have students work in small groups to prepare a poster that illustrates examples of manners that four- to six-year-old children might practice. Encourage students to design and illustrate the poster in a way that would be interesting to children in that age group. You might arrange to display students' posters in the kindergarten and first-grade classrooms. **L2**

Cross-Cultural Activity

Ask students if they are aware of any manners or customs in other cultures. How, for instance, do children address adults in other cultures? How does that compare to the way it's done in the United States? What are appropriate table manners in other cultures and in the United States? Have the class discuss how the different manners reflect different values. **L2**

CLOSE

Call on pairs of students to demonstrate a technique to teach manners to children four to six years of age.

CHECKING COMPREHENSION

Use the Summary and the Reviewing the Facts questions to help students go over the most important ideas in Chapter 15. Encourage students to ask questions and add details.

CHAPTER 15 REVIEW

Answers to Reviewing the Facts

1. Five.
2. Children feel caught between finding status in school and still feeling dependent.
3. By accepting the fear; allowing time for the child to express the fear without ridicule; helping the child feel able to face the fear.
4. By focusing on teamwork.
5. Fours and sixes have more conflict; fives are more likely to get along.
6. Six.
7. By making punishment for lying worse than the punishment for the original error.
8. Because the child might feel humiliated if criticized in front of others.
9. *Possible response:* By leading children away from television when young with other activities, parents can prevent them from making television a habit.

Summary

✔ Children four to six move from defiance to cooperation to defiance. (Section 15-1)
✔ Children four to six become less physical when they show anger. (Section 15-1)
✔ Competition can have both positive and negative effects on children. (Section 15-1)
✔ Peer acceptance grows in importance with children these ages. (Section 15-2)
✔ In this period, children begin to tell right from wrong. (Section 15-2)
✔ Parents can minimize the negative effects of outside influences. (Section 15-2)

Reviewing the Facts

1. At which age do children find it easier to finish what they have started? (Section 15-1)
2. Why is six a difficult age emotionally? (Section 15-1)
3. How should caregivers respond to a child's fears? (Section 15-1)
4. How can cooperation be fostered when children play competitive games? (Section 15-1)
5. Compare children at ages four, five, and six in terms of how they get along with each other. (Section 15-2)
6. Jeremy always seems to be fighting with his parents. Is he most likely to be four, five, or six? (Section 15-2)
7. How can caregivers prevent punishments from leading children to lie? (Section 15-2)

8. Why is it better to correct a child's behavior in private? (Section 15-2)
9. How can early training affect a child's television viewing? (Section 15-2)

Thinking Critically

1. **Analyzing.** Do you think it is possible to treat all children in the family in the same way? If not, how can parents prevent feelings of sibling rivalry?
2. **Drawing Conclusions.** Based on your own experience, do you think that competitive games are helpful or harmful for children? Be prepared to defend your position in a class debate.
3. **Applying.** What would you do if you overheard your five-year-old son and a friend exchanging gossip about another boy in their class?

Taking Action

1. **Teaching Values.** Suppose you are part of a group of adults setting up a league for six-year-olds to play a sport such as T-ball or soccer. Make a list of ten rules of behavior you want all players to follow. Make sure that the rules address the children's behavior, not athletic concerns. *(Leadership)*

CONNECTIONS

2. Avoiding Sibling Rivalry. With a partner, develop a list of ten things parents say that might cause five- or six-year-olds to feel jealous of a sibling. Working with the same partner, find more positive ways to express those thoughts. *(Communication)*

Cross-Curricular Connections

1. **Language Arts.** Write a story that begins with this paragraph: "Sandy came home in tears from her first day in kindergarten. She dropped her backpack and slumped on the floor at her mother's feet. 'I'm never going back there!' she said."

2. **Language Arts.** Read the story "The Boy Who Cried Wolf." Write a new version of the story for a five- or six-year-old. Update it to situations a child might encounter in your neighborhood. Include illustrations if you wish.

Workplace Connections

1. **Interpersonal Skills.** You work in a child care center and notice that in the past week four-year-old Callie has been blinking and spending more time alone. You also notice that Callie's father no longer comes to pick her up at the end of the day. What might be Callie's problem? Describe how you would handle the situation.

2. **Interpersonal Skills.** Suppose you were the head of a preschool. Write a list of rules you would expect children to follow in terms of their behavior with one another. Make sure the rules are appropriate for four- and five-year-olds.

Family and Community Connections

1. **Handling Outside Influences.** Ever since Jem started kindergarten, he's been talking about a video game that other children have. He wants it badly, but his parents have heard that it is extremely violent, and they don't want him to have it. Join with a partner to write and act out a scene between Jem and one of his parents when Jem asks for this game—and nothing else—for his birthday.

Technology Connections

1. **Ratings for Violence.** Television programs, movies, and video and computer games all have ratings that indicate the presence of violence or other possibly objectionable content. Research one of these rating systems and report on it to the class. If you don't think the system is effective, make suggestions to improve it.

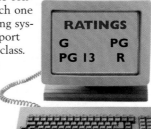

EVALUATION

1. Use the reproducible Chapter 15 Test in the *Teacher Resource Guide*, or construct your own test using the **Exam**View® Test Generator.

2. For an alternative assessment, assign the Chapter 15 activity in the *Authentic Assessment* section of the *Teacher Resource Guide*.

ENRICHMENT

Assign students either of the two activities in the *Enrichment Activities* booklet in the *Student Motivation Kit*.

EXTENSION

Ask a preschool or kindergarten teacher to speak to students about the social characteristics of their students and how these change during preschool years. Encourage students to ask questions.

CLOSE

Refer back to the activity in "Introducing Chapter 15." Have students review their predictions and verify or modify them. Take a new count of students who believe that child care professionals would agree or disagree with the statements. Have students explain their judgments.

CHAPTER 16 RESOURCES

Teacher Resource Guide
• Chapter 16 Test, p. 190
• Authentic Assessment, p. 287
Student Motivation Kit
• Observations, pp. 57-58
• Creative Activities, pp. 47-71,
79-101
Transparency Package
• CT-45 to CT-49
Effective Instruction CD-ROM

CHAPTER 16 OVERVIEW

In **Section 16-1**, students study
the characteristics of the preoperational stage of thinking, the different kinds of intelligence, and how
to encourage learning.

In **Section 16-2**, they learn how
to help children adjust to kindergarten, to identify possible speech
problems, and to help preschoolers
with special needs.

CHAPTER 16 OBJECTIVES

After completing Chapter 16,
students will be able to:

• Describe the characteristics of
intellectual and speech development of children aged four to six.
• Discuss multiple intelligences.
• Give examples of ways children
can learn from everyday experiences.
• Identify the effects of giftedness
and learning disabilities on children's school experiences.

CHAPTER 16
Intellectual Development from Four to Six

482 UNIT 5: The Child from Four to Six

RESOURCES TO EXPLORE

Encouraging Reading. Reading skills are clearly a key to school success, and many different
groups offer programs aimed at promoting
early reading. The Center for the
Improvement of Early Reading Achievement
(CIERA) views how reading is first taught as
the key to lifelong success at reading. CIERA
has a useful Website that includes information
on the group and the programs it runs, a list of
publications, and information on hot topics in
reading education. Visit this University of
Michigan site at www.ciera.org

Marcus patiently connected the blocks. He started with a long base and stacked medium-sized pieces atop it. After putting down a few pieces, he would stop and examine the results. Sometimes he pulled off a piece or two after these reviews, then quickly put others in a different position. On one side, the blocks rose like a wall with a gap in it. "What's that?" his father asked. "That's a window," said Marcus, not looking up from his work. He had trouble figuring out how to build above the window to reconnect the two sides of the wall, however. He couldn't find pieces that were long enough to bridge the gap. Marcus's father wanted to help, but he decided that it was best to let his son solve the problem on his own.

The solution would not come to Marcus right then, however. As he was still struggling with his problem, his father looked at his watch and said, "OK, Marcus, it's time for your bath."

"Sometimes Marcus would pull off a piece or two, then quickly put others in their place."

CHAPTER 16: Intellectual Development from Four to Six **483**

- Ask students to work with a partner to brainstorm a list of themes, such as family, friends, and nature, that would appeal to children ages four to six. Together, have them identify one creative activity for each theme on their list. Then ask them to explain how each activity stimulates a child's intellectual development.
- Have students look at the photograph on the page. **Ask:** What abilities besides small motor skills does a child need to build structures out of blocks? To what degree do children have those abilities before this age?

USING THE SCENARIO Have students read the story on this page of the student text. Ask them what actions show that Marcus was using a thinking process. Tell them that in this chapter they will learn about intellectual development in preschoolers.

KEY TO ABILITY LEVELS Each section gives skill-building activities. Each activity has been labeled for use with students of various learning styles and abilities.

L1 Level 1 activities are basic activities and should be within the range of all students.

L2 Level 2 activities are average activities and should be within the range of average and above average students.

L3 Level 3 activities are challenging activities designed for the ability range of above average students.

SECTION 16-1

SECTION 16-1 RESOURCES
Teacher Resource Guide
• Lesson Plan Organizer, p. 72
• Section 16-1 Quiz, p. 188
Student Motivation Kit
• Observ. & Case Studies
  (case study), pp. 129-130
• Reteaching Activity, p. 46
• Enrichment, p. 47
• Nurturing Brain
  Development, pp. 22-23,
  36-38, 80
Student Workbook
• Study Guide, pp. 128-131
• Deciphering Development,
  pp. 132-133
Transparency Package
• CT-45 to CT-47
Effective Instruction CD-ROM

FOCUS

MOTIVATOR

Ask students whether they learned to count and recognize colors or letters outside of school. Ask for a show of hands. Point out that caregivers have many opportunities to help children learn and apply these concepts.

VOCABULARY ACTIVITY

Pronounce the "Key Terms." Two of the words reveal the Greek and Latin roots of much of English. "Bilingual" derives from the Latin for language. "Phoneme" comes from the Greek for to speak.

484

Intelligence and Learning from Four to Six

Do you enjoy reading, art, or music? Think back to your first experiences in school. It's quite possible that your liking for these subjects started during this period of your life. When they enter school, children aged four to six become exposed to new people, activities, and ideas. These experiences have an impact on their growing minds.

KEY TERMS
bilingual
dramatic play
finger plays
intelligence quotient (IQ)
multiple intelligences
phoneme

OBJECTIVES:
• Identify signs of preoperational thinking in children aged four to six.
• Discuss different kinds of intelligence.
• Find ways to help children learn from everyday experiences.
• Use techniques to encourage children's interest in reading, art, and music.

484 UNIT 5: The Child from Four to Six

Preoperational Thinking

As you recall, Jean Piaget identified the time between ages two and seven as the preoperational period. In this period, children think in terms of their own activities and what they perceive at the moment. Four-, five-, and six-year-olds show by their thinking and actions that they are still in this period:

Observing & Participating

Have students give examples of the symbols that they use or encounter in their daily lives. Some examples that might come to mind readily are words, numbers, and traffic lights. Others include the national flag, religious symbols, or product logos. After two or three minutes of brainstorming, ask students what role symbols play in people's lives. How do they work as a code that makes it easier and quicker to send messages to one another? How do they think mastering this code helps children?

- **Use of symbols.** Children learn that objects and words can be symbols—that is, they can represent something else. A child this age can recognize that a stop sign means stop.
- **Make-believe play.** Children continue to learn through fantasy play and **dramatic play**, in which they imitate real-life situations, such as playing house or school.
- **Egocentric viewpoint.** In this period, children view the world in terms of their own thoughts and feelings. When the mother of a five-year-old wasn't feeling well, the child gave her mother her favorite stuffed animal for comfort.
- **Limited focus.** Children find it difficult to focus on more than one feature at a time. Suppose you show a child three white tennis balls and seven yellow ones. If you ask whether there are more yellow balls or more tennis balls, a four-year-old will probably say more yellow balls. The child can't focus on both the color and the type of ball at once. An older child would see that all the balls are tennis balls, of which only some are yellow.

INFOLINK

Preoperational Period

For more on *preoperational period*, see Chapter 10, pages 325-326.

In ages four to six, children learn that numbers represent quantity and letters stand for sounds. *What mental ability does this indicate?*

What Is Intelligence?

Although children these ages are still in the preoperational period, their mental abilities are clearly growing. Children learn to read and count in this period—the basis of later work in school. As children begin school, many parents wonder how intelligent their children are. Will they thrive in school? How will their school experiences shape their lives?

Traditional Views of Intelligence

Educators use formal intelligence tests to try to determine the thinking skills of children. The test results can help teachers, principals, and learning specialists understand and meet students' educational needs.

The first intelligence test was developed by a French psychologist, Alfred Binet, in 1905. In 1916, Lewis M. Terman of Stanford University made a major revision of the Binet test.

CHAPTER 16: Intellectual Development from Four to Six **485**

COMPREHENSION CHECK

1. What period precedes the preoperational period? What are its characteristics? (*Sensorimotor; children learn mainly through senses and own actions.*)

ACTIVITIES

Discussion Activity

Discuss with students how children show their egocentric viewpoint. Have them give examples of egocentric behavior that they have seen in four- to six-year-old children. **L2**

Critical Thinking Activity

Applying. Discuss with students the merits of pretend play for children. Then ask them to suggest how an older child, or an adult, might benefit from imaginative play. **L1**

Teamwork Activity

Have students work in groups to brainstorm examples of each of the manifestations of preoperational thinking listed in the text. Have them share their ideas with the class and discuss whether the examples fit in the category. **L2**

VISUAL LEARNING Using the Photograph
Answer: Ability to use symbols, part of preoperational thinking.

DID *You* **Know?**

Dramatic Play. Dramatic play has many benefits: (1) It provides an outlet for inner thoughts and feelings. (2) It helps children solve personal problems by acting out different possibilities. (3) It teaches children about roles in society. (4) It helps children expand their minds by using their imaginations. (5) It provides practice for language skills. (6) It helps children learn and practice courtesy, sharing, and cooperating.

ACTIVITIES

Critical Thinking Activity

Defining Terms. Have students generate their own definitions of intelligence. After writing their definitions, have them share them with the class. Have the class discuss the definitions. Do any definitions apply to all people who might be considered intelligent? How can intelligence be measured? **L1**

Discussion Activity

Do you agree or disagree with the following statement: "Every child should take an intelligence test before entering school." Why or why not? **L1**

Critical Thinking Activity

Evaluate. Give students the following situation: "Tran is a six-year-old who is learning English as a second language."
Ask: What might happen when Tran takes an IQ test? What does the test tell us about Tran's intelligence? **L2**

VISUAL LEARNING | **Using the Photograph**
Answer: They evaluate a child's development in more areas than just thinking skills.

Today the test is commonly called the Stanford-Binet, and it is one of many tests used to measure intelligence in children.

By having many children take the test, Terman created a mathematical formula that could be used to give a child's intelligence a number value. This **intelligence quotient**, or **IQ**, is a number obtained by comparing a person's test results to that of other children the same age. The average child of any age has an IQ between 90 and 110. Those who score higher or lower than this average are said to be of higher or lower intelligence.

Intelligence tests are composed of tasks and questions. These correspond to the expected abilities of children at different age levels. Two-year-olds, for example, cannot read. An intelligence test for them might include building a tower of blocks, identifying parts of the body, and fitting simple geometric shapes into corresponding holes.

There are several problems with using intelligence tests, however:

- No one test gives an accurate measure of a child's mental ability. Also, these tests only measure one kind of mental ability, ignoring other kinds.
- Many factors that have nothing to do with intelligence can influence test results. A child's physical or emotional state when taking the test can affect his or her score. Thus, test results are not consistent. The same test given to the same child at two separate times may show a wide difference in scores.
- The tests don't tell much about specific abilities. Two people with the same IQ may have very different strengths and weaknesses.

Because of these problems, educators must use intelligence tests cautiously. The

National Association for the Education of Young Children (NAEYC) warns that no decision about a child's placement in school should be made on the basis of one test alone. Today, preschools and kindergartens are more likely to use different techniques to gain an overview of a child's level of development in all areas, not just thinking skills. If the child falls outside the norms of development for his or her age, then an in-depth assessment of skills can be done. In this way, educators can identify problem areas and plan activities that will help the child.

Multiple Intelligences

In recent years, psychologist Howard Gardner has advanced a new way of looking

Before entering kindergarten, many children are given screening tests to assess their abilities. *Why are these assessments more useful than intelligence tests?*

The Developing Brain

Reversing Deprivation

Intellectual development is not permanently established by early childhood. Neither are scores on IQ tests. A child who has been deprived of stimulation may or may not fully develop intellectually. Some children who had less stimulating environments early in life improve their performance later, when new experiences provide a chance for the crucial brain pathways to develop.

Researchers have identified many different kinds of intelligence. **Which types are shown here?**

at intelligence. He argues that humans have **multiple intelligences**—many different ways of using the mind and body to experience the world. He outlines eight such intelligences:

- **Verbal-linguistic.** This is linked to language. A person strongest in this intelligence learns best through words.
- **Logical-mathematical.** This is shown by skill in arithmetic and many areas of science. People try to find patterns to connect facts and observations.
- **Visual-spatial.** This is shown by ability in drawing and construction. Learning is easiest through pictures and colors.
- **Musical.** This intelligence has to do with rhythm and sounds. Hearing rhythms and melodies helps promote learning.
- **Bodily-kinesthetic.** This intelligence is skill in moving the body through space. Athletes, dancers, and those who are skilled in crafts are high in this intelligence.

- **Interpersonal.** This intelligence has to do with social skills. A person with these abilities is good at communicating with and empathizing with others.
- **Intrapersonal.** This intelligence is revealed by a person who is more private and less social. A person who keeps a diary, has a strong will and much independence, and prefers to play alone has this intelligence.

---

1. How does someone show verbal-linguistic intelligence? (*Through skillful use of words.*)
2. How is a naturalistic intelligence exhibited? (*By an understanding of the natural world.*)

ACTIVITIES

Teamwork Activity

Divide students into groups, and assign each group one or two of the types of intelligence. Have the group members brainstorm to suggest other activities that would be appropriate for children with that kind of intelligence. How could such activities improve that intelligence in other children? Have them share their ideas with the class. **L2**

Critical Thinking Activity

Supporting Examples. Have students think of people they have known who seemed to be particularly strong in one of the eight multiple intelligences. Which intelligence did they have? Why would they classify the person that way? If the person was an adult, what did he or she do as a career? Did the particular intelligence lead to success in that career? **L1**

VISUAL LEARNING | **Using the Photographs**
Answers:
Left: Bodily-kinesthetic. *Right:* Musical.

MULTIPLE INTELLIGENCES

Many famous people exhibit multiple intelligences. Some examples are:
- **Bodily-kinesthetic:** Charlie Chaplin, Lindsay Davenport.
- **Naturalistic:** Jacques Cousteau, Jane Goodall.
- **Spatial:** Leonardo da Vinci, Stephen Spielberg.
- **Interpersonal:** Oprah Winfrey, Jimmy Carter.
- **Musical:** Garth Brooks, Wolfgang Mozart.

COMPREHENSION CHECK

1. Why do people need to be cautious of when using the multiple intelligence theory in working with children? (*They need to be careful not to label a child as being one particular way and then trying to focus on that area at the expense of others.*)

ACTIVITIES

Critical Thinking Activity

Synthesizing. Review the theory of multiple intelligences with students. Then ask the following: How could using this theory be helpful to a teacher?

Practicing Parenting

Have students describe ways they have seen parents focus on their child's intelligence and learning. Tell them that the feature will provide a variety of activities that parents could use to foster various types of intelligence.

Answers to Apply Your Knowledge

1. Interpersonal. Intrapersonal.
2. Visual-spatial.

• **Naturalistic.** This intelligence is revealed by an understanding of the natural world—plants, animals, and the processes of nature. A person who has naturalistic intelligence is likely to be interested in being outdoors and may enjoy books about animals.

Of course, people—including children—have abilities in various intelligences. Those who study multiple intelligences point out that caregivers shouldn't label a child as being one particular way and then try to enhance that intelligence at the expense of all others. Children need to grow in many areas.

Still, it can help caregivers to recognize a child's particular strengths in one or more areas. They can provide that child with opportunities in that area to challenge and interest the child in learning.

Practicing Parenting

Activities for Multiple Intelligences

Each type of intelligence can be fostered with particular activities:

♥ **Verbal-linguistic.** Word games and puzzles, reading, writing, jokes and tongue twisters, games involving memorizing.

♥ **Logical-mathematical.** Number games; chess and checkers; maps and diagrams; tests of logic; experiments.

♥ **Visual-spatial.** Play with pictures, drawing, modeling clay, construction toys, jigsaw puzzles.

♥ **Musical.** Toy instruments, household objects that can be banged, music tapes, music lessons.

♥ **Bodily-kinesthetic.** Physical activities such as gymnastics or soccer, using playground equipment, dancing.

♥ **Interpersonal.** Activities that involve other children such as joining clubs or other groups.

♥ **Intrapersonal.** Time to be alone and think, writing in a diary.

♥ **Naturalistic.** Opportunities to experience nature, such as gardening, walking in the woods, or watching birds.

APPLY YOUR KNOWLEDGE

1. What kind of intelligence is a child who enjoys cooperative play likely to have? What child would be least likely to join in such play?
2. What kinds of intelligences, other than logical-mathematical, do you think would be connected to playing chess or checkers?

Observing & Participating

Provide students with an opportunity to observe a preschool or kindergarten class. Have them observe the children, focusing on the kinds of intelligences evident among the children. Have them record the behaviors they used to infer the type of intelligence. After the observation, have them explain what intelligences they saw and what evidence they used to support their conclusions. Have the class discuss whether they agree with those assessments.

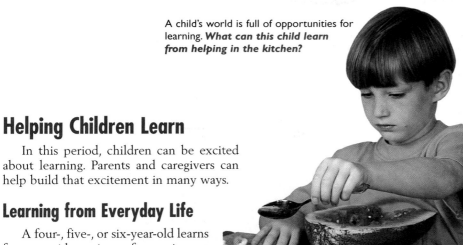

A child's world is full of opportunities for learning. **What can this child learn from helping in the kitchen?**

Helping Children Learn

In this period, children can be excited about learning. Parents and caregivers can help build that excitement in many ways.

Learning from Everyday Life

A four-, five-, or six-year-old learns from a wide variety of experiences, especially when a parent or other important caregiver shares them.

Talk with children about what they are doing. A few positive comments, such as "Wow, the building you are making is so tall—and it has so many windows!" can encourage interest. Questions help children think in new ways about what is happening and encourage them to organize their thoughts into answers.

Explanations and suggestions can also be helpful. You might explain in simple terms why water turns to ice. If a child is trying to lift a heavy box full of toys, you could suggest that pushing the box might be easier.

Asking a child's advice is another effective technique for promoting learning. For example, ask how to arrange the carrot sticks and radishes on the serving plate and then do so.

Trips and activities are important to learning. A ride on a bus, train, or plane can be an adventure that leads the child to discuss what is seen and to ask questions.

Nature walks are fun—and free. Everyone in the family can learn by looking closely at leaves, flowers, and birds.

Helping around the house provides great learning opportunities. Sharing such tasks also strengthens the family bonds and helps children develop responsibility, maturity, and independence.

Children of this age are curious to learn more about their own bodies and about where babies come from. Answer their questions in simple terms they can understand, and help them learn the correct names for body parts. Encourage children to have positive attitudes by answering their questions in an unembarrassed, natural way.

CHAPTER 16: Intellectual Development from Four to Six **489**

COMPREHENSION CHECK

1. How does asking children questions help children learn? (*It helps them think in new ways about what is happening and encourages them to organize their thoughts into answers.*)
2. What are three techniques that can be used to help children learn? (*Talk with children about what they are doing; give them explanations; ask for advice; use recreational and everyday activities to help them learn.*)

ACTIVITIES

Critical Thinking Activity

Applying. Have students give examples of how helping with the following activities could help students learn or reinforce such concepts as colors, shapes, counting, letters, or written words: shopping, cooking, setting the table. **L2**

| **VISUAL LEARNING** | *Possible responses:* About colors, numbers, food, nutrition, teamwork. |

| **ISSUES IN TEEN PARENTING** | If you have teen parents in your class, ask them how they spend most of their time. What proportion of time is used for different activities? Which of those activities do they perform with their child alongside or nearby? Ask how they can take everyday activities, such as shopping, cooking, and cleaning, and turn them into learning opportunities for their children. |

COMPREHENSION CHECK

1. Why is reading rhyming books to children important to their learning? (*Rhyming helps to develop an awareness of phonemes.*)

2. Why does being bilingual help in learning to read? (*Children who are bilingual seem to understand that printed words are symbols.*)

ACTIVITIES

Discussion Activity

Have students discuss the following statement: "In an age of television and computers, love of reading is not important." Remind students to give facts or examples to support their arguments. **L1**

Critical Thinking Activity

Making Inferences. How are children affected if they are not exposed to reading, art, and music? At what age does exposure to these areas no longer matter? **L2**

VISUAL LEARNING	**Using the Photographs**

Left—Possible responses: They are exposed to different stories; learn to pay attention.

Right—Possible responses: Covering floor, child's clothes to avoid paint ruining them.

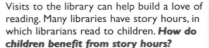

Visits to the library can help build a love of reading. Many libraries have story hours, in which librarians read to children. ***How do children benefit from story hours?***

Appreciating Reading

Developing an interest in reading is important. Books provide an opportunity to learn about and understand the world and the people in it. Children who enjoy reading will find learning easier—and more fun.

An important factor in learning to read is the ability to hear **phonemes** (FOH-neems), or the individual sounds in words. Rhyming words help develop this awareness, so reading rhyming books to children is a good learning activity. When a book becomes familiar, stop from time to time and let the child fill in the missing sounds.

Another way to develop this awareness is through alliteration—words that begin with the same sound. Many alphabet books provide an opportunity to hear alliteration because they collect many words that begin with each letter. After children have learned the sound, they will begin to connect the letter to it.

Research suggests that being **bilingual**, or able to speak two languages, may make reading easier. Children who are bilingual understand that printed words convey a particular meaning sooner than do children who speak one language. This may give them an edge in reading.

Choosing Books

Fortunately, young children love books and stories. If this interest is encouraged, children are likely to enjoy reading as they grow older.

Most communities have free public libraries that lend children's books. Many libraries also offer story hours for young children. Some schools and preschools allow children and families to borrow books for a short time.

When choosing books for children, use these questions to guide you:

- Are the pictures colorful, interesting, and easy to understand?

Management/Leadership Skills

Have students work in pairs. Give each pair an index card with the name of a place in your community. Have students find out what opportunities for learning this place can provide for children. Students might write a brief description of the place, explaining the kinds of learning opportunities available. Have students assemble the information in an illustrated list that could be made available to local parents.

- Will the story appeal to the child's interests?
- Does the story include action that will hold the child's interest?
- Will the child understand most of the words?
- Does the book use descriptive language that brings the story alive?
- Is the story short enough to read in one sitting?
- If you are considering buying the book, is it made well to stand up under hard use?

What kind of books do four- to six-year-olds like? Many like stories about experiences that are different from their own. Through books, city children can learn about farm life and children who live in rural areas can experience buses, apartments, and other parts of city life.

Children this age also enjoy humor, including funny rhymes, and unusual situations. When they giggle over the picture of a horse in the bathtub, they show that they are beginning to separate reality from fantasy.

Introducing Art and Music

Art helps children express their feelings, learn to control their body, and show creativity. Four- to six-year-olds benefit from using many different art materials, such as play dough, crayons, paper, paste, paint, and scissors. Even dried macaroni can be strung into a necklace or pasted onto a sheet of construction paper to make a design.

Children should be encouraged to experiment with art materials. Don't correct or criticize their work. Experiencing creativity rather than the product itself is what is important. Parents and other caregivers need to follow this guideline.

Children enjoy talking about their art—and this talking helps them build their ver-

Children enjoy experimenting with many different art materials. *If they are doing painting in the home, what precautions might a caregiver wish to take? Why?*

Language Arts Activity

Have students read a children's book and write a review of it. Ask students to use the checklist on pages 490-491 to evaluate the suitability of the book for a four- to six-year-old. **L3**

Art Activity

Collect a bag of items from around the house and yard, such as egg cartons, fabric, magazines, yarn, string, cans, pine cones, and small stones. Pair students and have each pair draw one item from the bag. Have students plan an art project a four- to six-year-old could make with the item and explain their ideas. **L2**

ISSUES IN CHILDREN'S HEALTH

Art Safety. All the materials children use in their art projects should be carefully checked for safety features. For example, paints, pastes, and other supplies must be nontoxic. Sharp objects, including sharply pointed scissors, should not be made available. Also remember that even carefully chosen materials are not safe unless the children know how to use them safely.

Parenting in *Action*

Parents and other caregivers can nurture children's artistic talent in many ways:
- Point out objects of interest and use visual words to refer to them—the tiny bug, the hairy dog.
- Ask questions that involve vision: What do you see that's blue?
- Ask children to point out similarities and differences in objects.
- Discuss pictures in art books.
- Provide art materials and a place for children to work.

CHECKING COMPREHENSION

Have students answer the Check Your Understanding questions. Answers appear at the bottom of this page.

EVALUATION

Give students the Section 16-1 Quiz in the *Teacher Resource Guide*.

RETEACHING

1. Assign Reteaching Activities, page 46.
2. Have students write a paragraph that completes this phrase: "A child learns best when . . . ."

ENRICHMENT

Have students research more about multiple intelligences by focusing on one and preparing a brief report about it. Ask them to specify which of the multiple intelligences they believe are their own strengths.

EXTENSION

Invite a music, art, preschool, or kindergarten teacher to your class. Have the teacher discuss music or art ideas he or she uses with young children.

CLOSE

Have students write a list of five suggestions for getting young children interested in reading, art, and music.

bal skills. Ask "How did you make that?" to prompt the child to explain the process used. Instead of guessing what a picture represents, ask the child to tell you. Then find specific aspects of the work that you can praise. For example, you might say, "I really like the bright colors you used for the flowers."

The Developing Brain

Math and music are interconnected. Researchers have found that children's reasoning about space and time improved when they had weekly piano lessons. That's the reasoning that underlies math.

All children respond naturally to rhythmic sound, which is a part of music. A boy rubs a stick against a fence as he walks, hearing the rhythm. A girl listens to her footsteps as she runs.

Three- to six-year-olds enjoy rhythm games and singing simple, repetitive songs. Many children are introduced to singing by **finger plays**, songs or chants with accompanying hand motions. "The Itsy-Bitsy Spider" is a finger play.

The opportunity to play simple instruments helps develop children's interest in music. Children enjoy using bells, drums, tambourines, or almost anything that makes a noise. There is no need to buy instruments; old kitchen pans and mixing spoons work well.

SECTION 16-1 REVIEW

✔ Check Your Understanding

1. List three signs of preoperational thinking.
2. What does an IQ score of 100 tell you about a child? What does it *not* tell you about the child?
3. What kind of intelligence is shown by a child who draws well? By a child who spends time riding bikes, practicing gymnastics, and swimming?
4. In terms of Gardner's idea, why would a teacher have to teach a lesson several different ways?
5. Name an everyday activity that could be used as a learning experience and explain how. Use an example other than those in the textbook.
6. What types of books can help children learn phonemes?
7. What are finger plays?

Putting Knowledge Into Practice

1. **Supporting a Position.** Some early childhood educators urge a stop to all standardized testing of young children. Do you agree with this idea? Why or why not?
2. **Analyzing.** When Dawn showed her father a drawing, he said "That's nice." What would have been a better response? Why?
3. **Observing and Participating.** Analyze your own abilities in terms of the eight intelligences. Using a five-point scale, in which 1 is low and 5 is high, rate how skilled you are in each area. Base your ratings on the activities you enjoy and how you learn.

492 UNIT 5: The Child from Four to Six

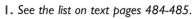

ANSWERS TO SECTION 16-1 REVIEW

1. *See the list on text pages 484-485.*
2. *Tells:* On a specific day, the child scored within the average for children of same age. *Does not tell (possible response):* Specific areas where child has abilities.
3. Visual-spatial; bodily-kinesthetic.
4. Children with different intelligences learn best in different ways.
5. *Possible response:* Doing laundry. Can be used to learn numbers and colors.
6. Books with rhymes or alliteration.
7. Songs or chants with hand motions.

SECTION 16-2

The Child in School

Sarah came home from kindergarten bursting with excitement. "We learned a new song today," she said. "And Mrs. Puhl told us about the leaves changing colors. Then we walked outside and picked up leaves. Then I helped serve the snack, but Janey wouldn't do it. After we ate, we made a drawing. Look!" Sarah thrust a paper into her mother's hand—and finally stopped for a breath.

KEY TERMS

attention deficit hyperactivity
    disorder (ADHD)
dyslexia
gifted children
learning disability

OBJECTIVES:

- Create ways to help a child adjust to starting kindergarten.

- Describe the speech development of children aged four to six, and identify possible speech problems.

- Identify ways to meet the needs of children with learning disabilities and gifted children.

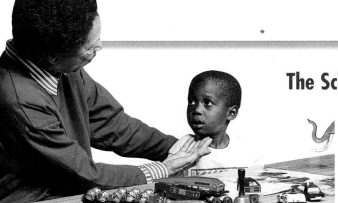

The School Experience

Since children attend school for many years, it is vital that they develop a positive attitude from the start. Children who have a bad experience with classmates or a teacher can develop negative feelings about school.

CHAPTER 16: Intellectual Development from Four to Six **493**

Observing & Participating

Have students interview kindergarten teachers about the issues children have when they first start school. Encourage students to develop a list of questions to ask prior to the interview. Students should focus on what the major issues are for the children and what the concerns are for the teachers. Students might also find out what suggestions the teachers have for making the transition from home to school easier for the children. Have the class discuss students' findings.

SECTION 16-2 RESOURCES

Teacher Resource Guide
- Lesson Plan Organizer, p. 73
- Section 16-2 Quiz, p. 189

Student Motivation Kit
- Observ. & Case Studies (case study), pp. 131-132
- Reteaching Activity, p. 47
- Enrichment, p. 48
- Nurturing Brain Development, pp. 10-11

Student Workbook
- Study Guide, pp. 128-131
- What Is Dyslexia Like?, p. 134

Transparency Package
- CT-48 Ready to Start School?

Effective Instruction CD-ROM

FOCUS

MOTIVATOR

Ask: What memories do you have of the transition from home to school? Students should focus on their reactions to sitting still, listening to the teacher, completing assignments, being with new children, and adjusting to the daily routine.

VOCABULARY ACTIVITY

Discuss the meaning of the term hyperactive. "Hyper" is a prefix meaning "over, more than normal, or too much." Hyperactive, thus, means "overactive." Ask for other examples of words with the prefix "hyper."

ACTIVITIES

Literature Activity

Have students examine books for young children about the preschool, child care, or school experience. Have them evaluate whether they think the book would help prepare a child for school. **L2**

Possible response: To make sure that the child can hear.

ISSUES IN
CHILDREN'S HEALTH

Maintaining Health Records. Keeping accurate, up-to-date records of children's immunizations and medical treatments is valuable to parents and other caregivers as children enter child care centers and schools. Since most institutions require proof of immunization, a medical history for each child provides instant access to needed dates and relevant information. Most doctors or health clinics provide a form that can be updated at each visit. Parents should maintain these records in an accessible place.

These feelings can keep them from learning as well as they might. To build that positive attitude, a smooth transition to school life is important.

Preparing for School

Many parents place their children in a preschool so that they can become used to being in a school setting. In preschool, children learn to pay attention, take turns, sit still for various periods of time, and interact with other children.

At age five or six, most children enter kindergarten. The standard for entering the public school system is usually when the child turns five years old. Most systems have a cutoff date, such as September 1 or December 31, after which the child must wait until the following year to enroll.

Many states require that a child have a physical exam by a physician before starting school. Parents also have to show that children have had all needed immunizations (see Chapter 18).

In the past, kindergarten was usually only a half day. Now, though, many school systems offer full-day kindergarten programs. Research has shown that children in full-day kindergarten programs perform better in elementary school.

Making the Transition

Starting kindergarten can be a major adjustment for a child—even one who has gone to preschool. The school is generally bigger than any preschool, and it includes children several years older. A child switching from a half-day preschool to a full-day kindergarten has other adjustments to make. For example many children begin riding on a school bus.

Parents can help their children adjust to this new experience in several ways:

- Be sure the child knows his or her full name, address, and telephone number.

INFOLINK

Preschools

For more about *preschools*, see Chapter 3, pages 107-108.

Some children need glasses so they can see the board. Having a hearing test is also a good idea. *Why would that be important?*

494   UNIT 5: The Child from Four to Six

Parenting in *Action*

Have students interview parents of school children about the first day of school. How did the parents prepare their children for the transition? How do they think the children felt about going to school? Students should ask whether the child had been in outside-the-home child care or preschool before school began. If so, how many hours a day and how many days a week? When students compare their findings, they should see whether child care or preschool had any impact on adjustment to school.

Ask the E**?**perts

Rachel Perkins
Child Development Technology
Instructor
Hinds Community College
Utica, Mississippi

READINESS *for School*

Q When should I start my child in school?

A The question of school readiness is a difficult one. Children born before the school system's cutoff date may enter school that year, but they do not have to enter. What should parents whose child doesn't seem ready do—put the child in school or wait another year?

For many years, experts said that holding a child out of school for another year would do no harm—and could help by giving a child time to develop more emotional maturity. One study showed that even children with high intelligence had emotional problems if they began school too early.

Another study, however, suggests that the opposite is true. In this research, children who started late had problems with behavior later in their school careers.

What, then, should a parent do? Many school systems offer screening tests for the children to take the summer before the school year begins. Parents who have their children in a preschool can talk to the teachers at that preschool. Those professionals can speak about the child's readiness based on what they have observed.

Parents can also look for certain signs. A child is ready for school if he or she can:

- *Communicate with adults other than his or her parents and be understood.*
- *Put on and take off coats and shoes and go to the bathroom on his or her own.*
- *Complete a task.*
- *Listen to a story and answer questions about it.*
- *Follow directions and take turns.*
- *Be willing to wait for a request to be met or a question answered.*

Thinking It Through

1. How can parents handle the conflicting results of different studies on the issue of school readiness?
2. Why do children need certain self-help skills to be ready for school?

Ask the E**?**perts

Introducing the Feature

Ask: What skills do you think children need to be ready to go to school? List students' responses on the board. Have them determine which two skills they consider most essential.

Answers to Thinking It Through
1. *Possible response:* They must make decisions based on their own child; they can get advice from preschool teachers.
2. *Possible response:* The child will have to care for him- or herself, not rely on the teacher, during the school day.

Applying What You've Learned

Have students find out what the cut-off date for entering school is in their district. **Ask:** What would you do if your child was born near to, but before, the cut-off date? Would you have your child begin school that year? Would you hold your child out for another year? Why?

LEARNING STYLES

Kinesthetic

Have pairs of students prepare a skit in which a parent and a preschool teacher are discussing whether the parent's child is ready for school. In each case, the preschool teacher should take the position that the child would benefit by delaying kindergarten for a year. The parent can either strongly believe that the child *should* begin school or be open to the teacher's suggestion but concerned about the child's well being. Have the pairs present their skits, then have the class discuss what issues arose.

COMPREHENSION CHECK

1. What is the extent of an average six-year-olds vocabulary (*Approximately 2,500 words.*)

2. Why are sounds represented by *j, ch, st, pl,* and *sl* the most difficult for children to make? (*They require the smooth coordination of the lips, tongue, and throat muscles.*)

3. What are some problems that may cause speech difficulties in children? (*Hearing and using only a limited number of simple words; speaking only a language other than English at home; moving from one part of the country to another; emotional immaturity.*)

ACTIVITIES

Discussion Activity

Point out to students the words listed on the page that could replace *go*. Ask students to suggest replacements for *big, pretty, fast,* and *good* when conversing with children.

- Explain what to expect at school. If possible, visit the school together before the child's first day. Some schools offer open house days for new students.
- Be sure that the child has plenty of rest by starting an earlier bedtime a few weeks before school begins.
- Let the child choose a lunch box or backpack and pick out the clothes to wear on the first day of school. With these choices, the child will link the new school to pleasant experiences.
- Above all, have a positive attitude. A parent's positive feelings will rub off on the child.

Speech Development

By the time they start school, children have gained an extensive knowledge of language just by listening. They probably don't know what an adjective is, but they can use adjectives confidently and correctly. As children grow older, their vocabulary increases. The sentences they use will become more complex. However, all the basic language forms have already been learned in the preschool years. For instance, children know how to use nouns and verbs to build a sentence, even if they can't label words as nouns and verbs.

A child's vocabulary should increase rapidly during this period. A normally developing six-year-old can understand and use approximately 2,500 words.

Articulation (clear, distinct speech) improves dramatically in this period as well. Three-year-olds typically say only about 30 percent of their words correctly. By age six, that has increased to 90 percent.

Much of this improvement depends on physical development. Some sounds are more difficult to make than others. The sounds represented by *b, m,* and *p* are produced simply by moving the lips. By three, most children can make these sounds. The *f* and *v* sounds, among others, involve both the lips and the teeth. Children may not master these sounds until age five. The most difficult sounds are those represented by *j, ch, st, pl,* and *sl.* They require the smooth coordination of the lips, tongue, and throat muscles. Some children may be six or seven before "pwease" becomes "please."

Speech Difficulties

Most children can develop good language skills at home. Some children, though, have problems with language. They may have plenty of opportunity to listen and speak at home, but hear and use only a limited number of simple words. Children need to hear—and be encouraged to use—language that is specific and rich in detail. For example, rather than using the very general verb *go,* encourage children to use a variety of specific verbs: The boys *race* across the field. The women *jog* every morning. The bugs *creep* down the tree.

Children who speak only a language other than English at home often have problems when they begin school. They must learn English language skills and, at the same time, keep up with their class. Children who move from one part of the country to another may also have difficulty because of differences in pronunciation.

Some children have physical problems that prevent normal speech. Others may be emotionally immature.

The Developing Brain

Speech Development

Young children are in an ideal position to learn more than one language—their brains are ready to understand a variety of sounds. Over time, it becomes harder for people to learn a second language because the brain is accustomed to processing only certain sounds. Knowing two languages is a valuable skill.

Some children with hearing loss are taught to communicate using sign language. *How would they benefit if other children learned to sign as well?*

All these situations may cause children to have difficulties at school. They may not be able to understand the teacher or to make themselves understood. As a result, learning becomes more difficult. This situation may cause emotional problems as well. Classmates are often unkind to a child whose speech is different. Teasing and jokes may add to a child's sense of isolation. Whatever the cause, children with speech problems need special help—preferably before they begin school.

Children with Special Needs

Some children have special educational needs. Two common causes of special needs—learning disabilities and unusually high intelligence—are discussed here.

Learning Disabilities

Not all children learn easily. For some, learning is made more difficult by a **learning disability**, a problem in a person's mental processes that prevents him or her from learning in a normal way. The Child Development Institute says that all the definitions of learning disability—and there are many—agree on four points:

1. People with learning disabilities have difficulty mastering academic work.
2. Development for people with learning disabilities is uneven, unlike that for other people.

INFOLINK

Children with Disabilities

For more about *children with disabilities*, see Chapter 19, pages 579-588.

Teamwork Activity

Have students work in small groups and make up a game for preschoolers to promote speech or vocabulary development. Arrange for students to play their games with a group of preschoolers.

VISUAL LEARNING — Using the Photograph *Answer:* They could communicate with others.

ISSUES IN CHILDREN'S HEALTH

Stuttering. About one-fourth of all children go through a period in which they stutter. Stress may trigger stuttering in a vulnerable child. To avoid creating stress-triggered stuttering:

- Maintain an easy and relaxed environment.
- Show interest in what the child says by listening carefully and maintaining eye contact.
- Avoid interrupting when the child is speaking.

By reducing pressure on the child, parents may help stuttering disappear. If it does not, the child's speech should be evaluated by a speech pathologist.

Management/Leadership Skills

Read the following situation: "Carlin is a six-year-old with a stuttering problem. Sometimes it takes him a long time to complete a sentence. Often people finish his sentences for him. 'Sometimes I just want to say it myself,' Carlin thinks."

Have students write a paragraph explaining Carlin's feelings and how they would help him. Call on volunteers to share their ideas with the class.

Critical Thinking Activity

Forming Opinions. Some children with learning disabilities are mainstreamed, or placed in a regular classroom, although they are taken out regularly for special help. Others go to a totally separate program for learning disabled children. Ask students what they think are the pros and cons of each method. What method would they prefer for their child? Why? **L1**

Critical Thinking Activity

Evaluating. Ask students to recall situations in which a child was treated unkindly by classmates because of a learning disability. Ask: How did the child react? How might that treatment have affected the child? **L2**

Critical Thinking Activity

Making Inferences. **Ask:** How do you think parents might feel if they suspect or find out their child has a learning disability? What might happen if parents ignore their suspicions? **L2**

VISUAL LEARNING | **Using the Photograph**
Answer: An imbalance of chemicals in the brain.

---

3. The learning problems these people have are not due to living in a disadvantaged environment.
4. The learning problems these people have are not due to mental or emotional problems.

A severe physical handicap, such as blindness, is not a learning disability. Being blind does make learning more difficult, but blindness is not a problem in how the brain processes information. Some children cannot understand what words mean or form their own thoughts into speech. If these problems result from problems in how the brain works, they are learning disabilities. From 6 to 10 percent of all children may have learning disabilities. Two are especially important.

- **Attention deficit hyperactivity disorder.** A child who is not able to control his or her activity or concentrate for a normal length of time may have **attention deficit hyperactivity disorder (ADHD).** Children who have ADHD often fail to finish what they start, don't seem to listen, and are easily distracted. They also may have difficulty staying in their seats or may always be active. Some of these children show signs of a lack of emotional control.

  Young children who first begin school and have difficulty sitting still do not necessarily have ADHD. Children from ages four to six simply need time to learn to settle down.

Children with ADHD can learn techniques to control their behavior so they can improve concentration and the ability to sit still. **What causes ADHD?**

Researchers think that ADHD is caused by an imbalance of chemicals in the brain. The problem has been linked to heredity—it runs in families—and to environment—taking drugs during pregnancy. Researchers have found they can use a special kind of brain scan to clearly tell whether a child has ADHD. This will help prevent cases of incorrectly diagnosing a child. The test is very expensive, however.

Some children with ADHD are given medication, but the practice is controversial. Studies are still being done. Children with ADHD can benefit by learning techniques that help them change their behavior and relax.

DID *You* **Know?**

Learning Disabilities. Early Childhood Intervention (ECI) programs can prevent years of frustration and failure for children who might not be diagnosed until much later, if at all. Language, coordination, and attention span can give clues to a problem. Speech should be understandable at least half the time by age three. By age three or four, a child should be able to sit and listen to a story. Problems do not necessarily mean a learning disorder, but a concerned parent should consult a physician.

CAREER OPPORTUNITIES

Special Education Teacher

A CONVERSATION WITH CARLA RANDISI

How did you become interested in becoming a special education teacher? I was studying for my degree in education. Through working with a scout troop, I became interested in helping children who have mental or physical disabilities.

What are the tasks and responsibilities of a special education teacher? We plan lessons that will help the children learn. Generally we teach each child individually—we have to develop methods of teaching that are suited to that child. We also keep parents informed of their child's progress.

What is the work environment like? We work in the school, either in our own classroom or in regular classrooms. Some teaching is done one-on-one, other times in groups.

What are the working hours like? We work a normal school schedule. After that we spend more time planning lessons and grading students' projects. We also meet with the regular teachers and with parents.

What aptitudes are needed to be a special education teacher? Like all teachers, we need to be well organized and good at planning and communicating. We also need to be flexible, and have patience, because students may take a long time to show progress. Self-control helps us handle students who have emotional problems.

SPECIAL EDUCATION TEACHER

Education and Training. Special education teachers have a bachelor's degree in education and often an extra year of training. All states require these teachers to receive a license before they can teach.

Career Outlook. The demand for special education is expected to continue to grow.

CONNECTING SCHOOL TO CAREER

1. **Thinking Skills.** Why do these teachers generally work with special needs children individually?
2. **Interpersonal Skills.** What do you think would be the most important interpersonal skill for a special education teacher? Why?

Building Career Skills

Information. Have students find out what education, training, and certification is needed to be a special education teacher in their school district. Students might also find out the starting salary for special education teachers in the district. They could also look into where these teachers work. Call on volunteers to report their findings to the class.

COMPREHENSION CHECK

1. What is the best way to teach reading to a child with dyslexia? (*Through the phonics approach.*)
2. How can parents help a child with learning disabilities learn? (*By removing distractions that might interfere.*)
3. How can the label "learning disabled" be as harmful to a child as the condition itself? (*They may be treated as if they are not capable of learning.*)
4. Who are gifted children? (*Children who have unusual intelligence or special talent in an artistic area.*)

ACTIVITIES

Discussion Activity

Are most parents good judges of whether their child is gifted? Why or why not?

VISUAL LEARNING | **Using the Photograph**

Explain to students that an MRI is made by passing radio waves through the body, which is inside a magnet. Body tissues vibrate due to the sound waves. MRIs, unlike x rays, can show "soft" tissues, such as organs, muscles, and blood vessels.

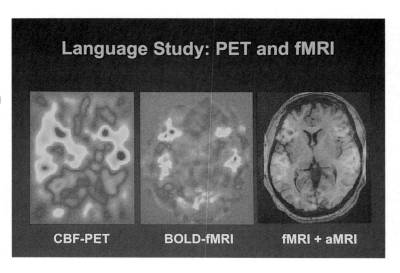

Language Study: PET and fMRI

Sophisticated medical tests such as the PET scan and functional MRI can be used to study and diagnose problems in brain function. This person was completing a language task during testing. The brightest colors show the areas of greatest activity.

CBF-PET   BOLD-fMRI   fMRI + aMRI

• **Dyslexia.** Another important disability is **dyslexia.** This problem prevents a person from understanding printed symbols in a normal way. Children with dyslexia are often intelligent, but their brains do not process some visual information normally. As a result, they have problems with reading, writing, spelling, and math. Children with dyslexia have difficulty understanding directions and repeating what is said to them. They may have problems distinguishing left and right as well.

Children with dyslexia need special help, particularly during the early school years. The best treatment for children with dyslexia, according to the Child Development Institute, is to use the phonics approach to teaching reading. This technique is based on learning to see that certain letter combinations stand for particular sounds.

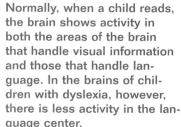

The Developing Brain

Normally, when a child reads, the brain shows activity in both the areas of the brain that handle visual information and those that handle language. In the brains of children with dyslexia, however, there is less activity in the language center.

Sometimes the label "learning disabled" can be as harmful as the problem itself. Children who have been found to have learning disabilities are sometimes treated as if they cannot learn. In fact, they can learn—but somewhat differently from most other children. They need special approaches tailored to their special needs.

ISSUES IN TEEN PARENTING

Point out to students that it is often not possible to know what has caused a learning disability. Severe head injuries and infections such as meningitis may be involved, or the problem may be a genetic one. Babies who are premature or of low birth weight are at risk for learning disabilities. This is of particular importance to teens, since prematurity and low birth weight are common in teen pregnancies.

Parents can find it difficult to accept that a child has a learning disability. One reason is that these problems often appear fairly late—when a child starts school. Until then, the parent was sure that the child was developing normally.

Parents can help these children overcome the disability by treating them with the same love and care shown to other children. Children should also have age-appropriate responsibilities around the house. Parents can help children with disabilities by removing any distractions that might interfere with learning. Finally, praise and reward for what is accomplished is important to these children. It took hard work!

Gifted and Talented Children

From 3 to 10 percent of the nation's students are **gifted children**, children who have unusual intelligence or special talent in an artistic area. Ramon, for example, has exceptional musical ability. Jennifer, though only four, shows remarkable artistic talent.

Educators once believed that gifted and talented children would thrive in any environment. It is now known that these children have special needs that must be met. They need recognition and acceptance—and they need challenging activities in which they can be successful. They benefit from playing with a variety of children, but

Children learn in different ways, based on their particular kind of intelligence. *What must teachers do as a result?*

CHAPTER 16: Intellectual Development from Four to Six **501**

Critical Thinking Activity

Making Inferences. Ask students if they think a gifted person is more likely to be successful than one who is not. Encourage students to give reasons for their opinions. **L1**

Discussion Activity

Ask students to suggest ways that a gifted child's education can be enriched. Why is it important to balance intellectual enrichment with physical, emotional, and social needs? **L2**

VISUAL LEARNING  Using the Photograph
Possible response: Develop lesson plans that can reach different kinds of intelligence.

DID You Know?

Gifted Children. **Some studies show that early creativity peaks at about age four, drops at five, develops again from grades one to three, and drops again at the beginning of fourth grade. Creative growth declines again at the beginning of seventh grade, and natural curiosity levels off by high school. To encourage creativity at all ages, children should be given the materials and freedom to create and to be different.**

MULTIPLE INTELLIGENCES

Organize students into small groups. Have students in each group plan activities that would provide gifted children with extra stimulation. The activities should be aimed at children who have special aptitude in one or more of the multiple intelligences. Have each group present their activities to the class, which should determine which intelligence the activity is suitable for and whether or not the activity would be beneficial and enjoyable to the children.

ACTIVITIES

Writing Activity

Ask students to think about some especially bright children they know. Have them determine what these children say and do to show their high levels of thinking and ability. Have students describe these characteristics in a written profile of that child. Emphasize that students should not identify the child they are describing. **L2**

VISUAL LEARNING | **Using the Photograph**
Answer: The child might not become a well rounded individual if he or she devotes too much time to one talent or interest.

DID *You* **Know?**

Highly Gifted Children. According to *Gifted Child Today Magazine*, the following traits are typical of more than 99% of highly gifted children: rapid learning, extensive vocabulary, and excellent memory. More than 93% display curiosity, excellent sense of humor, keen sense of observation, and long attention span as an infant or toddler. The mean age for beginning to read is age 4.

Recognizing and encouraging talent from a young age can enrich a child's life. *What might happen if a talent is overemphasized?*

they also need time with other gifted or talented learners.

Avoid overwhelming gifted and talented children with unrealistic expectations or goals. Instead, give these children encouragement and opportunities to explore their gifts.

Gifted children can easily become bored and frustrated in school. They may be labeled "problem children" because they don't follow classroom procedures, they give unexpected answers to questions, and they like to argue. Some gifted children who are not challenged at school become poor students. Most schools have special programs for gifted students. These may include enrichment programs within regular classes or special classes or even special schools for gifted children.

Most gifted children show recognizable signs by age two. They may talk early, using complete sentences, and show that they have an unusually large vocabulary. Many read before school age—some even by two and one-half. They are highly curious and ask challenging questions.

502 Unit 5: The Child from Four to Six

Management/Leadership Skills

Providing enrichment opportunities for children is often the basis for entrepreneurship. A gifted dancer or gymnast may open his or her own studio, a pianist may make a living by providing piano lessons for young students, and artists may instruct preschool and school-age children. Others might teach magic, computer skills, or science to young students. Ask students to share stories of people they know who are involved in enrichment programs outside of traditional classrooms. Collect newspaper clippings about such programs and teachers in your area.

Giving children opportunities in the areas that interest them can help build their talents.

ASSESS

CHECKING COMPREHENSION

Have students answer the Check Your Understanding questions. Answers appear at the bottom of this page.

EVALUATION

Give students the Section 16-2 Quiz in the *Teacher Resource Guide*.

RETEACHING

1. Assign Reteaching Activities, page 47.
2. Have students develop a chart in which they identify ways to meet the special needs covered in the section.

ENRICHMENT

Have students research dyslexia. What famous people have had dyslexia? How did they adjust?

EXTENSION

Have students research non-school programs available in their community for gifted children and share the information with the class.

CLOSE

Have students write a paragraph that begins with the sentence: "The most important thing for children with special needs is . . ."

SECTION 16-2 REVIEW

✔ Check Your Understanding

1. List two steps parents can take to prepare a child for kindergarten.
2. What are two signs of growing language skills among children of this period?
3. Why might children who only hear a language other than English in the home have problems in school?
4. Would deafness be a learning disability? Why or why not?
5. What behaviors are shown by a child with ADHD? By a child with dyslexia?
6. What do schools do to help gifted children?

Putting Knowledge Into Practice

1. **Analyzing.** Why do you think children who attend full-day kindergarten show better performance in school?
2. **Synthesizing.** How does a child benefit when he or she is diagnosed with a learning disability? What problems can such a diagnosis create for the child?
3. **Observing and Participating.** Describe your emotions when you first started high school. How did your earlier school experiences prepare you for high school? How would that compare to a six-year-old starting school for the first time? What could make that child's transition to school easier?

CHAPTER 16: Intellectual Development from Four to Six **503**

ANSWERS TO SECTION 16-2 REVIEW

1. *See the list on page 494-496.*
2. Larger vocabulary; improved articulation.
3. *Possible response:* They may have problems understanding directions and giving responses.
4. No, because it doesn't involve how the brain processes information.
5. *See the descriptions on pages 498, 500.*
6. Provide enrichment programs within regular classes or special classes or even special schools.

Ask students to recall what types of make-believe play they enjoyed when they were children. What do they think they gained from make-believe play?

TEACH

Discussion Activity

How does make-believe play show preoperational thinking? **L2**

Discussion Activity

What is the value of make-believe play? **L1**

Critical Thinking Activity

Making Inferences. Ask students to think about the role of adults in a child's make-believe play. Should a caregiver become involved in this play? Why or why not? **L1**

Language Arts Activity

Have students work in pairs to assemble a collection of simple props for a puppet show. Then have the students demonstrate a variety of ways the props can be used in make-believe play. **L2**

Parenting With Care

Encouraging Make-Believe Play

Between the ages of two and nine, children often engage in make-believe play.

This kind of play aids development in many ways.

What Is Make-Believe Play?

In make-believe play, children act out situations using their imagination.

They may engage in dramatic play, acting out what they see in the adult world. After watching an adult bake a cake, a child may pretend to bake a cake for a favorite stuffed animal. After spending a day at a parent's place of work, a child may play "office." Children might also use fantasy play, acting out a voyage to another planet or being a pirate.

The Benefits of Make-Believe Play

In make-believe play, children themselves choose what to play, and they create a situation over which they have full control. In this pretend world, they can be successful, feel important, and gain confi-

dence. They can make up their own rules and try out new activities without fear of failure or ridicule. Pretend play provides endless opportunities for trying out different roles. This play helps children understand and express their feelings. Stuffed animals, dolls, and puppets can all act as good friends—or perhaps enemies to talk to and act out feelings with.

Guiding Make-Believe Play

The best way to encourage make-believe play is to let it happen. Most children show an interest in this play at some time or another. Adults who allow it to take place naturally do the children a great favor.

Adults can also encourage this play by providing props. Kitchen equipment can help children playing house. A chalkboard and some books can turn a room into a school. Old

RESOURCES ON CREATIVE PLAY

Students interested in more information about the importance of make-believe play in a child's learning might contact the National Association for the Education of Young Children (NAEYC). This organization, made up of early childhood professionals and others, is dedicated to improving the quality of education programs for children from birth through age eight. Interested students can write to the NAEYC at 1509 16th Street, N.W., Washington, DC 20036; or visit the group's web site at www.naeyc.org.

clothes, jewelry, and shoes can be used for dressing up.

Caregivers should avoid limiting make-believe play. They can, however, let children know how they feel about certain situations. For example, suppose that a caregiver doesn't like shooting games. If children do begin to play such games, the caregiver might explain that he or she doesn't like to shoot people or be shot at. In this way, the caregiver reinforces a set of values without preventing the children from learning about aggressive behavior.

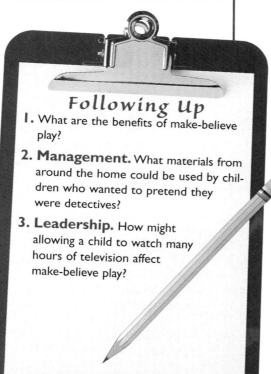

Following Up

1. What are the benefits of make-believe play?

2. **Management.** What materials from around the home could be used by children who wanted to pretend they were detectives?

3. **Leadership.** How might allowing a child to watch many hours of television affect make-believe play?

CHAPTER 16: Intellectual Development from Four to Six **505**

Writing Activity

On a sheet of paper, have students write a situation in which a child shows a negative emotion. Then ask students to exchange papers. Have them write an ending to the other student's story showing how make-believe play helped the child understand and overcome the feeling. Ask for volunteers to read their completed case study to the class. Discuss the solution. **L3**

Critical Thinking Activity

Applying. If possible, have students observe children from four to six engaging in make-believe play. What were the children pretending to do? How did they interact? How did the play end? Did other children join during the course of the play? If so, how were they accepted? Have them report to the class what they saw. **L2**

CLOSE

Ask students to write a response to this sentence: "Make-believe play for children is a waste of time."

CHECKING COMPREHENSION

Use the Summary and the Reviewing the Facts questions to help students go over the most important ideas in Chapter 16. Encourage students to ask questions and add details.

CHAPTER 16 REVIEW

Answers to Reviewing the Facts

1. Using symbols; learning through make-believe play; having an egocentric viewpoint; having a limited focus.
2. *Any one*: No test is reliable; test only one area of thinking; most rely on language and one particular culture; results can be influenced by other factors; tests say nothing about specific abilities.
3. *Possible response:* A person with interpersonal intelligence will be skilled at getting along with other people.
4. It can make learning easier.
5. *Possible responses:* Allows them to focus on the process, not the product; helps build language skills.
6. Physical exam and record of immunizations; age requirement.
7. Speaking simple words; speaking only a language other than English; moving from another part of the country.
8. *Possible response:* A physical disability may make learning more difficult, but a learning disability directly involves the way the brain processes information.
9. A child with unusual intelligence or special artistic talent.

CHAPTER 16   REVIEW &

Summary

✔ Children four to six are in the preoperational stage of thinking. (Section 16-1)

✔ One theorist emphasizes that there is more than one kind of intelligence. (Section 16-1)

✔ Parents and caregivers can lead children to appreciate reading, art, and music. (Section 16-1)

✔ Children starting school have to adjust to new situations. (Section 16-2)

✔ Between four and six, children have rapid language development, but some children need help. (Section 16-2)

Reviewing the Facts

1. What are the signs of preoperational thinking in children these ages? (Section 16-1)
2. List the disadvantages of intelligence tests. (Section 16-1)
3. Choose one of Gardner's multiple intelligences and explain what it means. (Section 16-1)
4. What positive effect does reading have on learning in general? (Section 16-1)
5. Why is it good to ask children about the processes they used to create art? (Section 16-1)
6. What do some states require before students start kindergarten? (Section 16-2)
7. What factors in the home might lead to language problems? (Section 16-2)

8. What is the difference between a learning disability and a physical disability? (Section 16-2)
9. What is meant by a "gifted" child? (Section 16-2)

Thinking Critically

1. **Making Inferences.** Lara is playing with her dolls by sitting them around a table with her. What kind of play typical of preoperational thinking is she playing?
2. **Analyzing.** How can an educator make a distinction between a child who is simply very squirmy because he or she is young and one who may have ADHD?
3. **Synthesizing.** What emotional problems might a gifted or talented child suffer? How might other children contribute to those problems?

Taking Action

1. **Making a Book.** Create a story suitable for a five-year-old about a child just starting kindergarten. Include some of the challenges that the child may face. Show how the child successfully met them. *(Communication)*
2. **Creating Finger Plays.** Think of a song that children enjoy and make up a finger play to go along with it. Show your creation to the class. *(Leadership)*

CONNECTIONS

 Cross-Curricular Connections

1. **Art.** Make a poster that explains the eight multiple intelligences.
2. **Music.** Listen to the recording of a singer or group that performs for young children. Perform the song, or read the words, to the class. Discuss why young children would find that song appealing.
3. **Communication.** Many children grow up in homes where English is not the primary language spoken. What programs are available for children four to six to improve their English skills? Suggest ways families, communities, and society can help this transition. Discuss how language impacts learning.

 Workplace Connections

1. **Resources.** Make a list of resources that you think should be on hand for art activities for kindergarten students.
2. **Interpersonal Skills.** With a partner, write and act out a scene in which a teacher informs a parent that his or her child has a learning disability or a speech problem and needs special help. Assume that the child has been tested to confirm the need and that the parent gave approval for the test.

 Family and Community Connections

1. **Learning in the Home.** Make a chart. At the top of each column, list such everyday experiences as cooking, cleaning, doing the laundry, or going shopping. Underneath, list ways that those activities can become learning experiences for children four to six years old.
2. **School Services.** Explore any special Early Childhood services that your school district offers to young children and their parents. Explain these services and their purpose to your classmates.

Technology Connections

1. **Internet.** Research gifted children, talented children, speech problems, ADHD, or dyslexia on the Internet, looking at government sites. What programs are suggested for children in these situations? Report your findings to the class.

EVALUATION

1. Use the reproducible Chapter 16 Test in the *Teacher Resource Guide*, or construct your own test using the **Exam***View*® Test Generator.
2. For an alternative assessment, assign the Chapter 16 activity in the *Authentic Assessment* section of the *Teacher Resource Guide*.

ENRICHMENT

Assign students either of the two extension activities in the *Enrichment Activities* booklet in the *Student Motivation Kit*.

EXTENSION

Ask students to match the eight multiple intelligences with careers that would be suitable for individuals with strengths in the respective areas. Examples might include accountants (logical-mathematical), salespeople (interpersonal), and architects (visual-spatial).

CLOSE

Have students create a brochure that details ways of enhancing the intellectual development of four- to six-year-olds.

After completing Unit 6, students will be able to:

- Explain the physical, emotional, social, and intellectual challenges of middle childhood and early adolescence.
- Demonstrate how to care for a sick child.
- Identify physical and emotional problems children face.
- Care for children and work in an early childhood classroom.

Chapter 17 covers the physical, emotional and intellectual changes of children between seven and twelve.

Chapter 18 discusses safety procedures and guidelines for general medical care for children of all ages.

Chapter 19 addresses the challenges children often face, such as disabilities, abuse, neglect, divorce and death.

Chapter 20 analyzes the responsibilities of a child care provider and the management of a preschool classroom.

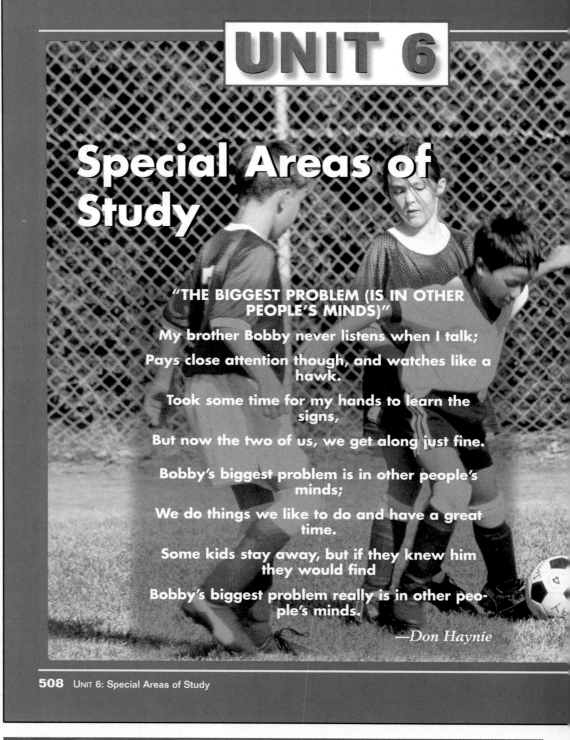

UNIT 6

Special Areas of Study

"THE BIGGEST PROBLEM (IS IN OTHER PEOPLE'S MINDS)"

My brother Bobby never listens when I talk;

Pays close attention though, and watches like a hawk.

Took some time for my hands to learn the signs,

But now the two of us, we get along just fine.

Bobby's biggest problem is in other people's minds;

We do things we like to do and have a great time.

Some kids stay away, but if they knew him they would find

Bobby's biggest problem really is in other people's minds.

—*Don Haynie*

508 Unit 6: Special Areas of Study

| USING THE POEM | Explore the ideas the poem presents. **Ask:** Who is the speaker? From what point of view are the ideas presented? What does the poem say about how children with special needs are treated by society? What does the speaker mean by "Bobby's biggest problem is in other people's minds"? In your experience, how are children with disabilities viewed by other people? Does the way disabled people are treated need to be changed? If so, in what ways? How can the change be accomplished? |

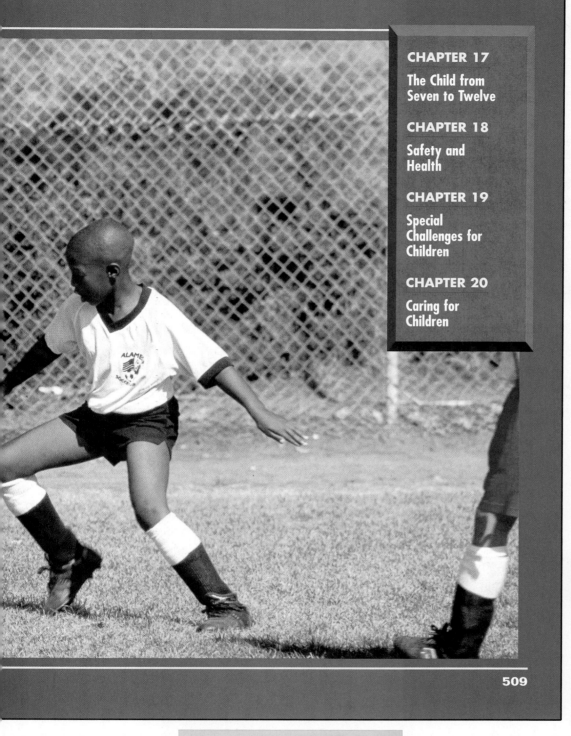

509

- Point to the titles of the four chapters in Unit 6. Ask students what they think each chapter will cover. **Ask:** How does this unit differ from the previous four units?
- Have students look at the photograph on these pages. Then have them look at photos of toddlers. Have them compare the children pictured here to those and to themselves. To which group do these children seem more similar? In what ways?

COMPLETING **UNIT 6**

EXTENSION

Have students investigate the work that UNICEF and the Children's Defense Fund do for the well-being of children. Ask them to choose one of the organizations and write a report of their findings.

EVALUATION

Use the Unit 6 Test on the Exam*View*® Test Generator or use the program to create your own test.

FCCLA Connection	**Preventing Bullying**

Divide students into groups. Have each group develop a skit that would encourage children (specify age) to practice care and inclusion, rather than belittling, exclusion, and other forms of bullying. Make arrangements for the groups to perform their skits for children of appropriate ages.

COMMUNITY AS CLASSROOM

Guest Speakers. The class could benefit by hearing from several professionals during the study of this unit. *For Chapter 17:* physical education teacher, nutritionist. *For Chapter 18:* visiting nurse, EMT. *For Chapter 19:* middle school principal, social worker. *For Chapter 20:* preschool teacher, home child care provider.

Field Trips. The class could take field trips to an outpatient clinic, an orthopedic doctor's office, a middle school, or a child care center to enhance their study of this unit.

CHAPTER 17 RESOURCES

Teacher Resource Guide
• Chapter 17 Test, p. 198
• Authentic Assessment, p. 289
Student Motivation Kit
• Observations, pp. 59-60
Transparency Package
• CT-50 Childhood Is a Time
for Growing
• CT-51 Ages & Stages: The
Child from Seven to Twelve
Effective Instruction CD-ROM

CHAPTER 17 **OVERVIEW**

Section 17-1 addresses growth,
nutrition, dental care, and hygiene.

Section 17-2 analyzes the development of personal identity and
guiding behavior.

Section 17-3 delves into the
social and moral concerns of children in this age group.

Section 17-4 looks at intellectual
development and the school experience.

CHAPTER 17

The Child from Seven to Twelve

RESOURCES TO EXPLORE

Mental Health. Children and young adults
suffer from mental illness just as some adults
do. Problems range from learning disabilities
to schizophrenia to autism. A good source of
information about mental health is the
National Mental Health Association (1021
Prince Street, Alexandria, VA 22314,
www.nmha.org). NMHA provides educational materials and referrals to local chapters and
community groups that provide services and
promote mental health.

Just before the curtain rose, the students on stage fought down their nerves. This was the big moment they had worked toward. Next year the sixth graders would be moving on to a new school. This would be their last performance at the old school, and they wanted it to be special.

Trisha thought about how much she had grown since she started in kindergarten. She remembered how big the school had looked then. In her first year at the school, the sixth graders seemed so grown up to her—big and knowing everything. Now she was one of them! She smiled when she remembered Mrs. Sanchez, who taught her how to read, and Mr. Nolan, who made social studies so interesting.

Trisha's thoughts were interrupted by Mrs. Robbins, who whispered from offstage. "OK, kids, we're going to raise the curtain now. Do a great job, I know you can!"

> **"This would be their last performance at the old school, and they wanted it to be special"**

CHAPTER 17: The Child from Seven to Twelve **511**

CHAPTER 17 OBJECTIVES

After completing Chapter 17, students will be able to:

- Explain the physical changes that puberty brings about.
- Analyze sense of self from seven to twelve.
- Identify how peer and family relations evolve.
- Contrast the thinking of children and young teens.

INTRODUCING CHAPTER 17

- Display pictures of children from seven to twelve. Ask what problems children of this age commonly face. Explore health, family, and social issues.
- Have students look at the photograph on these pages. **Ask:** How does the photograph reflect a changing orientation of children in this period?

USING THE SCENARIO Ask students to finish writing the story. Tell them to decide what point they want to make before they begin writing. Encourage them to maintain a consistent point of view (third person narrator with special focus on Trisha's thoughts). When everyone finishes writing, ask volunteers to read their ending and explain why they ended the story in that way.

KEY TO ABILITY LEVELS Each section gives skill-building activities. Each activity has been labeled for use with students of various learning styles and abilities.

L1 Level 1 activities are basic activities and should be within the range of all students.

L2 Level 2 activities are average activities and should be within the range of average and above average students.

L3 Level 3 activities are challenging activities designed for the ability range of above average students.

FOCUS

MOTIVATOR

Ask students what personal hygiene is. How is it related to good health? Why does hygiene become increasingly important as children enter adolescence? In what ways are teens different from children?

VOCABULARY ACTIVITY

Have students look up the Key Terms in the Glossary. Discuss the meaning of each word and explain how it is used. Then have students use each term in a sentence.

SECTION 17-1

Physical Growth and Development from Seven to Twelve

From seven to twelve, children go through two stages. The period from seven to ten is called middle childhood. In this time, children build on the growth and skills that began in early childhood. From ten to twelve, they are in early adolescence. These young teens or "pre-teens" stand poised to enter the path that leads to being an adult.

KEY TERMS

acne
eating disorder
fiber
orthodontist
puberty
saturated fat

OBJECTIVES:

• Describe average changes in height and weight during these years.

• Identify the physical changes that take place in puberty.

• Select foods that meet the guidelines for good nutrition.

• Explain how to fight acne.

Physical Changes

From seven to twelve, children go through a period of major physical change. A sudden spurt of growth adds to their height. Their bodies also change in profound ways as they begin to take on the physical signs of adulthood.

512 Unit 6: Special Areas of Study

Observing & Participating

Invite a physical education teacher to speak to the class about the normal range of physical abilities of children between seven and twelve. How do their motor skills develop during this period? Have students prepare questions for the speaker ahead of time. Then have students watch children at play on a playground or a school during recess. After that, have students compare what they saw with what they heard from the speaker.

From eleven to thirteen, girls have a growth spurt and begin to be taller than boys. **What brings about these changes? What happens afterward?**

Some disabilities affect the growth, as well as the development, of children. These differences may become more apparent as children get older. Children with Down Syndrome, for example, tend to be shorter than average. The physical effects of other diseases, such as Cystic Fibrosis, may limit a child's growth.

Height

In middle childhood, children grow an average of 2 inches (5.1 cm) each year. This gain is usually at a regular pace, but many children have spurts in which they grow very rapidly in a short time.

Growth speeds up in early adolescence. Young teens reach **puberty** (PYOO-burr-tee), the set of changes that gives a person a physically mature body able to reproduce. Young teens grow very rapidly, adding from 3 to 5 inches (7.6 to 12.7 cm) a year. During puberty, they add about a quarter of their adult height.

The chart on page 514 shows the average height of children from seven to twelve. Of course, these figures are averages. Children these ages differ greatly in height.

This growth takes place in different parts of the body at different times. Typically, hands and feet grow first, followed by arms and legs and then the torso. Sometimes one part of the body—perhaps the nose—grows faster than other parts. The child may feel awkward and uncomfortable. Fortunately, growth rates even out, and the differences disappear.

Because they grow so rapidly, some children have stretch marks on their skin. These whitish or purplish lines are caused by their skin being stretched. They fade over time.

Weight

On average, children gain about 6.5 pounds (3.0 kg) each year from age seven to twelve. At around age ten or eleven, a boy

CHAPTER 17: The Child from Seven to Twelve **513**

COMPREHENSION CHECK

1. What is puberty? (*A series of physical changes that turn a child into a mature adult able to reproduce.*)

ACTIVITIES

Discussion Activity

Ask: How can parents and schools structure children's lives so that they get a healthful amount of exercise? **L1**

VISUAL LEARNING

Using the Chart Have pairs of students use the information on the chart to create a line graph comparing the increase in height of boys and girls.

ISSUES IN CHILDREN'S HEALTH

Weight and Exercise. Between 25 and 30 percent of American children are overweight—they weigh 20 percent above the ideal weight for their height and age. Doctors do not believe reducing diets are appropriate for children. They recommend that a child do more exercise, decrease fat intake, and improve eating habits to let height catch up with weight. Only children who are more than 40 percent overweight may be put on special diets.

Average Height of Boys and Girls Seven to Twelve

AGE	BOYS		GIRLS	
	Inches	Centimeters	Inches	Centimeters
Seven	48.0	121.8	47.4	120.5
Eight	50.0	127.0	49.8	126.5
Nine	52.0	132.0	52.0	132.0
Ten	54.0	137.2	54.0	137.2
Eleven	56.3	143.0	57.0	144.8
Twelve	58.7	149.2	59.6	151.5

or girl may seem to be gaining more weight than that. This is typical just before puberty begins.

Heredity influences a child's weight, but environment plays a very important part, too. A child who eats food low in fat and high in nutrients is less likely to have weight problems than one who eats food high in fat and low in nutrients. Physically active children are less likely to have weight problems.

Some children—especially girls—become overly concerned about their weight. They see themselves as being fat when they really aren't. They may develop an **eating disorder**, a condition in which they starve themselves or eat large amounts of food at a time and then make themselves vomit.

Eating disorders can have a devastating effect on the body. They can even lead to death. These are emotional problems. A person with an eating disorder needs counseling from a trained professional.

─The Developing Brain─

Exercise helps the brain think, too. The tissue that connects the two sides of the brain benefits from both small and large motor activity. This tissue also plays a role in creative imagination and analytical thinking.

Changes of Puberty

Puberty usually starts about age ten for girls and about a year later for boys. The changes, which take place over many years, are usually completed by about sixteen or seventeen. Of course, some children begin puberty earlier and others do so later. There is no cause for concern if puberty is delayed for up to three years. If no signs of puberty show by the time a girl reaches thirteen or a boy fourteen, a doctor should be consulted.

Puberty causes profound changes to the young teen's body. For both boys and girls, hair appears under the arms and in the pubic area.

In addition, boys experience several other changes. Facial hair begins to appear, and their voice deepens. Sometimes the deepening doesn't take place smoothly, and the boy's voice may "crack," or change tones, from time to time. A boy's shoulders broaden, and muscles grow larger. Also, the boy's sexual organs develop and become capable of producing sperm.

Girls undergo several changes as well. Their breasts enlarge, their waist narrows, and their hips widen. The sexual organs develop and become capable of releasing mature eggs. Related to that change is the beginning of menstruation.

This is the monthly cycle in which the female's body releases an egg and the uterus prepares for a possible pregnancy. Most girls begin to have menstrual periods about two years after puberty begins. The average age for girls is about twelve or thirteen. Girls' menstrual periods may be quite uneven at first. They may not occur every month, and the amount of flow may vary greatly from month to month.

HEALTH TIP

Being Active

*A*merican children are less active than they used to be. As a result, about a third of them are overweight. Their physical skills have declined as well. In a fitness study, only 64 percent of boys aged six to twelve and 50 percent of girls that age could run a mile in ten minutes. Only 2 percent of the children tested could pass the fitness tests that are part of the President's Challenge award. Parents and educators are worried.

The National Association for Sport and Physical Education recommends that elementary school children need to be involved in active play at least one hour a day. More, says the association, is even better.

Children can take turns between vigorous activity that lasts ten or fifteen minutes and periods of rest. The association points out that the best activities are those that can be continued later in life. Walking, biking, swimming, and tennis are all examples. So are dancing, skating, and basketball.

FOLLOWING UP

1. Why do you think that children are less active now?

2. Why do you think lifetime sports like walking and biking are desirable?

Making Generalizations. Do children need to be prepared for puberty differently or more fully than for earlier physical changes? Why or why not? How? **L2**

Critical Thinking Activity

Making Connections. How do school physical education classes influence children's growth and development? **L1**

Teamwork Activity

Have small groups of students make two lists, one of activities they enjoyed at age seven and a second one of activities they enjoyed at age twelve. Tell the groups to compare the two lists and write a paragraph explaining the factors responsible for changes. **L2**

HEALTH TIP

What is the value of exercise? Does it have any benefits besides keeping a person physically fit?

Answers to
FOLLOWING UP

1. *Possible response:* Because there are so many other interesting non-physical things to do, like playing video games.

2. *Possible response:* They build good habits that can be followed throughout life.

Parenting in *Action*

Parental behavior can influence children's fitness and weight significantly. Children who see that their parents are physically active are more likely to be active themselves. The Jennings family's favorite activity is going to a movie on Friday nights and then out for a late dinner afterwards. Ask students to suggest other activities the parents might plan that would promote fitness for the entire family.

COMPREHENSION CHECK

1. How do children's motor skills change between seven and twelve? (*They gain increasing control of their muscles and greater coordination.*)

ACTIVITIES

Critical Thinking Activity

Analyzing. Do you think children between seven and twelve enjoy more activities that require small motor control than younger children? If so, what activities? If not, why not? **L1**

Teamwork Activity

Ask small groups of students to create menus for an entire day for children in this age group. Students may include snacks as well as the three regular meals. Discuss the menus as a class, analyzing them for nutritional value and for variety and appeal. After groups revise their menus, have them print them neatly and compile all into a booklet. **L2**

VISUAL LEARNING	Using the Photographs

This page: Have students compare these photographs to those earlier in the text. What physical skills do these children have?

Puberty brings about a growth spurt and many other physical changes. It also causes emotional changes.

Motor Skills

In the years from seven to twelve, children's motor skills improve greatly. As their bodies mature, they build more muscles and become stronger. Children these ages enjoy active play. They have fun running, using playground equipment, playing tag, in-line skating, and bike riding. Many enjoy playing on teams in organized sports.

They also have growing control over those muscles. Improved coordination shows in the greater ease and smoothness of their actions. It also shows in the complexity of the tasks they can perform. Seven-year-olds have trouble catching a baseball, but ten-year-olds can manage it.

Greater control extends to small motor skills as well. Around age seven, children's drawings become neater and more controlled. Younger children learn to write by printing, but around age eight they can learn cursive writing.

Caring for Children from Seven to Twelve

Children ages seven to twelve dress themselves and take care of their own personal hygiene. Parents need to ensure that

516 UNIT 6: Special Areas of Study

COMMUNITY AS CLASSROOM

Participating in sports should be fun for children, but that isn't the case when parents behave inappropriately at youth sporting events. Most students have witnessed such behavior. The National Recreation and Park Association (NRPA) sponsors a program called FUN FIRST! It is designed to help various youth sport providers in the community to educate parents about being a positive influence on their child's sport participation.

Nutrition

As at other ages, the key to good nutrition in these years is to plan meals using the Food Guide Pyramid. Children—and adults—should also follow the Dietary Guidelines to have a healthy diet:

INFOLINK

Food Guide Pyramid

For more about the *Food Guide Pyramid*, see Chapter 11, page 361.

- **Reduce the amount of fat in the diet.** It is especially important to limit the amount of **saturated fat** eaten. Saturated fat is animal fat that is solid when at room temperature.
- **Eat plenty of fiber.** Plant foods and products made from whole grain contain **fiber,** a part of plants that humans cannot digest. Eating fiber helps the digestive system work properly.
- **Limit sugar.** Sugary drinks or desserts have few nutrients.
- **Reduce the amount of salt.** Salt can contribute to high blood pressure and heart disease.

Children need to eat breakfast since it provides vital fuel to begin their day. Children who eat breakfast learn better, pay more attention, and are more likely to take part in activities than those who do not. A healthy breakfast includes two servings from the bread, cereal, rice, and pasta food group; one from the fruit group; and one from the milk, cheese, and yogurt group. National school breakfast and lunch programs help provide good nutrition.

Caring for the Teeth

In this period, children lose all of their primary teeth, and most of the permanent teeth appear. The first permanent teeth are a set of molars that appears around age six. Around age twelve, a second set of molars emerges behind the first set. The last set of molars—called the "wisdom teeth"—do not appear until age eighteen to twenty.

As they reach adolescence, children have even greater need for good nutrition, but many teens skip breakfast and eat many snack foods that are high in fat, salt, or sugar. *Why is having a healthy breakfast and choosing nutritious snacks so important?*

CHAPTER 17: The Child from Seven to Twelve **517**

Research Activity

Have students research government programs meant to improve the health and nutrition of children, including the National School Lunch Program, School Breakfast Program, Child and Adult Care Food Program, WIC, etc. What groups do the various programs target? What role do schools play in the process? What would be the anticipated consequences of discontinuing each program? **L2**

Discussion Activity

Explore how parents can motivate children to eat properly and take care of their teeth. **L1**

| **VISUAL LEARNING** | **Using the Photograph** |

This page—Possible response: Breakfast provides energy to start the day; promotes learning.

The Developing Brain

Anemia

Researchers have found that children who suffered from anemia early in childhood have a higher probability of developing mild to moderate retardation by age 10. The most common cause of anemia in young children is inadequate iron in the diet. A drop of a single unit in the hemoglobin count increases the chances of retardation by close to 30%.

| **LEARNING STYLES** | **Auditory** |

Ask students to create a feature story for a radio show discussing the physical changes children undergo between seven and twelve years of age. Suggest that they invent one or several fictional children for their story. The story can include commentary by "experts" and interviews with "parents." Students could include tapings of younger siblings or friends speaking the parts of the children. Remind students to rehearse their presentations.

they care for themselves in healthy ways, however. This is particularly important with nutrition.

The permanent teeth look different than the primary teeth. They are larger and somewhat more yellow. They are also more jagged looking, although the points wear down over time.

Teeth should be brushed at least twice a day and flossed at least once a day. A dental check-up and cleaning, at least once a year, help prevent decay.

Sometimes teeth don't come in straight. A dentist can suggest whether this is a potential problem. If so, the dentist may advise that the child see an **orthodontist**. This dental specialist can decide whether the child would benefit by having braces to straighten the teeth.

Personal Hygiene

Seven- to ten-year-olds sometimes resist keeping clean. It's not that they want to be dirty, they simply can't be bothered to take time out of their active lives. Parents can take various steps to prevent fights over hygiene:

- **Focus on essentials.** Make sure that the child washes before eating and after using the bathroom, but don't insist on the child bathing every day.
- **Give choices when possible.** Katrina lets Ashley choose when to shower, giving her some control over her life.
- **Send positive messages.** After he showered, Eduardo said how refreshed he felt. That signals his children that bathing brings benefits besides simply getting clean.

518 UNIT 6: Special Areas of Study

> **INFOLINK**
>
> **Permanent Teeth**
>
> For more about *permanent teeth*, see Chapter 14, page 438.

The lack of interest in hygiene changes around age ten. The timing is convenient, because the physical changes of puberty put new demands for cleanliness. With puberty, the body produces more sweat, so young teens may develop body odor. Washing, especially the feet and under the arms, can remove this odor. Also, the hair becomes more oily. This usually goes away over time, as the body's production of skin oil goes down. Until then, many teens need to wash their hair more often.

Acne

The oil glands bring about another condition as well. About 80 percent of all teens develop **acne**, a skin problem caused by these excess oils in the skin. The oil may plug a pore, or opening in the skin, and form a blackhead. Sometimes it collects below the skin and forms a whitehead. Some

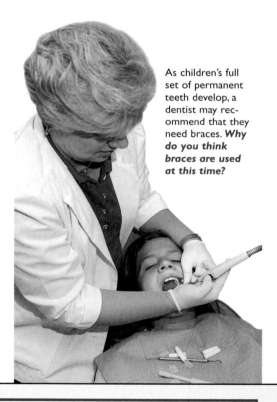

As children's full set of permanent teeth develop, a dentist may recommend that they need braces. *Why do you think braces are used at this time?*

Acne is a normal result of the physical changes of adolescence, but it can make young teens feel very self-conscious. They worry that pimples make them look funny or ugly. *What should a teen do if a case of acne is very severe?*

young teens have more severe forms, with infections forming below the skin. Acne tends to appear on the face, neck, and upper body.

Acne seems to be influenced by heredity. Parents who had serious acne are more likely to have children with the same problem. Diet doesn't affect acne in most cases, although some people find that certain foods worsen the problem. These can simply be avoided. Some makeup can also make acne worse.

Washing with warm water and mild soap is advised. With more severe forms, it may be necessary to see a doctor. The doctor may prescribe a special cream to be used on the face and antibiotics.

SECTION 17-1 REVIEW

✔ Check Your Understanding

1. What are the ages of middle childhood? What are the ages of early adolescence?
2. What changes in height and weight are typical in these years?
3. What is an eating disorder?
4. How do boys change in puberty? How do girls change?
5. What is better to drink, fruit juice made from concentrate or a fruit flavored soda? Why?
6. Why do some children need braces?
7. How do the changes of puberty increase the need for hygiene?
8. What causes acne? How can it be treated?

Putting Knowledge Into Practice

1. **Analyzing.** Why do you think girls are more likely to suffer from an eating disorder?
2. **Comparing.** Contrast the average ages of puberty for boys and girls. What social impact do you think these physical changes might have?
3. **Observing and Participating.** Compare the handwriting of children seven, ten, and twelve years old. What differences do you see? How do you explain those differences?

ASSESS

CHECKING COMPREHENSION

Have students answer the Check Your Understanding questions. Answers appear at the bottom of this page.

EVALUATION

Give students the Section 17-1 Quiz in the *Teacher Resource Guide.*

RETEACHING

1. Assign Reteaching Activities, page 48.
2. Have students create a web with the information in Section 17-1.

ENRICHMENT

Ask students to create a nutritious food product for children seven to twelve and write an ad describing how it helps them grow and develop.

EXTENSION

Have students assess their own diets or exercise habits.

CLOSE

Have students write a paragraph that begins by completing this sentence: "The changes caused by puberty affect a child . . ."

ANSWERS TO SECTION 17-1 REVIEW

1. 7 to 10; 10 to 12.
2. *Height:* 2 in (5.1 cm) a year until puberty; then a growth spurt of 3 to 5 in (7.6 to 12.7 cm) a year. *Weight:* About 6.5 lb (3 kg) a year.
3. People believe that they are fatter than they really are and starve themselves or eat too much and vomit.
4. *Changes are described on pages 514-515.*

5. Fruit juice; soda is probably sugary; juice is more nutritious.
6. The teeth do not come in straight.
7. The body sweats more; hair and skin are more oily.
8. *Cause:* Excess oils in skin. *Treatment:* Wash with warm water, mild soap.

**Emotional Development
from Seven to Twelve**

(pages 520-526)

SECTION 17-2 RESOURCES
Teacher Resource Guide
- Lesson Plan Organizer, p. 75
- Section 17-2 Quiz, p. 195

Student Motivation Kit
- Observ. & Case Studies
  (case study), pp. 135-136
- Reteaching Activity, p. 49
- Enrichment, p. 49

Student Workbook
- Study Guide, pp. 135-139
- Identifying Aspects of
  Personality, pp. 142-143

Effective Instruction CD-ROM

FOCUS

MOTIVATOR

Ask students to remember when they were in third grade. How would they have felt if someone said something critical about them, their clothing, or their toys? Would it have affected them the same way if it happened in the sixth grade? Why or why not?

VOCABULARY ACTIVITY

Have students match each term with the two related words or expressions in the following list: self-awareness, femininity, mentor, counselor.

Emotional Development from Seven to Twelve

At seven, Chloe often stayed in her room. At ten, she became more outgoing, and her parents adjusted to her new breezy manner and to her frequent shows of affection. A year later, she changed again. She became moody and had no interest in her parents at all. Chloe's emotional shifts are typical of the changes children go through between seven and twelve.

KEY TERMS

gender identity
role model

OBJECTIVES:

- Recognize signs of the child's growing sense of self.
- Identify a child's age based on his or her emotional behavior.
- Recommend strategies for living with children from seven to twelve.

A Sense of Self

One of the most important changes in this period is the developing sense of self. As children grow, they become able to think more abstractly. This shapes how they see themselves.

A researcher asked a girl who was five and one-half whether she could become the

Observing & Participating

Studies show that sports participation can increase children's self-esteem, ability to cooperate, motivation, and achievement. Children can develop a realistic sense of their physical abilities and the motivation to stay involved, which can transfer to other areas of life if parents and coaches are supportive and teach them to commit, communicate, and work together. Discuss ways of finding good athletic programs.

Children can build self-esteem by having pride in their accomplishments. **How can parents contribute to high self-esteem?**

family dog. The girl said no, but based her reasoning on physical traits. The dog, she said, "has brown eyes . . . and walks like a dog." When a nine-year-old was asked whether she could become her brother, she answered no for a different reason: "I'm me and he's him. I can't change in any way 'cause I've got to stay like . . . myself."

In this period, children see that they have a personality that is uniquely theirs. They see themselves as a mixture of many qualities. Some are based on their physical appearance, and others are based on talents or abilities. By ten, children can see themselves as highly skilled in one area and less able in another. By eleven and twelve, children also use personal qualities to define themselves —"I'm honest," or "I'm a good friend," or "I can be counted on."

They also see that they behave differently in different situations. Jeff thought of himself as friendly. Then he went to a party at his cousin's house. He didn't know anyone besides his cousin, and he found it hard to begin talking to anyone. As he thought about it, Jeff realized that he is shy with strangers. How could he be both friendly and shy? Jeff can reconcile these two opposite views by seeing that his approach to people changes as the situation he's in changes.

Young teens like Jeff also realize that different people may perceive them in different ways. This, too, is an example of their growing thinking skills. It shows that they can view themselves from other people's point of view.

CHAPTER 17: The Child from Seven to Twelve **521**

ACTIVITIES

Discussion Activity

Ask: How does choosing friends and role models of the same sex help children establish and confirm their gender identity? **L2**

Teamwork Activity

Divide the class into small groups and give each group sheets of paper with the headings "Middle Childhood" and "Early Adolescence." Have students pass the papers around the group and write examples of the emotional changes in the appropriate period. Then have groups review their lists and make corrections. **L1**

VISUAL LEARNING	Using the Photograph

Possible responses:
Religious leaders, community leaders, political leaders.

MULTIPLE INTELLIGENCES	To help intrapersonal and visual students explore their emotional reaction to

an experience such as taking a test, collect wrapping paper or fabric remnants. Cut these into small pieces and lay them out on a table. Have students choose a paper or fabric sample to represent their feelings *before* and another to reflect their feelings *after*, then paste them on a sheet of paper and write a caption explaining its meaning.

Being Male or Female

An important part of that growing sense of self is the child's **gender identity**. This is the awareness of being a boy or girl. Gender identity begins in early childhood and is usually firmly fixed by age four. In middle childhood and early adolescence that identity becomes stronger.

- Children spend more time with those of the same sex. The close friendships they develop are almost always with children of the same sex.
- They show an increased desire to act and talk like children of the same sex.
- They tend to choose adults of the same sex as their **role models,** the people they admire and who they wish to pattern their behavior after.
- In early adolescence, they begin to explore relationships with the opposite sex.

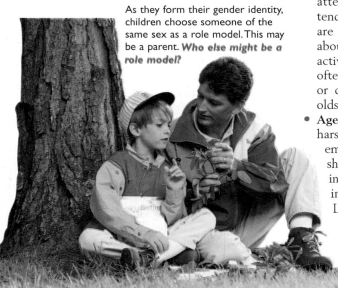

As they form their gender identity, children choose someone of the same sex as a role model. This may be a parent. **Who else might be a role model?**

Emotional Changes

Changes in intellectual development have an impact on how children see themselves. The physical changes of puberty also have a major impact on emotional life. While emotional development has characteristics at each age, a child's own temperament also makes a difference.

Middle Childhood

In middle childhood, how children handle their emotions varies from year to year. In some years, they are fairly negative. In others, they are often happy.

- **Age seven.** Seven-year-olds tend to be somewhat withdrawn and quiet. Many children this age worry a great deal—about all kinds of issues. Like many children aged seven, Jaquala is very sensitive to what others say about her.
- **Age eight.** Eight-year-olds direct their attention outward. Seven-year-olds tend to stay near home. Eight-year-olds are willing to explore and are curious about new things. They are lively and active—and very dramatic. Antuwan often exaggerates when telling stories or describing his feelings. Eight-year-olds take a positive attitude to life.
- **Age nine.** Nine-year-olds can be very harsh about their own failings—even embarrassed by them. They may also show signs of tension such as tightening the lips. They tend to be absorbed in their own thoughts. When Lamar's mother called, he didn't answer. She thought he was being rude, but he was concentrating so much on his own concerns that he simply didn't hear her.

RESOURCES TO EXPLORE

Internet Safety. Children of elementary and middle school ages enjoy online chatting and "instant messaging" friends. It is vital for parents to monitor their computer activities. *A Parent's Guide to Internet Safety* is offered by the Crimes Against Children program conducted by the Federal Bureau of Investigation. The FBI offers other helpful publications focusing on drugs and safeguarding children. The FBI's Website is www.fbi.gov/publications.htm

At age seven, children can be very gloomy. They often look at the negative side of things and say, for instance, that other people hate them. *What could parents do to help a child handle these feelings?*

Like nine-year-olds, young teens can be very absorbed in their own thoughts and concerns. They may pay little attention to others—except their peers. Peers are extremely important to young teens. They crave acceptance and become anxious if they stand out in any way from their peers.

Like nine-year-olds, young teens can be very absorbed in their own thoughts and concerns. They may pay little attention to others—except their peers. Peers are extremely important to young teens. They crave acceptance and become anxious if they stand out in any way from their peers.

Young teens can also hide their true feelings with a mask of not caring. This is a sign of growing emotional control. Younger children show the emotions they feel. Young teens are able to show the emotions they wish—to some degree.

Young teens are better able to verbalize their feelings. Many begin to write their thoughts in a diary. *What is another emotional characteristic of young teens?*

- **Age ten.** Ten-year-olds are more positive and happy. Many would agree with Whitney, who called ten the best age "because you're not too young and not too old."

Early Adolescence

The release of hormones into the body causes the physical changes of puberty. These hormones also bring about emotional changes. Young teens can move from happiness to anger, frustration, or sadness in minutes. These mood swings can just as easily swing in the opposite direction.

Critical Thinking Activity

Comparing and Contrasting. How do you think a seven-year-old would feel if he walked into a new classroom and was dressed totally different from his peers? How would a twelve-year-old feel? **L1**

Discussion Activity

How do the mood swings of adolescence make teens feel? **L1**

VISUAL LEARNING Using the Photographs

Top—Possible response: Help child learn to verbalize feelings.
Bottom: May pay little attention to others; may hide feelings.

DID *You* **Know?**

Sadness. **At this age, children's expanding world and their new relationships can bring on conflicts that make them sad. Unhappiness from the loss of a cherished person or pet—through death, divorce, or relocation—may require a long period of time to abate. Dissatisfaction with the way they look or act in social situations or with their performance in school or sports can also make children sad.**

LEARNING STYLES

Kinesthetic

Ask students to choose a typical everyday situation that seven- to twelve-year-olds find themselves in. It could relate to school or home or a sports team. Then have students choose a particular year of age and review its characteristics. Tell students to act out how a child of that age may go through that particular situation.

ACTIVITIES

Critical Thinking Activity

Analyzing. Why do you think some children continue to express anger through actions rather than words? Why do you think children frequently feel anger at this point in their lives? **L1**

Discussion Activity

Ask students to come up with a list of suggestions for resolving problems with others. Encourage them to explain what works for them and how they learned to work out conflicts with siblings. Discuss ways to compromise, to try to see things from the other person's point of view, and to listen to others without judging them. **L1**

VISUAL LEARNING	Using the Photograph

Ask students how they would handle sibling rivalry if they were the children's parent.

Specific Emotions

In early childhood, emotional life centers on the family. In middle childhood and the early teen years, the focus shifts to the wider world. People and events outside the family have more impact on the person's emotions than before.

Anger

As they leave early childhood, children gain greater ability to control their emotions. Still, from time to time, children feel angry—and let others know it. Even ten-year-olds, who are typically quite happy, show anger. When they do, though, it usually passes quickly.

The moodiness of young teens means that anger can erupt at any time. Often, though, occasions of anger are just that— eruptions that boil over and go away. The young teen may slam a door or noisily leave a room. Soon, though, the situation will be back to normal.

Many times, these outbursts have little to do with the small event or comment that triggered them. Courtney became very angry when her mother asked her to hang up her coat after school. Within minutes, though, she was cheerful. Courtney wasn't actually upset at anything her mother said. She was really angry because her friends went shopping without her.

By middle childhood, children generally know to use words to show anger. Sometimes, though, a child lashes out with aggressive actions. It is important to avoid responding in the same way. Setting a good example is the best method of teaching a child. In addition, caregivers can try these approaches:

- **Teach the child how to gain self-control.** Time-outs, counting to ten, or breathing deeply are all ways of helping children learn to calm down.

Eight-year-olds have very strong attachments to their mothers and may be jealous of other children in the family.

Management/Leadership Skills

Seven to twelve-year-olds often have to solve problems for themselves in the playground, lunchroom, and other settings. Yet the heightened emotions they often feel can magnify their problems. Discuss ways to teach children how to resolve their conflicts. Analyze ways to explore their own feelings to determine what is really important; examine other people's communications to determine what they feel and care about; and express themselves without hurting others. Finally, discuss what *compromise* means.

The mood swings of young teens can make them difficult to live with from time to time. Fortunately, negative feelings often quickly pass. *When children this age are angry, who is it usually with?*

- **Help the child learn how to resolve conflicts without fighting.** Working through problems at home—say with other siblings—can give a child the tools to settle conflicts at school.
- **Use rewards for controlling anger.** The reward reinforces the value of self-control.

Fear and Worry

Children's fears change during this period. Seven-year-olds may still fear some of the things they feared in early childhood, such as the dark. This can lead, with some, to problems going to sleep. Leaving a light on at night can help relieve this fear.

By age ten, these childhood fears have often disappeared. Many children may be like Summer, who simply announced one day that she was no longer afraid of dogs.

As childhood fears disappear, new worries may emerge. News reports of violent crimes or fatal car accidents or natural disasters lead some young teens to worry about these problems striking them or their families. More aware of the world around them, they realize that there are dangers in that world. They need to be reassured that caregivers will take all the steps necessary to protect them.

Other worries also appear. Most have to do with how others see them. Up to age ten, children may be concerned about how adults, as well as children, see them. By the young teen years, their focus is on the attitudes of their peers.

Living with Children Seven to Twelve

Living or working with children from seven to twelve can be difficult at times. The quiet, withdrawn seven-year-old may not be willing to talk about his feelings. The eight-year-old, though cheerful, often clings to her mother. Here are tips for preventing small emotional problems from becoming large ones:

- **Be patient.** Remember that the child still doesn't have full self-control. The

CHAPTER 17: The Child from Seven to Twelve **525**

CHECKING COMPREHENSION

Have students answer the Check Your Understanding questions. Answers appear at the bottom of this page.

EVALUATION

Give students the Section 17-2 Quiz in the *Teacher Resource Guide*.

RETEACHING

1. Assign Reteaching Activities, page 49.
2. Ask students to write an essay comparing emotional life in middle childhood and early adolescence.

ENRICHMENT

Ask students to brainstorm about societal factors that threaten the safety and well-being of children ages seven to twelve. Have them list at least five potential risks and highlight points about each one in outline form. Possible examples include bullying, gangs, family problems, abuse, and negative influence from TV, movies, video games, and the Internet. Have them offer measures that can be taken to reduce the risks.

EXTENSION

Invite students to interview their guidance counselors about the emotional problems children face that interfere with their schoolwork. Then have them report to the class.

Have students take the role of a child of any age from seven to twelve and write a diary entry expressing the child's emotional concerns.

526

anger young teens show often results mainly from the difficulty they are having adjusting to the changes in their bodies.

- **Avoid taking it personally.** A child who is angry or upset may say some pretty nasty things. Remember that the child doesn't usually mean what is said.
- **Keep the child under control.** Of course, the child also has to stay within acceptable limits of behavior. Actions that break the rules can and should be dealt with. If the problem wasn't too serious, talking through things may be enough. Remember that as they grow older, children have greater ability to understand abstract ideas and more complex explanations.
- **Listen.** Give the child a chance to explain what happened and why. The child may have a valid grievance. Admitting that does not lessen the force of saying you don't approve of how the anger was expressed.

SECTION 17-2 REVIEW

✔ Check Your Understanding

1. By eleven and twelve, how do young teens define their personalities?
2. How do early adolescents strengthen gender identity?
3. At what age is a child likely to be withdrawn and worry a great deal?
4. At what ages in middle childhood do children tend to be happy and positive?
5. What effect do the hormones of puberty have on the emotions of early adolescents?
6. What new fears may appear in middle childhood?

Putting Knowledge Into Practice

1. **Analyzing.** Charlie was reading when his brother asked for help with his homework. Charlie said, "I always help. Get Kim to help" and returned to his book. When his brother asked again, Charlie grew angry. "No one else does *anything* around here." Then he stormed off to his room and slammed the door. What age do you think Charlie is? Why?
2. **Applying.** What advice would you give a friend who has a seven-year-old sibling who frequently starts fights and tells your friend, "I hate you!"?
3. **Observing and Participating.** Write a paragraph describing what you were like at seven and another one describing what you were like at twelve. Evaluate how you changed and how you stayed the same.

526 UNIT 6: Special Areas of Study

ANSWERS TO SECTION 17-2 REVIEW

1. As a mixture of many qualities.
2. By spending more time with those of the same sex; talking and acting like those of the same sex; having same sex role models; and exploring relationships with the opposite sex.
3. Seven.
4. Eight and ten.
5. Mood swings.
6. Fear of real-life problems such as violent crime, car accidents, or natural disasters.

CAREER OPPORTUNITIES

Recreation Worker

A CONVERSATION WITH CHRIS O'BRIEN

How did you become interested in becoming a recreation worker? I've always liked sports and fitness, I enjoy working outdoors, and I love kids. This career seemed like a natural for me.

What are the tasks and responsibilities of a recreation worker? I teach the value of being fit, the basic skills of different sports, and how to be a good sport. All three are equally important.

What is the work environment like? I work at a local center that has a gym, a pool, and other facilities. During the school year, I teach younger children and adults during the day. We have classes in aerobics, swimming, and gymnastics. In the late afternoon, I head leagues for elementary school children. During the summer, I split my time between the gym and soccer and softball leagues.

What are the working hours like? The days are long and full. I work six days because our center is open on Saturday.

What aptitudes are needed to be a recreation worker? You need to be able to explain things to people. You need to have judgment so you can gauge what each person is capable of doing. The goal is not to make everyone a great athlete, but to help each person meet his or her full potential. You have to be well organized so that practices run smoothly. Kids hate standing around with nothing to do. Finally, you need a lot of energy and enthusiasm.

RECREATION WORKER

Education and Training. Most full-time recreation workers have a bachelor's degree, usually specializing in recreation.

Career Outlook. Many people compete for the jobs available in recreation work.

CONNECTING SCHOOL TO CAREER

1. **Thinking Skills.** Look at the three things O'Brien teaches. Do you agree that they are all equally valuable? Why or why not?
2. **Resources.** Why would having experience from summer jobs help someone who was applying for a job as a recreation worker? Where could you get that experience?

CAREER OPPORTUNITIES

Introducing the Feature

Ask students what a recreation worker is. Discuss the kinds of activities that take place in community centers and the kind of people who run them.

Answers to CONNECTING SCHOOL TO CAREER

1. **Possible response:** Yes, because they are all necessary to sports and fitness.
2. **Possible response:** Because it would give that person an edge over others who had no experience; at a summer camp or community center.

Applying What You've Learned

After reading the feature, ask students to think of other characteristics that recreation workers probably need. (*Possible responses: Ability to work with children and adults, adaptability, knowledge of the human body, understanding of many sports.*) Have the class discuss each suggestion.

Building Career Skills

Technology. Have students explore the Internet to find five recreational activities appropriate for children in middle childhood and five for children in early adolescence. Have students evaluate them for suitability and usefulness. Encourage them to review the physical and emotional characteristics and changes discussed in Sections 17-1 and 17-2 in preparation. Finally, ask students to design a chart listing and describing the recreational activities by age group.

SECTION 17-3

Social and Moral Development from Seven to Twelve

(pages 528-534)

SECTION 17-3 RESOURCES

Teacher Resource Guide
• Lesson Plan Organizer, p. 76
• Section 17-3 Quiz, p. 196
Student Motivation Kit
• Reteaching Activity, p. 50
• Enrichment, p. 50
Student Workbook
• Study Guide, pp. 135-139
• Handling Peer Pressure, p. 144
Effective Instruction CD-ROM

FOCUS

MOTIVATOR

Ask students to name the most important social and moral issues that face children between seven and twelve years of age. Have them discuss their reasons for mentioning those issues.

VOCABULARY ACTIVITY

Ask students to explain the relationship that they think exists between the two terms.

Social and Moral Development from Seven to Twelve

Jeannie and Carlton were neighbors. From the time they were two, they played together. First they played in the sandbox behind Jeannie's house. Later, they played on the same soccer team. When they were eight, though, Jeannie and Carlton began to move in different directions. Jeannie spent more time with the girls from school, and Carlton with the boys.

KEY TERMS
conformity
peer pressure

OBJECTIVES:
• Describe changes in friendship in these years.
• Analyze peer pressure.
• Explain changes in how children these ages get along with parents.
• Identify ways to help children learn to act morally.

528

Friendships

Children begin to play together early in life. By five, they speak of having friends, but these friends are simply playmates. In middle childhood and early adolescence, friendships change in character. They become much more personal, based on the children's thoughts and feelings, and they become deeper.

Observing & Participating

Have students go to a gathering place for youth in your community and take notes about where children in middle childhood and early adolescence meet and spend time together. At what age do they begin to do so? What do they do together? How much time do they spend together? How do they behave toward each other? Back in class, have students compare findings and discuss why they think children behave as they do. You might wish to have students compile their findings in graphic form.

Friendships are very important to young teens, but relations between friends aren't always smooth. Children may be upset if a friend seems to enjoy the company of another person. *How can children work these problems out?*

Beginning around age seven or eight, children see new reasons for friendship.

- Children value friends who are loyal. They appreciate those who stand by them when they are in a difficult situation or feeling low.
- They also look for friends that they can feel comfortable revealing inner feelings to. These older children share their thoughts and ideas with others. Close friends become those they feel they can trust—friends who won't pass these highly personal revelations on to others.

- Of course, they still look on friends as people they have fun with.

Not surprisingly, a common pastime of children these ages is talking. Children these ages still enjoy active, physical play, but they spend a great deal more time simply talking.

It is their development in other areas that brings about these changes. The physical and emotional changes of puberty raise new questions about dating and sexuality. Children talk to their friends as they try to think through these issues.

Their intellectual growth makes deeper friendships possible. Able to think abstractly, young teens can better understand how others see them. At the same time, they can more easily see other people's point of view and feel empathy for them. These new skills make it easier to relate to friends in a deeper way.

Friends of the Opposite Sex

As the story of Jeannie and Carlton shows, sex differences become important in these years. Even in early childhood, children are more likely to play with others of the same sex. Still, situations like Jeannie and Carlton's are not unusual.

As children grow older, though, they are more likely to play only with children of the same sex. This is true even though, as puberty begins, they become more interested in and preoccupied with children of the opposite sex.

CHAPTER 17: The Child from Seven to Twelve **529**

COMPREHENSION CHECK

1. Why do children from seven to twelve spend a lot of time talking? (*Answers will vary.*)

ACTIVITIES

Teamwork Activity

Have groups examine how children's friendships begin to change in middle childhood. Tell students to create a pair of "open mind" diagrams by drawing two large outlines of a human head. In the first, have them write words or phrases and draw symbols of the types of friendships and attitudes towards peers that four- to six-year-olds have. In the second outline, have them do the same for children seven to twelve. How do the diagrams compare? **L1**

Critical Thinking Activity

Selecting Supporting Evidence. Ask students to choose an example from their own lives that illustrates how children's friendships change over time. **L1**

VISUAL LEARNING	Using the Photograph

Answers will vary; students might offer suggestions based on their own experience.

Interpersonal

Have students form teams to debate whether peer pressure is a positive or negative force. Have the teams take turns presenting their side and responding to each other's arguments. Tell students to get together ahead of time and agree on the definition of all terms. Remind each team to state its position in a clear thesis with supporting reasons. Allow students sufficient time for research to obtain supporting evidence and for each side to meet to discuss their arguments.

How can belonging to a club or group help develop social skills?

One reason is that opposite sex friendships raise questions of being romantically involved. Many—perhaps most—eleven- and twelve-year-olds aren't yet ready for that step. They wish to avoid the teasing they may hear if they have a friend of the opposite sex.

How Many Friends?

Some children have many friends, some have a few, and some have only one or two. The number of friendships depends on the child's temperament—some children are private and quiet and simply don't need many friends. Another influence is environment. Children in after-school programs, clubs, or teams meet others more easily.

There is no set number of friends that a child should have. Still, young teens may use the number of friends as a way to measure their popularity. Those with fewer friends may feel that they fall short. They might feel unliked and unwanted.

The key to a healthy social life, though, is not how many friends a child has. It is whether a child has the social skills to form the friendships he or she wants to have.

Peer Pressure

Starting in early adolescence, peer groups become the most important set of relationships for children. Children this age loosen ties to parents and identify more with a group of peers.

Because of this, **peer pressure** becomes very strong. The desire for acceptance by children their own age leads young teens to adopt the words, behaviors, habits, and ideas of their group.

Peer pressure can be a powerful influence on a young person's life. It is important for young teens to join a peer group that

530 UNIT 6: Special Areas of Study

Ask the Eperts

Rachel Perkins
Child Development Technology
Instructor
Hinds Community College
Utica, Mississippi

TEACHING *Tolerance*

Q How can I teach my child to be tolerant of others?

A Children start out ready to be tolerant of anyone. Parents need to make sure that they continue to grow that way. One way is to avoid teaching them prejudice.

As with any moral teaching, parents do this best by example—by showing that they are not prejudiced. They can avoid making negative comments about people or groups who are different. If they do make such a remark, they can take it back in front of the child—and explain why it was wrong.

Parents can act in accepting ways towards other people. At work, at home, at school, or at play, they can show that they are willing to get along with anyone who behaves acceptably.

Messages in the media can counter the lessons that parents try to teach their children. Parents can fight those messages by pointing them out and explaining what is wrong with them.

Parents can help children to know and understand traditions of their own heritage as well as to know and respect the traditions of other cultures.

Teaching tolerance is not something that can be done once and then forgotten. Parents can raise the subject any time the opportunity presents itself. Reinforcing the message makes it more likely to be learned.

Thinking It Through

1. What should you do if a friend tells a joke that makes fun of a group of people?
2. Some people charge that taking tolerance too far can lead to acceptance of *any* behavior, even those that are wrong. Is that what tolerance means? If so, why? If not, why not?

CHAPTER 17: The Child from Seven to Twelve **531**

Ask the Eperts

Introducing the Feature

Ask students if they ever felt left out or out of place among a group of people. What thoughts ran through their minds? How did they feel? How did they respond to the situation? Has that experience had any effect on how they treat others?

Answers to Thinking It Through
1. *Possible response:* Tell the friend that you don't think such jokes are acceptable.
2. *Possible response:* No, somebody who does something wrong should be punished. Tolerance only extends to people who do nothing to harm others.

Applying What You've Learned

Ask small groups to create realistic scenarios for seven- to twelve-year-olds in which one or more children behave intolerantly towards another or towards a group. Tell them to explore different actions the victims could take and their probable consequences. Have groups present their scenarios to the class and discuss.

Parenting in *Action*

Helping children develop the self-motivation to do the "right thing" takes years. Parents need to do more than nag. One helpful approach is to treat children as if they already did the right thing to give them a positive self-image. Parents also need to create situations in which children experience the consequences of their behavior—whether rewards or sanctions. Finally, parents need to give plenty of positive reinforcement, so children will feel the satisfaction of knowing they did the right thing.

shows positive values. These values include staying free of drugs, tobacco, and alcohol and avoiding risky behaviors. It also includes tolerance for others who are different.

A child who is different from others can have a difficult time in this period. Young teens feel a strong drive for **conformity**—being like one another. The person who has different interests—music rather than athletics, gardening rather than video games—or who dresses differently may be ridiculed and teased by others.

How can they handle this teasing?

- Find others with similar interests and spend time with them. Clubs and other social groups can provide opportunities for sharing special interests.
- Recognize that the problem is with the others, not themselves.
- Avoid becoming upset when teased. People who tease are looking for a reaction. If there isn't one, they may stop the teasing. Try to release the frustration at home with a parent, rather than in front of the others.
- Try to break the situation up with humor. Making a joke can weaken the impact of harsh words—and show that he or she can't be picked on.

Parents can help such a child, too. By giving their love and support, they let the child know that he or she is not alone.

Family Relationships

With all the differences between seven- and twelve-year-olds, it's easy to see why family relationships change during this period. Development in all areas moves children from dependence toward more independence. The complex relationships within the family must reflect that change.

Family situations vary greatly. Some families have two parents in the home; others only one. Parents' work schedules make a difference in how much "family time" is available. The number and ages of siblings also affects family relationships.

With children, age does impact how they view their parents. Seven-year-olds depend on their parents but often challenge

When children have problems with their friendships, they may turn to their parents. *Name one good listening technique that parents can use.*

Management/Leadership Skills

There are ways parents can help their children cope with teasing.

- Tell them to act as if they don't hear or even see the teasers. Because the teasers are looking for a reaction, the best thing is not to give one. Teased children can walk away and express their feelings to trusted friends or family members in private.
- Support their self-esteem by praising courage, patience, or other qualities.
- Encourage them to join a youth group with others who share their interests.

Community service projects can teach children that people can make a difference. *What other lessons can they learn from these activities?*

parental authority. At eight, children tend to cling to their parents. But by nine, children sometimes ignore adults because they are wrapped up in their own thoughts. Ten is a smooth year, while eleven- and twelve-year-olds are critical of their parents. At twelve, children are again more cooperative.

Starting at age seven, children get along well with siblings who are very young or much older than themselves. They are helpful and protective of children under two. They tend to respect and admire siblings in their late teens.

Children often have difficult relationships with siblings closer in age. Fights are more often verbal than physical. They judge each other harshly. Parents need to help them develop empathy and a sense of cooperation.

Moral Development

As children spend more time outside the home, they more often face decisions about right and wrong that they must answer alone, without a parent being around. This is especially true starting in early adolescence, when children feel a growing need to be independent.

What will a child do when classmates tease someone else for not being a good ath-lete? What will he say if another child challenges him to smoke? What will she do if the group urges her to shoplift? With peer pressure being such a strong force in children's lives, the urge to go along with such wrong actions can be strong.

Parents can help prepare their children to make the right choice in a few ways:

- **Set a good example.** Showing tolerance to others and behaving in a moral way are the best way to teach a child to act in a moral way. If a cashier gives too much money in change, return the extra. That sends a powerful message to a child.

CHAPTER 17: The Child from Seven to Twelve **533**

CHECKING COMPREHENSION

Have students answer the Check Your Understanding questions. Answers appear at the bottom of this page.

EVALUATION

Give students the Section 17-3 Quiz in the *Teacher Resource Guide.*

RETEACHING

1. Assign Reteaching Activities, page 50.
2. Form students into groups of five and assign one of five topics to each student in a group. Have students with the same topics meet together and prepare a summary of it. Then have students return to original groups and teach the material to the others.

ENRICHMENT

Ask students to compile a book of wise sayings advising children how to handle the problems of these years. Encourage them to create sayings of their own.

EXTENSION

Have students interview a ten- to twelve-year-old about attitudes towards friendship.

CLOSE

Have students create a poster that illustrates the social or moral development of children from seven to twelve.

- **Support the child's growing conscience.** Sometimes the wrong thing can seem attractive. Joining the group, even if it's doing something wrong, can win acceptance. Remind the child, though, that doing the wrong thing can leave an uncomfortable feeling afterward.
- **Talk about situations that may occur.** Discussing "what if's" ahead of time can give a child coping strategies when confronted with difficult situations.
- **Reinforce empathy.** Joining in teasing another child can win acceptance by the group doing the teasing. Ask your child how he or she would feel as the object of that teasing. The child will probably remember that lesson in the future.
- **Use the child's sense of fairness.** Children these ages value fairness. That value can be used to lead them to the right decision.

SECTION 17-3 REVIEW

✔ Check Your Understanding

1. What characteristics do children look for in friends starting about age seven or eight?
2. How are deeper friendships in this period linked to changes in other areas of development?
3. What is peer pressure?
4. Why is conformity important to young teens?
5. Why do family relationships change during this period?
6. How do children from seven to twelve tend to get along with siblings?
7. Give an example in which a child's interest in fairness is used to lead him or her to make a moral choice.

Putting Knowledge Into Practice

1. **Synthesizing.** What social skills do you think a person needs to have in order to make friends?
2. **Analyzing.** What strategies would you recommend for coping with being teased over being different?
3. **Observing and Participating.** Think of an occasion in which you saw peer pressure at work. Describe what took place. Was the result good or bad? If it was bad, what could have been done differently to change the outcome?

ANSWERS TO SECTION 17-3 REVIEW

1. Loyalty, trustworthiness, sharing fun.
2. Physical and emotional development raises interest in sexuality; young teens talk about thoughts and feelings.
3. Desire for acceptance by others their age which leads young teens to adopt the ideas and behavior of a group.
4. Because they want to be accepted.
5. Because the children change.
6. They get along well with older and younger ones, but not close in age.
7. *Answers will vary.*

SECTION 17-4

Intellectual Development from Seven to Twelve

In middle childhood and early adolescence, children make many advances in their intellectual abilities. They find new ways of thinking and develop an awareness of how they learn. The emotional and intellectual needs of young teens are so special, educators have devised a special setting for them—the middle school.

KEY TERMS
conservation
hypothetical
transitivity

OBJECTIVES:
- Compare the thinking skills of children in middle childhood and early adolescence.
- Identify signs of intellectual development in children seven to twelve.
- Explain why middle school benefits young teens.

Thinking Skills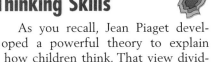

As you recall, Jean Piaget developed a powerful theory to explain how children think. That view divided thinking into four different stages. Children from seven to twelve fall in two of Piaget's stages.

CHAPTER 17: The Child from Seven to Twelve **535**

Observing & Participating

Invite a middle school teacher to speak to the class about what distinguishes middle school from high and elementary schools. What are middle schoolers like? What special concerns arise with children of this age? How do the teachers deal with them?

Do the many intellectual changes that take place during early adolescence affect the way they run their classrooms? Have students take notes and write a summary of what they learned.

SECTION 17-4

Intellectual Development from Seven to Twelve

(pages 535-541)

SECTION 17-4 RESOURCES

Teacher Resource Guide
- Lesson Plan Organizer, p. 77
- Section 17-4 Quiz, p. 197

Student Motivation Kit
- Reteaching Activity, p. 51
- Nurturing Brain Development, pp. 37-38

Student Workbook
- Study Guide, pp. 135-139
- Identifying Stages of Intellectual Development, p. 145

Effective Instruction CD-ROM

FOCUS

MOTIVATOR

Ask students what they remember about Piaget's theory of intellectual development. Review what skills were developed during the sensorimotor and preoperational stages.

VOCABULARY ACTIVITY

Have students write sentences using the terms. Then ask them to insert antonyms in their places and discuss how the meaning of the sentences changes.

COMPREHENSION CHECK

1. At what age do children begin to understand transitivity? (*Between seven and ten.*)
2. Define conservation. (*An object retains the same characteristics even if in a different form.*)

ACTIVITIES

Critical Thinking Activity

Identifying Effects. Ask students to explain how each of these thinking skills helps children master school-work.

VISUAL LEARNING | Using the Photograph
Possible response: For writing.

MULTIPLE INTELLIGENCES | Math and science projects are ideal for children between seven and ten.

Kinesthetic, mathematical, and visual learners enjoy building scale models or pouring equal amounts of colored sand into containers of different shapes. Auditory learners can count the length of tones and intervals in a melody. Interpersonal students can establish a schedule for a school day which they would lead other students through in order one day and then backwards the following day.

How are small motor skills used in school?

Concrete Thinking

Children from seven to ten are firmly placed in the stage that Piaget called "concrete operations." Their thinking works effectively on concrete objects. They can't yet understand abstract ideas, although they can generalize from their own experiences. A five-year-old probably can't draw a map of the route from home to a familiar landmark, even though the child is perfectly capable of walking the route. An eight-year-old can draw such a map.

INFOLINK

Piaget

For more about *Piaget*, see Chapter 10, pages 324-328.

During this period, children develop several important thinking skills. These abilities give them the basis for mastering school work:

- **Classifying objects.** Children as young as three can classify objects, or group them according to one similar characteristic. They can't sort out all the blocks that are both red and a certain shape. By age seven, they can handle two different characteristics at the same time.

- **Putting objects in a series.** In this stage, children can learn to put objects in a series from, say, largest to smallest. This is an important skill. As Piaget pointed out, all objects in the middle of the series have two properties at the same time. They are both smaller than some and larger than others.

- **Extending relationships.** Piaget said that children this age learn **transitivity**. This is the idea that a relative relationship between two objects can extend to another. If 3 is greater than 2, and 2 is greater than 1, then 3 must also be greater than 1.

- **Retaining basic qualities of an object.** Piaget said that in this period, children learn **conservation**. This is the idea that an object or quantity has the same characteristics even if there is a change in how it is presented. Piaget showed children two balls of clay of equal size. Then he rolled one into a long cylinder of clay and asked if one was larger now. Younger children think so—the longer piece of clay looks bigger, so they think it has more substance. By age seven, children see that the amount of clay hasn't changed.

LEARNING STYLES | **Kinesthetic**

Ask students to demonstrate how children's thinking changes from concrete to formal operations. Have them create a situation that a child between seven and twelve might face. Then invite them to role play how a seven-year-old and a twelve-year-old would handle it. Have them include speech showing how each child thinks about and tries to solve the problem.

Formal thinking doesn't begin until about age 12. Teens gain more experience dealing with hypothetical situations.

Formal Thinking

At about age twelve, children move into the formal operations stage. They now have the ability to think abstractly. They can visualize objects that are not in front of them. They can imagine **hypothetical** (HIGH-puh-THET-uh-kal) situations. That is, they can think about things that are not, but could be. This improves their ability to solve problems. It makes it possible for them to think about different situations and prepare for them before they occur. A young teen who begins to show this type of thinking is likely to use it only selectively at first—not in all areas and not at all times.

Other Signs of Intellectual Growth

Other researchers have looked at other aspects of intellectual growth of children from seven to twelve. They have found that children advance in many areas.

In this period, children's memory improves. This enables them to remember basic mathematical operations so they don't

Chapter 17: The Child from Seven to Twelve **537**

COMPREHENSION CHECK

1. How do children benefit from short study periods? (*These fit short attention spans.*)
2. Why is middle school a good setting for early teens? (*They are too mature for elementary, too young for high school.*)

ACTIVITIES

Teamwork Activity

After students take turns reading portions of text, give small groups large pieces of paper and magic markers. Then have group members write phrases and sketch symbols that summarize the intellectual development of early adolescents. **L1**

VISUAL LEARNING	Using the Photographs

Top—Answer: Formal operations.
Bottom—Possible response: They engage child's interest.

Some children learn best by physically manipulating objects. This is especially true of children from ages seven to ten, when they are in the concrete operations stage. **What is the following stage called?**

Computers provide new learning opportunities for children. **Why are learning games useful?**

have to count on their fingers. It helps them remember the spellings of unusual words or the names and capitals of the states.

Children also develop a better awareness of how they learn. They can find strategies that work for them. They can plan tasks and organize their work to complete longer term projects.

Other research shows that starting about age twelve, children's capacity for learning generally goes down for about two years. Researchers do not understand why, however. The rapid rate of learning picks up again in the mid teens.

A young teen's attention span also lessens. Children find it difficult to concentrate for long periods of time. They benefit if learning is broken up into small amounts.

As they learn to think abstractly, young teens often see things in sharp terms. They see complex problems, such as social issues, in terms of black and white and believe that the problems can be solved simply. They

538 UNIT 6: Special Areas of Study

Parenting in *Action*

Peer pressure, shortened attention span, and decreasing capacity to learn often result in lower grades for early adolescents. Parents may be concerned if their child has been a good student until then. If the child's grades are only down slightly, parents should not worry excessively. They can help him or her resolve social or academic problems. If school work suffers significantly, parents can meet with teachers and counselors at the school.

Many school activities call for group work. *How can children benefit from these projects?*

can't understand why people don't put these solutions into practice.

Along with this tendency, they also become very idealistic. They want perfection. They can't yet analyze their ideas to see if they are realistic.

Finally, young teens are interested in exploring. They like to become actively involved in learning, and they enjoy experimenting.

The School Experience

In middle childhood, children continue learning the basic skills that they need in order to succeed in school. In their young teens, they build on those basics and their new thinking skills.

The past few decades have seen a growing movement toward putting early adolescents in middle schools. Educators recognize that these children are too old for the approach of elementary school, in which the teacher is almost like a parent and students have the same teacher for most of their class work. Students this age are more independent and more able to take responsibility for their work.

At the same time, these students are too young for high school. In a high school, students have different teachers for all their classes. They may have an impersonal relationship with teachers. Young teens need more personal contact than that.

The middle school balances these two needs. Students typically have a homeroom

CHAPTER 17: The Child from Seven to Twelve **539**

ACTIVITIES

Critical Thinking Activity

Making Inferences. Why is it important to give a child a quiet space to do homework? What message does it send to the child? **L1**

Discussion Activity

How can parents encourage their child to meet school responsibilities without getting directly involved themselves? **L2**

Critical Thinking Activity

Applying Concepts. Explain how the developing intellectual abilities of early adolescents make it possible for them to take on long-term projects. **L2**

Teamwork Activity

As a review activity, ask students in small groups to take turns being "on the spot." Other group members call out topics or concepts studied in class. The student on the spot then gives all the information he or she recalls about it. **L2**

VISUAL LEARNING	Using the Photograph

Ask students how much time they think is appropriate for seven-year-olds to spend on homework. What about twelve-year-olds?

Homework gives students opportunities to practice their skills and to explore new areas of learning. Doing homework also teaches study skills and time management. Children vary in the amount of distraction they can handle while studying.

with one teacher who meets with them for a brief period every day. This teacher gets to know the students well and gives the students someone they can go to if a problem arises.

Most of the day is spent in a variety of classes. Some of those classes continue traditional subjects, such as English, math, and science. Others bring in new subjects, such as computers. In this way, young teens are prepared for high school.

Homework

As they begin school, children may be excited about the idea of homework. Bringing assignments home gives some children the feeling that they are growing up.

Along with that enthusiasm, though, they may also feel tired after a long day of schooling. They may need a mental break right after school ends for the day. After hours of sitting still at school, physical activ-

Management/Leadership Skills

Although many parents who work or care for family members would like to keep up with their child's progress at school, it is often difficult for them to make the time during school hours. Discuss practical ways in which parents can stay in touch with teachers, counselors, and school officials. Possible suggestions include using e-mail or voice mail, but students may have others. You might invite the school principal or a dean to the class to discuss the ideas.

ity can help work out their stored-up energy. This activity can also revive them, making the homework easier to get done.

Children work most effectively if they have a place where they can spread out their papers and concentrate on their work. Many children work best if the area is quiet and free of distractions.

Homework also becomes more complex over time. In the middle school years, teachers often assign projects that require students to plan over several days or even weeks.

Many parents wrestle with the question of how much help to give. Experts advise that parents remember that homework is the child's responsibility. Although younger children may need to be reminded to finish their work, by middle school children should be ready to take responsibility for their work themselves.

SECTION 17-4 REVIEW

✔ Check Your Understanding

1. How have children age seven advanced in their ability to classify?
2. How is the ability to put objects in a series linked to transitivity?
3. How does the thinking of early adolescents differ from that of children aged seven to ten?
4. How does having more awareness of how they learn help children learn?
5. In what ways is middle school different from elementary school and high school?
6. Give two reasons why children in this age group may need a break after school is over before they begin their homework.

Putting Knowledge Into Practice

1. **Making Inferences.** If hypothetical thinking is so advantageous for children, why don't they use it more often when they first acquire the skill?
2. **Creating.** Devise an experiment to test one of the four mental abilities that Piaget says children acquire in the concrete operations period. Write a description of how you would test this ability.
3. **Observing and Participating.** Watch a teacher in one of your classes. Identify ways that he or she tries to draw out students' ability to think in abstract terms.

CHAPTER 17: The Child from Seven to Twelve **541**

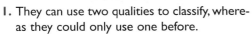
ASSESS

CHECKING COMPREHENSION

Have students answer the Check Your Understanding questions. Answers appear at the bottom of this page.

EVALUATION

Give students the Section 17-4 Quiz in the *Teacher Resource Guide*.

RETEACHING

1. Assign Reteaching Activities, page 51.
2. Ask students to make a booklet using pictures of children seven to twelve and adding labels describing their characteristics.

ENRICHMENT

Ask students to write a fairy tale in which a protagonist between seven and twelve has to master an intellectual challenge.

EXTENSION

Have students compile a list of Homework Do's and Don'ts to share with younger students. Ask students to interview peers for their input on the topic. Include a section of homework rules for students' parents to keep in mind.

CLOSE

Have students create a concept web highlighting intellectual development among children these ages.

FOCUS

MOTIVATOR

Ask students how they felt when their parents went to parent-teacher conferences in middle school. How did they feel about parent-teacher contacts in elementary school or preschool?

TEACH

Critical Thinking Activity

Interpreting. Ask students to explain how each of the listed activities affects a child. What does it say to a child about himself and his schooling? **L1**

Teamwork Activity

Have students create a cause-and-effect web to show how parental involvement in their child's education affects him or her. **L2**

Parenting With Care

Becoming Involved in a Child's Education

When parents get involved in their child's education, they send a very important message: school counts.

The children of involved parents are more likely to be engaged by school and to perform well in school. There are many different ways that they can send this message.

- **Meet the staff.** Many schools have a "back to school" or parents' night, when parents can visit their children's classes and meet their teachers. At these group meetings, teachers describe the curriculum for the year, their policy on homework, the behavior they expect, and the level of performance they require.

- **Talk to the teachers personally.** Many schools also schedule parent-teacher conferences. These are one-on-one sessions in which teachers describe the particular child's performance in class. Even if the school has no formal conferences, parents can call the school and arrange to talk to teachers.

- **Read any messages sent by the schools.** Teachers and principals often send home or mail important information about the school.

- **Review the child's homework.** Parents can judge a child's performance by reviewing homework. It is especially useful if they look at assignments that have been graded.

- **Help out with school activities.** When a class takes a field trip, schools usually ask for parent volunteers to come along. Taking part can give a parent a feel for what is going on in the school and how the child gets along with teachers and fellow students.

- **Join the parents' group.** In many communities, parents form an association that has monthly meetings. Often people from the school's faculty or administration speak at these meetings. Parents

RESOURCES ON EDUCATION

Parents who would like to get involved in their children's education and help their schools can get help from the National PTA. They can get referrals to state offices and advice on how to implement programs to promote the welfare of children. Already existing programs include education, the arts, and health and safety. The National PTA can be contacted at their headquarters at 330 N. Wabash Avenue, Suite 2100, Chicago, IL 60611, 800-307-4782, http://www.pta.org.

can learn a great deal about the school by attending these meetings.

- **Talk to the child.** Most important is to talk to the child about school. Dinner every night is a great opportunity to review the day. Students can describe the work they did and any important events that took place.

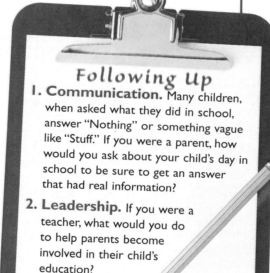

Following Up

1. Communication. Many children, when asked what they did in school, answer "Nothing" or something vague like "Stuff." If you were a parent, how would you ask about your child's day in school to be sure to get an answer that had real information?

2. Leadership. If you were a teacher, what would you do to help parents become involved in their child's education?

CHAPTER 17: The Child from Seven to Twelve **543**

CHECKING COMPREHENSION

Use the Summary and the Reviewing the Facts questions to help students go over the most important ideas in Chapter 17. Encourage students to ask questions and add details.

CHAPTER 17 REVIEW

Answers to Reviewing the Facts

1. *Before:* Grow 2 in (5.1 cm) a year, about 6.5 lb (3.0 kg). *After:* Can grow 3 to 5 in (7.6 to 12.7 cm) a year; about the same in weight (may have higher weight gain just before puberty begins).
2. *Charts should reflect the information on pages 514-516.*
3. Wash with mild soap, warm water, and washcloth. See a doctor if severe. Give up makeup or foods that aggravate problem.
4. Children see themselves as having unique personality, as a mixture of many qualities, as being different in different situations, and as being perceived by others differently.
5. By setting a good example; teaching techniques to calm down; helping the child learn to resolve conflicts without fighting; using rewards for good self-control.
6. *Age 5:* Friends are playmates. *Ages 7-12:* Children look for friends who are loyal, trustworthy, and fun.
7. *Possible response:* At least one to share thoughts and feelings with.
8. *Objects in series:* Shows child can think of objects in relation to more than one other object at a

---

CHAPTER 17   REVIEW &

Summary

✔ Once puberty begins, children undergo major physical changes. (Section 17-1)

✔ Children seven to twelve develop more of a sense of self and tend to be more emotional. (Section 17-2)

✔ In these years, children form deeper friendships than earlier. (Section 17-3)

✔ Young teens become capable of abstract thinking and have special needs for schooling. (Section 17-4)

Reviewing the Facts

1. How do height and weight increase before and after puberty? (Section 17-1)
2. Make a chart showing the changes of puberty for boys and girls. (Section 17-1)
3. What can a young teen do if he or she has acne? (Section 17-1)
4. What are the signs that a child has a growing sense of self? (Section 17-2)
5. How can parents teach children to control anger? (Section 17-2)
6. Compare friendship at age five and from seven to twelve. (Section 17-3)
7. How many close friends should a child have? Why? (Section (17-3)
8. Explain why Piaget said that putting objects in a series and understanding conservation were advances in mental abilities. (Section 17-4)

544 UNIT 6: Special Areas of Study

---

9. How does middle school prepare young teens for high school? (Section 17-4)

Thinking Critically

1. **Analyzing.** In what ways do you and your friends show conformity?
2. **Drawing Conclusions.** Why do you think children in these ages have more problems with siblings near them in age?

Taking Action

1. **Analyzing.** Identify the age that tends to be represented by the following behaviors: (a) telling exaggerated stories; (b) ignoring adults; (c) hiding feelings; (d) being sensitive to others' comments. *(Thinking Skills)*
2. **Memorizing.** Write two lists of random numbers from one to one hundred. Have six numbers in the first list and ten in the second. Ask a child seven to twelve to memorize both lists and repeat them back to you. Ask the child what strategies he or she used. Compare your findings to those of classmates and draw conclusions about how children use memory. *(Thinking Skills)*

---

time. *Conservation:* Shows child understands that changing shape does not change object's substance.
9. Gives them a variety of classes and teachers.

CONNECTIONS

Cross-Curricular Connections

1. **Language Arts.** Take the role of some-one who writes an advice column. Answer a letter from a parent who wants help handling a young teen who is frequently angry.
2. **Social Studies.** Research the work of Piaget. He used many different experi-ments to test different aspects of the con-crete operations period. Choose one of the experiments. Explain it to the class, then discuss whether you think the test is useful.

Workplace Connections

1. **Interpersonal Skills.** Suppose you coach a team of ten-year-olds. One child isn't a very good player, but he works hard at practice and cheers for his teammates during every game. The other children on the team make fun of this child every time he makes a mistake. What would you do to help his teammates learn to stop teasing him?

Family and Community Connections

1. **Planning Nutritious Snacks.** What snacks could you have in your home that would meet the guidelines on page 517 for a healthy diet?
2. **Sending Positive Messages.** Write a list of ten words or sentences that a parent could use to send reassuring messages to a child who is being teased by peers because he or she is different.

Technology Connections

1. **Television.** Think of a television show that focuses on the lives and concerns of a group of teens. Write the outline of an episode that shows peer pressure at work.
2. **Internet.** Search on-line for infor-mation about eating disor-ders. Create a chart that shows the causes and effects of this condition.

EVALUATION

1. Use the reproducible Chapter 17 Test in the *Teacher Resource Guide*, or construct your own test using the **Exam**View® Test Generator.
2. For an alternative assessment, assign the Chapter 17 activity in the *Authentic Assessment* section of the *Teacher Resource Guide*.

ENRICHMENT

Assign students either of the two enrichment activities in the *Enrichment Activities* booklet in the *Student Motivation Kit*.

EXTENSION

Have the class gather pictures and write text to make a "year-book" showing the physical, emo-tional, social, and intellectual development of children between seven and twelve.

CLOSE

Have students create a matching game, in which the characteristics of a given age have to be matched with a picture of a child labeled as that age.

CHAPTER 17: The Child from Seven to Twelve **545**

CHAPTER 18 RESOURCES

Teacher Resource Guide
• Chapter 18 Test, p. 204
• Authentic Assessment, p. 291
Student Motivation Kit
• Observations, pp. 61-62
Transparency Package
• CT-52 Keys to Outdoor Safety
Effective Instruction CD-ROM

CHAPTER 18 **OVERVIEW**

Section 18-1 highlights common safety hazards for children of different ages and describes rescue techniques and first aid for emergency situations.

Section 18-2 discusses the importance of health checkups and immunizations and gives suggestions for caring for a child who is ill.

CHAPTER 18 **OBJECTIVES**

After completing Chapter 18, students will be able to:

• Identify safety hazards and describe appropriate responses in emergencies.
• Discuss proper first aid for a variety of common injuries.
• Explain the importance of regular health checkups and immunizations.
• Discuss caregiver techniques for children who are ill or hospitalized.

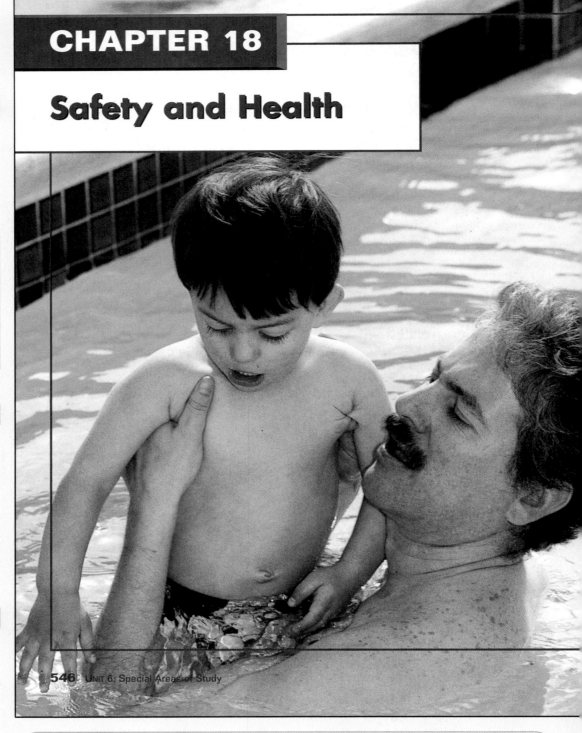

CHAPTER 18

Safety and Health

RESOURCES TO EXPLORE

Health and Safety. Children don't come with a manual explaining how to care for them, although at times many parents wish they did. Parents are constantly faced with questions and decisions such as: How do I protect my child against shaken-baby syndrome? Is the Hepatitis B vaccine safe and necessary? There is help. The American Academy of Pediatrics has numerous publications on a variety of age-specific topics. To order, write AAP Publications, 141 Northwest Point Blvd., P.O. Box 927, Elk Grove Village, IL 60009-0927. You can visit the organization's web site at www.aap.org

Max entered the water from the side without making too much of a splash. It was Noah's first trip to the pool, and he wanted to make it a positive one. Then he turned and held his arms up for his wife to hand Noah to him.

Max held Noah right at the surface of the water. He made sure that Noah could touch the water with his arms and legs without getting his face in it. Noah splashed happily as his father kept a secure hold. Max walked along the bottom of the pool so Noah could feel what it was like to move through the water. Noah spread his arms out and splashed some more.

"Isn't this fun?" Max asked. Noah grinned and agreed. "When you're a little older, we'll make sure that you learn how to swim. Would you like that?" Noah laughed, kicked vigorously with his feet, and responded with a loud "Yes." The surge of water hit his father's face, and Max called out in surprise and then he laughed, too.

"It was Noah's first trip to the pool, and Max wanted to make it a positive one."

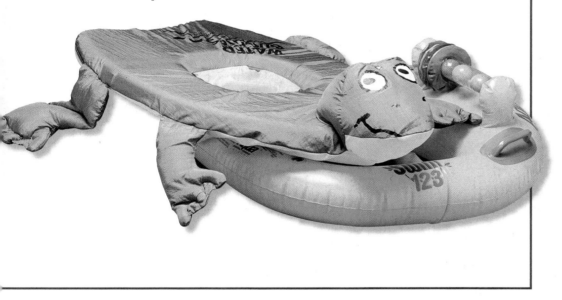

CHAPTER 18: Safety and Health **547**

- On the chalkboard write: "Feed a cold, starve a fever." Many people today think of it as no more than an old saying, but it actually has some credence. Begin a discussion about the meaning of the phrase. Write students' ideas on the board. Guide students to the conclusion that good nutrition is important for a healthy body, and it helps combat illness.

- Direct students' attention to the picture. Ask them to describe what is taking place. (*The father is helping his son acclimate to the water.*) **Ask:** What general principle of safety does this reveal? (*Safety is a learned behavior; children learn safe behaviors from caregivers.*)

USING THE SCENARIO Have students read the story in the student text. **Ask:** Is the father acting safely? How is the father helping his child learn safe water play?

KEY TO ABILITY LEVELS Each section gives skill-building activities. Each activity has been labeled for use with students of various learning styles and abilities.

L1 Level 1 activities are basic activities and should be within the range of all students.

L2 Level 2 activities are average activities and should be within the range of average and above average students.

L3 Level 3 activities are challenging activities designed for the ability range of above average students.

SECTION 18-1 RESOURCES

Teacher Resource Guide
- Lesson Plan Organizer, p. 78
- Section 18-1 Quiz, p. 202

Student Motivation Kit
- Observ. & Case Studies (case study), pp. 137-138
- Reteaching Activity, p. 52
- Enrichment, pp. 51-52
- Teen Parenting Skills, pp. 105, 108-109

Student Workbook
- Study Guide, pp. 146-150
- Taking the Right Steps in an Emergency, pp. 151-152

Transparency Package
- CT-52 Keys to Outdoor Safety

Effective Instruction CD-ROM

FOCUS

MOTIVATOR

Write different ages on the board. Ask for examples of things students would and would not allow a child in their care to do for each age. Discuss why.

VOCABULARY ACTIVITY

Have students work in pairs. Give each student four index cards, and have each student in a pair write four different terms and their definitions. (They can find the definitions in the Glossary at the back of the book.) Then have students teach the terms to their partners.

SECTION 18-1

Preventing Accidents and Handling Emergencies

"**A**n ounce of prevention is worth a pound of cure." That old saying is especially true when it comes to the safety of children. It's easier to prevent accidents than to cope with their effects. Anyone who cares for children, though, has to be prepared for possible emergencies.

KEY TERMS

artificial respiration
convulsion
CPR (cardiopulmonary resuscitation)
fracture
Heimlich maneuver
nontoxic
poison control center
sprain

OBJECTIVES:

- Identify safety hazards for children of different ages.
- Recognize emergency situations and plan appropriate responses.
- Demonstrate appropriate first aid for common ailments.
- Identify basic rescue techniques.

Safety

The safety of the child is the most important responsibility of every caregiver. Each age has its particular hazards because children of different ages have different abilities and interests.

Observing & Participating

Have students work in small groups to develop a safety checklist for outdoor play. Remind them that their checklist can include points about both facilities and behavior. Then have them observe children at play with their checklist in hand. Have them make notes on whether the safety principles they identified are being followed. Does watching actual children at play suggest other safety ideas? After discussing students' findings in class, have the class revise the checklist together.

Infants

Falls cause the most injuries among babies, and they account for many deaths. Even before an infant can crawl, wiggling can cause the baby to fall from a bed, a changing table, or an infant seat placed on a table. Babies tend to fall headfirst, which can result in brain damage. Because of these dangers, no baby should ever be left unattended on any kind of furniture where there's a danger that the child could fall.

Babies like to suck and chew on almost anything that comes within reach. This tendency produces three hazards:

- **Choking on small objects.** Anything that an infant might swallow—including small parts that might come off a toy—must be kept away from the baby.
- **Choking or suffocating on plastic bags.** Infants and small children should never be allowed to play with plastic bags. Don't use plastic bags as a protective covering for the mattress in a crib or playpen.
- **Poisoning.** Anything babies could place in the mouth—even the edges of furniture—must be **nontoxic**, or not poisonous. Some paints that contain lead are particularly dangerous for children. Many common household products are poisonous. The chart on pages 550-551 lists many of them. Any substances that are poisonous must be placed well out of a baby's reach.

What rule should caregivers always follow when infants are in water?

A small child should never be left alone near water, such as a tub or a wading pool. Drownings happen quickly, even in the time it takes to answer the phone or the door.

Careful crib selection and use are essential for infant safety. Review the guidelines on pages 210-211.

Car accidents cause more deaths among children than any other factor. Many deaths and injuries can be prevented if a baby is put in a child safety seat and an older child wears a seat belt. Regular adult seat belts cannot keep babies or young children safe.

CHAPTER 18: Safety and Health **549**

COMPREHENSION CHECK

1. What is the most important responsibility of a caregiver? (*The child's safety.*)
2. Babies tend to fall head first. What can be the result of this tendency? (*Brain damage.*)

ACTIVITIES

Discussion Activity

Falls cause the most injuries among babies. Have students brainstorm a list of measures that can be taken to reduce this hazard. (*Don't let the baby out of your sight, provide a space on the floor for the baby to play, place baby in a playpen or other enclosed area, block stairs, doors and windows.*)

Critical Thinking Activity

Decision Making. Have students identify a safe way to handle this situation: You are caring for a one-year-old. You are expecting a very important phone call. You put the child in the tub for a bath, and at that moment the phone rings. What do you do? Why?

 VISUAL LEARNING Using the Photograph *Answer:* Never leave the child alone.

LEARNING STYLES

Visual/Kinesthetic

Have available for the class the following objects (or pictures of the objects): a small marble, a tennis ball, a sharpened pencil, a stuffed animal. Direct students to imagine that they had to choose one of these items for children of the following ages: an infant, a two-year-old, a three-year-old, and a six-year-old. Have students give reasons for their choices.

COMPREHENSION CHECK

1. Do poisons always smell bad? Give examples to support your answer. (*No. Perfumes and aftershave lotions can smell good and still be poisonous if not used as intended.*)

2. Is it safe to leave a small child unattended the bathroom? (*No. A bathroom usually has access to water and possibly poisonous materials, such as shampoo or cleaning products.*)

3. What is the safety benefit of encouraging children to take small bites while eating, and not talking with food in the mouth? (*Helps prevent choking.*)

4. At what stage is it safe for a child to sit in a car seat that faces forward? (*Once a child is one year old and weighs more than 20 pounds.*)

VISUAL LEARNING	**Using the Chart**

Have students review the chart. Point out that most of the items listed are common household items. Have students list where these items are usually stored. (*Possible answers: Medicine cabinet, under the sink, in the bathroom, in the garage.*) Discuss what precautions could be taken to prevent children from having access to them. List their ideas on the chalkboard.

▶ **Common Household Poisons**

KINDS OF POISONS	EXAMPLES	TYPE OF CONTACT
Medicines	• Sleeping pills • Aspirin • Tranquilizers • Vitamins • Cold preparations	• Swallowing
Cleaning Products	• Ammonia • Automatic dishwasher detergent • Laundry detergents • Bleach • Drain and toilet bowl cleaners • Disinfectants • Furniture polish	• Swallowing • Skin • Eyes • Inhaling
Personal Care Products	• Shampoo • Soap • Nail polish remover • Perfumes and aftershave lotions • Mouthwash • Rubbing alcohol	• Swallowing • Skin • Eyes • Inhaling
Gardening and Garage Products	• Insecticides • Fertilizers • Rat and mouse poisons • Acids of all kinds • Gasoline • Paint thinner • Charcoal lighter fluid • Antifreeze	• Swallowing • Skin • Eyes • Inhaling

Continued on next page

Observing & Participating

Students—and their families—will benefit by observing where the common household poisons are stored in their own homes, and if they are stored safely. If not, encourage students, especially those with young children in the house, to reduce the risks by storing them safely. Remind students to double-check the list in the chart, since it is easy to overlook some common items thought to be safe.

Common Household Poisons Continued

KINDS OF POISONS	EXAMPLES	TYPE OF CONTACT
Plants	• Some wild mushrooms • English ivy • Daffodil bulbs • Rhubarb leaves • Holly berries • Poinsettias • Poison ivy and poison oak	• Swallowing • Skin

Parents must buy an infant car seat that meets current safety standards. Then they need to use it *every time* they put a baby or young child into the car, no matter how short the trip. This is the law in most states. Putting young children in the center of the back seat gives them the most protection. They should never ride in the front seat. Infants should face the back of the car.

Ages One to Three

One- to three-year-olds need very careful supervision. They are so mobile that they can quickly get into danger. Any area where they spend time should be carefully checked for safety. No toddler should be left unattended for more than a few minutes—and even then they should be within hearing distance.

Children can be taught to follow these safety guidelines to prevent choking:
- Stay seated while eating.
- Always take small bites.
- Chew all food thoroughly.
- Swallow before taking another bite.
- Don't talk or laugh with food in the mouth.
- Keep small toys and other small objects out of the mouth.

Some parents stop using child car seats after the child's first birthday. However, they are still essential. A different kind of seat is needed for older, heavier children. Once a child is a year old and weighs more than 20 pounds (9.1 kg), the child seat can face forward.

INFOLINK

Infant Car Seats

For more about *infant car seats*, see "Parenting with Care," Chapter 6, page 210.

CHAPTER 18: Safety and Health **551**

Critical Thinking Activity

Compare and Contrast. Provide students with labels from cleaning products that have warnings on them. Have students compare the first aid measures recommended, noting similarities and differences. **L2**

Social Studies Activity

Point out to students that almost 90 percent of one-year-olds are put in safety seats, but only 75 percent of three-year-olds regularly use seat belts. Have students research the law about safety seats and safety belts in your state. **L3**

Discussion Activity

Many states have a law requiring the use of child safety seats and seat belts. The number of serious injuries and deaths nationwide has been reduced because of these laws. **Ask:** Would it be better to have one law for the whole country? What are the benefits and problems of having different laws in different states? **L1**

Teamwork Activity

Have students work in pairs or groups to gather information on car seats. Students should find answers to questions such as: How many types and sizes are available? Do all car seats meet government standards? Can all seats be safely installed in all cars? What is the price range? Once all the information is available, have students determine which car seat is best and why. **L3**

DID You Know?

Accidents. Accidents are the greatest single cause of death in children between the ages of one and fifteen:
- Almost one-third of home accidents involve children under age four.
- At all ages, more males than females are involved in accidents.
- Stairs, windows, etc. are the second leading cause of accidents.
- Almost one-fifth of accidents involving children take place in the kitchen. The third chief cause of accidents is kitchen utensils, such as knives.

COMPREHENSION CHECK

1. What are good fire safety procedures regarding matches for children of all ages? Why is this so? (*All matches should be locked away. Many fires are started by children playing with matches.*)
2. What is the number to call for emergency help in your community?

ACTIVITIES

Critical Thinking Activity

Decision Making. Present the following scenario to students. Your six-year-old comes crying to you with a scraped, bloody knee. She says she was pushed off the swing. What do you do? **L1**

Safety seats and safety belts can also help prevent accidents while eating. *Why are infants and toddlers particularly at risk?*

Many young children are fascinated by fire. Even those who have been taught that matches are unsafe may experiment with them. As the match burns closer to the finger, the child often becomes frightened and may drop the match or throw it into a wastebasket. Many fires start this way. All matches should be locked away.

Ages Four and Older

Children from four to six spend a great deal of time in unsupervised play. They need to learn good safety practices. They won't always remember and follow all safety rules, however. They need frequent reminders and watchful caregivers nearby.

Outdoor play equipment, such as a swing set, should be firmly anchored to keep the set from tipping over. The ground should be covered with a soft material, such as shredded tires, to cushion falls. Caregivers should set and enforce safety rules. For example, there should be only one child on a swing at a time, and no pushing is allowed on a slide. A child riding a tricycle should wear a helmet.

Guidelines for Fast Action

If a child in your care does get hurt:
1. **Above all, try to remain calm.** This will help reassure the child and help you think more clearly.
2. **Evaluate the situation.** What seems to be wrong? You must know what's wrong so you can act properly.
3. **Make the victim comfortable.** If the injury is serious, keep the child warm.
4. **Call for help if necessary.** If you are not certain what the problem is or what to do, call for help. Keep emergency numbers at hand. Does your community have 911 emergency service?

   Know how to call the nearest **poison control center**—a special unit to advise and treat poisoning victims. Hospitals can also give advice.

   On the phone, clearly and concisely state the age of the child and the problem. Tell who you are and your relationship to the child. Follow instructions.
5. **Give the minimum necessary first aid treatment.** Give the most necessary first aid, then seek more qualified help.

If you have teen parents in your class, you might suggest that they begin a play group in their neighborhoods. Have them discuss the criteria for a successful group, such as:

- Children should be close in age.
- Parents should agree on safety rules and enforce them.
- The time of day and frequency of meetings should not conflict with other priorities.
- The location of meetings should be convenient.

Using Standard Precautions

Today, more is understood about the spread of diseases. Medical professionals have developed standard precautions to be used in caring for patients. Child care workers also need to know and follow many of these standard precautions to protect themselves and the children they care for. These include:

- Use of disposable gloves when changing diapers, dealing with bodily fluids (except sweat), or touching contaminated objects or surfaces.
- Thorough, frequent handwashing.
- Proper cleaning of surfaces and disposal of items which may be contaminated (such as disposable diapers and used gloves).
- Use of special devices for mouth-to-mouth resusitation.

First Aid

It is essential for anyone who takes care of children to be familiar with first aid procedures. The following guidelines are very general. For more information, contact the nearest office of the American Red Cross about first aid training classes.

Animal Bites

Wash the area around the bite with soap and running water. Tell the parents, who will probably talk to a doctor.

If the animal was a bat, fox, raccoon, skunk, dog, or cat that bit the child without being provoked, call the local health department. It will send someone to try to catch the animal so that it can be tested for rabies.

Playgrounds can be fun for children—but they can be dangerous too. *Name one safety guideline for playgrounds.*

CHAPTER 18: Safety and Health **553**

ACTIVITIES

Critical Thinking Activity

Synthesizing. Have students consider the following: They are taking a group of children to an amusement park. What should they pack in a first-aid kit? **L1**

VISUAL LEARNING | **Using the Photograph**
Possible responses: Don't push; walk, don't run, from one piece of equipment to another; walk a wide path around swings.

DID *You* **Know?**

Rabies. Rabies is a disease that exists primarily in wild animals, but can be contracted by domestic ones. Although rare in humans, it can be transmitted from a rabid animal by a bite or a lick on open skin, such as a scratch or cut. Once symptoms develop in a human, the disease is usually fatal. Anyone suspected of rabies exposure should receive immediate treatment. The sooner treatment is started, the better the victim's chances of survival. Prevention is the best means of controlling the disease.

LEARNING STYLES

Kinesthetic

Give groups of three students index cards. Have students write the name of an injury, such as a dog bite or scraped elbow, on one side of each card, and the appropriate first-aid action on the other. Each student will play one of the roles of: victim, caregiver, and monitor. The monitor will randomly choose one index card. The victim will pretend to suffer the injury indicated. The caregiver will take the appropriate action. The monitor will comment on whether the actions are correct. Students will switch roles until all have played all roles.

COMPREHENSION CHECK

1. What effect will firm pressure on a minor cut or scrape have? (*It will stop the bleeding.*)
2. What is a common treatment for bumps and bruises? Why is it done? (*Applying a cold cloth or ice pack; to minimize swelling.*)

ACTIVITIES

Discussion Activity

Have students skim the remainder of the section, looking at the headings. Have them identify which emergencies they feel prepared to handle. After reading the section, have them evaluate their preparedness again. **L1**

Discussion Activity

Point out to students that some states have "Good Samaritan" laws that protect those who provide first aid from any legal consequences if they are unable to help the victim. Have them discuss whether they think such laws are necessary and desirable. **L2**

VISUAL LEARNING | **Using the Photograph**

The Centers for Disease Control recommends that child care workers always wear gloves when giving first aid to anyone who is bleeding. Discuss how this protects both people. Do you think parents need to follow this practice with their own children?

This disease can be very dangerous. The child may need shots for protection from the disease.

Bleeding

The Centers for Disease Control recommends that child care workers always wear disposable plastic gloves when giving first aid to any person who is bleeding.

- **Minor cuts or scrapes.** Stop the bleeding by placing a clean cloth or gauze pad on the wound and pressing hard for ten to fifteen minutes without releasing. Once the bleeding has stopped, clean the area with soap and warm water. Apply a mild antiseptic, and cover it with a bandage.
- **Deep cuts or wounds.** These may need medical help. If the child's breathing is shallow and rapid, send for medical help. In a light-skinned child, the skin may turn pale and bluish. Continue to

554 Unit 6: Special Areas of Study

try to stop the bleeding until help arrives. Elevating the affected area may stop the bleeding. Do not apply a tourniquet. (A tourniquet is a bandage that cuts off the blood supply to a portion of the body.) An improperly applied tourniquet can harm the victim.

- **Nosebleeds.** Have the child sit down and lean slightly forward over a basin or sink. Using the thumb and forefinger, squeeze the child's nose firmly just below the bones in the nose. After squeezing for several minutes, check to see whether the bleeding has stopped. If not, reapply pressure for five to ten minutes. Sometimes putting cold packs on the nose and forehead also helps. If you can't stop the bleeding, or if the child becomes dizzy or pale, seek medical help.

Bumps and Bruises

Treat bruises with a cold cloth or ice pack to minimize swelling. An injured arm or leg can be elevated. If the child complains of pain for more than a day, call a physician. A fall or bump on the head can be serious. Call a doctor if the child loses consciousness, is drowsy or irritable, complains of a headache, or vomits.

To stop a nosebleed, have the child lean forward slightly. Firmly press above the nostrils and hold for several minutes.

DID *You* **Know?**

Bruises. The correct medical name for a bruise is contusion. This is an injury to tissues caused by a sudden impact or crushing. In a contusion, tiny blood vessels under the skin are ruptured, causing discoloration (the so-called black and blue marks) although the skin usually remains unbroken. Cold, wet compresses or an ice bag can help reduce pain and swelling. Salt-water ice, however, should be avoided. The salt in the water can lower the water's temperature, which, in turn, can result in further tissue damage.

Burns

How you treat a burn depends on what caused the burn and how bad it is. All but small surface burns are serious because they may cause scarring, infections, or shock. Burns are classified by degree.

- **First-degree burns look red and slightly swollen.** They may be caused by too much sun, hot objects, hot water, or steam. Cover the area with cold water or a cold, wet cloth until the pain stops. These burns heal rapidly.
- **Second-degree burns are deeper, redder, and blistered.** The burned area remains swollen and somewhat moist for several days. These burns may be caused by very deep sunburn, hot liquids, and flammable products like gasoline. Second-degree burns should be treated by a physician.
- **Third-degree burns destroy the skin.** These burns may look white or charred. There may be little pain at first because nerve endings have been destroyed. Third-degree burns can be caused by flames, burning clothing, hot water, extremely hot objects, or electricity.

    These burns are extremely serious and require immediate medical care. Cover the burn with a clean, dry cloth and keep the patient warm. To help ease the pain, elevate the burned area slightly. Get the victim to a hospital as soon as possible.
- **Chemical burns.** Household products such as toilet bowl cleaners, drain cleaners, and disinfectants can cause chemical burns. Using protective

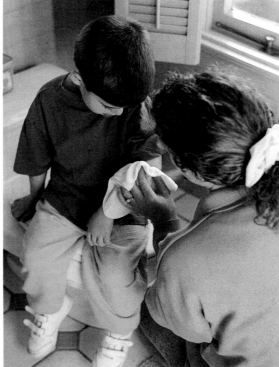

Minor burns can be treated with a cold, wet cloth and then covered with a clean, dry cloth. *What should be done with more serious burns?*

gloves or a towel, wash off the affected area immediately and completely with cold water. Remove any clothing with the chemical on it, unless the clothing is stuck to the skin. Apply a clean bandage, and call a doctor.
- **Electrical burns.** These burns may be deep, but they often appear minor, leaving only a small black dot on the skin. Cool the burned area with cold water, and cover it with a clean, smooth cloth such as a handkerchief.

CHAPTER 18: Safety and Health **555**

COMPREHENSION CHECK

1. What are the signs of choking? (*Inability to speak, breathe, or cry; bluish lips, nails, and skin; high-pitched noises; ineffective coughing.*)

Teamwork Activity

Have students work in pairs to practice rescue procedures for a child who is choking. Provide a doll for students to use as the subject. **L1**

Teamwork Activity

Have students work in pairs to practice the Heimlich maneuver's positioning. Emphasize that actual abdominal thrusts can cause internal injury and should not be performed unless the person is choking. **L1**

VISUAL LEARNING | **Using the Graphics** Focus students' attention on the illustrations. Review the steps. Discuss the effects the maneuvers have on the victims. Ask why the Heimlich maneuver is not recommended for infants.

Then have the patient lie down with legs elevated and head turned to one side. This prevents shock. (See page 560 for more about shock.) Take the child to a hospital emergency room, or call an ambulance.

Choking

Choking occurs when something is caught in a person's throat. The danger is that choking can cut off the supply of air. When oxygen is restricted, brain damage can occur within a few minutes.

First, recognize the signs of choking. They are an inability to speak, breathe, or cry; bluish lips, nails, and skin; high-pitched noises or ineffective coughing. If a person is choking, you must act quickly to dislodge the object that is blocking the breathing passage.

If an infant less than one year old is choking, follow the steps shown in the drawings below. With children older than one year and with adults, use the **Heimlich maneuver** (HIME-lick muh-new-vur). This technique uses pressure on the air in the body to expel an object that is blocking

Rescue Maneuver for Choking Infants

Step 1: Turn the infant face down over your arm.

Step 2: Using the heel of your other hand, give four quick blows between the infant's shoulder blades.

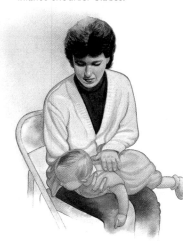

Step 3: Turn the infant over, supporting the head, neck, and back. Position your two middle fingers below the rib cage and above the navel. With your fingers in that position, give four quick thrusts toward the chest. Repeat these three steps until the object is expelled.

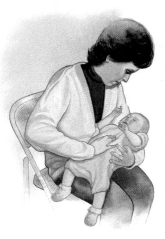

556 UNIT 6: Special Areas of Study

ISSUES IN CHILDREN'S HEALTH **Choking.** Each year, about 3,000 people in the United States die from choking. Almost two-thirds of these deaths are of children under age two. Choking occurs most often during eating, and meat is most often the culprit. There are four kinds of choking: (1) the feeling that something is in the airway; (2) an obstruction in front of the epiglottis; (3) an object behind the epiglottis; and (4) something caught in the lungs.

breathing. The drawings below show its steps.

The amount of pressure to use in the Heimlich maneuver depends on the age and size of the victim. Too much pressure can harm a young child. It is best to get training in using the Heimlich maneuver—before you need to use it.

If the child who is choking has lost consciousness or stops breathing, you must take different steps. First, call for emergency medical help. You can try to remove the object from the child's throat, but do so only if you can see the object and remove it safely. Use your thumb and forefinger to try to locate the object and pull it out. Then begin artificial respiration immediately. (See page 561 for more information on artificial respiration.) If you can't remove the object, try to help the person breathe until help arrives.

Heimlich Maneuver for Children One Year and Older and Adults

If the victim is standing or sitting:

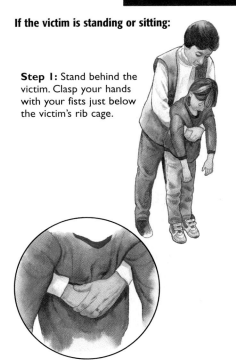

Step 1: Stand behind the victim. Clasp your hands with your fists just below the victim's rib cage.

Step 2: Press your clasped hands into the victim's abdomen with a quick upward thrust. Repeat step 2 if necessary until the object is expelled.

If the victim has collapsed:

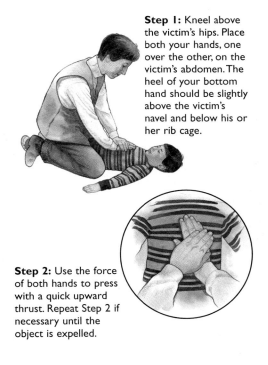

Step 1: Kneel above the victim's hips. Place both your hands, one over the other, on the victim's abdomen. The heel of your bottom hand should be slightly above the victim's navel and below his or her rib cage.

Step 2: Use the force of both hands to press with a quick upward thrust. Repeat Step 2 if necessary until the object is expelled.

Critical Thinking Activity

Hypothesizing. Ask students: If a child is choking on a foreign object, why is it advisable to attempt extraction only if the object is visible and can be removed safely using the thumb and forefinger? (*The foreign object may be pushed further into the airway.*)

Teamwork Activity

Have students work in groups to create a brochure about choking. They can outline the main dangers for choking and describe the procedures for helping infants and for performing the Heimlich maneuver. **L1**

Critical Thinking Activity

Making Inferences. Point out that many restaurants have posters describing the Heimlich maneuver. **Ask:** Why do they have them? Should displaying such posters be required by law? **L1**

Health Activity

Have students research epilepsy. Have them address causes, effects, and treatment. Ask them to describe how epilepsy is similar to and different from the convulsion described in the text (on page 558). Have them report on how others should respond when a person has an epileptic seizure. **L3**

ISSUES IN CHILDREN'S HEALTH

Fainting. Fainting in young children can be caused by a number of factors that are often radically different from those causing this condition in older children and adults. The causes include anemia, breath-holding, hyperventilation, extreme excitement (hysteria), drug reactions, illness or infection, and poisoning. Discuss with students the steps that need to be taken if a young child faints. **Ask:** Why would it be important to discover the cause of fainting? Why would an emergency room attendant be interested in the child's medical history?

COMPREHENSION CHECK

1. Why is it especially important to not move a child if a sprain or fracture is suspected in the ribs or back? (*You could cause further damage.*)

2. How much danger is usually associated with mosquito, ant, and chigger bites? (*Generally none.*)

Critical Thinking Activity

Making Assumptions. A child suddenly collapses on the playground. The child had been sweating, looks pale, and has cold skin. After a minute or two the child regains consciousness. What could be the problem? (*The child fainted.*) **L2**

ISSUES IN CHILDREN'S HEALTH

Lyme Disease. Lyme disease is a serious illness that can result from bites by deer ticks. It can cause such serious problems as arthritis, meningitis, and myocarditis. The first symptoms of the disease are headache, fever, and fatigue. Aches in the muscles and joints follow. Fortunately, there is a visual clue to the disease. Its presence is marked by a large red spot with a white center that appears where the tick bit. The severe consequences of this disease can be prevented with treatment. Parents living in areas where deer can be found should check their children for ticks when they come in from outdoors.

Convulsions

A **convulsion** or a seizure is a period of unconsciousness with uncontrolled jerking or twitching of the muscles. There are many causes of convulsions. They occur most often in infants, usually as a result of high fever.

If a child has a convulsion, place the child on his or her side on the floor. Move any hard objects out of the way. Don't attempt to hold the child down, and don't force anything between the teeth. After the convulsion stops, be sure the child's head is turned to one side to reduce the risk of choking. Check with a doctor for further instructions. If the convulsion lasts more than fifteen minutes, take the child to a hospital emergency room or call an ambulance.

Fainting

A child who faints loses consciousness. The child may collapse without warning, or he or she may first experience sweating, cold skin, nausea, or dizziness. A light-skinned child who is about to faint may look pale. Anyone who feels faint should lie down or sit with the head between the legs.

If a child has fainted, loosen any tight clothing. Position the child's head to one side. Check to be sure the child is breathing. If breathing has stopped, have someone call for medical assistance, and begin artificial respiration. (See page 561 for information on artificial respiration.) If the child is breathing, expect him or her to revive within a minute or two. If the child does not gain consciousness within two minutes, call for help.

Fractures and Sprains

A **fracture** is a break or a crack in a bone. A **sprain** is an injury caused by sudden, violent stretching of a joint or muscle. Both may cause pain, swelling, and bruising. It is often difficult to tell a sprain from a fracture without an X ray.

Sprained wrists are sometimes treated by wrapping the joint in an elastic wrap.

558 Unit 6: Special Areas of Study

Parenting in *Action*

As children grow older, they become more mobile, and their curiosity will put them in potentially dangerous situations. To keep the child safe, the caregiver may have to interact and participate in an otherwise dangerous activity. Some suggestions for preventing fractures and sprains are: holding the hand of your child while he walks along a wall and holding both of your child's hands while he jumps off a bench. This type of participation will help your child acquire the skill and dexterity to remain safe.

This symbol—called "Mr. Yuk"—is used to show small children that they should not eat or drink a substance. It can help protect them from taking in any poison.

If you suspect a fracture or a sprain, don't move the child until you know how serious the injury is. This is very important for injuries to the back, ribs, neck, or collarbone. You can cause further damage by moving the child. Head injuries are especially dangerous. Call for qualified medical help, and use artificial respiration if necessary.

You can treat a mild sprain by elevating the injured area and putting cold packs on it to help reduce the swelling. If the pain persists, check with a doctor.

Insect Stings and Bites

If a child has been stung by a bee, wasp, hornet, or yellow jacket, scrape off the stinger. Apply a cold cloth, an ice pack, or ice water to the area. Then cover it with a paste made from baking soda and water.

Some people are very allergic to insects. For them, a single sting can cause serious illness or even death. Anyone with a known allergy must be taken to a hospital or doctor immediately after being stung. The same is true of anyone who becomes dizzy, feels faint, has difficulty breathing, vomits, develops hives, or perspires heavily.

Ticks are small insects that cling to the skin or scalp. They carry diseases. If you find a tick, use tweezers to grab the tick as close to the skin as possible. Then pull the tick off in one smooth motion. Wash the area well with soap and water.

Mosquito, ant, and chigger bites are annoying, but most are not dangerous. A paste of baking soda and water or rubbing the spot with witch hazel or rubbing alcohol will give relief.

Some mosquitoes carry the West Nile virus. Most cases are mild, but some victims get seriously ill or even die. Use of an insect repellent is the best defense.

Poisoning

Recognizing that a child has been poisoned is not always easy. Here are some symptoms that may indicate poisoning:

- **From swallowed poisons.** Difficulty in breathing, unconsciousness, fever, burns in the mouth and throat, and vomiting may result from swallowed poisons or chemicals.
- **From skin-contact poisons.** Burns or rash on the skin can indicate the presence of these poisons.
- **From eye-contact poisons.** Look for burning or irritation of the eyes or blindness.
- **From inhaled poisons.** Choking, coughing, nausea, or dizziness all may result from fumes, sprays, and poisonous gases.

Insect bites and stings are a normal part of childhood. Especially those children who spend time outdoors are at risk. Discuss with students ways children can avoid some biting bugs. **L1**

Critical Thinking Activity

Problem Solving. Ask students why it might be difficult to determine whether a child has taken poison and what type of poison has been taken.

Critical Thinking Activity

Drawing Conclusions. Most poisonings occur in children under five. One in three take place when children are visiting grandparents. **Ask:** Why is that the case? What can grandparents do to provide better protection for their grandchildren? **L2**

VISUAL LEARNING | **Using the Illustration**

Point out to students that the Mr. Yuk symbol was developed at the Children's Hospital in Pittsburgh. Have them find out where parents can get these symbols in your community.

Poisonous Plants. Clothes that have come in contact with poison ivy and other plants that can cause severe skin reactions need to be washed before being worn again. If left unwashed, they can infect the wearer.

ISSUES IN CHILDREN'S HEALTH | **Treating Poisoning.** One of the most effective treatments for poisoning is vomiting. This process, which empties the stomach, is recommended for all poisons except those that are sufficiently abrasive to cause additional damage on the way back up. Syrup of ipecac is a common emetic, or solution that induces vomiting. This syrup is effective 97 percent of the time. Inexpensive, it is a good resource for the family medicine cabinet. Before using any emetic, however, contact a poison control center or physician.

ACTIVITIES

Discussion Activity

Discuss with the class that splinters can be more traumatic for some children than others. It is important for the caregiver to remain calm and find ways to entertain the child and keep him or her calm too. One approach is allowing the child to participate in the extraction process. Allow the child to observe as the needle and tweezers are sterilized. Have the child concentrate on holding the affected area very still, using additional support if necessary. Ask for other suggestions for making splinter extraction relatively painless. **L2**

Critical Thinking Activity

Decision Making. Give students the following situation: You witness an accident. It is clear that the injured child is having trouble breathing. You have read up on how to perform the appropriate rescue techniques. What do you do? Have students explain their decision. **L2**

Teamwork Activity

Have students review the situations described in this section. Have them make a list of the emergencies and rate each one on a scale of 1 (least severe) to 5 (most severe). Combine students' rankings and find an average for the class. Then discuss the rankings. **L2**

If a child is poisoned, take these steps:

1. Find out what has poisoned the child. If the child has swallowed something poisonous, try to learn how much he or she swallowed.
2. Phone the poison control center, hospital, or the child's doctor. Have the container that held the poisonous substance with you as you call. That way you can answer any questions you are asked.
3. Follow the directions you receive. Act quickly and calmly.

Anyone who has been poisoned must be seen by a physician. This is true even if emergency treatment has already been given and even if the victim shows no symptoms. Take the container that held the poisonous substance—or a sample of the substance—with you. This will help the doctor decide on the proper treatment.

Shock

When a person suffers a severe injury, the loss of a great deal of blood, or poisoning, the body goes into shock. Important body functions, including breathing and heart action, are impaired. The symptoms of shock include rapid pulse, clammy skin, shallow breathing, enlarged pupils, a glassy stare, and nausea. Sometimes a person in shock loses consciousness.

Shock can be serious. If you suspect a child is in shock, seek medical help immediately. Until help arrives, be sure the child remains lying down, and keep him or her warm.

Splinters and Thorns

Splinters are tiny pieces of wood, metal, or glass that become stuck in the skin. Thorns may also be treated as splinters.

Although splinters are not dangerous, they do hurt, and they can become infected.

If part of the splinter is above the surface, you can use tweezers for removal. Sterilize the tweezers in boiling water or in a flame. Grab onto the part of the splinter that sticks out and pull evenly. Put antiseptic on the wound and cover it with a sterile bandage.

If a nonglass splinter is just under the skin surface, you can take it out with a sterilized needle. Numb the skin over the splinter with a piece of ice. Use the needle to break the skin and lift the splinter out. Clean and cover the wound as described above.

Large or deep splinters and those caused by glass can be more serious. They should be removed by a physician.

Rescue Techniques

When an emergency situation causes the victim to stop breathing or the heart to stop beating, immediate action is vital. Learn the rescue techniques that will enable you to respond quickly.

Artificial Respiration

Artificial respiration (RES-puh-RAY-shun) is a procedure for forcing air into the lungs of a person whose breathing has stopped. Some emergency situations, such as drowning and electrical shock, call for artificial respiration. The technique to use with infants and small children is shown on page 561. Child care workers should wear gloves and use a special protective face mask when giving artificial respiration.

You can learn more about artificial respiration in a rescue training class. Taking such a class will also give you a chance to practice the correct techniques.

ISSUES IN TEEN PARENTING Ask any teen parents in the class to share their experiences with emergencies. Have volunteers share their feelings, fears, and concerns for their child. In addition to their own qualifications for handling emergencies, parents should inquire about the qualifications of any caregiver they contract.

Artificial Respiration for Infants and Small Children

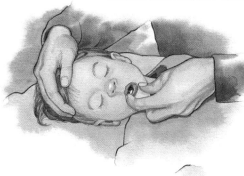

Step 1: Turn the child's head to one side. With your finger, carefully clear the child's mouth of any foreign objects or fluid. (If the victim is under a year old, do *not* put your finger into his or her mouth.) If there is an object caught in the child's throat, or to clear the mouth of the young baby, follow the instructions for aiding a choking victim, page 556. Be sure that you can see the object and remove it safely.

Step 2: Tilt the child's head back slightly. Put two fingers just under the chinbone and lift the jaw into a jutting-out position. Check for breathing.

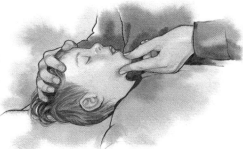

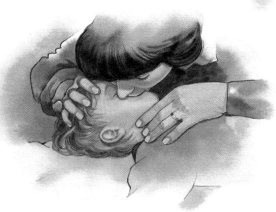

Step 3: If the child is not breathing, take a deep breath. Seal your lips around the child's mouth and nose. (If you can cover only the mouth, pinch the child's nostrils shut with your fingers.)

Step 4: Blow into the child's mouth and nose. (For an infant, use gentle puffs of air.) When you see the chest lift, remove your mouth and let the air come out. Then blow in again. Repeat 15 to 20 times per minute for a child, or 20 times per minute for an infant. Continue until the child resumes normal breathing or until help arrives.

CHAPTER 18: Safety and Health **561**

Discussion Activity

Discuss rescue techniques students have seen on television shows. Some shows will be more accurate than others. Why? Which shows are more likely to use correct procedures? **L1**

Teamwork Activity

Depending on class size, divide the class into two or four groups. These groups will become teams to play against each other. Have each team prepare two or three index cards with questions and answers on either side of the same card. Students can use the information on these pages to prepare their cards. All cards from the opposing teams are shuffled together. Teams and students take turns drawing cards and answering the questions. **L1**

VISUAL LEARNING Using the Illustration
Review the steps in the illustration with the class. Reiterate why each step is taken.

CHECKING COMPREHENSION

Have students answer the Check Your Understanding questions. Answers appear at the bottom of this page.

EVALUATION

Give students the Section 18-1 Quiz in the *Teacher Resource Guide*.

RETEACHING

1. Assign Reteaching Activities, page 52.
2. Have students write the descriptions of two accidents or injuries and then exchange papers with a partner, who should describe how someone should respond.

ENRICHMENT

Post a schedule of classes offered by the nearest American Red Cross chapter. Encourage students to sign up for an infant and child CPR course of a first aid course. Discuss the benefits with your class.

EXTENSION

Invite a public safety speaker to discuss safe procedures in weather-related emergencies.

CLOSE

Have students complete the sentence "The biggest safety worry for children is . . . ." Have them include suggestions for preventing serious problems from this danger.

CPR

CPR is the short name for **cardiopulmonary resuscitation** (CAR-dee-oh-POOL-muh-NER-ee ri-SUSS-uh-TAY-shun). This rescue technique is used to sustain life when both breathing and the heart have stopped. Special training from a certified instructor is needed to perform CPR. Many communities offer training programs. To find out where CPR training is offered in your area, call a local chapter of the Red Cross or the American Heart Association.

SECTION 18-1 REVIEW

✔ Check Your Understanding

1. Why should you put an infant or young child in a car safety seat?
2. What three dangers arise from the fact that infants often put things in their mouths?
3. List the five guidelines for responding to an accident or injury.
4. What is a poison control center?
5. What is the possible danger from an animal bite?
6. Briefly describe the three categories of burns.
7. What is the Heimlich maneuver?
8. What is the difference between a fracture and a sprain?
9. What symptoms call for artificial respiration? What symptoms call for CPR?

Putting Knowledge Into Practice

1. **Analyzing.** Why might it be difficult to remain calm if a child in your care was injured? Why would it be especially important to remain calm? What could you do to help yourself stay calm?
2. **Observing and Participating.** Visit a local park, and observe a group of kindergartners or first graders as they play. Describe the playground equipment used by the children. Are there any apparent safety hazards in the equipment? Are there any hazards in the children's behavior? Write a list of safety rules that you think should be posted at the park.

ANSWERS TO SECTION 18-1 REVIEW

1. To protect from injury or death.
2. Choking, suffocation, or poisoning.
3. Be calm; evaluate situation; victim comfortable; get help; minimum first aid.
4. Special hospital unit for poison victims.
5. Rabies may be contracted.
6. *See page 555.*
7. A method to force out an object that is blocking breathing.
8. *Fracture:* broken bone; *sprain:* violent pull to joint or muscle.
9. *Artificial respiration:* breathing stopped. *CPR:* both breathing and heart stopped.

CAREER OPPORTUNITIES

Emergency Medical Technician

A CONVERSATION WITH RON JACOBSON

How did you become interested in becoming an emergency medical technician? I wanted to be an EMT—that's what we're called—because I wanted to help people. I also like the excitement of meeting emergencies. It's tremendously satisfying to help save someone's life.

What are the tasks and responsibilities of an emergency medical technician? We respond to emergencies like car accidents or fires or a heart attack. We have to provide whatever immediate care the person needs, then get him or her to the hospital for further treatment. With us, it's often a life-or-death situation.

What is the work environment like? When we're not on call, we work on the equipment, study, and do paperwork. When an emergency happens, we could be called anywhere—and must get there quickly. We can be called any time of the day or night and in all kinds of weather.

What are the working hours like? In our station, we work eight hour days, six days a week. We have three shifts. Each of us works at least one weekend day every week. We often work on holidays, too.

What aptitudes are needed to be an emergency medical technician? The most important thing is to stay calm and think clearly under pressure. We need good dexterity to use the equipment. We need great teamwork skills. We have to be strong, too.

EMERGENCY MEDICAL TECHNICIAN

Education and Training. An EMT needs a high school diploma and special training. Workers must pass a certification test and retake the test every two years.

Career Outlook. The number of EMTs is expected to grow in the future.

CONNECTING SCHOOL TO CAREER

1. **Personal Qualities.** What do you think would be the most important personal quality of an EMT? Why?
2. **Technology.** What kinds of technology do you think EMTs use?

CHAPTER 18: Safety and Health **563**

Building Career Skills

Information. Emergency Medical Technicians need to know about first aid and rescue techniques to help people in need. They also need to know how to use certain medical equipment. EMT training programs are offered by universities and other organizations. Some people take such training to become rescue squad volunteers. Anyone interested in obtaining more information about this career can find it in libraries, the Internet, or a bookstore.

FOCUS

MOTIVATOR

Ask students to think about the last time they were sick. Was it an illness they "caught" from someone else? **Ask:** Why do you think people should stay home from school or work when they are sick?

VOCABULARY ACTIVITY

Have students work in groups to create a crossword puzzle using the Key Terms. Have groups exchange puzzles and solve.

Preventing Illness and Caring for a Sick Child

It is never easy caring for a child who is ill. Normal routines are upset. The child may cry often, demand attention, and have a short temper. However, the attitude of the caregiver can be as important as the medical treatment in restoring good health.

KEY TERMS

allergy
antibodies
asthma
communicable diseases
contagious
immunize
vaccine

OBJECTIVES:

- Explain how health checkups and immunizations help prevent illness.
- Discuss what allergies are and how they can be treated.
- Give basic guidelines for caring for children who are ill.
- Discuss how to help a child who is hospitalized.

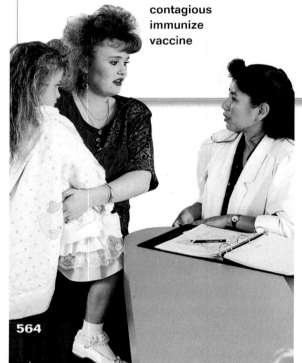

564

Regular Health Care

Children, like adults, should have regular medical checkups. These can often detect health problems in their early stages. Early treatment may prevent serious illness or serious damage to the child.

Newborns should be examined frequently during the first year. After the first year, healthy children need check-

Observing & Participating

Poll students to see who has had contact with a person who has had a lengthy illness. Ask: How did the illness interfere with that person's normal routine? Did it interfere with any other person's normal routine? Have students share their experiences about how long the illness lasted and how serious it was. Ask: How did the need to care for the person increase? How much more would that be the case if the ill person were a child? Why?

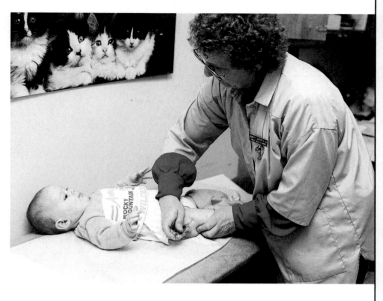
Immunizations have helped many youngsters lead healthier lives. *What diseases can be fought with vaccines?*

ups less frequently, but at least once a year. Because these checkups are so important, most cities have free or inexpensive clinics that provide good medical care.

Call the doctor's office if a child shows symptoms that concern you. In younger children, look for fever, lack of energy, prolonged diarrhea, constipation, vomiting, or difficulty in breathing. In older children, symptoms include fever, persistent cough, vomiting, severe headache, and dizziness.

Immunization

To **immunize** (IM-yuh-NIZE) is to protect a person against a particular disease. People can be protected from many **communicable diseases**—diseases that are easily passed from one person to another—by being immunized.

The most common way to immunize people against diseases is with vaccines. A **vaccine** (vak-SEEN) is a small amount of a disease-carrying germ introduced into the body so that the body can build resistance to the disease. After getting a vaccine, a person's body produces **antibodies** (AN-ta-BAHD-ees) that fight off the germs for that disease. If later exposed to the disease, the person already has antibodies that fight it.

That person will then either not get the disease or have only a very mild case of it.

The chart on page 566 shows what immunizations a child should receive and when. It's up to parents to be sure that children are given these immunizations at these times. They should keep a record of a child's immunizations.

Many states require immunizations for all school children. Many also require that children in a child care center be immunized. In fact, preschool children are most likely to develop complications from the diseases, so parents should not wait until elementary school starts to have their children immunized.

Some parents are afraid that a vaccine could hurt their child. In some extremely rare cases, a child does have a bad reaction to a vaccine. The chances of getting the disease are much, much higher, though.

CHAPTER 18: Safety and Health **565**

ACTIVITIES

Teamwork Activity

Have students work in pairs or small groups to devise a chart, or other method of record keeping, for a child's or family's schedule of immunizations and reactions to the vaccine, if any. **L1**

Language Arts Activity

Plagues, such as the Black Death during the Middle Ages, have at times wiped out a large portion of Earth's population. Students may enjoy reading *The Masque of the Red Death*, by Edgar Allan Poe. It recounts one man's effort to escape the plague. Have students who read this short story report to the class. **L3**

Critical Thinking Activity

Predicting Outcomes. **Ask:** Why might a doctor prefer to administer multiple doses of a vaccine to a child over a longer period of time rather than a single larger dose later in life? **L1**

VISUAL LEARNING — **Using the Chart** Have students focus on the chart. What are the youngest and oldest ages suggested for vaccines? At what age are most of the immunizations scheduled? Is there a pattern?

Schedule of Immunizations

Vaccine	Birth	1 mo.	2 mo.	4 mo.	6 mo.	1 yr.	15 mo.	18 mo.	4-6 yrs.	11-12 yrs.
Hepatitis B	1	2			3					
Hemophilias Influenzae Type b			1	2	3	4				
Diphtheria, Tenanus, Pertussis			1	2	3		4		5	6
Polio			1	2		3			4	
Pneumonia			1	2	3	4				
Measles, Mumps, Rubella						1			2	
Varicella (Chicken Pox)						1			2	
Hepatitis A									1	2

Note:

Hep A— Hepatitis A (2 doses at least 6 months apart; recommended in certain areas for children over 2 years)

Adapted from the Centers for Disease Control and American Academy of Pediatrics immunization schedules.

Timing for certain immunizations may vary according to doctor's advice. A short bar means the vaccine should be given at that age. The longer bar indicates an age range over which a vaccine can be given. The numbers inside the bars indicate the sequence in which the vaccine doses are given. Parents will need to provide documentation showing their children have received the necessary immunizations when enrolling at an early childhood center or school.

566 UNIT 6: Special Areas of Study

DID You Know?

Immunity and Allergies. The body protects itself against pathogens, including bacteria and many viruses, by creating antibodies when the pathogen enters the body. These antibodies remain in the body long after the infection has gone. If the person is exposed to the same pathogen again, the antibodies will fight off the invaders, making the person immune to the disease they cause. In allergic reactions, the immune mechanism "misfires," creating antibodies against substances that are not normally harmful, such as pollen.

Allergies

An **allergy** is an oversensitivity to one or more common substances. Individuals may have allergic reactions when they eat, breathe in, or touch specific substances, such as grass, molds, milk products, and pollens. Symptoms of allergic reactions may be mild, such as nonitching rash or a runny nose. Some allergic reactions, however, can threaten a person's life. Sometimes, for instance, the air sacs in the lungs can be constricted, which dangerously cuts the oxygen in the body.

Nearly half of all the children in the United States develop allergies. Specific allergies are not inherited, but the tendency to be allergic seems to be. If both parents have allergies, the child has a 70 percent chance of having at least one allergy.

Although allergies can't be cured, their effects are often preventable. For example, a child who is allergic to a specific food can avoid eating that food. Foods that commonly cause allergies in babies and children include milk, cereal grains, eggs, shellfish, nuts, fresh fruit juices, chocolate, and food additives.

A doctor may prescribe medication to help control an allergy. If the allergy causes severe problems, the child may be given a series of allergy tests to determine which specific substances are causing the problems. Then the child can be gradually desensitized to those substances.

Asthma

A growing health problem is **asthma** (AZ-muh). This condition affects the lungs, where air passages tighten, making it difficult to breathe. About 5 million children suffer from asthma.

Asthma attacks can be brought on by an allergic reaction. They may also be caused by a cold or flu. Cold air can bring on an attack, as can stress. Signs of an asthma attack include a tight feeling in the chest, a wheezing sound when the child breathes, and rapid breathing. The child may cough repeatedly but never be able to clear fluid out of the lungs.

Children with asthma can take medication to open their airways and breathe more easily. The medicine must be prescribed by a doctor. Children can be taught to take it when they need it. The doctor who examines the child can say whether or not the child needs to cut down on physical activities.

Asthma is a growing problem for children. **Can children with asthma still be active in sports?**

Allergies. The greatest single cause of chronic health problems among young children is allergies. Symptoms can range from the mildly annoying to the disabling and even life-threatening. In children, allergies often go hand in hand with asthma. As a rule, cases of asthma and asthmatic bronchitis contracted in childhood will lessen or dissipate by adulthood. In some children, a predisposition for asthma exists but remains dormant until adulthood.

Discussion Activity

Discuss with the class different allergies people suffer, the symptoms, and their severity. **Ask:** Why is it important to recognize and identify allergy symptoms, especially in the case of a child? If a food allergy is suspected, what steps can be taken to find out for sure? **L1**

Discussion Activity

Tell students to assume they have a child who has asthma. Attacks are triggered by an allergic reaction to dust mites. **Ask:** What changes will you have to make to make your child more comfortable? **L2**

Critical Thinking Activity

Making Decisions. Give students the following situation: "After a long night in the hospital with your sick child, the doctor tells you that your child has asthma triggered by cigarette smoke. Your child care provider, your aunt Linda, is a smoker. What would you do and why? **L2**

Housing and Health. Over 2.5 million families with children live in substandard housing. This is likely to increase as minimum-wage salaries grow more slowly than housing costs. Children in these families are more likely to suffer from asthma, lead-poisoning, and other long-term health problems.

COMPREHENSION CHECK

1. What is one way an infant or young child may communicate an earache? (*The child may pull on the ear and cry.*)
2. How long can a person expect to suffer from the flu? (*A week.*)

ACTIVITIES

Discussion Activity

Discuss how keeping a child inside and quiet for a while may help recovery. **L1**

VISUAL LEARNING **Using the Chart** Have students work in pairs or small groups. They will add a column titled *Immunization* to the chart. Students will need to find out how the vaccine is administered, at what age or ages, and whether or not it needs to be re-administered.

The Developing Brain

The Healing Power of Humor

Endorphins are produced in the brain. They are known as anti-stress hormones that relieve pain naturally and also make many of our organs healthy. Because they produce a euphoric effect on the brain, some people associate them with laughter, which in turn is then accredited with speeding up the healing process.

▶ Identifying and Treating Diseases

DISEASE	SIGNS	TREATMENT
Chicken Pox	A rash of tiny red, raised pimples or blisters appears first. It may cover the entire body. In a day or two, scabs form which fall off in 7 to 10 days. Fever is either absent or no higher than 102°F (39°C). Rash is irritating but child usually does not feel ill otherwise.	Rest in bed during feverish stage. Give acetaminophen to relieve fever, *but do not use aspirin*. Keep the child cool in loose clothing. Use powder or calamine lotion to relieve the itching. Recovery is usually within 7 days. Once scabs form, and no new pox have appeared for 2 days, the disease is no longer infectious.
Common Cold	Runny nose, sneezing or coughing, a mild fever of 101°to 102°F (38.3-38.9° C), lower appetite, and a sore throat.	Give the child plenty of rest and lots of liquids. Give acetaminophen to relieve fever. Don't give a cough or cold medicine to any child under three years of age unless approved by a doctor.
Ear Infection	An infant may pull at the ear and cry; an older child is likely to say that the ear hurts. There is usually a fever, which may go as high as 104°F (40°C).	The child needs to see a doctor, who may prescribe an antibiotic. You can use cool baths and acetaminophen to relieve the fever.
Influenza (Flu)	Sudden onset of fever, chills and shakes, tiredness, and aching muscles. After a few days, a sore throat and stuffy nose may appear. The disease may last as long as a week.	Give the child plenty of rest, lots of liquids, and extra food. Give acetaminophen to relieve fever.
Measles	Usually fever, sometimes as high as 105°F (41°C). The child may also have a cough, a runny nose, and inflamed, watery eyes. About 4 days later a blotchy, dusty-red rash appears, often seen first behind the ears or on the forehead and face. On day 6, the rash quickly fades and by day 7 all symptoms are gone.	The child should be under a doctor's supervision and kept in bed for the duration of the fever. The disease is most contagious during the few days before and after the rash appears. If the child's eyes are sensitive, keep him or her in a darkened room and do not allow reading or other close work.

Continued on next page

Medication. When caring for a child who is ill, it is vital to make sure the right medication is given at the correct time intervals and in the right dosage. Failure to do so could cause serious problems. Very young children cannot take medicine on their own, or may not be able to control a teaspoon for a liquid medicine dose. Two tools can help:
• Syringes are great for an infant who cannot yet drink from a cup. You just squirt the medicine in the back of the throat.
• Cylindrical dosing spoons are useful for children who spill when using a spoon.

DISEASE	SIGNS	TREATMENT
Mumps	Sudden fever, occasional nausea, abdominal pain, and swelling of one or more salivary glands, most commonly those located at the angles of the jaws. Swelling reaches maximum within 24 hours and may last 7 to 10 days. In boys, infection may also cause painful swelling in the testicles.	A hot water bottle and acetaminophen may ease pain. Fluids are easiest to swallow. Mumps is usually a mild disease, leaving no ill effects. However, sometimes deafness occurs.
Scarlet Fever and Streptococcal Sore Throat	Sudden onset, with headache, fever, sore throat. Lymph nodes usually enlarged. In scarlet fever a rash appears, usually within 24 hours, as fine red dots. The rash is seen first on the neck and upper part of the chest, and lasts 24 hours to 10 days. When it fades, the skin peels. The rash is the only sign that differentiates scarlet fever from strep throat.	A physician's care is needed. The child should rest in a warm, well-ventilated room. Patient usually recovers in a week, but watch for such complications as earache or inflamed neck glands.
Whooping Cough (Pertussis)	Begins with a cough that is worse at night. Symptoms may be mild at first. Characteristic "whooping" cough develops in about 2 weeks, and coughing spasms sometimes end with vomiting.	The child should take antibiotics under a doctor's care. Hospitalization is often required for infants. Rest is important, as is a diet that will not irritate the throat. Keep the child isolated from other children until antibiotics have been taken for at least 5 days.

Caring for a Sick Child

Children fall prey to illness from time to time. Caregivers need to recognize the signs of different illnesses. Of course, any caregiver who is unsure exactly what illness is bothering a child should talk to a medical professional. The child's doctor can also explain what treatment to offer the child.

Caring for a sick child often involves no more than keeping the child inside and quiet for a while. Often recovery takes only a few days. It may also be important to keep the child away from other children during the **contagious** period of illness. This is the time when a child can pass the germs on to someone else. A doctor can say how long the contagious period lasts.

CHAPTER 18: Safety and Health **569**

Discussion Activity

Discuss how many diseases on the chart share the same symptoms. What does that imply for caregivers? **L1**

Critical Thinking Activity

Analyzing. Give students the following situation: "Your child is ill. She has just come down with a cough, runny nose, and a fever." **Ask:** What would you do? **L1**

Teamwork Activity

Have students play a game of three-way-match. Have students copy each section of the chart onto separate index cards. Collect all the cards and then distribute them randomly to the class. Students must circulate among themselves trying to find their two matches. Take care to include the disease, signs, and treatment for each item to ensure complete matches. A disease can be used more than once if necessary. **L2**

ISSUES IN
CHILDREN'S HEALTH

When to Call the Doctor. The American Medical Association recommends that the doctor be called when the child has such symptoms as high fever; severe headaches; convulsions; loss of consciousness; paralysis of a part of the body; extreme tiredness or sleepiness; nasal fluid that is discolored or bloody; fluid discharged from the ear; red, watery eyes; diarrhea that is bloody; a cut or scrape that gives off pus.

ACTIVITIES

Discussion Activity

Have students brainstorm a list of quiet games and activities for children of different ages when they are ill. **L1**

Critical Thinking Activity

Hypothesizing. **Ask:** When a caregiver holds a sick baby, are there any risks for the caregiver? What steps can caregivers take to protect themselves? **L1**

Discussion Activity

Ask: Who should care for a sick child if both parents work? What factors influence the decision? **L1**

VISUAL LEARNING | **Using the Photograph**
Possible responses:
Because they are too young to understand what's happening to their bodies; because they can't use words to describe how they feel.

DID *You* **Know?**

Choosing Foods. A child who is constipated needs to eat less of foods that contribute to slow bowel movements, such as milk, cheese, and bananas, and more of high-fiber foods such as dried fruits, vegetables, and whole wheat breads and cereals. A child with diarrhea needs foods that are easy to digest such as bananas, rice, and potatoes. Giving water or flat (unbubbly) soda prevents dehydration.

Sometimes children need pain relief or a medicine to reduce fever. For children, doctors recommend using a medicine that contains the ingredient acetaminophen. Never give aspirin to a child with a fever. Although it happens only rarely, some children with a fever who take aspirin develop a serious illness called Reye syndrome. Also, be sure to use children's medicines, not products meant for adults.

Comforting a Sick Child

When a child is sick, try to maintain a calm and cheerful attitude. Treat the illness matter-of-factly. Remember, though, that from time to time the child may need some extra sympathy and love.

Children who are very ill don't have much energy for play. They spend most of the time sleeping. If children have only a mild illness or if they are recovering from a serious illness, however, they may be easily bored. Quiet play helps pass the time. Having a caregiver play along increases the child's fun!

Children of different ages have different needs during illness.

- **Infants.** Infants who are ill sleep much more than usual. They tend to be cranky and may want a lot of physical comforting. Gently rocking the baby, talking softly, singing, and holding the baby close (perhaps in a cloth carrier) can provide the needed comfort.
- **Ages one to three.** Young children are likely to need help keeping comfortable and occupied during an illness. Because children one to three are usually very physically active, staying in bed is difficult for them. The doctor will often allow a child who is warmly

Why is it more difficult to comfort very young children who are ill?

ISSUES IN TEEN PARENTING | A child who is ill can be difficult to manage, but when a teenage parent has to do it alone and juggle school and work too, that is even more difficult. Staying home every day the child is ill may not be an option for some teen parents. Some suggestions follow.

- Get your child immunized as early as possible to avoid some illnesses.
- Build a playgroup and support group who can help each other out in difficult times.

The school nurse may have information on where to find help.

Ask the Eperts

Dr. Van D. Stone
Pediatrician
Tupelo, Mississippi

NUTRITION *During Illness*

Q Can you give me any tips about feeding children who aren't feeling well?

By providing good nutrition during an illness, you can help a child feel more comfortable and often even encourage the child's recovery.

It's usually important to offer a sick child plenty of water and other liquids. The body needs fluids when fighting a fever, and liquids might be the only food that will stay down. A child with a fever should be encouraged to drink as much as possible.

However, if the child's stomach is upset, even water may cause vomiting. Offer very small, but frequent amounts of a commercially available rehydration fluid.

With some illnesses, the child's doctor may recommend a specific diet. In this case, of course, you should follow the doctor's suggestions as closely as possible. In all other cases, it's best simply to offer the sick child small amounts of regular foods. Remember, though, that it is never a good idea to force a child to eat.

In certain cases, a child's doctor may recommend a bland diet or a liquid diet. A bland diet consists of soft, smooth, mild-flavored foods, generally low in fat. If recommended, you might offer the child soups, hot cereals, puddings, gelatin, eggs, and mild cooked vegetables. A liquid diet provides foods in liquid form that can be more easily used by the body. If a pediatrician recommends a liquid diet, rehydration fluid can be used.

Thinking It Through

1. Should a sick child eat more, smaller meals, or fewer, larger meals? Why?
2. If the doctor recommends a bland diet, should a sick child be offered regular foods? Why or why not?

Ask the Eperts

Introducing the Feature

Good nutrition is vital to combating illness. Doctors recommend foods that are easy to digest. Foods can usually be grouped into three basic categories: liquids, bland, and regular. Prepare in advance a list of different kinds of foods, making sure to provide variety. On the chalkboard, have students group them according to the appropriate category.

Answers to Thinking It Through
1. *Possible response:* More frequent smaller meals will be easier to digest and help restore the child's energy.
2. *Possible response:* Only regular foods that are bland should be offered.

Applying What You've Learned

Have students work in pairs or small groups. Each group will make a chart listing symptoms, and recommended foods to eat. When finished, groups will compare charts and create a master list.

The Developing Brain

Television

It can be tempting to put a sick child in front of the television. Watching TV allows the child to be still, and entertaining programs can take the child's mind off the illness. Too much TV viewing, however, can produce lessened attention span, lack of motivation for learning, reduced creativity, and poorer thinking and problem-solving skills. The American Medical Association recommends one to two hours of television viewing per day.

ACTIVITIES

Discussion Activity

Discuss the value of a parent being with a child during the child's hospital stay. What effect on the child's feelings do you think the presence of a parent will have? **L1**

Critical Thinking Activity

Decision Making. Give students the following situation: "Your child needs to be admitted in the hospital. You think your child will be afraid. The hospital has given you the opportunity to visit the children's ward a few days prior to admittance. To do this, you would have to take a day off." What do you do and why? **L1**

Teamwork Activity

Have students work in pairs to prepare a list of questions to ask a hospital worker from the children's ward. They should include questions on ways the staff makes the children feel comfortable and not afraid. **L2**

If a child must be hospitalized, the doctor may suggest arranging a visit to the hospital beforehand to minimize fear.

dressed to play quietly around the house. Quiet play may include listening to stories, building with blocks, and playing simple games.

- **Ages four to twelve.** Preschoolers and school-age children can help care for themselves. They also have better verbal skills, meaning that they can more easily communicate how they feel. Children these ages can usually enjoy playing quietly with storybooks, stickers, puzzles, and games.

Going to the Hospital

A hospital stay is a difficult event for almost every child. Hospitalized youngsters may fear that their parents have abandoned them. They may be frightened that they will be hurt, or that they will die. Children have these fears because they don't understand what is happening to them.

A family that knows in advance that a child will be hospitalized can prepare the child for the event. The parents or doctor should explain to the child in simple words just what to expect. If possible, the parents should take the child to visit the hospital. Many hospitals have special tours that include a look in patient rooms and operating and recovery rooms. When the child is admitted, these things are already familiar—and less frightening.

The Hospital Stay

Hospitals realize that children recover better if a parent stays with them. Some

Parenting in *Action*

Children who are ill can be particularly cranky and fussy. When it comes to eating, the parent or caregiver must be creative, yet follow the guidelines set by the doctor. Liquid intake is very important when fighting a fever. As children sometimes will not be willing to drink as much as they should, it might be possible to convince them to eat a frozen pop. Homemade pops can be easily made by freezing juice in small plastic bags or ice cube trays.

move a cot into the child's room so that a parent can sleep nearby. Others have rooms with space for both child and parent. Even when there are no such arrangements, parents can often visit at any time. Of course, if the procedure the child needs is minor, he or she may have it done and go home the same day.

While in the hospital, a child often needs many tests and forms of treatment. When the child asks, "Will this hurt?" the parent should answer truthfully. Parents may be tempted to say, "Oh, no, this won't hurt." It is actually more helpful to the child to hear something more accurate, such as, "Yes, it will hurt for a while, but then you will feel much better. It is all right for you to cry when it hurts, if you feel like it."

If the child needs to go to the hospital for an emergency, it is important for a parent to stay with the child as much as possible. Being nearby can make a difficult situation less frightening to the child.

ASSESS

CHECKING COMPREHENSION

Have students answer the Check Your Understanding questions. Answers appear at the bottom of this page.

EVALUATION

Give students the Section 18-2 Quiz in the *Teacher Resource Guide.*

RETEACHING

1. Assign Reteaching Activities, page 53.
2. Have students list the benefits of regular health care.

ENRICHMENT

Have students research to learn more about how vaccines are developed or to learn how any one particular vaccine was created. Have them present their findings in a report.

EXTENSION

Invite a public health nurse to class to speak about local programs aimed at children who have to be hospitalized.

CLOSE

Have students create a list of the five most important health care steps they think parents can take.

SECTION 18-2 REVIEW

✔ Check Your Understanding

1. What diseases should a child be immunized against?
2. What is an allergy?
3. How does asthma affect a child? How is it treated?
4. What is the contagious period?
5. Why is physical comforting especially important for an infant who is ill?
6. Why is it particularly difficult to keep toddlers cheerful during illness?
7. What fears are common among young children who are hospitalized?

Putting Knowledge Into Practice

1. **Evaluating a Position.** Some parents fear the risks of giving their children a vaccine and don't have them immunized. What do you think of that practice?
2. **Applying.** Suppose you were caring for a sick two-year-old. Plan quiet activities for the child—enough to occupy an entire afternoon. What else would you expect to do with and for the child?
3. **Observing and Participating.** Write an account of a child's hospital stay from the perspective of the child. What would it feel like? How would the child react to being away from parents?

CHAPTER 18: Safety and Health **573**

ANSWERS TO SECTION 18-2 REVIEW

1. Hepatitis B; diphtheria, tetanus, pertussis; H. Influenzae; polio; measles, mumps, rubella; varicella.
2. An oversensitivity to common substances, such as grass, molds, and pollen.
3. Air passages in the lungs tighten. Medication opens airways.
4. The time when a person with a disease can pass the germs on to other people.
5. *Possible response:* They don't understand why they don't feel well.
6. They are normally very active.
7. That their parents have abandoned them; that they will be hurt or mutilated; that they will die.

Guide students to think about their own safety by posing questions such as: Would you be safe getting into a car with a stranger? Once students are focused on the dangers around them, remind them that children need to be taught how to recognize potentially dangerous situations and what to do to avoid them.

TEACH

ACTIVITIES

Discussion Activity

Encourage a discussion about why there is safety in numbers. Elicit descriptions of specific situations where children would be better off being in a group rather than alone. **L1**

Teamwork Actvity

Have students work in pairs or small groups to produce short skits representing situations where personal safety may be involved. The class will critique the skit and point out what actions kept the person safe, and which ones exposed him or her to danger. **L2**

Critical Thinking Activity

Making Inferences. Point out that many working parents have their children phone them at work when they get home from school. **Ask:** Why? **L1**

Parenting With Care

Teaching About Personal Safety

An important responsibility parents have is to teach children basic lessons of personal safety.

Without alarming children, parents should make clear that there are dangers in the world. Following safe practices can reduce the risk of those dangers touching the child.

Basic Safety Information
Each child should know the following information:
- His or her full name, address, and phone number, including the area code.
- The work number of any parents who work outside the home.
- The local number to call in the event of an emergency.
- How to recognize an emergency. To teach this, play the "What If?" game. Ask a child specific questions, such as: What would you do if you woke up at night and smelled smoke? What would you do if you heard scary noises outside your bedroom?
- If separated from a parent in a public place, such as a store or mall, go to a police officer or an employee and explain the problem.

Safety to and from School
To act safely as they go to and from school, children can follow these rules:
- Never go anywhere with a stranger.
- If approached in a threatening way, run in the opposite direction. If they are close to the home of a neighbor they know, go to that home for help.
- If the child walks to school, find the safest route and use it every day. Of course, the child should take care to cross streets only when it is safe. Usually crossing guards are posted to help children walk safely.
- It's safer to travel in numbers—not just to and from school, but anywhere. Parents may wish to ask an older child, either a sibling or a neighbor, to walk with a younger child.
- Avoid isolated or deserted areas.

574 UNIT 6: Special Areas of Study

RESOURCES ON SAFETY

Children are abducted and abused by strangers and estranged parents each day. Parents often worry about their child's safety in this regard. Teaching the child to recognize and avoid these situations is very important for his or her safety. Some parents, however, don't know how to approach the subject, and fear that such a discussion will frighten the child. Help is available. Run•Tell•Yell Ltd. offers workshops and lessons for private families and communities on ways to successfully avoid a potential problem. Contact them at: 1-888-543-7798.

- If traveling by bus, the child should enter and leave the bus only after it has reached a full stop. Don't do anything that might distract the bus driver during the trip.

When Alone at Home

Some children spend time home alone after school. They should follow these safety guidelines:

- Never enter the home if the door is ajar or a window is open or broken.
- Lock the door right after entering the house. Windows should be kept closed and locked as well.
- Check with the parent or a neighbor right after arriving home.
- Never open the door if a stranger comes.
- Never tell anyone at the door or on the phone that he or she is alone.

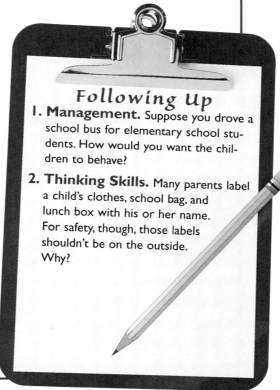

Following Up

1. **Management.** Suppose you drove a school bus for elementary school students. How would you want the children to behave?

2. **Thinking Skills.** Many parents label a child's clothes, school bag, and lunch box with his or her name. For safety, though, those labels shouldn't be on the outside. Why?

CHAPTER 18: Safety and Health **575**

Critical Thinking Activity

Making Inferences. What are the benefits of having your child walk the same route to and from school every day? **L1**

VISUAL LEARNING | **Using the Photographs** Have students look at the photographs on these two pages and describe how they demonstrate safe behavior.

CLOSE

1. Assign each team of students one age group: infants; ages one to three; ages four to six; ages seven to nine; and ages ten to twelve. Each team will draw up a list of personal safety topics for their age group. They will also include a method for teaching each topic.

2. **Extension.** Arrange for individual students or pairs to attend a child care center or a classroom. Students should note what safety and health rules have been established by the caregivers. Have them report their results to the class.

Answers to Following Up

1. *Possible response:* Stay in their seats while the bus is moving; no talking to the driver while the bus is moving; never throw anything inside or out of the bus; never put hands, arms, legs, or head outside of the bus while it is moving.
2. *Possible response:* A nametag on the outside could be read by a stranger who might use the information to fool the child into believing that he or she is someone who can be trusted.

CHECKING COMPREHENSION

Use the Summary and the Reviewing the Facts questions to help students go over the most important ideas in Chapter 18. Encourage students to ask questions and add details.

CHAPTER 18 REVIEW

Answers to Reviewing the Facts

1. *Cause:* Car accidents. *Prevention:* Using child safety seats and seat belts.
2. Teach the child the rules of safe eating; keep small objects out of the mouth.
3. Clean the area with soap and water. Apply antiseptic and cover with a clean bandage.
4. She may have taken poison.
5. Seek medical help immediately, keep the child lying down, and warm.
6. To detect problems early because early treatment can prevent serious illness or permanent damage.
7. Oversensitivity to common substances. *Treatment:* Avoid the substance, take prescribed medication.
8. A tight feeling in the chest; a wheezing sound when breathing; rapid breathing, a cough that doesn't clear fluid out of the lungs.
9. The child may develop Reye syndrome, a serious illness.

CHAPTER 18

REVIEW &

Summary

✔ It is much easier to prevent accidents than to handle the effects. (Section 18-1)

✔ The safety of the child is the most important responsibility of a caregiver. (Section 18-1)

✔ Emergencies must be dealt with quickly and calmly. (Section 18-1)

✔ Children should have regular checkups and should be immunized against certain diseases. (Section 18-2)

✔ The attitude of a caregiver toward a sick child can be as important as the care the child receives. (Section 18-2)

Reviewing the Facts

1. What is the leading cause of death among young children? How can it be prevented? (Section 18-1)

2. How would you try to protect a toddler from choking? (Section 18-1)

3. How would you treat a child who has a small cut? (Section 18-1)

4. Angela is having difficulty breathing, is vomiting, has a fever, and complains that her throat hurts. Nearby is an empty bottle of a liquid cleaner. What may have happened? (Section 18-1)

5. What should you do if a child seems to be in shock? (Section 18-1)

6. Why should children have regular medical checkups? (Section 18-2)

7. What is an allergy? How is it treated? (Section 18-2)

8. What are the signs of an asthma attack? (Section 18-2)

9. What is the danger of giving aspirin to a child with a fever? (Section 18-2)

Thinking Critically

1. **Sequencing.** Write the steps for rescuing an infant and a small child who is choking. Put each step on an index card. Use two separate sets of cards for the two different processes. Don't number the steps. Then shuffle the cards and give them to a partner. Have him or her put them in the correct order. When finished, your partner should do the same for you.

2. **Analyzing.** Why do you think people have to take special courses to learn CPR?

Taking Action

1. **Practicing a Rescue.** Using a large doll, practice artificial respiration for an infant. *(Leadership)*

2. **Categorizing.** With the class, brainstorm a list of ideas of activities that could be used with children who are ill. Write the ideas down as they are mentioned. When the list is complete, organize the ideas according to their appropriateness for children of different ages. *(Thinking Skills)*

CONNECTIONS

Cross-Curricular Connections

1. **Art.** Design and make a poster to increase parents' awareness of one aspect of child safety. If possible, display your poster in an area where parents are likely to read it.
2. **Language Arts.** Write a public service announcement that explains to child care workers the five basic guidelines for handling emergencies.

Workplace Connections

1. **Resources.** Develop a list of first aid supplies you think a child care center should have. Exchange lists with a classmate. Indicate on your classmates' list the situation for which each supply could be used.
2. **Information Systems.** Working with a partner, draw up a list of rules that you think a hospital should establish for children who are hospitalized.
3. **Thinking Skills.** Make a list of ways child care workers can protect themselves from on-the-job hazards. Which emergency situations carry the greatest risks? How can those risks be minimized? Should a parent take the same precautions?

Family and Community Connections

1. **Finding Emergency Numbers.** Make a list of emergency numbers for your family. Post it near each phone at home.
2. **Protecting Against Fires.** Design an escape plan that your family can use in case of a fire in your home.

Technology Connections

1. **Genetics.** Researchers are trying to find new ways of developing vaccines by using genes. Find out about this research and report to the class. Does this approach raise any ethical issues?
2. **Internet.** The Red Cross does more than run safety and first aid training. Use the Internet to find out what else the organization does and report to the class about it. How effective does this program seem to be?

EVALUATION

1. Use the Reproducible Chapter 18 Test in the *Teacher Resources Guide,* or construct your own test using the **Exam***View*® Test Generator.
2. For an alternative assessment, assign the Chapter 18 activity in the *Authentic Assessment* section of the *Teacher Resource Guide.*

ENRICHMENT

Assign students either of the two enrichment activities in the *Enrichment Activities* booklet in the *Student Motivation Kit.*

EXTENSION

Invite a health care professional to the class to discuss the personal qualities and training needed for that career. Have students prepare questions for the visitor in advance.

CLOSE

Have students organize a display on children's health and safety. They might make a first aid kit; create a poster on choking, hazards, and first aid; make a brochure about common household poisons or safety hazards; or create a public service announcement about immunizations.

CHAPTER 19 RESOURCES
Teacher Resource Guide
• Chapter 19 Test, p. 211
• Authentic Assessment, p. 293
Student Motivation Kit
• Observations, pp. 63-64
Transparency Package
• CT-53, CT-54
  (Also on CD-ROM)
Effective Instruction CD-ROM

CHAPTER 19 OVERVIEW

In **Section 19-1**, students examine the physical, mental, and emotional needs of children with disabilities.

In **Section 19-2**, students explore and recognize the severe and long-term effects of child abuse.

In **Section 19-3**, students learn that family stress situations affect children in profound ways.

CHAPTER 19 OBJECTIVES

After completing Chapter 19, students will be able to:

• Describe the needs of children with physical, mental, and emotional handicaps.
• Tell how parents and caregivers can assist and encourage children with disabilities.
• Explain what *child abuse* is and how to report it.
• Give strategies to help children handle various family stresses.

CHAPTER 19

Special Challenges for Children

578 UNIT 6: Special Areas of Study

RESOURCES TO EXPLORE

The National Down Syndrome Society (NDSS) supports research of Down syndrome and related illnesses, promotes public awareness, and provides services to affected families and individuals. Additionally, the society publishes a fact sheet entitled "Down Syndrome: Facts and Myths." For more information, write National Down Syndrome Society, 666 Broadway Street, 8th floor, New York, NY 10012. The society's Website is www.ndss.org

Florinda and Silvio Sanchez hurried to the first meeting of a group of parents of infants with Down syndrome. They were scheduled to talk to the group that evening.

After they had been introduced, Florinda said, "When I look at all of you, I see Silvio and myself sitting there just a few years ago. When you have a baby with Down syndrome, it seems like your world has shattered. I want you to know, though, that your outlook will change—now I laugh much more often than I cry. Our son Luis has made us a happier family."

Silvio continued, "Florinda and I have been actively involved in a local organization for mentally disabled persons. At first, we attended meetings because we needed information and we needed to talk to other parents in the same boat. We've become more involved because we enjoy it—and because we want to help other parents."

"Luis is such a lovable child," Florinda said. "We don't know just how much independence he'll be capable of as an adult. Right now, though, each of his achievements is cause for celebration."

" 'Our son Luis has made us a happier family.' "

- Ask students to identify circumstances of life that pose a challenge to children, such as having disabilities, abuse, or the divorce or death of parents. Have them suggest ways that children might be helped to cope with crisis situations.
- Have students look at the photograph in the student book. Point out that the picture shows a parent talking to another group of parents about her child, who has a disability. **Ask:** How can sharing information and experiences make it easier for people to cope with situations like this?

USING THE SCENARIO Have students read the story on this page of the student text. **Ask:** How can a child with a disability bring a family closer together?

KEY TO ABILITY LEVELS Each section gives skill-building activities. Each activity has been labeled for use with students of various learning styles and abilities.

L1 Level 1 activities are basic activities and should be within the range of all students.

L2 Level 2 activities are average activities and should be within the range of average and above average students.

L3 Level 3 activities are challenging activities designed for the ability range of above average students.

SECTION 19-1

Exceptional Children

(pages 580-587)

SECTION 19-1 RESOURCES

Teacher Resource Guide
- Lesson Plan Organizer, p. 80
- Section 19-1 Quiz, p. 208

Student Motivation Kit
- Reteaching Activity, p. 54
- Nurturing Brain Development, pp. 54-57

Student Workbook
- Study Guide, pp. 155-158
- Living with Children with Disabilities, p. 159

Transparency Package
- CT-53 Parenting Children with Disabilities

Effective Instruction CD-ROM

FOCUS

MOTIVATOR

Ask students if they have ever been concerned about a blemish or a scar. Encourage them to share and discuss their own experiences. **Ask:** What might a person with a physical disability say about such concerns?

VOCABULARY ACTIVITY

Ask students what support groups they are familiar with. Use the local yellow pages to locate specific groups in your area.

Exceptional Children

In the past, babies with disabilities often died at birth or soon after. Today medical science saves the lives of many of these children. With treatment many disabilities can be made less severe. Children can be taught to compensate for their disabilities. With proper care and treatment, disabled children can usually lead happy, productive lives.

KEY TERMS

behavioral therapist
inclusion
support group

OBJECTIVES:
- Describe the needs of children with physical, mental, and emotional disabilities.
- Develop strategies caregivers can use to help disabled children.

Children with Disabilities

The attitude of parents toward a child with a disability shapes that child's future. Parents can help the child become as independent as possible and accept the limitations that cannot be overcome. Parents who pity, resent, or overprotect a child with disabilities hinder his or her emotional and social development. The child may become angry and self-pitying and have difficulty living in society. A

Observing & Participating

To help students see how regular classrooms can be adapted to meet the needs of disabled children, have the class brainstorm a list of challenges that students with physical, mental, or emotional disabilities may face in a classroom setting. Write the suggestions on the chalkboard. Then create a second list of how teachers can adapt classroom activities or lessons to accommodate the needs of all students. Third, list the special-needs programs available at your school.

child with a positive attitude avoids these problems.

Many states require that public schools provide programs for disabled children and their parents. These programs may start right after the child's birth. Some states give children who have disabilities the chance to go to preschool.

Not all children with disabilities need to be in special programs. Many children do best when placed in regular classrooms. Both the children with disabilities and those without benefit. This approach, called **inclusion**, provides an opportunity for all the children to grow intellectually, develop social skills, and build empathy.

Practicing Parenting

Children's and Parents' Rights

In 1997, Congress passed and the President signed into law a new version of the Individuals with Disabilities Education Act (IDEA). The new law made several changes to the education of children with disabilities:

❤ Children have a right to a free public education that meets their needs.

❤ Parents must be notified if a school system plans to evaluate a child or change the child's school arrangement.

❤ Parents have the right to request that the school evaluate a child.

❤ Schools must ask parents to sign a form giving their consent to the initial plan for placing the child.

❤ Children must be retested every three years at least and their school situation must be reviewed at least every year.

❤ Children can be tested in the language they know best. Parents must be spoken to in the language they know best.

❤ Parents can request to see the child's school records.

❤ The school must draw up an educational program specifically for the child, and parents can take part in the process of developing that plan.

❤ Schools must make every effort to put the child, as much as possible, in a classroom with children who are not disabled.

APPLY YOUR KNOWLEDGE

1. What rights do parents have as a result of IDEA?
2. Why should the child's educational program be reviewed each year?
3. Why test the child in the language he or she knows best?

COMPREHENSION CHECK

1. Why do parents' attitudes to children with disabilities matter so much? (*They affect the child's potential to develop.*)
2. How does placing a disabled child in a regular classroom help all children in the class? (*Provides opportunity for intellectual growth, social development, and empathy skills.*)

ACTIVITIES

Discussion Activity

Exceptional children and their families need support from people they know. Have students discuss ways that others can provide that support. **L1**

Practicing Parenting

Ask: Why does Congress pass laws establishing civil rights for certain groups of people?

Answers to Apply Your Knowledge

1. *Students' responses should encompass the rights described in the feature.*
2. *Possible response:* to regularly check on how the plan meets the child's needs
3. *Possible response:* so the child has the opportunity to communicate in a familiar way.

Parenting in Action

Children with disabilities, like all children, need to feel loved and accepted. Parents need to find ways to keep such children involved in the family's life, through doing daily chores, going on special outings, and participating in fun activities. This also helps siblings who are without disabilities learn to be more tolerant. Correctly guided, children will learn to value how much people are alike, not how much they are different.

COMPREHENSION CHECK

1. When should parents seek a diagnosis of a child they suspect might be handicapped? (*As soon as possible.*)
2. What are the keys to helping a child gain independence? (*Special exercises, special equipment, understanding, and patience.*)

ACTIVITIES

Critical Thinking Activity

Comparing. Ask students to analyze the difference between having a physical handicap at birth and acquiring one later in childhood. How will adjustments be different for the child? For the family? **L1**

Discussion Activity

Have students brainstorm a list of movies they have seen or books they have read about people with disabilities. Ask them to describe the work, particularly how the person overcame adversity. **L2**

Discussion Activity

When a child with a physical disability is born, the baby may need lengthy hospitalization. **Ask:** How might this separation affect the interaction and bonding that takes place between a parent and child? **L1**

Special preschool programs give children with disabilities a chance to be with other children. *What law sets the rules for educating these children?*

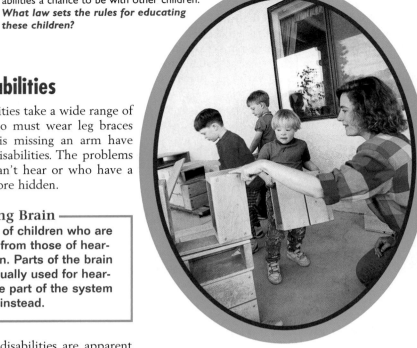

Physical Disabilities

Physical disabilities take a wide range of forms. A child who must wear leg braces and a child who is missing an arm have obvious physical disabilities. The problems of children who can't hear or who have a heart defect are more hidden.

The Developing Brain

The brains of children who are deaf differ from those of hearing children. Parts of the brain that are usually used for hearing become part of the system for seeing instead.

Some physical disabilities are apparent at birth, but others may not be revealed for months or years. Parents should seek a complete diagnosis as soon as they suspect that their child has a physical disability. If it is true, the child should begin treatment as soon as possible. Early diagnosis and treatment helps children reach their potential.

Each child with a physical disability has the need for individual care. Routines that others take for granted can be difficult or even impossible. For example, a three-year-old with poor coordination may be unable to dress or eat without help.

Special exercises, special equipment, understanding, and patience are the keys to helping children with physical disabilities learn to be independent. Sometimes surgery can help. Independence is essential, not only for the child's future but also for developing a positive self-concept. Self-care skills such as eating, dressing, bathing, and using the toilet are fundamental to this independence.

Learning Self-Care

Bathing is a good example of a self-care skill. A child should be encouraged to handle as much of the task as possible.

Begin by making sure the child feels secure during the bath. This can mean putting a nonskid mat on the bottom of the tub or installing rails on the sides of the tub. Some youngsters need an inner tube or inflated cushion to keep their head above water. For those who cannot sit indepen-

582 UNIT 6: Special Areas of Study

VISUAL LEARNING | Using the Photograph *Answer:* IDEA (Individuals with Disabilities Education Act).

LEARNING STYLES | **Kinesthetic**
Give students a chance to experience what it's like to be disabled.

Vision: Blindfold students. Have them leave the classroom and then return. Then have them pick up and manipulate objects.

Hearing: Have students put cotton balls or ear plugs in their ears.

Physical skills: Have students use a walker or crutches.

Ask students how they felt during the experience.

dently, the water level must be kept very low for safety.

Most children can perform some aspect of washing themselves. Children who have less coordination might participate by splashing water on themselves. Others might use a washcloth made into a mitt, which is easier to handle and less likely to be lost in the water. They can dry off using a towel with a hole cut in the middle. The child can slip the towel over the head to simplify the process of drying.

Parents and others who care for physically disabled children may need to develop similar adaptations for eating and other routine activities. Some children may need special help with only a few tasks. Others may need many adaptations because their physical skills are more limited.

Mental Disabilities

Children with mental disabilities do show some thinking skills. Their rate of development is slower than is typically the case, however, and it stops at a lower level. There are many degrees of mental disabilities. Some children simply have a harder time with normal tasks. Others may never progress past the mental abilities of babies.

Medical professionals can usually diagnose mental retardation early. They can offer some ideas about the child's learning potential, but they can't be exact. This is difficult to predict. Education and treatment must begin early to achieve the best possible results. Often doctors suggest special programs for these children.

Children with mental disabilities learn and respond best when they know what to expect. Directions for these children should be simple and direct. Showing the child what needs to be done and repeating the directions many times is usually the best way to teach.

The goal for children with mental disabilities is to help them become as independent as possible. Many can learn living and job skills that enable them to live alone or in a group home, support themselves, and perhaps marry and raise a family. Some depend totally on others their entire lives.

Some children with physical disabilities have a series of exercises they must do every day. *How do these exercises benefit the child?*

Ask the Eperts

Introducing the Feature

Explain to students that there are no easy answers when it comes to determining if your baby is behaving as most babies should. There is no set time—in terms of a definitive number of months and days—at which developmental activities should occur. Rather, there are ranges of time during which people master developmental tasks. Being overly sensitive to individual differences in development may cause parents concern.

Answers to Thinking It Through

1. *Possible response:* The use of language is often the first sign of complex mental activity.
2. *Possible response:* The pediatrician knows the child and has access to other health care experts.

Applying What You've Learned

Have students work in three groups: birth to one year; one to two years; two to three years. Have each group identify those developmental tasks that they think are most important for children of that age as a sign of normal development. Have each group report to the class and discuss their list.

Ask the Eperts

Jacqueline Mault
Director of Special Services for the Toppenish School District in Toppenish, Washington

IDENTIFYING *Children with Mental Disabilities*

Q How are children with mental disabilities identified?

A In many cases, parents are the first to suggest that a child has a mental disability. Usually, this is because they have noticed a delay in the child's development in certain areas. Often there are no signs until several months into the child's life. Physical development can proceed normally without there being any signs of problems with mental development. Many times, it is delays in language development that suggest to parents there may be a problem.

Usually, parents ask the child's pediatrician about their concerns. The doctor can comment on whether there does seem to be a delay in the child's acquisition of skills. He or she may not recommend any immediate action, however. If the delay is only slight, the doctor may feel that it is best to give the child a little more time.

Once the doctor feels that it is appropriate, he or she will suggest that the child be taken to a specialist in child development. That professional will give the child a series of tests.

The child's performance on the tests should identify whether he or she is mentally retarded. They should also show the child's strengths and weaknesses.

The tests will suggest how severe the child's problem is. It will also give hints as to what might be expected of the child's development in the future. These are only clues, though. It is impossible to make fully accurate predictions. With time and effort, with the help of professionals, and with the cooperation and dedication of parents, children can learn to master skills.

Thinking It Through

1. Why would language development often be a sign of mental disabilities?
2. Why do you think most parents take their concerns to a pediatrician?

584 UNIT 6: Special Areas of Study

Parenting in *Action*

Parents can help a disabled child make a successful transition to school by communicating frankly and openly with school personnel. It is also a good idea for the parents to visit the school with the child and help him or her become acquainted and comfortable with the new setting. At home parents can reinforce the skills learned at school and provide the child with opportunities to learn increased independence.

Being accepted by others is important for people with mental retardation. Children with mental disabilities should be taught grooming, manners, and acceptable social behavior. Learning these skills increases acceptance.

Emotional Disabilities

How can parents know when their child is emotionally troubled or needs professional help? The child's behavior is the best indication, but there is no clear-cut line between typical behavior and disturbed behavior. Some troublesome behavior may be a part of a normal stage of development. Sometimes, though, a child's behavior prevents typical development or disturbs the lives of family members. In those cases, parents should try to find out if the child has an emotional problem. Early intervention can help minimize problems.

Behavior that suggests an emotional disability usually becomes more noticeable and more disturbing over time. For example, at age two, Terry began to rock in his crib and bang his head over and over against the headboard. He resisted toilet training and had frequent toileting accidents. He stuttered. Terry's parents hoped that after starting school, Terry would improve.

In school, though, Terry fought with other children and upset classes with loud outbursts. The school suggested that he have a psychological evaluation. It indicated that Terry needed therapy.

Even when a child's behavior shows a pattern that suggests emotional problems exist—as Terry's did—parents may be reluctant to ask for help. They may be ashamed to admit they can't handle the problem themselves. For the sake of the child—and the rest of the family—they need to get help.

What to Do?

When a child does need help, parents need to find a **behavioral therapist**, a professional trained in helping people work through emotional problems. Pediatricians,

Where can parents go for help if they have a child with emotional disabilities?

CHAPTER 19: Special Challenges for Children **585**

COMPREHENSION CHECK

1. Why are parents reluctant to seek help when they suspect their child may have emotional problems? (*They don't want to admit their child has emotional problems.*)

ACTIVITIES

Social Studies Activity

Have students investigate how the treatment of children with disabilities has changed over the years. Have students develop a chart or time line to illustrate these changes. **L3**

VISUAL LEARNING | Using the Photograph
Possible responses: Psychologist, counselor, teacher, therapist.

The Developing Brain

Autism

Using brain imaging technology, scientists have identified regions of the brain that are abnormally small in children with autism. This finding, from research at Johns Hopkins University, is the result of imaging done on a pair of identical twin boys. The study suggested that family members of autistic children may have a milder form of the condition due to similar abnormal genes.

ISSUES IN CHILDREN'S HEALTH

Pets. Studies have shown that children can benefit from having a pet. New research suggests that pets may be even more important for children with emotional problems. In one study of the children with emotional disturbances, half of the children attended standard therapeutic activity groups. The other half played with a dog during therapy sessions. Those who received the pet therapy increased their ability to control impulses and understand others.

ACTIVITIES

Critical Thinking Activity

Making Inferences. Have students imagine that they are the parent of a six-year-old boy. Friends have a little boy who is mentally disabled. How would they prepare their son for the arrival of the mentally disabled boy for a visit? **L2**

Teamwork Activity

Have students work in small groups to write case studies that describe the emotional behavior of children. Each case study should focus on behavior that is either normal or disturbed. Have the groups exchange case studies and then analyze them to determine whether they think the behavior depicted shows normal or disturbed behavior. Have the groups read the case studies to the class and explain their analysis. **L3**

VISUAL LEARNING | Using the Photograph
Possible response: Neglecting other children.

---

school counselors, members of the clergy, or a local office of the Mental Health Association can suggest therapists to contact. Parents should take the time to select someone they trust and with whom they feel comfortable.

The therapist will ask for background information on the problem behaviors, get to know the entire family better, and observe the child in various situations. Then he or she will plan treatment for the child. The treatment may involve making a few changes in the ways family members interact. For example, the therapist might suggest that the parents spend individual time with the child each day or that the child be introduced to a special activity, such as gymnastics or music.

The therapist may find that emotional problems have physical causes. If so, the therapist may recommend that the child be examined by a doctor.

Often the therapist works directly with the child—and sometimes with other family members—to improve the child's self-concept and self-esteem. Therapy can change the way children view themselves and, as a result, the way they behave.

The results of therapy depend to a great extent on the child's parents. They must believe in and support the therapist's work. They must be available to listen and talk when the child is ready. They need to accept the changes that result from the therapy. Sharing the children's personal feelings, learning to understand them, and accepting children for who and what they are—not what parents expect them to be—all help children overcome their problems.

Raising a Child with Disabilities

The responsibilities and demands of raising a child with a disability can seem overwhelming. In accepting that their child has a disability, parents may feel guilt, sadness, anger, and frustration.

Children with disabilities are still children. They need to know they have their parents' love. *Since children with disabilities require a great deal of attention, what do parents of more than one child have to be careful about?*

DID *You* **Know?**

Depression. Scientists' findings show that children as young as five may become depressed, and that children's depression may last for several years. Depression is marked by thoughts of low self-worth, hopelessness, and helplessness. A study found that girls were more likely than boys to discuss their feelings. As a result, they were also more likely to get help.

They can get help for themselves in **support groups.** In these groups, parents get together with other parents of disabled children to share comfort, advice, and solutions to everyday problems. In addition, groups can keep members up-to-date on research and treatment options.

Support groups can also help parents find tools to meet the emotional needs of their children. Children who receive emotional support have a strong sense of self—positive self-esteem. This gives them the inner strength, patience, and courage they need to cope with their disabilities.

Children with disabilities can bring as much joy to a family as children without disabilities. Like others, children with disabilities give family members a chance to love and be loved, to give, to receive, and to share.

SECTION 19-1 REVIEW

✔ Check Your Understanding

1. How can parents' attitudes affect children with disabilities?
2. How do children without disabilities benefit when children who have disabilities are placed in regular classes?
3. Why is it especially important to encourage independence for children with physical disabilities?
4. Why should children with mental disabilities be trained in grooming, manners, and acceptable social behavior?
5. What signs suggest that a child may have an emotional disturbance?
6. How do self-concept and self-esteem enter into therapy for emotional disabilities?
7. How can support groups help parents of children with disabilities?

Putting Knowledge Into Practice

1. **Making Inferences.** Many children born with disabilities must remain in the hospital for the first weeks—or even months—of their life. How might this long period of separation affect the baby and the parents? What could the parents do?
2. **Observing and Participating.** Visit a preschool class in which some students are disabled and others are not. Describe how much the disabled children seem to be integrated into the classroom activities. What evidence do you see that all the children are learning empathy?

CHAPTER 19: Special Challenges for Children **587**

ANSWERS TO SECTION 19-1 REVIEW

1. *Possible response:* If parents are overprotective, he or she may become self-pitying. If they are supportive, the child's attitude will be positive.
2. They grow intellectually, develop social skills, and build empathy.
3. Helps develop positive self-concept.
4. More likely to gain others' acceptance.
5. Behavior becomes worse over time.
6. Therapy changes self-concept and self-esteem, and so the child's behavior.
7. Give parents a chance to explore feelings, share with others.

CAREER OPPORTUNITIES

Introducing the Feature

Ask students if they or someone they know has ever undergone physical therapy. Ask them to relate their experiences, such as the length of time in therapy, the type of exercises, and the results. Ask the class to brainstorm situations that might call for physical therapy.

Answers to CONNECTING SCHOOL TO CAREER

1. **Possible response:** They could use a stationary bike or an inclined walker to help a patient relearn how to walk.

2. **Possible response:** It could make demand go up because older people are more likely to develop medical conditions which benefit from physical therapy.

Applying What You've Learned

Ask students to list the pros and cons of this career in terms of what they are looking for in a career. What do they like? Dislike? Do they have the skills and attributes they need to carry out the duties of a physical therapist?

CAREER OPPORTUNITIES

Physical Therapist

A CONVERSATION WITH ALICIA WAGNER

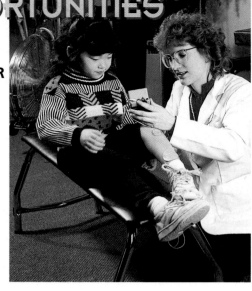

How did you become interested in becoming a physical therapist? I got hurt playing ball in high school, and a physical therapist helped me recover. We talked a lot while he worked with me. I realized that this could be a great career.

What are the tasks and responsibilities of a physical therapist? We try to help people recover the ability to use their bodies, which they've lost to an extent because of illness, or injury. We also help children with problems caused by some birth defects. To do this, we use massage, and exercise equipment like a stationary bike. We teach some patients how to use canes or walkers or artificial limbs.

What is the work environment like? I work mainly with children. Other therapists work in hospitals, sports medicine centers, or nursing homes.

What are the working hours like? I work forty hours a week.

What aptitudes are needed to be a physical therapist? Therapists have to be able to explain things clearly so that patients know what to do. They need to be very encouraging. With children, I try to make the exercises into games. Sometimes patients become frustrated when they don't make progress as rapidly as they'd like to. Therapists also need good writing skills because they have to write reports. They need to be fairly strong—sometimes it's necessary to lift patients.

Career Facts

PHYSICAL THERAPIST

Education and Training. Therapists need a bachelor's degree in physical therapy. They must also pass a licensing test to practice as a therapist.

Career Outlook. The demand for physical therapists is expected to grow much faster than average in the future.

┌─ CONNECTING SCHOOL TO CAREER ─┐

1. **Technology.** How might a physical therapist use exercise equipment?
2. **Thinking Skills.** How would the fact that the population is growing older affect the demand for physical therapists? Why?

588 UNIT 6: Special Areas of Study

Building Career Skills

Interpersonal Skills. Have the class brainstorm various situations requiring oral communication by a physical therapist. Suggest that not everyone is a cooperative patient. Divide the class into groups and have each group develop one of the situations by writing dialogue and then putting on a skit for the rest of the class. Have the class evaluate skills used and suggest alternatives.

Child Abuse and Neglect

Millions of children suffer from **child abuse** and neglect, also known as child maltreatment. The effects are long lasting. Abuse can affect the physical, emotional, mental, and social health of its victims throughout their lifetime.

KEY TERMS

child abuse
crisis nurseries
mandated reporters

OBJECTIVES:

- Explain what child abuse is and analyze why it happens.
- Discuss what can be done to prevent child abuse.
- Describe how to report suspected child maltreatment.

Types of Maltreatment

Approximately 3 million reports of suspected child abuse and neglect are made to state agencies yearly. Child maltreatment is defined by the Federal Child Abuse Prevention and Treatment Act (CAPTA). Each state, within its civil and criminal laws, has its own definitions of child abuse and neglect. Children of all ages are at risk, but those under age six are especially vulnerable.

CHAPTER 19: Special Challenges for Children **589**

Observing & Participating

Tell students to imagine they work in a setting where they interact with many young children, such as a child care center or a park district program. They suspect one of the children is being abused. Have students form pairs to discuss what next steps they will take, keeping in mind they need to be honest about suspicions but recognize they don't know all the details of the situation.

FOCUS

MOTIVATOR

Write the term *child abuse* on the board. Encourage students to discuss the reasons such incidents occur. Explain that parents may suffer emotional disabilities or be under extreme stress and that child abusers come from all groups.

VOCABULARY ACTIVITY

Ask students to define the word *crisis.* Explain that crisis nurseries are child care facilities where troubled parents can leave their children for a short time.

ACTIVITIES

Discussion Activity

Ask students to identify which type of child abuse might be the hardest to detect. Why? **L2**

Discussion Activity

Even when maltreatment is severe, it is common for abused children to continue to try to please their parents. Have students offer opinions on why children would respond in this manner. **L2**

Critical Thinking Activity

Evaluate. **Ask:** If abusive parents are criticized by other parents because their children do not behave, could this provoke an incident of abuse? **L2**

Critical Thinking Activity

Compare. Ask students to describe the difference between physical punishment and physical abuse. **L2**

VISUAL LEARNING	Using the Photograph

Possible response: Holding reassures the infant and builds trust, which fosters development.

INFOLINK

Physical Abuse

For information about *shaken baby syndrome,* see Chapter 8, page 270.

Regardless of how a specific state defines child abuse, there are four major types.

- **Physical abuse.** Injury caused by such mistreatment as shaking, burns, bites, or scalding water.
- **Neglect.** Failing to provide basic needs, such as food, clothing, shelter, health care, and education.
- **Sexual abuse.** This type of abuse ranges from fondling a child to pornography.
- **Emotional abuse.** Placing unreasonable or excessive demands on a child. Includes teasing and belittling a child and bizarre forms of punishment. Some children are deprived of the love they need for normal emotional development.

Child neglect is the most common form of abuse. Physical abuse occurs in about a quarter of the substantiated cases. More than ten percent involve sexual abuse.

Maltreatment typically involves a pattern of behavior. The longer it continues, the more serious the problem becomes. Health outcomes can range from poor growth and retardation to brain damage and mental health disorders. Hopelessness, depression, low self-esteem, and antisocial behavior are common among abused children.

Who Are Child Abusers?

Most child abusers are not monsters. They are ordinary people, usually parents or other relatives of the child, who don't intend harm. They are caught, however, in emotional situations that they can't handle.

Many abusive parents feel that comforting a baby who is upset will spoil the infant. *How does an infant benefit by being held?*

They are often people who feel lonely and can't cope with their own personal problems. They typically have low self-esteem. In many cases, they were themselves abused as children. When abuse is the only kind of parenting they have known, they repeat the behavior with their own children.

Child abusers come from all income levels, ethnic groups, and religions. Often, only one parent in a family actively abuses the children. However, the other parent may play a role by refusing to recognize it.

Why Does Abuse Happen?

Parents who abuse their children are usually easily provoked and unable to maintain self-control. When they are irritated, they respond quickly and violently, much as a young child does. A three-year-old who is angry responds without thought. The child may kick the cat, smash a toy truck, or

---

LEARNING STYLES	**Interpersonal**

Have students work in small groups to write suggestions on what they would do in the following situations:

- You observe your neighbor in the yard yanking on her child and telling him

how stupid and clumsy he is. This is a common scene with them.

- Your best friend often wears long sleeves in hot weather and will not explain bruises that she routinely has.

throw a doll across the room. An abusive adult displays the same uncontrollable emotions. An argument with a spouse, a car that won't start—almost anything—can trigger an incident of abuse. The child's words or actions are seldom the cause. The child is simply nearby, a defenseless target.

Abusive parents generally have certain beliefs that run against the facts of how children develop:

- They believe that infants will be spoiled if they are picked up and comforted when they cry. They don't recognize that this physical comforting is essential for the development of trust.
- They often have unrealistic expectations of what children can do. For example, they may tell a toddler to "sit up and eat right." They expect the toddler to do just that—promptly—even though the nature and skills of toddlers make this impossible.

- They expect young children to remember commands given only once. Of course, young children learn only after directions have been repeated many times. Abusive parents may see this as stubbornness, disobedience, or revenge.

What Can Be Done?

It is against the law to abuse a child. People who work with children—early childhood professionals, health care providers, and teachers—are required by law to report child abuse. They are called **mandated reporters.** Other citizens may not have a legal obligation, yet they should report child maltreatment to a child protective services agency. Every state has a child welfare agency, and most have hotline numbers to report suspected abuse.

Once an agency hears of suspected child abuse, it begins to investigate. If the child is in immediate danger, a court may place the

Counselors can help abusive parents understand why they are abusive and learn to change their attitudes and how they respond to situations.

CHAPTER 19: Special Challenges for Children **591**

Discussion Activity

Read the following to students: "Beth and Jason had been married for only two months when Jason first gave Beth a black eye. Five years and two children later, he is more abusive than ever. Last week, for the first time, after a night of drinking, Jason shoved two-year-old Natasha into the wall. Beth was gripped with fear. She has no job and no one to turn to. She wonders how much more she can take."
Ask students to analyze this situation. Why might Jason act as he does? Why does Beth let this go on? What should she do? Who will benefit from any action she takes?
L2

VISUAL LEARNING Using the Photograph
Ask students why it would be beneficial for both parents to attend these sessions, even if only one of them is abusive.

ISSUES IN CHILDREN'S HEALTH

Domestic Violence. The term *domestic violence* refers to violence as abuse against elders, spouses, siblings, and children. October has been designated as Domestic Violence Month. There is a national domestic violence hotline: 800-799-SAFE. The organization's Website is www.ndvh.org.

ISSUES IN TEEN PARENTING Parents who are involved in child abuse tend to be younger than average and to have children at a younger age. Teen parents, therefore, run a risk of becoming abusive parents. On the chalkboard, write *isolation, frustration, inade-quacy,* and *poverty.* Ask students to explain how these words relate to teen parents. How might these contribute to abusive behavior? Point out that, to combat the problems teen parents have, many schools and communities provide special programs that help teen parents.

CHECKING COMPREHENSION

Have students answer the Check Your Understanding questions. Answers appear at the bottom of this page.

EVALUATION

Give students the Section 19-2 Quiz in the *Teacher Resource Guide.*

RETEACHING

1. Assign Reteaching Activities, page 55.
2. Have students make a poster titled, "Hurting? Where can you call for help?" Have them finish the poster with information about where people who are abused can find help.

ENRICHMENT

Have students draft a bill of rights for children.

EXTENSION

Ask students to determine the definition of child abuse in your state. Have them visit the Website of the state agency that protects children and report on how it operates.

CLOSE

Have students give examples of how parenting education can prevent child abuse.

---

child in a foster home. If there is a history of past abuse or the child's injuries are severe, parents can be charged and tried.

Putting abusive people in jail does give the child temporary protection. It does not solve the problem of the abuse, however. In most cases, treatment and counseling are used in an effort to correct the cause of the abuse—and so bring the abuse to an end.

Most abusive parents must work harder to learn how to care for their children responsibly. There are many types of government, private, and volunteer programs available to help them. Parents Anonymous, one of the best-known groups, is made up of parents who help each other gain self-control.

Some communities have **crisis nurseries,** child care facilities where troubled parents can leave their children for a short time. Using a crisis nursery gives parents time to cool off and try to cope with their frustrations and anger away from their children. Workers at these crisis nurseries usually work with the abusive parents. They help parents understand their frustrations and resolve their problems. They guide parents in learning how to break the cycle of child abuse.

Many family problems, including child abuse, are directly related to poor parenting skills and to a lack of knowledge about child development. Classes like the one you are taking help give parents—and future parents—realistic ideas about what parenting involves. Are other parenting classes available in your community?

SECTION 19-2 REVIEW

✔ Check Your Understanding

1. What is child abuse?
2. Give an example of one of the categories of child abuse.
3. List three traits common among child abusers.
4. What quality do people who are abusive lack?
5. Where should child abuse be reported?
6. Is putting child abusers in prison the answer to the problem? Why or why not?
7. Who belongs to Parents Anonymous? What do members do?

Putting Knowledge Into Practice

1. **Supporting an Argument.** Child abuse is a personal problem. To what degree is it also a social problem? What can society do to try to solve this problem?
2. **Making Inferences.** How might understanding child development help prevent abuse?
3. **Observing and Participating.** Talk to a counselor or social worker about why people find it difficult to report suspected cases of child abuse. What particular problems would a person have in reporting abuse? Describe what you would say and do to encourage a close friend to report his or her suspicions of child abuse.

592 UNIT 6: Special Areas of Study

ANSWERS TO SECTION 19-2 REVIEW

1. The physical or emotional maltreatment of a child.
2. *See the list on page 590.*
3. They can't handle their situation; they have low self-esteem; they were abused as children.
4. Self-control.
5. To a social service or child welfare agency.
6. *Possible response:* No, parent needs counseling to change behavior.
7. Abusive parents; they try to help each other learn control.

SECTION 19-3

Family Stresses

Evan stared out the window. He didn't have the energy to do anything. He couldn't think of anything that would be fun. All he could think of was his friends in his old town—the town he and his family had just moved away from. He liked the new home, but he sure missed his friends.

KEY TERMS

addiction
co-dependency

OBJECTIVES:

- Describe the emotional effects on children of stressful family situations.
- Create strategies for minimizing these effects.

Children and Stress

During times of stress, children need even more support than adults. They are less capable of understanding the events that cause stress and lack essential tools for handling that stress. At these times, children should be encouraged to talk about their feelings.

CHAPTER 19: Special Challenges for Children **593**

Observing & Participating

Explain to students that each person experiences and handles stress in a unique way. Ask them to think of a time when they felt stress. Ask: How did you deal with your feelings? Did you talk with your close friends or confide in other family members? If you talked about your feelings, did that help you handle the situation? Ask for volunteers to share what techniques helped them cope with stress.

SECTION 19-3

Family Stresses

(pages 593-599)

SECTION 19-3 RESOURCES

Teacher Resource Guide
- Lesson Plan Organizer, p. 82
- Section 19-3 Quiz, p. 210

Student Motivation Kit
- Observations & Case Studies (case study), pp. 143-144
- Reteaching Activity, p. 56
- Enrichment, p. 57

Student Workbook
- Study Guide, pp. 155-158
- Thinking About Family Crises, pp. 161-162

Transparency Package
- CT-54 Coping with Change

Effective Instruction CD-ROM

FOCUS

MOTIVATOR

Have students brainstorm situations that might cause stress in families. As they respond, list their suggestions on the chalkboard. Suggest that they copy the list, add to it as they read, and take notes on chapter suggestions for helping children cope with stressful situations.

VOCABULARY ACTIVITY

Have students preview the definition of the terms by turning to the Glossary.

1. What is one sign that children are experiencing adjustment problems after a family breakup? (*Behavior problems.*)

ACTIVITIES

Critical Thinking Activity

Making Inferences. Discuss with students how children are affected by the way parents handle stress. What effect could this have on parent-child relationships? On sibling relationships? **L1**

Discussion Activity

Have students discuss how a divorce might affect celebration of holidays and other special occasions. Ask them to suggest ways of making such occasions happier for children and of minimizing stress or conflict. **L1**

VISUAL LEARNING | **Using the Photograph**
Possible responses: It makes the child feel bad; it puts the child in a position where he or she might feel compelled to choose between parents.

Divorce

Divorce is more common now than it used to be. Nearly 20 percent of children will have to face a family breakup before they turn eighteen.

If a family is about to break up, the children need to be told about the change in an honest and reassuring way. Experts advise using the following guidelines:

- **Truth.** The children should be told the truth about the upcoming changes. If possible, both parents should discuss the situation. All children, even toddlers, should be included. Young children often understand much more than parents realize. Parents can say something like this to their children: "We're having a hard time right now. We are going to live apart, for a while at least. Still, no matter what happens, we will both always love you and take care of you." The last point—that love will continue—is essential.

- **Elimination of blame.** Parents need to avoid placing blame for the divorce on one another, at least in front of the children. If the parents can't talk about the divorce without placing blame, they can ask a counselor or religious leader to help them. Each parent should remember that the children will continue to need both parents. It is unfair to children to place them in a position where they have to take sides with one or the other.

Children also need to be reassured that they are in no way responsible for the breakup. Parents should stress that they are separating because of their own differences, not because of anything their children have said or done—or failed to say or do. Most children feel guilty when their parents fail

Divorced parents should refrain from criticizing each other when the child is around. **Why?**

Parenting in *Action*

Divorce is hard on children, just as it is on adults. However, most child development experts believe that growing up in a family where there is constant bickering and unhappiness is even more damaging than divorce. Therefore, in such cases, it may not be best for parents to stay married just "for the sake of the children." After a divorce, children need to continue to build healthy relationships with both parents.

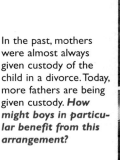
In the past, mothers were almost always given custody of the child in a divorce. Today, more fathers are being given custody. *How might boys in particular benefit from this arrangement?*

to get along. Parents should make a special effort to be reassuring on this point.

- **Reassurance.** Parents also need to reassure the children that they will continue to be loved by both parents. After a separation or divorce, children typically live with only one parent. They need to know that the other parent is still there for support and companionship.
- **No false hope.** The children shouldn't be encouraged to hope for a reconciliation if their parents are not considering the possibility. This false hope only delays the children's adjustment to their new situation.

After the divorce, children need stability and continuity. Their lives should be kept the same as much as possible. Siblings should continue living together if possible. Children will feel more comfortable if they don't change homes or schools. The absent

parent should spend time with the children often and regularly. Frequent contact with relatives from both sides of the family can help retain a sense of belonging. See the "Parenting with Care" feature on pages 600-601 for more suggestions about living with children after a divorce.

Many children begin to show behavior problems after the family breaks up. Even children who appear to adjust well may be hiding their grief and pain. If these problems continue, it is wise to seek professional help.

Death

The death of someone close causes special problems for a young child. The age of the child, however, influences the youngster's reaction.

- **Under age three.** Children this young cannot understand much more than a brief separation. Often, a toddler will

CHAPTER 19: Special Challenges for Children **595**

COMPREHENSION CHECK

1. What can parents do to help children deal with death? (*Possible responses: encourage children to talk about feelings, share memories of person who died, use simple and direct language about death.*)
2. In addition to sadness, children commonly experience what emotion when a parent dies? (*Guilt.*)

ACTIVITIES

Discussion Activity

Ask students why it might be difficult for a grieving adult to deal with a four-year-old's reaction to death. **L2**

Critical Thinking Activity

Comparing. **Ask:** How does the death of a family member affect the surviving family members? How can they help each other cope? **L2**

Discussion Activity

Ask students to consider how children would react to the death of a sibling. Would the response be different than that to the death of a parent? How? **L2**

VISUAL LEARNING	Using the Photograph

Answer: Disbelief; despair; reorganization.

Many children first experience death when a pet dies. *What are the three steps that children go through when dealing with death?*

react to a parent's death in the same way as to the parent's week-long vacation.

- **Ages three to five.** Children this age think that death is like sleep—you are dead, and then you wake up and are alive again. As a result, they may seem unfeeling when someone dies. They don't understand that death is permanent.
- **Ages five to nine.** As children mature, they accept the idea that a person who has died will not come back. However, they don't view death as something that happens to everyone. They don't recognize that they themselves will die.
- **Age nine or ten.** At this age, children begin to see that they, too, will die. This may make them afraid. At this age, children must come to terms with their fear and put it in proper perspective.

How Children Cope with Death

By age five, most children have had some contact with death and are curious about it. Perhaps a pet has died; or perhaps

it was someone in the extended family. Children go through a three-step process in accepting death. Caregivers who understand this process are usually better prepared to help children cope with death and their feelings about death.

1. **Disbelief.** In this early stage, children may express anger, hostility, and defiance.
2. **Despair.** Later, children are often withdrawn and depressed. Some may revert to babyish behavior during this stage.
3. **Reorganization.** Finally, children begin to adjust to life without the person who has died.

If a loved one dies, children should be told about it in an honest way. They may need an explanation of what death is. Children should then be encouraged to talk about their feelings. Parents, in turn, should let children know that they, too, miss the person very much. Sharing memories of the person who has died, looking at photographs, and talking about what made him or her special can help parents and children deal with the death.

LEARNING STYLES	Interpersonal

Have students write two questions that a four-year-old child might ask about the death of a family member. Do the same for a six-year-old and a nine-year-old. The questions should illustrate each child's level of ability to understand death.

Next, have students write the appropriate responses for each question.

Adults must be very careful about the words they use when discussing death with a child. Phrases like "passed away" or "gone to sleep" only add to a child's confusion. Use simple, direct references to death and dying. It's also important to remember that children understand most things in terms of themselves. For example, a child who is told that "Grandpa got very sick and died" may worry about dying the next time he or she gets a cold. The type of explanation an adult offers must fit the age and understanding of the child, but it should always be honest and direct.

When a Parent Dies

The death of a parent is the most tragic thing that can happen to a youngster. A child whose parent dies needs support for an extended period. Many children react with guilt. The child may think, "I wasn't always good when he wanted me to be" or "I wasn't quiet enough when she was sick." Children need the reassurance that nothing they did, said, or even thought caused the death. They also need help coping with their feelings of abandonment.

Even very young children should be allowed to take part in family funerals or memorial services. Doing so will help them heal and make the transition from the presence to the absence of the person who died. Children of any age are capable of mourning. Even infants go through a period of excessive crying and searching for a parent who has died.

Suicide

Some children feel that they can't cope with their problems any longer. They feel overwhelmed and without hope and try to take their own lives.

A person who is thinking about suicide needs help. Comments like "You'd all be better off without me" and actions like giving away prized possessions may be signs that someone is thinking about suicide. If you know of someone who shows these signs, talk to an adult. It may save a life.

Moving

Moving is stressful for children, because their familiar settings and routines are upset. Often, children don't want to leave their present home, where they feel secure and safe.

How might a child react to the death of a parent? A grandparent?

DID You Know?

Death. In the past, most people died in their own beds surrounded by relatives and friends. Children accepted death as normal because they were exposed to it. As dying became more isolated, children were often sheltered from death. When children feel adults are being evasive and withholding information, they become uneasy and worry. Children have the right to participate in the sorrows as well as the joys of life.

COMPREHENSION CHECK

1. Why is moving difficult for children? (*Possible responses: Leaving familiar surroundings, friends.*)
2. How should a parent discuss financial problems with a child? (*In simple, direct language; for example, the need to limit expenses for a while.*)

ACTIVITIES

Discussion Activity

Ask students to share experiences of moving. **Ask:** What was hard about the move? How long did it take you to adjust to a new place and find new friends? **L1**

Critical Thinking Activity

Planning. Have students work in groups to plan a hypothetical family move. What issues have to be dealt with? What arrangements have to be made? **L2**

Discussion Activity

Have students identify as many ways as possible that having someone in the household with a substance-abuse problem may affect children. Make a master list. **L2**

VISUAL LEARNING	Using the Photograph

Possible response: It helps them adjust by giving them control over part of the move.

Moving can be difficult for children, who have to adapt to a new school and find new friends. **Why should parents let children pack their own things?**

Parents can help soothe children's fears by encouraging them to talk about their feelings. Children should also be encouraged to pack their own belongings as much as possible. This activity helps them feel more in control and more involved in the move. Parents can also stress what the family—and the child—will gain from the move.

After the move, parents need to help the child get settled. They can take walks with the child around the new neighborhood and help the child meet nearby children. They can also take the child to visit his or her new school.

Financial Problems

When a family has financial problems, children sense the tensions even though they may not understand them. The parents may be short-tempered or pay less attention to the children than usual. Children typically believe that they themselves have done something wrong.

Children can't understand complex financial situations. Still, parents should talk to them about the family's situation. They may wish to point out a need to limit expenses for a while. Parents must work hard to avoid taking out their own fears and worries on their children.

Illness

When a family member is ill or in the hospital, the routine of family life is upset. Parents can help their children handle this kind of situation by explaining what is happening. If the illness is minor, the child can be reassured that the person will soon be well and everything return to normal. If the illness is serious or terminal, the child should be told the truth, but in a calm, reassuring way.

Children often worry that they will suffer a similar illness or injury. They may grow afraid of doctors or hospitals. Parents should take the time to explain how the relative's illness or injury differs from any the child is likely to have. As with other situations of family stress, parents need to show patience and reassurance.

Substance Abuse

Some people develop an **addiction** to a drug or to alcohol. When this happens, they

Management/Leadership Skills

Have students work in two large groups to investigate reasons why people suffer from financial problems. They might consider such questions as: Is it difficult for some people to stay on a budget? What if you lost your job? Do credit cards tempt people to live beyond their means? Have them also discuss steps someone can take to get finances under control. Have each group report its conclusions, and have the class discuss them.

crave the substance even though it has powerful and harmful effects on their minds and bodies. When people abuse substances, they cause many problems for their families.

Some parents who are substance abusers often begin to abuse their spouses or their children, causing further problems. If the drug or drinking problem becomes very serious, a person may lose a job or turn to crime in order to support the habit.

Members of the family often are well aware that a person has a substance abuse problem. They don't always admit it, though. Sometimes they show a kind of behavior called **co-dependency.** This means

they take on responsibilities that the substance abuser should be filling. In that way, they help the person hide the problem.

Substance abusers and their families need to face up to their problems. An abuser will not stop or seek help until ready to. Nagging or threatening won't make it happen. On the other hand, others in the family may need to protect themselves from the abuser's behavior. Groups like Alateen and Families Anonymous give support to the teen children and the families of alcoholics. Other groups are also available to provide help for the families of people who abuse drugs.

SECTION 19-3 REVIEW

✔ Check Your Understanding

1. List some guidelines for telling children about a separation or divorce.
2. What attitude toward death is typical of three- to five-year-olds? At what age do children usually begin to understand that death is inevitable for everyone?
3. Describe the signs of each of the three stages children often go through in accepting a death.
4. Twelve-year-old Danielle has a friend who has been very sad lately. One day, she gave Danielle all her CDs. What should Danielle do?
5. How can parents help children settle in after a move?
6. How might a family member's illness affect a child's own health?
7. What is co-dependency? How can it contribute to a substance abuse problem?

Putting Knowledge Into Practice

1. **Making Inferences.** Make a list of coping skills—techniques that families can use to handle problems such as talking honestly to children about a divorce. On your list, indicate which ideas would be especially effective with young children.
2. **Synthesizing.** When Curtis's grandmother died, his parents said, "Grandma went on a long trip." Was that an effective message to give their five-year-old? Why or why not? If not, what could the parents have said instead?
3. **Observing and Participating.** Think of how you handle stress. Would your techniques be suitable for a child? Why or why not?

CHAPTER 19: Special Challenges for Children **599**

ANSWERS TO SECTION 19-3 REVIEW

1. Tell the truth, avoid blame, reassure child that parents are still there
2. Death is like sleep; nine or ten.
3. *Disbelief:* anger, hostility; *Despair:* withdrawn, depressed; *Reorganization:* adjusting to life without the person.
4. Talk to an adult because friend may be considering suicide.
5. Walking around neighborhood with child, helping child meet new friends, visiting school with child.
6. May fear getting same illness.
7. Taking on the responsibilities of an abuser. Adds to problem by hiding it.

Introduce this feature by asking students to think about how their mothers and fathers are similar and different in respect to the following: attitudes, behaviors, parenting styles. Which ones do the students feel more comfortable with? Agree with?

TEACH

DISCUSSION ACTIVITY

Ask: How difficult is it to negotiate rules for two separate households. Who should get the final say? How do stepparents and stepsiblings enter into the picture? **L1**

Teamwork Activity

Have students work in pairs to act out a conversation between divorced parents who have joint custody. They should focus on a specific situation that may likely occur, such as a difference in attitude toward the child doing household chores. How do they resolve the situation? Have the class discuss whether the solution would be good for the child. What alternatives can other students suggest? **L2**

Parenting With Care

Living with Children After a Divorce

When parents divorce, one parent is often given custody of the children.

In the past, that parent was almost always the mother. Now, most courts base the decision on a judgment of which parent can provide a loving, stable home.

In more and more families, parents take joint custody—they both agree to take responsibility for children. The children usually split their time between their two parents' homes. Either way, parents can take certain steps to make their children's lives easier:

- If the court orders a parent to send money for child support, that parent must comply.
- The parent whom children don't live with should visit the children as often as possible to maintain healthy relationships.
- Follow the same routines in both homes to help the child feel comfortable.
- Follow the same rules in both homes so that children have consistent standards of behavior. This also prevents the child from being able to play one parent against the other by saying "Daddy lets me watch that show" or "Mommy lets me eat that."
- Use guidance in the same way as before the divorce. Avoid being too harsh or too lenient with the child. The health and welfare of the child should be most important.
- The parent with custody should keep the other parent informed about the child's life. He or she should share news about school events or recent illnesses, for example.
- Both parents should avoid saying negative things about the other. Criticisms of the other parent can let a child feel caught between love for one or the other.
- If parents fight whenever they see each other, use another adult—such as a grandparent—as a go-between.

RESOURCES ON CHILD SUPPORT

Many parents, mostly fathers, are delinquent in their child support payments. Sometimes these parents leave the area without information on where to contact them. This is against the law, but the judicial system alone can't find and enforce payments from all the delinquents. The Child Support Network can help locate missing parents and collect court-ordered child support payments. The CSN can be contacted at 212 E. Osborn Road, Suite 210, Phoenix, AZ 85012 and can be found at www.childsupport.com.

- Give extra comfort to the child just before he or she is ready to spend time at the other parent's home.
- Don't be surprised if the child begins to revert to the behavior of a younger child. Children do so in an unconscious desire to restore life to an earlier, happier time. Show patience while still making it clear to the child that appropriate behavior is expected.

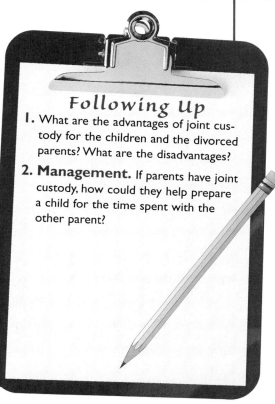

Following Up

1. What are the advantages of joint custody for the children and the divorced parents? What are the disadvantages?

2. **Management.** If parents have joint custody, how could they help prepare a child for the time spent with the other parent?

Writing Activity

Have students write three diary entries from the point-of-view of a child of eight whose parents have joint custody. The child's mother is remarried for two years and the stepfather has a ten-year-old daughter who visits on weekends. The child's father is still single and rents out the upstairs of a two-story house. **L2**

Critical Thinking Activity

Describe the following situation to students: "Rico lives with his mother during the week. Because his mother works weekdays, Rico helps by making his own lunch, doing the dinner dishes, and cleaning the house. He spends weekends with his father. His father never asks Rico to do any chores." **Ask:** What impact might these different circumstances have on how Rico relates to his parents? **L2**

CLOSE

1. Have students explain the positives and negatives of joint custody.
2. **Extension.** Have students research custody laws in your state and prepare a report. They may visit a local university or government law library.

Answers to Following Up

1. *Possible responses: Advantages*: Chance to spend large amounts of time with both parents, greater chance of seeing both extended families. *Disadvantages*: Possible confusion over rules; possible disruption of routine.
2. *Possible responses:* Have a large calendar and mark off the days.

CHECKING COMPREHENSION

Use the Summary and the Reviewing the Facts questions to help students go over the most important ideas in Chapter 19. Encourage students to ask questions and add details.

CHAPTER 19 REVIEW

Answers to Reviewing the Facts

1. Parents who pity, resent, or coddle a child with disabilities hinder his or her development. The child may become angry and self-pitying and have difficulty living in society.
2. Learning self-care fosters independence.
3. They are more likely to receive the social acceptance they need.
4. Determines whether a child has emotional disabilities and devises a program for treatment.
5. The physical or emotional maltreatment of a child.
6. They are caught in emotional situations they can't handle; they have low self-esteem; they were often abused themselves when they were children.
7. Mandated reporters are required by law to report it.
8. Parents should tell children in as honest and simple a way as possible.
9. *Under age three:* Think of death as a brief separation. *Ages three to five:* See death as similar to sleeping; want to know when the dead person will awake again. *Ages five to nine:* Understand death, but do not understand it happens to everyone. *Age nine or ten:* Understand that everyone dies.
10. Co-dependency.

Summary

✔ Some children have serious disabilities that make their lives more difficult, but they can usually have productive lives. (Section 19-1)

✔ Treatment and counseling can help abusive parents learn to cope with their problems and stop patterns of abuse. (Section 19-2)

✔ Children need extra support when facing stressful situations. (Section 19-3)

✔ When the family faces problems or stresses, children should be told about the problem honestly and in a way suited to their level. (Section 19-3)

Reviewing the Facts

1. How do parents' attitudes affect a child who has a disability? (Section 19-1)
2. Why should a child with a physical disability be taught self-care? (Section 19-1)
3. Why is it suggested that children with mental disabilities learn manners and cleanliness? (Section 19-1)
4. What does a behavioral therapist do? (Section 19-1)
5. What is child abuse? (Section 19-2)
6. What are the emotional characteristics of people who abuse children? (Section 19-2)
7. What responsibility do people have if they see signs of child abuse? (Section 19-2)
8. Who should tell children that their parents are divorcing? How should they be told? (Section 19-3)

9. Contrast how children of different ages understand death. (Section 19-3)
10. Kevin does all the shopping and cleaning and cares for his younger sister because his mother has a drinking problem. What is Kevin's behavior called? (Section 19-3)

Thinking Critically

1. **Analyzing.** Children with disabilities are more likely to be abused than children without disabilities. Why do you think that is true?
2. **Synthesizing.** Which do you think would be better for a child, living in a home in which the parents often fight or having parents divorce? Why?

Taking Action

1. **Making a Poster.** Make a poster that contains advice for young children whose parents are divorced. *(Communication)*
2. **Helping Out.** Find a local group that offers help to families with any of the problems described in this chapter. Find out what people your age can do to help out. Create a fact sheet that describes the group and the help they are looking for. *(Leadership)*

CONNECTIONS

Cross-Curricular Connections

1. **Social Studies.** Stage a debate in which you argue for or against the idea that parents who abuse children should lose all rights of custody for those children.
2. **Language Arts.** Write a story about a five-year-old child whose family just moved.

Workplace Connections

1. **Basic Skills.** Suppose you wrote a newspaper advice column. A parent writes you to say that her spouse is dying of a serious illness. She wants advice on how to explain his illness and upcoming death to their children, ages six and four. Write a reply to the letter.

Family and Community Connections

1. **Help for the Abused.** Gather information about the work of a group in your area that helps spouses or children who are abused. What kind of help is offered?

2. **In the School.** Learn more about the Individuals with Disabilities Education Act (IDEA). What does the act require of schools? Of parents and children? Write a summary of your findings.

Technology Connections

1. **Internet.** Search online to find a group that provides support to families who have a child with a disability. What kind of help do they give to parents? Write a summary of what you find.
2. **Internet.** Search online to find a group that provides help to those who abuse substances. Examples are Alcoholics Anonymous and Alateen. Choose one of the following issues: alcoholism, crime, mental health, co-dependency, impact on children. Report your findings to the class, and suggest steps society can take to try to solve the problem you addressed.

EVALUATION

1. Use the reproducible Chapter 19 Test in the *Teacher Resource Guide*, or construct your own test using the **Exam***View*® Test Generator.
2. For an alternative assessment, assign the Chapter 19 activity in the *Authentic Assessment* section of the *Teacher Resource Guide*.

ENRICHMENT

Assign students either of the two enrichment activities in the *Enrichment Activities* booklet in the *Student Motivation Kit*.

EXTENSION

Identify local support groups and government agencies involved with mental retardation. Find out what services they offer.

CLOSE

Have students divide into two groups: one will be a panel of experts and the other will be participating audience members. Each audience member must come prepared with three questions that relate to the content of this chapter. The panel will then handle the questions or respond to opinions and other comments audience members may have.

CHAPTER 20 RESOURCES

Teacher Resource Guide
• Chapter 20 Test, p. 217
• Authentic Assessment, p. 295

Student Motivation Kit
• Observations, pp. 65-66

Transparency Package
• CT-55 Learning Centers
• CT-56 On-the-Job Communication

Effective Instruction CD-ROM

CHAPTER 20 OVERVIEW

In **Section 20-1**, students read about the responsibilities of a child care provider and the skills and abilities needed to care for children of different ages. They also review safety tips for child care providers.

In **Section 20-2**, students learn more about the early childhood classroom, including its physical organization, health and safety procedures, and the importance of schedules and activity plans.

CHAPTER 20 OBJECTIVES

After completing Chapter 20, students will be able to:

• Describe the responsibilities of a child care provider.
• List the skills an effective child care provider should have.
• Discuss methods for organizing early childhood classrooms, for planning activities, and for promoting positive behavior in class.

CHAPTER 20

Caring for Children

604   Unit 6: Special Areas of Study

RESOURCES TO EXPLORE

Child Care Entrepreneurs. Some teens might be curious about how to start a child care business. Suggest they read *The Child Care Notebook* (Cornell University Cooperative Extension). In it, they will learn how to assess the child care needs of their community, what kind of equipment to buy, and strategies for handling licensing, insurance, and food preparation. To obtain a copy, write The Media Services Resource Center, Cornell University, 7 Cornell Business and Technology Park, Ithaca, NY 14850.

Mrs. Slater told the children that it was time to finish up their projects and put their materials away. They had been making an art project using construction paper, glue, and paint. Mrs. Slater told the children where to put their projects so they would dry in time to take them home after school. She didn't have to remind them where to put the glue and extra paper—the children knew from practice where those went.

As the children put things away, there were the usual interruptions. Alex objected to Brock telling him what to do. Lisa needed to go to the rest room. Eventually, though, the picking up was completed.

Mrs. Slater herded all the children to the reading area and said, "OK, kids, it's time to hear more of our story." Shawna came up with the question about her art project, but the children soon settled down on the floor. "Who remembers where we left off yesterday?" she asked. Immediately, hands were raised and the children called out, "I do."

"OK, kids, it's time to hear more of our story."

INTRODUCING CHAPTER 20

- Have students take the role of the parents of a child under six. They need a caregiver to watch the child three days a week. Have them write an advertisement listing the qualifications they require.
- Have students look at the photograph on the previous page. **Ask:** Based on what the children are doing, what social skills have they learned?

USING THE SCENARIO Have students read the opening scenario. Then ask students to list several aptitudes that a child care provider must possess, based on the information in the opener.

KEY TO ABILITY LEVELS Each section gives skill-building activities. Each activity has been labeled for use with students of various learning styles and abilities.

L1 Level 1 activities are basic activities and should be within the range of all students.

L2 Level 2 activities are average activities and should be within the range of average and above average students.

L3 Level 3 activities are challenging activities designed for the ability range of above average students.

Providing Short-Term Child Care

(pages 606-611)

SECTION 20-1 RESOURCES
Teacher Resource Guide
- Lesson Plan Organizer, p. 83
- Section 20-1 Quiz, p. 215

Student Motivation Kit
- Reteaching Activity, p. 57

Student Workbook
- Study Guide, pp. 163-166
- Identifying Learning Opportunities, pp. 167-168

Effective Instruction CD-ROM

FOCUS

MOTIVATOR

Write the word *babysitter* on the chalkboard. Ask students to say the first thing that comes to mind when they hear the word. Write their responses on the chalkboard. Guide students to see that responsibility is a key attribute of babysitters.

VOCABULARY ACTIVITY

Ask students to consider how the words *authority* and *power* might be related. Why might a babysitter need authority? Why shouldn't a babysitter abuse his or her authority?

Providing Short-Term Child Care

The most common first child care job is **babysitting,** caring for children for a short time while parents are away from the home. Actually, *babysitting* is not a very accurate term. When you undertake this job, you are really providing care for children. The job allows little time for sitting—unless the children are asleep!

KEY TERMS

authority
babysitting

OBJECTIVES:
- Determine what personal qualities are needed to be a good babysitter or child care provider.
- Describe the responsibilities of a child care provider when caring for children of various ages.
- List safety guidelines that are especially important for child care providers.

Making Arrangements

Whenever you arrange a babysitting job, agree in advance on the rate of pay. Ask how long the parents intend to be gone and discuss how you will get to and from their home. Before you leave for the job, be sure your own family knows the name, address, and phone number of the people you will

Observing & Participating

Ask students who have been babysitters to describe their experiences. What were their duties? What did they enjoy about the job? What did they dislike? Ask students who have been cared for by babysitters in the past to share those experiences from the child's perspective. What do children like in a babysitter?

be working for and the approximate time you will return.

The first time you provide child care for a family, arrive about 20 minutes early. This will give the children a chance to get used to you while their parents are still home. It will also allow you enough time to find out any additional information from the parents. Obvious questions to ask include when bedtimes are, where the parents will be, how the parents can be reached, and emergency procedures.

Caring for Children of Different Ages

When parents are gone, child care providers are completely responsible for the safety and welfare of the children. Good caregivers:

- Are interested in the children, not just in the money they are earning.
- Can behave responsibly.
- Have patience, especially with small children.
- Understand children's physical, emotional, social, and intellectual needs.
- Are flexible and prepared to meet the needs of children of different ages.
- Have a sense of humor.
- Come prepared to meet the children's needs.

Teens who take a babysitting job should be sure to find out what the parents expect them to do in caring for the children. Will they have to feed and bathe the children? Do the parents want them to play with the children? Knowing this in advance will make the babysitting experience satisfying for everyone concerned.

Babies

Babies need a great deal of physical care and protection. This means that when you agree to care for an infant, you should have the necessary skills and understand the characteristics of babies.

INFOLINK

Caring for an Infant

For more about *caring for an infant*, see Chapter 8, pages 268-291.

COMPREHENSION CHECK

1. Why should a new babysitter arrive early for the first job? (*To give the children a chance to become accustomed to them and to review last minute information from the parents.*)
2. Which age group probably needs the most care and attention? (*Possible response: Babies.*)

ACTIVITIES

Critical Thinking Activity

Drawing Conclusions. Have students write a few sentences in answer to the following: Why does a good caregiver possess a sense of humor? Patience? Flexibility? Have them share their answers and discuss them as a class. **L1**

VISUAL LEARNING | **Using the Photograph**

Have students work in groups to write a list of specific questions a child care provider should ask before parents leave the house. Then ask the members of different groups to share and compare their lists.

Management/Leadership Skills

A babysitter needs to know:
- What the child may eat or drink.
- Hours of bedtime or nap time.
- Not to open doors to strangers.
- Where the exits to the house are.
- How to lock doors and windows.

- What play activities the child enjoys.
- What activities are not allowed.
- What parts of the house or grounds are off-limits for children or the sitter.
- How baby equipment works.
- What to do in case of an emergency.

COMPREHENSION CHECK

1. Why should a babysitter never leave a toddler alone? (*Their curiosity may lead the toddler into a dangerous situation in which the child could be hurt.*)
2. For what reasons might an older child pose a behavioral problem for a babysitter? (*May be jealous of a younger sibling; may think they can misbehave when their parents are absent; may feel they don't need a babysitter.*)
3. How should a babysitter handle misbehavior, both with the child and the parents? (*Use reasonable punishment; tell the parents what happened later.*)

ACIVITIES

Critical Thinking Activity

Identifying Alternatives. Present the following situation to the class: "Robin arrived early for her first job at the Watson home watching two-year-old Molly. Unfortunately, Molly began crying even before her mother left and screamed in response to Robin's every suggestion. Ms. Watson won't be home for another four hours."

Have students list Robin's options. Then have them write a paragraph explaining what they think she should do and why. **L2**

Remember to follow ~~five~~ three most important rules of caring for infants:

- When handling a young infant, hold the infant firmly, and always support the baby's head and neck.
- Never leave a baby on a bed, sofa, or other raised surface. Even a tiny baby can wiggle enough to fall off.
- Keep harmful objects out of the reach of crawling infants.
- Never shake a baby. Even a few moments of strong shaking can cause permanent damage to the baby's brain.
- Use the time when a child is awake for positive, loving interaction.

When a baby cries, find out what the problem is. Is the baby too cold or warm or perhaps hungry? Is the diaper wet or soiled? Remember, too, that except for very young infants, babies cry when they are lonely. If that is the problem, a few minutes of cuddling will help.

Changing diapers is a frequent duty of child care providers. Be sure to gather all needed supplies so that they are nearby before you start changing the diaper.

Child care providers aren't usually asked to bathe a baby. However, a qualified care provider should be able to undertake this task. Before you agree to do it as part of a child care job, review what is involved and practice bathing a baby while an adult watches.

Toddlers and Preschoolers

Because toddlers and preschoolers sleep less and are more adventuresome, they require more watching. Don't leave them alone—even for a minute—while they are awake. They are also more sensitive than infants to their parents' leaving and may need comforting. They like being read to, played with, or talked to.

Sometimes babysitters have to feed the children they care for. **What can they do to help promote self-feeding?**

Management/Leadership Skills

Have students suppose they are caring for two children aged five and eight. The parents plan to return by 11:00 P.M. Have students describe how they would respond to the following: (1) The five-year-old hits the eight-year-old with a metal truck, causing bleeding. (2) A neighbor phones and asks to borrow something. (3) A man rings the doorbell and says he accidentally dented the fender of the car in front of the house, which is your car. (4) By 11:30, the parents have not returned or contacted you.

Following the child's normal routine can make bedtime easier when you are babysitting. *What would you do if a child says that parents let him or her stay up later on nights that there is a babysitter?*

Bedtime may be a problem. Toddlers and preschoolers usually don't want to go to bed. Try to follow the child's regular bedtime routine. Ask the parents in advance what bedtime activities the child is used to so you can follow the normal routine.

During the night, a young child may be awakened by a bad dream. Providing a bit of comfort will help the child go back to sleep. Later, tell the parents about the bad dream—and anything else unusual.

School-Age Children

Some older children try to give caregivers a difficult time. Some are jealous of the time and attention given to younger siblings. Others try to get away with behavior their parents wouldn't permit. Still others may feel they are too old for a babysitter.

Get the relationship off to a good start by making friends with older children. If you show interest in their possessions, games, or activities, you'll win over even the most independent youngsters.

It helps if before the parents leave, they make clear to the children that you have **authority**. This means you have the right to make decisions in their absence.

At no time is your maturity as a care provider more important than when a child deliberately misbehaves. You will have better control of the situation if you remain calm. Be fair—but firm and consistent.

No matter how a child behaves, never use physical punishment. Bribery and threats don't work well, either. If you feel you need to punish a child, use reasonable punishment, such as no TV. Be sure to describe the situation to the parents when they return. Tell what the child did, how you responded, and why. Ask if the parents would prefer you to handle such situations differently. In the future, then, you can act accordingly.

INFOLINK

Guidance

For more about *guidance*, see Chapter 3, pages 88-89.

CHAPTER 20: Caring for Children **609**

Critical Thinking Activity

Applying. Have students develop creative projects and games to play while babysitting. These could include arts and crafts, such as puppet-making, or active games, such as paper cup bowling. Write students' suggestions on the board and have the class discuss how suitable each one is. **L2**

VISUAL LEARNING | **Using the Photographs**
Left—Possible response: Give finger foods. *Right—Possible response:* Say what your instructions were from the parents.

DID You Know?

Bedtime Routines. One researcher found seven common features of bedtime routines: stalling, increased use of the child's name by the parents, increased use of the word "my" by children, increased affection, specific sequence of activities, a bedtime story, and conversation that moves from past (what happened today) to future (what will happen tomorrow). Awareness of these common rituals can help babysitters handle this part of their jobs more easily.

ISSUES IN TEEN PARENTING Teen parents who opt to babysit other people's children often find they have two advantages over teen babysitters who are not parents. First, they are more accomplished at the skills needed to care for a young child. Second, older children in their care will no doubt respect the babysitter's status as a parent and will be less likely to think they can take advantage of them.

COMPREHENSION CHECK

1. What is the best way to prevent serious safety problems while babysitting? (*Give the job your full attention; be on the scene quickly when things happen.*)
2. What is a babysitter's first responsibility in the event of a fire? (*Leading the children to safety.*)

ACTIVITIES

Critical Thinking Activity

Analysis. Have students make a list of what topics should be covered in a first-aid course for babysitters.

Teamwork Activity

Have groups of students write, perform, and audiotape public service announcements for radio that present a specific tip for child care providers. Members of the group should assign the following roles: "idea" people, writers, performers, technical experts.

VISUAL LEARNING	Using the Photograph *Answers will vary.*

Safety Tips for Child Care Providers

Caring for children requires your full attention. If you are alert and on the scene when something starts to happen, you can usually prevent serious problems. You should never let anything distract you from your primary job—watching the children.

One of the most dangerous situations you might meet is a fire. When you begin a child care job, locate all the outside doors. Note escape routes from various parts of the home. Find out whether the house has smoke detectors and a fire extinguisher. Ask whether the parents have a family escape plan to be used in case of fire. If they do, have them review it with you.

If a fire does break out, remember that the children are your first responsibility. Lead or carry them to safety. Then alert anyone else who may be in danger, and call the fire department. After calling the fire department, notify the parents.

INFOLINK
Accidents and First Aid
For more about *accidents and first aid*, see Chapter 18, pages 548-562.

How Do You Rate as a Care Provider?

Successful child care requires thoughtful attention to the children. You will rate

When you are babysitting, ask for a phone number where the parents can be reached. **What kind of situation would require a phone call to the parents?**

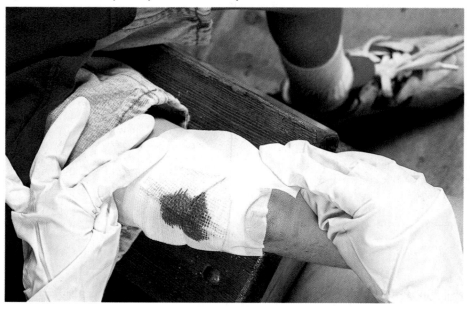

LEARNING STYLES	**Auditory** Assign students the task of performing a one-person play in which the star performs the role of a babysitter. Students can dictate the subject matter, as long as it touches on section content	in a relevant manner. Give students time to script the performance. When they have finished, allow the rest of the class to review the performance through class discussion.

well with parents if the children are well cared for, safe, and happy. Parents also want a care provider to arrive on time and follow the routines or directions provided. In addition, parents appreciate a care provider who straightens up, making sure that toys, books, and games have been put away and any snacks or meals have been cleared away. Ask ahead of time about any food a child may or should have.

You will rate well with children if you are prepared to spend time with them in activities that appeal to them. Buying toys and bringing them with you is not the only way—or even the best way—to keep children amused and happy. More important are your interests, imagination, and enthusiasm. An attentive care provider with a headful of stories, rhymes, songs, tricks, and games is more welcome than toys. These activities can make a child care job a pleasant and worthwhile experience.

SECTION 20-1 REVIEW

✔ Check Your Understanding

1. What arrangements should be discussed when taking on a babysitting job?
2. List five qualities of a good care provider.
3. What are the five basic rules of caring for an infant?
4. Patricia is babysitting a six-month-old who begins to cry. What should she do?
5. What should a care provider do to help make bedtime easier for a toddler or preschooler?
6. What three steps can a babysitter take to be prepared in case there is a fire?

Putting Knowledge Into Practice

1. **Giving Examples.** How can parents make clear to their children that a babysitter has authority?
2. **Applying.** Imagine that you are providing care for a family with an eight-year-old. The child is clearly interested in finding out how much she can get away with. How would you encourage the child to behave in appropriate ways?
3. **Observing and Participating.** Write down a list of qualities and skills you think a babysitter should have. Then interview at least two parents of small children to ask what qualities and skills they look for. Compare your list to the parents' responses. What differences are there? Why?

CHECKING COMPREHENSION

Have students answer the Check Your Understanding Questions. Answers appear at the bottom of this page.

EVALUATION

Give students the Section 20-1 Quiz in the *Teacher Resource Guide.*

RETEACHING

1. Assign Reteaching Activities, page 57.
2. Have students make posters to illustrate the basic responsibilities of child care providers. Display the finished work in the classroom.

ENRICHMENT

Have students design and create a Babysitter's Manual for younger students who are beginning their babysitting careers. Make sure that safety precautions are covered.

EXTENSION

Invite several parents with young children to visit the class to discuss what they look for in a child care provider.

CLOSE

Have students complete the sentence "What I expect from a babysitter is . . ."

ANSWERS TO SECTION 20-1 REVIEW

1. How much you will charge; how long the parents will be out; transportation.
2. *See the list on page 607.*
3. *See the list on page 608.*
4. Find out what the problem is and then try to resolve it.
5. Follow the normal bedtime routine.
6. Identify escape routes; locate smoke detectors and fire extinguisher.

CAREER OPPORTUNITIES

Introducing the Feature

Ask students how many of them are considering a career as a child care center worker. Have those students share their reasons with the class. If no one in class is considering this career, have students read the feature and then check again to see whether anyone is now interested.

Answers to CONNECTING SCHOOL TO CAREER

1. **Possible response:** A good deal, because they have to work together to plan lessons and to share their observations about the children.
2. *Answers will vary but should be supported by sound reasoning.*

Applying What You've Learned

Have students write a help wanted advertisement for a child care center worker using the information they learned in the feature.

INFOLINK

Child Care Workers

For information about *background checks*, see page 634.

CAREER OPPORTUNITIES

Child Care Center Worker

A CONVERSATION WITH SHANNA RUTHERFORD

How did you become interested in becoming a child care center worker? I started babysitting at fourteen, and just loved it. I mean, young children are so incredibly alive. I wanted to be one of those people to give them a good start in life. I'm a child care aide now, but am working on my college degree.

What are the tasks and responsibilities of a child care center worker? First, care for their physical needs—we need to keep them safe and healthy. Next, give them chances to learn and develop their physical skills, their minds, their language skills, how they get along with others. You name it!

What is the work environment like? Noisy, and fun, and demanding, and exciting. We try to have as much structure as possible so the children know what to expect, but the children make every day a surprise.

What are the working hours like? I work eight hours a day, five days a week. It's a long eight hours, because I have to be alert and upbeat all the time.

What aptitudes are needed to be a child care center worker? I always tell my friends that the main thing is energy. Next is enthusiasm. Being soft spoken and gentle is important. So is having patience. There are so many things, it's hard to narrow the list!

CHILD CARE CENTER WORKER

Education and Training. Child care workers need at least a high school education. They can also take courses in early childhood education at two- or four-year colleges. Degrees are needed for higher-level positions.

Career Outlook. The outlook for child care workers is expected to be good.

CONNECTING SCHOOL TO CAREER

1. **Interpersonal Skills.** How much do you think workers in a child care center need to cooperate with one another—a lot or a little? Why?
2. **Resources.** Do you think that child care workers should have to pass a skills test to earn a license? Why or why not?

Building Career Skills

Information. What background data would a child care center need to keep on each child enrolled at the center? Have students list the information on an index card, then exchange cards with a partner. Ask the pairs to discuss any differences between their two lists. What information should be considered confidential?

Participating in Child Care and Education

As a part of your class in child development, you may have the chance to participate in an early childhood classroom. The following guidelines will help you get started and suggest ways that both you and the children can learn together. These skills can help you move toward a career in child care.

KEY TERMS

circle time
learning centers
transitions

OBJECTIVES:

- Explain the benefits of different learning centers in early childhood classrooms.
- Discuss how to promote health and safety in early childhood classrooms.
- Analyze what makes activity plans effective for young children.
- Discuss how to promote positive behavior.

The Early Childhood Classroom

Classrooms for young children need to be designed to meet their special needs. Think about all you have learned about the physical, social, emotional, and intellectual development of young children.

SECTION 20-2 RESOURCES

Teacher Resource Guide
- Lesson Plan Organizer, p. 84
- Section 20-2 Quiz, p. 216

Student Motivation Kit
- Observ. & Case Studies (case study), pp. 145-148
- Reteaching Activity, p. 58
- Enrichment, pp. 58-60

Student Workbook
- Study Guide, pp. 163-166
- Testing Your Safety Ideas, pp. 169-170

Transparency Package
- CT-55 Learning Centers
- CT-56 On-the-Job Communication

Effective Instruction CD-ROM

FOCUS

MOTIVATOR

Have students call out ideas for the different areas that would be needed in an early childhood classroom, such as a reading corner, an art center, or a music area. Write their ideas on the chalkboard. Then ask: What advantages would a classroom in a large space have over one in a small space?

VOCABULARY ACTIVITY

Ask students to hypothesize about the meanings of circle time and learning centers in relation to the early childhood classroom.

Observing & Participating

Have students suggest techniques for separating different learning centers and providing transitions between activities in an early childhood classroom where space is limited. For example, students may suggest that children sit in chairs for art time, but on the floor for reading time. In this way, separate areas would not be necessary for the two activities. Clearing away tables and chairs provides children with a transition between art and reading time.

COMPREHENSION CHECK

1. What are the benefits of learning centers? (*They offer children choices, allow them to explore different areas of knowledge, and develop skills.*)
2. Why is a low table useful in a science center? (*It provides the children with a convenient place to work.*)
3. Why should a language arts center not be placed near an active play area? (*The active play would interfere with the quieter activities of the language arts center.*)

ACTIVITIES

Critical Thinking Activity

Evaluating. Have students identify the kinds of skills that can be developed by each of the different learning areas. Write the learning areas on the board and solicit suggestions from students, writing each under the appropriate heading. **L2**

VISUAL LEARNING | **Using the Photographs**
Possible responses: Top photo is organized and has child-size furniture; bottom photo has equipment anchored to ground.

The first requirement is for the classroom environment to be child-sized. This promotes independence because children are able to use the materials without having to ask adults for help. This independence allows the child to feel successful. Chairs should be low enough to allow children to sit with their feet touching the floor. Shelves should be low so that children can get and return materials on their own.

A classroom for young children must be designed for their activities and needs. Discovery centers should have interesting objects to explore. Play areas must have sturdy equipment. *How do the areas shown here meet these standards?*

Management/Leadership Skills

Have students develop a list of activities or materials for the early childhood classroom that will help children learn to use each of the following senses: visual, auditory, kinesthetic, tactile, and olfactory. Both kinesthetic and auditory stimulation, for example, may be provided through a game such as musical chairs. Pair students after the initial brainstorming so that they can come up with a combined list consisting of their best ideas.

Learning Centers

Early childhood classrooms are usually divided into **learning centers.** These are areas of the classroom meant for certain types of play and learning. Learning centers offer children choices. They can select activities, explore different areas of knowledge, and develop skills through hands-on experiences.

The number and type of learning centers varies. The illustration on pages 616-617 shows one arrangement of centers in an early childhood classroom. Guidelines for materials learning centers are described in the "Parenting With Care" feature on pages 626-627.

Early childhood programs use guidelines such as these in setting up learning centers:

- Use different colored floor coverings, wall decorations, low shelves, or storage containers to separate different learning centers.
- Separate noisy centers from quiet centers.
- Place the art center near a source of water. The floor should be easy to clean if it gets wet.
- Leave a large, open area for large-group activities such as dancing to music.

Health and Safety

Ensuring the health and safety of the children is the first responsibility

of the staff of an early childhood classroom. Workers must follow health care routines to prevent illness, make sure the environment is safe, and supervise play.

Health Care Routines

Health care routines prevent the spread of illness. They also help make sure the children are well nourished and rested.

As children enter the classroom, staff members usually look for any obvious signs of illness. Children who are sick or become sick aren't allowed to stay with the group.

Children who attend a child care center for a half-day should have a snack in the middle of the morning or afternoon session.

Critical Thinking Activity

Making Inferences. **Ask:** Why does the art center need to be near a source of water? Are there other centers that could make use of water? **L1**

VISUAL LEARNING — **Using the Photograph** **Ask:** Why do children need a snack at these times? (Because their stomachs are small, they need to eat more frequently than adults.)

DID *You* **Know?**

Language Arts Centers. Because many children in today's early childhood classrooms do not speak English as their first language, language arts centers need to be more and more responsive to this trend. Educators can provide an optimal learning environment for these children by providing materials that teach in several languages, as well as those that enhance the English speaking and pre-reading abilities of non-English-proficient (NEP) or limited-English-proficient (LEP) students.

Management/Leadership Skills

Some centers use themes, or topics of special interest, as a means of carrying out their curriculum. A theme is used to link the various activities around a focal point or area of interest. Some themes include family, transportation, nature, seasons, animals, and plants. Have students choose a theme and develop learning activities around it. In addition, have students suggest decorations for the classroom based on the theme. Ask students to present their ideas in an oral or written report.

ACTIVITIES

Critical Thinking Activity

Making Inferences. **Ask:** Why is it important to mark each learning center off from other centers? How does it help the children? How does it help the teachers?

| VISUAL LEARNING | **Using the Graphic** Have each student design a floor plan for a children's classroom that includes at least five learning centers. Then let students share, discuss, evaluate, and display their floor plans. |

DID You Know?

Computer Learning Centers. Early childhood educators who are considering including a computer learning center in their classroom should strive to keep the use of this equipment as equitable as possible. Researchers have found that girls tend to use computers less often than boys. Some teachers use computer time as a reward for good behavior, rather than a learning opportunity for all.

Learning Centers in the Early Childhood Classroom

1 Block Center

Include small and large blocks, building logs, trucks and cars, and people and animal figures. Placing the block center on carpeting cuts down on noise. ▶

2 Science Center

The science center allows children to explore their world. Include magnifying glasses, scales, magnets, and specimens—rocks, leaves, and other natural objects—for children to use. Have a low table to give children a place to work. ▶

 Math Center

In this area, children can learn such concepts as matching, sorting, classifying, and counting. They can also learn about colors, sizes, and shapes and ideas such as before and after or over and under. ▶

4 Music Center

This area can include musical instruments such as tambourines, finger cymbals, triangles, and drums. It can also include records, CDs, audio tapes, and equipment to play them.

| LEARNING STYLES | **Logical/Mathematical** Have students design a math center for an early childhood classroom. Their plans should indicate the materials that would be available in the center and the skills that would be taught. Students should assume that their classroom | includes children from three to five years old. Ask students to include answer to the following question: How would you make mathematics interesting to preschoolers? |

Form students into groups and assign each group one of the learning centers on these pages. Have them review the materials listed for their center and create a list of activities that children could do with those materials. Have them share their ideas with the class. **L2**

Art Center

8

The art center allows children to be creative and exercise their imagination by drawing, painting, and working with clay and fabric. It should include paper, scissors and paste, crayons, paints, chalk, clay, and fabric. There should be smocks for children to wear when they work with these materials.

Active Play Area

7

In this area, children exercise their large muscles. It can include bean bags and streamers for throwing; areas for climbing, tumbling, and sliding; and a work bench for hammering.

Language Arts Center

6

This area includes materials related to speaking, listening, reading, and writing. It should be a quiet area with good lighting and comfortable chairs or throw pillows. The area might include a computer as well.

Dramatic Play Center

5

This area provides children with opportunities for make-believe play. It can include clothes and hats for dressing up, a play kitchen and related equipment, material that can be used to play office or grocery store, play money, and a telephone.

CHAPTER 20: Caring for Children **617**

MULTIPLE INTELLIGENCES

Because children are more comfortable learning in a particular way—perhaps visually, kinesthetically, or otherwise—they are likely to gravitate toward the same sorts of activities when given a choice. Auditory learners will choose listening to a story as it's read aloud, while visual learners will prefer to read the story themselves. This is fine, but it is the caregiver's responsibility to broaden the children's skills by drawing them into activities they might shun. Encourage the kinesthetic learner to sit and read and the visual learner to jump rope. Some early childhood programs give preschoolers "tickets" to different learning centers on different days.

Management/Leadership Skills

Have students form "Safety Patrol" teams whose mission is to eliminate needless injuries to children. Have them draw up a safety checklist and an advertisement that explains their purpose. Then, if possible, have them visit a local child care center or playground to check for safety hazards. After their visit, students should write an evaluation of their findings.

COMPREHENSION CHECK

1. What are three health care habits that children should be taught, in addition to hand washing? (*Proper hygiene when blowing the nose, no sharing of personal items, no sharing of eating and drinking utensils.*)

2. What requirements must be met for a balanced schedule in the classroom? (*Activities for individuals, for large and small groups, and for each area of development.*)

ACTIVITIES

Art Activity

Have students make posters reminding children of the importance of hand washing or showing children the proper way to wash their hands. If possible, donate the completed posters to child care centers. **L2**

Discussion Activity

Guide students in discussing how the design of a classroom can affect children's safety. For example, what problems might result if the block center were near a major traffic lane? (*Children might trip over the blocks and get hurt.*) What other potential problems can students identify? **L1**

Careful hand washing in one of the best ways to prevent he spread of disease. Children should be taught to wash their own hands thoroughly with warm water and soap, then dry them with a clean paper towel. Hands need washing after using the toilet, after blowing the nose, and before cooking, eating, or playing with materials such as clay.

Make a habit of washing your own hands often, both to protect everyone's health and to set a good example. Be sure to wash them after helping a child in the rest room, after you use the rest room yourself, after using a tissue to wipe a child's nose, and before handling food.

Children should learn several other important health care habits as well:

- To blow and wipe their nose and to dispose of the tissue.
- To cover their mouth when they cough.
- To use only his or her own comb, brush, or head wear—never those of another child.
- To avoid taking bites of each other's food and not to share the same cup or eating utensils.

Safety

To keep young children safe, make sure the environment is childproofed. Check the children's classroom and outdoor play areas for any possible safety hazards.

In addition, you need to supervise the children closely as they work and play. There should always be an ade-

INFOLINK

Health and Safety

For more about *health and safety*, see Chapter 18, pages 546-577.

quate number of teens or adults present to watch the children in each area. If an emergency arises, some caregivers should stay with the children in the classroom while someone goes for help.

Planning Appropriate Activities

Planning plays an important role in providing appropriate learning experiences for young children. The daily schedule should provide a balance of activities for individuals and for small and large groups of children. Activities also need to provide opportunities in each area of development. Of course, activities must be appropriate to the age and skill levels of the children too.

Learning Through Play

As you plan activities for young children, remember that the more involved the children are and the more realistic their experiences are, the more they learn. A story about a fire truck isn't nearly as effective a learning tool as a trip to the fire station and a chance to climb on a real one.

Children need play experiences that focus on these areas of development:

- Thinking and problem solving.
- Movement of large and small muscles.
- Creativity, including music, dance, dramatic play, and art.
- Relationships with others.

Children need a variety of activities that involve different kinds of experiences. When several children sit at a table each working on a puzzle, they are playing individually but alongside one another. Sometimes children play alone, perhaps looking at books by themselves. Children

Parenting in Action

Most parents are upset when they hear of a child being hurt by a caregiver. Such fear has given rise to the use, in some states, of fingerprinting and criminal background checks for volunteers and others who work with children. The effectiveness of such measures is open to debate. Most experts maintain that a strong relationship between parent and child and active involvement of the parent in the child's social life are the best prevention against child abuse.

Ask the Eperts

Pat Brodeen
Teacher and Teen Parent Coordinator
at Theodore Roosevelt High School in
San Antonio, Texas

WHAT TO *Look for in a Child Care Program*

Q How can I know that I'm choosing the best child care program for my child?

A Child care is very important and often a very difficult choice for parents to make. Let me suggest an effective approach to making this decision. Once you have found a program that is convenient and affordable and that offers the hours and services you need, approach that program from the child's point of view.

I want to spend my time with a loving person. Will the caregiver here love and appreciate me? Does he or she know how to communicate with me? Will the caregiver give me gentle but firm guidelines for my behavior? Does the caregiver have a high tolerance for my noisy activity level? If my caregiver's children are also here, will I get the same treatment? Has the caregiver had any educational preparation to work with me? Does he or she treat me the way my parents do, so I will have consistency in my day? Do I really like this person?

The facility where I will stay is also important to me. Are there few enough children so that I can feel secure in getting plenty of attention? Is the food nutritious, attractive, and tasty? Will I get regular meals and snacks, so I won't ever feel too hungry? Will I be safe here? Will I be encouraged to explore and learn, to be creative, to use all of my muscles, to pretend, and to laugh? Is this place clean and attractive? Will I get to go outside often and play on different kinds of equipment? After I have played and am really tired, will there be a special place for me to rest—a spot with soft, clean sheets that only I use?

Of course, these questions are just a start. You know your own child best, and you are the person who can most fully adopt your child's perspectives and interests in selecting a child care program.

Thinking It Through

1. Think of three more questions to add to the list. Explain why they are important.
2. How can a parent try to find out about a child care center to be able to answer these questions?

Ask the E perts

Introducing the Feature

Ask students if they are aware of any child care programs in your area. Then ask them to express an opinion about which program they would choose for their child, and why.

Answers to Thinking It Through

1. *Possible responses:* What are the other children like? Will I get along with them? Are they friendly? These questions matter because the child will spend a lot of time with other children in the program.
2. *Possible responses:* Visiting the center to watch children and child care workers interact; talking to the workers; having the child stay at the center for a day or two to see how he or she responds; talking to other parents.

Applying What You've Learned

Have students suppose they are the author of a weekly column in the local newspaper. The column is similar to a restaurant or movie review column, except that it rates child care programs. Have students select an imaginary program and write a review of it for this week's column.

ISSUES IN	
TEEN PARENTING	

Ask teen parents to make a list of their top ten requirements in a child care program. Then ask them to pick six of those items on which they would not compromise, and four on which they would compromise if necessary. Discuss students' choices. Which items are on their list due to necessity, such as cost or location? Which items are personal preference?

ACTIVITIES

Discussion Activity

Ask: Why schedule quiet activities after outdoor play? (*To give children chance to rest.*)

Critical Thinking Activity

Making Comparisons. Ask students whether they spend any part of their day playing. If so, what activities constitute play? Then ask them to name various ways in which adults play. Finally, ask them to write a paragraph in which they compare teen or adult play with the play of young children. In what fundamental way do they differ? **L2**

Critical Thinking Activity

Analyzing Information. Present the following daily schedule for students' consideration:

12:45-1:00	Arrival
1:00-1:15	Snack
1:15-1:45	Outdoor play
1:45-2:30	Learning centers
2:30-3:15	Small-group activities
3:15-3:30	Large-group story
3:30-3:45	Large-group music activity
3:45-4:00	Departure

Ask: What problems does this schedule create? How would you alter the schedule? Why? **L2**

A field trip gives the children a chance to have new learning experiences. **What places can you think of to take children?**

also play in small groups. Sheera, Kyle, and Tessa are pretending they are going to the store. Large group music or movement activities are usually guided by a teacher. The group as a whole may join together in **circle time,** in which a large group sits together for such activities as show-and-tell or story reading.

The Developing Brain

The brains of young children benefit by hearing nursery rhymes. The patterns formed by rhymes and rhythms prime them for later learning of reading and math. Working puzzles has the same benefit.

The Daily Schedule

The daily schedule is the master plan for how the children will use their time. Good schedules for young children in group settings feature a balance of active and quiet activities, small- and large-group activities, and teacher-directed and child-selected activities. Here's a sample schedule for a three-hour session:

8:30-8:45	Arrival and free play
8:45-9:00	Circle time
9:00-9:30	Small-group activities
9:30-9:45	Large-group activities
9:45-10:00	Toileting and hand-washing
10:00-10:15	Snack
10:15-10:45	Outdoor play
10:45-11:15	Learning centers
11:15-11:30	Large-group story time

A good daily schedule allows time for **transitions,** periods during which children move from one activity to the next. During a transition, the children need to conclude one activity, put their materials away, and get ready for the next activity. Always let them know a few minutes ahead of time that they will soon have to make a change. Whenever possible, use a song or a game to help children move from one place to another or from one activity to the next. For

Management/Leadership Skills

Have one student organize the writing of a detailed planning chart for a four-hour schedule. The student should supply the basic schedule. He or she should then assign other students to complete the following tasks: type of activity; objective of each activity; materials needed; procedures; evaluation. Students can complete the chart in a round-robin fashion, passing it to the next student when they have completed their section.

Why is a warm welcome a good start to a child's day?

Planning activities for each day will help make your work with children more successful. **What could happen if you didn't plan?**

example, you might sing a special cleanup song as you and the children put away materials after learning center time.

Writing Learning Activity Plans

A daily schedule outlines the children's day in general. The lead teacher then must plan specific things to do during each activity period. There are two types of forms that can be used to write these plans.

The first form—the planning chart—works from the daily schedule. This form lists the activities that will take place in each learning center during each period of the day. Suppose you are preparing a one week overview based on the daily schedule on the previous page. If so, you would note which outdoor activities would take place each day and which stories you would tell during story time each day.

The second form allows you to record detailed information about each planned

CHAPTER 20: Caring for Children **621**

COMPREHENSION CHECK

1. What are transitions? What should take place during a transition? (*Periods in which children complete one activity and prepare for the next. They need to put all materials for first activity away and get ready to begin a new one.*)

ACTIVITIES

Teamwork Activity

Have students work in groups to write a daily schedule for a two-hour program of after-school activities for first-graders, as well as for a four-hour program for preschoolers. In what ways should these schedules differ? Why? Have each team prepare an explanation and justification for their schedules. **L2**

VISUAL LEARNING	Using the Photographs

p. 620: *Answers will vary.*
p. 621 Left:—*Possible response:* Shows children they are welcome. *Right:*—*Possible responses:* May not be enough materials for all children; may not have good variety of activities.

DID You Know?

Planning Activities. When planning activities, it is important to consider the ages of the children in the center. Activities that excite a two-year-old may bore a four-year-old. In addition, planners need to know the attention span of children at particular ages. A half-hour activity for children with an attention span of 15 minutes will not succeed.

COMPREHENSION CHECK

1. What guidelines should a caregiver follow when establishing classroom rules? (*Limit the number of rules; state rules in a positive way; be sure each rule has a clear purpose.*)
2. When is positive reinforcement ineffective? (*When it is given in an absentminded or insincere manner.*)

ACTIVITIES

Discussion Activity

Ask: Is it necessary for teachers and other care providers to be good role models at all times or only in the classroom? Why? **L1**

Teamwork Activity

Have students work in groups to discuss methods of presenting rules to young children. Have the members of each group select one of the listed rules and plan an activity that would help teach that rule to a group of preschoolers. **L2**

VISUAL LEARNING | **Using the Photograph**
Possible responses: Running is not allowed inside; don't take anything being used by another child.

Putting away is a basic rule that teaches respect for others. **Name another.**

activity. On this form, you would include specific information under these headings:
- Title of the activity.
- Objective, or purpose, of the activity.
- Type of activity (for a learning center, small group, or large group).
- Materials needed.
- Procedures to be followed.
- Evaluation—a recap of the success or problems with the activities.

The form you use isn't as important as the fact that you do have written plans.

Writing out plans ahead of time helps you think through the appropriateness of each activity. It also provides a list of everything you need so that the materials can be set up before the children arrive. Written plans give workers materials they can discuss with the children's parents. Finally, having a written plan will give you a reference source you and your co-workers can consult when it is time to start the activity.

Promoting Positive Behavior

For a classroom to function smoothly, rules need to be established for the children to follow. Child care providers also need to use positive reinforcement and act as role models. Strategies must be developed for dealing with unacceptable behavior in a safe and nurturing manner.

Establishing Classroom Rules

Young children need classroom rules, but too many rules can overwhelm them. The classroom rules should be stated in positive terms. That is, each rule should tell the children what they should do—not what they shouldn't do. Each classroom rule should also have a clear purpose. Rules should also be appropriate for the age of the children involved. The younger the child, the shorter and fewer the rules should be.

LEARNING STYLES | **Visual/Spatial**

Have students design a planning chart form that caregivers can reuse each week. Give them the following guidelines: planning charts should include the specific information listed on page 622; planning charts should be attractive and well organized; planning charts should allow for flexibility in the daily schedule. Have students make a model of their planning charts. Then display their finished work around the classroom. If desired, allow other students to review and critique the charts.

The following list shows one possible set of rules:

1. **Use your hands gently.** This discourages hitting or pushing.
2. **Walk, don't run, inside the classroom.** This prevents accidents from falls.
3. **Put materials away when you are finished.** This keeps the room well organized and allows children to find materials when they want them.
4. **Use an inside voice in the classroom.** This prevents the classroom from being too noisy.
5. **Be a friend to other people.** This builds a pleasant atmosphere.
6. **Keep your feet away from others.** This prevents injuries and falls.

Provide activities that help the children understand the rules. For example, for "use your hands gently," you might have a collection of pictures showing friendly touching and hurtful touching. By asking the children questions, you could help them understand what each type of touching feels like. Make it very clear that hurtful touching is not allowed in your classroom.

Using Positive Reinforcement

Children enjoy being recognized and rewarded with attention. They tend to repeat behaviors that are rewarded. To make this technique effective, however, you must be sincere in your response to a child's behavior. If you give only automatic or inattentive comments and praise, the children won't see them as rewards.

Caregivers can reinforce the purpose and importance of basic rules through stories and conversation.

CHAPTER 20: Caring for Children **623**

Have students write a brief opening statement to be made to a preschool class on the first day of school, explaining the kind of behavior expected in the classroom and the rules of the classroom. Remind students to keep in mind that the audience is a group of young children, who find it difficult to sit still and pay attention for long. **L2**

DID *You* **Know?**

Guiding Behavior. When children are restless and the potential for misbehavior seems high, caregivers can try the following suggestions:

- **Change the pace** by suggesting a new activity.
- **Use a timer** to help teach sharing if a squabble over a toy seems imminent.
- **Involve children in a "meeting,"** and ask for ideas of how to solve the problem.
- **Be sure** that you are not causing the behavior with inattention, irritability, or other inappropriate behavior.

Management/Leadership Skills

Have students suggest how they would respond to the following instances of behavior in a preschool classroom:

- After repeated unsuccessful attempts to cut a piece of paper, Cory throws the scissors across the room.

- In spite of two reminders, Zoe continues to color on the table, not on her sheet of paper.
- After being told five minutes ago that it was time to clean up their paints and get ready for story time, several children continue to paint.

COMPREHENSION CHECK

1. For what type of misbehavior is a time-out an appropriate response? (*Answers will vary.*)

ACTIVITIES

Discussion Activity

Discuss the following scenario as a class: "Sondra has twice warned Johnny to stop grabbing the toy car from Eliza. On the third grab, Sondra places Johnny in the seat reserved for time-outs. He immediately gets up and walks away." What should she do?

Teamwork Activity

Have students take turns playing the roles of caregiver and child. Give two or more "children" three minutes to discuss a situation to present to the caregiver that involves misbehavior. Then allow these students to act out their roles, while the "caregiver" responds as he or she thinks appropriate. After the scenario is played out, have the rest of the class comment on how well the caregiver handled the situation.

Child care workers need to communicate with parents. *Do you think they should tell parents every time a child does something wrong? Why?*

Being a Good Role Model

In the classroom, your own behavior has a powerful influence on children. Children are more likely to do what you do—not what you say. If you want the children to use inside voices, then you must always use a quiet voice indoors. If you want them to treat each other with kindness, you must treat them and co-workers kindly.

Dealing with Misbehavior

Of course, children will from time to time behave in unacceptable ways. You need to know in advance the program's guidelines for handling such situations. The children should also understand what will happen if they behave in unacceptable ways.

In most cases, a simple statement of what you want the child to do is effective. If a child is using too loud a voice, for example, simply say, "Taylor, please use your inside voice. I can't hear well when you are shouting." In other situations, you may offer the child a choice of more acceptable activities. If a child is not playing well in the block center, you might say, "Qiuhong, you may choose to go to the dramatic play center or the art center. I can't let you stay in the block center because you are still trying to take Emilio's blocks." Notice that each

624 UNIT 6: Special Areas of Study

Parenting in *Action*

Some child care centers now offer parents the opportunity to log onto the Internet to view live pictures of their child. The pictures are updated frequently throughout the day, perhaps as often as every 30 seconds. Parents feel more in touch with their child, although they don't necessarily feel more secure about leaving them in child care. Concerns focus on unauthorized access and a generation of children who think that video surveillance is the norm.

example includes an explanation of why the child's behavior was unacceptable.

For some types of unacceptable behavior, a stronger response is necessary. Behavior that hurts other people or property must not be permitted at any time. Children who break this type of rule should receive an immediate and consistent response. One effective approach is to give the child a time-out. Of course, you need to continue to show that you care for the child—but that the actions aren't acceptable.

INFOLINK

Time-Out

For more about *time-out*, see Chapter 3, page 97.

SECTION 20-2 REVIEW

✔ Check Your Understanding

1. What are learning centers?
2. How can you separate learning centers from one another?
3. When should young children wash their hands? When should child care workers wash theirs?
4. Study the sample schedule in this section. Are the different activity periods long or short? Why?
5. What are transitions? How can teachers help young children feel comfortable during transition times?
6. What elements need to be listed in an activity plan?
7. How lengthy should a child care worker make any explanations about why a child is being disciplined? Why?

Putting Knowledge Into Practice

1. **Analyzing.** What makes an activity plan effective? Why does a caregiver need to look at other plans for the children to do in the same day in order to evaluate an activity plan?
2. **Applying.** Working in a group, brainstorm a list of possible rules for an early childhood classroom. Share these rules with the rest of the class and develop a class list.
3. **Observing and Participating.** Visit a child care center. Describe how attentive the adults seem to be. Do you feel the children are receiving personal, loving care? Why or why not?

CHAPTER 20: Caring for Children **625**

ASSESS

CHECKING COMPREHENSION

Have students answer the Check Your Understanding questions. Answers appear at the bottom of this page.

EVALUATION

Give students the Section 20-2 Quiz in the *Teacher Resource Guide*.

RETEACHING

1. Assign Reteaching Activities, page 58.
2. Present a list of preschool activities. Have students arrange the activities in a sequence that provides a balance of activities.

ENRICHMENT

Have students compare and contrast daily schedules from three local preschools and, on that basis, rate the programs.

EXTENSION

Arrange a class visit to an early childhood classroom. Have students draw a floor plan of the classroom and list the equipment and supplies in at least two learning centers. Later, ask students to write an evaluation of the classroom.

CLOSE

Have students complete the following sentence: "Workers in a child care center can help children by . . . "

Have several students describe the "equipment" that furnishes their bedrooms at home. What factors went into choosing these materials?

COMPREHENSION CHECK

1. Why is ease of cleaning even more important in the classroom than in the home? (*Because the materials will be used by many different children.*)
2. Why is it important that the classroom have ample storage space for all materials? (*Poorly stored items or a cluttered classroom can cause a tripping hazard.*)

ACTIVITIES

Critical Thinking Activity

Formulating Questions. Have students suppose they are teachers in a preschool classroom. A salesperson is visiting to try to sell them a new item for the classroom. Ask students to write a list of five questions they would ask the salesperson about the item. **L2**

Parenting With Care

Choosing Materials for the Classroom

*T*he materials chosen in different learning centers have to be chosen carefully.

These materials can be expensive, and educators can't afford to waste money. They must meet special requirements because they will be used by many children of different ages over a long period of time.

*H*ere are some guidelines for choosing materials for the early childhood classroom:

- Are they safe? Edges should be rounded rather than sharp. Paint must be nontoxic since children often put objects in their mouths. Will they withstand heavy or rough use by a group of as many as twenty children? Are the materials durable?
- Will the materials be easy to clean? This is even more important in the classroom than in the home since materials are used by many different children.
- Does the classroom have sufficient storage space for the materials? Are there storage containers available?
- Can children of different ages use the materials?
- Do the materials encourage cooperative play rather than aggressive play?
- Do the materials encourage creative play? Can they be used for more than one purpose?
- Do the materials encourage children's active play rather than passive participation? Will it hold a child's interest?
- Will children learn basic concepts while using the materials? Will the materials support program goals? Will they reinforce curriculum themes and objectives?
- Will the materials allow children to learn from their senses?

- Could both boys and girls use the materials? Are the materials free of racial, cultural, and gender stereotypes?
- Will children have fun with the materials?

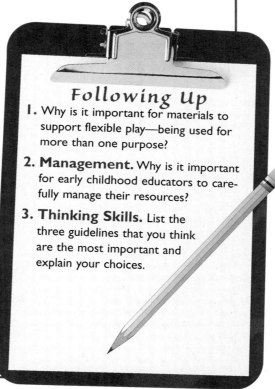

Following Up

1. Why is it important for materials to support flexible play—being used for more than one purpose?

2. **Management.** Why is it important for early childhood educators to carefully manage their resources?

3. **Thinking Skills.** List the three guidelines that you think are the most important and explain your choices.

CHAPTER 20: Caring for Children **627**

Teamwork Activity

Have students work in groups to devise a list of basic materials for the early childhood classroom. Then have groups exchange lists and check for the appropriateness of the listed items based on the guidelines given in the feature. **L1**

CLOSE

1. Have students choose one of the guidelines in the text and think of an item that does not meet this requirement. Ask students to write a brief paragraph describing the item and explaining its shortcomings.

2. **Extension.** Have students speak with an early childhood educator to find out how that professional went about selecting items for the classroom. What state or local requirements had to be met? What other requirements were considered? How much money could be spent? Have students report their findings to the class in a written or oral report.

CHECKING COMPREHENSION

Use the Summary and the Reviewing the Facts questions to help students go over the most important ideas in Chapter 20. Encourage students to ask questions and add details.

CHAPTER 20 REVIEW

Answers to Reviewing the Facts

1. Gives the children a chance to get used to the person, parent to give information.
2. Adventurousness leading to danger; sleeping problems.
3. Show interest in games, possessions, or activities.
4. Get children to safety; alert others; call fire department; call parents.
5. Area of the classroom for certain type of learning.
6. The children's health and safety.
7. *Any three:* Wash hands after using the toilet, blowing the nose, or helping a child in the rest room; wash before cooking or eating; dispose of soiled tissues; do not share personal items; avoid sharing food.
8. *Possible response:* Learn about autumn by gathering leaves and naming colors.
9. Title of activity; objectives; type of activity; materials needed; procedures; evaluation.
10. Establishing classroom rules; giving positive reinforcement; being a good role model; dealing with misbehavior appropriately.

CHAPTER 20 REVIEW &

Summary

✔ Babysitters take responsibility for caring for children for a short time. (Section 20-1)
✔ Caring for children requires being prepared to meet the needs of children of different ages. (Seciton 20-1)
✔ An early childhood classroom includes different learning centers and must be healthful and safe for children. (Section 20-2)

✔ The classroom should stimulate learning by children. (Section 20-2)
✔ Early childhood staff must promote positive behavior. (Section 20-2)

Reviewing the Facts

1. Why is it important for a babysitter to arrive about 20 minutes early the first time he or she works for a family? (Section 20-1)
2. What problems must a babysitter be prepared for when watching toddlers and preschoolers? (Section 20-1)
3. What can a babysitter do to get along more easily with an older child? (Section 20-1)
4. What should you do if a fire breaks out where you are babysitting? (Section 20-1)
5. What is a learning center? (Section 20-2)
6. What is the first responsibility of the staff of an early education classroom? (Section 20-2)
7. List three practices that contribute to health in the classroom. (Section 20-2)

8. Give an example of how being involved in an activity can help children learn. (Section 20-2)
9. What information should be included on an activity plan? (Section 20-2)
10. What are the methods staff can use to teach children appropriate behavior? (Section 20-2)

Thinking Critically

1. **Diagramming.** Make a chart of important skills a child care provider should have to care for children. Put each item under the heading "Infants," "Toddlers and Preschoolers," and "Older Children."
2. **Analyzing.** Evaluate the following sequence of activities. If you think it is not effective, make changes to fix the problems: Arrival and free play; dancing; story time; outdoor play; art activities; snack; toileting and hand-washing; resting.

Taking Action

1. **Making a Book.** Create a cartoon-like book or a series of posters that can teach young children the benefits of basic safety habits. *(Communication)*
2. **Easing Transitions.** Make up a song or game that you could use in an early childhood classroom to ease children in the transition from one activity to another.

CONNECTIONS

Demonstrate the song or game to others in the class and ask for suggestions to improve your idea. *(Leadership)*

Cross-Curricular Connections

1. **Language Arts.** Write a help-wanted ad that a parent might write for a babysitter. The child to be watched could be of any age from birth to eight years old. What qualities would the parent be looking for?

Workplace Connections

1. **Resources.** Make a schedule that could be used for a half-day program for three-year-olds. Be sure to vary activities aimed at different developmental areas and different ways for children to be involved.

2. **Basic Skills.** Take the role of the supervisor of an early childhood classroom. Write a memo to new staff members that explains how children can benefit from each of the learning centers in the classroom. Choose any six centers to write about.

Family and Community Connections

1. **It's in the Bag.** Make a "care provider bag" of materials you find around your home that you could bring with you on

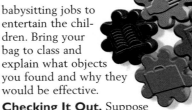

babysitting jobs to entertain the children. Bring your bag to class and explain what objects you found and why they would be effective.

2. **Checking It Out.** Suppose you were the parent searching for an early childhood classroom for your four-year-old. Create a checklist of what you would look for.

Technology Connections

1. **Internet.** Search online for information about health in early childhood classrooms. Choose one issue that you find in your research. Develop a list of procedures that could be followed in a classroom to meet the recommendations.

2. **Technology.** Search online or in the library to find out how the computer or other technology is being used in the early childhood classroom. Evaluate the uses described—what impact might these uses have on small motor skills, for instance?

EVALUATION

1. Use the reproducible Chapter 20 Test in the *Teacher Resource Guide,* or construct your own test using the **Exam***View*® Test Generator.

2. For an alternative assessment, assign the Chapter 20 activity in the *Authentic Assessment* section of the *Teacher Resource Guide.*

ENRICHMENT

Assign students either of the two enrichment activities in the *Enrichment Activities* booklet in the *Student Motivation Kit.*

EXTENSION

Have students videotape children at play in a child care center. (If videotaping equipment is unavailable, ask students to prepare photographs or drawings.) Use the videotapes as a basis for discussion, noting classroom organization, schedule planning, and approaches to promoting positive behavior.

CLOSE

Have students write diary entries that describe a young child's day at preschool. Entries should address the caregiver's personality, health and safety in the classroom, learning centers, and guiding behavior.

Career Success Handbook

Your career is stretching out before you. That may feel both exciting and a bit unnerving. Section 1-4 gave suggestions on choosing and preparing yourself for a career. This Handbook focuses on entering and succeeding in the working world.

Your first jobs may be part-time or summer jobs while you are still in school. They could simply be jobs that are convenient and available or ones that lead to your career goal. Every job, however, can enhance your employability skills.

It all begins with finding a job that's right for you. Next, you need to do that job well. When it's time to make a career move to another job, you will want to leave on good terms with your former employer.

This Handbook can help guide you through that process. It explains the "rules" of employment and gives tips for achieving career success.

When you follow up on job leads by phone, it's what you say that makes a first impression.

Finding a Job

You may be lucky enough to be in the right place at the right time and be hired for the perfect job. You may be fortunate to have an internship or a part-time job that turns into a full-time position. Most people, however, must devote a considerable amount of time and effort to their job search. They spend time finding job openings, contacting employers, and interviewing.

Plan to make that investment of time and energy in your own job search. After all, you will be spending many hours at work each week. Your working relationship with your employer should be mutually beneficial—you should be an asset to your employer and the relationship should benefit you, too.

As you start your search, be organized. Create a job search notebook or computer file. Use it to record names, addresses, and pertinent dates. For instance, you might record the date you responded to a newspaper ad for a position as a summer camp coordinator, the date you were contacted by the agency's director, the time and location of your interview, and the date you sent a follow-up letter.

Finding Job Openings

The Internet and classified ads from the newspaper are excellent ways to find job openings, but they are not your only resources.

Finding a job often begins with a tip from a friend or associate. Spread the word that you are job hunting. Enlist the aid of your circle of acquaintances. This includes your friends' parents and relatives.

Perhaps your neighbor's sister-in-law is a Girl Scout leader who knows that the organization will be looking for a new program director soon. Maybe your brother's roommate knows of an opening for a teacher at the preschool where his girlfriend works. The more people who know you are seeking a job, the more job leads you will hear about. This practice of using your personal and professional contacts to further your career goals is called "networking."

Does your community have job fairs? Sometimes they are sponsored by a local community college or university. Employers with current or future job openings meet with prospective employees. You may not land the perfect job by attending the job fair, but you will be able to make valuable contacts for your job search by meeting some of the exhibitors.

Preparing a Résumé

A résumé is a concise document that provides a summary of your education, work experience, and accomplishments. Your résumé gives you a chance to put your best foot forward as you conduct your job search.

Think of it as an advertisement of yourself. A sample résumé on page 632 shows the sections that are traditionally included in a résumé.

The first section—the job or professional objective—consists of one or two sentences stating the type of position you are seeking. It should convey a sense of purpose and direction. It's good to customize the objective for each specific potential employer.

The next section, education, lists your most recent educational institution or program first. Honors or awards may be included in this section. If you have several, you may add a separate listing for "honors."

Choose carefully what to include and emphasize in your résumé. If you don't have much work experience, focus on your skills and education. Be sure to include volunteer jobs. That conveys to potential employers that you are reliable and have a positive attitude toward work.

Here are some additional tips for preparing an effective résumé.

- Be concise, keeping the résumé to one page if possible. Two pages is the maximum length.
- Always be truthful. Don't misrepresent your work history, accomplishments, or education.
- Use action verbs to describe accomplishments. Consider these possibilities: achieved, developed, reorganized, coordinated, produced, led, and conducted.
- Proofread the document carefully. Have someone help you if necessary. Poor grammar or misspelled words may eliminate you from consideration.
- Keep it simple. Don't clutter your résumé with pictures and graphics.
- Ask any references for permission before including their name and contact information. References may be listed on your résumé or on a separate page.

Chris T. Revoir
6412 W. Main St.
Arlington, Texas 76000
682-555-1234
CTR81@anymail.com

Objective:	To work with children as a teacher's aide in a Bilingual Education program
Education:	Associate in Applied Science degree, 2003 Ashton Community College, Dallas, Texas
	High School Diploma, 2001 Whittier High School, Arlington, Texas
Skills:	Excellent organizational skills Fluent in Spanish and French Ability to work without direct supervision

Experience:

2001-Present **Photography Assistant**
Angelface Photography Studio, Dallas, Texas.
Assist children's photographer with studio sittings; schedule appointments.

1999-2001 **Foreign Language Tutor**
Spanish and French.
Tutored 4-5 high school students each semester.

1998-2000 **Counselor**
Far Hills Equestrian Camp, Round Rock, Texas.
Supervised 8 campers each session.

Honors: FCCLA State Vice President of STAR Events, 2001
American Legion Award, 2000
National French Honor Society

Membership: Family, Career and Community Leaders of America (FCCLA)
4-H (Chairperson of Horse Leader's Conference)

References available upon request

6412 W. Main St.
Arlington, TX 76000

June 15, 2003

Michelle Baldwin
Director, Human Resources
School District 184
Garland, TX 75001

Dear Ms. Baldwin:

I am replying to the ad in the *Dallas Morning News,* seeking a teacher's aide for the Bilingual Education program at the Early Childhood Education Center. I believe my skills are an excellent match for this position.

As a high school and college student, I enjoyed courses in child development. I have been successful working with children of all ages—as a camp counselor, tutor, and active member of FCCLA and 4-H. Currently, my job as a photography assistant involves working with preschool and grade school age children. My other main interest is foreign language. In 2001, I was fortunate to participate in a month-long exchange program in Mexico. I speak Spanish fluently and have five years of credit in French. As a language student at Whittier High School, I frequently assisted with special events in an ESL classroom.

As you review my résumé, I believe you will see I have the interest and ability to succeed as a teacher's aide. I would appreciate learning more about your program at the Early Childhood Education Center.

I am available for an interview any morning of the week. The best time to reach me at home is before noon. My telephone number is 682-555-1234. My e-mail address is CTR81@anymail.com. Thank you for your consideration.

Sincerely,

Chris T. Revoir

Chris T. Revoir

Writing a Cover Letter

Many employers have dozens of résumés cross their desks. An interesting cover letter can set yours apart from the rest and result in a request for an interview. See the sample cover letter above.

This introductory letter, sent with your résumé, is your initial opportunity to make a good impression. It should explain how your talents and skills would benefit the program or company, prompt the employer to read your résumé, and ultimately result in an interview.

Keep these points in mind:

- Highlight your skills and background, but don't repeat everything in your résumé.
- Limit the cover letter to one page.
- Make sure the letter doesn't sound like a form letter. Tailor it to fit the particular situation.
- As with the résumé, make sure your spelling and grammar are flawless.
- Try to address the letter to an individual rather than "to whom it may concern." You may be able to call the employer to find the name of a contact person or the person's title. This information may also be on an employer's Website.
- Use high-quality white or cream paper and sign your name legibly in black ink.
- Some companies require computer-scannable résumés. Ask for specific formatting guidelines.

Filling Out an Application

Most employers routinely ask applicants to fill out a job application. Application forms serve as a screening tool to determine which applicants deserve further consideration.

Make a good impression by being well groomed and neatly dressed when you go to fill out an application.

As you complete an application, read and follow the directions carefully. Print neatly and answer questions truthfully and as positively as possible. If a question doesn't pertain to you, write "NA" in the blank for "not applicable." Some applications ask for the salary you require. "Negotiable" is a tactful way to respond.

Whenever you expect to be filling out a job application, bring along your job search notebook or printouts from your computer file. You will need specific information about your educational background and work history, including dates and locations. Also take a printed list of your references. This information will help you complete the application quickly and accurately.

Most applications ask when you would be available to start working. If you aren't currently working, you may be able to state "immediately." Otherwise, you may write "upon two weeks' notice" if you must resign from your current job.

Before you may be hired for a position in early childhood care and education, your state probably requires that you pass a criminal background check. Job candidates who have been convicted of a crime against a child must be rejected.

Interviews

The thought of a job interview makes many job seekers nervous. You can reduce your apprehension by being well prepared for interviews. Think of the interview as your chance to let the interviewer see you as more than a name on a piece of paper.

Consider these components of the interview process.

- **Preparation.** Learn as much as possible about the company or program before the interview. Study the employer's Website if there is one. Talk to anyone you know who is familiar with the employer.
- **Rehearse.** Ask someone to help you practice for the interview. See commonly asked interview questions on page 635. You may wish to videotape the rehearsal. Look for any mannerisms that you want to avoid, such as slouching, twisting your hair, or saying "You know."
- **Dress appropriately.** Try to match your outfit to the job. Looking your best will help you feel confident. Take a modest, conservative approach. Avoid very baggy or tight clothing. Keep jewelry to a minimum.
- **Arrive early.** Allow for possible traffic delays and arrive a few minutes early, but not too early. It may be wise to have a trial run the day before to see how long it takes to get to the interview site at that time of day.
- **Greet the interviewer.** Shake the person's hand firmly. Try not to appear anxious or overeager. Don't call the interviewer by his or her first name. Once invited to sit down, keep your possessions in your lap rather than setting them on the interviewer's desk.
- **Listen carefully.** Pay attention to the questions you are asked. Maintain eye contact. Don't attempt to change the subject or interrupt the interviewer.

- **Ask appropriate questions.** When the employer asks if you have any questions, try to find out as much as possible about the position to see if you're truly qualified and interested. You might ask about the nature of the job, its responsibilities, and the work environment. Don't bring up the topic of salary and benefits at a first interview unless the interviewer does.
- **Leave gracefully.** The interviewer may signal the end of the interview by saying that you will be contacted later. Be sure to thank the interviewer and to shake hands as you leave. Don't prolong the process. The interviewer may need to start the next scheduled interview.

Following Up After an Interview

After every job interview, promptly send a follow-up letter to the interviewer. Thank the person for taking the time to meet with you. Reinforce how your skills would be an asset to the position. Confirm your interest in the job.

Many job seekers become frustrated with the waiting game they must play. If the interviewer says that you will be hearing from them within two weeks, wait that length of time. Then it's permissible to call and politely ask about the status of your job application. You might ask,

Commonly Asked Interview Questions

What are your weaknesses? Can you answer that question? Before going to a job interview, you should have a ready reply. The interviewer is likely to ask that question, among others. You will have a clear advantage if you can anticipate questions that are likely to be asked. Here are a few standard questions that might be asked:

1. Why would you like to work for this company (or organization)?
2. What are your qualifications for this position?
3. What are your strengths and weaknesses?
4. What do you want to be doing in five years (or ten years)?
5. How would you describe yourself?
6. Why did you leave your last job?
7. What are the most important rewards you anticipate in your career?
8. Why did you choose this career?
9. How do you work under pressure?
10. What two or three accomplishments have given you the most satisfaction? Why?
11. What is a major problem you have encountered at school or on the job? How did you deal with it?
12. How creative are you? What are some examples of your creativity?
13. Have you been a member of a team or club? What did you like best and least about the experience?
14. Why should we hire you?
15. You seem overqualified for this position. Are you?
16. What is the hardest job you have ever performed?
17. What questions do you have about the job or this company/organization?
18. Are you opposed to drug testing?

"Could you please tell me what the next step is in the hiring process?" The employer might request that you come in for a second interview, or you may learn that someone else has been hired.

It may be tempting to ask why you didn't get the job, but be gracious in accepting the news. The employer is not obligated to tell you why you were not offered the job.

Above all, don't be discouraged. Your qualifications may not have been the right match for this particular job. Learn from the experience of the interview. If you felt you stumbled when answering a particular question, practice a better response before your next interview.

Evaluating a Job Offer

You may think that the most important factor in deciding whether to accept or reject a job offer is the salary. Of course you want to receive adequate compensation, but there are other factors to consider.

Perhaps the company is one that could provide you with a bright future. Many employees have started at entry-level positions simply to "get their foot in the door" at a desirable company or school. If there is potential for advancement, try to avoid thinking that a job is beneath you. In the early years of your career, remember that you are building a work history.

When you do receive a job offer, you don't need to give an answer on the spot. It's permissible to ask for a day to think about the offer. Avoid putting off responding, however. Make a list of pros and cons, if necessary. Consider the benefits that you would receive in addition to your paycheck. Health insurance and tuition reimburse-ment are two benefits that may be especially attractive to you. If the salary is lower than you expected, you might request a somewhat higher salary.

If you feel that you would probably remain at the job for just a short time, it may be best to decline. Changing jobs frequently is not an asset on your résumé.

Be gracious in turning down any job offer. If you have a specific reason for declining, such as a demanding travel schedule or working at night, ask the employer to keep you in mind for another position that might become available.

Building Your Career Skills

Beginning a new job is an exciting time. You will be learning new skills and practicing the ones you have already acquired. Whether you're working with the Head Start program or at a children's museum, there will be new people to get to know.

A positive attitude will help ensure success in the workplace. Never assume that you can get by with doing the minimum requirements of the job. Impress your supervisor by displaying a strong work ethic. Show that you possess good communication and human relationship skills. It's vital that you be able to get along with others. Display your ability to work as part of a team.

Communication Skills

Communication skills are key to every employee's success at work. The way that you speak, listen, and write will have an impact on your success in the world of work.

- **Speaking skills.** Do your best to speak clearly so others will understand you. Avoid speaking too rapidly. This is especially important when you are working with young children.
- **Edit your vocabulary.** Some words that weren't spoken in polite company 20 years ago have become almost commonplace in today's society. That doesn't mean they're acceptable in the workplace, however. It's not possible to appear professional at work if you use "bad language" and slang.
- **Avoid gossip.** The things that you *don't* say can impact your success at work. Resist any temptation to speak negatively about your employer, coworkers, or clients. Being kind to others is not only the right thing to do, it will help advance your career in the long run.
- **Writing skills.** Depending on your position, you may be required to communicate in writing with parents, coworkers, clients, and possibly the press. This may involve e-mail, memos, letters, press releases, or notes sent home to parents. Consider the audience to whom you are writing. Make sure your correspondence is free of errors. Keep your computer skills up to date.
- **Listening skills.** Good listening skills involve more than hearing what a person is saying. It often involves responding to the speaker's message. As you listen to a child or another adult, try to ignore distractions if possible. Maintain eye contact with the individual. Read the speaker's body language, as you listen to what's said.

Human Relationship Skills

Whenever a group of people must work together, there is the potential for conflicts. Problems that people have at work stem often from relationships they have with other employees. Success in the workplace requires respect for others. Make every attempt to treat your coworkers the way you wish to be treated. Keep the following concepts in mind.

- **Respect differences.** You will be working with people with various personalities and strengths. If you dislike a coworker, don't let it show. Keep your personal feelings separate from the job that you both must do.
- **Understand workplace hierarchy.** Choose appropriate behavior by realizing there is usually a hierarchy at work. Your supervisor is the person to whom you report. Your colleagues are at the same level of responsibility as you are. Subordinates are employees who are under you. Of course, coworkers at every level deserve your respect.
- **Communicate in a positive manner.** Be encouraging and supportive of coworkers. Make sure that your nonverbal communication, or body language, matches your positive words. Consider the comment, "I'd be happy to work for you the day after Thanksgiving." Imagine if it were said with a scowl, through clenched teeth, or with arms crossed. The nonverbal communication would contradict the spoken words.
- **Resolve conflicts.** Use compromise and negotiation to resolve conflicts. If you

think about conflict as a mutual problem to be solved, it's easier to find a solution. Analyze what points are most important to you and which ones you can be flexible about. Try to keep your emotions out of the process.

- **Avoid dating coworkers.** Romance in the workplace is not unusual, but it is seldom a good idea. Dating a superior or subordinate is especially ill advised. Coworkers may feel that you are getting preferential treatment. There is also a risk of sexual harassment claims.

Leadership

Leadership skills are necessary for numerous careers that relate to children. After all, children look up to the adults in their lives for guidance and leadership. Family members of the children you serve in your capacity as a teacher, counselor, social worker, or agency employee will also regard you as a leader. When asked to supervise other employees or volunteers at work, you take on a leadership role.

As an effective leader, you must exhibit integrity. What other traits do people in leadership roles possess? Here are a few qualities of good leaders. Can you think of others?

- **Decision-making ability.** Informed decisions have to be made in a timely fashion. Others will be counting on their leader to ensure that progress is being made.
- **Ability to delegate.** Good leaders don't attempt to do every task on their own just to make sure it's done their own way. When necessary, leaders must be able to delegate responsibility to other people who can get the job done.
- **Trustworthiness.** Coworkers have to be able to respect and trust their leader. The ability to keep information confidential is a key component of trustworthiness.
- **Fairness.** Leaders earn the respect of the people they lead when they treat them fairly. Showing favoritism toward certain employees will be noticed.
- **Consideration.** Effective leaders take time to listen to ideas expressed by others.
- **Self-confidence.** Leaders must be self-assured to perform the duties of their jobs.
- **Positive attitude.** Negativity will not inspire others to do their best work.

Involvement in a professional organization is an ideal way to hone your leadership skills. For high school students, an excellent choice is FCCLA (Family, Career and Community Leaders of America).

Teamwork

Do you enjoy working on group projects at school or in your community? Have you been a member of the band or an extracurricular or sports team? Hopefully you learned the value of teamwork long ago, because it will continue to be essential as you work with a variety of people on the job.

What personal traits do you think are necessary for teamwork to occur? In addition to the human relationship and leadership skills discussed in the previous sections, the ability to follow rules and regulations is important. Dependability, responsibility, honesty, and a desire to do your best are also essential. Team members have to "be there" for one another.

Jared is known as a great "idea person," but repeatedly forgets to show up for committee meetings and work sessions. Later he offers outlandish excuses for his absence. As creative as he is, would you want Jared on your team?

At work, your team's goals will reflect the goals of your employer. Remember that the good of the group comes before your own personal desires. Imagine that you and your coworkers set a date for the annual preschool open house. Later you realize that's the night you wanted to attend a basketball tournament game. What would you do?

Managing Multiple Roles

Throughout your career you will assume a variety of roles. It will be necessary to juggle work, family, social, and community obligations.

You may be an employee, a supervisor, a son or daughter, a parent, a spouse, neighbor, volunteer, and friend. Consider Laura Jackson, a teacher and mother of two. Currently she is supervising a student

What skills and characteristics do you have that make you a valuable team member?

teacher in her kindergarten classroom. That makes Laura a teacher, supervisor, employee, mother, and wife—just to name a few of her roles.

At age three, Laura's youngest child was diagnosed with juvenile diabetes. To provide the care she needed, Laura took "family leave" for the final 12 weeks of the school year. The following school year she was able to job share and work half days, teaching the morning class only. Now that her daughter is in school, she is able to teach full time once again.

While Laura was able to find workable solutions to her family crisis, that isn't always possible. Sometimes it is necessary to find a different job to allow you to handle your most important responsibilities. Coworkers can pitch in and help during a personal crisis for a short time, but completing your work is ultimately your responsibility.

Pressure from multiple roles can lead employees to feel they're not doing an adequate job in any of their roles. Learning to prioritize, manage time effectively, and handle stress can help workers feel in control of the demands on their time. It may be necessary to relax personal expectations somewhat. Parents may want to serve their children a homecooked meal every evening, but may settle sometimes for baking a frozen cheese pizza and serving salad from a bag.

Sometimes it's necessary to change or give up an activity. Brittany Corso has volunteered for two years at her community's women's shelter, usually taking the overnight shift on Mondays. Now that she's running the "Kidcare" program at a resort hotel, Brittany can't afford to lose a night's

sleep. To continue her volunteer work, she plans to conduct a children's story hour at the shelter on her afternoon off.

Learning from Performance Evaluations

Wherever you work, expect to have periodic performance evaluations. Also known as reviews or job evaluations, these evaluations should not be regarded as personal criticism. Think of the performance evaluation as an opportunity to see where you stand. A good boss will comment on things you are doing well and point out areas to work on improving. This practice should help you grow in your job.

Instead of filing away your performance evaluation permanently, make a point of referring back to it occasionally. Are you making progress in any areas that were defined as weak? Working on your shortcomings can help you advance in your career.

A poor performance evaluation can signal that your job is in jeopardy. Let your actions show your supervisor that you are working very hard to improve. Ask for feedback and advice.

Continuing to Learn

You may thoroughly enjoy your job, but chances are that you will want a different or added challenge next year, in five years, or in 10 years. Even if you remain in the same job, you will probably have to grow with the position. For example, as a preschool assistant teacher, you may choose to work toward the Child Development Associate

(CDA) credential. As a service agency employee, you may decide to pursue an MSW degree—master's in social work.

You will want to show initiative and take advantage of opportunities for continuing education. Your employer may even be willing to pay for all or part of the cost. Perhaps your performance evaluation noted that your computer skills are limited. A computer class, or even one three-hour program, could boost your job performance.

Continuing education can take the form of attending a weekend conference or workshop, earning credentials through a professional organization, or taking college classes. Many colleges and universities now offer distance learning courses that may be completed online. Reading periodicals published by professional organizations will also help you keep up with advancements in your field.

As you learned in Chapter 1, it's vital to be a lifelong learner. What if, in 1985, a secretary had said, "No, I'll just use the typewriter. I don't really want to learn about computers."? Obviously that person's career would have been stalled!

Leaving a Job

The days of staying with the same employer until retirement are a thing of the past for most American workers. It is highly likely that you will change jobs—and perhaps careers—a number of times during your lifetime. Attempt to make the transition from one job to another as smoothly as possible.

Typically it's a poor idea to quit one job to look for another. Many employers are more interested in potential employees who are currently working. As you conduct a job search, make sure you do so on your own time, however. It is unethical to use work time to interview for another job. Don't spend company time writing or printing your résumé or contacting prospective employers.

Your Responsibilities

Make every effort to leave your current job under the best circumstances possible.

Follow any established procedure for notifying your employer of your intent to resign. Typically, a resignation is put in writing. Give as much notice as possible so your employer may find your replacement. A two-week notice is typical.

Continue doing your job well. If you are asked to train your replacement, strive to give that person the best possible start. You may well cross paths with your coworkers in the future. You may even want to return to this employer later in your career.

Take home any personal items, but leave everything that belongs to your employer. That includes any clothing or equipment that you were issued.

Your Employer's Responsibilities

There may be a time when you leave a job, not because you want to quit, but because the employer terminates your employment. When the local or national economy is poor, your job may be cut through no fault of your own. You may be entitled to state unemployment benefits and to continued health insurance at your own expense.

Jason had been running the youth fitness area at Lakeview Health and Racquet Club for two years when his employment was terminated. Although Jason's reviews had been excellent, the club's membership had declined when a new health club opened nearby. Lakeview simply could not afford to keep him on the payroll.

Naturally, Jason was worried about making ends meet without a job, but realized that he would receive unemployment benefits while he searched for new employment. (If, instead of being terminated, Jason had quit his job, then he would not have received unemployment compensation from his state.)

Another concern was Jason's lack of health insurance until he was informed about COBRA coverage (Consolidated Omnibus Budget Reconciliation Act). Jason could pay the insurance premium for up to 18 months and be covered by the same group insurance he had as a Lakeview employee. The monthly premium was costly, but Jason was confident that he would find another job within a few weeks or months.

Jason was encouraged when he heard a statement that many others who have suffered job setbacks have found to be true: "Sometimes when a door closes, a window opens." Jason had a feeling that there was an even better position waiting for him. Now it was his job to find it.

Ongoing Employability

As you proceed along your own career path, make sure you remember the keys to your early employment success. Commit yourself to excellence. Continue learning. No matter how high you climb on the career ladder, a strong work ethic is always desired.

That work ethic is your commitment to do your very best. It includes reliability, flexibility, teamwork, honesty, and taking responsibility. Make sure you have what it takes to succeed in the world of work in the 21st century!

APPENDIX

A basic knowledge of how the female and male reproductive systems work is a key to understanding pregnancy. Information on family planning shows methods for preventing or spacing pregnancies.

The Female Reproductive System

The female reproductive system has three functions. They are to produce and store eggs; to allow fertilization to take place; and to provide a place where the fertilized egg can grow and develop. The illustrations on page 632 show the parts of the female reproductive system and the role that each plays in these processes.

About two years after reaching puberty, a female begins to have a menstrual cycle. She will continue to have cycles for the next thirty or forty years. The average length of a menstrual cycle is 28 days, although individual women vary.

The cycle begins when an egg cell develops in the ovary. Hormones that are released into the body prepare the lining of the uterus in case the egg is fertilized. About the fourteenth day of the cycle, the mature egg is released. If fertilization does not take place, the uterus sheds its lining. It leaves the body as a bloody flow—often called a "period"—that passes through the vagina.

Females can use tampons or sanitary napkins to absorb the blood of the menstrual flow. These should be changed regularly. Using tampons may bring about a serious infection called toxic shock syndrome. Women who use tampons should change them every four or six hours to avoid this problem.

Some women use a product called a "douche" to clean the vagina during menstruation. This is not a good idea. By changing the balance of chemicals in the vagina, these products increase the chances of the women developing an infection.

If a woman notices an unusual discharge coming from the vagina, she should see a doctor. It could be the sign of an infection.

The Male Reproductive System

The male reproductive system has three functions also. It produces, stores, and transports sperm cells. The illustrations on page 633 show the parts of the male reproductive system and describes their role in these processes.

Males should avoid wearing underwear or pants that are too tight. They should also wear protective cups when they play contact sports. Males should also see a doctor if they notice any unusual discharge coming from the penis. They should also check their testicles from time to time. If they find swelling or soreness, they should see a doctor.

The Female Reproductive System

Ovaries: Each woman has two ovaries (OH-vuh-rees), which produce and store eggs. All the eggs a female will have are present at birth. Until they mature—which happens first when the female reaches puberty—they cannot be fertilized. Normally, each month one egg will mature. The ovaries also have two hormones that control the menstrual cycle.

Fallopian Tubes: Near each ovary is a fallopian tube (fuh-LOH-pee-uhn). When an egg is released by the ovary, it enters the fallopian tube. If fertilization takes place, it occurs in the fallopian tube. The fertilized egg then moves down the tube to the uterus.

Vagina: The vagina is a tube that leads from the uterus to outside the female body. When a male's sperm enters the vagina, pregnancy may occur. It is through the vagina—sometimes called the "birth canal"—that the baby must travel in childbirth.

Uterus: The uterus is the organ where the fertilized egg grows and develops.

Cervix The cervix is the opening of the uterus.

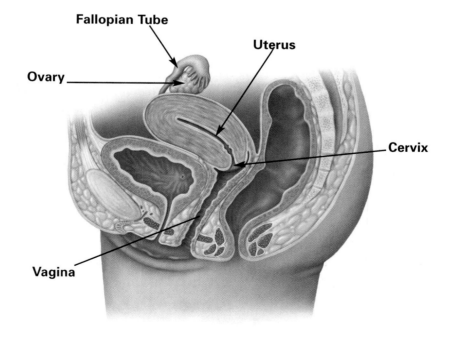

Fallopian Tube

Uterus

Ovary

Cervix

Vagina

The Male Reproductive System

Seminal Vesicles, Prostate Gland, and Cowper's Glands: The two seminal vesicles (SEM-uh-nuhl VES-uh-culs), the prostate gland, and the two Cowper's glands all produce semen (SEE-muhn), a liquid that helps nourish and transport sperm cells.

Vas Deferens: Leading from the epididymis is a tube called the vas deferens (vass DE-fuh-runz), which carries the sperm to the urethra.

Testes: Males have two testes (TES-teez), which are the organs that produce sperm. They are also called "testicles." They sit outside the body in the scrotum (SKROH-tuhm), a sac.

Urethra: The urethra (yoo-REE-thruh) is a long tube that carries urine or semen outside the body.

Epididymis: Behind each testicle is a network of tubes called the epididymis (ep-i-DID-uh-mis). These tubes store the sperm, allowing them to mature.

Penis: The penis (PEE-nis) is the external male sexual organ. The urethra is inside it.

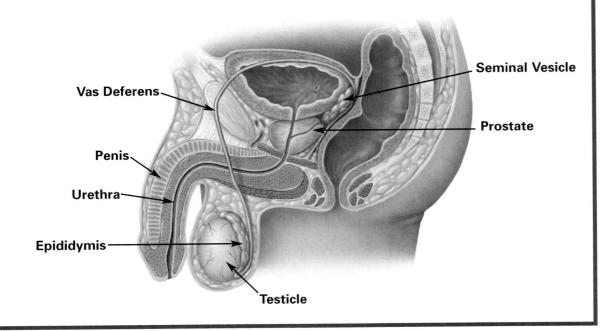

Vas Deferens

Seminal Vesicle

Prostate

Penis

Urethra

Epididymis

Testicle

Family Planning

The only sure way to prevent pregnancy is abstinence—avoiding sexual activity. There are various other methods of contraception, which help prevent pregnancy.

Most methods do not prevent sexually transmitted diseases (STDs). Abstinence is the best method for preventing STDs as well.

Most methods of family planning have the possibility of side effects. These are problems that develop among some, but not all, users of the method. The chart below compares various methods of family planning and indicates if there are side effects. Check medical reference books for complete listings of side effects.

Effectiveness is given as a percentage. A method that is 100 percent effective—such as abstinence—works all the time. If a method is 80 percent effective, there is a one in five chance that a pregnancy could occur when that method is used.

▶ Methods of Family Planning

METHOD	CHARACTERISTICS
Abstinence	Only method that is 100% effective.
Birth control pills	Some side effects; 97%–98% effective.
Cervical cap	Small latex thimble must remain in place 8 hours; increased risk of infection; 82% effective.
Condom	Available for females, but more frequently used by males. Helps reduce spread of STDs. Effectiveness 86% to 90%; should be used with spermicide.
Diaphragm	Diaphragm is used with spermicide; increases risk of urinary infections; 84–90% effective.
Hormonal implants	Capsules placed under skin of upper arm; 99% effective for up to 5 years.
Hormonal injections	Hormones given by physician monthly or once every 3 months; may cause irregular bleeding; up to 99% effective.
Hormonal patch	Thin patch worn on skin 3 weeks each month; similar side effects to birth control pills; 99% effective.
Intrauterine device (IUD) and Uterine Implant	May cause discomfort and side effects first 3 months of use; up to 99% effective.
Natural family planning	Known as the rhythm method, 53% to 80% effective.
Spermicide	Foams, creams, gels may cause allergic reactions; 74% effective; should be used with condom, diaphragm, cervical cap.
Vaginal implant	Ring worn internally for 3 weeks each month. Effectiveness rate not available.

GLOSSARY

A

abstinence Avoiding sexual activity. *(4-1)*

accreditation A formal process in which the National Association for the Education of Young Children reviews a child care facility's staff, programs, and environment to see if they meet the association's strict standards. *(3-3)*

acne (AK-knee) A skin problem caused by excess oils. *(17-1)*

addiction (uh-DICK-shun) Craving a substance, such as a drug, even though it has powerful and harmful effects on the mind and body. *(19-3)*

adolescence (AD-uh-LES-unts) The stage of life between childhood and adulthood. *(1-2)*

adoption A legal process by which children enter a family they were not born into. *(2-1)*

age appropriate Suitable for the age and individual needs of a child. *(10-2)*

allergy (AL-ur-jee) An oversensitivity to one or more common substances. *(18-2)*

alternative birth center A facility separate from any hospital that has homelike rooms for giving birth. *(6-3)*

ambidextrous Able to use both hands with equal skill. *(14-1)*

amniocentesis (AM-knee-oh-sen-TEE-sis) A prenatal test performed by withdrawing a sample of the **amniotic fluid** surrounding an unborn baby and testing that fluid for indications of specific birth defects or other health problems. *(5-3)*

amniotic fluid (AM-knee-AH-tik) Liquid that surrounds and protects the developing baby in the uterus during pregnancy. *(5-1)*

anecdotal (AN-ek-DOE-tuhl) **record** A method of writing observations in which the observer writes down all the behaviors that have to do with one issue only. *See also*

developmental checklist, frequency count, running record. *(1-3)*

anemia (ah-KNEE-mee-ah) A condition caused by lack of iron that results in poor appetite, tiredness, and weakness. *(6-1)*

antibodies (AN-ta-BOD-ees) Substances produced by the body to fight off germs. *(18-2)*

Apgar scale A rating system used to evaluate a newborn's physical condition and applied shortly after birth. *(7-2)*

aptitudes A person's special talents and abilities. *(1-4)*

articulation The ability to use clear, distinct speech. *(13-2)*

artificial respiration (AR-tuh-FISH-ul RES-puh-RAY-shun) A procedure for forcing air into the lungs of a person whose breathing has stopped. *(18-1)*

asthma (AZ-muh) A condition affecting the lungs in which air passages tighten, making it difficult to breathe. *(18-2)*

attachment The bond between a parent or caregiver and a child. *(9-1)*

attention deficit hyperactivity disorder (ADHD) A learning disability in which a person is not able to control his or her activity or concentrate for a normal length of time. *(16-2)*

attention span The length of time a person can concentrate on a task without getting bored. *(10-1)*

authoritarian style A parenting style based on the idea that children should obey their parents without question. *See also* **democratic style, permissive style.** *(3-1)*

authority The right to make decisions. *(20-1)*

axons (AKS-ons) The parts of neurons that transmit instructions from the cell body of a neuron to another neuron. *See also* **dendrites.** *(8-2)*

babysitting Caring for a child for a short time while parents are away from the home. *(20-1)*

baseline A **frequency count** taken before any steps are taken to change the behavior being counted. *(1-3)*

behavioral therapist A professional trained in helping people work through emotional problems. *(19-1)*

behaviors Ways of acting or responding. *(1-1)*

bilingual Able to speak two languages. *(16-1)*

birth defects Problems babies are born with which threaten their health or ability to live. *(5-3)*

blended family A family group that is formed when a single parent marries another person, who may or may not be a parent as well. *(2-1)*

bonding Forming strong emotional ties between parent and child. *(7-2)*

budget A spending plan used to help people set financial goals and work toward them. *(6-2)*

cardiopulmonary resuscitation (CPR) (CAR-dee-oh-POOL-muh-NER-ee ri-SUSS-uh-TAY-shun) A rescue technique used to sustain life when both breathing and the heart have stopped. *(18-1)*

caregivers Parents and others who take care of children. *(1-1)*

cause and effect The idea that one action results in another action or condition. *(10-1)*

cervix (SIR-viks) The lower part of the uterus. *(7-1)*

cesarean birth (si-ZARE-ee-uhn) The delivery of a baby by making a surgical incision in the mother's abdomen. *(7-1)*

child abuse The physical or emotional mistreatment of a child. *(19-2)*

child care center A facility in which staff provides care for children whose parents are not available during working hours. *(3-3)*

child development The study of how children master new skills. *(1-1)*

Child Development Associate (CDA) credential A document given to someone whose competency in specific areas of child care has been certified. *(1-4)*

childproof Taking steps to protect a child from possible dangers in the home. *(10-2)*

chorionic villi sampling (CORE-ee-ON-ik VI-lie) A prenatal test for specific birth defects performed by sampling small amounts of the tissue from the membrane that encases the fetus. *(5-3)*

chromosomes (CROW-muh-soams) Tiny threadlike particles in the nucleus of every cell. *(5-2)*

circle time A period in a child care facility during which a large group of children sit together for such activities as show-and-tell or story reading. *(20-2)*

closed adoption A type of **adoption** in which the birth parents do not know the names of the adoptive parents. *See also* **open adoption**. *(4-1)*

co-dependency The actions of a member of the family of a substance abuser, in which the person takes on responsibilities that the substance abuser should be fulfilling. *(19-3)*

colic (COL-ik) A baby's being extremely fussy every day. *(9-2)*

colostrum The first milk produced by a woman's breast after childbirth, which is easy to digest and rich in antibodies to protect the baby against disease. *(7-2)*

communicable diseases Illnesses that are easily passed from one person to another. *(18-2)*

conception The union of an ovum and sperm, resulting in the beginning of a pregnancy. *(5-1)*

concepts General categories of objects and information. *(13-1)*

concrete operations period Piaget's third stage of learning, during which children can think logically but still learn best from direct experience. *See also* **formal operations, preoperational period, sensorimotor period**. *(10-1)*

confidentiality (CON-fuh-den-shee-AL-uht-ee) Privacy. *(1-3)*

conformity Being like other people. *(17-3)*

conscience (KON-shuns) An inner sense of what is right. *(3-2)*

conservation The idea that an object or quantity has the same characteristics even if there is a change in how it is presented. *(17-4)*

contagious The period during which a **communicable disease** can be spread to another person. *(18-2)*

contraction The regular tightening and release of the muscle of the uterus during labor. *(7-1)*

convulsion A seizure or a period of unconsciousness with uncontrolled jerking or twitching of muscles. *(18-1)*

cooperative play The situation in which children actually play with one another. *See also* **parallel play.** *(12-2)*

cortex (CORE-teks) Part of the cerebrum, in the brain. *(8-2)*

cradle cap A skin condition of infants in which the scalp develops patches of yellowish, crusty scales. *(8-4)*

creativity A mental ability in which the imagination is used to produce something. *(13-1)*

crisis nursery Child care facilities where troubled parents can leave their children for a short time. *(19-2)*

D

delivery The birth of a baby. *See also* **labor.** *(6-3)*

democratic style A parenting style in which parents allow children some input into rules and limits put on their behavior. *See also* **authoritarian style, permissive style.** *(3-1)*

dendrites The parts of neurons that receive messages from other neurons. *See also* **axons.** *(8-2)*

deprivation The lack of an enriching environment. *(3-1)*

depth perception The ability to recognize that an object is three-dimensional, not flat. *(8-1)*

developmental checklist A method of writing observations in which the observer identifies a series of specific skills or behaviors that a child of a certain age should master and checks off those that are observed in a particular child. *See also* **anecdotal record, frequency count, running record.** *(1-3)*

developmentally appropriate Tasks that are suitable to a child given his or her age and interests. *(11-1)*

developmental task Challenge that must be met or skill developed at a particular stage of life. *(1-2)*

dexterity The skillful use of the hands and fingers. *(11-1)*

diaper rash Patches of rough, irritated skin in the diaper area. *(8-4)*

directed learning Learning that results from being taught. *(13-1)*

dominant The gene that dictates the way a trait is expressed. *See also* **gene; recessive gene.** *(5-2)*

dramatic play Play in which children imitate real-life situations. *(16-1)*

dyslexia (dis-LEKS-see-uh) A learning disability in which a person is unable to understand printed symbols in a normal way. *(16-2)*

E

eating disorder A behavioral problem in which people think they are fat when they really aren't and, as a result, starve themselves or eat large amounts of food at a time and then make themselves vomit. *(17-1)*

embryo (EM-bree-oh) The developing baby from about the third to the eighth week of pregnancy. *See also* **fetus, zygote.** *(5-1)*

emotional development The process of learning to recognize and express one's feelings and to establish one's identity as a unique person. *(9-1)*

emotional maturity Being responsible enough to consistently put someone else's needs before your own. *(2-2)*

empathy The ability to put oneself in another's place. *(12-1)*

entrepreneurs People who are self-employed or own their own business. *(1-4)*

entry-level job A position for beginners in a field, one which requires limited education and training. *(1-4)*

environment (in-VY-run-munt) The people, places, and things that surround and influence a person. *(1-2)*

extended family A family group that includes relatives other than a parent and child who live with them. *(2-1)*

F

failure to thrive A condition in which the baby does not grow and develop properly. *(9-1)*

family child care A child care situation in which an adult cares for a small number of children in his or her own home. *(3-3)*

family life cycle A series of stages that families live through. *(2-1)*

fetal alcohol effects (FEE-tuhl) A condition less severe than **fetal alcohol syndrome** that still results in damage to the developing baby caused by a pregnant woman drinking alcohol. *(5-4)*

fetal alcohol syndrome (FAS) (FEE-tuhl) A condition that includes physical and mental problems that result from a mother's drinking alcohol while she is pregnant. *(5-4)*

fetus (FEE-tuhs) The developing baby from the eighth or ninth week of pregnancy until birth. *See also* **embryo, zygote.** *(5-1)*

fiber A part of plants that humans cannot digest; eating it helps the digestive system work properly. *(17-1)*

finger plays Songs or chants with accompanying hand motions. *(16-1)*

fixed expenses A cost that cannot be changed, such as payments for housing, taxes, insurance, and loans. *See* **flexible expenses.** *(6-2)*

flammable Easily burned. *(13-2)*

flexible expenses A cost over which people have some control and which can be cut back if necessary, such as food, household maintenance, clothing, recreation, and similar expenses. *See* **fixed expenses.** *(6-2)*

fluoride A chemical that strengthens the outer coating of teeth. *(14-2)*

fontanels (FON-tuh-NELLS) Open spaces in a baby's head where the bones have not yet joined. *(7-1)*

forceps Specialized tongs made from bands of surgical steel that are molded to fit the shape of a baby's head. *(7-1)*

formal operations period Piaget's fourth stage of learning, during which children become capable of abstract thinking. *See also* **concrete operations, preoperational period, sensorimotor period.** *(10-1)*

formula A mixture of milk or milk substitute, water, and nutrients that can be fed to a baby. *(6-2)*

foster children Children who enter a family temporarily because they need a home until their parents can solve their problems or until the children can find a permanent adoptive home. *(2-1)*

fracture A break or crack in a bone. *(18-1)*

frequency count A method of writing observations in which the observer tallies how often a certain behavior occurs. *See also* **anecdotal record, developmental checklist, running record.** *(1-3)*

G

gender identity The awareness of being a boy or girl. *(17-2)*

gene The unit that determines inherited characteristics. *(5-2)*

gifted children Children who have unusual intelligence or special talent in an artistic area. *(16-2)*

grasp reflex The automatic response of a newborn's hand to close over anything that comes in contact with the palm. *(7-3)*

group identification A feeling of belonging. *(14-2)*

guardian Adult who takes all financial and legal responsibility for raising a child when the child's parents die. *(2-1)*

guidance Using firmness and understanding to help children learn to control their own behavior. *(3-2)*

H

hand-eye coordination The ability to move hands and fingers precisely in relation to what is seen. *(8-1)*

Head Start A federal government program that sets up locally run child care facilities designed to help lower-income and disadvantaged children improve their readiness for school. *(3-3)*

Heimlich maneuver (HIME-lick muh-NEW-vur) A technique for rescuing a person who is choking that puts pressure on the air in the body to expel an object that is blocking breathing. *(18-1)*

heredity (huh-RED-uht-ee) The passing on of certain characteristics from earlier generations. *(1-2)*

hormones Chemicals in the body that cause changes. *(4-1)*

hygiene Personal cleanliness. *(11-2)*

hypothetical (HIGH-puh-THET-uh-kal) Imagined; used to describe things that are not but could be. *(17-4)*

I

imitation Learning that occurs by watching and copying the actions of others. *(13-1)*

immunize (IM-yuh-NIZE) To protect a person from a particular disease, usually by means of giving the person a **vaccine.** *(18-2)*

incidental learning Learning that is not planned. *(13-1)*

inclusion Placing children with disabilities in regular classrooms. *(19-1)*

incubator A special enclosed crib used for premature babies in which the oxygen supply, temperature, and humidity can be closely controlled. *(7-2)*

infertility The inability to become pregnant. *(5-2)*

initiative Motivation to accomplish more. *(15-1)*

intelligence The ability to interpret or understand everyday situations and to use that experience when faced with new situations or problems. *(13-1)*

intelligence quotient (IQ) A number obtained by comparing a person's score on an intelligence test to the scores of other people the same age. *(16-1)*

interpret To find meaning in, explain, or make sense of something. *(1-3)*

J

job shadowing Spending time on the job with someone whose career interests you. *(1-4)*

L

labor The process by which the baby gradually moves out of the uterus into the vagina to be born. *(6-3)*

large motor skill An ability that depends on the use and control of the large muscles of the back, legs, shoulders, and arms. *See also* **small motor skill.** *(11-1)*

lay midwife A person with special training in the care of pregnant women and normal deliveries, but who does not have a nursing degree. *(6-3)*

learning center Areas of the early childhood classroom meant for certain types of play and learning. *(20-2)*

learning disability A problem in a person's mental processes that prevents him or her from learning in a normal way. *(16-2)*

license A document issued by a state which shows that caregivers meet health and safety standards. *(3-3)*

lifelong learner Person who spends his or her entire life learning new information and skills. *(1-4)*

M

mandated reporters Those in child-related occupations required by law to report cases of suspected child abuse. *(19-2)*

maternity leave Time off from work that allows a women to give birth, recover, and begin to care for a new baby. *(6-2)*

miscarriage (MISS-care-uj) The unexpected death of a developing baby before 20 weeks of pregnancy. *See also* **stillbirth.** *(5-3)*

Montessori (mon-tuh-SORE-ee) **preschool** A facility for the education of children aged three to five that uses special learning materials and follows the ideas of Dr. Maria Montessori. *(3-3)*

moral development The process of gradually learning to base one's behavior on personal beliefs of right and wrong. *(15-2)*

motor skills Abilities that depend on the use and control of muscles. *(8-1)*

multiple intelligences Many different ways of using the mind and body to experience the world. *(16-1)*

myelin A waxy substance that coats **axons,** making it easier to transmit information from one neuron to another. *(8-2)*

N

nanny Trained worker hired by a family to provide live-in child care. *(3-3)*

negative reinforcement A response aimed at discouraging a child from repeating a behavior. *See also* **positive reinforcement.** *(3-2)*

negativism Doing the opposite of what others want, a normal behavior for a young toddler. *(12-1)*

neurons (NER-ons) Nerve cells. *(1-2)*

nontoxic Not poisonous. *(18-1)*

nuclear family A family group that includes a mother and father and at least one child. *(2-1)*

nurse-midwife A registered nurse with advanced training in normal pregnancy and birth. *(6-3)*

nurturing Giving a child opportunities for encouragement and enrichment and showing love, support, and concern for the child. *(3-1)*

O

objective Using facts, not personal feelings or prejudices, to describe things. *See also* **subjective.** *(1-3)*

object permanence (PURR-muh-nens) The idea that objects continue to exist even when they are out of sight. *(10-1)*

obstetrician (AHB-stuh-TRISH-un) A doctor who specializes in pregnancy and childbirth. *(6-1)*

open adoption A type of **adoption** in which birth parents are told about the adoptive parents and may even get to meet them. *See also* **closed adoption.** *(4-1)*

orthodontist A dental specialist who sees whether a child needs braces. *(17-1)*

ovum (OH-vum) Female cell, or egg, needed for reproduction. *(5-1)*

P

pacifier (pass-uh-FIE-uhr) A nipple attached to a plastic ring. *(9-2)*

parallel play The situation in which a child plays independently near, but not actually with, another child. *See also* **cooperative play.** *(12-2)*

paraprofessional (pare-uh-pro-FESH-uhn-uhl) A worker with education beyond high school that trains him or her for a certain field. *(1-4)*

parent cooperative A child care situation in which part of the care is provided by the parents of children in the program. *(3-3)*

parenthood The state of being a parent, which begins when one has a child by birth or adoption. *(2-2)*

parenting Caring for children and helping them develop. *(3-1)*

paternity Legal identification of a male as the father of a child. *(4-1)*

pediatrician A doctor who specializes in treating children. *(6-2)*

peer pressure The influence of people one's own age. *(4-1)*

peers People one's own age. *(15-2)*

perception (purr-SEP-shun) The ability to learn from the senses. *(10-1)*

permanent teeth The set of 32 teeth that replace the **primary teeth** but will not themselves be naturally replaced, which begin to appear at about six years. *(14-1)*

permissive style A parenting style in which parents give children a wide range of freedom, with children being able to set their own rules. *See also* **authoritarian style, democratic style.** *(3-1)*

phonemes The individual sounds in words. *(16-1)*

placenta (pluh-SEN-tuh) A tissue in the **uterus** of a pregnant woman that is rich in blood vessels and plays a role in bringing food and oxygen from the mother's body to a developing baby. *(5-1)*

play group A child care arrangement in which parents take turns caring for each other's children in their own homes. *(3-3)*

poison control center A special unit that gives advice for and treats victims of poisoning. *(18-1)*

positive reinforcement A response that encourages a particular behavior so it will be repeated. *See also* **negative reinforcement.** *(3-2)*

postnatal The period after birth. *(7-2)*

postpartum The time after a baby is born. *(6-3)*

premature Babies born before 37 weeks of development and weighing less than 5 pounds, 8 ounces (2.5 kg). *(7-2)*

prenatal development Physical changes that take place before a baby is born. *(5-1)*

preoperational period (pree-OP-ur-AY-shun-ul) Piaget's second stage of learning, during which children think about everything in terms of their own activities and what they perceive at the moment. *See also* **concrete operations, formal operations, sensorimotor period.** *(10-1)*

prepared childbirth A method of giving birth in which pain is reduced through the elimination of fear and the use of special conditioning exercises. *(6-3)*

preschool A facility that provides education programs for children aged three to five. *(3-3)*

primary teeth The first set of teeth that a baby gets, which usually start to appear about six or seven months of age. *See also* **permanent teeth.** *(8-1)*

professional A worker who has at least a degree from a four-year college or technical school in a particular field. *(1-4)*

proportion The size relationship between different parts of the body. *(8-1)*

puberty (PYOO-burr-tee) The set of changes that gives a child a physically mature body able to reproduce. *(17-1)*

R

recall The order of the Consumer Protection Agency to take a product off the market or bring it back to the manufacturer for needed repairs because it is not safe. *(10-2)*

recessive The gene that is expressed as a trait only if paired with a matching recessive gene. *See also* **dominant gene; gene.** *(5-2)*

reflex Instinctive, automatic response, such as sneezing or yawning. *(7-3)*

Rh factor A characteristic of the blood indicating the presence or absence of a certain protein. *(6-1)*

role model A person that someone admires and wishes to pattern his or her behavior after. *(17-2)*

rooming-in An arrangement in which a newborn baby stays in the mother's room in the hospital day and night. *(7-2)*

rooting reflex A newborn's automatic response, when touched on the lips or cheeks, of turning toward the touch and beginning to suck. *(7-3)*

running record A method of writing observations in which the observer writes down for a set period of time everything observed about a particular child, group, or teacher. *See also* **anecdotal record, developmental checklist, frequency count.** *(1-3)*

S

saturated fat Animal fat that is solid at room temperature. *(17-1)*

sealant Thin plastic coating applied to the teeth that prevents plaque from developing. *(14-2)*

self-centered People who think about their own needs and wants. *(12-1)*

self-concept How you see yourself. *(12-1)*

self-discipline Children's ability to control their own behavior, learned through **guidance.** *(3-2)*

self-esteem How you value yourself. *(1-2)*

sensorimotor period (SEN-suh-ree-MOE-tur) Piaget's first stage of learning, during which babies learn primarily through their senses and their own actions. *See also* **concrete operations, formal operations, preoperational period.** *(10-1)*

separation anxiety A child's fear of being away from parents, familiar caregivers, or the normal environment. *(12-1)*

sequence A step-by-step pattern. *(1-2)*

service learning A program that combines some form of community service with schoolwork. *(1-4)*

sexuality (SEK-shoo-AL-uht-ee) A person's view of himself or herself as a male or female. *(4-1)*

sexually transmitted disease (STD) An illness spread from one person to another by sexual contact. *(4-1)*

shaken baby syndrome A condition caused when parents severely shake a baby, which can lead to damage to the baby's brain and perhaps other problems. *(8-3)*

sibling rivalry Competition between brothers or sisters for parents' affection and attention. *(12-1)*

single-parent family A family group that includes one parent and at least one child. *(2-1)*

sleeper A one-piece stretchy garment with feet, meant for an infant. *(8-3)*

small motor skill An ability that depends on the use and control of the finer muscles of the wrists, fingers, and ankles. *See also* **large motor skill.** *(11-1)*

social development The process of learning to interact with others and to express oneself to others. *(9-1)*

socialization The process by which young children gradually learn to get along with other people, first in their own families and then in groups. *(12-2)*

speech-language pathologist A specialist trained to detect and correct speech problems. *(13-2)*

sperm Male cell needed for reproduction. *(5-1)*

sphincter muscles (SFINGK-tur) The muscles that control elimination. *(11-2)*

sprain An injury caused by sudden, violent stretching of a joint or muscle. *(18-1)*

startle reflex A newborn's automatic response to a loud noise or a touch on the stomach, in which the legs are thrown up, fingers spread, and arms are first extended and then brought back rapidly while the fingers close in a grasping action. *(7-3)*

stillbirth The death of a developing baby after 20 weeks of a pregnancy. *See also* **miscarriage.** *(5-3)*

stranger anxiety A baby's fear of unfamiliar people, usually expressed by crying. *(9-2)*

subjective Using personal opinions or feelings, rather than facts, to judge or describe things. *See also* **objective.** *(1-3)*

subsidized child care Programs usually for low- to middle-income families through which the government or social service agency pays part of the cost of child care. *(3-3)*

support group A group that gives people with problems a chance to explore and accept their feelings. *(19-1)*

surrogate A substitute. *(5-2)*

symbolic thinking (sim-BOL-ik) The use of words and numbers to stand for ideas. *(10-1)*

synapses (sin-AP-suhs) Gaps between neurons over which messages are sent between neurons. *(8-2)*

synthetic fiber Manufactured thread, made from chemicals rather than natural sources. *(11-2)*

T

temperament A person's style of reacting to the world and relating to others. *(7-3)*

temper tantrums Occasions when a child releases anger or frustration by screaming, crying, kicking, pounding, and sometimes holding his or her breath. *(12-1)*

time-out A short period of time in which a child sits away from other people and the center of activity after he or she has misbehaved. *(3-2)*

toddlers Children from age one to three, so named for the unsteady steps they use when they first begin walking. *(11-1)*

training pants Heavy, absorbent underpants that can be worn in place of diapers. *(11-2)*

transition A period during which children move from one activity to the next. *(20-2)*

transitivity The idea that a relative relationship between two objects can extend to another object. *(17-4)*

trial-and-error learning Learning that takes place when a child tries several ways of solving a problem before finding one that works. *(13-1)*

U

ultrasound A prenatal test performed by using sound waves to make a video image of an unborn baby to check for specific health problems. *(5-3)*

umbilical cord (um-BILL-uh-cuhl) A long tube that connects the **placenta** to the developing baby during pregnancy; carries food and oxygen to the baby. *(5-1)*

uterus (UTE-uh-rus) The organ in a woman's body in which a baby develops during pregnancy. *(5-1)*

V

vaccine (vak-SEEN) A small amount of disease-carrying germs introduced to the body on purpose so that the body can build resistance to that disease. *(18-2)*

values What is important to people. *(2-1)*

W

weaning The process of changing from drinking from the bottle or breast to drinking from a cup. *(8-3)*

work-based learning A program in which students combine in-school and on-the-job learning. *(1-4)*

work environment The physical and social surroundings at the workplace. *(1-4)*

Z

zygote (ZY-goat) The fertilized egg. *See also* **embryo, fetus.** *(5-1)*

Credits

Interior Design: Nio Graphics

Cover Photo: Stock Market, Kunio Owaki

Infographic Design: Peter B. Getz, Circle Design

Design Photos (Realia): Andrew Yates Photography

Arnold & Brown, 141, 179, 215, 229, 249, 246-247, 294, 295, 318, 319, 346, 347, 344-345, 376, 406, 407, 457, 464, 482, 483, 511, 547, 570, 575, 607
Joel & Sharon Harris, Articulate Graphics, 632, 633, 261, 262, 263
Artville/Burke/Triolo, 362
Jim Ballard, 429
Roger B. Bean, 42, 101, 196, 202, 205, 226, 236, 236, 296, 305, 382, 408, 425, 580, 581
Marshal Berman Photography, Design Office, 91, 106, 127, 129, 269, 334, 378, 403, 424, 468, 488, 520, 554, 555, 589, 591, 593, 596, 606, 612, 613, 614, 621, 623
Keith Berry, 135, 168, 172, 219, 235
Children's Hospital of Pittsburgh, 559
Pete Christie, 366
Carol A. Spengel, Circle Design, 220, 254, 143, 144, 148, 149, 151, 146, 147
CORBIS, 47, 336, 341, 502
    Laura Dwight, 421
    Ted Horowitz Photography, 476, 521
    Tom & Dee Ann McCarthy, 258, 470
    Roy Morsch, 567
    Jose Luis Pelaez, Inc., 28, 298
    ROB & SAS photography, 377
    Norbert Schaefer, 108
    Ariel Skelley, 280, 604- 605
    Tom Stewart Photography, 231

Straus/Curtis, 540
Larry Williams and Associates, 460
Ghislain & Marie David de Lossy/Getty Images/The Image Bank, 537
K.D. Dittlinger, 626
Everett Collection Inc., CSU Archives, 324
FPG International
    Chris Bartlett, 437
    Ron Chapple, 447
    Bill Losh, 440
    Jacob Taposchaner, 445
    Telegraph Colour Library, 434, 432-433
David R. Frazier Photolibrary Inc.
    David R. Frazier, 57, 94, 392
    Jeff Greenberg, 104
    Trent Steffler, 51
FoodPix, 187, 361
Tim Fuller Photography, Morgan Cain and Associates, 60, 134, 393, 548, 564, 582, 583
Ann Garvin, 315, 362, 362
Mark E. Gibson, 620
The Gorilla Foundation, 297
Linda Henson, 363
Image Bank
    Mike Quon, 13, 59, 537
Image Club Graphics, Digital Vision Collection, 449, 450
Index Stock Photography
    Mark Gibson, 508-509
Ken Karp, 608
Robert F. Kusel, 194, 211, 213, 360
Elyse Lewin/Getty Images/The Image Bank, 61
March of Dimes, 180
McGill University, Montreal Neurological Institute, McConnell Brain Imaging Centre/Dr. Denise Klein and Dr. Bruce Pike, 500
Mead Johnson Nutritional Group, 216, 268
Lawrence Migdale, 9, 510, 522, 524, 525, 527, 530, 538, 542, 546, 552, 571, 578, 579, 595, 605, 609, 624
Ted Mishima, 7, 24, 465, 474, 528
Monkmeyer Press

Das, 9, 614, 615
Kopstein, 600
LeDuc, 584
Merrim, 590
Shackman, 622
Siteman, 586, 594
Ullman, 627
Photodisc, 12, 24, 53, 60, 71, 79, 92, 104, 106, 115, 123, 137, 163, 177, 182, 195, 213, 229, 238, 245, 273, 293, 307, 317, 338, 343, 352, 370, 375, 382, 400, 405, 413, 415, 431, 437, 440, 441, 442, 444, 445, 446, 447, 448, 452, 453, 455, 474, 481, 488, 495, 507, 531, 545, 571, 577, 581 584, 603, 619, 629
Photo Edit
    Bill Aron, 505
    Bill Bachman, 501
    Billy E. Barnes, 341
    Vic Bider, 131
    Robert Brenner, 71, 80, 88, 91, 273, 275, 327, 329, 366, 379, 423, 471, 572
    Michelle Bridwell, 117, 118, 290, 307
    Myrleen Cate, 69, 76, 90, 142, 163, 184, 232, 237, 239, 252, 259, 302, 309, 340, 351, 354, 380, 389, 390, 395, 410, 413, 420, 423, 460, 478, 489, 516
    Cindy Charles, 167, 394, 399, 459
    CLEO, 178, 276, 477
    Paul Conklin, 417
    Gary Conner, 412
    David K. Crow, 57, 68
    Mary Kate Denney, 23, 105, 128, 137, 175, 383, 479, 485, 498
    Laura Dwight, 4, 27, 150, 162, 252, 258, 291, 309, 314, 321, 331, 337, 341, 333, 343, 353, 356, 370, 398, 475
    Amy C. Etra, 169, 192, 258, 332
    Kathy Ferguson, 84
    Tony Freeman, 38, 102, 109-110, 201, 291, 301, 325, 381, 383, 386, 405, 409, 415, 462, 472, 479, 487
    Jose Galvez, 62
    Robert W. Ginn, 243, 422

Spencer Grant, 267, 563
Will Hart, 495, 499
Richard Hutchings, 135, 428, 490
Bonnie Kamin, 487
Felicia Martinez, 98, 259
Phil McCarten, 131
Tom McCarthy, 251, 254, 264, 272, 494
Michael Newman, 43, 19, 63, 65, 74, 82, 116, 164, 165, 171, 182, 185, 190, 199, 200, 230, 233, 259, 269, 271, 272, 279, 282, 284, 285, 299, 302, 304, 308, 311, 312, 334, 358, 380, 397, 410, 463, 470, 491, 535
Jonathan Nourok, 64, 240, 241, 309, 317
Tom Prettyman, 157, 350
A. Ramey, 153
Mark Richards, 96, 125, 206
Elena Rooraid, 367
Robin L. Sachs, 426, 431, 497, 507
James Shaffer, 132
Rhoda Sidney, 204, 211
Frank Siteman, 419
Barbara W. Stitzer, 77, 123
Merrit Vincent, 77, 123
David Young-Wolf, 7, 51, 87, 93, 119, 140, 152, 174, 186, 191, 208, 218, 234, 265, 269, 287, 288, 293, 300, 302, 313, 381, 384, 400, 403, 461, 466, 505, 517
Elizabeth Zuckerman, 381
Photo Researchers
    CNRI/Science Photo Library, Science Source, 161, 177
    Petit Format, Science Source, 146
    Petit Format/Nestle, Science Source, 146
    Neil Bromhall/Genesis Films/Science Photo Library, Science Source, 147
Liz Purcell, 286
Stock Boston
    Tom Cheek, 543
Stock Market
    Roger Ball, 155, 269
    Paul Barton, 18, 212, 120, 181, 243
    Joe Bator, 373
    Peter Beck, 45, 439
    C/B Productions, 355
    Sandy Clark, 212
    DiMaggio/Kalish, 124
    George DiSario, 55
    John Feingersh, 37, 156, 89
    Ted Horowitz, 106, 227
    Ronnie Kaufman, 64
    Michael Keller, 170, 183

Rob Lewine, 368, 375
Don Mason, 33
Tom and DeeAnn McCarthy, 20, 26, 95, 193, 436
Bill Miles, 130
Roy Morsch, 22, 97, 438
Mug Shots, 29
Jeffry W. Myers, 338, 44
Kunio Owaki, 211
Jose L. Pelaez, 32, 72, 103, 113, 126, 217, 435, 21
Mark Richards, 54
Chuck Savage, 65, 85
Norbert Schafer, 195, 145, 145, 145, 223, 245
George Shelly, 212
Ariel Skelley, 30, 64, 77, 70-79, 86, 112, 113, 138-139, 364, 387, 451, 453
Tom Stewart, 35, 222, 456
David Stocklein, 175
William Taufic, 63
A & J Verkiak, 81
David Woods, 50, 65
Jeff Zaruba, 56
Jeffrey J. Stoeker, 115
Tony Stone Images
    Chris Cheadle, 619, 629
    Churchill & Klenr, 523
    Ken Fisher, 601
    Charles Gupton, 585
    Billy Hustace, 621
    Mitch Kezar, 588
    Dennis O'Clair, 549
    Andy Sacks, 601
    Terry Vine, 531
    David Young-Wolff, 518
Dan Grossman, Stony Creek Studio, 556, 557, 561
Unicorn Stock Photos
    Jean Higgins, 533
    Karen Holsinger Mullen, 565
V.C.L./Getty Images/Taxi, 630
Mary Vogel, 309
Dana White Productions, 1 ,4, 6, 16-17, 71, 92, 100, 153, 207, 238, 242, 250, 255, 256, 260, 274, 278, 283, 306, 308, 308, 315, 328, 337, 348, 349, 352, 353, 359, 365, 402, 414, 418, 429, 443, 449, 458, 469, 484, 486, 493, 503, 504, 512, 515, 610
Jim Whitmer Photography, 523, 529, 532, 536, 538, 539, 543, 513, 545, 575, 597, 627
Gloria Williams, 372, 373
Nancy Wood, 5, 320, 330
Craig D. Wood, 516, 519, 574, 558, 577, 598, 603
Duane R. Zehr, 210

Acknowledgements: Greater Peoria Family YMCA Childcare Center, PALS Preschool and Kindergarten, Friendship House, A Child's World, American Red Cross, St. Francis Medical Center, Murray Language Academy.

Models and fictional names have been used to portray characters in stories and examples in this text.

Poetry Acknowledgments

17: Excerpted from the book *Children Learn What They Live*, © 1998 by Dorothy Law Nolte and Rachel Harris. The poem "Children Learn What They Live" © 1972 Dorothy Law Nolte.

130: "Some Things Don't Make Any Sense," reprinted by permisson of Atheneum Books for Young Readers, an imprint of Simon & Schuster Children's Publishing Division, from IF I WERE IN CHARGE OF THE WORLD AND OTHER WORRIES. Copyright © 1981 by Judith Viorst.

344: "Everybody Says" from *Everything and Anything* by Dorothy Aldis, copyright 1925-1927, renewed 1953, © 1954, 1955 by Dorothy Aldis. Used by permission of G. P. Putnam Sons, an imprint of Penguin Books for Young Readers, a division of Penguin Putnam, Inc. All rights reserved.

432: "The End" by A. A. Milne, copyright 1927 by E. P. Dutton, renewed © 1955 by A. A. Milne, from *Now We Are Six* by A. A. Milne, illustrated by E. H. Shephard. Used with permission of Dutton's Children's Books, an imprint of Penguin Putnam Books for Young Readers, a division of Penguin Putnam, Inc. All rights reserved.

508: Copyright © Free To Be Foundation, Inc. Used by permission.

INDEX

P